Forty Years to Life
by
Brenda Bradford Ward

Forty Years To Life

Brenda Bradford Ward

Ordering Information:

For orders and inquiries, please contact:
1-888-404-1388
www.goldtouchpress.com
book.orders@goldtouchpress.com

Printed in the United States of America

Author's Statement of Authenticity:

This work's content is original, except where attributed, and is the whole truth to the best of her knowledge and belief. Where text is based on, or quoted from, other sources, those works are cited and believed to be reliable.

Scripture taken from the New American Standard Bible, (c) Copyright The LOCKMAN Foundation 1960, 1962, 1963, 1968, 1971, 1972, 1973, 1975, 1977, 1988. Used by permission.

DEDICATION

This work is dedicated to my
wonderful family and friends who
consistently provided support and
stability during a most challenging
transition period, even with a
few challenges, questions, and
doubts of their own; and to several
extremely competent and caring
professionals whose skills, through
the centuries, might have saved
and improved countless lives.

Acknowledgments

Many psychiatrists and psychologists have dedicated a large part of their research and/or practice to helping "transgendered" people and, to those who assert that the term refers to something that has happened, I argue that the condition's biological cause is of an in utereo origin so, clearly, it would have to be. Mental health professionals have helped to establish and advance Standards of Care for treating the condition. While acknowledging the need for, and utility of, such standards, however, a special few of these professionals have realized that the standards are a guide for helping people rather than for insisting that people must be forced to fit those standards. The professionalism and dedication of these relative few, both to their patients and their field, have been an immeasurable blessing to the transgendered people they have helped when other practitioners would find the risk of deviating from their profession's cookbook daunting or inhibiting to the point of inertia. I will always be grateful that I found such people when I most needed them. The World Professional Association for Transgender Health (WAPTH) now in its 7th edition (WPATH 2012) has undertaken this mission.[1]

Drs. Milton Diamond and Keith Sigmundson have shown the essential role that practitioners of science must play in attempting to rectify the effects, however well-intentioned but nonetheless errant, of theories and/or practices propounded by others who have attempted to practice science without rigorously adhering to the essence of its method. They have argued persuasively that extensive attempts to alter the direction indicated by any subject's internal gender identity compass consistently and spectacularly have failed. Their efforts lend substantial support to this work's argument regarding the condition's extant innate nature. Without the efforts of such dedicated professionals to test and refute their discipline's missteps, research and the practice of the science of the medical arts would be reduced to little more than shamanism.

Those who have established, contributed to, and maintain the online Internet Movie Database (http://www.imdb.com/) have provided, and continue to provide, its users with a link of inestimable value to their own pasts. The database is an organized wealth of information about those who have used the transforming power of film and television to help viewers interpret, measure, and shape their lives and the world they share. The Sarasota County Public Library system ranks among those which have repeatedly demonstrated the competent commitment to access to and dissemination of knowledge that helps make local libraries the invaluable tools they can be in perpetuating and improving the intellectual health of our communities and nation. The genealogical work by at least three generations of my mother's family has helped to clarify the dates when, and places where, various family members made their homes and built their businesses.

The work of copy editor Roderick de Asis and reviewer Christine Gerra was most helpful in preparation of an earlier version of this manuscript. Their careful reading and the efforts of each of the associated personnel of Goldtouch press helped make this work possible. As one of countless beneficiaries of the labors of these, and all of the above-mentioned, wonderfully dedicated professionals who have sought to improve their society, I gratefully acknowledge their contributions.

Contents

6. A "Normal Boy"

7. For Higher Learning

8. Key Relationships

9. Lessons of Self and Gender

16. Popular Misconceptions

17. A Call to Action

18. Following the Plan

19. A Closing Word:

20. Definitions and Conventions Used In This Work

1. The Terminology War

"The" Science

Like millions or billions of other science students I learned that every
one of the nearly eight-billion people who now share our planet required human
ovum and sperm to begin life. Quibble as we might about how many parents,
how parent is defined, test-tubes, matters of marriage if any, ambiguous genitalia,
and a dictionary of other possible terms and considerations; the unequivocal
fact remains that union of sperm and egg account for every person living on, or
near, planet earth and has done so since the dawn of humankind. This certainly
is not meant to suggest that genetic ambiguity never occurs at birth, and those
who insist that a sex-at-birth standard should determine gender have no valid
argument here. The pressure that any medical professional should and must feel
to attempt to create a whole person with functioning genitalia in cases of at-birth
deformity could be crushing.

To discuss reasonably the physio-biology of the above large number of
"normal" people on an individual basis usually means using such commonly-
accepted terms as boy and girl, man and woman, male and female. The ice under
foot seems firm to this point. Empirical analysis and conclusion regarding the
above billions of people must be dispositive to any but the most obtuse observer
regarding nature's common reproductive process, those frequent at-birth
ambiguities (and ideally at one that number is too many) notwithstanding.

The most unfortunate view of many people that gender is and must be
fundamentally and even divinely ordained as congruent with sex-at-birth see a
clear division of male on one side of a line and female on the other. That clear
differentiation would mean that all "males" are masculine and all "females"
are feminine. I can find no substantial support for the argument that there are
multiple genders or sexes nor that anyone moves back and forth among a group
of genders or sexes, transition due to gender identity conflict notwithstanding.
The principle of gender fluidity would deny the breadth of the correct definition
of "gender". Rather than a single dividing line between two distinct sets either
of "sex" or "gender", in both matters a bell curve should apply, although actual

tail populations presumably would be unable to produce their own children. Statistical analysis tells us that the arithmetic mean plus and minus three standard deviations in a "normal" distribution leaves very small but intriguing tails that include a great variety of extant intriguing psychology and physiology, and the ice is getting thinner. Add gender expression, sexual attraction, and/or partner preference and suddenly all ice has disappeared. Tales of the bell curve distribution's tails taken individually have filled, and could well continue to fill, volumes of compelling research regarding individual brains, bodies, and their interactions. MtF women occupy our own very small space in one or each of those softly waving tails. Right or left tail depends upon the sample's labeling, but "cis-gender" people (sample subjects who have no gender identity conflict) land closer to the center of the "sex" curve while their "gender" position depends on how closely their true gender expression conforms to the mean.

Feminine vs Female

A critical failure in much extant literature is an abject failure to define "gender" with sufficient breadth. The "masculine" male who wishes to have carried and/or breast fed his children while otherwise being wholly masculine is very near to one end of the curve. The FtM transitioning female whose womb is used to carry the couple's child might define the other end. Still another tail occupant might be the "feminine" female who nonetheless longs to stand while urinating, to have impregnated her husband, and be the sole provider for and defender of her family.

This work is an exposition of at least part of the transgendered condition from the perspective of someone who has known it intimately. No one else could tell this particular story and it needs desperately to be told. Society still is far from having a generally accepted and accurate understanding of this condition that powerfully affects, directly and indirectly, an unknowably large but significant number of people. Those who have dedicated a substantial portion of their lives to the study and treatment of the condition and, perhaps especially, those who are skeptical or cynical regarding its nature should benefit from this personal recounting of actions, anguish, discovery, joy, and faith. The future of medicine well may hold the ability to prevent gender identity conflict or to treat it before its nascent victim even is aware of the need for treatment. Yet, the struggle of male-to-female (MtF) transgendered people will have afforded the rest of humanity a deeper understanding of societal, familial, and egocentric expectations for each person's living his, and especially, her richest and fullest-possible life.

By writing about life as a transgendered person, I am not implying that there are not hundreds or even thousands of world problems at least as important. I would not suggest that a transgendered person's life is necessarily more harshly cruel and tragic or more arduous than the life of anyone else. However, the unique set of circumstances this condition visits upon those and the families of those who have it, and society's reaction, or lack of action, regarding it, warrant this and other serious efforts thoroughly to address the condition. For its own sake, society needs both to enhance public and professional knowledge and understanding of the condition and to encourage greater systematic efforts to alleviate the suffering it causes.

Many of my recounted experiences will seem familiar to other transgendered women. To the extent that this narrative shows similarities with, and differences from, the accounts of other MtF women, this work should be useful in refining the ability to diagnose and treat others who approach and then experience transition. While not comfortable with the inclusion of every personal aspect and element in this work, I believe omission of them would have resulted in an incomplete account that could reduce its utility. There is also a reticence in writing parts of this work because they could be misunderstood or taken out of context and used specifically to thwart the work's primary purpose of trying to help others with the condition. Some people with other identity questions or psychosexual disorders might present my experiences as their own in sessions with their counselor(s) from a mistaken notion that the deceit will help them obtain a desired, but possibly inappropriate, professional action. If successful, they not only could aggravate their conditions and jeopardize their own lives, but they would threaten the future of the professional practices of those who were trying to help them. Yet, the importance of trying to help those who might otherwise see decades of their lives only partly lived by resisting public disclosure and who might even deny to themselves the existence of their own conflicting gender identities makes this effort worth these and other risks.

The Double Life

Any reader might know, or know of, an MtF woman who is in, or has gone through, transition. Of possibly greater interest, though, is the person who the reader believes is a relatively normal male friend, co-worker, family member, trusted professional, a pseudo stranger who often shares a seat or cabin during a morning commute, or a more distant but readily recognized acquaintance, but she is actually an MtF woman. She is living both a public "male" life and an intensely secret private life closely guarding her conflicting gender identity out of confusion, fear, shame, and concern for people about whom she cares.

During an hypothetical shared morning commute or trip to the barber, your seatmate holds "his" newspaper quite normally and appears relaxed, but her breathing is shallow and her pulse is rapid. She has not started to reread the same paragraph for the fifth time because she is suddenly having difficulty with the language. Perhaps triggered by someone she saw, an ad in the paper, or an unbidden thought about some of the clothing she keeps carefully hidden, she is hoping, as she has so many other times in her past, that the present intense urge to alter her appearance will pass. She again hopes that her conflict will just go away, be cured by some always-illusive power of reason, or continue to be a barely manageable but still fiercely suppressed other self.

These "men" appear to be someone's son, brother, uncle, cousin, and even father, but they have gender identities that are constantly at *war*, for lack of a stronger term, with the rest of their lives. They buy their clothing "necessities" or "gifts for her" in stores, from catalogues, and online in nervous dread that someone will discover that the items are really intended to satisfy all too brief manifestations of their own true gender identities that they otherwise continue to suppress. Transvestite males buy these things too, but I cannot know what the entirety of the experience is for them. The suppressing transgendered person's dread is surreal, readily understandable, and occurs each time "his" carefully crafted and assiduously maintained façade again comes perilously close to its calamitous destruction.

Your transgendered casual acquaintance, co-worker, lifelong friend, or close relative may very recently have experienced another in her long history of such episodes. If the wounds were physical, the incessant and frequently severe bleeding would induce even the most unsympathetic, callous, or self-centered person to intervene, if only to keep her or his shoes dry. Yet, the hemorrhaging, though real, is intangible, and it stealthily affects all people with whom she comes in contact. Worse still is her inhibiting conviction that any fate would be preferable to the unbearable shame and embarrassment of discovery by people about whom she most cares or who are important to her for other reasons.

When an MtF woman's gender identity no longer can be suppressed, her life and the lives of those closest to her finally contend with the reality of a conflict that, at present, has only one known effective, though imperfect, treatment. However dramatic and eventful might be the acknowledgment for herself and the revelation to others, the resulting and nearly indescribable freedom of no longer suppressing who she really is releases the incredibly large genii from her impossibly small, but carefully crafted and diligently maintained, bottle. For her entire life to that time, she maintained dual and seemingly bizarre fantasies. One was the other-gendered self she was compelled to approximate in secret and to become in incessantly recurring imaginings. The other was the seemingly whole but fabricated shell-person she let others think she was. Both false but real pseudo persons finally reach their long overdue end. The penultimately demanding role of acting from an early age as a convincing male, and even trying to convince herself that she can surmount her obsession and be the male she pretends to be, has seen its last performance.

The metamorphosis to a new reality for an MtF woman comes by her accepting and admitting, to herself and to other people, the person she had always resisted appearing to be. The newly unfettered self finally shatters the impossibly thick, yet transparent, barrier through which she viewed the lives of others, but that had separated her from a whole and real life of her own. The longer she postpones transition, the more of that life passes half-lived as someone else. She lives as a shadow person who is not complete and whose gender identity is different from her physical and publicly perceived biological or anatomical sex. While not being able physically to be the woman a part of her has always seen herself as being, she can live more completely as that woman than she ever thought possible and far more completely than she could as an irreparably incomplete man.

Gender Identity Conundrum

Relevant history, media coverage, much academic literature, and personal experience show that, while almost every adult has heard about the transgendered condition, few have an accurate understanding of even the most basic of its aspects. Most people are unaware, for example, of the distinction between a transgendered person who is suppressing her gender identity before transition and one who has acknowledged and affirmed it during and after transition. The distinction is paramount. People who, through no fault of their own, are suppressing their gender identities are the primary focus of this work, but most of society is not even aware that gender identity, as a "thing", actually exists.

Gender identity conflict is viewed from three vantage points as a basis for proposing a new effort at more effectively addressing this pivotal aspect of the lives of thousands of Americans. A similar effort applied elsewhere could help an unknowable number of other people around the world. The life experience of a transgendered person includes uniquely shared elements among the populations of MtF women and FtM men, to a greater or lesser extent, depending upon her or his age at transition, and that is described in this work from a most personal perspective. The condition as others have seen it, primarily from a scientific and a pseudoscientific vantage point, is the second view. Society's contention with transgendered people in law, through its institutions, and through broader culture and religion is the third approach. Through much of the work, all three perspectives have some bearing, and a subject's consignment under one heading is intended, by no means, as exclusionary.

An unfortunate, persistent, and occasionally intentional ambiguity permeates discussions of the transgendered condition and compounds the task of those trying to understand it. Often, when attempting to differentiate between matters of physiology and behavior, conventional use of "sex" refers to the former and "gender" refers to the manifested identity of the subject. Thus, a suppressing MtF woman would be described accurately as being physically male and exhibiting masculine gender, even though her gender identity is feminine and female. Thus, "sex" would be so thoroughly devoid of heart, soul, and mind that it refers solely to a test-tube kind of process (and not to identity). The confusion is exacerbated by those who do not accept the existence of gender identity and its bearing on gender identity conflict. The usage described in its *Definitions and Conventions* section has been followed throughout this work.

Identity suppression

The following chapters include, among exposition of other aspects of the condition, an account of an undetected and undisclosed deception of more than forty years duration. Very lengthy secret lives are an unfortunate and dreadfully common part of the existence of each suppressing transgendered person and of the journey each one makes to her or his climactic and shattering disclosure. This account includes elements unique to my own experience but others common to transgendered and/or homosexual people. While not certain into which category every kind of experience should fall, I have attempted to include as much information as might be useful in categorizing them. Where random samples of various populations repeatedly show common characteristics, researchers still must determine which cause, which result from, and which are largely unrelated to the sample's universe. Also included are references to the accounts of other transgendered people, primarily regarding their encounters with the courts. The tentatively positive direction suggested by recent enlightened judicial rulings abroad and an increasing number of domestic rulings show that wide variance between or among national populations still is likely.

Abigail Shrier's recent work "Irreversible Damage (Shrier 2020)" is a wonderful exposition of the horrendous harm done to those not suffering gender identity conflict, but who were treated socially and professionally as though they were.[2] Ms. Shrier shows the other side of the coin regarding the all too easy lesson learned so convincingly by those who become determined to hide their conflict. That lesson once learned, and reinforced by all of the child's surroundings, regarding what is, and is not, accepted gender behavior will not easily be changed.

Despite evidence that at least some aspects of the transgendered person's experience may be as old as humanity, society's effort to contend with these people has only relatively recently begun to include serious investigation into the condition, especially regarding analysis of its likely genesis and its most effective treatment. The problem's occurrence apparently has not been bounded by time nor geography, and different political entities have reacted to it in a variety of ways. These struggles are examined both from an historic view of the condition and the way in which it has been handled by various courts.

Where the United States Government and state governments ultimately rest along the continuum of reaction is of more than passing interest to many people in local, national, and the international communities. The manner in which America accommodates an almost infinite number of distinct, yet overlapping, minorities is arguably one of its greatest strengths. Continuing unrest over the correct legal definition of marriage colors American public discourse. Its definition may ultimately include any two people, any three or more people, or even a person and a pet or plant. Without due recognition of the primary importance of gender identity to and in defining that pivotal inter-personal relationship, any legislated privileges and prohibitions will be based solely on grossly insufficient determinations regarding each one's physical anatomy rather than an essence much more important and fundamental to each person's humanness.

Estimates of persons likely to be transgendered in a given population seem to differ as widely as do the people making the estimates. While I would count only those individuals whose identity conflict demands, has demanded, or will demand surgical resolution and as complete a transition as possible; some people would include a broader spectrum of gender dysphoria, and still others even would include intersexed people who honestly profess gender consonance and have no gender identity conflict. Unless otherwise indicated, when I refer to MtF women and FtM men throughout this work I am referring to the first set of individuals. Britain has approximately 5,000 post-op transgendered people with 3% to 18% questioning the appropriateness of their surgery (Batty 2004)[3] from its estimated population of 60,270,708 (Central Intelligence Agency 2004).[4] Excluding those questionable surgeries, still an average one in every 12,427 to 14,700 (.007%-.008%) people in Britain transitioned appropriately. If the British model applied to the United States, between 20,408 and 24,054 people of all ages, races, creeds, etc. already would have transitioned here. With well under one-percent of America's population directly affected, we clearly can be persuasive solely on principle.

If public support for reasonable efforts to help this population, however defined, rests on whether there are 20,000, 200,000, or 2,000,000 transgendered people in the United States, an effort to determine the condition's incidence still would be essential. Incidence also would be essential for accurate estimates of the cost of effective intervention. Regardless of actual frequency of occurrence, its impact for each transgendered person, her or his family, and to a lesser extent each affected community is, as I will attempt to show from a very personal perspective, preeminently significant.

Extant public accounts show that MtF women have begun transition at a variety of ages including in young adolescence, in their teens, and during their twenties. Their fortitude is commendable. I might envy the timeliness of their effective familial support and/or the lack of critical restraining influences, their more effective and efficient introspection, the increasing availability of appropriate resources, and/or other factors that have facilitated their transition. Yet, I cannot say with confidence that the nature of the mechanism that caused their gender identity conflict was either very different from, or similar to, my own. Whether anything other than mere chance causes some MtF women to suppress the conflict for decades while others transition much earlier still is a matter of speculation and hypothesis rather than established fact.

Much about the condition remains a mystery, perhaps with more unknown than known, for both the scientific and medical community as well as ethical, moral, and spiritual theorists. Whether by intuition or logic, though, the process by which many "experts" either accept or reject the premise of the condition's early biological origin is invariably tinted by a filter of predisposition toward or against that genesis. Those opposing innate origin for religious reasons see the condition as another wrongly chosen alternative to the single dichotomous female or male Biblical model where gender and sex are synonymous. For them, the combination is properly oriented solely to the production and dedicated rearing of children. Others are predisposed to the acceptance of any honest expression of individual personality as long as it does not involve physical violence or other harm to another person. These people are likely to assert that transgendered people have merely chosen to live in a less conventional manner. They would argue that such choice should not be restricted, perhaps simply because they see challenges to conventions as essential to preventing society's stagnation and lethargy. I attempt to respond to these very different views by explaining the nature and content of my own experience and, especially, the sum of nearly half a lifetime's frustrating efforts to rationalize, eradicate, compartmentalize, and otherwise tame what seemed an insatiable obsession.

The introspection reflected in the title of this work was unavoidable in relating life experiences and the circuitous path I took to resolution, but that is not in the least a part of the purpose of this work. If there were no other suppressing transgendered people in the world, then relating these experiences might do little more than tease the same curiosity that was fed by sideshows of an earlier era's carnivals. The biographical information I have included is intended to show the physical, familial, and social influences that suggested the roles considered appropriate to females and males during my childhood, adolescence, and all the years prior to transition, as well as my interaction with those influences. I believe that observation, rather than speculation, supports the contention that gender identity informs every aspect of each one of every human's interpersonal associations.

A transgendered child's sense of gender identity may be ambiguous, deeply felt but concealed, or even asserted but not resolved. Yet, in each case, her or his gender identity is in conflict with that child's biological sex. It must be virtually impossible for such a child to establish the kind of enduring, meaningful, and complete relationships with parents, siblings, other relatives, friends, and others that are essential to her or his growth as a whole person. Some growth occurs as inevitably for humans as it does for weeds in an untended field. The direction of that unavoidable growth for a transgendered person runs parallel to, rather than intersecting with, the more complete lives of those whose consonance of gender identity and physical sex make fulfilling perceived societal expectations for their behavior far less confusing.

Whatever the incidence of gender identity conflict, it is a terrible experience for each suppressing transgendered person and a tragic loss for the society which both perpetrates the unhealthful fraud of inappropriately assigned gender and which loses the greater contributions that might have been made by those people who endure it. Suppressing transgendered people half-live a secret real life, which seems like a fantasy to them before transition, while they present an elaborate fantasy that is perceived as real by everyone else. An acute awareness that "normal" people can and do form meaningful and fulfilling associations is a constant reminder to transgendered people that there is a major difference between their hidden selves and other people around them. Some suppressing transgendered people even will commit themselves to marriage in an attempt to claim the coveted intimacy that is denied to their secret selves. A deeper understanding of the nature of gender identity conflict and of society's role in exacerbating, rather than alleviating, the problem are essential to the development of an effective means of more efficiently addressing the condition.

This work concludes with a multi-faceted program that, if implemented, would address effectively most aspects of the problem. Whatever productive or constructive benefits come to those who suppress their gender identities for decades of their lives, those benefits come at an horrendous cost to transgendered people and an inordinate opportunity cost to society. Reasonable efforts to avoid those costs are not merely an opportunity for society, as the U.S. Constitution, Preamble says, "...to form a more perfect union..." (Kashner 2007, 499)[5] but they are an obligation to which the United States legally has bound itself.

To borrow from one of the most American of pastimes, this work's adding, however modestly, to a wider understanding of what it means to be a transgendered person would be comparable to getting a game-winning runner to home plate. The work's series-winning "homer" would be helping to bring about the earliest feasible and least traumatic transition for the greatest-possible number of present and future suppressing transgendered people

2. A Matter of Perception

Appearing Normal

Millions of Americans shared aspects of a boomer childhood similar to the ones I have described. They remember playing the board games, sharing similar outdoor experiences with friends, watching the television programs, experiencing scouting, were educated in a different era's public education system, etc. Most or all of those people will doubtlessly realize and should readily admit that none of these does, nor do they collectively, cause or prevent a person's being transgendered. As aware as I was of the similarities between other children and myself, the significance and power of my differences from them were at least as inescapable. The disturbing sensation of being an acutely interested but uninvolved spectator on a different perceptual plane is not sufficiently descriptive. Other children my age who were supposedly like me seemed to act and react much differently with their friends, family, and in daily life, but I did not understand why that should be so.

Everyone feels awkwardly out of place at times, but there is a substantial difference between an occasional sense of not belonging and an observable but unintended chronic and consistent pattern of divergent social interactions. The essence of that divergence is that the suppressing MtF child's comments and actions are filtered by her intent to preserve and perpetuate an image of a male self. Wholly spontaneous expression of open and sincere emotions, beliefs, and reactions would threaten that image. Openness and sincerity are fundamentally incompatible with hiding one's conflicting gender identity. Aspirations for a married life, her own children, and vocational fulfillment are but a few of the tantalizing gems strewn on open ground on the other side of an unbridgeable chasm. Those things seem attainable for the person an MtF child pretends and is perceived to be, but the essence of that chasm is an at least nagging inkling that she is unable to commit fully to being a man, husband, and father. Yet, at least partly because of her determined effort at suppression, the possibility of her becoming a wife and mother is almost unimaginable.

Commitment to a spousal relationship presents challenges that occasionally are overwhelming even for people who fervently desire to meet or exceed their spousal obligations and who are not transgendered. However spousal roles are defined by, or for, each generation, either set of roles constitutes unattainable goals for a suppressing MtF woman. If she marries before transition, personal, spousal, familial, and societal expectations must foster an unrelenting psychological torment for her. Her gender identity wars unrelentingly against the man she is trying to be for her spouse, her children, and others.

Other people in one's community, memorable characters in literature, reporters and those covered in their stories, formal education, religious training, and life-experience must have much to do with each person's determining what is, and what is not, appropriate behavior for oneself and others in a nearly infinite set of circumstances. Acquisition of an important component of that framework is virtually impossible for a suppressing MtF woman. She longs for the feminizing socialization of being recognized, accepted, and treated as female by all those around her but knows of no way to make or help that happen, nor of any way to rid herself of that longing.

I experienced, second-hand, some of the extremes of pain and pleasure my sisters endured as part of that socialization, but I was unable to share directly in its more mundane lessons. I would not have enjoyed the things they did not enjoy, but those experiences are part of the women they became, and they would have been so for me. So much of those experiences color the way we see others and ourselves either by forming and reinforcing a sense of identity or by exacerbating any irreconcilable differences.

Responding To Appearance

Long before the earliest humans realized they were doing so, they must have been seeing, and drawing conclusions about, other people and creatures approaching them. As sophistication of other mental faculties increased, human powers of observation and development of strategies to influence what others saw became an increasingly important part of human life. History did not record the circumstances surrounding use of the earliest equivalent of the Trojan horse, but human intent to influence the perception of others would date back, at least, to that time. There may be an innate component to human knowledge regarding attempts to appear threatening or non-threatening. Schoolyards across the country have moved generations of more contemporary children to learn whatever part of that skill was not innate. The art to interpreting "body language", as well as practicing its transmission is both an acknowledgment and a refinement of those early skills. At some level concern for outer appearance and attempts to communicate nonverbally must be indistinguishable in effect if not intent.

One can only imagine how long it would take to consciously catalog the things she or he observed, wanted to remember, and chose to ignore about each new acquaintance. For most people, a new acquaintance would be across the room meeting someone else by the time they located their notepad and pen. An almost endless list of physical characteristics, such as apparent gender and sex, attained age, and style of clothing would fill several pages of the pad. Less obvious details such as accent, mannerisms, clues about level and nature of acquired formal education, and apparent shared and differing interests would consume more pages. More notebooks would soon be needed to cover the person or people with the new acquaintance and, perhaps, many other strangers in the room. Each note taker would be too busy writing to notice many of the most obvious or important items about everyone else. The inefficiency of such a process contrasts sharply to the mix of innate and learned practices that glean key facts while missing occasional abstract data, such as names.

The physical setting for the encounter, the presence of others and their association with the observer, the meeting's purpose if there is one, and other clues help each person anticipate the new acquaintance's being a friend, an adversary, or competitor, but she or he will still do the assessment. Time constraints may add to the cursory nature of the appraisal. When so important but abstract a datum as a name is easily lost, less obvious data will certainly be missed in favor of more tangible realities such as relative stature, hair and eye color, apparent health, tone of voice and inflection, and whether the new acquaintance is armed and pointing a weapon. During that assessment, almost certain to be missed in someone determined to hide it, is that person's true gender identity.

The above spectrum illustrates briefly the analytical process of evaluating possible threats that pose a complicated set of choices for people who may not have sufficient time to consider them. Often welcomed as non-threatening are people whose appearance suggests the simple treasured dichotomous heterogendered model of a 1950's television family. Ironically, the fantasies of many MtF women were to live their lives as the wives, sisters, or daughters of that model. Those perceived as being more threatening are people who seem to be the antithesis to that model.

Much of the suspicion evoked, however unintentionally, by people outside the model is triggered by a preconceived belief that the threat from transgendered and/or homogendered people neither is physical nor readily apparent, but it is no less real. Extra-model people are thought to have deliberately chosen or inadvertently contracted an unacceptable pattern of thought and behavior that might be passed to other people. Further, the entire extra-model population is presumed to have an interest in promiscuous and frequent sexual activity that corrupts the body as it has corrupted the mind. The presumption persists despite the fact that peer-reviewed literature does not support it. That persistence is not explained by religion, bigotry, or other belief. The presumption persists because people choose to believe it.

To the extent that "responses" are related to preconceived belief and presumption, they may be triggered by an encounter but are not perceptions based on it. Given the power of such bias, a suppressing transgendered person is unlikely to be discovered and a transitioned transgendered person's honest indications of gender identity are apt to be rejected. The consuming complexity of the friend or foe analytical process means that important characteristics of the appearance and manner of a new acquaintance are almost certainly going to be missed.

Filling the Slots

There is a frustratingly persistent and all too human tendency to attempt to add a few precious moments to days that are too short by hastily deciding into which mental slots a new acquaintance must fit. Each carefully crafted extant container already is defined by its catalogue of previously determined characteristics. All of each slot's attributes will be ascribed to people to whom that container's label seems appropriate. The containers and the characteristics of their prospective inhabitants are formed from parental comments, expressed biases of other relatives and friends, the content of printed or viewed media, and/or her or his life experience.

Once formed, that mental vault of biases is likely to either facilitate or impair each person's relationships throughout her or his life. The facility comes from the enhanced ability to quickly familiarize oneself with and remember people one has just met. The impairment comes from not getting to know new acquaintances as the individuals they really are because a comment, mannerism, or element of appearance has triggered a slot assignment. Fortunately, some people have discovered that the panoply of humanity does not include a single person with whom they agree about everything. Whatever the differences, these people are loathe to consign anyone to a broader "them" slot because their "us" slot is so large, and application of its "us" label so encompassing.

Yet, even these people who are determined to resist the expedient of labeling are far from being immunized fully against its use. As soon as sufficient data has been gleaned to consign someone to a slot, the remaining time with them is filtered heavily to confirm the accuracy of the assignment. The rapidity with which the newly consigned person confirms and validates each of the elements in the container's set of characteristics is almost as breathtaking as it is subjective. The sometimes rapidly-fabricated, but always carefully maintained, slots are constructed of the most durable material our minds can manufacture. The slots' escape-resistant boundaries would be a worthy challenge to the world's most gifted escape artists because once consigned to a slot, few people escape and even fewer willingly are released.

The efficiency and durability of these biases suggests strongly that their use is as old as human consciousness. Human resistance to accepting as true each of two incompatible ideas means that whatever the newly consigned acquaintance actually says, the listener is unlikely to hear anything that conflicts with a slot's assigned characteristics. A slotted transgendered person's revelation of gender identity readily becomes the listener's additional evidence of a repugnant "choice". The slotting device seems so essential in helping each person make sense of, and function in, a world of conflicting priorities that its use is unbounded by inconvenient constraints such as race, creed, an/or age.

Seeing as a Child

One of the reasons my most unpleasant encounters since transition have been with those under age 18 must be the inordinate significance younger people so often ascribe to superficial appearance. If their close proximity to puberty has given them a heightened sensitivity to a prospective mate, they are quite likely to commence assigning slots on sight---even to the point of immediately announcing that assignment at the top of their voice to anyone within earshot. Children and teenagers must know that most people, including themselves, would like to change one or more obvious physical characteristic(s), but there is a maturity-shaded component to the intensity of that desire. Regardless of age, one might wish to be taller, shorter, thinner, have more hair, less hair, have hair where they do not have it, and not have it where they do, etc. Apart from their own desire for themselves to be different, however, young people often are stubbornly unwilling to acknowledge that, since they know they cannot easily change certain of their own physical characteristics, they must know other people are similarly constrained. If they would acknowledge such constraints for others, perhaps they see them as an infuriating reminder of their own limitations.

Clothing, body piercing, hair, and other teen fads not only represent an outward display of non-conformity to adult conventions but as a physical kinship with others of their own age. There is a confusing sense that many of them want to be different, but different in the same, or a similar, way. When some younger people dress in an unusual manner, they do so to show that they feel as though they are unusual. They experience a compulsion to honestly manifest a core self that is akin, but only remotely, to the suppressed desire pre-transition MtF women feel to reveal their gender identities.

When some younger people adopt the mode of attire they would ascribe to people with whom they disagree, they are attempting to show that they do not believe in identification by appearance, even though they have just done that very thing themselves. They would assert, by their attire, "I am dressing the way people dress when they are trying to make this point about appearance". Especially troubling is the fact that younger people, by definition, lack the years of life experience that greater maturity might give them about how misleading appearance-based judgments can be. Adults who judge solely or primarily by appearance cannot use their own attained age as a valid excuse, even though they may share a similar lack of life experience with people who are quite different from themselves.

When encountering a tall transgendered woman, appearance-obsessed young people might see her either as being tall in an intended slight to other tall women or as a reminder to shorter women that they are short, when the fact is she is "doing" neither. As a rudimentary understanding of basic science should have made blatantly obvious, she is "being tall" because her innate and unaltered biochemistry, aided by ample nutrition, made her that way. If they would assert that she is too tall to be a woman, they would have to accept the corollary that some men must be too short to be men. There are many men of smaller frames, shorter stature, with higher pitched voices, or larger breasts than some women have. Such men probably were teased when they were younger and still may not be at peace with themselves as adults. If their gender identities are masculine, however, they have no gender identity conflict. If their gender identities are feminine, most MtF women would consider them exceptionally, if not enviously, fortunate.

While sharing diminutive characteristics of physically smaller men might have eased my own transition, the essence of the process still is the resolution of conflict. The "Serenity Prayer" of disputed authorship and used in numerous contexts asks, "God give me the serenity to accept the things which cannot be changed; Give me courage to change that which must be changed; and the wisdom to distinguish one from the other" (Niebuhr 1950, 276).[6] While the prayer was never intended to apply specifically to transgendered people, it is apropos because it speaks to a common human need. Many people would prefer that the prayer's author had substituted "must improve" for "must change" since actions taken solely in pursuit of change could cause great harm. Praying for the courage to cause harm for the sake of change ill befits any acceptable concept of religion. The prayer also is a reminder to transitioning women to be judicious and restrained in their efforts at finally realizing their dream as fully as reasonably is possible.

The Importance of Being

A keen awareness of, and concern for, each person's own appearance may be as innate a human trait as is consciousness. Altering aspects of her physical self that are contrary to manifesting her identity is an important, but not the central, matter in an MtF woman's transition. I did not realize the whole of that truth before or during transition, but I began to learn the lesson after it. I do not mean to diminish the importance of any aspect of the electrolysis, hormone therapy, and surgery because, for most MtF women, those are an essential part of transition. Reconciling herself to attempting to convey true gender identity through, rather than being controlled by, her physical self, though, is the primary impetus to her resolving her conflict. The Harry Benjamin Standards of Care "real life" test required prior to surgery may be intended, at least partially, to awaken this realization. Despite my having tried to alter the covering of my body in childhood and adolescence by wearing my mother's or my older sister's clothes, I had always accepted my physical characteristics as being unalterably male. Only a much later realization of the primacy of gender identity over physiology freed me from that unacceptable limitation. The meaning and implications of that realization came more as a process than as a flash of insight.

During childhood and adolescence, I was at least as tall as most of my male classmates, and nothing else about my appearance suggested femininity. I had no desire to appear to be an effeminate male nor to appear to be female while being dressed and behaving "like a boy". I also had no desire to disclose what I thought were intolerably shameful but obsessive thoughts and desires to people who would not understand them any better than I did. I attempted to affect what I thought was an average male appearance of non-aggressive self-confidence. I did this, not primarily as part of an intentional masquerade, but because I knew no one else was aware of my perplexing obsession and because I saw no reasonable alternative.

Being "diminutively challenged" meant my larger physical stature was sufficient to discourage the senseless teasing many relatively smaller children experience from their classmates. I did receive the same messages as other children my age, however, in the informal but bluntly unmistakable language of youth that there were harshly adverse consequences for any "boy" who might appear to be different in a socially unacceptable manner. Scorn, taunting, and other physical and verbal abuse were waiting in unavoidable and unremitting abundance for anyone whose appearance or mannerisms were perceived to diverge excessively from certain generally accepted norms. Such abuse might have been gratifying if it replaced my guilt-ridden self-condemnation for the constantly reoccurring aberrant thoughts so inconsistent with my appearance. The appearance and mannerisms that would have invited that abuse, though, also would have meant my not appearing to be the good son, brother, and grandson that seemed so important to the parents, sisters, and grandmother who were a major part of my daily life.

While confronting physical threats with a physical response is less likely to be an effective, or at least painless, strategy for a physically smaller person, it was all but essential for those of relatively equal or greater stature to avoid incurring more threats. The playground pacifist of any size could expect taunting or worse. The typical schoolyard bully would not attempt to taunt a larger person if a smaller one, female or male, was nearby. Attitudinal and verbal responses learned through years of observation and interaction with other women and men prepare most females to function effectively but differently in society. The intimidation and vulnerability many women seem to feel as a result both of being encouraged to express themselves verbally rather than physically and their growing up among mostly male contemporaries much larger than they is a reality to which they can adjust by adopting and refining a variety of behaviors I never had reason to try to learn.

Departure for a planned vacation trip to the New Jersey Cape one summer had been delayed so that I might participate in a church choir concert. While driving across the Pennsylvania Turnpike I stopped at a rest area and waited in line for counter service. A much shorter gentleman in front of me told the order clerk that he thought he better place his order quickly because he would not want to antagonize me. I had not said anything to anyone nor had I been unusually anxious for service, and I was embarrassed by his comment. I told him and the clerk that they might be surprised to know of my participation in the previous day's church music program. The combined chorus had performed in a church whose air-conditioning was not working. The heat index in the choir loft must have been in the high nineties. He said something gracious about jumping to erroneous conclusions based on perceptions of appearance, but he also had provided an example of the reflexive and deftly disarming preemptive defensiveness often practiced by shorter people.

Those techniques, or at least having learned them the way other women do, are another component largely missing from my femininity. Such techniques may be a useful defensive weapon in the arsenal of possible responses for physical males of smaller stature, but I do not know if having learned the techniques differently for suppressing MtF women helps or hinders them during and after transition. Those who transition early enough would have the advantage of acquiring, by conscious effort or osmosis, this set of feminine skills when, and in the same manner as, other women do. During a more youthful transition, transgendered children would have more than ample opportunities to acquire a full set of physical, verbal, emotional, and other responses to other children and to adults who do not understand or accept their transitions. Although I would envy the overwhelming benefits inuring to those who transition earlier, I devoutly wish those transgendered people could be spared the need to develop and practice the patience, as they endure the lasting stress, of these confrontations. At any age, the experience of transition imparts a special sense of vulnerability and the self-discipline necessary to accommodate it.

Society's perpetuation of the concept of women's constructive vulnerability has been reinforced in overt, as well as subtle, ways. So much of women's "tall-sized" clothing is described as being appropriate to a height range of five-feet-seven-inches to five-feet-eleven inches. The inference is that women might be, in an extreme case, five feet eleven and ten-elevenths inches tall, but they never would be, or admit to having reached, the decidedly unfeminine height of six-feet. Perversely, the shorter woman's being perceived as physically vulnerable or unlikely to be a physical threat can be an asset because those she encounters may pay more attention to her intellect and personality. Where the perceived inability to be a threat means the smaller woman can be safely ignored however, the taller woman would have the advantage.

In each case, her selection of clothing, perhaps subconsciously, may be intended to influence the way she is perceived. The shorter woman does not wish to appear to be unusually short nor the taller woman unusually tall. In what could be construed by a paranoid statistician as a massive conspiracy against her or against the center of her profession, most women probably consider themselves to be shorter or taller than average. Each woman in the latter group well might see her greater stature as unintentionally, but no less embarrassingly, intimidating to others and as her least feminine feature.

I accept that my appearance never will be what I would have wished, but it is much more satisfying than I ever had thought possible. When wearing gender identity-appropriate clothing ("dressing") at home before beginning transition, the wigs, artificial nails, make-up, and clothing occasionally suggested an acceptably feminine appearance that I always found welcome. My height, weight, and physical structure, however, always made those welcome perceptions seem grossly inadequate to constitute an acceptable whole for others. Doubt about how others would perceive and react to me coupled with a general disappointment with various, and what I saw as nearly impossible-to-change physical attributes served as an additional impediment to, or a convenient excuse for, not even attempting to realize my "fantasy" of transition. If my appearance might be acceptable during or shortly after transition, the apprehension about how I might appear ten, twenty, and thirty years after transition was still another reason to postpone action. When I occasionally would express doubts about prospects for a successful transition to my psychiatrist, he would inquire whether postponement or inaction toward attaining my goal was possible, and I would reply that it was not. Repetition over time of such a verbal game of tag may be a useful technique for achieving certainty in a diagnosis.

The reservations I expressed were appropriate to my situation and might be a factor in any MtF woman's choices about how to transition, but they should have no bearing on the decision for it. Such questions only are about the adequacy of physical appearance; they are not about attempting to resolve gender identity conflict. While occasionally encountering pronoun problems over the telephone because of the sound of my voice, I never would have believed it possible that I could be so readily accepted by those around me. With the exception of a few children, and a few more teens, the hundreds or thousands of people who have seen me in stores, airports, churches, etc. have not responded negatively. The laughter, stares, fainting, or any of the other anticipated embarrassing reactions that I had so feared before transition, for the most part, have not occurred. Had they occurred frequently, they would have been a continual reminder of failure to be accepted as the person I am.

Concern that those I frequently encountered would accept my appearance as reflecting my identity is at least as important to me now as it is for anyone else. Appearance is more important to a post-transition MtF woman than to those motivated by vanity, though, because rejection of the "new" self can be felt as a rejection of her newly-disclosed essential identity. I feared not only that my appearance might fail to augment existing relationships, but that it could cause those relationships to end and would interfere with my establishing new ones. Ironically, desired post-transition relationships are much more real and valuable to an MtF woman than those established through her previous and fraudulent male persona because she wholly is the person who engages in them.

A few friends I have known for many years still apparently have irreconcilable problems with my appearance and/or transition, but these friends have not become unfriendly. They can serve as a reminder of the occasional need each person has for moderate, but not consuming or destructive, introspection. However well-adjusted a paroled prisoner might be, her or his visits with a probation officer must feel much like encounters with these friends, although I feel no guilt for having acted to finally resolve my conflict. Honest disagreement about the very existence of gender identity, and hence of gender identity conflict, means rejecting the current standards of care for treating that conflict. These people are adamantly opposed to participating in, or even acknowledging, what they see as a new fraud resulting from transition. They assert that, because each person usually is born with only one apparent physical sex, that natal sex must also be the person's gender. For these deniers, there is no such thing as gender identity, and the so-called "transgendered" person is simply failing to accept her or his correct gender from shear perversity, a yearning for attention, a means of escape, or some other grossly inadequate excuse.

This view probably constitutes as fundamental a disagreement as anyone can have regarding transgendered people and their self-knowledge. The assertion is not an argument primarily based on perceptions of height, voice, carriage, or other matters of physical appearance, but it simply is their effort to call the essence of a tall plant with limbs and leaves a tree. Indeed, each tree may have a sex, but it does not have a mind, a soul, nor a gender identity. The object is called a tree because the essence it communicates to humans, as well as any tree can project its essence, is received by humans as being a tree. It is not reasonable that deniers react so much differently and less graciously to transgendered people. Transgendered people who no longer are suppressing their gender identities are attempting to reveal and convey their own essential selves. They should be treated with at least as much respect as that afforded a plant.

The possibility of my appearance and essence being considered attractive by a heterogendered male to whom I might be attracted remains theoretical. It is difficult to imagine how a man I would find attractive could see me as his ideal woman and a prospective spouse. I understand, though, that many other women have had a similar reservation and have been persuaded by a man whom they believe that it has happened. Not only have other MtF women satisfied themselves that one such male exists however, but they are certain, perhaps with good reason, that there actually are many such men. One might wonder whether each of these women has reached her conclusion through having established an honest relationship with these men, or if she merely has presented a new gender identity-based, but false, image to them. She may aspire to an honest and lasting relationship with one man but present an appearance that only encourages brief infatuations. Such MtF women must know, at least at some level, the extent of their limited candor or practiced deceit. Again, this has been beyond my own experience.

If there is a biophysical reproductive component to mutual attraction, it is likely that it would be most active during the years when humans likely to produce their own children. Other components must be involved in mutual attraction, or couples beyond the average childbearing years would not marry. Whatever the components of attraction, the fact that most people through history have been monogamous strongly suggests that at least one of the genes involved in mutual attraction is coded for longevity. The trait apparently is not uniquely human since some pairs of animals do mate for life.

An old saw of questionable rationale asserts that couples even grow to resemble each other as they age. The couples themselves probably would disagree. The observation may well have originated with younger people who did not find people older than themselves to be sexually attractive or who saw all older people as looking very much alike. Couples who have been married for fifty years and more often profess that they love each other at least as much as they did when they were first married although, perhaps, differently and more deeply. It is unlikely that they would say that about someone whom they did not find attractive.

Appearance reasonably cannot be a lasting substitute for common interests, perspectives, and ambitions. The romantic importance of appearance must be that, if it is sufficiently attractive to another person, that other person would risk the possibility of embarrassment and the disappointment of rejection in an attempt to become part of a relationship. Dr. John Money's hypothesis regarding "lovemaps" puts this more strongly. He suggested that when any person finds someone who closely approximates her or his firmly established ideal prospective spouse, and that sentiment is reciprocated, there is little that would keep them apart (Money 1970, xv).[7] Alarmingly, this mutual perception-driven infatuation has nothing to do with either person's essential identity. The attraction, whether wholly dependent upon physical appearance or a deeper perception of appealing values, personality, intellect, voice, mannerisms, and a host of other attributes, is a grossly inadequate basis for a lengthy relationship. The image comparison for these unfortunate couples does not depend on shared or valued non-physical attributes. Where the relationship is based only on image, the relationship would be harshly and adversely impacted by dramatic changes in appearance and the prospective mate's virtually inevitable meeting someone who shares real desired attributes. However important an attractive physical, intellectual, emotional, or any other attribute(s) might be to the establishment of intimate relationships, appearing to be of the appropriate gender and having the requisite gender identity must be high on the shortest list.

The Substance of Appearance

A mapping that compared a prospective ideal mate's richly detailed gender identity as a substitute for appearance or other mapped tangible characteristics could be as valid an hypothesis. If a woman perceived that a prospective mate did fit her gender-mate map, whether innate or developed from reason and experience, of how her ideal husband would think, feel, act, and appear, she might desire a relationship with him. This variant on Dr. Money's "love map" hypothesis might explain why some MtF heterogendered women have been able to marry women to whom they were, at least initially, attracted, and who reciprocated. The pairing would occur without regard for obviously incongruent physical attributes and the MtF woman's suppressed awareness that each of their gender identities was female.

In a perverse twist on mapping and gender identity, a suppressing MtF woman might be attracted, perhaps subconsciously, to a woman she sees as being like her fantasized version of the self she is suppressing. She would be trying in effect to embrace through marriage a separate embodiment of her own gender identity. This cannot be narcissism because she has never known the whole of her identity or, figuratively, seen the whole of her entrancing reflection.

She would continue to affect her male persona while being almost constantly reminded of the suppressed gender identity her wife represents. Perhaps long after beginning her marriage with that woman, she would admit fully and finally to herself what she had done, even as she found continuation of the farce no longer tenable. Never having been part of such a relationship, I can barely imagine how difficult such knowledge without-acknowledgment might be, but I can readily imagine the nature of the moment of her disclosure.

The realization might be gradual and even mutual, but the impact on the lives of each member of the "wife's," the "husband's", and each woman's biological family would be horrendous, especially if a young child is, or children are, involved. Whatever the apparent initial reaction of a young child to that event, the entirety of her or his young life had been built on the confident perception of a firm foundation of constancy and dependability afforded by two caring but quite different parents. Disclosing to the child that the foundation is and always was far different from the perception risks the future capacity of that child ever to trust again those closest to her or him. Even as a substitute or modified replacement is offered, saying in essence "I still love you, but I am not who you thought I was," must be nearly as traumatic for that child as the loss of a parent. That altered relationship even is difficult for most adults to understand.

Telling the child that she or he must ultimately be self-reliant could not ameliorate, but would aggravate, the blow's harshness. Children are acutely aware of their lack of the physical and intellectual capabilities necessary to cope with a sometimes harsh and hostile world. The buffer that parents normally represent suddenly would become the source of the child's emotional pain and uncertainty. The very mechanism usually relied upon by children for coping with unpleasant realities would be altered at the precise moment they most feel the greatest need for it. The disclosure would mean that the structure formerly relied upon had been unintentionally false and that now even the false structure might change dramatically. The potential of being responsible for such emotional trauma might have helped prevent my becoming involved in a serious relationship with another woman, although I never consciously made that choice. I do not know why the same potential did not prevent other transgendered people from permitting themselves to become so involved.

It would be a gross mischaracterization to construe this argument as meaning that transgendered people are incapable of being superb parents. Indeed, courts have determined in some cases that post-transition transgendered people are better prepared than their former spouses to care for their children.

There is nothing about any phase of the transgendered condition that would impair its victims' ability and capacity to love their children. The irony, however, is that while the condition is least discernable to others, it has the greatest potential to cause emotional harm. Non-transgendered people occasionally inflict emotional harm on those closest to them and can fail to be the people others expect them to be. The difference, though, is the specific capacity conferred by the fraudulent personas of suppressing transgendered people that is common only among that population.

Since I was not interested in a romantic relationship with a male and would not risk discovery of my fraudulent male persona by a female before transition, I avoided potentially "serious" relationships. As cold as that seems on paper and was in fact, it was habitual before transition. Yet, like a psychic paper-cut that does not heal, the absence of romantic involvement in a world of other people having such relationships can be very much a painful part of the suppressing transgendered person's experience. Incomplete understanding of her conflict can still provide sufficient self-knowledge for the suppressing MtF woman to realize that such emotional isolation is necessary until the conflict is resolved.

An earlier transition might well afford opportunities for MtF women to meet men on a romantic level and to compare experiences with other women regarding a healthy conventional heterogendered pairing. I can never know how much different would have been those irretrievable years spent before transition. The youthful interactions I would have had with other students and young adults if I had both appeared to be, and was perceived as being, female could not happen. As wonderful as renewal of past acquaintances can be after transition, those experiences cannot replace memories of a shared past that were never formed. Speculation regarding what might have been could be as limitless as it is unproductive, except for the insight such introspection provides regarding possible future encounters. Since I had a physical appearance opposite to my gender identity, all my interactions with both females and males were predicated on my seeming to be the male persona I affected. Resulting relationships were formed, and others failed to form, at least partially due to my failing to act as others might have expected and an unsettled set of my own expectations regarding their actions and reactions.

Transgendered people who accept their gender identities at an early age and decide they must express them have only to contend with disclosing their conflict and seeking a means to its resolution. They probably do not consider themselves fortunate, but their earlier efforts at revelation and transition are the envy of most, or all, of those who transition at a later age. An earlier transition still means enduring the difficult struggle with "who, when, and how" questions of revelation, counseling, and the means of transition. The merciless taunting of clueless contemporaries, and even of some physical adults with immature perception and/or intellect, might be more traumatic for younger people who have not had time to develop the emotional and rational maturity that would help minimize the damage from such assaults.

The transition of younger transgendered people shares important similarities with those who transition later, and their success is a real concern. Their experience, however, was very different from mine. Of even greater concern, though, are those transgendered people, and especially MtF women, now alive and others yet to be born who are attempting, or will attempt, to hide their true identities. It is not only possible, but likely, that those who transition later will do so as a result of greater understanding that precludes the continuation of the fraud they previously were able to abide.

To continue to suppress their conflict, those who transition later must construct a bearable compartmentalization that sequesters episodic manifestations of their gender identities. Their temporary realizations of gender identity are usually, if not exclusively, expressed only under the most guarded of conditions. For most or all suppressing MtF women, the makeup and "dressing" are a staging of reality for themselves alone as both actor and audience.

The best actresses and actors convince their audiences that they really are the characters they portray for the length of time they are on stage or in front of a camera. A script is provided that tells the performer who the character is, what will be said, reveals the course of interactions, and suggests why the characters are doing what they are doing. A suppressing MtF woman however does not have an offstage time with other people until she is finally willing, or feels compelled, to disclose her identity. The harm of that deceit to herself, her friends, relatives, co-workers, and others is not just the false nature of the relationships that are formed, but at least as significantly, the real relationships that are not. There can be a wonderful opportunity for growth for everyone involved in the disclosure of transition, but that comes at the expense of a lengthy deceit and the honest relationships that would have been established earlier. Every MtF woman has physical attributes that will either facilitate or impede her transition. A set of less-masculine features may help others begin their transition sooner and may bear on other aspects of transition, but I can imagine no feature, or set of features, sufficient to counter the realization that one's gender identity conflict must end.

Experience is a most convincing teacher of the fact that outward appearance and perceived expression often are misleading. An MtF suppressing woman's fraudulent identity is always misleading until she begins transition. Beginning, during, and after transition, her appearance means much more to her than a mere covering. Her hypersensitivity to her appearance and to the reaction to it of everyone she encounters is part of her new striving to be perceived as the woman she is and to her finally rejecting the conflict that occupied for so long a huge part of her life. She dresses as she does during and after transition to reveal, rather than conceal, an appearance she finds appropriate to her true self.

When anyone refuses to accept the female self an MtF woman presents, whatever else of her they would accept is, at best, incomplete and, at worst, the remnants of a sham. Anyone clinging to a remembered familiarity with the affected persona previously presented is attempting to hold on to something that never was real and that exists only in memory. Expecting an MtF woman to continue to live a life that she knows is false is something like asking an actress to live her life as one of her characters. Before transition, whatever part of myself was real still is the essence of who I am now; but I no longer am willing to hide or disguise the remainder.

The importance of one's sense-of-self has not been overstated, but that does not mean the rejection of an MtF woman's appearance, even by someone she knows and respects, necessarily is crushing for her. Decades spent living as a female in fantasies, daydreams, as conscious thoughts in otherwise idle moments, and in very private "dressing" episodes are a most convincing means of discovering that however intensely an MtF woman pursues her aspirations, she rarely will experience a sense of fulfillment. Doubtlessly, every parent can recall an instance of heartbreaking awareness when her or his child was rejected by other children. Those children did not accept and appreciate the special gifts of her or his child, or found those gifts to be inadequate. Christians will recall a profound "Holy Week" rejection showing Christ's inability or unwillingness to be what others would have had Him be. Resolution of gender identity conflict on a much smaller scale can be a powerful contributor to the self-confidence necessary to the weathering of such rejection.

Each person's honest assessment of self should be neither overly generous nor excessively harsh. The assessment reasonably would include an inventory of interests, abilities, character traits, and habits. It should include a special focus on things that, with motivation and effort, might be changed if that change is desirable, but the assessment also would examine the essential self that is unlikely or even impossible to change. The vast majority of non-transgendered people would say they completed such an exercise repeatedly while in their teens and, at a later age, would consider such introspection to be a poor use of precious time and unlikely to result in any substantive improvement. A far smaller number might realize that the effort never had been made with honesty, intensity, and understanding.

As people attempt to establish, or revise, and pursue goals that demand the most of their talents, abilities, and opportunities, they may have attained, or be near attaining, some intended accomplishment without ever having decided whether they can abide the whole and parts of the life they chose. Without advocating, in the slightest, any form of narcissism, I submit that an opposite stasis of attempting to avoid or suppress one's essential self is at least as unhealthful. A person who does not like herself or himself must find it nearly impossible to speak, act, and exist with appropriate confidence.

The Image in the Mirror

There is an intimate link between the person one honestly intends to present to other people and the person she or he is perceived as being over time. Feigned self-assurance, for example, eventually would fail even to convince its perpetrator, and the insecure person would be seen as insecure. After transition, MtF women want to appear as the whole, honest, and confident women they always have longed to be. That desire may conflict with their pressing need to present a satisfying feminine appearance. To avoid acquiring a new obsession, and one of their own choosing, they reasonably would pursue moderation regarding their appearance. Having ended the long charade of presenting their male personas, most, if not all, MtF women would eschew garish, forced, or contrived alternatives. The perceptions, fantasies, and aspirations of a lifetime before transition reliably can guide them during and after transition.

For decades, I secretly wore a wide variety of clothing and makeup that I thought never would be seen by anyone who knew me. I constantly sought to find acceptable manifestations of my gender identity without realizing that recognition was its real purpose. During her countless episodes of temporary release, the suppressing MtF woman finds mirrors an essential tool. Her reflection approximates the real gender identity that she knows intimately but does not fully comprehend. The experience might be compared to an expectant mother's seeing a sonogram. When I would find a satisfying reflected image, that image always resonated with my fundamental self. The "dressing" experience never had anything to do with attempting to look like anyone else, or even like a dreamed of, or fantasized, self. Each episode was an attempt to discover and reveal my most attractive and feminine self which almost seemed to live on the other side of the mirror.

This matter is so much more than an exercise in semantics. Despite perceptions of others and sublime self-delusion, the suppressing transgendered person cannot become the person projected as her or his conflicting persona. People with severe physical deformities do not develop grossly distorted personalities to match their appearance. Those disfigured by terrible accidents may alter their attitudes and temperament, but they do not become fundamentally different people. Like transgendered people, their difficulty is especially harsh when they cannot appear to others as the selves they know themselves to be. Whether others accept you as who you are is not really a negotiation; their acceptance, rejection, or mid-level attitude certainly affects how you feel about them.

Until I finally sought professional help, I did not understand that my "dressing" episodes were desperate attempts freely to present my true appearance. The most satisfying attempts always were bittersweet because the transformations were temporary and incomplete. Such "dressing" episodes were something like what happens when a vibrating tuning fork touches a firm surface and produces its audible tone. There was an intense feeling of wanting to be the person I saw in the mirror, or of seeing the person I could or should be, but that reflection was not the persona I had accepted. Because the image seemed more fantasy than reality, it would not be limited by the possible. I could have imagined the mirror's image as that of almost anyone, and especially a successful, younger, and happily married mother of two or more children. The image, though, was sufficiently grounded in reality that I did not ascribe names, faces, or characteristics to any possible relationships. For the same reason, I would not construct and dwell on scenarios based on what my life might have been if I had always been, and been seen as being, either fully female or male. Again, these potentially realizable fantasies almost certainly were an attempt by my suppressed self to obtain its final release.

Each of my "dressing" episodes was a vicarious trip that assumed a complete post-transition self living a full and "normal" life after transition; but I was certain such a transition and a post-transition life never could happen.

None of my pre-transition imaginings ever seemed close to being attainable, but that was not particularly disquieting because an implausibility built on an impossibility meant that my puzzle had no real solution. This erroneous conclusion always seemed so obvious and familiar that continually revisiting the puzzle was almost maddening, yet the visits kept proving to be unavoidable.

Accounts of some suicides describe an apparent intent to go beyond the fact of the perpetrator/victim's having decided to end her or his life, because she or he chose to inflict as much damage as possible to some part or all of the body. From a sense of bitter disappointment and rage, the person apparently acted to end her or his struggle against a perceived, persistent, and seemingly irremediable failure of a physical self to achieve one or more desired goals. The facts that other people face as great or greater physical challenges and that even the most challenged person is an amazingly complex possessor of the gift of life are lost for such people. They also lack sufficient regard for their surviving family and friends since introspection and overwhelming despair leave room for nothing else.

This kind of frustration and anger readily applies to those who experience gender identity conflict when they might resolve to smash the tangible matter that has been home to their seemingly inescapable and irresolvable obsession. A lesser motivation to suicide is anxiety regarding appearance and the prospective inability to interact with a variety of other people, especially those most important to them, during, shortly after, and long after transition. However much one might wish to inflict harm upon that part of herself that has perpetrated or perpetuated, as well as endured such conflict; suicide also would harm, for the remainder of their lives, those about whom she most cares, and those who care about her. Surely that must be considered as an unacceptable level of "collateral damage". Even as a selfish, excessively simple, and faith-devoid solution to obsession and anxiety, suicide seemed a more attractive option when I realized I no longer could avoid transition. Instead of death as an alternative to contending with continued suppression, it had become a possible alternative to transition.

Anxiety regarding the inadequacy of my feminine appearance was an important, but certainly not the most important, element in the set of concerns triggered by my deciding that I had to begin transition. Coping with transition's anxiety may have been as acute a problem as the obsession had been chronic. Neither state was healthful but each was unavoidable. As long as the incessantly recurring obsession continued to follow its well-established course, there was no apparent reason to believe it would get worse. The cost of the forgone deeper and richer life a whole person seeks in a full spousal relationship, or the cost of not even entering a relationship that might lead to marriage, was bearable at least partly because I was giving up something I never directly had experienced. When the course relatively few people have trod reached its unanticipated and climactic barrier in my journey, the choice was either to accept the journey's end or to eliminate the obstruction.

Whether the manner in which the expression and suppression cycle, then crisis, revelation, and transition is experienced by all transgendered people remains unknown. A younger transgendered person who never tries to hide the conflict may skip the intervening phases and pursue transition with familial and/or professional support. Formal education, character, family, and other influences must affect each of the condition's phases that are experienced. The direction and power of each of those influences must vary, especially with respect to attained age at transition. How each of these is the same or different for MtF women and FtM men is another question more easily asked than answered. Research to begin to answer accurately these questions and more has been increasing at an increasing rate, but there are still many more questions than definitive answers.

Since I was not the first person to have contended with gender identity conflict, I had resources and procedures available to me that made my transition less difficult. None of those things happened by themselves. The gender identities of each of the people involved in making them available colored those resources and procedures, as did the providers of them. Similarly, the gender identity and personality of each transitioning transgendered person makes unique her or his own experience with some part of each element. MtF transgendered people desperately seek full participation in their society, but they must do so as the women they are. The gender identity component of each person's essential self colors every one of her or his actions and interactions. Gender identity's significance, as a critical component of identity, is at least as great as any other aspect of any person's being human.

3. A Manner of Being

Gender and Society

Gender identity is much more than a matter of which restroom a person would use in a public setting. The Federal Aid to Education Act, Title Nine amendment is an attempt to eliminate adverse gender and sex bias in education. First enacted in 1972, that effort has helped to produce dramatic increases in the participation of women in all phases of education. This important extension of governmental protection has meant that no person may be denied educational opportunity simply because she or he appears to be female. The current iteration of protection centers on dispositive natal physical sex or true gender identity.

Those correctly using the French, Spanish, and other languages will recognize gender differences in objects such as tables and doors that may not be apparent to anyone else. An American-English exception is use of the terms "female" and "male" by plumbers and electricians to describe materials used in their work. Foreign or not, these and many other instances are attempts by elements of society to acknowledge fundamental differences between females and males in an acutely sex-conscious world. Even the most obvious of physical sexual and gender references is also a tacit recognition of differences in gender identity, or the physical differences would have no deeper meaning. Since gender differences refer to actions as well as apparent thoughts, they have been seen intuitively as showing that the minds of females and males do function differently and often produce demonstrably, if subtly, different results. More recently, real differences have been, and continue to be, substantiated by functional magnetic resonance imaging (fMRIs).

The Equal Rights Amendment to the U.S. Constitution has nearly the number of votes needed for ratification. Without regard for all of its unknowable consequences, amendment proponents seek to require that demonstrated differences associated with sex (and presumably gender) must be ignored in matters of law. As appears to be its purpose, the effort would obtain by court interpretation the overturning of *stare decisis*, common, and enacted law that justly reflected the will of the majority. That would be anathema to supporters of the country's founding principle of representative government. It would be comparable to Afghanistan and Iran under their constitutionally empowered mullahs.

Difference in physical sex would be treated like racial differences as a proscribed reason for discrimination. Faith in the basic principle of equal justice is compelling where that is the only salient matter at hand. That principle is abused, however, if it is used to demand treating as equal two parties who are fundamentally equal-but-differently regarding a central matter at issue. Without extensive consideration of the ways in which preponderant gender identity implications of sexual differences are unlike any other differences, legislatures of the majority, but not the requisite supermajority for adoption, of states already have voted for ratification. Since the unratified amendment specifically refers to equality based on sex, its failure to address gender identity is a serious deficiency. Acceptance of the amendment's text so long ago may explain but not excuse that deficiency.

The real possibility that gender identity and/or sex differences might need to be recognized and protected in law must be a significant part of the resistance to ratification. Perceived adequacy of extant civil rights protections and reluctance to afford the courts endless opportunities to interpret the amendment would account for much of the rest. Interpretation of the amendment could make a wide variety of common practices illegal and require a rewriting of state and sub-state laws and policies to remove all references to gender and sex. The U.S. Supreme Court seems to have decided that the U.S. Constitution does not permit an opposite-sex requirement for legal marriage. While such potential changes are lauded with justification in some circles, it is irresponsible to ignore possible adverse and even chaotic consequences of these actions.

Nothing in this work is intended to suggest that women or men are inherently less virtuous. Perhaps, in an attempt to understand the unpleasant experiences they have had, some MtF and other women have made disparaging remarks about their perception of a common lecherous tendency among all males. They have asserted that, if men are not engaged in sexual intercourse, they are thinking about it. This absurd characterization should be as unacceptable in public discourse as the suggestion that some women have that same tendency. One of the most absurd things about the assertion regarding men is that, based solely on the characteristic of apparent gender, it implies that hundreds of millions of people are incessantly self-centered and concerned only with their own transient "happiness" to the exclusion of all other thought. If this characterization were valid, there would be no rationale for the entertainment, cosmetics, and clothing industries' attention to provocative attire and manner.

An MtF or other woman frequently will notice and often comment on attractive aspects of manner or appearance exhibited by another woman to a third party and, almost as often, directly to the woman observed. There usually is nothing gratuitous about the proffered comment. The act of sharing the compliment seems at least as important as the observed feature for any or all of several possible reasons. Women may be seeking to assure themselves and others that they are dedicated to a life of nurturing and caring. By exercising this behavior and evidently enjoying it, women foster the same behavior in others. A feeling of strength and confidence in their own lives forms a figurative reservoir from which women can impart the same feelings to others. In attempting to reassure others, they pass along a lesson other women have shared with them; most women thrive in and desire an expansion of an ever stronger, more confidently secure society. The ones who do not must prefer a foreign ideology.

I would not suggest by the above that women are incapable of envy, ambition, avarice, or other less generous and more selfish forms of behavior; but women may have adopted a general tendency toward mutual support as a more effective strategy for survival, especially when their male counterparts occasionally have exhibited a prodigious capacity for aggression and competition. Western society has careened at what seems an increasing rate from women's suffrage and basic property rights to an inexorable collision with an unknowable future contingent upon expanded gender neutrality in custom and law. By doing so, society seeks to continue along an evolutionary path where it has acknowledged the existence of substantial gender identity differences but has been unable to determine how to accommodate them. In some respects, the results of its determinations may be counter-evolutionary.

As someone who ardently would attest to the power of a suppressed gender identity, I share the concern of those who question the wisdom of failing to accommodate appropriately so fundamental a part of humanity in law. Society's prudent legal protections will not, however, be based merely on customs or perceptions advocated by self-appointed or widely heralded holders of "the truth". Society should indeed reject distinctions in this area that are not justified by real differences in gender identity, but it should preserve and strengthen those provisions that protect all gender differences essential to each person's being the person she or he really is.

No one could possess an incontrovertible and all-inclusive list of such differences and the necessary text for enactment of their protections. Any effort to begin that process, though, appropriately would begin with fundamental identity. To anyone who has spent decades suppressing her gender identity, it is patently absurd to suggest that essential identity begins with anything other than gender identity. A woman or man, regardless of age, might precede by any number of adjectives a personal description of her or his essential self, but identifying oneself as a person without any concern for or sense of gender identity is a lie of omission, whether that person intends self-deception or to deceive others. However subtle or overt the implications for each person's own actions and interactions with other people, concepts, and things; each person's sense of identity will either manifest itself or war within herself or himself as long as she or he suppresses it.

The arbitrary nature of accommodating gender identity differences would seem to place the matter squarely and suitably in the legislative arena, bounded by an extant and powerful judiciary dedicated to protecting the constitutional rights of all people within its jurisdiction. Each person might well favor protection of her or his set of differences, and a few sets would be similar or even identical. The political system in America is ordered in a manner favoring majority-held views, not because those views are necessarily the most virtuous and inclusive, but because the majority must live under the same rules and suffer for themselves and their descendants the adverse consequences of their decisions as well as any burden of rejected but superior alternatives.

Of possibly greater concern than any person's or group's concept of the nature and extent of acknowledged differences are those people who would advocate excluding all legal accommodations regarding gender identity at one extreme, and those who would draw strictures and protections based on belief rather than knowledge at another. Though the matter might never be resolved with finality, later-transitioning MtF women readily would attest to the substantial harm done when core elements of gender identity and its expression are suppressed. This is as important a matter for women who are nurturing their own families and/or others as it is for men concerned about their own families, the society in which they live, and their society's future.

For some women, an instinct to nurture may be so ingrained that they will assume all women possess it, and they may be correct. These women seem to expect other women to share their willingness, need, and determination to share. Two members of a women's church or social group might well have the following conversation:

> Sally: "Alice, we are having the youth group
>
> over Saturday and we'd really like for you to
>
> help us by baking four- dozen cookies."
>
> Alice: "Gee, I have a recipe I would love to use,
>
> but it only makes three dozen. Maybe I could
>
> double it."
>
> Sally: "That'll be wonderful, Alice. I'm sure the
>
> kids really will enjoy them."

Two men with a similar purpose might have the following conversation:

 (Jack and Bill are collecting the equipment used after coaching the youth group's softball practice:)

> Jack: "You know, Bill, Sally and I are having the
>
> kids group Saturday and we'd really appreciate
>
> some help with snacks. Do you think you could
>
> help us out?"
>
> Bill: "A sign in the window of the new bakery
>
> over on tenth says they have a good deal on
>
> cookies.
>
> If you buy three dozen the fourth is free this
>
> week.
>
> Lend me twenty bucks and I'll see what they've
>
> got."
>
> Jack: (handing Bill twenty dollars) "This was
>
> not exactly what I had in mind, Bill. I hope you
>
> remember where that twenty came from."
>
> Jack: (to himself) "(At least Bill will be picking

up the cookies.

Every time Sally goes near that place it usually

costs a lot more than twenty bucks.)"

(later, at Bill's home.)

Bill: (to his wife) "Hey Alice, how about

making four dozen cookies for that kids thing at

the Stewart's on Saturday?"

Alice: "Certainly, dear. I was going to call Sally

to see if she wanted some help. I've got Mom's

recipe for oatmeal

fudge cookies and a new one for chocolate-

covered pecan and cherry nougat that I've been

wanting to try."

Bill: (to himself) "('Looks like I just made

twenty bucks, yay!

And what the devil is pecan nougat?')"

Before transition, I frequently encountered examples of a quite different kind of "nurturing" behavior among men, and it occasionally was directed at me. It usually would include a male who was trying but failing to do something or he was not doing it in the precise manner another male thought he should. If the assertive male intended to display leadership or dominance, his position was either validated or rejected depending on the reaction of the other male. Such exhibitions easily could be seen as ambition or competitive instinct masquerading as nurturing behavior. Women often exhibit the same assertive instinct by a gushing display of undesired and inappropriate assistance or effusive concern. Whether this behavior by women stems from a yearning to feel needed or from genuine concern, it may be as unwelcome as their male counterpart's instruction but more warmly received and regarded. Such dichotomous observations of apparent gender differences are not original. Having lived in each camp though, I believe their accuracy has seen frequent confirmation.

The disgusting habit some men have of spitting as though they were animals marking their territory especially, but by no means solely, when they are engaged in athletic competition, may be nothing more than a non-verbal expression of a similar kind of assertiveness or competition. Finding that kind of assertive behavior among women would be as salutary as instances of female animals mounting males. Depending on where the spitting occurred, "non-politically correct" women present would be apt to see which of them was fastest in getting to the gloves, paper towels, and disinfectant. They would not do so necessarily from a need for competition but from a general concern for health and sanitation.

From such motives, women and men have performed innumerable nurturing acts of selfless generosity throughout history including material sacrifice, organ donation, and even laying down their lives. The number of acts, their moral weight, and their economic value may be roughly equal among women and men, but the two often perform different acts and perform the same ones differently. I firmly believe that men are as much committed to the nurturing of their own families, other people, and society as are women but they are, in innate, learned, and/or in a mixed set of ways, generally inclined to express that commitment quite differently.

Some people who should know better will argue that, because male nurturing behavior is provided in a manner different from traditional feminine behavior, commitment by men either does not exist or has negligible value. The sacrifices women make for their families and others are denigrated by those who resent the injustice implicit in society's perceived demand that their sacrifices are a duty while those of men are a choice. Others suggest that women make such sacrifices because they cannot be, or are unwilling to be, independent. It is ironic that those making such arguments may do so from the same nurturing instinct that moves the people they criticize. Where the commitment to nurture is part of the nature of women and men, suppressing it or disparaging it is inviting chaos. It is arguing that people must be singularly self-centered and must define their focus narrowly. Rejecting the instinct to nurture is contrary to the whole history of pivotal and essential bonds of humanity. It is, in essence, inhuman.

The sacrifices men make to provide emotional, financial, and other support for their families and others are real, but gender critics argue that only because men are making those sacrifices, they must be acting as a matter of choice. This circular logic is like saying that the reason something is true is that it is true. Why the same kind of social pressures are deemed coercive to women but not so to men is puzzling. If the point were merely part of a causal dinner conversation, it easily could be dismissed. Anecdotal indications and some academic work regarding an increasing ratio of female to male college enrollments and a higher average age for marriage, however, suggest greater cause for concern.

If more men are forsaking academic life in favor of vocational educations at the potential cost of lower lifetime earnings and, more pertinently, eschewing marriage for an uncommitted emotional state, some would laud that freedom and independence. That absence of commitment though, if it becomes the predominant choice in a community, comes at the high cost of a new and arguably inferior social order that would deny the monogamous nature of humanity. A community bereft of enduring spousal relationships built on mutual support and shared experiences cannot be stable and strong. By definition, the choice for independence made by young adults precludes early marriage and parenting. In retrospect, each such adult well may become keenly, bitterly, and remorsefully aware of the priceless worth of the irreplaceable relationship she or he has forfeited.

Forsaking early traditional relationships strikes a familiar chord with suppressing and post-suppression transgendered people. Ruing unfulfilled and incomplete lives is the bane of gender identity suppression. That lack of fulfillment cannot easily be forgotten and miraculously attained when suppression ends. The suppressing MtF woman's twist on maiden aunts and "old maids" is that she was not afforded the opportunity to experience the potential relationships other women see through the normal course of their lives. Except for hypotheses suggesting an infinite number of concurrent realities with respect to time and choice, few people can be certain what would have followed had they made different choices. Even the certainty of those few must fade over time. For most MtF women the need to exercise their nurturing natures as biological mothers goes unfulfilled.

Whether MtF women or FtM men have a separate set or sets of innate inclinations regarding their relationships with others is another of the myriad things about populations of transgendered people that warrant further study. If inclinations regarding nurturing are innate for non-transgendered people, the utility of such studies could be increased by reversing their focus. A person's innate attitude toward aspects of nurturing may help determine whether she or he is transgendered. I have not attempted to separate my own inclinations, interests, and behaviors into those that are innately feminine and those that comprise a rearing-induced masculine set. Decades of having been perceived as a man have made reaching for gender identity-specific innate sensations and inclinations in some areas like trying to see first-generation galaxies through a pair of seven-power binoculars. The objects are or were present, but they are not easily characterized even by the wonder of the James Webb Telescope.

As a post-op transgendered person, if I find something interesting, humorous, irritating, inspirational, etc., I do not first consider whether my reaction is gender identity-appropriate or expected by others before reacting. Prior to transition though, I habitually was careful not to show reactions or emotions that might jeopardize acceptance of my male persona. My genuine emotional responses are the same now as before, but I am far less reserved about showing them. I never had a sense that I was other than one person, so I believe my sentiments were and are as feminine as my gender identity demands and permits. My singing voice never will be sufficiently feminine but when singing, my focus is on the words and music, the action of singing, and whether I am doing it correctly, rather than whether the sound is excessively or decidedly masculine. If the music and words elicit thoughts and emotion, as good music does, that content will be as naturally evident in my singing as if the words were spoken. A hymn I have sung as part of quartets both pre- and post-transition always evokes additional emotion as the lyrics and my memories of those performances converge.

The power of the vocal aspect of nurturing is not easily overstated. When appropriate gender is not conveyed as part of oral communication, a part of varying importance is missed and the effectiveness of that communication is diminished. Years after transition, I am still concerned about, and occasionally disappointed by, the sounds and effect of my voice. Since each such disappointment is a failure to express my gender identity effectively, it is gratifying when someone perceives my voice as feminine over the telephone. Placing an order for a carryout meal is a mildly disappointing experience when the call ends with "thank you, sir." The same misperception regarding an expression of sympathy would be far more disturbing. Its significance would not be quantifiable, but the failure to convey the whole of the message does harm to both the speaker and the listener. Though not usually characterized as nurture, the sharing of an enriching graphic, dramatic, or musical artistic experience, whether of religious or secular emphasis, embodies many of the attributes of nurturing by attempting to support the sharing and reinforcement of common virtues. An unintended expression of inappropriate gender would diminish the power of the exchange.

Realization that the nature of nurturing must evolve is inescapable. The process has adapted through time to accommodate mothers who work outside of the home, single mothers, those in non-traditional relationships, changes for parents and children resulting from advancing technology, etc. Evolution also applies to the maturing and, especially, to the growing independence of each child. As the nature of each relationship progresses, demands of time, effort, clarity of action, and all else except intended commitment can change dramatically. Such lessons come not only from being a parent but from recalling each person's interactions with her or his own parents, seeing those parents with their parents, the experiences of friends, etc. Those manifestations of nurturing can be studied and adopted or discarded, but the need to practice the art seems an indelible part of each woman's and man's being.

Gender and the Workplace

Regardless of their expectations before marriage, married men share and have shared a partnership with their wives in pursuit of common goals. Men also have known women as their mothers, sisters, aunts, other relatives, friends, etc. Despite that experience, many men see women much differently in the workplace. Female co-workers, whether superiors, subordinates, or bearing similar responsibilities, are often regarded as having a substantially different, and often inferior, set of capabilities. While visiting a bank with which ours had a correspondent relationship, one of its officers and I were discussing a procedure for securing a collateral interest and the officer said "Just have a girl do it." The inflection clearly implied the task was within the limited capabilities of an almost human subspecies called "girls" (regardless of their age). At that time, more women than men were employed in banking's minimum-wage positions, and they were doing work essential for banks to function. The willingness of women to accept a lower relative wage had been part of an earlier generation's reallocation of positions formerly held by men. Instead of appreciating the capacity of women to perform those duties at lower wages, some male supervisors have regarded them as members of an undedicated mass of easily replaceable and interchangeable lesser beings.

Borrowing again from the vocal arts, the confident expectation, determination, and daring that such singers as Cecilia Bartoli and Juan Diego Flores have exhibited in performance, especially when singing a most demanding aria, were essential to their success. Yet, these singers produced quintessentially feminine and masculine results. The power and beauty of their work occur despite a multitude of differences including sex, age, height, weight, vocal training, life experience, etc. Many of these differences add to the unique and spectacular nature of each performance.

Some people argue that because of the similar demands of their work and the stellar quality of the results, they should receive equal remuneration. Other things being equal, if weekly demand for their performances is 7,000 in one case and 6,000 in the other, the market is indicating that the value of their work is not equal. For sponsoring organizations, the ability to attract an audience is a major factor in deciding how much a performer can be offered. For each of the two singers cited, a sell-out audience would be virtually assured, but for other performers there will be a difference.

In musical or athletic performance, medicine, business, the law, teaching, etc. females and males do produce satisfactory and even spectacular results. Functional magnetic resonance imaging (fMRIs) of female and male brains have shown significant differences in respective function when accomplishing identical tasks, but they do not show either group as more or less capable of performing them. In a test of working memory, there was little sex-based difference in performance test results, but significant sex differences appeared in respective brain patterns (Goldstein 2005, 512-3).[8] Such studies reinforce the fact that women and men often do many things differently while still getting them done, and they often do so with a perceptibly feminine or masculine method and result.

If the gender difference of the result is significant to the effort's success, as is argued regarding some tasks in the military for example, it is not reasonable to resent the gender difference but prudent and even laudatory to acknowledge the ability that makes accomplishment of the worthwhile task possible. The same argument would apply to other essential tasks where a difference in intellect, height, age, or any other characteristic improves efficiency or makes prospects for success more likely. It would make no sense to say that height must be excluded as a factor when hiring a basketball player, nor would it be reasonable to make height the sole factor in selecting a surgeon. One can only imagine how a male might give birth, but that does not mean he cannot be, or that a female can be, a fantastic father.

Nurture and Competition

Application of Title IX to public financial support for athletic programs for women has been spectacularly effective at increasing the opportunities for high school and college females participating in competitive sports, even at the possible cost of eliminated marginal programs for males. Fostering a competitive and team-centered focus may help some of these girls become women who attain substantial vocational success. If that happens and is fulfilling for them, or if it contributes to strengthened, desired, and healthier family relationships, then the effort will have been richly rewarded. If these programs help other girls know they can receive favorable attention for pursuing attractive alternatives to becoming teenage mothers, then the effort will have proved even more worthwhile. When young women know that a need to be a biological mother is not part of their nature, a society that prizes liberty reasonably would neither compel nor encourage them to become one. Such women, like every other member of society, should seek the whole of that classical good which brings them fulfillment. For young women who do feel that personal need though, subordinating, ignoring, or postponing it for transient and superficial ambition is likely to mean, as it is for their male counterparts described above, an irredeemably forsaken opportunity for enduring peace, happiness, and fulfillment.

Those forces empowering and encouraging young people to pursue mold-shattering choices are like someone who sends a rider-less wagon full of irreplaceable possessions careening over a cliff. While millennia of human history have proven a need for the enduring strength of a family-centered, supportive, and life-affirming set of interpersonal relationships and connectedness; no set of comparable data portends success for its opposite. A general concern for the continued strength of society is inescapable. A specific concern for the imminent proliferating melancholy of forsaken mutual commitment is very much a part of the legacy of the suppressing transgendered experience. This has nothing to do with a "set-in-concrete" reverence for immutable stereotypes, but everything to do with accepting and expressing innate identity-based gender.

A Nurturing Act

One day while working at the bank, I was driving home for a late lunch and saw two teenage boys fighting less than a block from my home. A crowd of middle school students was gathered around the boys, but no one seemed willing or able to stop the fight. A member of the crowd later told me that the two who were fighting were two of the biggest boys in the school and that none of the students alone was able to stop the fight. At the time, I was angered by the idea that at least one of the boys did not want to be involved and that the fight was happening on the sidewalk of my great-grandfather's home. I stopped the car suddenly in the middle of the street, jumped from my seat, and asked which of the boys wanted to fight with me. Whatever their perception of my appearance, they must have seen that I was serious. They did stop fighting and slowly resumed their walk home from school.

I am certain that no one saw anything overtly feminine and nurturing about my actions, and I have no idea how I would respond to a similar situation today. I would not offer to become a substitute combatant, but I would be just as angry about their fighting. My inclination to act would not have changed, but the way in which I acted almost certainly would be different. Another person would intervene using her or his own physical, intellectual, religious training, or other capabilities to achieve the desired purpose. Not only might most men respond differently from most women, but some women doubtlessly would respond differently from other women.

Women may be more aware, both consciously and subconsciously, of the physical differences that separate them from other women and men but their awareness would not share the potential-threat assessment perspective of men. The taller woman might envy the shorter one's petite figure and her wearing a shorter skirt to make her legs look longer. The shorter woman may regard the taller one as being graceful and elegant in her floor-skimming gown. A suppressing MtF woman is much more conscious of such comparisons since she feels so strongly compelled to end her identity conflict, even as she fails to self-diagnose it, and to appear as much as possible to herself and everyone else as the woman she is. After transition, the shorter and slighter MtF woman, who was taunted as a youth because of her size and who envied her larger classmates, may be seen as more fortunate by an MtF woman who played football as a defensive lineman and was seldom, if ever, intimidated by larger classmates.

The Matter of Self

The incessantly recurring process of human self-assessment is much more than a "grass is greener" comparison. Each person continually considers those personal physical attributes that easily or reasonably can be improved either from a self or altruistic interest. This is especially true for MtF women. Admiring attractive characteristics or features in others is not the same as envying or coveting them for themselves. The difference is that non-suppressing MtF women attempt to be the best, most expressive, and most effective people they can be; but they do so differently from the people they had been seen as being . They do not wish merely to copy or to take anything away from an admired person. MtF women, as well as most people who are aware of their authentic selves, want to use their bodies to say things about and as the people they are.

The entire meaning of attempted communication will be more readily received and understood if the intended listener finds the presenter's appearance appealing or at least consistent with the message. From an emotional standpoint each person wants others to find her or him attractive as a means to achieving more meaningful interaction with them. If the message one is attempting to convey is of a romantic nature, the other party's finding that person attractive would seem essential. Appearance at best though, can reveal only some, and arguably less important, aspects of a person's identity. Appearance should never become or be confused with the whole of any person's identity, although it often is.

The line between wanting to make reasonable changes to accommodate identity and to becoming obsessed with an interminable process to alter one's appearance is anything but distinct. The MtF woman seeks ultimately to be honest and may best achieve her goal by just being the person she is. Her surgeries should not become a substitute statement that she must be female because of the procedures she has endured. Ironically, the importance of physical change can become a pseudo capitulation to the argument that one's body does determine gender identity while its opposite must be true. The test of whether a surgical change would bring someone closer to a greater ambition and/ or enhance important interpersonal interactions can help each person find the area code of the dichotomy's necessary, versus excessive, boundary. Discerning the precise location of the line though, must depend on the acuity of the involved mental health professional's expertise.

A significant part of the self-awareness of any MtF woman is the fact that she has been around other women all of her life, but prior to transition, she was not seen as feminine. She knows both that other women did have that experience and that she did not. The harmony of gender identity and physical appearance that MtF women only begin to experience after transition is an unquestioned constant for most women.

While contending with a variety of insecurities throughout their lives, the essence of most women's self-awareness or self-knowledge can begin with the confident statement "I am a woman who...". Even when being mistaken for a male over the telephone, in an unusual social setting, or during an intended ambiguity of dress and manner: the center from which most women can explore the rest of their identities and interact with other people begins from that certainty. Women whose natal sex is female well may find the harmony so complete that they never have doubted, or even questioned, its existence. All other important aspects of each one's identity can possess her thoughts with doubts, ambivalence, and certainties about who she is, what she wants to accomplish, and how she wants to live her life. Through any or all of that, she can confidently begin the statement defining herself with that "I am..." phrase. The experience may be much the same for non-transgendered men whose absence of gender identity conflict also frees them to define themselves as the men they are and to decide what they wish to accomplish.

An MtF woman may be uncomfortable using the phrase "I am a woman..." in the same sense because she keenly feels that "woman" refers to a completeness that she has always thought was impossible for her to achieve. Some of the earliest writings about human history include accounts of those who exhibited gender identity or sex characteristics deemed inappropriate to them by their contemporaries. MtF women today, like their predecessors, may still qualify that "I am a woman..." phrase because of their uniquely awkward history of struggle and discovery, a sense of incompleteness, and the knowledge that their physiology raged against, rather than confirming, who they are. That same physiology influenced the people around them and prevented societal reinforcement of their normal growth and maturation as women. Other attributes or characteristics an MtF woman might admire about another woman not withstanding, every non-transgendered or "cis-gender" woman they encounter has a core element of historic identity that MtF women never can possess at their center.

The self-defining statement of MtF women during and after transition affirms that they have the same essential gender identity as other women. They can add, with the confidence that comes from the experience, that they have struggled with, firmly decided to end, fully disclosed, and moved to resolve, to the greatest possible extent, their discordant physical identity. Their honest statement may seem excessively heroic or congratulatory to others, but there is no other earthly presence inside them but themselves; and they are intimately familiar with the road they have traveled. While there may be a plethora of other core facets to explore and resolve for every person, a transgendered person's finding and employing the answer to gender identity harmony that had always eluded her or him provides an immensely calming and stable foundation.

In a room occupied by 10 or 1000 other women, I may look for another one nearly my height or sharing other physical characteristics, but I do not feel in the least as though I do not belong there. If a discussion turns to the experience of feminine childhood and adolescent rivalries, to early sexual experiences, pregnancy, the joys and sorrows of motherhood, menopause, or other uniquely feminine experiences that I have not shared, I may listen with rapt attention. I am very much intrigued by these aspects of womanhood that have not been part of my own life experience, but they do not seem inappropriate and certainly are not irrelevant to the person I am. As a child I never thought that making such a statement aloud or in print would be possible.

During my childhood I shared the lack of knowledge and experience common to most of my peers to form and attempt to answer essential and very personal questions about who I was, what kind of life I wanted to live, and what work I hoped to accomplish. My childhood was filled with learning about people, things, and ideas outside of myself, and I was told about or could infer my own connectedness to them. At so early an age, the idea that a child might have an identity that is independent of that learning, and yet has to be defined in terms of it if it could be defined at all, would have seemed the equivalent of attempting to contemplate living on another planet. Later, I would learn that discovering the essence of my own separate identity was not only possible, but that it had become paramount.

Those defining terms of my early experience were learned from interactions with family, friends, and classmates, but they also were learned from children and adults in Scouting, public school, our church, and the community. I could not understand what being a transgendered child meant, and I was unwilling to trust anyone who might help me understand. I was apprehensive about what might happen within our family if I revealed that I was not the person they thought I was, and I feared embarrassment and ridicule outside of my family if the condition was discovered or disclosed. For all of these reasons I hid my incredibly persistent obsession from every one of these people.

If there is virtue in honesty, it would not be found in instances of convenience, ease, or advantage. Even the most dishonest person would be honest at such times if only to increase the likelihood of her or his being believed when attempting to deceive someone for gain. Honesty, as a virtue, would require disclosure of all material information regarding a given situation as soon as possible to everyone affected, especially when doing so is a disadvantage to the person making the disclosure. If a necessary component of being dishonest is an attempt to gain something from someone else at that person's disadvantage, my deceptions in attempting to acquire gender-inappropriate clothing hurt only myself and materially enriched those selling things to me. The fraud perpetrated by society's assigning a male gender identity to me based on my apparent sex was well underway by the time my complicity mattered.

Attempting to fulfill the expectations of others came relatively easily since I was determined to hide my embarrassingly shameful secret, especially when I did not understand that I had a gender identity and sex conflict. I do not believe that I attempted to deceive anyone to that person's disadvantage, including my own, about my having a feminine gender identity. I revealed, as gently and expeditiously as possible to those affected by my transition, as much as I could and as soon as I could after I began to obtain a diagnosis from a most competent professional.

I take no pride, perverse or otherwise, in the fact that I had so completely deceived everyone I most care about for so many years, but I am also no longer ashamed of it. It is no more reasonable to expect an unaided young child to be responsible for discovering that she erroneously is being encouraged to be, and to grow to become, a male than it is to expect anyone spontaneously to grow an extra limb. The fraud perpetrated is surely not the fault of the child. As an adult, I did attempt to resolve or self-diagnose my obsessive behavior, but I did not seek professional help because I knew of no one who might provide it. I dared not risk my secret's discovery by asking for a referral. I could not seek professional assistance anonymously. Speaking with anyone who might help would have meant disclosing a nearly life-long secret that was as impossible to divulge as it seemed unlikely to be resolved.

The inertia that lies behind a closely guarded secret life seductively assures the suppressor that it is better to live with the anguish that is known than to risk an unknown potential humiliation of disclosure. The U.S. Declaration of Independence includes the words "...all experience hath shown that mankind are more disposed to suffer while evils are sufferable than to right themselves by abolishing the forms to which they are accustomed" (Kashner 2007, 496).[9] The paralyzing inertia to which he referred apparently is most acutely felt and constraining when the importance of the matter it regards has become paramount. That especially is true of the desperate moment when it no longer is possible to suppress one's gender identity.

4. Encounters of Youth

Exceptional Differences

A deeper understanding and wider perspective regarding what is normal and whether deviations are reasonable, objectionable, and/or call for some action on our part come from a variety of sources. Books, prose, plays, experiences with close friends and family, and casual acquaintances provide a wealth of opportunities to make comparisons. People learn from normal routine and from unusual events. Those people who seem so objectionably different from us that we seek to avoid having any future contact with them can teach us about things we thought we knew and about things we did not know existed.

My experiences with our family, my closest childhood friend, and his parents fell easily into the category of warm personal relationships. Singular events that, of their own weight as well as being a catalyst for our own and the actions of others, can have an overwhelming influence on the voyage of our lives. A beautiful autumn day saw the advent of such an event in the life of our family. Adventures with Scouting and my attending public school provided numerous opportunities to experience the other kinds of acquaintances.

A Friend's Family

I met the boy who would become my closest childhood friend when he was four years old and I was five. I was playing in the ditches prepared to receive the footer of a new field house on the other side of the high school in the block north of our house. He was playing in their driveway and yard that complemented the ell design of their home. For the next seven years, I spent almost as much time with him as I did at my own home. Their home was one of the two oldest homes in the area and its construction predated the founding of our hometown. The house was spacious with a large recreation room added at its north end, a pantry with its own exterior door beside the kitchen door off the smaller back porch, and two stairways to the second floor. The entrance hall was used for storage because the home fronted on what had become the primary north-south route through the state and there was no paved sidewalk in front of the home. We spent little time in the living and dining rooms except at Christmas, when the season's decorations made the living room almost irresistible. Part of what had once been a large farm had been acquired by the county's board of education. The farmland behind the house had become a parking lot for the high school's new field house, a football field, an off-loading area for school busses, and the city park.

My friend's mother and her two brothers had lived in the house before her marriage. When we were older, she operated a kindergarten that my younger sister attended in the large recreation room and later, she became superintendent of our church's Sunday school. Her enduring interest in working with children, despite a lack of advanced formal training, made it even easier for me to be her son's friend. The boy's father was a steelworker who coached our "Little League" baseball team and, shortly before or after his military service, he had pursued a career in professional baseball.

This father's interests were not restricted to athletics and, when he and his wife got an upright piano to help their son study piano, he asked me to help him learn to play a scale. The fact that any adult would ask me to provide this kind of help was stunning, but he was not hesitant or embarrassed to ask. I thought I was far too young to be a teacher. Even though I had been studying piano for several years, I had not really thought about how muscles, with practice, can consistently do what is expected of them. Watching him expect his large fingers to learn to move fluidly and capably over a keyboard was a lesson for me. It also taught me that one of the best ways to learn more about, and to test one's knowledge of, a subject is to try to teach it. This man's knowledge of the training and use of larger muscles to throw a ball, swing a bat, and to use the fingers collectively to "handle" a ball was not transferred easily to moving his fingers independently. He was much more diligent in trying to teach me about baseball than I was about trying to help him with piano. At our respective ages, he knew much more about his subject than I did about mine, but he was interested in what I did know about piano that might help him.

The son of these caring parents shared my interests in games and movies but he was a much better baseball player. He had no evident performance anxiety when practicing or playing the game, and little or no concern for the possibility of damaging his hands and impairing his ability to play piano. Part of his aptitude for and interest in the game may have been innate, but his father's ability, attitude, and support were a clarion summons for him to engage in that most American of sports. The question for baseball people was not whether the ball would be caught but where to through it after catching it. Similarly, with an assumption that the ball would be hit, the batter should attempt to place the ball where runners might be given the best chance to advance. Their interest in baseball meant that, if I wanted to spend time with them, I was going to have to play baseball. I did so but at a performance level that was decidedly less than stellar.

When he knew I was going to be playing, Dad got a glove, baseball, and bat for me at a small store in town. Despite having had two brothers they, or at least he, did not play much baseball. The glove he bought was for softball and was about as useful for fielding a hardball as a block of wood. My friend came over, and he, Dad, and I went to our backyard. The three of us were roughly 20 feet apart and Dad tossed the new ball to me. Showing, literally, incredible athletic prowess, I stood motionless and watched the ball as it struck me squarely in the center of my forehead before it dropped to the ground. As I began to cry, I realized that playing baseball might not be my sport.

I do not remember how much time elapsed before I picked up the glove and ball again, but my friend and I did get them broken in. When we were both old enough, we were enrolled in our town's "Little League" and played on the same team his father coached. The team did well for the three or four years I was on it but its success had nothing to do with me. At first, I enjoyed the activity and played well enough during team practices but I did not play well during games. My friend's father had known me for several years by then and tried to help when he, his son, and I went to the field alone to practice. I had little difficulty hitting the balls he threw and fielding balls he hit.

During a subsequent practice, I had reverted to my norm for playing when people might be watching me, and he took the mound. I stood frozen in a batting stance while he shot three baseball bullets waist-high across the plate and then told me I was "out." I am sure he had no idea why I did not react the way he expected so he could not know what else to do. At the time, I rationalized that I did not want to have any part of me in front of a hard object thrown with such force. I did not want to risk injury to my hands trying to hit the ball and, if I did hit it, I had no control over where it would go and did not want it to hit him. Those excuses ignored the fact that he not only wanted me to swing at his pitches but to hit them. We had unrelated goals. He thought I wanted to play or learn to play baseball. I just wanted to be his son's friend.

From an early age I attempted to avoid situations where my carefully crafted and maintained image might be questioned. Those few childhood confrontations in which I engaged occurred where the unacceptable alternative was a public and embarrassing surrender that would have invited more confrontations. However well prepared by education, practice, and experience for a competition, contest, or performance, seeing myself as a likely victor seemed impossible. Rather than trying to use such visualization as a tool to improve performance, I saw that imagery as a fantasy similar to my awkward images of suppressed gender identity. The distraction of performance anxiety and an imperative to seem male were far more powerful than any desire to win. I thought I knew something about myself that, at least subconsciously, always meant that I did not deserve to win. After years of introspection, I wondered if not being honest about the person I was could make committing that self in successful competition impossible. The curiosity was anything but idle, yet wondering about it did not lead to any acceptable plausible prospective solutions.

The conflict between my suppressed real identity and its projected male persona produced incredibly inconsistent behavior. My ability to play baseball when it was a game with friends but not when I played as a team member in uniform is one example. My stalemate in my first competitive chess-team match despite having had a huge lead was another. During a judo club session at college, students paired with each other and attempted to use any of several holds they had learned to throw their partners. Even that "friendly" competition seemed like something I should not be doing until my opponent's irritating stiff-arm technique helped replace my reluctance with anger. Before transition, I did not realize that I reacted differently to threats or challenges to my persona and threats to me. In college, I thought there was a distinct difference between competition and learning. Even learning about physical activity was an academic pursuit. I spent much of an earlier judo session being thrown in a graceful arc over the head of a partner who had mastered the throw and we each enjoyed the experience.

My performance anxiety regarding "Little League" baseball became so acute that I had severe headaches lasting more than an hour after each practice. I had become increasingly aware of tension in a "game" that was something other than recreation. Every "performance" on a baseball field, during a piano jury, singing a sacred music solo, or any activity in which I was engaged where people might be assessing my performance was a new opportunity for someone to find a flaw in the maleness I presented. Before one team practice, I endured some taunting and then chased the worst offender into the outfield, tackled him, and, not knowing what else to do but intending to embarrass him, I spanked him. There was less taunting after that but my baseball playing did not improve. Only when something seemed to threaten the edges of my male persona would that threat be fully addressed. The strategy employed was whatever was most likely to defeat, remove, or diminish the threat.

A couple years after "Little League," my advantage of relative height, depth perception, and coordination gave me an edge in basketball. The absence of the sting of a hard-thrown baseball or successfully swung bat helped make basketball my preferred sport. Yet when I played basketball on our school's eighth grade team, I had little more success than when I played baseball. The games were enough to occupy the mind without a player becoming so self-conscious and self-inhibiting that relying on practiced skills is almost impossible.

I also enjoyed throwing, catching, and kicking a football but neither tackling nor being tackled was at all appealing. Bowling and tennis were later additions to my list of favorite sports, but the only contact sport I enjoyed was judo when practiced for sport rather than competition. My opportunities for engaging in competitive sports have been limited since transition, but I now *let* myself play piano more than I ever did before transition. That approach has helped me to enjoy playing more than I had ever thought possible. If such a change were the test for proving the success of transition as a cure for adolescent performance anxiety, I would immodestly claim a perfect score.

My friend and I often explored a narrow but deep hollow between his home and the town's drive-in theater, always finding something of unusual interest, whether natural or manmade. During one trek, we found a decidedly scary looking red and yellow crab-like creature that was, at first, much more frightening than its diminutive size would warrant. Its apparent speed was proportional to its diminutive size, so apprehension gave way to curiosity until preoccupation with the absence of an answer to this natural puzzle was replaced by an interest in the next discovery. Another excursion provided an encounter with several salamanders, one of which was injured and was chewing some of its own damaged tissue. This biological lesson seemed important but not philosophically comforting. I will never know if the creature survived, and if so, for how long.

As an only child, my friend was bereft of the joys and trials of sibling rivalries and had undivided parental support. His homemaker-mother always seemed to have time for a chat and, as I grew older, I talked more with her than with him. Because of his home's proximity to the drive-in theater, my summer sleepovers often included a visit to that theater. He and I would sit on a bench in front of the drive-in's concession stand enjoying the enticing aroma and occasional helpings of well-cooked hot dogs, popcorn, and other treats while listening to and watching the family-oriented fare. When I was eleven years old, he and I saw a film about "Atlantis". It included a scene where a mysterious rotating crystal transformed men into subhuman creatures who performed slave labor. I did not understand the reason but found the possibility of so extensive a physical transformation exciting and compelling. Distrusting that excitement and perplexed by its presence, I never discussed that interest with anyone. The film's blatant statement that men are made to become, and are treated as being less than, men when they are enslaved was lost on a child who was enthralled with the mechanics of the transformation. In retrospect, the tantalizing clues about suppressed gender identity and the futility of an MtF woman aspiring to a wholly male role are infinitely more clear after transition than they were to an eleven-year old.

For daytime and cold weather entertainment, there were three indoor theaters in the town across the river and each was readily accessible via regional bus service. When old enough, this friend and I would come home by bus after his or my parents took us to one of the theaters for a Saturday or summer-day afternoon's entertainment. We enjoyed such films as *Phantom of the Opera* (Lubin 1943),[10] *The Werewolf* (Sears 1956),[11] and *Dr. Jekyll and Mr. Hyde* (Fleming 1941).[12] We also saw film trailers for *The Mummy* (Fisher 1959)[13] and *Darby O'Gill and the Little People* (Stevenson 1959).[14] None of the films we saw frightened me as much as those two trailers. Either the unstoppable mummy in the first trailer or the fearsome banshee in the second was so frightening that I was certain the creature would soon find its way to my bedroom, sparing every other room in all of the homes in the valley. The logic of a child reasoned that it would come to my room because that was where I was. When I complained at bedtime, Dad saw nothing of which to be frightened, and said so. After I complained to my mother of chest pain and painful breathing, she took me on one of our infrequent trips to the family doctor.

The doctor had been a classmate of my great-aunt and seemed to enjoy cigarettes at least as much as any other smoker of the day. His reserved and patient, yet efficient, manner endeared him to most of the people in town. As he performed his examination, he asked if I had been having a problem with someone at school or if anything of a troubling nature had been happening in the neighborhood and I said no. He said it was evident that I had been frightened by something, and this was several days after my having seen the trailer. I neglected to ask if he had seen any other children with a similar problem, probably because I assumed no one else would have found those images as disturbing as I did.

The possibility of a similar event or of any unanticipated incident so frightening or harming my child is one of the few things I would not miss about the experience of being a parent. However much assurance is offered and self-confidence is taught, the reality of such fear may bear no evident proportional relationship to its cause. Most of the films my friend and I saw were not frightening, even if they were intended to be or were so characterized in their promotions. I do not know what seemed so frightening to me about a movie screen image and I do understand why my father would simply insist that there was no reason to be frightened. Fearing things that appear to be dangerous must be a primal part of being human, though, and telling a child not to be frightened must be almost as practical as telling the wind not to blow.

I did not understand that the fear I felt was far more harmful to me than the thing depicted on film. I needed to apply reason to control the emotion of fear but I was obviously missing something in the process, or failing to apply it properly. Countering fear with knowledge or understanding means analyzing the thing that was encountered and, if it poses a threat, accessing the nature of the threat and how best to counter it. Whatever the threat, the fear someone feels still should be proportionate and appropriate. However that lesson is learned, it should be learned for self-protection and the protection of other people. The lesson reasonably would apply to movie mummies, banshees, and neighborhood transgendered people.

The cited version of *Phantom of the Opera* was a particularly memorable film. Its audiences may not always have understood the story as the director intended. My sympathies primarily were with Claude Rains as one of the film's leading characters because of his love of, and life in, music. The story's other musicians primarily projected academic, performance, career, or business interests. As a young piano student and even more so when I began to study voice, I did not understand why a violinist would become so dedicated to the career of a young soprano. The story might have made more sense if the "Phantom" had been another singer at the opera, but apparently that was not appealing to the film's creators. The director, producer, writers, and others may have considered most singers incapable of composing a concerto, thought any violinist *de facto* interested in great singing, or believed that audiences had a bias either for the abilities of violinists or against the abilities of singers.

Another troubling aspect is the unusually amoral aspect of the story. The audience can see the "Phantom" as a dangerous, but also a daring, challenge to law enforcement and the opera company. Subjected to trials more sudden than

Job's, the respected, gentle, and generous violinist might have been expected to lash out violently against some person or thing. The pecuniary perspective on the "Phantom's" murders as an inconvenience to the opera company is also unlike American films released during W.W. II. Rather than focusing on the "Phantom's" moral and legal guilt for the publisher's murder, the film's focus became the "Phantom's" psychotic obsession for Christine's success.

The alleged criminal insanity of Lon Chaney's "Phantom" (Julian 1925)[15] could be blamed for specific behavior and his having been tortured in the cellars of the Opera House would explain anything else. Understanding the Chaney "Phantom", though, does not mean empathizing with him. Claude Rains' sane, if eccentric, "Phantom" seemed to command sympathy. I responded with such sympathy that only after seeing the film many years later did I realize that the publisher's death and the "Phantom's" burns were not accidents resulting from their struggle.

At the end of his career as a performer, the violinist does not lament his fate following his many long hours of practice, his first lessons, his instructors, early performances, later triumphs, and favorite works. The cascade of misfortune he experiences includes a diminished capacity to play the violin and loss of his employment, his apartment, his protégé, and his concerto. As a final blow, he loses his identity as a civilized human when he strangles the publisher. Ironically, the final loss is self-inflicted.

It is puzzling that the result of these losses is the sudden willingness repeatedly to commit murder. The transformation purportedly occurs despite, or perhaps ironically because of, his years of discipline and training in music. He spent his life creating and recreating music but, in response to misfortune, he readily turns to taking the lives of others. The black-hat and white-hat simplicity of American westerns or, more generously, an American concern for individual responsibility in each person's interactions with others, is not satisfied in this story. Given the opportunity to comment, Mark Twain probably would have noted that the original work was, after all, a story originally written by a Frenchman about another Frenchman living in France.

Ayn Rand's *The Fountainhead* finds its creator/hero innocent of criminal charges for destroying the remains of his desecrated opus, while the "Phantom"/ antihero is destroyed after he and his creative efforts fall victim to a similar kind of theft (Rand 1943/1993, 687).[16] Creators of the 1943 "Phantom" may have cared little about the role of the state in protecting copyrights, perhaps sharing Thomas Jefferson's pessimism regarding their worth to society. They might have argued, even more objectionably, or have been satirizing the view, that it is the obligation of people to serve the state and not the state to serve its citizens. Americans who have achieved remarkable success, especially economic success, have reversed the service ethic. They have discovered something uncommon, even about something quite common, and enriched themselves by being wholly dedicated to exploiting the observation.

Discovery of the opportunity, dedication of substantial resources, and application of sound business principles have often been richly rewarded. When they have not, failure and bankruptcy have given countless entrepreneurs second, third, and more chances to succeed. The American economic system was not designed to favor specific individuals but to achieve in perpetuity the greatest good for the greatest number with consumers as the ultimate arbiters of what good means. By preserving opportunity and challenge for each competing entrepreneur, the American system encourages individuals to enhance public good by pursuing individual goals. In *The Fountainhead,* Ms Rand's hero could not be more opposed to the fascist view when he says he A...does not exist for any other manCand he asks no other man to exist for him" (ibid., 683).[17]

Its 1943 release date does not necessarily mean that anyone associated with the film intended to convey a political message. It is likely, though, that Ayn Rand would have wanted that screenplay written far differently. Her performer/composer would have been much younger, disdainful of his work as "just" another of the violinists in the orchestra, and hailed by true lovers of music for his composition's originality of form and style. Ms. Rand's regard for anyone who created great art could be seen as the epitome of art appreciation. Regard for artistic effort without the utmost regard for its author would have been an unacceptable hypocrisy. She would have seen original work as being immeasurably more worthy than any act of destruction by others; that is the focus of tension when her architect destroys the result after his work was altered without his permission. Her regard for the individual, even to the point of virtually worshiping her or his own goals, is contrary to the selflessness of the Christian ethic, but her focus was government constrained by philosophy and not by religion. The 1943 "Phantom's" credited writers were Samuel Hoffenstein and brothers Hans and John Jacoby (Lubin 1943).[18] They were apparently determined or encouraged to show the violinist's ruin by his interaction with the society in which he lived. Rand also would have agreed that the individual's interaction with an improperly constituted state could be, or even was inevitably, destructive but that this was a strong argument *per se* for establishment of the proper state.

My friend did not seem to find many of these film details nearly as interesting as I did. I had been disappointed because I was sympathetic to the "Phantom" and thought he had been treated unfairly, at least until he repeatedly committed murder. My friend had enjoyed going to the theater and viewing an entertaining film, but then he was ready to do something else. His actions and reactions to almost everything were more typical of other boys in our neighborhood, and I was especially aware of the differences when he and I were with other "boys". If he ever noticed those differences, and he almost certainly did, he never asked me about them. He and I were not alike in many respects but we were friends. He, my family, and others I cared about provided nearly constant opportunities for comparing my inclinations, actions, and reactions to their own.

A Like-aged Neighbor

A friend next-door was my age and also enjoyed bike riding, playing as cape wearing super-heroes, and the "cowboy and Indians" games of early childhood. We collected soda or "pop" bottles from beneath the bleachers at the high school football field in the next block. We redeemed them at the gasoline and food store in the next block and received two cents per bottle. Hard-won proceeds of the endeavor usually went quickly for candy or soda. One of us decided to pool our money and use it for a pack of cigarettes. We were chain-smokers of Lucky Strikes for almost two weeks before he was caught by his mother and punished. Whatever his punishment, it was evident that there was a high cost to smoking that had nothing to do with a surgeon general. I was a cigarette smoker for almost two weeks and have never again been tempted.

At age seven, I received my twenty-six-inch "Rollfast" bicycle for Christmas; this was the wondrous device of inestimable worth mentioned earlier in other contexts. The two-speed Kelly-green bicycle with thin white accent stripes on its fenders, white cushioned handle grips, a green and white seat, and green chain guard must have made me one of the happiest children in town and it quickly became my most prized possession. I sat on its seat and pretended to ride that bicycle in the house for weeks as it rested against the upright piano in our hall. After warmer weather finally arrived, I was anxious to try riding it outside but when Dad helped me onto the seat, the ground now seemed so much farther away than the hall floor had been and, rather than enjoying the thrill of that first ride, I could think of nothing else but how I would stop. I landed abruptly in the soft grass of a neighbor's yard without physical injury to me or the bicycle, but I waited for more than a month before trying to ride it again.

My neighbor and smoking partner had a much shorter bicycle and, when he was available, we would swap bikes for some part of each day. He probably fell off my bike as often as I would have but he just kept getting back on it. The scratches and dents my bike acquired were ones I should have been adding and ones that might have been marks of accomplishment at my own learning. One Sunday when he was later getting back from church, I finally decided to try riding my own bike again. The first effort lasted about ten yards and I had anticipated a rough landing every inch of that brief journey, but this time I was determined to try again. The second effort became a conventional ride around our block until I stopped at the front steps of our house. I mastered the art of keeping my balance as I swung my leg over the seat to get on and off the bicycle several days after this momentous ride, but trying to find conveniently located curbs or steps in the interim was problematic. The briefly entertained idea of taking our front steps along would have been a greater problem.

I remember well the immediate and growing sense of accomplishment at having mastered my bike on that ride; it was really much easier than I had feared. I realized that, had I made this discovery sooner, the dents and scratches that marked my friend's use would not have occurred. Had I committed to riding that bike sooner, its scratches would have been a representative history of my use of this prized possession. I felt much of the same mixed sense of accomplishment and regret after purposefully and with essential professional help, confronting my gender identity conflict.

When I ran inside our house and announced my riding achievement, Mother's comment was that she and Dad repeatedly had been telling me, but I would not hear or heard differently, what I finally had discovered for myself. I did not know then that Dad had bought his sturdy "Fox" bicycle with earnings from a newspaper route when he was a high school freshman in Richmond, Virginia, nor that my mother desperately had wanted but not gotten one because her father was afraid she would be hurt while riding or falling from it. My parents' fifteen to twenty-year-old memories of having wanted a bicycle did help them understand and want to satisfy my desire for one, but those memories also magnified their disappointment when I so readily participated in an exchange that left my bicycle in someone else's care. I knew that my friend had not deliberately harmed my bicycle, but I also realized that he was more willing to accept the chance of falling from it. Each person's image of the consequences of daring, whether salutary or disdainful, must color her or his view of the action.

The important lesson of valuing success in some things enough to risk failure, heavily weighted by values, abilities, and interests does frame and inform our perspective on appropriate daring.

School is Elementary

At age five, I had been permitted to walk three blocks from our house to greet my sister on her way home from the elementary school that was roughly four blocks from home. Several members of our church lived on that street, and I visited with a few of them during some of those afternoons. One autumn day about a month before my sixth birthday, it was finally my turn to begin attending school. The morning of that first day, Dad, as he had done for several years and would for the next twenty-six years, walked the block to my grandmother's home to get her car, she met him at the garage, and they drove to our house for my sister and me. The four of us picked up a bank employee on the way, my sister and I got out at the school, and the three adults continued on to the bank. I staged some feeble protest about entering the building, but my older sister was concerned about getting to her class on time. With encouragement from the car, she helped me up the steps and into one of the four classrooms in that building.

The routine of the morning car pool using my grandmother's car lasted throughout the six years of our county's elementary school, but the three daily trips home for lunch, back to school, and then home after school meant walking those four blocks through rain, snow, cold, and sun. There were approximately fifty concrete steps with a sloped walkway and railing to traverse a hillside between home and the elementary school. I climbed those steps at lunchtime and after school nearly every school day for six years. The first bell rang from the larger building's tower ten minutes before the second bell, when all students were to be in their respective classrooms. While a several students walked as far as my sisters and I did, very few walked farther. Students who were closer to the elementary school walked the longer distance I had when they attended the high school only two doors from my home.

I attended first, third, and fourth grade in the building that had once been the town's high school. A second and larger building on the same grounds contained eight classrooms, and is where I spent grades two, five, and six. The restrooms were in the basement of each building and were cool, dark, damp, and malodorous. The larger building also housed a cafeteria where children in town who walked to school were permitted to eat only if they were recovering from illness or had other special permission. Students who rode in the busses to school were not expected to go home for lunch and might, on rare occasions, have walked to a friend's or relative's home as a welcome respite from cafeteria fare. I never discovered how such dispensations were arranged and do not recall anyone's having come to our home for lunch with me. The time allotted for lunch was sufficient but not excessive; the purposeful trips home and back to school with a short time for eating demanded almost as much discipline as was enforced in the cafeteria. The difference, though, between internal motivation and external coercion, I always believed, favored those of us who walked home in some freedom, rather than those who were policed in the school's cafeteria.

Highpoints to each elementary school year included Valentine's Day, Halloween, and a year-end school picnic at the town's park. Valentine's Day was observed by our decorating shoeboxes with slots cut into their lids. Each student brought her or his box to class and deposited small cards for each of the other students in their boxes. Halloween even afforded a day's break from classes as we donned costumes and met in our classrooms, then paraded through town. The school picnic was always a wonderful way to spend the year's last day of school. Except for the organized walk from school to the park, there was no regimentation that day, which was the point. Seeing teachers and students outside of the school meant seeing them in a figurative new light.

During one walk home after school, my cigarette-smoking neighbor and another boy pushed me into a hedge along the sidewalk of Main Street and sat on me. I do not remember what reason, if any, precipitated their action, but I did find the experience as unpleasant as I believe they intended. I pinched my neighbor's leg and can still hear him telling the boy sitting on him to "Get up! GET UP!". He did but they seemed to think that I was the one who had acted inappropriately. Despite the provocation, real boys apparently did not pinch other boys.

Elementary school mornings began with Dad shaved, dressed, and ready to head downstairs to prepare his breakfast while listening to a local radio news broadcast. Unless we were ill, he expected us to get up at his single summons. Dad did not have a snooze button and I do not remember even considering the possibility of feigning illness. One frequent and irritating advertising jingle on that radio station reminded prospective patrons that at a certain finance company (car horn, car horn,) they could borrow more money that they might from any other lender. Their jingle seemed to haunt the mornings of my entire elementary school experience.

Throughout the last three of our six years of grade school, I would try to be downstairs in time to check the coat pocket of my younger sister's sitter. Each weekday, she faithfully brought a packet of plastic wrapped popcorn and margarine. When I would get home from school, the sitter would pop the corn over a kitchen burner and the whole day invariably improved. This marvelous sitter occasionally baked and iced cinnamon rolls that seemed to reach astronomical heights and to create an almost unimaginably wonderful aroma. They tasted even better.

With breakfast over and the sitter greeted, Dad would tie his tie in front of the hall mirror. The wall-mounted hexagonal hall mirror was hung above a black ceramic table lamp that featured a deer, a trough suitable for smaller house plants, coin, pens and pencils, or other essentials, and a large dark maroon shade Soon after buying our house, my parents acquired the lamp from a neighbor who was moving away. That lamp has now been in our family for more than fifty years. The fact that it is an imposing, if not especially interesting and attractive, focal point at the entrance to their home is an indication that my taste in lamps differs markedly from my parents, of the tenacity with which my parents retain many of their possessions, or both.

I was in third grade when my older sister shared the less than pleasant experiences she and her classmates endured throughout their fifth grade year. There was an even chance that I would be assigned to the same teacher but that became my lot. With great trepidation I attended that first dreaded day of fifth grade. When someone from the principal's office told the teacher that he had one too many students in his class and that someone must be chosen to go to the other class, he looked quickly over his entire class roster. Without looking up from it he said in a raised voice, "Ward! You're out of here!" I felt an immense and immediate elation and feared he might change his mind. My feet barely touched the floor as I flew from the rear of the room to the hall outside.

The other fifth grade class shared its teacher and her classroom with sixth grade students. I was seated beside an older student who was repeating fifth grade. It must have been terribly hard for that boy to have been held back from sixth grade and then have to spend every school day with sixth grade students. His boredom with the repeated material led to his finding or creating a variety of distractions that were almost always interesting. I saw them as unscripted additions to, rather than replacements for, what we were supposed to be learning.

A large two-sash window behind my desk had a pane broken by a ball someone had thrown through it. On a blustery early spring day, the dark sky, mist, and wind threatened to pour through that broken window. As the cracked but mostly intact pane rattled and wavered in the wind, I told our teacher of my concern. She did not think the situation was dangerous and told me to return to my seat. When a one-foot square section of the pane started to fall, I managed to jump from my seat before it plummeted to the floor next to my seat. I had always gotten along well with that teacher and did not understand why she would so willingly accept responsibility for the possibility of my being seriously injured. She did have 30 other students to worry about.

The Millionaire (Brahm 1955)[19] was a popular television show about a fictional philanthropist who anonymously awarded a one-million dollar check to a different unsuspecting recipient each week. The philanthropist opened each program describing to his assistant why the payee should receive a check and closed the introduction with the line "... our *next* millionaire, Mike." In current dollars, the award would be roughly $5 million. When "Mike" delivered each check, its recipient reacted unpredictably and occasionally involved "Mike" in the ensuing events. The philanthropist's diligence was such that the recipients occasionally used or obligated all of the funds by the program's end. When the sixth-grade class was studying math, the teacher asked that class, and then anyone in the room, to write the number one-million on the blackboard. I was apparently the only student who had counted the zeros in the program's introduction and I wrote the correct number on the board. This was the only instance I remember of having directly applied something learned from the era's "family" programming.

When the same teacher talked about when the air force was formed, I knew it had been part of the U.S. Army during W.W. II and said so. She disagreed and I took Dad's wallet-sized laminated miniature of his discharge from the U.S. Army Air Corps to school, proving the point. In the 1950's, finding and correcting any adult's error was a daring and discouraged challenge to authority. The established order required a general mix of veneration for, and fear of, those on the "adult" side of a distinct line. Familiarity occasionally ameliorated the extremes regarding certain adults.

One of the most pleasant contradictions of the adult/superior and childhood/inferior dichotomy was the appreciation expressed annually by the American Automobile Association (AAA) toward the "patrol boys" in our valley. Four "male" students were chosen each elementary school year to be patrol boys. These students accepted the responsibility to be at school each school day five minutes before the sounding of the first of the two bells summoning students to class. We stayed at our posts until the second bell sounded, so that we were always a couple minutes late for class. The bells applied to bussed students as well as those within walking distance of the school since students in either group might be engaged in playground activity instead of going prematurely to their classrooms. Patrol boys wore a white belt and shoulder strap fastened at the waste, a badge, and a whistle. They each carried a wood pole with a red flag on one end. They also left class a couple minutes early at the end of each school day and took positions on each side of a heavily-traveled street abutting school property. I held that job with three classmates while we were in fifth and sixth grades. Occasionally, our presence was augmented by the city's police chief or a police deputy and we were not hesitant to use the whistles if a car was traveling much faster than the school zone's posted speed limit.

AAA expressed its appreciation by chartering two commercial busses each year to pick up the "patrol boys" from area elementary schools and transport them to Pittsburgh's Forbes Field for a Pirates baseball game. In addition to getting the tickets, arranging for the day away from school, and furnishing transportation to and from the game, AAA also provided money for snacks or souvenirs. It seemed odd to be thanked, especially in such a generous manner, for having done something I enjoyed. Even after my sister's accident, I did not think that we were making substantially safer the lives of children as much as five years younger than we were.

Passive Influences

It is deceptively easy for children to assume that everyone must be like them sometimes and that no one else is like them at others. For an ashamed transgendered child, it does indeed seem that no one else could have the same problem. The awareness that something is different, and different in a way that threatens the fragile sense of one's life with those around her or him, is an inescapably isolating feeling. The blessedly infrequent occurrence of the condition for the rest of the population means an exacerbated sense of profound loneliness for the MtF child hiding her seemingly incomprehensible compulsion. It cannot be surprising that these relatively few children would attempt to escape the realm of aberrant thoughts by engaging in activities which otherwise occupy the mind and by trying harder to be the person those they care most about seem to want them to be.

Reading books about children who were emotionally attached to, and cared for, animals were one means of escape. Even so, I was keenly aware of the apparent gender of each character. I never dared ask for books where the central character was female so the central characters in the books I received were invariably male. Works about circus life, people and horses, and a book my father had read as a child about the early days of aviation were horizon-broadening food for my imagination, even if the entirety of any particular story was less satisfying.

The ending of *The Call of the Wild* (London, 1903/1995)[20] was disappointing because the dog at the story's center, having experienced both kind and harsh human masters, heeded the wild's call after the murder of its loving and last owner. London's writing about the dog as though it were human challenged the diametric opposite of current understanding that dogs accept humans as being like them and belonging to their pack. The author satisfied a primitive form of justice by having the dog kill his last owner's killers, but there was no such resolution regarding the dog's original owner. The devoted owner who would not rest until she or he recovered a cherished pet would not have helped make London's point about nature and identity.

My bias for humanity demanded that the dog become re-associated with at least one person to give greater value and meaning to the animal's life. The dog's finding fulfillment as a super-wild being with a mythic and feared status among men was unsettling to me as a child, although I might have empathized immediately if I were a dog. The dog's own identity was firmly held relative to its time and place and independent of its association with any other being. Yet it savagely attacked those responsible for its last master's death as though it had been dependent on their relationship. In the end, its sense of self was liberating rather than confining; it thought and acted, and could be defined by the result.

Unlike some suppressing transgendered people, Mr. London's hero acted without pretense or intent to deceive. It did not bend to fit any prior definition. Hedonists, libertarians, and others might laud this approach but so too would Adolf Hitler, Idi Amin, and Saddam Hussein. Each of the latter trio who ruled by whim and fiat held power after London's work was completed, but history of London's day was not devoid of similar examples. A virtuous society could not long endure if a common sense of justice and morality, stronger than any citizen who opposed them, were not firmly established at that society's core.

It also had not occurred to me that nature's summons to the dog was closely akin to my incessant conflict with suppressed gender identity. To analyze the story's elements accurately readers should remember that the work was written by an adult with a message intended for a mature audience. A child's superficial and incomplete comprehension of that message might serve as a cautionary warning regarding society's apparent adoration of youth. While a more youthful perspective is less constrained by personal history and experience, it is also less informed by them.

I had expected a human author, like so many others before him, to write about the special relationship people have with their pets. The Scots of Edinburgh have remembered and honored Greyfriars' Bobby for more than one hundred years (Edinburgh Scotland Tourist Information).[21] English poet Lord Byron had a large monument built, and he penned a tribute to honor his faithful dog "Boatswain" (Byron 1808).[22] Countless others have written testaments to the very special and enduring bond formed between them and a treasured pet. None of these could have inspired Jack London to write as he did. If such realizations do not occur to a young reader, they are still very much a part of the experience of reading because an author's words can remain long after the work was first read.

Children's television was another frequent diversion. Its fare, especially on Saturday mornings, included animals, cowboys, cartoons, and super heroes. Going outside with a few props let me play out variations on the storylines without leaving our yard. Two corners of a bath towel fastened around the neck by a safety pin transformed the material into a cape of fantasy capable of imparting magical powers of flight enabling at least the imagination to leap into the air and soar to the farthest visible point. Cowboy hats and six-guns served as sufficient armament to help a pseudo *Lone Ranger* (Morse et al. 1949)[23], *Roy Rogers* (Blair et al. 1951)[24], or *Cisco Kid* (Davis et al. 1950)[25] chase bad guys, ward off attacking Indians, rescue hostages, and otherwise help to tame the West before returning home for lunch. *Sky King's* plane (Copelan et al. 1951)[26] carried him wherever he was needed and enabled him to perform daring feats and rescues while his daughter helped coordinate efforts via radio from their base station. The towel/cape or a holstered pair of six-guns permitted youthful minds in active bodies to imagine interacting with fantasy environments at least as real as today's virtual reality of computer gaming.

As stimulating as these programs were to the imagination, they also influenced attitudes toward established norms of "sex-appropriate" societal roles. Many contemporary films intended for teenage audiences portray a physical union, often of short duration and devoid of any suggestion of long-term mutual commitment, as the major reason two people become a quicksilver couple. These films often strongly suggest that one or each partner is thinking, "I'll love you forever, darling --- unless that great-looking person across the room will go out with me." An urge for sexual, but not emotional, intimacy is treated as ubiquitous. Satisfying that urge is merely answering a need as fundamental as hunger for food or desire for rest.

The message is that answering a purely physical need, rather than acknowledging a need for lasting affection and more complex emotional fulfillment, is what is important. In the coldest examples, the fact that some fleeting pleasure is related to the activity is almost coincident to the mechanics of satisfying the need. The fact that by the end of their lives almost all women in the United States will have been married at least once is not important to, or reflected in, these films. The inference is that a longer-term relationship may result from a mutually satisfactory and essentially physical sexual union, but it is only transient satisfaction of that immediate need that is the primary and preeminent basis for beginning the relationship.

With a film industry employing vast resources to promote or reinforce such a message in an apparently accurate reading of market demand, it is readily understandable, if not excusable, that viewers of such films might miss the distinction between gender identity and physical sex. The message of most television programming and films after World War II was quite different. If establishing relationships at that time was less complicated, there was still a compelling need for them, often as subtext, that brought and kept couples together. How that programming found an audience is evident when, after winning a world war and while fighting a "cold war", much of American society accepted virtue as central to the success of liberty. The current self-policing film industry's attempts to utilize film codes shows that the idea is not dead.

If yesterday's male lead was predominant on one program, another program would arise with a different emphasis. Neither being a father nor a mother seemed a superior or preferable role to me. I did not wish to be a mother more than a father, or the reverse, but to be fully one or the other. I hopefully expected that my conflict would disappear and I would become a father in a most natural and, as my relatives and some of our neighbors suggested, seemingly unavoidable course of events. Television programs such as *Father Knows Best* (Russell and Tewksbury 1954)[27] and its pseudo feminine answer *The Donna Reed Show* (Bellamy et al. 1958)[28] were centered on families with strong parental characters who were capable and dedicated adults caring very much for and about their children. The stories always seemed to take place in their homes with the families, as a unit, drawing upon, and giving to, each other as the plots unfolded. *The Honeymooners* (Satenstein 1955)[29] let comically inept character "Ralph Kramden" show a transcendent aspiration to become a successful husband with the strength to observe at each program's end that his wife Alice was Athe greatest". Like Donna Reed's character, Alice could ultimately meet each new challenge with creative and intelligent imagination, marshaling and allocating requisite resources to meet the current crisis. In *Father Knows Best*, father "Jim Anderson" had the intellect, common sense, and practical experience to know how to handle almost every problem, including the wisdom to know when he did not know enough or just could not solve a particular problem alone.

Sharing childhood with such television families did provide a benchmark for how well my own and other families were coping with daily life. The absence of any character with whom I could fully identify did not prevent my assimilating the programs' intended lessons. Jim Anderson's son "Bud" had an older and a younger sister with age differences close to my sisters and me. He usually got along well with each and both parents, but his experiences were very different from my own. His actions and reactions were much like those of boys I knew. While I preferred the role of "Bud's" older sister, her life was not like mine. Donna Reed's husband on her program was a doctor whose office was part of their home but he often was not as adept at resolving the plot's crisis as she. It was obviously not his program. Barbara Stanwyck in *The Big Valley* (Vogel et al. 1965)[30] was a pseudo programming contrast to Loren Greene in *Bonanza* (Claxton et al.1959)[31], with each program showing surviving spouses owning large ranches and attempting to guide their adult offspring. With such notable exceptions as Donna Reed and Barbara Stanwyck, Dale Evans as wife of cowboy "Roy Rogers" played almost as important a part in his show as his horse "Trigger." Trailblazer *Annie Oakley* was a rare western series for cowgirls that reversed the dominant gender role with a clearly inferior one for her brother Tagg. Even his name suggested an unnecessary appendage to something or someone more important.

Neither of my parents professed to have, nor did my sisters or I ascribe to them, all the knowledge and/or power to resolve, or help us resolve our lesser childhood crises and wants. I sought help from whichever parent seemed most likely to help meet each need. Mother was usually more willing to provide funds for something I thought I very much wanted, although I was never encouraged to believe there was anything automatic about the process. One exception was a desire for several small metal cap pistols that also worked but made a far softer sound without caps. As a fan of the television show *Yancy Derringer* (Sale and Claxton 1958)[32], I wanted several of those small pistols to hide like the weapons the program's hero always had within reach. The premise of an undercover riverboat gambler as hero seems strange now but it was quite plausible to a nine-year-old.

To Grandma's House

During the first phase of our home's remodeling to add a second bath, a study, a larger kitchen, and attached garage, I was home from school with one of several minor childhood illnesses. I do not remember whether it was chickenpox, mumps, measles, etc., but the ailment did not diminish the excitement of our family's temporary move to be with Grandma (we never called her anything else). My parents and my grandmother had agreed that the five of us would live with her for a couple months until the major part of the renovation was completed. I was nine years old, ill, and at home when Dad came from work on moving day, wrapped me in my favorite, yes, pink quilt and carried me down the stairs and out to the car. He drove the block to my grandmother's house and carried me inside to the sofa in her living room. The sofa was under three contiguous windows against the north wall of her living room and her television was against the opposite corner of the room's east wall. This was my first experience with the extravagance of watching television while "in bed" and was easily worth being ill. When Dad returned to work, I was alone in the house for the first time and, despite the tube's distraction, immediately noticed every thump and creak.

During the years before cable television was available, our black and white set only received passably strong signals from one NBC and one CBS station. The stations reversed their network affiliations at least once but are still located roughly twenty miles apart in Steubenville, Ohio and in Wheeling, West Virginia. Pittsburgh's stations were not far away as a crow might fly, but no crow could carry a signal through the hills surrounding our small town. However significant the contributions of Pittsburgh's KDKA to the world of television, we saw none of its broadcasts until cable television was available in our valley.

Those early days of television taught an interesting lesson about the short-lived weekly broadcast of a circus. While the first program had a large audience, programmers soon realized that even audiences that were relatively new to television would quickly tire of essentially the same circus pageant and animal acts repeated weekly over the small screen. Why a circus quickly could become boring and lose its audience while so many other predictable shows could hold theirs suggests that there is, or was, a narrow range between familiar characters encountering a variety of situations and unfamiliar characters performing similar acts that become tedious. An elephant wearing a green harness instead of a red one would not be interesting in color but would not even be noticed in black and white. People in the new industry of television did know this from literature, radio, and film. It is ironic that while an almost infinite number of shows probably could have aired successfully about the performers, animals, and managers that made up the circus, viewers quickly tired of viewing the culmination of their collective efforts. The children's television series *Circus Boy* (Archainbaud 1956)[33] showed that a circus setting could be fertile ground for stories with interesting plots about appealing characters.

From the comfort of my grandmother's sofa I was able to participate vicariously in the cited *Yancy Derringer* episodes using the small pistols Dad had bought. The pistols were less useful aids for enjoying *Lawman*'s Marshall "Dan Troop" (Bare 1958)[34] who did not carry as many guns. I liked the dresses *Lawman*'s female lead wore. Her character had the *Gunsmoke*'s "Miss Kitty" part (Meston 1956)[35] on *Lawman*. The actress's appearance and the roll she played were as appealing as her wardrobe. Why a seemingly normal nine-year-old boy would prefer her role to that of the marshal in the program is confusing enough to an average adult but was even more so to me as a young "boy". The parts these two women played in their respective westerns were those of intelligent, capable, physically attractive, modestly successful women, and they were helpful, if not romantically committed, supporters of the male leads. This subordination of the supporting roles of women to their male leads was standard fare for much, but not all, of that era.

The mothers on *Lassie* (Beaudine Jr. 1954)[36] and *My Friend Flicka* (Clark 1956)[37] were often on screen but were seldom central to the stories. Whether helping the boys on *Fury* (Salkow, Selander, and Nazarro 1955),[38] *Flika, The Adventures of Rin Tin Tin*, (Bellamy 1954)[39] and *Circus Boy* or playing the leads on *Gunsmoke, Bat Masterson* (Conrad et al. 1958),[40] *Wanted Dead or Alive* (Carr 1958),[41] *The Bounty Hunter* (De Toth 1954),[42] *The Rifleman* (Boetticher 1958),[43] *Have Gun - Will Travel* (Meadow 1957)[44] and *Cheyenne* (Adreon 1955),[45] male leads of the 1950s and 1960s were usually quite human but strong, capable, and determined heroes. Intelligent use of their strength usually brought about satisfactory conclusions to the stories' conflicts. The programs with roles for children were also peopled by caring and youth-centered adults who still saw and met their other responsibilities. I understood that, as a "boy", I should hope to emulate the mature behavior of these characters, if not the actors who played them. *The Rifleman* was an unusual mixture of a series focusing alternately on adults, youth, and their interactions, but it had few roles for females. Even if the heroes in these programs were not always successful, they were portrayed as capable conscientious people with worthy motives who probably would have been recognized by audiences of early Greek morality plays.

I Love Lucy, *Make Room For Daddy*, and *F-Troop* were shows with far less powerful, less effective, usually bumbling, and unequivocally inept anti-heroes who were often barely able to influence, much less control, their environments or the people in them. Such programs, as an indictment of existing culture, would have been a logical result of, rather than precursor to, the ubiquitous anti-establishment attitudes so popular on college campuses in the late 1960s. I did not understand the popularity among my peers of Clint Eastwood's "Rowdy Yates" character on *Rawhide* (Post 1959).[46] The program's writers seemed to follow a formula requiring "Rowdy" to earn his name anew in each episode. The character's occasional challenges to authority probably appealed to many of my classmates for psychological or philosophic reasons, but more than a few girls in school just thought he was "cute". I preferred the show's trail boss/authority figure "Gil Favor," who often accepted some of the responsibility for and helped to resolve problems that "Rowdy Yates" and/or other cowboys had either instigated or exacerbated when they were not directly involved in their primary duty to herd cattle. I thought the "Rowdy" character, at least in earlier episodes, was written as a youthful, impulsive, and occasionally rebellious antagonist. The adults from whom I most sought approbation had a low threshold of tolerance for activity that was not constructive.

My childhood Saturday mornings included generous quantities of television briefly interrupted by dairy, bakery, and laundry deliveries. The local dairy supplied milk in glass bottles to a foam-insulated box on our front porch. The bread man brought our weekly order of bakery products to the door. I usually ate several of the dozen fresh cinnamon rolls that were a delicious part of that order in addition to, or in place of, breakfast. A man from the local "Star" laundry picked-up and delivered dry-cleaning consisting primarily of Dad's clothes for work. One or more of these deliveries seemed always to interrupt a favorite program at a climactic moment. This television fare included westerns, westerns with animals, and cartoons. *The Lone Ranger*, *Roy Rogers*, and *The Cisco Kid* were typical westerns. *Rin Tin Tin*, *My Friend Flika*, *Fury*, and *Circus Boy* emphasized animals. *Mighty Mouse* and *Heckle and Jekyl* typified the cartoon shows. Lessons the programs taught always reinforced those gleaned from parents, reading, school, church, and other sources regarding the rightness of established truths and the strength they possessed to assure ultimate, if not immediate, success.

The hypothetical and fantasy environments imagined by such people as Stephen Hawking, Stephen King, and Steven Spielberg prove that a person's interacting physically with such worlds is not essential to contemplation of the creation, enjoyment, and implications of their ascribed attributes. Those attributes can facilitate communication of concepts, perception, and higher truths unbounded by mundane constraints. The fantasy world a pre-transition MtF transgendered person creates and to which she devotes so much time, energy, and other resources is not one of theory, escape, relaxation, or enjoyment. I do not know if transvestite men see their "dressing" episodes that way, but the suppressing MtF transgendered person's fantasy is the only means by which she can fully express her identity.

The odd juxtaposition of being a make-believe "male" person in a real world and a real female person in a fantasy was as at least as unsatisfying as it was unavoidable. One more article of clothing of a different color or fit, a different application of makeup, some new fantasized encounter, and a thousand other variations were like the pallet of an artist who is never satisfied with her most important canvas. While a graphic artist might get closer to her or his goal with each successive stroke of the brush, as a transgendered person before transition and despite tremendous effort, I had really barely touched the canvas. In retrospect, the effort of that cumulative and seemingly futile decades-long struggle to understand is staggering.

5. A Singular Event

Playing in the Leaves

Our neighborhood had more trees lining its streets than did any other part of town. Residents of the fifteen homes that lined both sides of our street enjoyed covered front porches that spanned the width of each home. Each porch afforded a shaded view of the maple-canopied lightly-crowned brick street that an earlier era's workers had meticulously laid. The workers' precision produced an impressively, evenly artistically, smooth surface. When wet, though, the light-brown bricks were slippery and made stopping a bicycle dangerous. As comforting a sight as the maple trees provided for so much of the year, their colorful autumn display always meant that the annual raking season soon would be at hand. The minor inconvenience of that work was usually insignificant compared to the beauty and shade the trees also provided. The task of raking those leaves on a cold and breezy day, though, always made that less pleasant present seem to outweigh past and future seasons of green.

The fallen leaves also confirmed the passing of each carefree summer. The bright colors of early autumn meant the nearing of a full winter's shorter, clouded, dreary, and cold days. With a figurative salute to the first primitive ancestor whose advancing intellect registered an awareness of a cycle of seasons, countless generations of people have come to that same realization. Yet, it was new for each one of them. That realization is not something learned in the way people are taught "b" follows "a" or that "Spot" can run, but it is known in a fundamentally sensory way as it is experienced by each person. For each person it is something she or he knows differently, however small the difference, from everyone else. The intimate way in which a suppressing transgendered person comes to know her or his conflict shares this characteristic. The confusion, shame, sense of guilt, fear of discovery, etc. are intensely experienced by each suppressing transgendered person in desolate isolation, however many people are nearby.

I had begun helping with leaf raking and snow shoveling when I was tall enough to handle the implements properly but Dad, despite his grass allergies, reserved management of the gasoline mower until I was several years older. A few weeks after my tenth birthday on another cold but clear autumn day, I was again engaged in the annual ritual of leaf harvest. My five-year old sister was more interested in playing in the leaves than helping to rake them, but we agreed to sit in a pile of them at the curb if she would let me finish raking.

With comic book in hand, I sat in the street with my back against the curb while my sister sat across from me. We both saw the neighbor's car come up the street at the end of the block and turn onto our street. We recognized the car as belonging to the neighbor a couple doors further down and on the far side of the street, and we saw that its driver was headed for the spot in front of their house where he usually parked. This, however, was a Friday afternoon and the high school's football team had a home game scheduled for that night. The town council had decided that there would be no parking on the neighbor's side of the street on game nights to facilitate flow of traffic, especially of emergency vehicles if they were needed, and white paper "No Parking This Side" signs were stapled to the trees on that side. The neighbor rounded the turn, saw the signs reminding him not to park in his usual spot, and turned straight toward us from a distance of a few car-lengths. Mother and my older sister had just come out on our front porch to call us to get ready for dinner.

This all happened in less time than it takes to describe it. I saw the car's front bumper as being almost certain to crush me between it and the curb, but I rolled up over the curb just as the car began striking my sister. A little girl who weighed fewer than fifty pounds was knocked over by the bumper and then run over by both the front and rear wheels of nearly two thousand pounds of automobile; one wheel going over her head and the other over her chest. The same blond-haired and blue-eyed child had stood on my grandmother's front porch less than a year earlier and shouted at the top of her young voice to anyone who could hear, and several neighbors did, "I love everybody!" Clearly, accidents happen even to such children.

Anyone who has not had such an experience can barely imagine the sensation of an irresistible force pushing her head into the maple leaves and against the uncompromisingly solid brick street. If, as many people who have experienced traumatic events assert, time seems to slow to a crawl for its principals, we can sense her palpable horror at the realization that a great force has just threatened to crush her head, that she is bumped by another part of the moving vehicle, and then that second wheel is going to and does roll over her chest. If her conscious mind could not process and assimilate all the sensations of such unprecedented abuse, the information must still have been rushing to her brain.

Mother was unable to scream as she saw two of her three children in such peril; then saw one escape unscathed while the other did not. My older sister ran to my younger one, picked her up, and carried her to Mother on the porch. Mother's hands were full of the tufts of hair she had just torn, apparently without sensation, from her own head as she had just witnessed what she was certain was the death of her youngest child. Mother carried her into the house, placed her on the living room sofa, and began tearing at my sister's clothes looking frantically for any signs of life-threatening injury she might alleviate. She could not believe that my sister was still alive. Mother raced to the wall by the dining room phone and pounded on it desperately trying to organize her thoughts. She told the telephone operator there had been a horrible accident, asked for our family doctor who still made house calls, and then phoned Dad at the bank.

The doctor quickly traversed the several blocks between his office and our home and arranged for my sister's reception at one of the hospitals across the river. After an examination in its emergency room, another ambulance took her to another hospital twenty miles south. Mother would stay with her in that hospital for the next two weeks as the doctors re-inflated most of a partially collapsed lung, helped reduce severe swelling of my sister's nose and face, fought a case of pneumonia and high fever, and treated numerous surface abrasions. Every single leaf, my sister's clothing, and, we are convinced, an incredible Power had spared my sister's life. Cynics and skeptics might contend that fortune, coincidence, and/or simple physics prevented her being killed, but they will not find a receptive audience among the event's witnesses.

When my sister got home, I attempted to give her a welcoming hug but was told "NOT TO TOUCH HER!" What Mother had meant as a cautionary warning to a ten-year old boy to be especially careful with a still-sick child was accepted as partial admonition for my involvement in the accident. I might have joined my sister under those wheels but there was not time, nor did I have sufficient strength, to grab her and pull her with me over the curb. Had she been seated beside me, if we had switched places, if the driver had been later coming home, or had any number of other possible variables been altered, the accident might never have happened. None of that could alter what happened to her mind and body.

In Need of Help

The victim of the accident was a traumatically abused, small, incredibly sweet, and very vulnerable child who had somehow survived an horrendous encounter with a large part of roughly a ton of moving machine, but she was not the only person deeply affected by the experience. The car's driver had a daughter almost my sister's age and was married to one of my mother's lifelong friends. The hardest thing this man probably ever would do was to admit to himself and to anyone else that he had been driving that car. The farthest thing from his mind as he neared his home has to have been the possibility of what was about to happen. His wanting so desperately to believe that he could not have been driving a vehicle that ran over a child ended cruelly when his family found strands of her hair caught on the underside of the car. His torment must have been nearly unbearable. One of the few times our neighbors saw another neighbor, and owner of the local hardware store, wear a formal suit was during his visit to my recuperating sister after her stay in the hospital. Our minister, other neighbors, and many other people shared prayers, cards, and other expressions of concern for her.

At the height of the cold war, when the paranoia of the McCarthy hearings was an all too present memory and fear of mind control was a small skirmish in the battle against the ideology of Communism, much of society and many in the medical community had little respect for what was seen as the pseudo sciences of psychiatry and psychology. This dismissiveness abounded despite the disciplines' sharing of a history dating from the dawn of man. Every normal healthy person of any intellect and level of emotional maturity was deemed capable of calmly applying reason and understanding appropriate to her or his age to any stressful event, and was expected to accept and adjust to the event's reality. Anyone having difficulty coping with the reality and aftermath of a shattering experience, those attempting to cope with a chronic condition, or those having faced an unusually challenging situation simply needed more time, more faith, and/or common sense, and the caring attention of family and friends. Only horribly confused, or "weak-minded" people, or people who had presumably never been quite "right" from birth were thought to require help from dubiously qualified practitioners of this questionable art; and even after such help these people would never be considered to have achieved the coveted status of "normal".

If such professional help were too scarce and/or expensive to be readily available, that was just additional impetus to and further indication that people were meant to handle such matters on their own or with the help of family, clergy, and friends. After Michigan's Governor George Romney described himself as having been "brainwashed" on the subject of Viet Nam during what had been a budding effort to be the 1968 Republican Presidential nominee, his campaign never recovered. When Senator George McGovern's running mate in 1972, Senator Thomas Eagleton, admitted to having sought help and supposedly gotten it from a mental health professional, despite the continuing support of Senator McGovern, Senator Eagleton had to resign from the campaign, and the remaining ticket still suffered one of the worst defeats in the history of presidential campaigns.

Although much less prevalent today, there remain certain mindsets, organizations, and cultures, especially those tracing their origins to the 1950s, that cling to, and perpetuate, the "man as an island" myth. For growth and for perceptual or emotional stability, they would deny themselves access to the divine spark and essential humanity in others, as well as access to the professionally competent expertise of practitioners whose study, training, and licensing are an invaluable tool for and product of civilized society. For much of the time before my transition, I would have agreed with those deniers, at least partly, because I knew most people seemed different from me. I did not understand, and therefore could not trust, what constituted and sustained that difference. I was not antisocial but certainly might have become so if I had had different parents, friends, and life experience.

Where people diminish themselves by eschewing those resources that are some of the Creator's most precious gifts to each person, the tragedy is unfortunate but self-inflicted. Where people act to deny needed counseling or mental health services to others, those actions are or should be illegal. Denial of psychological and, especially, psychiatric remediation is not importantly different from denial of any other critically needed remediation, whatever the economic system established to provide it. Moderate popular skepticism regarding accepted standards and qualifications can be beneficial and even necessary to the encouragement of a reasonable degree of humility and diligence among a profession's membership, improvement of standards and enforcement among licensing and policy boards, and as a cautionary warning to prospective clients. That skepticism clearly crosses an important line and becomes unreasonable, counterproductive, and harmful to everyone involved when it impedes or prevents those needing qualified professional services from obtaining them.

Shortly after returning home from the hospital, my sister began having bouts of internal hives that would usually impair her breathing. Her hives were always preceded by a swelling and stiffening of her fingers, and a pronounced puffiness around her eyes and over the bridge of her nose. This claxon call of swelling could sound anywhere and at any time, and always necessitated our getting her to the nearest prearranged medical facility as quickly as possible. Although she had never had such a problem before the accident, she was sent to an allergist. She had begun a strictly controlled diet of gradually reintroduced foods, had various clothing materials presented and others withheld, and observed a carefully planned routine in an attempt to discover the offending allergen(s). The alarmingly obvious proximate cause of something that was happening after the accident that had never occurred before the accident was apparently not obvious enough even to trained medical professionals. Either they would not consider, or were dissuaded by exogenous factors from considering, the possibility that so young a child's intimate inspection of the underside of a neighbor's moving car had left deep and lasting mental and emotional scars on that child that were every bit as real as her physical ones, and which would heal much more slowly. It should surprise no one that no hive-inducing allergen was ever found and her frightening attacks continued for years.

After terrorists so viciously attacked the Pentagon and World Trade Center school students across the country were encouraged to seek professional counseling to help them cope with the rumors, images, and stories of the widely reported but distant events. Yet in the aftermath of my sister's harrowing accident that so powerfully impacted the lives of a child, her family, their neighbors, and lifelong friends; the only specialist recommended for anyone following her hospitalization was for her to see an allergist. Finding the cause of my sister's attacks was literally as important as whether she could breathe. The absence of the services of a qualified and capable psychologist or psychiatrist meant that she would continue to endure her life-threatening hives episodes long after the accident.

The unrelenting mental anguish of the driver must have been excruciating. To avoid the unacceptable stigma of having obtained help from a mental health professional, each one of the accident's principals was expected to accept and adjust as well as she or he might alone or with family, as though what had been experienced was little more than a bad dream or a bout of sniffles. Since professional therapeutic counseling was not deemed, by anyone who might have recommended it, to be appropriate in this instance to repair some of the event's psychological aftermath, it is difficult to imagine a scenario under the same standard where it would ever be seen as appropriate.

Love as Strength

My mother had received a form of therapy in having so closely observed and aided in the miraculous healing of so terribly abused a small, fragile, and yet resilient physical frame. She did fight initially to keep my sister awake and later permitted her to take short naps, fearful that any deeper sleep would mean my sister's never waking. My sister would later remember her not being permitted to sleep soundly, even in her steamy oxygen tent, as almost being worse than her trip under the wheels. Mother argued with my sister's doctor to obtain an older favored medication that did finally lower a pneumonia-induced fever when the fever stubbornly refused to yield to the doctor's newer, and surely better, medication. Mother confronted an incredulous insurance company representative who first challenged the idea that my sister had even been injured and then could not believe that Mother only sought payment for my sister's immediate medical expenses.

Mother's nearly incessant communication with my sister included daily readings that attracted other children who were patients in nearby hospital rooms. Every mother worthy of the appellation would doubtlessly understand the level of maternal desire, determination, and commitment that was focused on securing the clearest possible path to my sister's fullest possible recovery. The fact that the path afforded my mother scant opportunity for sleep bothered her far less than even the slightest hint that she even consider leaving my sister's room without my sister.

Sis's amazingly short and successful two-week hospitalization was just as unlikely as had been her initial survival. Mother would spend as much time at home as possible with her that fall, but Mother did ease back into her part-time and then full-time teaching responsibilities. I do not know when the first attack of hives occurred, but my sister was far from well when she was released from the hospital and it is difficult to imagine anything that might have made it more difficult for Mother to go back to work. That winter and the following spring did see a gradual return to better health but her weight was unchanged for a year after the accident.

To the Shore

Most of our family spent the summer following the accident in a small town at the New Jersey shore. My sister's doctor had recommended sea air to help heal her partially collapsed lung and Mother would have carried her to New

Jersey by herself if that had been the only way to get her there. One of Dad's cousins knew a man who had just completed construction of a six-unit apartment building in Sea Isle City. When the school year ended Mother, Dad, my sisters, and I packed a summer's living essentials into the trunk of the family car and headed for our new home for the summer. My bitterly plaintive objections about missing a summer with my bicycle, my best friend, and the city pool did not delay our departure; nor did the similar complaints of my sisters. Assurance that those things we thought we would miss so terribly would still be in town when we returned was little consolation. I knew I would be almost eleven years old when we returned and would be missing that essential summer experience at home that had preceded each previous birthday.

Dad stayed with us at the shore for only a few days before flying back home to work but he would return for July 4th, his vacation in August, and to assist us in our family's return home at summer's end. My parents had not had to be apart since their marriage fifteen years earlier and that summer would be an uncomfortably long one for each of them. Dad would tell us later that he had never been so aware of just how loud the ticking of our living room's "sunburst" clock could be before that especially long summer. As important as it was for Mother to be with my sister during her continuing recovery, we were acutely aware that our family's economic future was closely tied to the bank and Dad was committed to helping to ensure its success.

Our new "home" was the first unit at the top of the stairs on the second floor of the Silver Sands Apartments. The beach abutted a two-foot wood seawall at the edge of the parking lot behind the building and no air-conditioning meant we were almost constantly exposed to as much salt as the Atlantic could release into the air. My sisters shared one double bed, Mother and Dad would share the double in the other bedroom, and I slept on a bolster bed in the living room. A single bath and eat-in kitchen completed the apartment. There was slatted glass and a screen on the front door and at least one screened window in every room that provided fresh air, if it was not raining, and a beautiful view of life at the ocean's edge.

Absence of air-conditioning was not unusual for us since few people we knew had it in their homes at that time and we spent most of the summer not realizing that the apartment also did not have a television. We were far enough from Philadelphia that reception would have been poor and cable and video recordings were only available in science fiction stories. Our previous shore visits had always been sans tube, and not watching summer reruns seemed quite natural in this new home away from home. The unpaved parking area behind the apartments did not feature the slightest hint of anything green but the owner, who spent much of the summer in the first floor apartment at the other end of the building, battled constantly to keep a lush green lawn in front of the structure.

Although our family had vacationed at the shore for a week or two from my earliest memory, we had never spent more time than that near the ocean. Despite the reason for our being there, my sister's aforementioned recurring and life-threatening bouts of internal hives, and our initial complaints about missing a whole summer at home; much of those months spent in that small ocean-side town provided experiences that are among my fondest of memories. I spent as much of each day as possible either in the surf or on the beach.

One blond-haired boy became a particularly close friend. We were the same age and loved the beach and ocean. He and I would explore a rock jetty two blocks north of the apartments that collected an amazing variety of sea life and shells but, as some of that life had ended with each receding tide, emitted a most unpleasant odor. We teased blue crabs that had buried themselves in the sand around the posts that supported the boardwalk, and others posts supporting a large house that had either been built right on the beach or too close to an eroding one. Between this house and the rock jetty was a second house surrounded on three sides by a concrete wall. At high tide, and especially on days with rougher seas, the waves would strike the face of the wall and splash impressively higher than the top of the wall. Each of the homes showed one of two methods of attempting to preserve a home sited so close to the water's edge, and each would prove to be spectacularly unsuccessful.

The beach patrol awarded t-shirts with two lines of red felt S I C B P Mascot (Sea Isle City Beach Patrol) lettering to boys who had spent at least half of the summer in town and who knew the first names of at least thirteen lifeguards. Those t-shirts were, or were among, the most coveted items in town for young boys. Our informally assigned responsibilities consisted of helping to move the lifeboats as the tide required, handing things up to the guards on their stands, and doing anything else that might occur to them that they probably could have done more quickly and easily themselves. The beach was supposedly closed to swimming after the guards left at 5:00 P.M. but I could usually get in almost another hour of body surfing and simply enjoying the ocean before being called for dinner.

The boardwalk had been much longer prior to one or more of the violent storms that occasionally strike the shore. By this particular summer, though, the walk had been reduced to only a few blocks in length beginning two blocks south of the apartments. Diagonally across from our apartment was a large home with a small store in its basement. Tony sold delicious Italian Ice there, and sold much less of it to us than we would have liked to consume. My family did not even care that he thought West Virginia meant western Virginia. The few other staples and candy he sold were of far less interest to us than his "snow cones".

Across from Tony's was the "Casino" lounge and it, too, lacked air-conditioning. Its open doors and live music until midnight or later may have been one of the reasons I still do not care for the sound of a saxophone. My parents had always taken us to family restaurants and never to places that served wine or beer. The people who visited the "Casino" were different from us just in being permitted to be in the place. Our open windows taught me that trying to sleep to the sounds of soft jazz must be an acquired taste that I never acquired. Whether I liked the music or not, I have always found it nearly impossible not to listen to what is playing. The best chance for me to get to sleep came at the end of each set.

In the next block was the Pennsylvania Hotel which had survived harsh storms that destroyed many similar of the island's hotels. This large wood building had a wide covered porch on which different people were always comfortably seated. Another half block south was a small restaurant that assembled delicious submarine sandwiches. I had never had a sandwich like these before that summer but would have gladly had them three times a day after the first one. Across that next street was the Braca Theatre where I saw several films that were popular at the time. One of these was *The Savage Innocents* featuring Anthony Quinn as a credible Eskimo (Ray 1960).[47] The juxtaposition of the film's arctic setting and the shore's summertime heat was no more strange than Mr. Quinn's having been cast as an Eskimo but they were each enjoyable. A second theater off the boardwalk was built on piling that extended into the surf. The "Madelyn" was a large theater that actually swayed slightly with the wave action at high tide so that watching a film there was often a "moving" experience regardless of the feature. I saw Disney's *Pollyanna* (Swift 1960)[48] in that theater with an audience of children near my own age. The fact that Hayley Mills was also close to my age when she made the film may have had something to do with it, but I loved her accent almost as much as I enjoyed her performance.

Sea Isle City's boardwalk also featured a bumper car amusement ride that let me control my first powered vehicle, at age ten. While other riders seemed to enjoy bumping into as many cars as possible and getting caught in the unmoving jams that often resulted, I always tried to make the thrill of an uninterrupted drive around the floor last as long as possible. When rentable time on trampolines was added to the walk's options, my older sister and I were anxious to try them. We were unschooled in the necessity of keeping our knees flexed. Our first and only experience with jumping on those trampolines was followed by our spending most of the next day in bed. How too much of something we had expected to be so much fun could make us so uncomfortable was an important lesson we would try to apply to other seemingly enticing new things.

One novelty many children in the area found far more attractive than we did was the jeep that fogged to suppress mosquitoes. If we were home and heard the vehicle coming, we would race to close the windows before the insecticide could reach us. We thought the kids who would run as closely behind the jeep as they could were doing something that was dangerous but the driver's efforts to dissuade them were always unsuccessful. The fogging needed to occur at dusk because that was when the mosquitoes were most active. Dusk was also the time when children so inclined could get in their last moments of committed outdoor play. If the fog were as effective in reducing the insect population as it was in attracting some of the kids, there would have been far fewer mosquitoes. There was a mile or more of marsh between the barrier island and the mainland, which made mosquito control on dry land a never-ending, Herculean, and futile task.

I was able to capture some of the town's images during that and the following summer with a Kodak Instamatic 100 camera I bought at the local drug store. Subsequent models of that small camera would use a "flash cube", but the "100" had a popup flash that used readily available bulbs, was more compact, and it was fun to play with. Color film for the series was available some months after the new line of cameras was introduced, but my pictures from those shore years are black and white. That camera is still one of the most tangible of the memories of those long-ago days at the shore.

I used that inexpensive camera for more than fifteen years taking color pictures at the New York World's Fair, in the Hawaiian Islands, and on a tour of England, Scotland, and Wales. Kodak's announcement that it would no longer make film cartridges for its Instamatic series was another of those bittersweet indications of technology's relentless progress. I have used digital cameras and sent their modified images by email moments later but no other instrument shares my first camera's history. Earlier generations may well have felt the same way about their console radios, comfortable surreys, Clovis points, or stone tools.

The Rain Must Fall

We stayed in the same apartment in Sea Isle City for six weeks the second summer after the accident, and were to spend four weeks there in 1962. The storm that struck the Jersey Cape and the Mid-Atlantic region March 5-9, 1962 is known as the "Ash Wednesday Storm". Causing more than $200 million (in 1962 dollars) of damage from North Carolina to New York, the storm destroyed or damaged 45,000 homes in New Jersey alone, and was the twentieth century's strongest nor'easter (N.O.A.A. n.d.).[49] Applying the gross domestic product price deflator adjusts the $200 million in 1962 dollars to an equivalent of over $962 million in 2001 dollars (Council 2003, tbl. B-3).[50] Because of the increased residential and commercial building density that has increased at a frenetic pace on barrier islands since that storm, the economic loss of a storm of similar magnitude today easily would run into billions of dollars.

The endlessly fascinating and wondrously beautiful Atlantic of so many of my youthful and later summers had wrought horrible devastation upon our small barrier island. My father's parents celebrated their forty-eighth wedding anniversary at their home in Kingston, N. Y. in April, 1962, and we returned home from its commemoration by way of the New Jersey shore. Our reaction to the incredible destruction must have been some of what London's blitz survivors felt on having witnessed the almost total destruction of what had been their homes and neighborhoods, except that the tremendous losses in Britain had not been caused by nature.

The ocean's surge over the barrier island had pushed Silver Sands apartments into what had been that assiduously maintained front lawn and the receding flow had canted the remaining structure back toward the ocean. The cottage the owner had built in what had been the parking lot was lifted from its foundation and dropped on one crushed corner. The two homes on the beach had each vanished without a trace. The swaying theater on piling and everything that had been part of the boardwalk were gone. Parts of a few homes on the mainland-side of the island had been carried far into the marsh. The Pennsylvania Hotel, like so many other buildings all along the shore, was unrecognizable rubble. Unlike that of so many Sea Isle City's residents, our loss was not a financial one, nor did we share the emotional attachment to the entire community that must have been felt by some of its longer-term residents. My family had spent an important summer and half of a second one in this second home. We felt a small part of the community's deep sense of loss as our own.

As Sea Isle began to rebuild, the few blocks around what had been our summer home were transformed. Two large buildings with roughly one hundred condominium units were built behind a paved barrier of boulders. On the seaside of the boulders, the return of a natural structure of sand dunes was being encouraged. All of this was located where the beach homes, our apartment building, and a skating rink had once stood. The economic pressure for beachfront housing from residents primarily from the Philadelphia area helped developers utilize almost every possible inch of property on which anything might be built.

A large guesthouse further down the island in which we had stayed for parts of six or seven summers in some of the years following the storm was replaced by an unattractive but most utilitarian condominium. It is probably coincidence but the increasing penchant for turning almost any structure into a multi-unit condominium seems to have coincided with the telephone company's discontinuing use of four-sided phone booths. A reluctance or inability to adopt and enforce lower maximum occupancy limits and greater property setbacks helped to transform a quiet seaside community into one that felt much more urban. Sharing the shore with so many more residents means that each resident now has a different experience from that earlier and less harried day. There may have been at least a few residents who had resented the advent of Silver Sands Apartments to an area of predominantly single-family homes, but that building would easily have been dwarfed by the huge units that now stand so close to where our apartment once did.

What seems certain and regrettable is that ten-year-olds do not have today, and will not have for the foreseeable future, the experience of large, shell-covered, and uncrowded beaches and an innocent, trusting, and vulnerable openness to the natural forces of sky, wind, and sea that so permeated those summer days of my childhood at the New Jersey Shore. The friends I met there did add to my experience of comparing similarities and differences with people who enjoyed the same seaside offerings, proximate interests of chess, movies, and skee-ball, and the pursuit of Sunday school attendance pins that I did. It was easier to find friends at the beach because so many other children were also away from home and were seeking friendship.

Being away from the forced nature of public school class associations and our home's location in the neighborhood had facilitated finding new friends and avoiding people I thought might be less friendly. At the end of our visit to the shore, our return home meant spending time with my best friend and seeing my grandmother who, because of her work in the bank, was almost never able to vacation with us. I quickly became reacquainted with the things I enjoyed at home, and being in the home where I thought I belonged. Yet, our return also meant revisiting forced associations of school and my attempting to meet expectations I knew I could satisfy but could not do so in a natural manor. The ease of association or separation, the freedom from formal responsibilities, and the independence from the role each person plays to, for, or in the lives of others must be one of the most refreshing aspects of vacations. For many people at greater peace with their normal lives, the interdependence of daily life and of associations formed and strengthened over many years may be missed while traveling, as one misses the sense of community and of belonging.

The role public school plays in encouraging the essential development of social skills that enable us to interact with, learn from, attempt to persuade, and otherwise coexist with those whom we would rather avoid was at least as important for me as for anyone else. Many of those whom I would have preferred to avoid were simply much better at being male than I was. Without knowing what this was and why it bothered me, I tried to avoid them or accept their avoiding me, and otherwise ignore the problem. The sentiment was really more one of failing to understand, rather than of jealousy. Trying to accept school, the neighborhood, and other people with whom I spent time as choices I made would have been a wise and healthful thing to do, but I did not feel as though I had the power of choice. I did not realize how internal a matter choice is and, since I was suppressing my identity, that suppressed self was not free to choose anything.

6. A "Normal Boy"

The Young Scout

Having a general interest in Scouting was not the common denominator it might have been to forging closer ties with other people my age. To the extent that troop meetings and activities offered a less regimented use of time than did public school classes, they afforded members an opportunity to obtain a much richer appreciation for some of the variety of human aptitude, ability, and experience present even in a relatively small homogeneous community. Appreciating some of that variety was often more of a challenge than I was prepared to meet or willing to accept, and it was more than evident to me that many of my contemporaries were quite willing to abide my absence. I was sufficiently comfortable with my own interests and attitudes, as borrowed or affected as they were, that differences from some of these peers were acceptable, if not desired. Becoming more comfortable with the available variety and enjoying differences through conversation required a maturity that was sorely lacking in my earliest interactions. When I joined our troop, several higher-ranking Scouts were much more at home with nature, camping, and sports than I, but rather than my trying to be accepted by them and to learn from them, I chose the inertia of my own interests. I missed the knowledge they and the process of getting to know them might have imparted.

The greater wisdom and experience of the men who organized and assisted with troop activities was much more welcome to me, even though they seemed quite different from my parents. Their volunteering to spend time helping young Scouts was substantially different in character and content from the commitment of other adults such as public school and Sunday school teachers. While still being adults with commensurate authority and responsibility, the troop leaders also seemed, in another sense, like older boys and especially like the people described in the Scout manual. They made what had seemed an immense barrier of age and experience which might have separated them from young boys seem like little more than a different perspective on the same world. I did not really see them as older peers but thought that they made the seemingly immense gulf between the acutely felt limitations of youth and the maturity, independence, and responsibility of adults take on shrink to still large but defined proportions.

Our Scout troop's initial meeting place was in a real log cabin located a short distance down a steep hill behind a popular tavern. The cabin could be, and often was, heated by a classic pot-bellied wood burning stove whose fire was almost never started until after the opening of our meetings. Each Scout sat on any of several long wood benches that nearly filled the small cabin. After our standing for a recitation of the Pledge of Allegiance, the Scout Oath, and the Scout Laws, Scouts sat on those cold uncovered wood benches as we heard about planned troop activities, reviewed requirements for individual advancement, learned survival skills, and increased our general knowledge of the natural world and our place in it. The information about first-aid and camping would be quite useful to someone intending to hike or go on a camping trip but were less useful for those who only imagined being latter-day frontiersmen. To a transgendered child, the idea of spending much time in the woods was as appealing as being a cowboy or a husband and father, but I had no plans for taking any of them beyond the stage of thought.

A new concrete block "cabin" was built on more level ground about two miles from the tavern about a year after I joined the troop. The new cabin lacked the rustic feel of the old one and seemed to transform the troop into a more contemporary organization. There were wild blackberry bushes near the new cabin. The berries ripened and, after one early-summer meeting, Scouts were encouraged to take some of the berries home. One of the men gave me a small paper sack that I filled. When I got home, Mother washed that sack of berries and rested them comfortably in a dish with a little milk and sugar. They tasted like a touch of heaven. Contemporary Scouting, or at least the new cabin, thus was transformed into a clearly superior version of the more rustic model.

As a faithful Scout, I read my handbook frequently and enjoyed comparing it to my father's. His had been in our attic for almost ten years and seemed more like a museum artifact than something a contemporary Scout might use. World War II had been fought in the twenty-plus years since their respective publications, and a shift from a more rural to a more urban focus was reflected throughout my manual in its greater emphasis on first aid, civic activities, and color illustrations versus the earlier edition's larger sections on dressing wild game, identifying berries, and camping. Much of the remaining content seemed similar. While opportunities for practical application of the nature-oriented content were sparse, it was not difficult to fantasize about its use.

Scouting's popularity among some of my acquaintances, the numerous and varied activities of our troop, my father's having been a Scout, and even the uniform Scouts wore were some of the reasons I wanted to join. Having decided on the necessity for becoming a Scout, I cornered the troop's Scoutmaster at a court of honor and, when he was not sure which questions comprised the test for "tenderfoot" classification, I suggested many of the questions as well as reciting their answers. I probably have not attempted to tie most of the knots that I remember being a part of that test since I passed it so many years ago, but learning to tie them was a potentially helpful form of initiation into the group. I repeatedly was disappointed that most troop members did not consistently seem to exhibit the manners and character traits supposedly inculcated by our study of the Laws, Oath, and handbook except during the more formal part of meetings, but I did enjoy many of the activities the dedicated leaders arranged for us.

One such activity was an all-day hike that taught us an interesting fact about cattails. The Scouts stripped the seeds from at least fifty of the pods into a large pile in the middle of a dirt road. With everyone a reasonably safe distance away, a match or burning wad of paper was tossed into the pile, igniting it into a sudden, intense, and huge fireball that quickly consumed the seeds but caused no other damage. The idea to do this did not originate with any of the leaders, but they did permit our indulging in the experiment. The men and fathers who were our leaders walked an occasionally fine line between being responsible adult supervisors and being the curious, active, and athletic role models that young boys might wish to emulate.

After several hours of hiking we prepared and ate the lunches we had brought with us as we rested on a hilltop which overlooked the river valley, the mills, and several of the local bridges to Ohio. Night was falling when the hike ended near the home of one of the leaders. As the troop climbed a rise behind his home I slipped on some soft and moist soil and, rather than offering a hand, the other members passed me. Instead of getting up and following, I convinced myself I could not climb the last few feet to level ground. A few of the others had a little difficulty near that spot and had helped each other to prevent their slipping. A combination of being a tired kid and my determination to see which of the troop members was the helpful, kind, and cheerful Scout of the handbook kept me fixed to that spot on the rise.

Someone did finally give me a hand and I still remember who he was but I was embarrassed by the ease with which I took those last few steps. I thought I was discovering that if something was rather easy I could count on someone's finally being willing to help but if something was more difficult I needed to be self-reliant. It is alarming that children might so easily misconstrue such events that occur regardless of the child's intelligence and character. The conflict between the terror of some of the responsibilities of parenting, the possibilities for failure, the inability to control extraneous forces and events, and the joy of involvement in a child's development are some of the things I really have missed about not having been a parent.

The grounds of the county park, located among the hilltops of the highest spot in our county, included a large old barn that is now a theater, a pool, and a lake stocked with fish. On another outing, the troop spent an early spring night at this park. The night's low temperature was not expected to dip into the 40's but it seemed to go much lower. All Scouts had been assigned spaces for our sleeping bags in the tents gathered from a variety of sources. Sometime after we had bedded down while wearing our coats and clothes inside the sleeping bags, one or more Scouts decided it would be great fun to bring one, and then all, of the tents down. If there was a conspirator in our tent, he experienced the same loss of sleep as his victims.

By morning, all of the tents were down and I was the only Scout to have spent the night in, or quite literally under a tent but not as anyone had really expected. Everyone else had found space and tried to sleep in a park shelter which had a concrete floor and a large fireplace at one end. Above the three-foot block wall up to the roof, though, the shelter's other three sides were open to the weather. Since the concrete floor and open shelter provided nothing to hold heat, I probably had the most comfortable accommodations and got the most sleep. This time, the feeling of not fitting in with the group had seemed an appreciable advantage.

After crawling out of my sleeping bag and the collapsed tent, I joined the others in the shelter as we waited for sunrise. At my mother's insistence, I had brought a foil-wrapped and buttered potato from home with no idea of how to bake it. One of the leaders tossed it into the ashes in the shelter's large fireplace and said it should be left there awhile. About an hour later, I enjoyed one of the best-tasting baked potatoes I have ever eaten. For baking potatoes, that leader had also proven to be a master chef.

The leaders probably had expected to spend the night in their vehicles until the tents started coming down. In addition to interfering with what would have been a meager night's sleep, the Scouts also provided a bit of drama. While chopping some wood for the fire, a troop member had his foot on a log to steady it as he swung his hatchet. The tool glanced off the log and found his leg. There were more than enough leaders present for someone to help him into a car for the ten-mile ride to the nearest emergency room. Several years later, that Scout became one of the best cross-country runners in our high school without the slightest indication that he had ever had a misadventure with the hatchet. An almost anticlimactic game of capture-the-flag, where the flags were roughly a mile apart, seemed to last much longer than the hour or so it consumed that Saturday morning, and after we went home in the early afternoon, most participants probably enjoyed a suitably long nap.

Another of our outings was a visit to the Steubenville, Ohio television broadcasting facilities. The studio and broadcast facility where in one building on a valley hilltop. The facility's location must have been nearly impossible to reach after a heavy snow or in freezing rain, but I do not remember the station's ever being off the air. Before the community had cable television, this most local of the two area stations was the source of much of our non-print news, weather, and entertainment. The stool-mounted projector that reversed images shot from the other side of the screen would seem quite primitive to a digital station receiving a remote feed today. The people who read the news and weather had not really seemed like people when we had only seen their two-dimensional images on our sets at home. After seeing and understanding how the station did so much of its work, the hardest part of that work seemed to be the consistent, repetitive, and time-driven regimentation necessary for their daily broadcasts.

For several Saturday mornings during one winter many of our Scout troop members visited a nearby Y.M.C.A. for a swim and some basketball. This was my first experience with an indoor pool. While I was a child, I spent as much of each summer in the town's swimming pool as I could, and I loved the Atlantic's waves during our annual New Jersey shore vacations. The new experience of swimming indoors on a cold winter day was a great boon to the imagination; what had been an exclusively summertime activity was no longer bounded by the calendar. Similar strictures regarding time, place, and other activities might also be less inhibiting in an appropriate setting. While I could imagine a variety of scenarios where and when my own appearance might be quite different even as a child, these imaginings were always little different from daydreams. When our allotted "Y" time expired, it still was winter outside of the building and I still looked very much as I had when I entered.

The "Y's" recreational basketball period was not an organized competition and there were enough hoops available to afford a variety of troop member combinations to use them. A neighbor's garage-mounted basket had let us practice shooting and I played on our seventh-grade team. I never quite understood or accepted the grave seriousness and primacy some fellows seemed to attach to competition. It has been generally accepted and anecdotally evinced that women have tended toward collaboration in groups instead of competition, and have been more disposed to oral, rather than physical, confrontations than men. That was certainly the prevalent view when I was in public school. It also seemed evident in our inter-faith bowling league.

Not in the Handbook

At a Boy Scout "jamboree" in a local National Guard armory one weekend, our troop presented an exhibit of rope-making featuring a machine one of the members had acquired. We spun strands of string into ropes of varying lengths and thickness. We enjoyed the thrill of making something potentially useful and our perusal of the projects of other area troops. One of the exhibits demonstrated first-aid techniques that were included in the Scout manual. To illustrate treatment of deep cuts, someone used melted wax from a candle dripped generously onto the skin. A sharp knife pressed into the wax simulated the cut. A mixture of iodine and hand lotion was dripped over the wax. The result was an excellent reproduction of a very recent and severe wound. My grandmother had a small brown bottle with a screw top and brush that I filled with the crimson concoction. I fabricated wounds for friends and family as play but never actually needed to use the manual's first-aid lessons. I still have the bottle of mixture that looks as it did so long ago even though it has not been used for more than 30 years.

While I enjoyed many of the lessons and activities of Scouting, I also learned that membership did not confer or impart a *de jure* bond among troop members acknowledging a common understanding based on shared values of intellect and purpose, despite the handbook's contents and our troop leader's intentions. Scouting afforded an opportunity to learn about civic responsibilities and required members to commit to acting in a generally civil manner, but it did not include specifics about what was to be done and what consequences would attend failure to keep that commitment. The recitation of the Scout Oath, Scout Laws, and Pledge of Allegiance which opened each meeting demanded each member's familiarity with substantive concepts worthy of contemplation, but interpretation of these generalities was limited only by the Scout's imagination and benchmarks for progress were also left to the member's discretion.

Millions of adults can still recite them, but a dull recitation by dispassionate youthful Scouts could be hollow and empty. The content could be deemed to obligate Scouts only to a vaguely distant mass of people whom we might like and with whom we might agree if we ever saw them. Our troop's recitations were never performed in a circle and there seemed to be an unwritten imperative to avoid eye contact with other Scouts while making these promises. That avoidance may be a common characteristic among most boys not yet in their teens, be geographically specific, or may have been more common in that era, but it was an effective exercise in avoiding the forging of a common bond among a group of disparate members. The wonderfully generous men who devoted so much time and other resources to the group were dedicated and sincere, but they were not teachers or pastors by vocation. They seemed to focus more on what troop members did and could do rather than what we thought or felt about ourselves and the group.

Our squad worked at accumulating merit badges and I especially remember the first aid and railroading sessions. The first-aid badge was achieved after our squad met with the local Chief of Police at his home. His daughter helped us as much as he did and that seemed acceptable even in a guys-only setting. The squad meeting's focus was the badge's requirements for learning first aid, even if we learned from a non-male instructor. The requirements for the railroading badge were met at the home of one of the squad members whose father worked with trains serving one of the mills. He explained some of the operation of the track switches, the capacity of the railcars, and the meaning of the train whistles. After the squad session and as we were leaving his home, I heard three of the rougher members of our small squad making plans to "get" me. I did not know what they had in mind but knew it had nothing to do with anything in the Scout manual. Reaching the last of the steps from their home, I ran off around the nearest bend heading away from my home. I heard one of them ask "Where did he go?" and I kept running away from my home for roughly twenty minutes. At that later hour on a cold dark evening, there were few, if any, people outside of their homes. It did not occur to me that, if the trio spread out enough to search, they would no longer be in a group for their attack, but I was not interested in a hostile confrontation with any of them.

If my gender identity conflict left me feeling as though I should be punished, I knew I had not let the squad know anything about it. I would not cede to them an opportunity to inflict punishment for some other imagined or contrived wrong. I found a vantage point where I was concealed but could watch for anyone approaching from any direction. Having seen no one for more than ten minutes, I cautiously approached my home from the direction opposite what had been the most direct route home. I knew my fellow Scouts might have stayed together and approached or regrouped near my house but I thought they would tire of waiting in the time that had elapsed since the end of the meeting. I carefully approached my home, entered quietly, and was most relieved to find myself safely inside. I had returned home that night later than usual but had also missed confronting those squad members.

I never learned the reason for their hastily planned attack. I had not trusted a couple of the squad members and a few of the other troop members, apparently with good reason, and they may have known how I felt. Nothing in the leader's lessons, the manual, or other Scouting experiences suggested that a ten or eleven year old boy should consider this a normal or acceptable part of childhood. The experience of having felt so threatened probably was more memorable than an actual confrontation would have been. An episode of such fear or an unanticipated threat seems at least as memorable a childhood experience as a more tangible encounter.

I tried to be sure that there would always be at least one adult present for future Scout meetings but eventually lost interest in the organization. Later, I told my father that I was no longer interested in Scouting primarily because the other kids were not like the ones described in the manual. He asked what I intended to do the next time I was part of something in which people did not behave in the manner I thought was appropriate, and I replied that it probably would depend on the circumstances. He obviously was disappointed that I did not intend to continue with Scouting, but he did not insist that I attend any more meetings.

The Reason for the Group

I joined another organization at age fourteen that did encourage its members to think more deeply about many of the same virtues espoused by Scouts. Its study of the life of an aged French martyr, who was executed one thousand years ago, had nothing to do with crafts, merit badges, or camping. Its primary focus was the reverse of Scouting's emphasis on activities. Members learned lessons that they might begin to apply immediately as well as throughout their lives. As our chapter's leader for a year, I was afforded an opportunity to experience the constraints and responsibilities such a position entails. A childlike view of leadership as power to compel performance and to satisfy one's own whims would not survive the briefest encounter with its practice. I realized that achieving the cooperation of volunteers in pursuit of the organization's goals depended almost entirely upon the members' abilities and their degree of commitment when asked to participate, rather than upon any supposedly implicit authority conveyed or acknowledged by a title.

One extremely capable member declined each opportunity to "rise" through the ranks. He set a wonderful example of service for the entire membership by flawlessly keeping the chapter's records throughout his association with the chapter. His dedication to the organization was beyond question even if others regretted the underutilization of his talent for more formal leadership. One of the reasons this organization was exceptional is that its members were dedicated to attempting to pursue a variety of worthwhile principles. All of its functions and activities were organized around that pursuit.

My sense of never fully being a member of groups like the Scouts and our "Little League" team contributed to a more general mistrust of less formal social groups, whether or not they seemed to accept me as a member. I could not commit the developing human resources and experience other group members possessed but I did not, and some members probably realized that deficiency. I did not empathize with other group members who might have been feeling just as insecure about their connectedness to the group. There were few groups, clubs, or teams in our six-year elementary school from which to feel isolated but that made belonging to, or being separated from, one of them seem even more important.

The brief outdoor "recess" periods during each school day often meant the hasty organizing of two softball teams by their teacher-appointed captains or the selection of team members by the teacher. When captains chose their teams, the popularity contest was always uncomfortable. Softball games in winter meant playing over the frozen mud footprints of the previous day's teams. Our hard-soled shoes were not suited to such uneven terrain, and I often had a sore and swollen ankle just from playing on the playground. Trying to catch a cold softball with bare hands was even less fun and fortunately, I seldom had the opportunity to try. Sore hands and ankles was a frequent condition for many of the playground's veterans, but that was a readily paid price for playing.

The reason a group formed and my dedication to its purpose became an excellent predictor of my likely success in numerous high school associations but trying to join informal gatherings of students was usually less successful. I grew up with the reinforced belief that work had value but play did not. An inferred corollary was that, since most adults worked and most children did

not, adults were easily more valuable and important than children. As a child
and adolescent, my view of this relative worth could not endear me to my
contemporaries unless I found the few who had the same understanding. I never
discussed this view with anyone but must have expressed it nonverbally when
I deemed unimportant those things many of my classmates found compelling.
Non-inclusion by those classmates was less difficult to accept if an adult's
approbation occasionally was forthcoming.

When I visited the homes of more popular children, I realized that their
parents seemed to accept as very important those things that were important
to their children. This seemed like a wonderful arrangement but I could not
reconcile it with a religious and economic system that not only valued work over
play, but it provided substantially greater financial rewards for some work than it
did for other, seemingly harder, work. Surely, rationalizing morality, priorities,
and values with a market economy is not a problem unique to children. My peers
embraced a separation between themselves and adults, and accepted that their
own system of social rewards could be separate. By relying primarily on the
approval of adults for success in defining my affected male persona, I rejected the
rewards system of my peers. That was just one of the ways I was different from
so many of them. They were much farther along in deciding for themselves, often
in conflict with adults, what they thought most mattered.

The classmates whose company I sought usually were people who also
did not seem as readily accepted. I learned that these people offered something
besides a very important friendship; their different experiences and interests
helped broaden my own. The fact that I did not believe I could disclose my secret
obsession to these friends may have given them a sense that I was not being
completely honest with them, although none of them ever suggested it. Their
generally guileless behavior did not lead me to the logical possibility that they or
some other of my classmates might not have been honest with me.

I do not know of any other transgendered people who were members of
my graduating class or of any among the nearly 1,200 students in the six grades
of that school the year I graduated. I will never know what effect knowing of
someone's transitioning while I was in grade school or college might have had
on my life. I doubt that it would have led either to an accurate self-diagnosis
or to my seeking professional help in attempting to resolve the matter. I
probably would have found some aspect of their experience to be so challenging,
frightening, or repulsive that I would have envied them but continued to hide my
interest.

A Good Friend

My closest friends were boys who believed I was a boy. I enjoyed their company as we shared common interests in humor, non-competitive athletics, intellectual discussions, chess, fishing, bowling, and other activities but usually with only one friend at a time. My associations were almost never with more than one friend at a time and were usually with the same friend over a longer period. In retrospect, these friendships could almost be described as my attempts at dating, but I would not have accepted that characterization at the time and those friends would have vehemently rejected the suggestion with complete justification. There was never anything remotely romantic or sexual about those friendships and they nor I believed they were unusual. They were excellent examples of the best part of the nonsexual aspects of a heterogendered relationship, except that there was no reciprocated sense of commitment. If I did derive any gender identity satisfaction from these friendships, it was purely subconscious in its instigation and fulfillment.

One of these friends was a classmate who lived a block from my home. He and his parents moved to our area when we were in high school. The change of schools for sixth to seventh grade students meant that I was seeing my closer childhood friend far less frequently. A precursor of today's quick-stop gasoline and grocery stores was located near his home and he got a job there. At Mother's request, I often got bread, milk, or ice cream in that store and I believe that is where I met him   His easy, confident, and capable manner facilitated his associations with co-workers and customers. His interest in a variety of activities was a welcome change from my sedentary pursuits of piano and chess. We often passed and kicked a football on the field across from my home and probably spent some time with a baseball and gloves on the same field.

We rode our bicycles to a creek south of town carrying our fishing rods and taking bits of bread and cheese for bait. The creek met the Ohio River under a bridge that was part of the town's main highway. We fished recreationally under that bridge for "bluegills" and anything else that would take the bait but we never caught anything worthy of the effort. The long bicycle ride, interesting location, and fishing were still a wonderful way to spend a summer afternoon.

During colder weather, we took turns shooting paper targets with my b-b gun, played ping pong, or threw darts in my basement. We liked to bowl at a couple of the several alleys in the area. One Saturday, his mother took us to a bowling alley on her way to work and we planned to return home by bus. After bowling three games, we walked outside to what we had thought was a route stop.

We were glad we had used rented equipment because it was a two-mile walk to the actual bus stop.

We did not play cards or board games and rarely, if ever, watched television together. Like my parents, his mother and father worked outside of the home. He was as much at home in the kitchen as I was, and his delicious French-fried potatoes could have caused weight problems if we had not been growing and active teenagers. We discussed a variety of subjects, often related to school. He shared the interest in, and curiosity about, girls that was so important to other boys his age. His mother, a nurse, had explained enough about physiology and anatomy that his perspective was refreshingly mature. If he ever wondered why I did not seem more interested, he never mentioned it. His reserve was part of what I thought was his more mature attitude. He knew that I planned to go to college and I may have said that I thought that was soon enough to begin "looking."

Music had not been part of his background and, when we talked about it, he said he thought he was tone-deaf. I told him I thought that condition was as rare as total color-blindness. I played a note on our piano and asked him to sing it. He was off by more than an octave. I played a scale and the dominant to tonic, asked him to think for a moment, and try again. He was right on pitch. I think he joined our high school chorus but he certainly had learned that he was not tone-deaf.

Several years after my college graduation, I met his wife and him while shopping in an area store. When I said we should have kept in touch, he replied that his mother had told him I would "not know him" after I went to college. I did not know his parents well but liked them. Whatever she may have meant by her statement, a negative interpretation would have meant that she had greatly underestimated her son and me. Nothing about him, at any time, would have led me to wish I did not know him. The facts that I went to a school four hundred miles from home and that he entered military service had everything to do with our losing touch. I had felt much closer to him than to many of my other high school classmates and always enjoyed his company.

Goals, Performance, and Achievement

An apparent friction exists among those in education who emphasize group, rather than individual, performance. As a student, I believed that academic or intellectual achievement required individual effort in most instances. I would still disagree with those in education who assert that every class can collectively out-think any of its members because the members of the class still think as individuals. Assessment of performance in athletics highly favors the superior results of individual effort even in team sports. This has certainly been true in the recruitment of male athletes for higher education and professional sports. It has increasingly applied to women athletes in public education as Title IX requires equal opportunity in team sports, and standouts are rewarded with college scholarships.

Determination to do one's best, for women as well as men, is separate from, and probably independent of, an urge to defeat an opponent. While involved in competitive athletics, one may feel compelled to perform at a higher level than she or he thought possible, but this may still be a constructive effort at attempting to win rather than an effort to harm inadvertently or intentionally and defeat an opponent. The difference in attitude toward recreation for exercise and amusement versus a higher-stakes participation in competitive sports would not necessarily be gender identity related. The former may involve a sense that nothing is at risk while the latter often calls for the application of, and tests one's commitment toward, espoused philosophical, moral, and ethical beliefs in addition to applying her or his physical abilities.

Joining the Boy Scouts, playing a snare drum in the high school band, and being part of the five percent of my junior class selected for National Honor Society membership were my primary goals as a child and adolescent. I did attain each of them but found them to be different from what I had expected. Few have known the elation that must have accompanied each of the astronauts as he took his first steps on the lunar surface, or the depth of sadness and despair that might have been briefly felt by each of those who have perished in the space program. Non-astronauts can have some understanding of the resolve and determination that these extraordinary people possessed as they were found qualified and could progress toward their goals. In the sense that tossing a paper airplane might be compared to flying an SR-71 "Blackbird", each person's setting and attaining far less lofty goals teaches her or him about similar lessons of applying ambition, dedication, and abilities to her or his interests. The process also teaches that a few things are subject to our control and influence but a host of other things is decidedly beyond them.

My second goal as an adolescent was to play a snare drum as a member of the high school band. Before adoption of the current four-four-four public school system and construction of a large consolidated high school, our county had a six and six division of the county's twelve grades. The county supported two rivaling high schools roughly three miles apart. The division between grades six and seven meant that our town's "junior high" band could not include any members from grades five and six, or any of roughly 150 students. The senior band consisted almost entirely of members from grades nine through twelve. The 1,200 students in the latter six grades supported a junior band of about 60 members and a senior band membership of roughly 100 students.

Fifth and sixth grade students had been able to schedule weekly sessions with the high school band director and/or arrange for private lessons in preparation for joining a band in high school. Because I had begun receiving the director's instruction in fifth grade, I was able to join the senior band a year early. A tenor drummer had graduated and I could either fill that position or wait for my coveted snare drum slot the following year. Rides to football games and parades in the band buses were afforded to tenor drummers as well as snare drummers and, after being assured that I could switch to a snare drum the following autumn, the choice could not have been much easier.

Because I was studying piano, I was one of the few drummers who could read a key signature, which helped me become the band's "concert season" timpanist. The idea of anyone's meekly or tentatively playing tympani is unlikely to occur even to the most timid or introverted soul, including a most determined suppressing transgendered person. I especially enjoyed playing the arrangement the band used of the movie theme from "Lawrence of Arabia". The forceful and tonally strong rhythmic tonic-dominant-tonic opening was wonderfully therapeutic. It would be as ridiculous to play it tentatively as to thank a favorite performer by applauding with one hand.

While there is a positive aspect to playing tympani, that privilege carried a heavy responsibility. Our band's two tympani did not have wheels and I was responsible for transporting the drums from the band room to the adjacent field house, to the instruments truck, or over other short, but usually not short enough, distances. By grabbing a lug on each side of a drum (or tympan) and swinging it upward, the tympan could be carried on one's back. This might be called a timpanist's version of the "fireman's carry", but is arguably of far less therapeutic value than playing the drums. A miscalculation could have meant falling on one's nose in close proximity to a briefly airborne tympan. While that experience escaped me, it would be unlikely to happen to anyone twice.

The less-desirable aspect of "marching season" was the inclement weather through which we sometimes marched. One Christmas parade began on a Saturday morning with a temperature below 10 degrees. As band members waited for the parade to begin, some of us stood behind cars whose engines were running to warm our feet under their exhaust pipes. Since drum sticks tend not to stay in a drummer's hands if gloves are worn, we did not wear gloves. Unlike other instrumentalists, we played almost constantly while the band was in formation, so the additional working muscles did keep us warm enough, at least, under some very cold skin.

A statewide band competition involved a trip to the central part of the state where our band filled a hotel for much of one weekend. The competition almost seemed incidental to the experience of supervised independence, anonymity, and adventure. No gangs appeared to resist an invasion of their territory. The small quiet city was an excellent site for that competition. A trip to the New York City World's Fair included our band's staying in a Columbia University dormitory, a bus tour of the city, and a visit to the United Nations Complex. The band played in parades in cold, hot, rainy, or snowy weather, followed the football team to away games, and endured frequently noisy band rehearsals. The experiences were far more enjoyable than I had hoped they might be. The band's concert in the state's pavilion was scheduled for the same time as a Marine Band performance in the U.S. Pavilion next door. Our audience consisted of the few passers-by who did not know about the Marine Band performance and a few loyal parents of band members.

I forfeited the opportunity to use the band's newest pearl-blue snare drum as a favor to a friend who was a year older, firm in the understanding that I would have a turn with that instrument during my senior year. The following year, the band implemented new policies. The informal, but previously accepted, seniority system for drum assignments was abandoned in favor of a system of merit awards. The merit test favored another student and I objected.

This lesson about rule changes sometimes adversely affecting those who had been living under the previous set is interesting from the standpoint of political theory but was a lesson I would rather have learned another way. After I marched for several days without a drum, it became evident that, in the absence of an effective appeal or acceptable compromise, the only alternative to acquiescence was my departure. With the school principal's sympathies, I left the band and was assigned to the first one-hour "study hall" period of my high school years.

It was little consolation to hear another student say that the activity I had so anticipated as an adolescent and enjoyed as a teenager for more than four years had also become less enjoyable for others. Using different methods to recognize individual merit, however that was defined, the band's new system rewarded individual performance and/or capability and fostered competition among its members. It did this, though, at the risk of a reduced level of group performance, a diminished sense of unity, and a possible reduction of pride in belonging to the organization. A student would still be a band member but would march and wear a uniform that labeled that student as either a greater or lesser member of the band. The informal awareness of ability that each member had for others in her or his section, and even for other section members, became formal and was evinced by non-uniform uniforms, assigned marching positions, and instrument assignments. Emphasis on perceived individual merit was apparently intended to employ ambition and competition to lead to improved individual, and then overall performance. Better performance might also mean better morale.

Because of the focus of the disciplines, psychology and sociology offer different perspectives on attempting to harmonize individual and group achievement. Management studies, organizational behavior classes, and other disciplines encourage study of past and extant major corporations as each pursued and pursues, respectively, an optimal model to meet efficiently the expectations of its customers. The General Motors' intra-competitive corporate model of its Chevrolet, Buick, and Pontiac divisions, and Proctor and Gamble's competitive brands have often been cited as examples of efforts to spur competition among company divisions as a means to maximizing overall organizational performance. The responsibility for effectively managing an organization often impels managers to implement a system of incentives and rewards intended to balance individual and group performance.

The subjectivity inherent in some aspects of assessing merit invites resentment from those deemed to have less of it, and organizational cohesiveness can be harmed as a result. Individuals who believe that their above-average performance has not been fairly and suitably recognized should be expected to take exception to the process. The quality of performance of those whose internal and historic inclination has always been to perform to the best of their ability is not readily affected by these systems. The focus of these people, however, may change dramatically as they gain a more precise understanding of their employer's expectations, the nature of the performance that is rewarded, and the accommodation necessary to conform to their own sense of self-respect.

While many athletes in team sports walk a fine line between individual performance and teamwork (with a few stellar exceptions,) the latitude for individual performance in larger musical groups is usually quite constrained.

Where the athletic team has a plan and strategy to face the uncertainty of competition, a musical group usually has practiced and will perform a known work, and expects to do so in the manner that has been well rehearsed. As ardently as I would argue in support of individual liberty and independence, there are many situations where independence of group members can make attainment of a shared goal nearly impossible.

Choral and symphonic works are, in this sense, an inescapable metaphor for the inseparability of freedom and responsibility in action. Where a soloist can perform the entire work, she or he has a virtually unlimited freedom to paint the best sonic picture of which she or he is capable. Concomitant responsibility for the performance's success or failure also rests primarily with that performer. Where there is a shared goal of attempting the best possible rendition of a work requiring more voices and/or instruments, there is a more limited individual responsibility for a positive contribution to the whole performance and a limited freedom to use one's understanding and ability to meet that obligation.

In a fascist system, each citizen exists solely to serve the state. Her or his right to exist is dependent on an ability to contribute to the state. Each person is worthwhile, entitled to the few protections of citizenship, and has moral and ethical significance only so long as she or he serves the state. A transgendered person in that system cannot own her or his identity so, in theory, she or he can have no gender identity conflict. In theory, one might as constructively deny the existence of air. The concept of citizens as state property is the antithesis of most religious doctrine regarding the worth of every individual. Asserting that all human rights are only those granted by government is a direct contradiction of the U.S. Declaration of Independence's phrase "endowed by their creator..." (Kashner 2007, 496).[51]

Fascism's dehumanizing rationale for enslaving people to the state, and to the elite which controls it, does not perceive citizens as Thomas Jefferson's individual sovereigns who must organize and reorganize government that is accountable to them. Fascism's citizens must be subjects of a possibly capricious but all-powerful perpetual government. America's founders contended that man without liberty is not man. Jefferson wrote "The God who gave us life gave us liberty at the same time: the hand of force may destroy but cannot disjoin them" (Jefferson 1774/1996).[52] Any system that would deny the liberty of any of its citizens without just cause must be, by definition, inhuman. Everything created within that system's borders belongs to the state. Since only the state is sovereign, no citizen can have a valid claim against it.

Some people would argue that the liberty of transgendered people to express their gender identity should be constrained; that there is a social obligation to suppress gender identity conflict for a shared goal of a stereotypical norm of peace and order. Transgendered expression is a dissonant threat to the work and purpose of the whole of society. This may not be an exquisitely concise definition, if one exists, of quintessential fascism, but it should be considered close enough to alarm those and their families who sacrificed so much of their lives to oppose it.

A high school band seeking to recognize, encourage, and reward individual achievement, even at the risk of compromised unit performance, could hardly be accused of practicing fascism because it would be zealously pursuing its opposite. I did not have this perspective when I complained about drum assignments. The instrument I had anticipated playing for several years was going to be played by someone else. My response was at least as emotional as rational. The psychology, political theory, and business perspectives I would later acquire have helped in understanding the much greater value of that life-lesson.

An Indispensable Honor

My third goal was honor society membership during the first of the two years for which students were eligible. The lesson of this experience was augmented by the trial of patience endured by all class members who waited for the reading of names of the selected students. Membership status that year was altered when a student many thought should have been inducted was not. The harshness of that lesson was at least comparable to my experience with the band, even though I was not directly affected by it.

At least partially because of a pseudo rivalry with my older sister, her class's salutatorian, I dreaded the inevitable and horrendous feelings of failure and embarrassment I knew would attend my not being one of my class's ten students selected for the society's membership. Until someone actually began reading the names of those selected during the student assembly, I do not think I realized how important I had let that moment become. I overheard a few students seated in the row behind me discussing students they thought might be selected. When one of them mentioned my name and another agreed, I thought it was a gracious compliment and was embarrassed that they might see how anxious I was. It is ironic that people are often encouraged to want such things but discouraged from appearing to want them.

Psychologists might suggest that I missed a singular opportunity for growth by not having had to learn to contend at that time with so dreaded a failure. One's character may be strengthened by the experience of living through such failure, and failure may be a more effective teacher of some lessons than success, but failure must be less effective in feeding aspirations. The opportunity for students to learn about themselves through an important individual achievement or failure must be, at least partially, behind efforts to organize such events. Surely part of the lesson from such an experience is intended to be the importance of making a substantial commitment of personal resources to any attempt at obtaining whatever a person has decided is important. As pleasantly rewarding as was this experience for those who were chosen, it must have been as intensely difficult for those students who were not; many of whom I knew, including my few closer friends. My father's presence would have told me, before the announcement, that I had reached this goal, but he and other parents were carefully hidden by the event's organizers. The elation at hearing my name read was at least as much due to an intense relief at having not failed as to having achieved something worthwhile.

Despite the large enrollment of the high school, our 200-plus member graduating class included between 40 and 60 students with whom I attended all 12 grades, and a smaller number with whom I shared most of the "academic" (versus a "commercial" or "general") tract of classes. One of these classmates was liked and respected by most students, a member of our church, and one of the first-year honor society members. His parents seemed to know all of his friends and to deem everything he did as important to them. I occasionally misunderstood his self-confidence as an inappropriately boosted ego and only later realized that he did not regard adults or others as being less important, but he would not accept a less important status for himself and his friends. When one's own sense of self has been borrowed from others, the concomitant insecurity of unavoidable self-doubt makes suspicion of the apparent ease and self-confidence of others inevitable. After separation from the high school band, I finally attended a high school football game with him, his parents, and another of his friends. These people were all gracious without condescension, and wonderful companions for watching that, or any, ball game. The band and I were proving we could get along well enough without each other and I thoroughly enjoyed the game from the non-band section of the viewing stands.

When I talked with this classmate during a reunion following my transition, we had not seen each other for more than ten years. He did not seem embarrassed by my appearance nor did he seem to think that I should be, and he readily introduced me to his children. Although he never seemed reluctant to state what he sincerely believed, he did not tell me what he thought about the transgendered condition but was only concerned about how I felt. I told him how liberating the experience had been and that I knew it was right for me. He agreed that was important and we changed the subject. Once again, he had shown why so many people have valued his friendship.

Another high school student with exceptional ability was apparently self-assured and took special interest in the fact that my interactions with most students seemed emotionally sterile. This student chose to analyze that perceived sterility for me, and for the few other classmates present, during a senior year unsupervised hour when we were supposed to be doing something else. Many people will recall a comparable incident in their own high school experience and this student may also have had one, but those thoughts did not occur to me at the time. The lengthy analysis by this intelligent student exhaustively examined each of my perceived failings to manifest an acceptable social personality. The fact that the perceived failings were ones of omission, rather than commission, was of little consequence.

That this student could so volubly assess my perceived imperfections bespoke an unusual ability that almost certainly has been put to a far more constructive use. As much as the embarrassing assessment stung, I saw no remedy, nor was a plausible one offered, for altering any aspect of the alleged egregious behavior. That enthusiastically presented analysis of presumed ills was easily the most complete catalogue of my possible social failings as a high school student that I would ever receive, but the manner of its presentation prevented its effective use by me or anyone else. Aside from the embarrassing experience of the assessment, its tone, but none of the critique, was memorable and it had not occurred to me to take notes. Delivered in another setting or manner of presentation, that assessment might have led to my seeking a professional and competent elicitation and analysis of my suppressed identity. It became, though, merely another of the rather common and unpleasant encounters that occur with distressing frequency for many teenagers. Like most of those other teens, I was determined to forget the experience as quickly as memory would permit. My continuous searching and introspection would not let that happen.

7. For Higher Learning

A Freshman Again

When other high school students were determined to discover their own identities and what was important to them, I thought the exercise was silly. Barring an unforeseeable calamity, my family would remain involved in business and our community. I thought my continued involvement with the bank was both necessary and inevitable, at least through my twenties, which was almost a lifetime from my teenage perspective. While more certain of their immediate post-high school plans, most classmates saw their twenties as presenting much greater uncertainty but posing welcome opportunities and a few menacing threats. Youthful optimism usually meant that opportunities seemed easily to outweigh threats and any threats that materialized would be confronted and overcome. Still, I was certain that my first years of post-college life would be spent behind the window of a teller's "cage." I was seventeen years old and would be off to Michigan for my freshman year at college.

Dad was behind the wheel one day during that pre-college summer as he and I pursued a bank errand. I offered a disparaging assessment of the noisy *Sturm und Drang* of my contemporaries' search for identity. I was sure he would say something favorable about how well grounded I was, credit my more mature clear-sightedness, or at least agree that I probably was right but he responded quite differently. He pointed to the inherently quirky nature of life, the fact that any number of things might change before my presumed, but not certain, college graduation, and even the possibility that I might not really know myself as well as I seemed to think I did. I might have asked him about his own or his contemporaries' struggles but I was stunned by his reply. Later, I thought his time after high school graduation was too long ago to be relevant or that I would not understand his experience any better than I did the widely publicized self-searching of some of my generation's "dropouts." I felt neither a preoccupation with the prospect of college's independence and personal responsibility nor the slightest inclination to seek companionship with a group of my era's "flower children."

New parents doubtlessly await with some anxiety their child's first defiant demonstrations that she or he is not a mere obedient parental appendage but a unique person determined to act independently. The child may find that the color and motion of flame are attractive and decide to touch the intriguing object. The startling parental "No! Don't touch!" might be sufficient to prevent the child's being burned. On another occasion, the child may be asked to do something and will unexpectedly issue an emphatic "No!" with the same inflection hastily imparted earlier and since forgotten by her or his parent. After innumerable episodes of this drama and despite the legal, cultural, moral, emotional, intellectual, and other responsibilities parents bear for their offspring, children often express their displeasure at not having been consulted about, much less having agreed to, the entire arrangement. Having been the arrangement's primary financial beneficiary without concomitant responsibilities, at least in its earliest stages, for many years, when the child is old enough to do so, she or he often attempts to negotiate an even more one-sided arrangement. Children seem inevitably bound to exhibit independence and individuality that is often surprisingly different from the expectations of their parents. Its being different sometimes seems to be the only explanation for the exhibition, but at other times, it will be a direct application of something a parent said in a totally different context.

There must be a tremendously empty feeling waiting for those who have done a thing only because they were told they should not do it. There can be no sense of having approached or attained a worthy and desired goal. The story of Eden suggests this and much more. License masquerading as "liberty" in a drug-friendly subculture and the general questioning of "establishment" rules and institutions during the late 1960s and early 1970s also buttress the point. President Kennedy's inaugural address included the words "...the torch has been passed to a new generation of Americans..." (Kennedy 1961/1997).[53] Many students and others on those campuses would have replied, "Passed, yes, but do not hold it too tightly. Just pass it along to us immediately, if not sooner." The accusatory justification for haste would be, "No one could do worse than the members of your generation." The assertion that age should be the primary determinant of who should hold power and that anyone over age 35 would abuse power is contrary to the social conventions of other societies and to a human history showing that, in most instances, no single physical characteristic should "qualify" or disqualify any person as a leader. I had many reasons to feel a part of the generation expressing the desire to seize and exercise political power but had invested the whole of my affected persona in the order that was being challenged.

During that summer of 1967, parts of Detroit and other cities experienced violence attributed to racial tensions and protests regarding the increasing numbers of American servicemen who died in Viet Nam. These events seemed a media reality that did not bear, or bear directly, on my immediate plans. A naive lack of circumspection that sustained a detached focus on my own smaller world meant that, if no person is an island, then some of us could, at times, permit ourselves to be connected to the rest by only the most narrow of isthmuses. It is apparently all too human a trait that some people will struggle to maintain their detached but treasured fantasies however persistent might be the reality that attempts to intrude. I did not feel compelled to attempt to affect those conflicts as a student nor did I see any reason why those events should alter my plans for obtaining a college diploma. I expected my college experience to help me prepare for whatever I would do after college.

I thought that some naive detachment was justified. My formal and social high school education, character, personality, and other assets seemed grossly inadequate resources for attempting to make a significant contribution to the lessening of racial tension in America or to helping to resolve the strife in and about Viet Nam. Yet, there were people my age who found ways to try to influence national policies. The conviction that motivated and sustained them was at least partially attributable to their sense of who they were and what they expected of themselves regarding national and world events. Even when I disagreed with their positions, I knew they were different from me in their certainty, passion, and confidence.

"Spending" Money

Like thousands of other students, I was employed as a dormitory switchboard operator in each of the two dorms I lived in while attending Alma. The work helped provide income for the seemingly endless wants and needs of a college student. A dormitory with only two campus phones and one pay phone per floor doubtlessly seems quaint to graduates and current students who had or have computer hookups and a phone or two in each room. In the days before personal computers and the telephone monopoly's breakup, however, manual switchboards were the norm. Each dormitory had its own switchboard supervisor whose compensation for the extra work of training, scheduling, and tracking hours worked was a higher hourly rate for her or his own hours at the switchboard. The supervisor's additional responsibilities often meant having less time to work at the board so that, on a monthly basis, she or he was among the lowest paid of the whole staff.

This perverse compensation system equating more authority and responsibility with less compensation may have made sense to philosophy, sociology, and/or psychology majors, but I was not majoring in any of those. I neither sought the position nor served as a supervisor, but if I had, I would have planned to work as many hours as most other operators. The occasional sorting of campus mail, placing and retrieving memos, paging quad recipients of incoming phone calls, and placing students' outgoing calls through the campus phone system was an enjoyable means of earning money. Students had more privacy if they used the pay phone located on each floor but there was no additional cost for local use of the school's phones. I had figured out how the underutilized recording interface of the public address system in the dorm lobby worked, and received several favorable comments for playing a recording of Elgar's *Enigma Variations* one afternoon as former students and parents visited the dorm during homecoming. Given the reportedly cool reaction of some of Elgar's friends to the variations they inspired, I have often wondered what reaction I might have gotten if I had instead played a recording of Mussorgsky's *Pictures at an Exhibition*.

I also worked for the library's audio/visual (a. v.) department showing films, not on video cassettes or disc players but using real-to-real film projectors. The a. v. department scheduled all films for the school's classes, student government, and organizations that met on campus. Showing class films was an extremely interesting means of supplementing my enrolled course work. Films of involving psychological research and testing were especially interesting. During one of the films about autism in infants, the narrator's voice disclosed the caring concern she felt for the trials' "subjects." In another film, a dog's reaction to a "visual cliff" kept it from walking on a solid but transparent surface. Curiosity about why some people do what they do was obviously not the sole province of political science, philosophy, religion, or any other discipline.

The art department arranged showings of sophisticated film projects submitted by advanced students from other schools. The collections usually included 10 to 20 productions that ran in a two-hour time slot. The evident talent and skill of the students was inspiring as some wrote, directed, and starred in their own films. Showing a series of foreign films was another horizon-broadening experience indicating how great the cultural differences are between the United States and some other countries. I showed major commercial films on Friday and Saturday nights under the auspices of the school's student government, which led to my having a key to the science building auditorium's projection booth. The informal passing of a key to that booth occurred every two or three years as a graduating projectionist gave it to his successor. The key's origin was shrouded in secrecy and few people new of its existence, but without it, the school's practice of keeping doors locked to rooms not properly scheduled for use would have delayed or prevented innumerable showings.

The science auditorium had a thirteen-foot grand piano in one of its wings that could be played legitimately with the permission of the music department, and I received that permission. When the auditorium was locked, I could get into the projection booth, out through one of the larger windows in the front of the booth, into the auditorium, and over to that piano. With the auditorium doors still locked, I frequently could play that magnificent instrument without interruption. A friend and fellow "projectionist" was in the auditorium with me after one of us ran a film one evening, and everyone else had left. I went to the piano and began playing. My friend went to the circuit panel and turned off all of the auditorium's lights. He was surprised that I could keep playing without missing a beat and apparently did not realize that I would still know where the keys were. That sense of "geography" might be compared to use of a computer keyboard, and missed notes would correspond to typographical errors. Any similarity of technique, however, would certainly not favor the pianist.

One of the most gracious compliments I ever received was offered while I was playing that grand. A campus security guard, who was a favorite of many of the students and instantly became mine, heard my playing and wanted to know how I had gotten into the room. When I told him I had been showing a film, he said he had just been over at the student union where the amplified music was terribly loud, and most students there did not seem to be listening to it. He said those students should have been here, in the auditorium, listening to me. I had heard students say that, although he was old enough to be their grandfather, he enjoyed talking with them. If he helped other students feel as good as he helped me to feel that evening, his being so well liked surely cannot be a mystery.

The Virtue of Honesty

At the end of my sophomore year, I learned that dormitory resident assistants (R. A.s) did not pay room fees and I thought the job might be interesting. The sizable reduction in the cost of college, rather than an overwhelming urge to assist fellow students, impelled me to schedule an interview for one of the positions. Instead of being asked why I thought I might be a good R.A., I was asked to describe myself and, because of insufficient experience with interviews, I hesitated. A perceptive interviewer asked me to describe what I thought someone who knew me well would say. The only part of the brief response I recall was that I hoped she or he would say that I was honest. I might have professed so strong a desire to help other students that I would have been willing to serve in the position even if the room fee waiver were not offered, but that would not have been honest and I am gratified that it did not even occur to me.

Rather than mentioning a breadth of academic and social interests, including an interest in the lives of other students, my rather stilted response regarding honesty and several analogies to music almost certainly left the impression that I was not the kind of "people person" the position required. The reference to honesty might have been understood to mean that I did not believe other applicants were as concerned about that virtue as I was, implying that I was distrustful or suspicious of other students. The reference might also have suggested that, since honesty was the only quality I remember mentioning, some aspect of it might be particularly troubling for me. I did not think then, that suppressing my gender identity was a matter of conscious honesty or dishonesty, but there may well have been some subconscious screaming about the matter that occasionally did reveal itself in so subtle a manner.

The honesty trait was an attribute that I believed was roughly equivalent to the heart of anyone's worth as a person. With regard to maintaining personal financial records, the financial affairs of others, general veracity, and the keeping of commitments, that virtue seems not only essential from the perspective of self-worth but as an essential basis for an effective and efficient society. My parents and grandparents not only imparted this view but practiced it. Someone with this belief and background walling off a section of her life and deciding "but not this part of my life" cannot easily do so. Each time I bought gender identity-appropriate clothing, I practiced relative dishonesty. I did think that I was the only person who might be adversely affected by the act, while exposing my secret might harm or disturb so many others that I cared about. This rationalization did not mean being dishonest was acceptable but there still seemed to be no bearable alternative.

American society's treatment of Santa Claus might be a wonderfully imaginative way for its children to learn that, from beneficent intent, the people they most care about and who most care about them will, inevitably, tell them something that is not wholly true. Such well-intentioned dishonesty is not intended to harm or to obtain unfair advantage. Its purpose is to strengthen, instruct, and protect, and it stems from loving concern. In a sense, it is even a religious lesson since some people are taught not to put their full faith in other people but in God, alone. Still, the result is a practiced deceit whose discovery is keenly felt by each child. By the time most children learn about the true nature of Santa Clause, they have already had extensive experience with truthfulness and its opposite.

I was dishonest with my sister from the first time we played my favorite game called "Janet and Joanne". It involved my wearing one of her dresses and pretending to be her girlfriend. I am not certain which of us was Janet but Joanne was the name of her favorite doll and, while neither of us thought of me as her doll, I believe I was Joanne. As much as I enjoyed the game, our playing it always seemed to be my sister's idea. It was not until I talked with two other transgendered women during the early stages of my transition that they assured me, and I accepted, that the original game or, at least, its repetitions were definitely not my sister's idea.

Even as an adult, my sister remembered that game as something she always initiated and somehow coaxed me to play. While I was still suppressing my gender identity conflict and maintaining my male façade, I did not attempt to dissuade her from that contention, and I even accepted her assertion as truth. The efficacy of this gender identity fraud, so carefully constructed by a young child and reinforced by family's expectations and social interactions, is an indication of how enduringly manipulative and deviously deceitful the condition's imperative of secrecy can enable and compel a suppressing transgendered person to be.

My sister was one of the earliest victims of the fraud since she felt, or was helped to feel, responsible for inducing me to do something that was so obviously inappropriate for a young boy. By expressing my obsession so indirectly, I was able to play for brief intervals as a young girl without anyone else's knowing, and without admitting to myself, that it was much more than a game. There was not a single instance, from earliest childhood until my crisis point more than forty years later, when I was willing to confide in anyone who would have been able to help me resolve the conflict. I was even less likely to disclose my conflict to someone who did not present that potential.

The Modern Art of Compromise

Roommates my freshman, sophomore, and junior years, and an absence of suitable transportation had precluded my acting on impulses to buy gender identity-appropriate clothing. Toward the end of my junior year, I acquired a car that my parents had intended to trade. The balance of that year, my senior year, and an extra term to complete requirements for an additional major finally provided numerous opportunities to acquire clothing I had thought I might never own.

The excitement occasioned just by thinking about these clothes was electrifying. After college, my pulse and breathing could quicken dramatically, even when I was hundreds of miles from my secret "things", at the thought of one more brief release of my suppressed self. In college, the perplexing heart-pounding reaction to the thoughts, the humiliating dishonesty of wanting to acquire, and of actually buying, the clothes, and the confusing mix of emotions and thoughts while wearing them had always been overwhelming. Those intense feelings were usually followed by feelings of guilt, a sense of compromised honor, self-reproach for an apparent waste of time, effort, money, apprehension about the possibility of being discovered, and of remorse for having yielded to a compulsion I could not understand.

Some of the emotion preceding each episode might be akin to sexual tension and excitement, although it was not sexually exciting for me. It might also be compared to the thrill of a gambling addiction when its victim places a large wager she or he is almost certain to lose. The suppressed part of one's identity freed at such moments becomes more familiar but its release also feels like an irresponsible abrogation of responsibility for maintaining the male façade. The unaided suppressing MtF woman may never realize that her hidden self is the truth and the assiduously maintained male façade is the lie. I only began to realize the extent of that difference after I had begun transition. As carefully as I planned and rehearsed each acquisition and dressing episode, there was always the danger of an unanticipated element leading to embarrassment or a shattering disclosure. That risk was greatest during my first purchases in college and it diminished but was never eliminated after graduation.

The onset of each obsessive episode was always uncompromising. Thoughts about class work or piano, the act of writing to family members, conversations with classmates, or any other deliberate distraction always eventually yielded to the intensity of the obsession. The probability that no one else on campus and, possibly, on the planet seemed to have this same desire was irrelevant. When I knew that the only impediments to my obsession were those I constructed, each one inevitably fell. The absence of an inhibiting roommate as a constraint, the availability of transportation, and the funds I had saved helped make resistance to each summons futile. After repeated unsuccessful efforts to control or extinguish each outbreak of obsessive thoughts, only by acting as quickly as possible to satisfy the desire could I hope to accomplish something worthwhile during the remainder of the day. Critics might ask, "Wasn't that a convenient compromise between desire and determination?" In post-transition hindsight, the MtF woman would answer, "Yes, and an unavoidable exercise of dubious merit."

The first of these indulgent trips was to a town a few miles south of Alma. I had been through Ithaca on several occasions before I had gotten my car, and thought it was a small, pleasant, and thoroughly American part of Michigan. I drove by a dress shop that did not seem terribly busy, and then drove past it again from the opposite direction. Hoping that no one I recognized was near the store, I parked around the block's nearest corner. Deciding one last time that there was no alternative to acting on the compulsion, I locked the car and went to the shop.

Two unusually kind and helpful older women seemed to think my awkwardness was understandable embarrassment. When I did not know the size of the bra "she" wanted, they suggested a couple possibilities that could as well have been binary room dimensions. When I hesitated, they invited my use of their phone and I offered an excuse about why I could not call "her." As though waking from amnesia, I suddenly "remembered" that one of the sizes they suggested was the one "she" needed, paid for the bra, and left. Despite their warmth and apparent understanding, I hoped I would never see either of them again. I wanted to put the bra on immediately but realized that was at least a little more foolish than what I had just done.

The drive back to school was uneventful but seemed to take forever. When I got back to my room and put the bra on, the mix of feelings included a fleeting moment of satisfaction, disappointment that so much thought, effort, and anxiety had resulted in so little, self-reproach for having indulged in the exercise, and realization that the beast I was trying to feed had a much greater appetite. I also noted things that did not happen. My purchase of the bra invoked or possessed no power to feminize my voice, soften my features, lengthen my hair, or cause any other wished-for physical change. Almost at the same time as I was acknowledging the waste of time and effort, I was wondering how many more such towns, dress shops, and helpful clerks I might find within a short drive from campus. As I was nearing completion of the requirements for three college majors, I was now earnestly engaged in attempting to address an interest with a far more compelling nature.

The obsessive thoughts about acquiring and wearing natal-sex inappropriate clothing can be seen as temptation to which acquiescence is a moral failing. I am not aware of any comparable, enduring, and unrelenting compulsion similar to the war to suppress gender identity conflict. If there is one, it would certainly be appropriate to consider it in a moral and religious context. People with problems of physical health or with addictions know that there is an essential mental attitude that acknowledges the problem. The attitude either calls and permits them to control their own lives or it cedes that control to the affliction. It is inviting but inaccurate to see gender identity conflict in that light. Morality and religion are the staff of life for most transgendered and non-transgendered people alike. For many people, the soul and spirit are sufficiently separate from the matter that makes up their tangible physical selves that they seek spiritual guidance for the former and scientific knowledge to deal with latter. The difficulty comes in separating those aspects of each issue.

I would not suggest that prayer is, in any way, inappropriate to the mundane or tangible aspects of each person's life, or to any matter about which someone feels a need to pray. The same God who created earth and humanity apparently did so according to rules, or in a way from which rules can be deduced. He also gave humanity an ability to understand that order and symmetry, however imperfect may be its understanding. Science is not that set of rules but the process by which its practitioners attempt to discover and decipher the rules. Those who dedicate their lives to the process apparently have great curiosity, patience, or both.

Some would argue that a chronic or acute illness is a moral test or punishment. That view is really a vestige of medieval thought that saw matters of health as contest. Resistance or susceptibility to an illness was dependent on the person's strong or weak spirit. Ostensibly, succumbing is due to a lack of sufficient faith or is a form of divine punishment of the person's soul or spirit, and not a matter of a physical assault by injury or disease on one's mind or body. Such reasoning is akin to superstition and a fear of spiteful ghouls and goblins that visit affliction upon their hapless victims. This view is supported neither by careful studies of the etiology of health problems nor is it validated by sound theological argument. Like "trial by ordeal," this view can be seen as an attempt to control God. In a test of innocence or faith, made so by the thought or act of man, God must act in a prescribed and timely manner or His inaction indicates guilt or insufficient faith.

This or similar reasoning, knowledge, and beliefs preceded, coincided with, and followed each of my "dressing" episodes for the four decades between childhood and transition. I did not know whether my obsession was, or was a symptom of, a bizarre chronic illness. Its constancy was that of a powerful and familiar adversary. It was capable of a significant, if limited, level of destruction but it had no separate identity. No line of reasoning would moderate the urge to act. The puzzle's essential key that I needed but had not even heard of before beginning transition was innate gender identity.

Still searching for that illusive key, I answered another of the obsession's calls with a drive from college to a Saginaw, Michigan department store and bought a girdle and two pairs of stockings. The forty-five minute trip had been one more opportunity to consider how ridiculous my actions seemed and to question, again, why I was doing it. If no new insight or revelation presented itself before I parked the car, another episode of buying, wearing, and purging would be underway. I knew of no laws that prohibited my buying, for my own use, clothing that I could buy legally for anyone else, nor any Biblical proscription against the purchase of sex-inappropriate clothing, although neither prohibition would have quieted the desire. In a repressive country where an MtF woman who temporarily released her otherwise suppressed gender identity would be severely punished, I am certain she would still find a way to express her gender identity. Few needs are more fundamental and uncompromising.

I headed for a counter in the women's department so intent on my purpose that I lost track of which of the store's entrances I had used. My apparent unease or an insufficient knowledge regarding the garment's style or size caused the first clerk I encountered to be reluctant to help with the purchase. I said, with a determination that even surprised me, "There is no reason to make this any more difficult than it already is". I had intended the statement as an assertive "male" indication of irritation at a delay in executing my errand "for her," but "this" could have been understood to mean either the sex-appropriate purchase "for her" or the gender identity-appropriate purchase for me.

A second clerk nearby quickly came to help and seemed to have little or no difficulty getting what I wanted. I left the store certain that the actual cost of my purchases had been far greater than the currency used to pay for them. Expenditures for such clothing were the only ones that did not find their way into the financial diary that I faithfully maintained throughout my college years. I knew the exact cost of my room, board, tuition, books, entertainment, transportation, and incidentals for the thirteen terms spent at college, but I kept no written record regarding my clandestine purchases.

During the trip back to campus, I took a detour over increasingly more rural roads looking for the best place to put on the new paneled girdle and stockings I could wear under my slacks. If desire had not been sufficient motivation, wearing them under my clothing also meant not having to carry them into the dorm. I found a place to stop off a dirt road next to a fence where a farmer drove his tractor to and from his field. The intense thrill of owning and donning the clothes, hurrying to minimize the chance of discovery, and my anxiety over the possibility of being discovered, conspired to produce a set of cardiopulmonary numbers that probably would have pegged the meter. The dishonesty of, at least implied, misrepresentation that was a necessary part of acquiring the clothes and my awareness that I dare not betray the maleness of my façade were in stark and irreconcilable contrast to the sense of appropriateness that was part of owning and wearing the items.

There was no harrowing encounter with the farmer and, after my pulse and breathing moderated, I made the rest of the trip back to campus uneventfully. My customary self-reproach included awareness that another several irreplaceable hours of a beautiful spring day had been spent in a seemingly futile attempt to satisfy my insatiable obsession. The time, effort, and resources appeared not merely to have been wasted but spent destructively from the ego-bruising standpoint of my misrepresentation in the store, hiding in my outdoor "dressing room," and smuggling my treasures back into the dorm.

The girdle and stockings were stored in an enclosed overhead area above my room's dresser and mirror. I had left one of the compartment's sliding doors open when I prepared a glass of instant lemonade. A classmate, who almost never did so, came by for some casual conversation. I do not recall what we discussed at least partly because I wanted to get him away from that compartment or, at least, close the storage door without arousing suspicion. I carefully but quickly retrieved a beverage mug from that shelf, closing the door in the same motion, and walked out of the room to a nearby water fountain, talking to him all the way. If he noticed the clothing or anything unusual in my actions, he was gracious enough not say so.

At first I had only worn my treasured possessions in the locked confines of my dorm room, but I eventually yielded to the temptation to wear them under my clothes outside at night and then to an afternoon's college choir practice. The dark slacks I wore should have hidden the lace-like trim on the leg of the girdle, but whether the material was too thin or the lighting was wrong, a choir member seated beside me saw the garment's ruffled leg. When I realized what had attracted his attention, I mustered my most stern expression but said nothing. To his very much-appreciated credit, he never mentioned the incident to me or, to my knowledge, to anyone else.

I considered the possibility that, in buying the clothes and wearing them where the act might be discovered, I might subconsciously be seeking that discovery. I was at least tempting or defying the prospect. In this latest of so many rounds of self-analysis, I could not see how discovery would be helpful or how it would lead to anything other than humiliation. The observant choir member was the first person outside my family to have seen me wearing sex-inappropriate clothing since the incident with my robe-wearing childhood friend.

Emptying the Closet

That night I sat on the bolster bed in my dorm room with the lights off as I stared at the garments and tried to imagine again how I might end this ongoing struggle with my obsession. The girdle and gartered stockings were a perfect part of a wardrobe I had longed to possess, but I also knew I wanted my life to be about more than the fleeting enjoyment of wearing such things or the longer-lasting excitement of thinking about them. The possibility of further discovery and unacceptable embarrassment was an additional consideration helping me decide to dispose of them.

Realizing that I would almost inevitably seek their replacement, I placed the things in a brown paper bag. It was midnight. I quietly left my room but did not lock the door because of the noise it would make. I got into my car and drove to a picturesque roadside park and lake roughly fifteen miles from campus. Unsurprisingly, the park was deserted. I paused once more to consider the action, and then threw the bag as far out into the lake as I could.

There was no cathartic vision, no freeing sense of relief, and no music of angel choruses or blaring trumpets heralding this minor and temporary victory in my lifelong war. I felt no great satisfaction that anything had been resolved. It was late, I still had schoolwork to do, and I was several miles from the dorm. The entire exercise and the reason for it seemed stupid, wasteful, and sick.

When I got back to the dorm, I found that the door to my room I had closed so quietly had not latched. The door had swung open slightly. On the rug in the center of the room was one of the stockings I somehow had failed to secure in the bag. I was certain I had placed it in that bag and, in a science fiction film, it would still have been wet from its visit to the lake.

Its presence could have been accepted as an omen of my inability to rid myself of the obsession. Instead, it symbolized exasperating frustration. I picked up the stocking, wadded it with some scrap paper, and tossed it down the garbage chute. Three dorm floors, ten rooms per quad, thirty rooms per trash chute; surely, no nosy sleuth, however motivated, could trace the thing back to me. If anyone else saw the incriminating stocking, he (or they) never told me.

Each four hundred mile drive back to school was an opportunity to acquire one or more items I could wear during the term. I did not even consider purchasing makeup because the dorm's common bathing areas afforded no assurance of privacy for removing it. My preferred route meant driving through Toledo, Ohio, which minimized the amount of time those purchases added to my trip. I would not plan to purchase anything when I left home but, after a couple hours on the Ohio Turnpike, my dormant gender identity would waken. As I would near the Toledo exit, "dormant" was the least accurate description possible for my hyperactive obsession. These purchases were always things that I could wear under my male attire. I did not begin buying other clothing and makeup until after college graduation.

Since I spent the summers of my college years working in the bank, my secret clothing did not have a chance to get old. I would not risk taking home anything that would be difficult to explain, or worse, that might be discovered after an accident en route. There was no suitable place on campus to hide the things, nor anyone with whom I was willing to leave them.

The satisfaction derived from having my secret and treasured possessions could not surmount the prospect of their being discovered, either while I was in transit or after I was home. There was a remote chance of discovery in having the clothes in my dorm room but, until the incident during the unexpected classmate's visit, I had thought no one would have an opportunity to find them in my single room. Each purging attempt was intended to include everything associated with the obsession. One of those bundles was deposited in the trash bin of an A. & W. Restaurant after I had enjoyed a carryout lunch from a sack large enough to accommodate the bundle. The fact that the restaurant's sack was larger after my lunch than before I started drew no apparent notice.

A Friend for Life

A library secretary scheduled the showing of all films using the library's equipment, so I saw her almost daily regarding that schedule. She shared my interest in music, birth month, a link to my home state through her father's hand-blown glass making, and a lively interest in a wide range of other subjects. While in her teens, she had traveled with one of her brothers, singing with him in churches and for other gatherings. Our visits for film-showing assignments were rarely brief, and we continued an active correspondence for decades until her death. In more than twenty-five years of conversations, cards, and letters, we had touched on innumerable topics but, especially, discussed details about her family and mine. Although the brother with whom she had sung survived over a year of captivity when Iranians seized the U.S. embassy in Tehran, she believed that episode shortened his life.

When I wrote to her about my change of name, transition, and sex-reassignment surgery, the new chapter in our correspondence suddenly became much richer. She wrote, for the first time, about some less pleasant and most personal experiences that had been difficult for her but said she had somehow found the determination to get through them for herself and those closest to her. Her notes and cards always included a reference to an encouraging verse of scripture. Just before my college graduation, she had given me a book about success as a promise of faith. She strongly believed in and practiced that message.

Self-Diagnosis

The genie I had attempted to keep firmly corked in its bottle kept emitting instant reminders of its presence, primarily in the form of urges to acquire and wear gender identity-appropriate clothing and makeup. The seeming importance of wearing the clothes and makeup made it all too easy to believe that my problem was solely the intense desire to have and wear them. It did not occur to me to wonder why, despite my determination to hide my obsession, I wanted to be around other people in that guise. Reading Jan Morris's *Conundrum* while in my early twenties did help me erroneously decide that, because of the many ways in which I was different from her, I was a transvestite and not transgendered (Morris 1974).[54] Her accounts of attempting to overcompensate for her gender identity inclinations by appearing to be unquestionably male were not part of my experience. Her confidence and comfort during and after transition were almost impossible to imagine because I was still convinced that my cross-dressing was a capitulation to an improper desire. Her diminutive physical stature relative to mine and to larger males seemed to facilitate her construct of her gender identity and was a physical attribute I wished I shared but knew I did not.

Another work, on the history of transvestism, was similarly unhelpful in my attempt to obtain an accurate self-diagnosis. I remembered my mother's telling me that cross-dressing as a child could lead to one's *becoming* a transvestite even though my obsession was always present. I did not even consider the nature or nurture argument since I did not understand my problem. Seeking a professional opinion even to evaluate the transvestite condition had never seemed an option. To do so would have meant talking with someone about my obsession. I do not know from whom I would have sought a diagnosis nor am I certain the diagnosis rendered would have been accurate. It still seemed more important to keep the obsession secret than to find an effective or alternative means of resolving it. Had anyone been able to tell me that, without a correct diagnosis, my condition would continue unabated for the next twenty years, I cannot know how I would have responded. Accepting that prospect would have been most difficult, if not impossible.

As a self-diagnosed transvestite, I knew I could find relief and even erotic satisfaction with the modest expenditure of one or two hundred dollars each year to buy make-up and clothing and wasted hours spent wearing and thinking about wearing them. Since I expected to be the only person seeing the incomplete result of their use, spending more than that rather modest amount would have been pointlessly extravagant. The facts that I was content with neither the incompleteness of my transformation nor the knowledge that I was the only person aware of my attempts were not addressed in my self-diagnosis. I believed that if the compulsion, or addiction, or whatever my condition was could be managed so inexpensively, it was something with which I could continue to live. I also accepted, because there seemed to be no acceptable alternative, that there was an additional non-monetary cost to the secret life I was maintaining but dared not share.

The line from the Christmas carol "Don we now our gay apparel..." always evoked an ironic response. I knew that other like-aged, and especially male, singers were bemused by the awkward wording and alternative meaning of the phrase, but my secret apparel had nothing to do with homogendered inclinations. It was too easy to believe that, because I seemed obsessed by the desire to wear those things, I must be a transvestite. I had progressed from wearing my sister's and then my mother's clothing at home to the daring and embarrassing purchase and wearing of my own sex-inappropriate clothing at school. I wore those first purchases in the "single" room of my college dorm and then, occasionally, under my regular clothes on campus. I bought and hid other garments and wanted increasingly to wear other things on short drives, in malls, and everywhere.

No one was given an opportunity to explain to me, and I had not discovered, that my repeated enactment of wearing the clothes and make-up was an expressed desire rooted in unacknowledged gender identity. I had not even heard the terms "gender identity" and "gender identity conflict" before beginning the process of transition. The tormenting internal conflict and a lack of understanding were real and perplexing, but I had no sense of warring personalities. I did not feel as though I was someone else "trapped" in my body, nor did I feel like a female and a male living in one body. It was the fact that the unit's physical and mental components were essentially incompatible that was incessantly troubling. While wishing I could change so many things about my body or, ideally, have that body magically transformed to be, if not to always have been, female, I never had any illusions or doubts about the oneness of my existence.

One of the reasons I could accept postponing my transition while in my 20's was that I saw no reasonable counter-argument to my own question about how I could hope to be seen as a woman among a population of women who had spent their first twenty-plus years learning to be the women they are. The answer I finally accepted to that question, after waiting another twenty years to formulate it, was that it would have to be whatever it was. I would have to be and accept the woman I had learned to be. What was inconceivable to me before transition was that most mature people of whatever physical age seem to respond to the sincerity and substance presented rather than solely to an unusual or superficial appearance. My living quite openly now means no longer having to try to be the male person I never was, nor being self-conscious about my appearance. I told one neighbor that I no longer felt as though I was dragging a thousand-pound weight with me. The self new acquaintances now see and respond to is partly suggested by my appearance, but that appearance now introduces and enhances who I am instead of contradicting it.

I had no desire to be, or be like, any of the women in our family, or to be any other real or imagined person. I never wanted or pretended to be essentially different from the person I was or to seek radical change as an escape from a general or specific disappointment with my professional or personal life. Such often-repeated descriptions of MtF transgendered people are most inaccurate and misleading. These descriptions are, like so many other fallacious explanations, poor substitutes for describing the reality of gender identity conflict. In the center of a crowd of thousands of people or alone on a raft at sea, I would ultimately and honestly want to be myself, and to know who that self is.

Before transition and after college graduation, I thought I did have some control over the compulsion and could exist, if not live fully, as a self-gratifying transvestite. Unlike those pensive moments contemplating the sex-inappropriate garments in my college dorm room, I sought to accept, as a more mature adult, the inevitability of the obsession and the limitations that behavior would impose on my developing sex-appropriate social relationships. The few attempts at dating that I made were much like a dance in which each person waits for the other to lead. Lack of a sincere interest in dating during and after college probably was apparent, although its basis in identity conflict certainly was not.

In 1973, while attending a "banking school" for commercial-bank correspondents of one of Pittsburgh's banks, I stayed in that city's now demolished Carlton House. I bought a pair of red "baby doll" pajamas, shaved my legs for the first time, and crawled into bed as the most female version of myself I could imagine. I felt more feminine that evening than I had at any earlier time, until I again began cataloguing excesses and deficiencies in my appearance and noting the hour by which the fantasy must end. In an exception to my self-imposed traveling rules from my college years, I brought those things home, hid them, and occasionally wore them.

My intellectual wanderings in search of the condition's resolution found few clues in the behavior of other people. I could neither experience the feelings of, nor instinctively react to, situations and events like the gender identity-consonant females and males around me. Each situation or event immediately placed me at a relative disadvantage to the people around me because it was safer to appear not to react. I was comfortable around my contemporaries of both sexes when gender identity ostensibly had little to do with our being together, but I lacked an innate and perceived affinity for either sex. I did feel envious of girls who were not compelled to suppress their identities. Appearing to be male without the natural mental and instinctual inclinations of a male meant accepting relegation to a form of social isolation that would necessarily impede formation of most associations. Inherent and learned components of an appreciation for honesty did not encourage an alternative affected masculine extroversion, which probably would not have been convincing and sustainable if it had been attempted.

A general awareness of the unpleasant consequences for my male peers and a native or learned aversion to effeminate males who sought unusual associations with groups of girls precluded any attempts to join in their activities and discussions. Given my physical appearance, they would have been unlikely to welcome my participation. Lacking the necessary female physical attributes and not foreseeing any opportunity to redress the deficiency, I could not share the physical changes and new experiences of other girls. I would not feign what would have had to seem a homogendered interest in boys to learn from that aspect of their discussions.

8. Key Relationships

Two Selves

When each person looks in a mirror or is seen by other people, evident facts of external appearance such as height, weight, gender, eye color, taste in clothing and its situational appropriateness are instantly gleaned and assessed. The mirror shows a two-dimensional image of a surface with an illusion of depth but does not show what is behind or beneath that surface. The additional dimension of that person's depth, including such facets as intellect, character, and projected personality, is conveyed through actions, discussions, reputation, etc.; any and all of which are not instantly apparent. The importance of the superficial image, both physical and the projected personality, is not easily overstated.

Popular entertainers have dramatically influenced both public policy and private industry, and they have helped foster an immense media industry based largely on public perceptions of their two-dimensional television and/or movie screen images. On various issues of social prejudice, physical and mental health, the Nation's energy policy regarding alternative fuels, etc., the special status afforded to entertainers and used by them has been effective. Some people question whether President Ronald Reagan would ever have reached public office if he had not established a memorable film and television presence. While his subsequent elections cannot reasonably be attributed to appearance alone, his use of his public image has proven the potential power of that resource.

For more than forty years, the image I usually saw and presented to others was the result of my inability or unwillingness to confront a reality. While my real gender identity conflicted with that image, the image for everyone other than myself was the perceived reality. As carefully as I did work at maintaining, projecting, and even trying to be the person that image seemed to reflect, the effort was misdirected. Surely, sound mental health is at risk for any person who pretends always to be someone she or he is not, and cannot, be. Regardless of evidence appearing to support the fiction, that "proof" should not delude others and cannot be wholly convincing to the perpetrator. Those who suggest that transgendered people should continue to suppress their gender identity cannot understand what they are asking.

Professionals whose responsibilities require accurate assessments, including psychiatrists, psychologists, and agents of law enforcement, cannot fulfill their duties if their assessments are based solely on perceptions of a superficial image. Shortly before my mother left teaching, she was Dean of Women for one of four "centers" at the local consolidated high school. Her responsibilities included dealing with excused and un-excused absences. During her last years of teaching, this experienced professional said it had become nearly impossible for her to tell when some students were lying. Their statements of altered truth or fantasy were being related with sufficient conviction to virtually assure their being received as truth.

A student who falsely says AI had to stay home yesterday because I was ill" is not at all comparable to an MtF woman with a masculine appearance, a birth certificate saying she is male, and a history of having been raised as a male whose legal name is John. The magnitude of the difference between these misstatements and what each statement represents is immense. The former statement is an intentional deception to avoid punishment for another intentional misdeed. The latter is a brief summary of an horrendous fraud perpetrated from the initial mis-assignment of her gender at birth. Ironically, though, the latter case is the more difficult to assess or to expose in someone determined to hide it.

Hiding the conflict is far from pretending it does not exist. I never wanted to be another woman, and I never felt as though I were another person trapped in my body or "the wrong body." Although I would dispute its accuracy, the often heard "wrong body" characterization may be useful for two reasons. Surely, those who use it are exhibiting a sense of self that is different from their apparent physical selves. Further, the phrase may be more common to those who have a different sense of the nature of their conflict and they may pursue an earlier transition. It is far more than semantics to refer to a physical sex that differs from the mind's conception of its gender identity. Because gender identity is part of the non-physical self, it does not have specific physical requirements. As long as it exists on earth, one's essential self resides in the body it was given. The essence of my conflict was that my body did not reflect my identity and I knew of no way, despite decades of trying, to make it do so. Yet, I do not recall a single dream where I was still myself but in a different body.

If it were possible to capture an image from a special mirror's reverse, or otherwise to look beyond the reflection it shows, that view might be a complete and an accurate image of who the reflected person really is. Years ago, such a mirror's image would have served as a diagnostic tool beyond price. It would have provided evidence to support my beginning transition decades sooner. Conventional mirrors in my home reflected an image that I modified with clothes and makeup. That image always brought intense momentary satisfaction if it appeared sufficiently feminine, but it also brought disappointment at the least failings in the alteration. When dressing as a male for school, work, and other aspects of a normal male routine, the mirror was just another useful grooming tool. As an aid for temporary female transformation, mirrors were an essential element, if not a gateway, to my world of fantasy. While never being a window to the soul or even the subconscious, each reflected image of partial transformation turned an obsession and continuing fantasy into an incomplete, and far too ephemeral, near reality. As satisfying as these brief sessions were, they always seemed fleeting and a singularly unproductive use of time. Any work attempted while dressed nearly always seemed to take much longer, as though each release of my gender identity-genie became an end, rather than the means to an end. I did not realize the whole meaning of that release until after transition. Neither confronting and resisting nor acquiescing to makeup and "dressing" were, nor could they be, tamers of the obsession.

If there were a magic mirror on whose reverse transgendered people might see their true selves and they could show that image to others, it would prove how fundamentally and inevitably female the lives of MtF women ultimately must be. Life on the face of such a mirror is a grossly incomplete pseudo reality that excludes from a whole life the individual's essential self and her or his (for an FtM man) potential. A suppressing MtF woman cannot fully realize the talent, abilities, and opportunities that help comprise a whole person's life. The sum of those attributes cannot be reflected in a two-dimensional image that a mirror's face reflects. In the absence of the equivalent of that elegant mirror, society must know that, despite the care, expense, and other resources MtF women commit to their appearance, they cannot be judged accurately merely by the result of those efforts. No one should be able to assert successfully in a court of law that they can.

A Personal View of Reverence

While there may be people whose daily communication with God is so distinct that they seem to correct each other's grammar, it is also possible that the voice they hear does not come from God. Most people who have professed their faith and trust in Him believe that God speaks to them, and in a variety of ways. He communicates regularly with those who will hear Him through His Word, through other people, and through the imprint He left on the heart of everything He created. On rare and very special occasions, that communication will be direct, powerful, and unmistakable. Those instances do not happen on the supplicant's timetable but on His. People communicate with Him through their actions and prayer. Those who seek structured confirmation or correction of the message(s) they perceive will seek the established institution and company of those who have shared and continue to share a common statement of faith. They will find great warmth and comfort among that company, as well as occasional and relatively minor disappointments.

When Sunday school and church services were so much a part of my childhood and adolescence, I accepted the lessons, scripture, hymns, and religious community as part of a normal and natural order. I did not realize that many young people, including many of my peers, grew in more secular, or less structured, environments where such constancy and sense of belonging were absent. I have often reflected on the worth of my training, and I regard that part of my past with great fondness and gratitude. Although I cannot claim a Constantine-like moment of revelation, I do not feel slighted. I memorized and accepted as a child our catechism statement regarding the chief end of man. While my understanding of that statement has deepened and my perspective has changed greatly, attempting to glorify God and to enjoy His presence forever has been, and remains, unrivaled as an insurmountable objective. It might be possible to experience such a childhood and to act either from habit or to satisfy someone else, so that an honest professing of faith is postponed indefinitely and, perhaps, fatally. Any MtF woman who contends with her suppressed identity, however, has almost as powerful a need to share that burden as the compulsion she feels to hide it. My sharing that burden in prayer helped make bearing it possible.

Most of the world's major religions, including Judaism, Islam, and Christianity, acknowledge the existence of God and attempt to describe Him as the one who was revealed to the prophets. God's message, from their accounts, was about His capabilities, His creation, and His relationship with humanity. Each person was created in His image, which doubtlessly includes the ability to contend with her or his own life and interactions with the rest of His creation. Part of that interaction, for most people, includes procreation.

The whole of humanity is described as children of the God who knew them before they were born but their bodies do have human parents. The obvious reality is that the God who is infinite, eternal, unchangeable, and omniscient, does not need a husband or wife to create a lot of successor gods as children. The male gender identity ascribed to God may be mankind's re-creation of Him in an attempt to discover more about who He really is and what a relationship with God should and can be. If God does have a divine gender identity, it must not be related to the human concept of procreation.

Many Christians believe that Christ's birth to a human mother was God's becoming human in a world that would have been even less receptive to His message had Christ been female. If there would be real and substantive differences in perception, preference, morality, comprehension and insight, etc. were God to have a different gender identity, those differences would be unimaginable to inheritors of the faith of Abraham since they would harshly conflict with the history of their spiritual reality. God as Father and Creator, but not each person's biological father, suggests that human gender identity, sexual identity, and procreation are inextricably bound, at least as they relate to the earthly lives of humans.

In attempting to deal with recent revelations regarding the tragic, immoral, and illegal interaction between some priests and their young parishioners, several priests and some laity have asserted that the vow of celibacy is at fault as a root cause of or contributing factor to the priests" misdeeds. Each sexual contact between priests who have taken a vow of celibacy and any other person would certainly seem to have a psychosexual component oriented to something other than fathering a child. The Church has traditionally regarded any sexual interaction as sinful where the intent, or at least an acknowledged small possibility, of creating a child is not present. The priest engaged in illicit sexual activity is failing to follow scripture, is dishonoring his calling, and disrespects the Christian's sole need of a continuing spiritual relationship, rooted in gratification and adoration, for the gift of salvation. This greater spiritual need pertains to anyone who would profess both a desire to live a Christian life and to possess an aversion to any force of spirit or thought inconsistent with that life.

The rationale that, because a person has vowed to deny to herself or himself a traditional gender identity-appropriate spousal relationship, that person would be more inclined to establish an aberrant or abusive sexual relationship is counterintuitive and seems absurd. If a desire for a traditional relationship were so strong that a priest felt compelled to act, it seems much more likely that he would seek, or permit himself to become part of, a traditional spousal relationship, even though it meant breaking his vow. A priest's becoming involved in any sexual relationship is sometimes seen as a capitulation to human emotion, to a dark internal impulse or external force, or even to Satan. It is much more logical to presume that he found the need to be part of a traditional human family, possibly like the one in which he was raised, to be stronger than his willingness to separate himself from having that life. He may even believe his call to be an integral part of his own human family is a Divine calling.

A few acquaintances have suggested that my own efforts to resolve an unbearable dissonance between the spiritual/intellectual self and my physical self were actually a capitulation to a malevolent influence. They do not, and perhaps cannot, accept that transgendered people know intimately the essence of their conflict is between their physical and non-physical selves, even as they may spend decades attempting to resolve that conflict. The conflict is not the result of any external influence. However much of the non-physical self is affected by gender identity, the gender identity of MtF women is female. If the essential self has separate components of soul, intellect, and emotional capacity, then gender identity must have some interaction with, or be a part of, each of them. Although the prospect is most unlikely, it could be fascinating to witness, if unbearable to endure, a lengthy conflict among a spiritual, emotional, and intellectual self that had provably different genders identities. So powerful a dissonance among those primary aspects of each person's essence, which I believe are inseparable in life, would make life impossible for its victim.

It is much more likely that each person's gender identity colors, and is colored by, the way her or his mind relates to the physical self, and by extension, to other people. Whatever are any person's frustrations with being unable to establish and maintain her or his desired relationships, it is unfathomable that such frustration would directly lead to an undesired relationship. Inability to obtain something intensely desired would logically feed either an obsession to obtain it or the resolve to eschew it. It is not reasonable to assert that an undesired thing would be sought in its place. Surely, a person's seeking something to which she or he is averse would promise failure or worse.

Accepting a substitute for what is ardently desired is different from seeking that substitute but, if the desired thing was important, abiding its substitute is also likely to fail. Mental health counselors doubtlessly contend constantly with patients who live their lives in misery because they are not pursuing what they really want. Discovering or accepting what that desired thing is may be the critical key to assuaging, and not continually suppressing, that misery. I do not believe that God will make that journey for his followers but there is no substitute for His making the journey with them.

The Ernest Prayer

Some faithful followers profess to know a sense of constant shared presence with God so strong that they see no distinction between prayer and living. If so, unlike so many people described in scripture, they must not see prayer as the separate and distinct act . For Christians, Matthew 6: 6 advises "But whenever you pray, go into your room and shut the door and pray to your Father..." (Division of Christian Education 1989)[55] Others may preface every conscious action with prayer, but either their actions are few or their days are longer than twenty-four hours.

In addition to praying thankfully about their own lives, members of the community of faith also pray about their own needs and the needs of others. Because "needs" is a relative term, each person's prayers are probably unique. While some decisions are prefaced by prayer others, such as which coin to put in a parking meter or attempting to save one's child from an imminent threat, are so spontaneous that it would not occur to someone to pray for guidance. A bank customer once proclaimed confidently that God protected her checking account. She may well have been correct because I do not recall that the account ever was overdrawn but, if it had been, the notice would have been sent to her. The parent who rescued her or his child, though, would express gratitude in prayer.

Our church treasurer once said that there had been many times during her tenure when available funds were insufficient to meet looming expenses, yet when the bills were due, there was always enough in the account to pay them. No corporate financial officer could expect to remain employed under a similar scenario. Even some responsible for administration of church finances might take to chewing their nails and growing gray hair at such times, but others would argue that the funds belong to His Church, the people have faith, so there is no insurmountable problem. The latter group would be living the words of Luke 12: 22-31 and Matthew 6: 25-33 (National Council 1989).[56] This group too probably would find a chronic insufficiency of needed funds to be a suitable matter for prayer. While finance may be an often-sighted tree in the forest of prayer concerns, it is by no means the only, and for many people is the least appropriate, subject about which to pray.

Whether to wear the red or the blue dress would seem an even less appropriate subject for prayer. When an MtF woman contemplates exiting her home in broad daylight and being seen by, and intending to see, people who have never seen her wearing a dress, that matter would easily pass through the finest of filters for suitability. Still, whether the color, shape, style, etc. of components of appearance matter at all is secondary to the decision of whether and when to take that first public step. Having stepped from the airplane, the parachutist is appropriately unconcerned about how the parachute's color is perceived by bystanders below. As I struggled with the immediacy of my impending actions and my psychiatrist's advice that my secret life would have to become public if I intended to continue on transition's path, I did wonder if it was possible finally to do what for so long had been fantasy.

A few months before taking my first public steps, I had written some questions, doubts, and troubling thoughts on the notepad at bedside in an attempt to remove them from conscious thought so I could sleep. The attempt failed and then an increasingly agitating sense of desperation was making sleep impossible. That sense continued to build as though it might reach some explosive point until I suddenly "heard" a voice of calming reassurance like none I had before encountered or have since experienced. The voice said "It will be alright". "Said" is inaccurate, but I was aware of the words as something I had just heard rather than felt as an unbidden thought. Some would say that I let myself hear what I most wanted to hear, but that does not explain the sense of another presence and the stunning power of the experience nor its effefct.

While there seemed to have been a voice, I could not describe it because the event had occurred so suddenly and unexpectedly that I did not immediately understand what had happened. There were no blaring trumpets, fluttering angel wings, or flowing robes. The voice did not say that I would have no more questions, doubts, and fears. It did not promise freedom from embarrassment or insult. It did not provide a lesson on the essence of mankind's purpose in the universe and how a transgendered person's experience might fit into that plan. Its completely unexpected presence, simplicity, clarity, and the immediate sense of calm assurance it provided helped me accept its origin as divine.

The trite or precious tale about the two sets of footprints that become one, or countless and more elegantly related testaments to an otherwise inexplicable solace or encouragement that was suddenly present when it was desperately needed apparently refers to similar experiences. I had never had such an experience before that night, and have not had a comparable one since. Its effect was real and immediate. Although astonished by it, I gratefully accepted the assurance, was immediately more at ease, and soon fell asleep.

In *Sergeant York* (Hawks 1941),[57] a sudden breeze turns the pages of a Bible held by Alvin York (impressively portrayed by Gary Cooper) to a verse containing the words he accepts as the solution to a conflict between understanding his faith and a duty to enter military service. My experience was certainly less visually dramatic than the scene in that film, and it did not lead to anything approximating the heroic actions for which Sergeant York was decorated. I do believe, and especially so after that experience, that at such moments, regardless of the nature of the fears with which we contend and when we are earnestly seeking a sense of direction that we seem unable to find within ourselves or in others, we can find that we are not really alone.

When I told a minister/friend about that moment, he did not offer an explanation, possibly because he was consistently determined that I would always be male. His accepting that "voice" for what I believe it was and what I thought it meant, would have been contrary to his own determination. A line from the Prayer of St. Francis de Sales says, "He will either shield you from suffering or will give you unfailing strength to bear it" (de Sales n.d.).[58] That line occurred to and comforted me then, and must be a continuing comfort to others who also believe those words. To those who do not, I am sure there will come a time when their own powers, even with the help of others, are insufficient to meet their circumstance. If they cannot accept and rely on faith, I cannot imagine how they will survive the experience.

Love and Obligation

Mother's two-year old sister and her maternal grandmother died the year before my mother was born. As devastating as the losses were for her mother, my mother does not recall a single instance when she thought that her childhood was different because of them. She has always felt close to her younger sister but especially so because of a life-threatening illness her sister had in childhood. Aware of the loss of her older sister, Mother prayerfully and desperately sought to avoid the loss of her younger one. When, after months of battling the illness, her sister recovered, Mother accepted the recovery as a special gift to her.

When she was older, Mother was urged to help her father at work while she pursued her formal education. Her father perceived his abbreviated period of structured learning as a disadvantage and did not want either of his daughters to feel similarly constrained. Despite an abiding interest in music, Mother studied business and seriously considered attending law school. At the end of her sophomore year in college, increasing concern for her father's health helped her decide to transfer from a school farther from home that had an excellent music program to one closer to her home that had a better business program.

Her academic change of direction probably was inevitable. Her sense of love and obligation predominated even, or especially, when they conflicted with her own ambitions and interests. Her choices were not made because she had an irresistible martyr complex but because of her genuine caring concern for her family and the knowledge that she was willing and able to do what she knew they wanted her to do. When some members of society seek escape, fulfillment, quicksilver elation, etc. from alcohol or illicit drugs, others, like my mother, through commitment, a sense of obligation, and a grounded awareness of propriety are not tempted in the least by such substances.

If Mother had stayed at the more distant college, she would not have met my father and, almost as certainly, would have led a very different life. That life would have belonged to a very different person who would not have changed schools to be closer to the parents and sister she loved. Yet, Mother knew who she was and what she wanted. When the man who would become my father proposed to her from Florida, Mother considered her parents' request to wait until the War's end. She knew she wanted to marry this man, accepted his proposal, and they were married in Florida.

Throughout my childhood and adolescence, I knew I could talk with her about things not related to my suppressed gender identity. If I wanted something, I could talk with her about it but, if she said no, she meant it. Restating the request or asking her to change her mind did not invite punishment but my older sister and I knew the effort of repetition was unlikely to be rewarded. After my younger sister's accident, a slightly different set of rules seemed to apply to her but I was never tempted to share an experience like hers to qualify for that new set. If, when Mother thought about saying "no" to her, she saw that small child in an oxygen tent with her terribly swollen face and her condensation-soaked hair sticking to the abrasions, it must have been almost impossible to deny my sister's requests. Many of my sister's requests were simply for Mother to stay within arm's length or nearer.

The school system's increasingly urgent calls for my mother to return to teaching and my sister's impending attendance at first grade made separation necessary before either felt wholly prepared for it. Mother's knowing who she was and what she wanted did not always make such decisions easy. Had my mother been certain that my sister was not ready for school or that she needed to stay with my sister, few forces could have prevailed against her. She also wanted my sister to have a "normal" education and Mother was dedicated to teaching. Despite the difficulty, Mother knew it was time for that limited separation to begin.

A less difficult decision for her was permitting me to begin to study piano, even though it meant obligating additional time out of her already heavily burdened week. After my older sister had begun studying piano, I wanted lessons too. Mother knew I was too young and said, that if I still wanted to study in a year, she would permit it. At age six, I was already acutely aware that there were acceptable, and even expected, ways to be different from my older sister and ways that seemed unacceptable to me or to other people. For me, wanting to study piano was easy. My mother played piano. My older sister was learning to play. I thought it was important and something I wanted to be able to do. Only after beginning lessons, though, did I realize how much difference there was between wanting something and the tedious discipline necessary to achieve it.

Later, Mother's commitment of time and her endurance of winter cold and summer heat were almost minor travails compared to persuading me to take the lessons for which I had not prepared, and there were too many of those. Mother would explain patiently that the timing of my concern was misplaced and insist that, if I was unprepared, I would have to suffer the consequences. My teacher also was patient and, perhaps, excessively lenient because I would leave the lesson with "very good" or "excellent" written on the notebook I carried with my music.

The effort these two women expended to help secure for me some part of the gift of music often was greater than I had expended. Yet, I never suggested that I thought it was their responsibility to help me do something I wanted, and occasionally resisted wanting, to do. They acted from their own sense of love, dedication, and obligation to perpetuate appreciation for something important to them. They did not expect that I would appreciate their gift at the time. They typify a generosity of spirit that is almost assumed by people who misunderstand and demean such willing sacrifice. That love and dedication are not earned or commanded but are either given or withheld as a choice that discloses identity. This brief summary grossly understates my mother's influence on my life and the lives of my sisters, but it shows the nature of a critical component of my upbringing.

From the "Garden" State

My father, the oldest of four children, was born in New Jersey and spent his first eight years there. His father worked for the U.S. Department of Agriculture which ordered his transfer to Richmond, Virginia just as Dad was to enter high school. In addition to leaving his hometown and friends at such an important time for adolescents, Dad also had to adjust to the unexpected and profoundly significant discovery that he was from the north at a time and in a place where that was not deemed by others his age to be a good thing. Through four years of high school, Dad would often hear the word Yankee but almost never without a certain four-letter word preceding it. As an added insult, he was learning German with a Dixie accent. His sister and two brothers were similarly informed of their less than esteemed status by their peers, but they did not share the onus of Dad's leadership role as the oldest sibling. In addition to his schoolwork and family responsibilities, Dad delivered newspapers and took accordion lessons. Those experiences are so much a part of him that he kept the labeled canvas newspaper bag he used and his accordion until his death.

Customary wisdom would count it an odd trait for any employee of the U.S. Government, and especially so for the stereotypical bureaucrat, but Dad's father had little patience for lengthy explanations and a knack for briefly summarizing long and seemingly complicated discourse. If brevity is the soul of wit Granddad's tenacious grip on that soul might have made Satan envious, but I wonder what might have been his version of a suitably abridged encyclopedia or a worthy literary collection. Dad inherited that economy of language and always seemed especially fond of the phrase "talk is cheap." Never fond of lengthy explanations, he would rather show how something was to be done.

A childhood spent in the Great Depression, his Richmond experience with other teens, a father disinclined to discussion, and World War II gave Dad a generally serious demeanor and little interest in recreation. When I attempted to share my close childhood friend's interest in baseball, Dad took me to a local sporting goods store to get a ball, bat, and glove. I did not realize for several years that the glove he bought was a softball glove but when I did, I thought Dad should have known the difference. I would not understand until much later that, at the time when Dad was interested in that most American of team sports, many of his contemporaries would have wanted "that damn Yankee" to be the only player on the other team. Their reason had nothing to do with personality, abilities, or disposition, but everything to do with bias and geography. Further, a large family and weak American economy meant that there was not a lot of money in their household for things like sports equipment.

When asked, Dad readily answered specific questions about his youth, but I did not learn until after my college graduation how the plans he had made as a high school student to attend a four-year college in Virginia were dashed by his family's move to New York. At several pivotal times in his life, my father acceded to the vagaries of fate or fortune, forsaking carefully made plans that had promised a vastly different and desired future. After revising his plans for college, he found employment in manufacturing. These new plans were altered drastically, along with those of millions of others, by the Empire of Japan on December 7, 1941. Dad knew himself well enough to adapt quickly to each of these new realities.

Although his employment in the making of molds for metal castings qualified him for draft deferment, he enlisted in the U.S. Army Air Corps (which did not become the U.S. Air Force until after W.W. II) and spent the next five years in uniform. He practiced some of the free enterprise for which he was fighting by selling his allotment of cigarettes and duplicates of photos he took and developed of places his unit encountered outside of the U.S. When a transport ship on which he served was returning prisoners of war to Italy, a mine came perilously close to ending all of his plans and those of everyone else onboard.

My favorite photograph of him as my father was taken when I was four years old. He was kneeling on one knee beside me, wearing his sport coat and tie with one hand at his side and the other near me as though he thought, if he held me too closely, I would break. The picture is of a very proud young father with his "son" and Dad looks as though he could not have been much happier. Every son of a loving father probably has at least one such photo and counts among his most fond memories the circumstances under which it was taken. While the child I was looks very happy in that photo, I was too young to remember its being taken. I still like what it said though about my father.

During my youth when Dad was not working in the bank or attending meetings of various organizations, he often worked at his workbench in our basement fixing something that had broken or servicing some item to make it work at least as well as it should. He spent time cleaning the tubes in our old radios using some of what he had learned in the Air Corps, but he never tried to transfer that skill to our television set. He assembled and painted several plastic models of airplanes and automobiles, and tried to help me assemble a few. While his completed versions always looked like the picture on the package, mine seldom did. Dad wanted me to watch him as he worked with his tools in the basement, but I would quickly decide that I thought I understood what he was doing, he would do what needed to be done, and something else must be more fun. The care he took and patience he expended in working with his hand tools or assembling a plastic model seemed limitless but those projects were very taxing for a child who wanted to be more, or more independently, active.

When a friend of my older sister's was sharing a summer evening's meal with us, Dad was comfortably dressed in a sport shirt, shorts, and sandals. Neither my sister nor I would have said anything to admonish Dad but she said she thought he had spilled corn kernels on the floor. Dad immediately replied "That isn't corn, those are my toes". Whether we had expected Dad to reply more harshly or were just surprised to hear his humorous response, the three children at that table could not have been more delighted by his remark. The friend's laughter was particularly engaging and we all giggled and laughed through the rest of the meal.

I do not know if Dad would have been considered an especially strict disciplinarian but he and Mother did let us know that there were rules that would be enforced, usually employing corporal punishment, if they or either of them thought punishment was necessary. During a bout with chickenpox I may have felt immune from punishment either because I was sick or because I was told that the small blisters, if broken, would form scars. I do not recall what I said but Dad's response broke my illusion of immunity and one of the blisters. Although quite faint, the mark is still present and serves as a reminder both about illusions of immunity and the breaking of rules, and about the indelible affect each person's actions sometimes have on others.

Dad's admonitions were not always administered corporally. He may have inherited, but definitely perfected, a glower through practice in influencing the behavior of his two younger brothers. His stern stare was instantly and unmistakably inhibiting for my sisters and me. It was, and probably was intended to be, intimidating, uncompromising, and showing a momentary but complete absence of love, compassion, kindness, warmth, and understanding. Unlike its customary colloquial application, the trite "if looks could kill" phrase would aptly apply to that stare, although the person receiving it might prefer to be hit, shot, or stabbed. The effectiveness of such a device most likely was dependent upon the necessity of his maintaining a continuing relationship with its recipient.

Were Dad to administer "The Look" to a misbehaving dog, a robber, an officer giving him a traffic ticket, or another driver who had "cut him off" in traffic; it probably would have little effect. Dad's youngest brother asked during a phone call whether Dad still could generate "The Look". This decorated World War II combat veteran of U.S. Navy air artillery service, and a hero who would reserve use of that term for those who died in or as a result of battle, was attesting to his acquaintance with, and memory of, its enduring power. His was our first indication that the expression had a lengthy history, and its effectiveness had not been diminished by age.

As cold as was that stare, Dad also could and often did generate a warm and gracious smile. His laughter was not loud but genuine and obviously was something he enjoyed. While in my teens I had reached an impasse with him where he or I seemed constantly to irritate the other. My older sister remembers this as the time I realized that I could make him laugh. I would argue that he had to be willing to laugh but I had learned that judicious use of wit could occasionally elicit a non-confrontational release of tension. We rarely seemed to want to do things the same way but our differences could be entertaining as well as informative.

I prized things associated with his youth and even thought I looked like Dad in a picture of him taken when he was in elementary school. Although his bicycle was far heavier than mine, I enjoyed riding the one he had used for delivering newspapers and that his brothers also had used. With his permission, I played his accordion using one of the songbooks he kept in its case. Affection for him and liking things that belonged to him though did not mean that I could be like him. My suppressed gender identity would permit me to attempt to be the person he wanted me to be but there were limits beyond which I could not, or would not, go. Although I was not close to resolving impediments to acceptance of my own identity, I could not completely accept my father's expectations nor the identity he would have had me fulfill. The continuing struggle well may have been as difficult for him as it was for me, albeit in a far different way.

The First Child

Before my younger sister was born, my older sister and I were not just siblings but close friends who played together in our home and outside it. She originated a short-lived tradition of our hand-crafting Christmas presents for our parents using scissors, paper, crayons, etc. on Christmas morning. In addition to playing my favorite game of wearing her clothes and pretending to be her girlfriend, we played with our dolls (my two were male, of course,) board games, and with a variety of toys. When her largest doll was to "marry" my three-foot tall doll with a rabbit's head, she insisted that, before they could be married, we had to remove my rabbit's ears. This modification of the doll's anatomy for what we considered a worthy purpose might well have been portentous but I reluctantly agreed to her performing the surgery.

Our toys were never held in common. We knew which things were hers and which were mine and did not use something belonging to the other without permission. I do not know how we came to that understanding but the Tablets of Moses contained no more inviolable law. We readily understood and accepted that if something supposedly belonged to both of us, it did not really belong to either of us.

When I was five years old, my parents gave me a large metal wagon in which I could ride by sitting with one leg inside it and under me, while propelling myself and the wagon with the other leg. For a person reaching a certain height, that feat becomes nearly impossible, and it happened to me quite early. My peddle-driven red metal "car" presented a similar problem much sooner. In less than a year, I went from being barely able to reach its pedals to not having enough room between the pedals and the underside of the hood for my knees. I was still young enough to want to play with the toy but so tall I could no longer use it. That very early lesson in the fleeting nature of youth reinforced my knowledge and understanding that some things just cannot be changed. The car was a one-person toy but I could transport my sister in the wagon rather easily down the slight grade of our block's sidewalk. I reluctantly ceded the trip back up the walk to the greater force of gravity. Using the wagon this way became one of our shorter-lived diversions.

My older sister began taking baton lessons under the tutelage of the high school principal's daughter and I insisted that I wanted to take lessons too. I wondered why no one questioned my interest until I realized that I was expected to practice a different routine. Instead of being taught how to be a majorette, I was expected to aspire to becoming a "drum major." Rather than having a slim and shiny knurled baton with gleaming white knobs at each end, I had a short and stout dull gray metal tube with a red ball on one end. It is not difficult to imagine what Dr. Freud might make of that comparison but I quickly lost interest in the lessons.

During a childhood spat I had with my cigarette smoking co-conspirator, my sister came to my defense with a forceful vocal argument that he answered by throwing a rock that hit her head. The blow gave her a mild concussion as she was forced to pay a high price for attempting to protect me. He no more expected his action to cause serious injury than my sister expected a physical reaction to her oral argument. My relationship with the neighbor returned to its less adversarial state the same day, having healed much more quickly than my sister or her view of acceptable public discourse.

If very many children in our neighborhood were playing together and my sister was present, a game of "school" was likely to begin with my sister as its teacher. I never stayed for the game. My sense of "sibling rivalry," although I had never encountered the term, would not accommodate the difference in status between teacher and student despite my sister's being two-and-one-half years older than me. During one of these school sessions at another friend's home, his mother, an English teacher at the local high school, helped set up a pseudo classroom in their garage. I remember neither how long the session lasted nor whether one or more sessions followed sometime later, but I felt as though a nebulous force of fairness should have prevented that appropriation of *my* friend's home. When seen outside of my rivalry bias, of course, that use of the garage was entirely appropriate.

While I was in bed with a childhood ailment on an otherwise idyllic midsummer evening, I heard my father and older sister outside riding bicycles. Dad was riding my bicycle and my older sister was riding hers. The incident seemed a most unfair compounding of my misery. I was unable to be outside and did not feel well, but my traitorous bicycle was providing pleasure to someone else. Further, Dad was actually participating in outdoor recreation, which occurred much too infrequently, and I could not be included. I did not construe this instance as a missed opportunity to compete with my older sister for parental attention. Rather, it seemed as though someone had decided that fun would be available in abundance just outside my window but I would not be permitted to share in it. Later that evening, Dad read again to me the *Better Homes and Gardens* version of how a certain elephant's "child" got its trunk (Kipling 1902/1950, 101-5).[59] The creature in the river still would not let go of the young elephant's "dose" until it lengthened and the odd-sounding name of the Limpopo River was still fun to hear and repeat, especially with the author's alliterative set of adjectives preceding it. My earlier feelings of profound misery had been quickly and easily ameliorated.

Several years later, a love of Latin and a willingness to teach led my sister to attend her high school Latin teacher's alma mater but, after my sister's enrollment, the school eliminated that major. The study of this "dead" language, which had helped its students acquire a quasi-built-in dictionary for defining many unfamiliar words and had given clues to their use, lost yet another battle in its war to continue to play an important part in formal education. In Dr. Asimov's "The Last Question", the essence of human consciousness and analog computer answers the question generated by a dying universe's faint trickle of remaining energy with the singularly momentous "Let there be light", (Asimov 1974/1956, 157-169)[60] As a quintessential antithesis to Dr. Asimov's answer, the once-great language of Roman civilization would whisper only "condominium." This remnant language from a culture that had spanned the known world and spawned the Pax Romana is so diminished that today's thundering roar from Latin's fired cannon would be followed several seconds later by the smallest of pebbles rolling feebly from the barrel and falling softly to the ground. A contemporary John Wilkes Booth might leap to the stage and incinerate a Latin textbook declaring "like, sic semper any vernacular not heard nightly on commercial television, *know* what I'm sayin'". The event would pass with nothing approaching the original performance's aftermath. Leaving the theater, Booth would encounter a rush of enthusiastic fans waving the world's few remaining Latin texts and waving boxes of matches. No one ever will know how important a contribution my sister might have made as a teacher of Latin because she and her prospective students were not afforded the opportunity to make it.

My sister's appreciation of Latin was not the only subject about which we differed and some of the differences may have been, at least subconsciously, contrived. While still a child, I began to cry when I overheard my mother telling my great aunt that she saw a developmental difference favoring my sister. She attributed at least some of the difference to sex. As one woman talking to another woman about a third female, my mother had concluded that there were observable developmental differences between a girl and a "boy" at the same age. Two women engaged in a casual discussion about the perceived superiority of female aptitude or ability might be forgiven for not being entirely objective. That generous observation, however, would not come readily to a young child regarding comments by her or his mother. I was unwilling to accept a verdict of native impairment or deficiency, in any respect, in a sibling rivalry that increasingly became a contest for the attention and affection of my younger sister. Between the natural rivalry for parental attention and the contest regarding our younger sister, my older sister became, at least for me, as much a competitor as a companion. People who contend that team sports are a requisite experience to an understanding of competition must have been raised in the absence of siblings and other children.

At first, my sister did not recognize our competition, but her being older and my being seen as a male in the 1950's and 1960's contributed to the virtual inevitability of the contest. She remembers the contest as a series of individual disagreements and not as a campaign of long duration. She has said that if I had been older than she and male, our relationship probably would have progressed more amicably. Had we been able to grow as sisters, our early common experiences might well have outweighed, or at least moderated, the rivalry.

My perception of the male role and of the behavior expected by others during disagreements, or at least that aspect of each contest, would not have occurred. I knew the role of inferior or subordinate male was not well tolerated by my youthful contemporaries and, while I did not expect their acceptance or friendship, I would not abide their disrespect. The consequences of accepting an inferior or subordinate status would not merely have included a harshly enforced isolation but an at least partial crumbling of the façade of my male persona. However well-deserved I believed that exile might be, I could not imagine a bearable existence if my persona were compromised. I already knew that the other-gendered self I had previously expressed was not acceptable to my parents when they thought, and I had accepted that, I was a boy.

As my sister welcomed the arrival of our younger sister, she had no way of knowing how our relationship would change. She saw another sibling as an additional opportunity to share a close and loving relationship. Our unintended and unwelcome competition kept a part of that from happening. Some of the time that might have been consumed by those sibling relationships was spent, with parental approbation, on my sister's academic pursuits. That focus eventually helped her discover her love of Latin and led to her being one of the top two students in her 200-plus class at high school graduation. Being a serious student may have become as important to my sister's definition of her own identity as maintaining my male persona was to defining mine.

Her serious attitude toward scholarship was undiminished as an undergrad. She pursued a teaching certificate and major in English with the dedication she had hoped to apply to Latin. Much like my father's changes of direction as an undergrad from Richmond to Syracuse and from industry to military service, my older sister adapted to a plan that had been altered by forces beyond her control. While authors of fiction can draw their characters as heroically and victoriously adapting to the winds of fate or single-mindedly pursuing their unchanging course, reality makes such choices more difficult. If a different major and/or school had meant her having a different husband and daughter, I am certain that my sister would not have changed either.

A Younger Sibling

Despite my younger sister's traumatic encounter with the underside of our neighbor's automobile, her outgoing personality has consistently been among her many endearing qualities. Even the hives-induced episodes of facial swelling did not reduce her popularity among her classmates. While I rarely spent time with more than one friend at a time, she was frequently with two or more of the girls with whom she went through school. She usually would have one, two, or three of her friends with her at our home, if she was not with them at one of theirs. They never seemed to exhaust their list of topics for conversation and rarely, if ever, had serious disagreements.

When my older sister and I were riding on an uncomfortable "amusement" ride in New Jersey that we were certain was going to collapse and fatally injure one or both of us, we melodramatically took turns bequeathing our possessions to this sister. Her ability to attract friends followed her to the New Jersey shore and occasionally spawned lighter friendships with people with whom she had little in common. At such times, she invariably waited for them to realize the extent of their differences.

During family visits with me at college, she noticed that almost everyone we saw on campus exchanged greetings with me and she welcomed that contrast to her perception of my older sister's experiences at her alma mater. My younger sister followed two siblings through public school and I wanted her to have a unique college experience. After seeing several other schools, she decided she could have her own experience at my alma mater and proceeded to prove that she was right. She met the man she would marry there; he also had followed an older sibling to the school.

Her innate compass would not permit her to be defined by her childhood accident and, as important as her friends were to her, they, too, could not assign a different identity to her. Her sense of self and what was important to her would determine, and not be derived from, her chosen path. Her charted journey accommodated inevitable diversions, but when those ended or required a choice, she would invariably revert to her original course. That marvelous elasticity meant that, for example, instead of considering only those schools that had extensive course offerings in her chosen field, she attended the school she preferred with the appropriate department's assurance that she could pursue her desired major.

She shared the family preoccupation with the English language.   While

I felt fortunate to have reduced my areas of focus to three, this sister had tentatively chosen a single major before leaving high school. My older sister majored in English, I enjoyed writing and theater, and she studied speech. Her interest in live theater grew while she was in college but she was particularly interested in those who had difficulty with oral communication. That interest seems a logical extension of her concern for other people. Difficulty or inability to express oneself separates anyone from those with whom she or he would communicate. That isolation is anathema to those who find human interaction compelling.

The variant of separation transgendered people experience is that the gender identity of their oral communication often is not heard correctly or clearly by their listeners. That partial inability to communicate effectively is not a speech therapist's concern because the transgendered person's speech is correct, given the physical apparatus used to produce it. The purpose of the therapist's training is to correct errant use. While empathizing as people, therapists would violate the canons of their profession if they deliberately trained people to abuse their voices. This view is my own, and not necessarily that of my sister.

Some therapists may see their responsibilities differently and be quite willing to help transgendered people manipulate their voices to achieve a desired effect. To some extent, these therapists might say, all human speech depends on adaptation of physiology that was originally used for a far different purpose. Vocal abuse, however, refers to use that is likely to lead to such problems as nodules, muscle strain, or other irritation.

After more than a decade of work with impaired students in her county's facility to help those students, her state determined the system demanded change. When resulting changes to her work schedule would clearly be less advantageous, she again employed the wonderful elasticity that enabled her to continue to practice in her field but with an improved schedule. While she would argue that there has been nothing automatic about charting her path, she has held to that path with a consistency that precludes chance as its driving force.

Great-Relatives

One of maternal grandmother's sisters-in-law had a voice that sounded much like the late Everett Dirksen, U.S. Senator from Illinois. She shared recollections in that rich voice with its unusual accent, and the effect would have made sharing of the driest of memories interesting. When she spoke about what people used to wear and what they did, each detail had greater meaning because of that wonderful voice. Her reserved manner and her educated and experienced perspective added to each account, even though I usually did not know many of the people in her stories.

My great uncle's voice was not as accented or as colorful but his style of delivery and the nature of his stories more than compensated for not having a dramatically unusual voice. His recollections regarding the community's early history, his work in area funeral homes, and his experiences as an undertaker in rural southern West Virginia were endlessly fascinating. One of the more memorable tales was about his having been summoned regarding a death in a remote part of the State. He was asked to drive to the end of a dirt road and then to follow a streambed to its end. He followed the stream until it became a trickle and was met there by a man with a horse. He rode the horse until they got to the house where the body was. He was told he could do anything necessary to prepare the body but he was not to remove the body from the house. Since the men who surrounded him were all roughly twice his size and he was a long way from his car, he prudently decided that he would accede to their wishes. A door was removed from its hinges, the body was placed on the door, my great-uncle prepared it, and then left the way he had come. He understood that the body would be buried behind the house but he had no interest in joining it.

My great-uncle had worked for the military's Graves Registration in Hawaii at the end of World War II and did similar work after the Buffalo Creek disaster in West Virginia's Logan County in 1972. He did not talk very much about his experiences in Hawaii or those involving Buffalo Creek, but the flood received wide coverage. A dam failed and the breach sent a roiling mass of water more than 25-feet high through a narrow valley. The sudden flood killed more than 100 people and left roughly 4,000 people homeless (Dotson-Lewis 1972).[61] The dead included several infants less than a year old. Primarily because of his work in Hawaii, my great-uncle was asked to help assemble and identify the bodies. As grateful as society must be to have people who can and are willing to do such work, the horror of their seeing and working with the remains of those young children would have to exact a high toll. Perhaps the only position more difficult to bear would be that of the people responsible for the dam's construction or its continued existence. People so intimately involved with the aftermath of the disaster would find it impossible to talk dispassionately about the experience, especially when whole families were among those killed. My great-uncle's silence spoke volumes.

A Paragon

I wrote earlier of my maternal grandmother's work in the bank, her service to the community, her interest in books, etc., but those were almost part of a separate life away from her family and her home. Before I was in high school, most of those outside activities were an important part of her life, but they only touched the periphery of mine. During the innocent years of my childhood, she seemed an ever-present family member who happened to have her own home in the next block. My earliest memories include my grandmother staying with my older sister and me while my parents enjoyed an occasional evening out and, when I was almost four and one-half, during the birth of my younger sister. Child sitting may have been the least challenging of her many roles.

She had been a church organist when she was too young to reach the instrument's pedals. The pedals fed the bellows that powered the organ and "knee swells" altered its sound. That organ must have given new meaning to the terms "manual" and "manual labor." Perhaps only a child would dare try to play such a thing. Her great interest in church music, especially Welsh hymns, stayed with her throughout her life.

Shortly after moving to my hometown, she became the church choir's director. A list of its members suggests that the choir was so large relative to the size of the loft that they stood through much of each service before taking seats in the congregation for the sermon. Her service to the Church also included being its Sunday School treasurer for more than 30 years. After the children's offering was collected, it would be placed in a brown cloth bag bearing the Bank's name. I spent part of many Sunday afternoons counting that offering with her at her newspaper-covered kitchen table. The fact that the deposit would be counted again at the Bank the next day, including use of a coin-counting machine, did not dissuade us from the exercise.

When choir directing became someone else's responsibility, Grandma sat with her family in the second row from the back of the church, in the large center section, and on its left side. My parents used the same pew, and there just never seemed a reason to change. Grandma's church attire usually included a suit, tight-fitting lace gloves, and a hat with a small lace veil over its front. Among the hymns she loved to sing were settings of Welsh tunes such as "Cwm Rhondda" or "Aberystwyth", and she quickly grew impatient with any organist who played them too slowly. Her abiding faith had no room for hymns of praise or even solemn hymns played and sung as mournful dirges.

Grandma prepared the Sunday meals we enjoyed at her house after church. She had a two-burner gas stove in her basement on which she would start a roast of lamb, pork, beef, or chicken early on Sunday mornings. This was a compromise of convenience for her since her mother and grandmother always did their cooking for Sunday the day or night before. They reserved Sunday for more solemn matters. In Grandma's youth, Sundays were days to refrain from swimming, playing loudly, or otherwise acting in a manner considered inappropriate to the Sabbath.

For several years, if we did not change our clothes at home first, we went to Grandma's house from church. My sisters and I always enjoyed being with her for any occasion but, however strong the temptation, she neither contradicted our parents in our presence nor suggested that a different set of rules applied in her house. We would wait hungrily, helping where we could, as she prepared the mashed potatoes, cauliflower in cheese and cream sauce, and green beans, peas, broccoli, or lima beans. Then the roast was placed on its serving dish, always seeming at least as appetizing as the aroma that filled the house.

After the meal, my sisters and I might play, do unfinished homework, or chores at home in the afternoon, but we would return to Grandma's for an evening meal of potato chips and sandwiches of white bread, meat left from the noon meal, tomato, lettuce, mayonnaise, and cheese. A favorite cheese for the sandwiches was a sharp tasting version of something only she seemed to buy, but her favorite for most other occasions was mild Colby longhorn. Before the age of microwaves and non-stick pan coatings, Grandma would melt chunks of Colby in a metal pie pan on her range and drizzle the result onto a piece of toast topped with a slice of tomato. This culinary wonder was always a welcome snack. An evening in front of her television usually completed the day.

Her stories of an earlier era included walking through snow nearly a mile to school in her small Ohio hometown. She occasionally made that trip in warmer weather on their horse. She never forgot the horse's temperament. He would wait until she was near the gate, then turn and run as fast as he could to the opposite side of the corral. She might well decide it would be easier and faster to walk. The oldest of five children, though, if she walked, they did too.

The Family

Once each day, my family gathered for dinner. This daily reaffirmation said that we were a family and not merely a loose association of quasi-autonomous individuals sharing a common roof. We tacitly acknowledged at each meal that we were part of something real and important, even as we were aware how much we differed from each other. At the time, I knew other people did not share our custom, and I envied their independence. Only later did I realize the price they paid for that freedom in terms of missed conversation, the habitual common experience, and the strengthening sense of belonging. Homemakers dedicated exclusively to their occupation also pay a high price to afford that experience to their families. As they arrest, postpone, or forsake their careers outside of the home, these women relinquish financial, social, and psychological rewards for participation in the economic engine that powers the country. They freely make a different and important contribution to all of society for which they receive non-monetary compensation. The single consistent exception to our nightly evening meal was Sunday evenings. After each Sunday morning's church service, the family walked the block back to our home or, in later years, to Grandma's house, and later still, drove to family restaurants. While there were occasional exceptions to, or variations in, this routine, it was the norm for most of my first twenty years.

Enjoying that after-church meal at a favorite restaurant occurred with increasing frequency during, and after I left, high school. For about a year, the family's restaurant of choice was Oglebay Park's Wilson Lodge in Wheeling, West Virginia. The area of the Lodge that served elegant meals on white linen tablecloths was on its second floor above a gift shop and the service desk for Lodge guests. Renovations and expansion of Wilson Lodge have relegated that old restaurant area to the negligible status of a minor passageway but when I was a teenager, it was a very special place to dine. When I received my first pay envelope from the Bank, it was an incumbent responsibility to pay for the family's dinner at the Lodge. The remaining half of that month's pay was spent more gradually.

Another favorite after-church dining spot was the modified hall and living room of the Biddle residence located on a major two-lane highway twenty miles west of Pittsburgh. Biddle's Restaurant served meals throughout the week, although we only ate there on Sundays. The same guests, also still dressed in church attire, returned weekly to one of a dozen tables. The familiarity of the people and the intimacy of the experience always helped make those meals even more enjoyable. In winter, the appearance of the fireplace added more to the ambiance than its modest heat did to the interior temperature. The wooded view through the windows at the back of the house accented each passing season. Aunt Biddle's nephew "Jim," his friend, or one of several waitresses over the years, would take our order for their delicious ham loaf with mustard sauce, moist and very tender roasted chicken, velvety roast beef au jus, stuffed pork chop, or one of a few other special menu choices.

Jim was not only a gracious host but, in addition to his other business responsibilities, was an excellent waiter. He and his aunt lived on the restaurant's second floor and must have enjoyed the wonderful aroma of her delicious cooking for most of their lives. There were several cabins for rent behind the restaurant but after the hilly and winding two-lane major highway was bypassed by a four-lane divided highway, the cabins drew fewer tenants and the restaurant served fewer dining guests until the business closed in the mid 1970's. Jim was a wonderful example of someone whose grace, dignity, and dedication could help transform a small family restaurant into a uniquely wonderful place to dine. Mother corresponded with him regularly from the time the restaurant closed until his death, but that was long after a most pleasant weekly routine had seen its end.

This strong sense of family was common in our valley at the time and is still, for many, an indispensable resource. It prevailed over divergent interests, friendships, academic demands, social and vocational obligations, and other distractions. It was reinforced by societal attitudes, much of the media, and the experience of common worship. For nurture advocates attempting to explain the transgendered condition, nothing in this family history or environment encouraged cross-gendered behavior, but there was consistent and overwhelming support for behavior appropriate to assigned gender. Where assigned gender was correct, that kind of support and reinforcement must have been gratifying.

9. Lessons of Self and Gender

As a Dog

The delightful amusement of watching each of our family's dogs wholly dedicated to the vigorous pursuit of its tail has often been accompanied by curiosity about what the dog would do when the tail was caught. The tail already belongs to the dog so the chase seems pointless to humans, or at least to adult humans less concerned with the importance of play. The dog, though, does have a clear objective toward which all of its energy and abilities are directed. The only thing that might make even less sense to people, and perhaps to dogs too, would be if a dog were trying to run from its tail. By attempting to avoid my gender identity, I was like this latter dog. Wherever I might go and whatever I would do, that identity would still be with me because it was a fundamental part of me. The conflict that now seems so obviously inescapable needed resolution, but it first had to be acknowledged for what it was. However the conflict might be addressed, an escape from, or suppression of, the obsession was the quintessential fool's errand with the same hope and prospects for success as a dog fleeing its tail. The dog, at least, would know what it was fleeing.

Insufficient regard for the importance of discovering my essential identity facilitated my being defined by the expectations of those I cared about or who made themselves important to me. I did not "get it". This was not like sitting down to a four-star dinner without an aperitif, a menu, or a fork; the whole restaurant was missing. I did not understand that the "Who am I" question actually was primary and essential because it must be the precursor to deciding the person each of us would have ourselves become. The determination or discovery of the purpose of one's life, the shaping of adult relationships, and the formation of other associations flow honestly from the answer to that basic question. Not trusting the self who was obsessed with physical sex-inappropriate clothes meant accepting almost any reasonable alternative suggested by those closest to me. Mistrust of my inclinations and obsession made me firmly determined not to risk more fully becoming the person they called me to be. The self of compelling desires seemed someone I did not want to be and would not dare become; that self would have to contend with questions and problems I could not answer and did not want to accept.

By adopting the expectations of those closest to me as my own, I attempted to avoid being that suppressed self with its incomprehensible and ultimately irrepressible obsession. Having made that too common error, I concluded that I could be a slightly modified, or more personalized, version of the person defined by my family and other people. My degree of success in meeting their expectations would determine whether I was a good person. The failings of that adopted self, when they occurred, could be shared by whoever had helped create it. I even accepted assurances that I would eventually and inevitably become a husband and father.

Such a shallowly defined self lacked conviction because, while I knew other people's expectations of me and even some of the things that seemed fundamentally important to me, that knowledge was not built on the foundation of a whole essential self. I knew that, whoever I was, I did have some talents and abilities, but their use needed more focus and direction than a borrowed vision of my future could provide. Whoever that adopted self might become seemed less important than just not being the person my obsession called me to be.

By Another Name, a Rose

Comparing the condition of transgendered people to life in royal families probably would not occur to most members of either group. There must be far more differences than similarities between them and the word "queen" carries considerable baggage for anyone with gender identity conflict. Dissimilarities aside, it is difficult to imagine how Queen Elizabeth II or any of her family could have anything close to a conventional opportunity to discover their own identities. While their carefully scripted lives might have allowed a three-week period during the month of August in their thirteenth year for rebelling, they would have known that on the first day of the fourth week they must resume their regular duties. If British citizens occasionally accuse members of the Royal Family of acting as though the country belongs to them, the Royal Family probably would argue that it is they, more than any other of their countrymen, who are possessed by their country.

Whatever independence might be presumed to accompany royals who exercise great influence and have enormous wealth, history arguably indicates the greater functional accuracy of its opposite. These people cannot live as though they freely discerned and pursued their chosen professions as one of the most important things in their lives. Producing something that has substantial commercial and/or artistic value of its own merit and for which they might be esteemed is an economic or esthetic validation of human existence that has been denied to them. A vocation pursued from an altruistic motivation might have provided a wholly different, but at least as important, feeling of accomplishment they cannot experience. Royals are also denied the confidence and satisfaction that comes from discovering exactly who they are and were meant to be. There was no structured competition with other qualified candidates for their positions that would help them understand how much they wanted to be next, fourth, or eighth in the line of succession, and "...succession for what?" never would occur to them. However capable they might be in any endeavor and despite their accomplishments as royalty, they must bear a wearing suspicion that they have not really earned their position. They know they have paid a high price for it, but that is more akin to a transaction acquiring a great work of fine art than to remuneration for contracted labor.

These people may share a similar void with transgendered people and others who have suppressed their identities. Their inability freely to pursue identity means that Royals may also have missed the opportunity to build and strengthen an incredibly important part their humanity. I know of no instance when a member of the British Royal Family suppressed her or his gender identity. I can readily imagine, however, how King Edward VIII would discover that who he was as a person, rather than as an unthinking and unfeeling object with a title, and his desired relationship with Wallis Simpson were sufficient reasons for his abdicating the British throne.

Americans often seem to feel an obligation, beyond their First Amendment right, to exercise freedom of speech. A similarly common feeling among their "subjects" is compounded by tradition and ceremony in Britain. These present an impossibly divergent and fluid set of demands to a family whose accident of birth places them in positions where they must respond, even if only by calculated and deliberate inaction. The response further alters the set of demands influencing or commanding their behavior. My parents and the rest of our family had no experience of similar scope but the person my family's expectations for me seemed to describe, and which I adopted, was at least as inappropriate to my essential self as it was consistent.

Defining Union

The apparent gender and sex of each person's prospective life partner are usually so quickly and naturally determined that she or he is not even aware it occurred. Other attributes and characteristics are consciously and more purposefully gleaned. Still other aspects of personality and character may be discovered and/or evolve in an interactive process that will consume the balance of a lifetime. For suppressing transgendered people and those with whom they interact, however, even the first step is problematic. They see as, and are seen by others as being, their fraudulent personas.

As a teenager, the suppressing MtF woman becomes acutely aware that many others of her apparent age and sex repeatedly express an interest in having sexual encounters, ostensibly with almost any opposite-sexed person and with anything from farm animals to food containers. Talking about such things may merely be intended to project or protect a hyper-male image for these teens but there is a reason why that image is deemed worth the effort. At least some of the interest is real. The suppressing MtF woman's awareness of her conflict is exacerbated. Her circumspection, the biology of her own male hormones, confusion about her suppressed obsession, her own life experience, and concern for her whole family can create or augment a paralyzing social inertia.

No innate self-awareness separates an MtF woman's sense of self from her presumed male future; she does not know where her identity ends and her aspirations begin. The fact that ultimate resolution of her obsession resides in her suppressed identity, even if it occurred to her, would seem impossible. However much she would desire a conventional marriage and family, she may see no way to attain it. A woman attracted to the MtF woman's affected male persona may well share her conventional desire but be completely unaware of the MtF woman's inability wholly to be a husband.

A hallowed concept of, and appreciation for, traditional marriage is ubiquitous, though not universal. Many of those who would participate in the current discourse about marriage view their own unions, those of their parents, and the potential unions of their children as among the most important matters of their lives. Married people have known the joys and disappointments, successes and failings, and support and sacrifice their relationship provides and demands. Many of them see the whole of their marriages as being demeaned, and the institution's potential value for their children diminished, by any change to, or extension of, the term "marriage" beyond its traditional application. These status quo defenders see cohabitation by unmarried couples, the high incidence of divorce, and unmarried women bearing children as an already existing, unintended, but collective assault on an essential institution of society. Sanction of non-traditional marriage is feared as the potentially fatal blow to the worth and power of the relationship at the historic core of strong families.

As an honored religious and civil commitment, marriage has been critical to ensuring the future of a structured and nurturing society. To the extent that a society is more than the simple sum of the people who live in it, that society's regard for, and perpetuation of, institutions such as marriage, law, a system of politics and of education are essential elements of its character. If these institutions are weakened or destroyed without providing a superior replacement, its people might survive but that society is diminished if not mortally wounded. If they wish to preserve the essence of their society, its members have an obligation not only to protect but to support and strengthen its major institutions. Effective strengthening though is critically dependent upon a common and accurate understanding of the thing being strengthened.

A marriage license engraved in granite would be stronger than one printed on tissue paper but the underlying relationship would not be strengthened. Whether performed by one minister or twelve, held in the largest cathedral or the smallest chapel, accompanied by the grandest pipe organ or the small voice of a child, the continuing commitment of the couple united in marriage will determine the strength of their union. The fundamental issue is the identities of the two people making the commitment and to what they are committing themselves. If they want substantially different things from their union, its future can hardly be promising. The matter of identities is at least as important.

Having made a spontaneous, and even instinctive, assessment of a prospective partner's gender identity and sex, each person's subsequent observations would tend to reinforce, rather than contradict, that assessment. As instinctively as such assessments occur, they are not always correct. While popular thought would assert that lies of commission, omission, or both are an escapable part of contemporary dating, that would make as much sense as two strangers relying on their surrogates for a date. It is difficult to imagine why anyone would spend time with someone in whom an at least rudimentary level of trust was not vested. If one is unprepared or unwilling to disclose truthful information, surely that is not acceptable justification for saying something that is not true. Those who say they would never lie about anything important are implying that they always know when something is, or might become, important. By the time an acquaintance might have become a prospective life partner, mendacity may have doomed the relationship.

When a suppressing transgendered person is intent upon preserving an opposite-gendered persona, detecting her or his authentic gender identity might be impossible even for a qualified mental health professional. A cursory or instinctual assessment is unlikely to reveal true, rather than affected, identity even when an initial assessment is supported by a wealth of subsequent encounters. The transgendered person is not lying by affecting a persona when she or he does not understand the obsession she or he struggles to suppress. Still, her or his inability to rely on gender identity as the basis for marriage is equivalent to making a commitment she or he is irreparably unable to keep.

If opposite gender identities are not the basis for the relationship of a couple seeking a traditional heterogendered union, their castle may be built on, and of, sand. For an MtF woman and non-transgendered woman who legally marry, each wants unequivocally from her marriage something it cannot provide. The fact that children have been born to such unions clearly indicates that a *pro forma* sexual intimacy is not the missing component. Whatever else such couples seek from their marriage, each spouse has a gender identity expectation for her mate that is not confined, and may only be distantly related, to procreation.

Civil Unions

By failing to define accurately the terms "woman" and "man" in their efforts to prohibit homogendered legal unions, advocates and opponents are debating packaging but ignoring content. Focus of the marriage debate needs to be changed from form to substance. Recent voter initiatives and voter-approved marriage definition amendments, however, indicate that establishing enlightened sensitivity to gender identity as the basis for legally binding unions will not be easily achieved. States and status-quo defenders continue to attempt to prevent official sanction of single-sex legal unions by focusing on purely physical and woefully inadequate criteria. Legislatures have not addressed the paradox of physically heterosexual couples who have the same gender identity, nor have they appropriately resolved the status of unions that include two transgendered people. Without agreement on terminology and common acceptance and clear understanding of gender identity, all of this effort is like trying to swim in one inch of water. Yet current *stare decisis* has determined that marriage is a right that cannot be denied on the basis of biological sex at birth. Where this might go in the future is unknown.

Interest in preserving the nature and status of marriage for each person's own family and progeny compels most people to venerate and advocate an exclusive family model. In their view, only a natal physical female should be permitted legally to marry a natal physical male. The legal rights and responsibilities incurred and pledged in marriage by and to each spouse, these advocates would assert, must be reserved solely for the physically whole natural female and male couples who wish to be united in that officially sanctioned traditional relationship.   Marriage's rights and responsibilities are, by this definition, denied to people whose gender identity and physical sex have been in conflict and who wish to wed based on opposite gender identities and mutual attraction. This is an unjust denial of the right to possess oneself and to commit that self to another person in an appropriate, authentically traditional, and loving relationship.The honestly desired gender identity and physical sex of any person's prospective mate are at least as inappropriate to defining that person's gender identity as they are essential to characterizing accurately the fundamental nature of the union of two people. Gender identity is an inalienable part of one's essential self, whether that self is alone or among thousands of people. Honest partner preference flows from one's knowledge of self; it does not precede it. Identity and preference are as different as cause and effect. Failure to acknowledge that difference abounds, and even predominates, in society and the political arena.

It is readily understandable why people wish to reserve application of "sacred marriage" as a term and form of relationship only to traditional families. The virtue that the current and historic practice of marriage holds for society is evinced by the nurturing stability successive generations have found in its embrace. Surely, so esteemed an integral part of American society and all of civilization commands each person's respect first, as a child, and then as a possible spouse and parent. Yet, same gender identity and single sex couples also unite in pursuit or continuance of their sincere desire to establish and sustain a strong, and even child or children-centered, family. Those unions do far more to further the concept of family than the *de jure* marriage of a heterogendered couple who were not, or are no longer, committed to each other and their family.

The sincerity of their mutual dedication and commitment, same-gender identity and single sex couples would argue, can only strengthen the meaning and institution of "marriage" if that term is legally applied to their union, but that argument is often inexplicably unheard or conveniently ignored by their opponents. From a social, if not political, perspective, pursuit of the traditional commitment to family would seem more firmly grounded than an asserted but contested civil right. Yet, committed same gender identity and single sex couples are as unwilling to accept a term other than "marriage" to encompass their relationship as would be most heterogendered couples. Clearly most, if not all, same-gender identity couples seeking to sanctify through a recognized ceremony of commitment their sense of oneness as a family do not intend to be irreligious or anarchical. To the contrary, they seek to profess publicly and ceremonially the enduring mutual bond they have felt and shared privately. They seek also to avail themselves of all of the legal rights, privileges, and responsibilities that status conveys in our society.

Whether society is prepared to grant or acknowledge a "right" to same-sex unions, it has a continuing need for stable and supportive families, even if those families cannot fit the "ideal" or stereotypical model demanded of them. Extant homogendered (same gender identity and single-sex) parents have raised the natural or adopted children of one or both parents in family relationships at least as strong as those of single-parent families. In some instances, these less conventional families include adopted children who otherwise would not have been adopted. Surely, these relationships should receive the support and have access to the mechanisms that society has established to protect families, whatever term is applied to them. Still, the public debate over lawfully issued licenses remains framed as a matter of civil rights versus traditional marriage, with marriage depicted as a critical relationship under constant assault from a popular culture often seeming to embrace anything that is not traditional.

When issuing driver licenses, states appropriately discriminate based on age, ability to process information, level of coordination, etc. While many drivers allegedly drive like children, a child cannot be granted a license even if she or he met every other requirement. Similarly, those who cannot pass a written test or control their vehicles with a minimum required proficiency also are denied licenses. States place legal hurdles in the path of people intending to engage in any other licensed activity. Each hurdle discriminates between those who surmount it and those who do not. Those barriers are necessary for the public purpose of assuring minimum standards of performance. If a licensee fails to operate a vehicle within established standards, the license can be revoked. Failure to love and honor one's spouse usually leads to the license revocation of divorce. Supporters of traditional marriage often argue that the Defense of Marriage Act affords each member of a same gender identity and single-sex couple the same non-discriminating right granted other couples to marry someone of the opposite sex. By focusing solely on indications of physical sex, though, these supporters would ignore the essence of the relationship they purport to defend.Each successful attempt to win from the courts what is difficult or impossible to obtain through the legislature is a demonstration of the protection of established individual rights guaranteed to every person.

That protection is especially evident when exercised in opposition to a majority that would deny unjustly any of those rights. Friction occurs when the Court recognizes a "right" not acknowledged by a substantial number of people as lawful or constitutionally protected. Single-vote U.S. Supreme Court majority decisions can be seen, not as the result of careful constructions of fine distinctions in relevant law but as the law becoming what enough judges say it is. If the legislature fails to be sufficiently precise in its work, the legislature abrogates its responsibility and enhances interpretive judicial power.

A narrowly decided ruling discerning a protected right not recognized by a substantial portion of the population can be seen as a challenge to majority rule, especially where judges do not regularly face the electorate. Judges who stand for election allegedly are less likely to protect the rights of minorities but a preponderance of peer-reviewed studies probably would not support that view. Since each person is a member of one or more minorities, she or he would certainly resist relinquishing any rights based on that status and would support courts that protect those rights. A corollary is that circumspect judges need, and must be sensitive to, that support to thwart potential encroachment on the judicial branch by the legislative or executive branches of government. As each branch of government contends daily with the press of intensely partisan issues, it appropriately considers potential longer-term consequences of its actions on the perceived and real need for changes in the government's balanced powers. Ultimately, each branch's surest protection is the fullest-possible exercise of its legitimate powers, even, or especially, regarding protection of the most precious of chosen human relationships.

Those favoring establishment of same-sex mutual commitments as legally delimited "civil unions" would recognize the right of two same-sex adults willingly to obligate themselves and their possessions to a binding and enduring relationship. Heterogendered individuals would have the same right as homogendered individuals to unite in these newly delimited relationships, just as homogendered individuals currently can legally marry someone of the opposite physical sex. Both the U.S. Constitution, Fourth Amendment right of each person to be secure in her or his person and property and the Fifth Amendment prohibition against the taking of private property without just compensation are guarantees of the principle of individual sovereignty (Kashner 2007, 504).[62] They are recognition by the nation's founders and American society that the right of each person to own property, including the implied right to obligate oneself without becoming a slave, is fundamental if not unlimited. The U.S. Constitution's framers specifically protected the arguably less important rights to ownership and security of property but they did not specifically protect a right to pledge oneself in marriage. It is no more likely that they would have thought it necessary to delimit marriage than to delimit the similarly perceived natural events of birth and death. The framers indicated in the Tenth Amendment that their intent was not to address every important matter through the U.S. Constitution (Kashner 2007, 504).[63] They realized that they could not create an inflexibly static and sustainable democratic government. They provided a mechanism to address important issues where law was deemed appropriate, even if that action faced substantial organized and ardent opposition. The framers established a dynamic government of structured flexibility, and they trusted to succeeding generations its use or abuse.

If Congress would establish civil unions, the U.S. Supreme Court still might then hold that they are, in effect if not intent, an unconstitutional form of discrimination. Proponents of civil unions might respond by adding them as part of, or in addition to, an amendment to define legal marriage. The sympathies of the framers certainly would seem to be with those advocating a legal right to civil mutual commitment for any couple, since any reasonable definition of privacy and private property implies a fundamental right to share or transfer that ownership. Similarly, dissolution of established relationships and disposition of property under law would be impossible if a prior lawful relationship, ownership, and possession could not be proven.

Nobler to Bear

If the primary requirement for a couple legally to marry is the ability to produce children naturally, then marriages where one or the other of the couple is sterile would be prohibited. To preclude the possibility of sterility, a child and DNA evidence proving parenthood could be required to qualify for a license. Rather than discouraging births outside of marriage, society would require them. Failure to apply such a requirement to all couples would deservedly bring suits alleging illegal discrimination.

Persons who developed a procedure to enable MtF women to bear their own children would doubtlessly count among their least achievements the enabling of transgendered women to pass so absurd a test. That development almost certainly would result from efforts to help women whose natal physiology was female and would be impossible to perform for MtF women over a certain age. Adaptation of the procedure to help MtF women would be reminiscent of, but far more challenging than, the adaptation of hormone replacement therapy.

Unlike that adaptation, though, the purpose of enabling women to become mothers would be unaltered.

Like other women, no MtF woman would accept a term for her union with a man other than "marriage" because she is intending fully to commit herself to be her husband's wife, and expects her betrothed to commit fully to being her husband. If a post-transition MtF woman were to unite with a man under provisions for a civil union, each partner would be acquiescing to the view that she is not a "real" woman despite her real gender identity, medical certification, and corrected government-issued documents. The possibility of producing children is an important, but must not be the overriding, statutory basis for marriage. Age and health reasons, especially those related to attained age, preclude many couples from raising their own biological children, and some couples have agreed for any or all of a variety of reasons that they do not intend to become parents.

For a heterogendered transgendered person or any other circumspect heterogendered person, her or his marriage is a matter of joining two people whose gender identities are opposite, regardless of natal physical sex. Most same gender identity partners, however, see their committed union as joining two people of like gender and physical sex. Unlike heterogendered transgendered people, by definition those desiring same gender identity and single-sex relationships do not present an even remotely theoretical ability to produce their own biological children. The crucial common ground between the very different family models of single-gendered and opposite-gendered couples is the shared, sincere, and enduring commitment each person makes to her or his partner and family.

In *Lawrence versus Texas*, an arguably conservative-leaning U.S. Supreme Court ruled, with two justices dissenting, that whether two people sharing a sexual relationship in an apartment are heterogendered or homogendered is a moot point under the Constitution (*Lawrence v. Texas* 2003).[64] Whether the people involved call themselves a couple, a family, a trio, or an avocado seems equally moot. An amendment to the U.S Constitution might specifically prohibit the same underlying activity but, even if the prohibition were ratified, it probably could not be enforced. Were laws enacted and amendments adopted that were not intended to be enforced, the resulting muddled dichotomy of enforced and not-enforced laws would threaten each person's liberty by inviting rule by those who choose which laws to enforce (an anathema to the Framers), rather than everyone's living under the rule of law.

Lawrence did not represent a seminal change. The U.S. District Court of Appeals' 11th Circuit upheld Florida's prohibition of adoption by homogendered people. This court affirmed that Florida's right to decide who could adopt children in its care must prevail over the possible right of any prospective parents to adopt (Lofton et al. 2004).[65] The right of U.S. citizens to commit themselves to each other was deemed substantially different from a state-granted right to adopt children into that relationship. If a state wishes to permit adoption by unstable and abusive heterogendered couples while prohibiting it to stable, caring, and committed homogendered couples, it cannot escape responsibility for its decision through federal judicial review. Even if the court concluded that the practice was unwise or even abhorrent, it held that the power to regulate adoption belongs to the state. While this apparent abuse of state power has not stirred the political will necessary to prohibit further abuse, the will to define nationally what constitutes marriage may be nearing such a moment.

In anticipation of the Supreme Court striking down the "Defense of Marriage Act", proponents of a constitutional amendment to define legal marriage see its passage as essential. Because of the importance of marriage to legislators, their families, and their constituents, its prospects for eventual ratification would seem favorable. Same gender identity and single sex marriages lawfully performed prior to ratification of the amendment probably would have to be recognized, but legal claims arising from those marriages made after ratification (such as disposition of dependent children and decedent estates) might be denied. This speculation leaves most people as avid spectators, if not ardent advocates, in the arena of continuing current events. The legislature may be avoiding further action from apprehension that any new law would aggravate, rather than resolve, current tensions. Clearly, apprehension cannot suffice to absolve legislators of their constitutional responsibility to act. Whatever the reason, where the legislature is or the people are unwilling to act when action is necessary, even greater harm is done to the whole of government and the society it serves.

A Female Father

All of nature proves the importance to every living thing of its ability to reproduce. Even living things without the least capacity to reason exhibit tremendous capacity to reproduce. Unfortunately, pre-transition reproductive capacity would not enable transgendered people to become the parent their gender identities demand that they be. This may be one of the strongest arguments that gender identity conflict is a disorder, instead of a "choice," since resolving the conflict, at present, means relinquishing the ability to become either natural parent. The reproduction argument, however, may also be one of the strongest rationales for the independent embryonic formation of gender identity and reproductive physiology. Part of that argument centers on whether human reproduction is seen as a single act, a lifetime commitment, or both.

Nature reasonably would impart a strong sense of gender identity to each person since that identity would tend to enforce dedicated and responsible parenting. That characteristic of gender identity is undiminished in transgendered people but it urges each of them to become the wrong parent. It may well be that the same anthropological development that led to the higher powers of human thought is also responsible for independent formation of gender identity and reproductive physiology. That separation would also explain why instances of consistent transgendered behavior among individual animals are not readily observed in nature. From a religious perspective, this clearly would mean that the same Divine Hand that uniquely created mankind also created the potential for gender identity conflict. Interpreting this as suggesting that God is to blame for gender identity conflict is a poor and false interpretation. Assigning blame requires judgment and, even if attempting to affix blame were appropriate, no person reasonably and meaningfully can judge God.

As forcefully as I have argued for acknowledging the distinct significance of each person's innate gender identity, if there were no physical means to articulate it and to express it in other ways, gender identity could have little significance. Each person's gender identity, or the mind's image of the entirety of her or his sex, and that person's physical sexual self can be seen as two halves of the same whole. One without the other would be grossly incomplete. To argue that there is no meaningful distinction between the two, though, is to fail to separate aspect and physical characteristics from essential but non-physical ones. Gender identity is the fundamental and uniquely human part of sex and sexuality that underlies much of civilization. No parallel is evident in the non-human reproduction of plants or insects, and it may not be characteristic of the Hedonistic sexual activities of contemporary pseudo Epicureans. It certainly has been characteristic of the historic and traditional nature of the family whose relationships are established and perpetuated by the nurturing aspects of those harmonious and complementary, rather than unison, identities.

Even a couple's sexual intimacy, where every effort to minimize the chance of pregnancy has been made, still suggests, if fleetingly, the creation, sustaining, or strengthening of a nurturing environment into which a child might be born. Those who assert that the entirety of the significance of human sexual acts or impulses can be separated from their possible consequences and obvious natural purpose are attempting to redefine and debase humanity. Their argument is like suggesting that sight can be separated from color, form, and dimension; taste from food, drink, and nutrition; smell from a myriad of enticing aromas and repugnant odors; hearing from the most soothing of musical passages and the most startling of alarms; touch from the most tender caress and the most vicious assault; or faith from worship of its Creator.

The idea of being a parent was as attractive to me as any aspect of my becoming an adult. Fatherhood was the most likely prospect but committing myself to be my wife's husband and then our jointly committing ourselves to be a child's parents were obligations I was never wholly prepared to undertake. I cannot know from personal experience what moves some pre-transitioning MtF women to promise to be another woman's husband, and then to attempt to have a child or children with her. Those choices might be the ultimate test for the male persona affected by suppressing MtF women who marry. However much she wished to be "normal" and to share a loving relationship with someone, though, the suppressing MtF woman must be aware of her unrelenting obsession even if she does not understand it. The biological possibility of an MtF woman fathering a child is undeniable. Her being the child's real, whole, committed father and everything that word implies is just as emphatically impossible.

This defense of authentic gender for mothers and fathers does not mean that transgendered people who have their own children are not, and have not been, dedicated, loving, and worthwhile parents. Throughout its history, though, humanity has overwhelmingly favored the traditional and historic innate honest gender identity differences of each parent as essential to the strength of families and their children. Those gender identity differences either are authentically present or absent as an important part of a child's daily life from birth. Many children have survived much harsher deficiencies, and I would not presume to suggest that anyone should not become a parent. Clearly though, fathering a child when one cannot be that child's whole father, however strong the intent, seems like making a commitment one cannot wholly fulfill.

Whatever the conclusion from attempted self-diagnosis or however intense the denial or suppression of gender identity, when someone professes love for another and seeks to wed, her or his actions must come from an honest assessment of identity and what that person wants and is prepared to strive for throughout life. It is certainly possible that a suppressing pre-transition MtF woman would carefully preserve her meticulously constructed and maintained illusion of her "male" shell as long as nothing made that suppression impossible. Her pledging that carefully crafted illusion in marriage, however, would require either a fully engrossing self-delusion or a nearly tangible desperation to resist transition that goes well beyond concern for merely preserving the fraud. MtF women who have done this may have hoped that marriage could extinguish her suppressed self. Even if that were possible, however, she could not know who or what would be left in that self's place.

A suppressing transgendered person's marriage proposal probably would be worded as "Lets get married", "Do you want to get married", or even "Will you marry me" instead of the more assertive "I want to marry you". The three interrogatives afford the excuse that there was equivocation and agreement based on a compromise of, or yielding to, mutual sentiment, or acknowledged partnership. A declaration, though, indicates that the speaker has thoroughly assessed her or his own position or feels an overwhelming emotional compulsion to act. The assertive suitor has at least a general idea of the nature of a strongly desired future and is saying, in essence, "you may feel differently but I know I want to be married to you". In the absence of personal experience, I cannot imagine how a transgendered person, however well intended, would enter into such an arrangement but, clearly, many have. The simple human need to become a spouse or parent, regardless of gender identity, may be a significant part of that motivation. As much as I would like to have been a parent, I was not by gender identity able to be a father, and I could not by physiology be a natural mother.

Perverting a Gift

It is ironic that when life expectancies are twice what they were at the beginning of the twentieth century and women are increasingly able, with medical assistance, to bear children later in life, there is such high incidence of teens and even preteens having sexual intercourse. For a planet inhabited by billions of people, this makes as much sense as a drowning man pleading for a glass of water. In anticipation of death, male Islamic extremists are encouraged to anticipate a heaven where they are almost constantly engaged in an endless series of physical sexual encounters with different women, but the possibility and utility of those acts in a spiritual realm is certainly questionable at best. The minds, hearts, aspirations, and other aspects of the nature of those women is not considered. It would be instructive for such a man to imagine instead that he would be female and all of those other people were males. The lives of such men must be so devoid of other meaning that their understanding of the classical "good", of human worth, and their essential selves is replaced by an exclusive interest in endless repetitions of a single, presumably pleasurable, act.

In this fantasy, the sexual experience where an infant might result is grossly abused and distorted through a shift of focus. A physical act requiring little intellectual involvement that is a minor part of the lifelong endeavor of creating and building families is reduced to a hedonistic celebration of the act of sexual intercourse. An act intimately connected to the creation and propagation of human life is perverted as an expedient to extinguishing human life. For centuries the "Midas" fable has taught that some things are more precious when they are extremely difficult to obtain, but they lose much if not all of their value if they become available in profusion.

The diamond market is an excellent example of an application of this concept, especially regarding something that Americans and others associate with an unequaled expression of sentiment. In their unique role of representing love and devotion, diamonds have been given the perverse characteristic that the greater their price, the more and deeper emotion they are presumed to represent, even at the cost of jeopardizing that new family's financial stability. That devotion and commitment also are expected to extend to any subsequent expansion of the family. It is ironic that Christian religious symbols of commitment for baptism and communion, including water, bread, and wine, have the same meaning regardless of the monetary value of any of those common elements. As a symbol of *The New Covenant*, grape juice from a discount store or the most rare bottle of imported wine have equal value to a professing Christian. These ritualistic elements arguably come closer to representing the intangible "beyond price" value a loving parent has for her or his child than does the commercial value of a diamond.

Many couples trying to have children have gone to great lengths to bear their own biological children or to adopt children domestically or internationally, while some teens and preteens who did not even realize a pregnancy might result produce unplanned and unwanted children with distressing frequency. Society and civilization place a high value on human life in very real terms in custom, religion, and law. They do so in less tangible terms by defining and protecting interpersonal relationships. Thus, it is reasonable to expect that high human value would be ascribed to every sexual act from which a pregnancy might ensue. Some people of faith would argue that pregnancy is the only appropriate goal whenever a couple engages in sexual intercourse. Others might imagine that marriage and a financial plan showing everything from mortgage payments and dental braces to college tuition and retirement would precede each act of sexual intimacy. However prudent that practice might be, experience indicates that is far from the norm.

One might expect that the continuing phenomenon of early sexual behavior resulting in parenthood would only occur where an area's population is in steep decline, people anticipate some great danger like war or pestilence, or there is a plan to colonize some vast and vacant place. Pressure on water and other natural resources is already a concern in large parts of the world and is a danger posed by every growing population that faces finite resources. Whatever else is the rationale or motivation for this earlier sexual activity, the act even precedes the acquisition of life experience, and the formation and development of the requisite relationship that would give it real meaning. An introductory handshake would seem to have more meaning than some premature sexual activity. While this argument could be seen as expressing the sentiments of millions of antecedents, its focus is still the rationale, or the lack thereof, behind the actions.

There also is a difference, at least in American culture, in the understanding of this matter from an intellectual, moral, emotional, and psychological perspective. If the most intelligent 12-year-old student, who has excelled in biology and been carefully schooled in when such behavior is appropriate, still engages in it, her or his behavior may be attributable to nothing other than immaturity. If an intelligent married adult in a position of power and responsibility similarly engages in extra-marital sexual activity, another rationale must apply. The adult's rationale would likely be any one of many unsatisfying excuses for behaving irresponsibly. In each case, if a child is produced, there has been a serious abuse of a process that has an important meaning for a civilized society. The abuse may be most keenly felt by those who do not have the ability to bear their own children, which presently includes all MtF women.

It seems as though God, evolution, or nature would have provided an overpowering awareness, something like the pain response when touching a flame, that procreation or the act that can lead to it is only appropriate and gratifying under certain conditions. Conscience or social pressure have not been an effective substitute. The power to reason and a sense of responsibility also have failed to protect children. In contemporary society with its increasing life expectancies, the consequence of ever-younger mothers is absurd from an educational, moral, financial, sociological, and other practical perspectives. Even for pedophiles, if the basic urge were a biological imperative to procreate, it would reasonably be impossible that the words "sex" and "with children" could even appear in the same sentence. Yet, that terrible connection has been made and apparently remains with the abusers throughout their lives. I do not know what percentage of abusers of children if any might be transgendered but if there are any, it must be despite, rather than because of, their being transgendered.

Shadow People

My view during childhood and adolescence of a person as an appendage of the hopes of others is a convenient way to rationalize not accepting responsibility for the choices I might make. Could anyone possibly live all of her or his long lifetime in such an illusion? The answer may be one of degree. In retrospect, my living a life primarily defined by response to the perceived expectations of others seems in some ways similar to what might happen each time a dog's owner nears her or his pet. The dog often stops what it is doing and immediately becomes fully attentive to its owner's actions. This would not seem the behavior of a self-assured being who pursues her or his own well-defined goals such as chewing that stuffed toy three more times. Since the first dog crawled into his master's cave, or the reverse, the dog's goals surely would include attempting to protect a reciprocating master. A confident goal-oriented dog with additional priorities would decide when and how he showed that loyalty, respect, and affection for his living partner, and would occasionally and appropriately indicate "I am coming but not just this minute. I smell something awfully interesting under the sofa".

By so defining myself and living only to realize my perception of the expectations of other people, I was also errantly pursuing what Dr. Paul Elbin called *The Paradox of Happiness.* His observation was based on years of study and his having been a college president, fulfilling pastoral responsibilities, presiding over a symphony, writing, etc. He wrote that many people pursue what they think will make them happy, but they discover that their pursuit has left them unhappy and possessing few things of real value despite having expended precious time, energy, and other resources. He realized that those who pursued something else of worth, especially those who saw themselves as, and were seen by others as being, remarkably successful found happiness during and resulting from the pursuit of that worthy thing (Elbin 1975/1981 161-3).[66]

For those sharing the perception, the whole of human history is evidence that a providential and incomprehensible intellect, even the Creator, ordered for each person a constant interaction between her or his essential self and certain physical capabilities and limitations. That interaction was ordained as both a challenge and an opportunity for each person to live in the best way possible, however "best" is defined, with the just expectation that she or he must be responsible for the result. For each MtF woman, an extremely important and difficult part of the challenge before transition is projecting her female gender identity through a genetically male physiology. That challenge for most transgendered people is comparable to attempting to force the proverbial camel through the eye of a fine needle. In another sense, though, that challenge is simply a matter of their being themselves; their appearance, voice, rearing, and other considerations notwithstanding. While years of suppression and denial may make their physical appearance even more important to MtF women than appearance is to other people, MtF women can prevail and pursue their aspirations just as have countless other people who endured lengthy and difficult conflict.

Identity and aspirations are obviously and intimately connected but they are not the same thing. Enlightened pursuit of self-discovery means that each person's essential self is fixed and she or he must discover who that self is. Deciding what she or he wants to accomplish means each person has the power of choice but that power is not unlimited and it is constrained by identity. People are most likely to be happy, not when they choose to pursue happiness or the goals of others, but when they pursue their own authentic ambitions. Things that intellectually and emotionally speak to and appeal to them, things they find repulsive, their concepts of order, honesty, and beauty, and their sense of purpose are indications of authentic interest. Those things are less obvious and accurate indicators, however, for people who are suppressing their gender identities or any other aspect of their essential selves.

Over one hundred years ago Henley wrote:

> I thank whatever gods may be for my unconquerable
> soul...
>
> I am the master of my fate; I am the captain of my soul"

(Henley ca. 1900).[67]
The sorely tested author must have considered and discarded numerous alternatives to the word "captain." "Originator" or "owner" might appeal to those who reject the soul's divine origin. "Guardian" or "keeper" might have

been chosen by devout and more passive authors who saw their pledged souls as subject to unrelenting temptation. Henley, though, knew his ultimate fate was dependent upon the course he charted. His lines wonderfully describe the responsibility for their own discontent that those who are self-indulgent, often at the expense of others, would appropriately feel because of their actions. An accurate definition of hell must include the constant torment one might expect to experience at having knowingly, willingly, and selfishly chosen an irremediably wrong path. Knowingly and willingly would be crucial, though, because a sense of divine grace and justice suggests that ultimate judgment would consider each person's level of comprehension and choice. Reasonable people would accept that they are obligated to discover, to the extent possible, what their path should be.

As my soul's captain, I may have little or no influence on the other vessels and condition of the sea around me, but I am still fully responsible for holding my ship to the course I have charted. Some would argue that the self each person would become is a much more important question than who she or he is. Yet, it would be impossible to chart any meaningful journey without first knowing its starting point and destination. Gender identity is an inescapable and fundamental part of that starting point. Anyone might attempt to abrogate responsibility for discovering her or his own identity but people are not made in a way that permits them to do that throughout their entire lives. If ultimate judgment depends on the way each person lives her or his life, a just God will not let anyone escape this informed responsibility.

If only because of their new, growing, and dying cells, humans do not die in the same mature bodies into which they were born. The essence of each person, those she or he cares about, and others cannot be their physical selves. That ultimately responsible self must be the extant essence residing in, and acting through, each constantly changing person, even as those actions and interactions help reflect who each person is and influence who she or he may become. People do have considerable, and yet limited, influence on the characteristics and abilities of their physical selves but they have far greater control over the way in which their abilities are used. Things great artists and athletes do amaze and inspire others but no one has been able to add and subtract ten years of age or a foot in height to her or his body at will.

Most people are assigned an officially sanctioned gender at birth based on their apparent natal sex. For medical reasons in other instances, sex is surgically assigned. Like the authority of those who assign it, the power and influence that assignment holds is virtually unquestioned and absolute. The setting of expectations and development of goals and strategies are strongly influenced by that official assignment. An innocent new person, the child's parents, an entire future and its constellation of life events will interact through the victories, defeats, and learning of everyday life without questioning the accuracy of that assigned gender, except when profound dissonance of identity demands it. The fallacy, though, is that assigned gender results from an informed guess, not a flawlessly determined diagnosis. If grass is painted red, it is still the paint that is red, not the grass. Only when a transgendered person acknowledges the existence of gender identity conflict and then chooses the path to resolve that conflict does she or he finally begin to honestly assess how her or his essential self can best accommodate unavoidable revelation and transition.

Consonant gender identity and expressed physical sex is not merely important; it is essential to each person's whole life. Yet, the essential nature of that consonance still is not well understood. Historically, "hermaphrodites" or intersex newborns rarely have been thought to pose an ethical dilemma for the medical community. Natal sexual ambiguity usually has been resolved in favor of surgical assignment of female sex because that anatomy is easier to construct (Reiner 2004).[68] Further, the behaviorist model of imposing gender was established in the late 1970s ((Reiner and Gearhart 2004, 338-9).[69] Concern for possible innate gender identity was virtually nonexistent regarding these surgeries. Due especially to the efforts of dedicated professionals and others, though, that may finally be changing. People in a variety of disciplines have attempted to contend with the ethical, moral, and legal aspects of such surgery but in no instance, could there be enough evidence at birth to deal with its psychological aspects, and the medical community still lacks sufficient understanding to do a genetic, biochemical, x-ray, or other definitive test for gender identity.

The reaction and continuing sentiment of postoperative patients who far later learn of their early surgeries has been astounding. The people contacted in the above report were concerned that the surgery had been done without their consent, rather than whether it was or was not appropriate to their gender identities! After reflection, it occurred to me that the reason these post-surgical patients were not concerned about appropriateness must be that they did not feel the slightest hint of gender identity conflict. The surgery left most of them with a physically female sexual anatomy that was completely consonant with their own gender identities.

These patients probably would have been dismissive of, or confused by, questions about the gender identity appropriateness of their surgery. People whose natal anatomy and belatedly- informed surgical status begged the obvious "female or male" question did not even seem to be aware of the question. Gender identity has always been my primary filter regarding anything of a sexual nature, even when I did not understand what it was. Gender identity is the ever-present, if unmentioned, figurative elephant in the room acutely sensed by transgendered people because their lives have been harshly influenced by its conflict. Frequently those who have not experienced that conflict, whatever their physiology, not only fail to perceive the elephant but they may even deny that such a creature exists.

Whether a blessing, a curse, or both, humans usually see the world so much through their own eyes that they cannot know what life is really like for someone whose life has been significantly different from their own and, in some way, almost everyone's life has been that different. Many argue that all humans are essentially alike and that too much is made of slight differences. Yet, disagreeing with that view is one more proof of its antithesis; the ways in which people are not alike are occasionally so significant that the contrary argument will seem absurd. The wonderful or terrible irony is that one of the things humans most have in common is their being so different from each other.

Genomic similarities and differences may reveal much about the history of life on earth. Humans share more than ninety-seven percent (97%) of their DNA with chimpanzees and smaller percentages with other living beings (Culotta 2005).[70] In one sense, this is no more remarkable than a similar statement about racecars and washing machines. In another sense, though, it indicates the tremendous complexity of the genetic sequencing similarities and differences among humans. Recent work even shows that parts of human DNA originated in near-human beings for which history has found no record. The smallest differences might be the unique tangible evidence of the matter through which each human soul interacts differently with her or his earthly self. Those slight genetic variations would account for physiology-based differences in personalities, character, intellect, attractions, aversions, and every other way in which each person is so different from everyone else. Further, some similarities might be compared to the structure of large-capacity thumb drives. Mapping a drive would reveal little about the intricacies and possible combinations of the data it contained, and each drive's user would be responsible for its use. However helpful any given map, even a genomic map, its utility is finite and what it cannot reveal may be at least as important as what it shows. Having achieved the extraordinary benchmark of the mapping of the human genome, science is far from having mapped the capacity and potential of the human soul and mind.

Sharing Responsibility

David Reimer's reported treatment through Johns Hopkins is compelling. The boy refused to accept the inappropriately assigned sex and eventually underwent extensive surgery to restore some of what had been taken from him without his consent. His ultimate rejection of extensive attempts to cause him to act and be treated as female evinces the unsuccessful effort of the applied resources of one of the nation's foremost research institutions to change the gender identity of a child by surgical, chemical, and psychosocial means. It is a stellar triumph for the human spirit that any individual, but especially a child and adolescent, withstood such influences and ultimately proved the undeniable failure of the attempt (Diamond and Sigmundson 1997, 298-304;[71] Colapinto 2000).[72]

The case is a wonderful testament to the strength and persistence of the innate self, which will evidently resist the most persistent of urgings to reverse its direction. It would be interesting to elicit the thoughts of Thomas Hobbes on this matter. If he were revived and afforded an opportunity to consider this failure of extra-personal forces to sway one child, his preference for the firm hand of a controlling central authority might change. He might argue that gender identity is a component of the innate and ultimate controlling central authority for each person, even though he had argued that was contrary to human nature. The souls of humans after death may well have no gender identity but, in the face of such supporting evidence, gender identity's primacy in determining how humans define themselves on earth eventually must become undeniable.

However small the part of each person that accounts for individual characteristics, its power and significance is not easily overstated. Despite the well-intentioned persuasive influence of family and of divergent extra-family forces, the incessant urging of gender identity as a primary component of essential self will not be assuaged. The suicide of the subject of this ordeal after having belatedly manifested his masculine identity was surely not the outcome desired by any of the other parties involved. That death is one more indication of the gravity of this subject.

In correspondence with a long-time family friend whom I had just told about my beginning transition, he wrote, essentially, that it is wrong for a man to wear women's clothes. My reply was that it is not wrong for a woman to do so. A woman does not usually wear women's clothing only because she likes the clothes but because she is a woman. By denying the appropriateness of my new appearance he was rejecting my identity. People are not defined wholly and accurately by their actions, but they will be identified by them. An MtF transgendered person does not don other-sex attire to become someone else but to reflect more accurately the person she is.

As society has gained experience through encounters with its transgendered people, transition becomes less arduous an ordeal, at least in some matters of law and forms of public interaction, for each successive transgendered person. The determination Christine Jorgensen had to have must have come from an internal compass that would no longer permit her to hide her identity. The incredible pressure to resist the forces determined to make her remain physically male are similar to the ones faced by the errant Johns Hopkins efforts in the other direction cited above. The undeniable and colossal failures to force a woman to continue to live as a man in the first case and to compel a man to live as a woman in the second should convince the most adamant skeptic that the book is not determined by its cover, but the appropriate cover will reflect its book. These examples should also serve as unwavering beacons for any individual who must ultimately chart a course against seemingly overwhelming social and institutional forces. Each person's sense of her or his own gender identity will ultimately be manifested when hiding, suppressing, or repressing it is no longer bearable.

The confusion and conflict created by an inappropriately assigned gender are a horrendous wrong perpetrated by society against a relatively small group of entirely innocent newborns. Inadvertently complicit participants in the socialization of a transgendered person exhibit a virtually absolute faith in society's infallibly assigning gender based on apparent natal sex. If this were a prosecutable crime, these people would be guilty as active, though arguably unwitting, conspirators in perpetuating a fraud of immense psychological proportions for each affected individual. In both the Reimer and Jorgensen cases, the subjects' efforts to disclose and assert their gender identities met with determined opposition. Ideally, strident unwitting-ness would be at least as awkward in practice as its use is grammatically questionable.

A society wishing to preserve, and acknowledging the necessity for, a system of comprehensive justice should try to make whole the immediate victims of its mis-assignment and strive to prevent, to the greatest possible extent, creation of future victims. Prevention, in time, might mean effecting a manipulation of DNA, inhibiting an RNA reactive process, or achieving some other genetic intervention. More immediately, though, prevention means ascertaining that gender identity recognition by family and society is accurate. If that accuracy cannot be assured, mechanisms must be implemented that afford effective and efficient means of helping each person reveal her or his own gender identity before an extrinsic and possibly fallacious assignment makes that revelation inordinately more difficult.

The public interest in avoiding the injustice of mis-assigned gender should easily justify the expenditures necessary for counseling and basic remediation at the earliest possible age. The greater economic costs for electrolysis, hormone therapy, and reassignment surgery after puberty might be considered prohibitively high. Government requirement of a declaration of natal sex (and implicit gender) on birth certificates and its use of official documents that demand an indication of sex make government responsible for the adverse effects when those documents are wrong. To a still unresolved extent, legal conflicts caused by, and resulting from, mis-assigned gender are resolved at the transgendered person's expense through processes she or he initiates. Nothing in those processes requires an admission of responsibility by others for mis-assignment of her or his gender nor demands restitution for the act.

To attempt to argue that an official indication of sex is not an assignment of gender is like attempting to avoid responsibility for the damage caused by a bullet after firing the weapon. Rectification of mis-assignment, since authority to, and responsibility for, doing so have been abused, is an obligation of the governments that require and encourage the assignment. Some would offer the defense that government has an interest in using sex designation as a necessary means of identification. The all too obvious fallacy of this straw man is that, thankfully, people are not asked to display their genitals for purposes of identification. Even after the tragedies of September 11, such an intrusive requirement would be contested immediately on the grounds of the U.S. Constitution, Fourth Amendment's personal security and unreasonable search provisions and of public decency laws (Kashner 2007, 504).[73] Clearly, the gender identity manifested by each person is intended by those requiring such identification to be an identifiable characteristic. The fact that a person's evident physical sex and her or his gender identity apparently coincides for most people has facilitated this oversight in the use of evident physical sex for identification, but that cannot excuse its abuse when the two are in conflict.

Representative government has been granted authority and responsibility that, in the extreme, could exceed its means. Redress for the fraud and torment of mis-assigned gender cannot bind government to a prohibitively and possibly unending series of expenditures for medical and psychiatric or psychological remediation. The economies of a single and virtually painless lethal injection supplied to all transgendered people would appeal to some as an attractive alternative. The ultimate cost of applying that extreme measure to an inevitably increasing number of arbitrarily selected conditions would be fatal for that society's sense of its own right to exist. At the very least, society must end the practice of mis-assigning gender.

Much of society seeks to continue to avoid its responsibility for that initial act and its iterations of reinforcing mis-assignment by stubbornly continuing to support the initial false assertion. While consistency usually is a virtue in the practice of something worthwhile, it means unremitting suffering when practiced to affirm inappropriately assigned gender. Ultimately, society can no longer continue the abuse when each transgendered person is no longer willing or able to endure her or his participation in the farce.

There is nothing so perplexing to a transgendered person as the failure of others to understand that gender identity is a fundamental part of each person's essential identity, and not something determined by anatomy. Yet, this failure of understanding is different from the intentional abrogation of responsibility asserted by those insisting that a person's biological sex establishes immutably her or his sexual self. This latter group will accept the concept of a non-physical self but would constrain that self to precise physical limits set by or inferred from her or his body. For these physical body-bounded individuals the amazingly gifted cosmologist Stephen Hawking, because of his physical challenges, might be compelled to limit his thought to a universe no larger than Cleveland, Ohio. As tragically limiting as would have been that injustice to a great man, those limits would have meant a far greater loss for science and humanity.

An MtF woman's emancipation of that non-physical self means reaching accommodation with her physical self that reflects to the greatest possible extent the person she is. As transition became an increasingly real prospect, I became more acutely apprehensive about my appearance. I was very much concerned that I would be perceived only as a pathetically embarrassing and embarrassed man wearing a dress. That could easily have been a self-fulfilling expectation if I behaved as though the expectations of others determined who I was. Transition, though, was not about perpetuating a façade but about ending one. My appearance is much more gratifying than I ever thought it could be but less satisfying than I would like it to be. Yet, I realized during and after transition that I was not dressing and appearing as a woman to seem more like one but because I wanted to be recognized as the woman I am. When told that women do not do something I had just done, I replied confidently that this woman does. The core of such certainty comes from essential identity but it is nourished and supported by faith, love, and understanding. That trio is occasionally a virtually indistinguishable whole that can be experienced through great works of nature and inspired works of man.

10. Music Discovered

What We Hear

History shows that what is currently called "music" evolved over thousands of years. An early cave dweller may have struck several objects, marveled at the sounds, and thought, "I have discovered music!" but the case for evolution is much stronger. Its actual origin probably does date to shortly after, if not at, the dawn of man. A pleasing collection of sounds may well have stirred or fed humanity's earliest sense of consciousness and invited repetition, replication, or augmentation. On hearing some compositions and/or performers, listeners might sarcastically opine that not all humans have been so stirred. The ostensibly "musical" sounds occasionally produced are anything but pleasant, and they are not always intended to be. Music's objective and subjective elements aside, my "discovery" of music refers to an awakening to a heightened sense of awareness regarding the incredible beauty and meaning a gifted person's arrangement and presentation of sounds can convey.

In his previously cited book *The Paradox of Happiness,* Dr. Paul Elbin wrote convincingly that if humans believe or accept that God is in them, then they must also believe God is in other people. If God is in people as His creations, then He is also in the world and everything He created (Elbin 1975, 43-46).[74] The words in James 1: 17 "Every generous act of giving, with every perfect gift, is from above, coming down from the Father of lights…" make a similar point and may have been in Dr. Elbin's thoughts as he wrote those pages (National Council 1989).[75] With God as the author of beauty, great composers either add their interpretation to a divine image, or otherwise reflect that image in their work. To experience that work is often to feel an assurance that its composer virtually touched and/or was touched by God during the work's creation. The beauty of some musical passages thus would evoke an acute emotional response for which there really is no adequate release.

Tears may be the most visible response on hearing a work of great beauty. Those tears though are grossly insufficient tangible evidence for the listener of the whole of the transforming, encompassing, and wonderful whole that existed too briefly as a performance but after, it can linger as a memory that lives as long as the listener does. Those memories must have been much more vivid and resilient before improved recordings and ubiquitous devices to play them may have reduced their power. Following an exceptional performance, the listener might feel a sense of the loss a reluctant earth-bound ex-astronaut feels on seeing another space shuttle lifting off, the void one feels at the passing of a beloved person or pet, or the longing to return to a favorite time and/or place of one's past. The reluctance to return to life described by people who have had near-death experiences might also be akin to the sense of not being able to remain in the wonderful place to which a marvelous work has taken its listeners. The brief life that each note has, as it is heard, is a reminder of the mortality of the existence of every living thing. There is a conflicting sense of elation at experiencing a great work's beauty and sadness at its passing that may leave listeners in a wonderful, yet unsatisfied, state. Certainly, not all music has been composed to reflect such beauty or to evoke that response. "America", "The Star-Spangled Banner", madrigals, movie themes, etc. are written to fulfill other important purposes, and often do so quite powerfully, but the works that speak to convey the above sense of the presence and loss of great beauty place themselves, by their nature, in a unique category. In doing so such music makes no pretense and does not deceive. It is or is not beautiful. Beautiful and enduring passages often seem not only to have been inspired by God but to have been written by Him and merely transcribed by their "composer."

Part of the Music

To participate in a work's performance alters the above calculus since, while in motion, the performer is actually part of the transient, living, but intangible, existence of the work. From my limited experience with voice and piano, I have found that performers usually know their audiences want them to succeed. The possibility of not succeeding vies with the desire and determination to be successful. The edge a performer's proper use of energy can provide when encouraged by an audience is misdirected when that energy interferes with the performance. That is not the fault of the audience but the performer. Some performers have successfully sought help from hypnotists, others are calm during a performance but nervous after it, and still others are prevented from performing at all.

It is easier to say than to do but keeping focused on the work, rather than on oneself, and trusting one's technique can relieve anxiety as the musician prepares for a performance. The performer should acknowledge the virtual certainty that something or some things will not happen as planned and that inappropriate tension makes that more likely. Thinking about something unrelated to, or that will follow, a performance helps maintain perspective. A few performers are so confident of their ability and mastery of material that they are anxious to perform instead of being anxious about performing. The contest between a desire to succeed and the fear of failure means something is at risk. That must be lacking, perhaps noticeably so, in a supremely confident performer. If that line is crossed, the egotist, and not the musical work, becomes the event's focus.

Each work lives, perhaps eternally, as long as it can be given voice. This wonderful form of immortality may be one of the greatest enduring accomplishments of humanity. A performance of a great work recorded today might now be nearly immortal but not so the whole of each person who wrote, first performed, or heard the original work. The meaning of the work is new to each new listener whether the performance is new or old. Live or recorded, the power of its beauty is at least temporarily transforming. A great work is capable of filling its audience with wonder and a reverence for its temporal author and her or his Creator. Part of the elation on hearing a wonderful performance may be each listener's perception of the work's immortality. The listener may be filled with determination to attempt to ensure the work's continued survival.

Mother, her sister, and their mother, Dad, my sisters, and I each studied music differently. I still remember Mother's playing piano pieces, accompanying herself singing, and playing for other women on our old upright piano at home and in rehearsals for their club's programs. Mother and her mother directed our church's choir. Dad studied accordion when he was a teenager and, with two other past-master Masons, comprised roughly half of the male part of our church choir for many years.

When I expressed an interest in studying piano, at least partly because my older sister was taking lessons, Mother attempted to help me with some keyboard fundamentals. Although Mother was a public school teacher for over thirty years and was involved in a variety of music-related activities for much of that time, her efforts at teaching piano to me were not satisfying for either of us. She was no more successful teaching me than she had been with my older sister. My formal piano lessons began when I was seven years old and I continued formal study of piano through my junior year in college. As a child, I studied privately in the home of a church pianist who had taught piano to my mother, my older sister, and many other area residents. This gentle sole was always encouraging and seemed not to notice when I stole time from practice, which must have been evident during each following lesson. Toward the end of her life, heart medication impaired her gait and speech, and she reduced her teaching schedule to a few students. She continued to teach me until her death. After her passing, I pursued further study of piano and added study of voice with another of my mother's former teachers. I continued studying with her until my high school graduation.

This second teacher's approach to voice could not have differed more from that of a friendly rival of hers with whom I would later study. When I complained to my mother about tense or sore throat muscles after trying to follow her teacher's instruction, I neither understood, nor did anyone explain to me, that muscles cannot be forced to work for long before they exact a toll in rebellion. Abused muscles will stiffen and eventually refuse to work, they will transfer their tension to other muscles, or they will cause problems that require prolonged rest and/or medical intervention. Although I envied other children who were bike riding, playing baseball, or were otherwise more physically active outdoors on a pleasant summer day while I practiced piano, I did not realize the common connection among these quite different but still physical activities. I was amazed when a first-string football player told me about his having studied piano. It took me far too long to realize Aristotle's "arts" and "athletics" were never intended to refer to separate and rival extremes of mutually exclusive memberships but, at least ideally, they should be two seamlessly blended parts of a well-balanced whole for each person. The dichotomy was a superficial separation of activities with which everyone should have some degree of familiarity and between which everyone must find a suitable balance.

My college piano professor hailed from Canada and constantly carried part of Vancouver with him. A mural covering a wall in his studio was a beautiful rustic scene in British Colombia. The scene did not remind me of the hills of my valley home but studying piano in the heart of Michigan's flat Lower Peninsula was incongruous with thoughts of the hills of either locale. I auditioned for this professor when I first visited the school and he asked, quite reasonably, what I hoped to accomplish from my study there. While having begun studying piano at an early age, I did not have what I considered to be a well-developed, or even suitable, keyboard technique. I asked him if we could work on that and he said there would not be sufficient time to do that and build a requisite repertoire. The technique I had acquired to that point would have to suffice. Ten years later, I resumed studying voice with the highly recommended "rival" of my previous voice teacher. I immediately began to learn more about how to have muscles do what I wanted them to do than I had learned in my previous twenty years of studying piano.

This second voice teacher, Mrs. Helen Elbin, prized a yellowed program from an early recital during which she had sung to Eleanor Steber's piano accompaniment when both were students. Mrs. Elbin had studied piano with a teacher who taught nothing but keyboard technique. Her spacious studio included her impressive grand piano, a pipe organ, two massive audio speakers, and other audio equipment whose use she and her husband shared. Her study of piano, brass, and voice had given her an encompassing approach to the proper use of the body. Its use to make or realize music demanded a constant emphasis on encouraging and expecting but never forcing muscles to work. Proper vigilance especially during vocal eases served as the rearview mirror that showed if what was supposed to happen actually did. The emphasis on suggesting and letting, rather than on forcing and demanding, permits muscles to act. I studied voice with her for more than twenty years and told her on numerous occasions that I never left her studio without feeling as though I had learned something important. Her husband's use of the room included playing the organ and listening to recordings to write album reviews. Together they gave to music at least as generously as they received from it.

A Style of Singing

My lengthy study of *bel canto* singing was not merely pursuit of a specific goal but attempting proper pursuit of that goal. This approach to voice requires a natural use, as closely as possible, of the organs of vocal production without manipulation or attempted placement. Imagery feeds anticipation of the desired result and proper physical support of the breath sustains tone. As insufficient as this brief description must be to summarize so many years of study, the heart of the approach is a non-manipulative vocal technique. Transgendered women I spoke with about transition seemed confident that feminizing my voice would come easily to anyone who studied voice. They did not realize that attempting to manipulate my voice to approximate a feminine sound would mean doing the opposite of what I had been studying for so many years.

During that study, I never considered wanting to sing well to be either a feminine or masculine endeavor. Mrs. Elbin's students included roughly as many women as men. The proper result of the effort, though, is a decidedly feminine or masculine sound. My interest in singing as a physical male was never an attempt to reveal my gender identity. I was pleased to create as authentic a tenor performance as possible with the full realization that the textual aspirations of most secular songs called for some extra imagination or acting on my part. Music with a romantic theme called for my imagining, rather than recalling, an authentic relationship.

Average women and men sing, play piano, rake leaves, and do many of the same things differently, however small those differences, because of the physical structure of their bodies. Athletes of each sex have seemingly endless variations of bone length and/or density, body type, lean muscle mass, etc. that enable some to perform certain activities at a much higher level of skill than their competitors. A small number of those born physically female may even have characteristics similar to mine. Probably no woman has a physical makeup that would enable her to sound like I do without substantial manipulation of her voice. I have a similar disadvantage when attempting to "discover" my feminine voice.

In Shakespeare's *Twelfth Night* none of the characters seems confused by the voice of the sister acting as her brother. Understanding that a male would have played that part in Shakespeare's day makes consideration of what should have been a major problem easier. The aural sense people use daily to interact, especially over the telephone, tells them much about the people with whom they are speaking. The characteristics of each person's pitch, tone, inflection, etc. usually convey to the listener whether the speaker is angry, pleased, disappointed, etc. The need to include that expressiveness in one's speech is as fundamental as the need to communicate. People who have been deprived of the use of their voices for long periods have been severely depressed to the point of suicide when they have been unable to convey orally their desires and intentions. In 1978, 21-year old fireman Timothy Heidler had an accident while riding his motorcycle. He struck a steel cable that had been strung between two trees and irreparably damaged his larynx. He regained an ability to communicate orally using an electrolarynx but twenty years later he was willing to risk his life in a widely reported and successfully performed larynx transplant that restored his ability to speak normally (Cleveland Clinic 2001).[76]

The importance to each person of her or his own speaking and singing voice is difficult to overstate. Beyond its mere function in communication, one's own voice tells the speaker and the listener that she or he is not merely alive but is also experiencing life and exchanging discoveries and perceptions of the experience with fellow travelers in real time. Her or his voice not only affirms those aspects of reality for the speaker but it becomes the aural embodiment of that person to others. When someone dies, her or his stilled voice is one of the most tangible of memories. In *Twelfth Night* the audience readily understands the sister's willingness to be taken for her brother while wearing a disguise. In a romantic setting with someone she cared for, however, she would no more want to sound like her brother than her partner would want her to sound like him. Few physical characteristics are as personal, expressive, flexible, and effortlessly natural as the properly used human voice.

As difficult as it was to attempt vocal success as a tenor, the physical structure necessary for me to be a soprano is far beyond the skill of any surgeon. I still enjoy singing in a congregation where my voice is just one of many in worship but I cannot visualize an acceptable image for my tenor voice with a most non-tenor appearance. Some women sing tenor parts in choirs around the world, but that probably is as appealing to most singers as is cross-dressing. A wider range of performance is accepted in the speaking voice, and it is tremendously satisfying for me to be taken immediately as female over the telephone. My speaking voice frequently demands conscious thought to avoid its sounding excessively masculine. At such times, I do not attempt to force muscles to behave differently but review my expectations and trust my vocal technique. The result should be authentic. After decades of affecting a masculine persona, I have no desire to affect a feminine one.

Beauty by Another Name

Although I remember being too young for much of my mother's music to speak to me, music did begin to speak with a clarion voice that I could not ignore when I was about twelve years old. My family had delightful recordings of Broadway musicals but I enjoyed at least as much our smaller collection of such "classical" recordings as Beethoven's symphonies and a 12-record set of great works by noted composers. *A Smattering of the Better-Known Works Written by a Small Number of the World's Greatest Composers* would have been an accurate title for the 12-record set, but it probably was discarded because of its modesty and length. While much of this section will seem uncomfortably common or offensively precious to those who were intimately familiar with "the standard rep." by age eight, they should know that many or most Americans did not share that childhood experience and never remedied the deficiency. Those who come to know and love great music with a more mature ear may well know them differently.

Schubert's "Unfinished" 8th Symphony, Mendelssohn's *Hebrides Overture* and *Italian Symphony*, and Beethoven's 3rd Symphony, *Eroica*, were favorites in this latter set. I had enjoyed the Beethoven-ness of that composer's "Alleluia" from *Mount of Olives* when singing it as a senior in college. When two church choirs performed that work as part of a special program more than ten years later, the piece seemed more appropriate to a sporting event than a church service. Beethoven may not have counted that chorus among his most beautiful works. The wonderful choir of which I was a member then performed Evensong services that included the "Credo" and "Gloria" from Bach's Mass in B Minor and the romantic Faure *Requiem*.

The incredible beauty and sadness of such passages as the adagio restatement and development of the second movement of Beethoven's 3rd symphony, "Surely He Hath Borne Our Griefs" in Handel's *Messiah*, and the Mozart Requiem's "Lachrymose" show that tremendous beauty can be built on or from great grief and sorrow. Among the descriptions of Heaven from someone who would seem to have been there must be Faure Requiem's "In Paradisum" and the Brahms *Requiem's* "Wie Lieblich Sind Deine Wohungen." The celebration of vibrant life in Claude Debussy's *Prelude A L'Apres-Midi D'Un Faune* is a hymn to creation and a testament to life and nature. The determination for victory of the character portrayed by a trained and talented tenor singing Verdi's "Nessun Dorma" can be powerfully stirring and inspirational. Ralph Vaughn-Williams's *Fantasia on a Theme by Thomas Tallis* has remained a favorite piece of simply beautiful music from the time I first heard it roughly thirty years ago. This brief list of works that I have found stirringly beautiful and which evoke a variety of emotional responses infers nothing about works that were not included. Other listeners and musicians would cite quite different examples and disagree with my descriptions or perceived quality of the works but that does not diminish in the slightest the enduring beauty of those cited.

By explaining how these works have spoken to me, I am not suggesting that every listener or even any other listener would necessarily hear the same thing. These works speak though and speak powerfully in their own voices to attest to their composer's vision. Like any great work of art the created image comes to its audience on a firm foundation of occasionally different language in the composer's time, to the contemporary listener's ear, or both. Each work wondrously conveys the composer's conceptions of strength, beauty, harmony, and/or other virtues. The message can be repeated to countless generations of listeners who could not even have been imagined by its composer but because of the composer's effort they can see, however imperfectly, that ephemeral creation.

The questionable clarity of the image or its meaning to its audience is apparent in
the recently developed fashion of dancing in chorus-line style to July 4th "pops"
concert performances of Tchaikovsky's *Overture 1812*. People participating
seem to enjoy the activity, but I cannot imagine what they hear that makes
their action seem appropriate. If still loving to hear that work or even Rimsky-
Korsakov's *Scheherazade* repeatedly over the past decades means my musical
tastes are plebeian, my capacity to continue to enjoy them is not diminished in
the least. A college friend who regularly attended symphony concerts in his youth
wondered how much our school's music students knew about their subject. He
chose as an example my professed appreciation for *Scheherazade* and asked
what I thought it meant. He seemed satisfied when I replied that it could be
appropriate theme music for a nautical cartoon. I should have added, though,
that despite or its thematic nature, I still loved the piece.

These few glimpses of evident special visions seen by incredibly talented
people give each listener a connectedness to what other humans have perceived,
so that to a small extent, the listener can share in the perception. The level
of achievement great composers attained in their work is one to which any
human can reasonably aspire. As often as I have used the word "transform" or
variations of it in this work, each hearing of a great work does transform, in a
quite different sense, the listener into a better self. Without contemplating an
encompassing but unendingly debatable definition of "great work", listeners must
know that when such a work is heard, the listener has been fed an aural food of
the highest nutritional value, if not a super-vitamin for the spirit. Such power is
so marvelously pure, unreserved, munificent, and dynamic that any distortion or
abuse stealing from its ability to convey its message cannot endure as long as the
abused version does not permanently replace the original.

I once naively complained to a cousin that time and energy I spent
attempting to perform a musical work could not be sufficiently satisfying
because there was no substantial material evidence of anything having been
accomplished. A recording in this context was served as a pale imitation of
a live performance and not equivalent to the experience of performing, or of
witnessing, a live performance. What I was failing to realize was that as soon as a
live performance is preserved in material form, that form, at least in some minute
way, begins to deteriorate. A great work is eternal in that it can live again each
time it is performed. It can be brought back to life as long as people are capable
of giving life to it or making it live through them. The most capable performer(s)
can show an audience a richly detailed contemporary view of a demanding work.
An amateur attempting the same work, like one of Plato's shadow-viewing cave

dwellers, can get close to the more polished performer's thrill of realizing the work's latest reincarnation.

My enthusiastic appreciation for some of these works is far from universal. In our family, everyone else's preferences have tended to more varied or lighter fare. Although I have attended many musical events with my mother, including opera performances at Pittsburgh, Pennsylvania's Heinz Hall both before and after transition, her preferences have been more eclectic but her responses less enthralled than my own. My more intense, positive, and consuming emotional reaction to some parts or the whole of some performances, tepid response to other music, and aversion or revulsion to other works or their renditions are more visceral than might be expected from the mere hearing of a fleeting aural event. I do not know what, if any, useful conclusions might be drawn about those who respond more intensely to music versus those who are less affected by it, although those who practice, as well as those who have been helped by, music therapy can attest to the potency of its power. Those who question the relative worth of the works cited here, or to my characterization of them, are reinforcing this point about the power music has for them.

After the restatement of the second movement's theme in Beethoven's above mentioned *Eroica*, the composer wrote a nearly perfect, if not wholly perfect, and incredibly beautiful treatment of something that is, at first, familiar but develops quite differently. Listeners recognize the restatement of the theme but it does not go where they expect and the new direction expresses and explores great sorrow. Perhaps as a depiction of the composer's hearing loss, the development could not be more vividly descriptive of the horrendous anguish felt at the loss of something deemed only slightly less dear than life itself. Although I have listened to that part of his symphony countless times without having thought of the comparison, an MtF woman could easily feel that desperate loss at her separation from the persona she had affected for all of her pre-transition life. She would be more likely, however, to regret the lost opportunity to have lived fully as herself much sooner. The affected persona is not merely her loss but a loss shared by all who thought they knew her. While she knows intimately the path she has trod and that it had to end, her future is far from certain as she takes the first steps on the path that will affect everyone she knows.

Beethoven trod a similar path. He seems to have grappled with almost overwhelming grief and he emerges from the battle as a stunningly resilient victor whose sense of strength and gratitude are characterized by the elation of the symphony's next movement. His symphonic portrayal of the voyage from the deepest emotional despair to its polar opposite of great joy might be heard as encompassing a thing in each person's life that was terribly important but which could not happen, or happen as she or he wanted. Yet, the desired thing is incredibly and ultimately obtained or achieved. That journey must have been central to Beethoven's view of life because it appears repeatedly in his work. The composer must have traveled the whole journey before writing *Eroica*, regardless of the order in which he actually composed the parts of the symphony, because the grief, acceptance, and then elation are a depiction of a whole whose each segment is colored and set in place by what follows, as well as what preceded, it. Beethoven might have written about the elation he finally, and perhaps most unexpectedly, experienced before deciding how it fit into the whole but he did experience and his composition reflects that whole. How anyone could remain unaffected by an aural expression of so powerful a human experience must be nearly incomprehensible to the transported listener vicariously sharing the composer's voyage.

For an unfathomable reason, contemporary variations of some of these works have found an audience. Some of these "updated" versions are offered purportedly to induce a younger or wider audience to be more receptive to the originals. This seems little different from a depiction of the *Mona Lisa* sporting a "spike" hairdo, brow-piercing studs, a tank top, arm tattoos, cut-offs, and sandals. *The Last Supper* might be reproduced as a bar scene with contemporary clothing, beer, and pizza. Such reproductions would not attempt to replicate the beauty and meaning of the originals and probably would not find wide appreciative audiences. Why abuse of beautiful and powerful works of music has met a different fate is mystifying.

Having watched television variety shows whose audiences were filled with screaming, mostly female, fans of popular music groups in the 1960s, I knew the audiences were hearing, or thought they heard, something considerably different from what I heard. As intense as have been some of my own reactions, they never approached anything like the frenzy of those fans. In high school and college, my preferences in music often were something that separated me from, rather than strengthening bonds with, other students. Simple sharing may be a large part of popular music preferences so that my rejection of most contemporary fare was perceived as a rejection of other students. That was never my conscious intent and there was no such separation in band, choir, music classes, and lessons.

Describing my own reactions to music whose beauty I find nearly indescribable is preferable to attempting to characterize the raucous reception given some performances of contemporary works and, especially, by youthful performers before younger audiences. The different reactions, though, is striking. Absence of comparable fainting, hair-pulling, or screaming responses to performances by Leontyne Price, Frederica Von Stade, Placido Domingo, Sherrill Milnes, Itzhak Perlman, or Vladimir Horowitz clearly was not because these performers were less skilled. Thunderous ovations from appreciative audiences certainly have followed these performers throughout their careers but not so the frantic and almost frightening adulation offered by some youthful audiences. If these very different audience responses share common ground, it must be the intent to show appropriate appreciation for each performer's accomplishment. If the responses are fundamentally different, that difference may relate to a different regard for the performer than the music in one case, and respect for the whole in the other.

This comparison of responses is intended to be neither flattering nor disparaging to those who have apparently enjoyed musical events I avoided whenever possible. Having enjoyed many wonderful performances, I have never exhibited a self-indulging effusive response, however, nor do I understand why other people have been so inclined. My lack of empathy with so many of my contemporaries regarding their musical preferences, which so starkly contrasted with my own, often meant my feeling disconnected from people with whom I had so many other things in common. I would later learn that the things we had in common and our means of dealing with them were at least as interesting as the nature of our differences.

Caring for the Instrument

Summer concerts at an area amphitheater have included solo, concerto, and symphonic programs of great beauty in a magnificent natural setting. I enjoyed innumerable performances there since childhood. A single performer, though, was memorable for a different reason. The pianist, known for an aggressive keyboard technique, seemed to see the instrument, not as an ally or neutral object but as his adversary. His apparent goal was not harmony or beauty but victory without mercy. This performer's almost vicious approach to playing what is accurately described as a percussion instrument was the diametric counter to Vladimir Horowitz's contention that a piano could be played almost as one plays a harp. The performance seemed terribly inappropriate to the beauty and history of the setting and to what had been my high regard for any pianist afforded an opportunity to play there. The spectacle was so disturbing that it remains the only performance on which I ever "walked out."

Several years ago, I heard a symphony concert at London's Royal Albert Hall. After the performance of a newer work whose composer stood for his verdict, many in the audience voiced their displeasure with what they had heard. I asked an usher if the reaction was unusual. He explained that many people in the audience were students who could scarcely afford the price of admission and they expected great value for that price. They had obviously been disappointed and were not reluctant to show it. That same regard for the better use to which such superb resources might have been employed had helped move me to walk out on the earlier belligerent pianist's concert, but it would not have occurred to me to be even more rude.

Even America's allegedly materialistic society does not generally revere objects. If someone abuses a piano the way the performer above did, one might mourn for the disrespect shown toward the craftsmen who made the instrument, those who paid for it, and future performers using it whose efforts might be diminished as a result of that abuse. No major religion suggests that innate things have intrinsic worth that people are obliged to respect. People would not argue that the piano felt pain or was insulted by the pianist; assaulted perhaps but not insulted. Objects are valued for the sentiment their previous owner imparted when giving them to another, for other memories attached to the object's acquisition or past use, or for the use to which they might be put. The craft, artistic ability, and vision of the object's maker can be gratifying and inspiring.

From another perspective, a responsibility of stewardship is inherent in civilization to preserve an object's potential utility or "value" for its present, or a subsequent, owner. This responsibility is part of ownership, however transient or fleeting, of things under the user's control. Common acceptance of that responsibility is offended when an object's user deliberately misuses or abuses the object, just as that same sense is intensely gratified when an artist applies great skill to create great beauty using an otherwise inanimate instrument. There is a difference in magnitude but little difference in kind between the terrorist pilots on September 11, 2001 and someone's deliberately ruining a great work of art, but there can be no commonality between the creation of a great work and an act causing that work's destruction.

The Gender of Music

Languages other than English seem almost preoccupied with gender. The association of gender with such objects as a window, a door, or the world of music is puzzling. Surely, none of these things has a gender identity so, if they have a gender, it must have been given to them. Most symphonies, concerti, instrumental solo works, and sacred music have never seemed to have, or to reflect, gender. Their composers and performers certainly have gender identities and they would reasonably be expected to have affected their work. The very real and human emotions evoked by performances of instrumental and vocal works can be as intensely experienced by the most feminine females and the most masculine males. A piece's evident color of emotion does not tell listeners if the composer's inspiration was uniquely feminine or masculine, even in works portraying traditionally female or male activities, whether the compositional style is baroque, classic, romantic, etc.

Yet, the gender identity of a performer seems an intrinsically essential component of a vocal, and instrumental, performance. I have heard at least one male singing convincingly as a mezzo-soprano, and not as a countertenor, who must have or have had great difficulty finding non-sacred works for his voice. Since love is so important to every human, it is difficult to imagine a world where a vast store of secular music would not exist to express various hues of sentiments ranging from elation to anguish that people have felt throughout their emotional, and especially their romantic, lives. Although instrumental music does not usually seem to have a gender and there are composers, arrangers, performers, and others of a full spectrum of gender manifestation, many works for voice would be inappropriate, hilarious, absurd, and worse when performed by a person of the wrong apparent gender.

If the *South Pacific* roles were reversed for the song "Some Enchanted Evening," the female lead would sing "...and fly to [his] side and make [him] your own..." (Logan 1958).[77] As much as millions of listeners have enjoyed hearing Placido Domingo and Luciano Pavarotti sing works appropriate to their beautiful voices, neither of them would sing *Show Boat*'s torch song "Can't Help Lovin'" ... as it was written. One might imagine a slight lyric young soprano on the back of that film's "Cotton Blossom" singing "...you gits a little drunk and ya lands in jail..."(Sidney 1951).[78]

Unless offered in parody, the prospect of such renditions should trouble the most ardent of gender abolitionists. Devoid of their gender, the scenes could be filmed and the lines sung lightly by anyone to suggest "I love someone" in the first examples and "I feel melancholy" in the third. While the abolitionists might cheer that small victory, American English would have lost its power to convey a large amount of additional information. That loss would inure to every user of American English, including the abolitionists. The half-measure of altering lyric pronouns would be as appropriate as a painted goatee on the Leonardo da Vinci's *Mona Lisa* or cut-offs affixed to Michelangelo's *Pieta*.

Show Boat's torch song paints a vivid image of a woman of a particular era devoted to the man she would marry. From other of their performances, it is evident that each of the above tenors is more than capable of expressing romantic love in song. Since they love as men, and not as women though, no one could reasonably expect either of them to sing credibly about the way in which a woman loves a man. Still, it is arguably the words to the song, and not the music, that infers gender. The questionable psychological health of a woman whose day is sunny anytime her philandering partner returns is another matter, however much she thinks she loves him.

With the rest of a small audience, I enjoyed hearing a live performance of basso Les Young singing *Show Boat's* "Old Man River" to a piano accompaniment. His harshly stunning "Hey, You! Lift that bale!" powerfully conveyed the profound sense of disdainful and degrading humiliation one would feel as an enforced social outcast. Mr. Young portrayed a supervisor whose unbridled contempt for his charges showed that they were regarded more as unwanted burdens than as respected human beings. Whatever the imagery or life experience that helped Mr. Young accomplish the task, he did it with a seemingly effortless grace and natural energy that characterizes truly artistic performance. Many performers seem to practice the reverse, as though short and simple phrases demanded the exertion of a sprinter. Mr. Young exhibited the artist's economy of motion that, even in so animated a moment, meant that each movement conveyed additional meaning and enhanced his performance. While Mr. Young's deep, rich, and powerful voice so effectively conveyed the intended sentiment, with no mean credit due the performer, it would be difficult or impossible to separate the power of the piece that comes from its lyrics from that which comes from its music.

When great singers sing great music, and even more so for singers with less ability, the music they might perform that was written for women cannot speak to its audience with the powerful message intended if sung by men, the above male mezzo notwithstanding. Similarly, music written for male voices does not convey the same message when sung by women. On this point, I would willingly wear the hat of a sexist if the term really is appropriate, but this seems more a matter of observable fact than belief. Even with the wide range of differences in physical stature among people, it is not reasonable to expect a tuba to sound like a trumpet, a cello to sound like a violin, or Cecilia Bartoli to say the same thing and in the same way as Jerry Hadley in songs relating to gender. Even if they could, though, their respective audiences would almost certainly be, uniquely, disappointed.

In the film *White Christmas* (Curtiz 1954),[79] Bing Crosby and Danny Kaye sang what was intended to be an hilariously unconvincing rendition of a song about being sisters to build their characters and further the romantic interest of the story. It is difficult to imagine Bing Crosby, Danny Kaye, or any man's having seriously attempted to approximate Nancy Kwan's performance of "I Enjoy Being a Girl" in the film *Flower Drum Song* (Koster 1961).[80] Since my first hearing of that piece when I was in high school, and especially after having seen Ms. Kwan's performance on film, I wished that I might credibly be able to live out the verses of that song. I have admired, as many other women must have, the actress's ability to have performed that piece as well as she did. I will never know if I might have sung "I Enjoy Being a Girl" more empathetically and believably had I transitioned earlier. By writing about the experience, I sincerely hope more MtF children and adolescents will achieve an earlier transition that permits them to achieve the song's sentiment as a full part of their lives.

It would be impossible for an MtF woman to establish a successful career singing romantic music prior to her transition. However seductive and feminine her appearance and however pleasing the voice, an essential element would be missing. Surely, the best interpretation, however that is defined, is not added to a piece but comes from the singer's knowledge of, reaction to, and feelings about the music. An MtF woman may try to convince herself that she is a man. Many MtF women have convinced women they married that they would be good husbands and fathers. Still, a practiced deceit that could extend to a convincing but feigned sincerity sufficient to satisfy numerous audiences and critics consistently, were it possible, would have little utility. Even if an MtF woman loved another woman and drew on that emotion in performance, especially when that engine would encompass the essential attraction and relationship between two people upon which the whole of human history and civilization are based, a consistently convincing application would seem to require superhuman or nonhuman ability.

I will never have the physical capacity, even if I had the richest of emotional experiences upon which to draw, to sing professionally about a real or imagined ideal male mate. Such an aspiration would not be unlike that of the diminutive athlete who would wish for a career as a professional basketball player or the defensive lineman on a professional football team who secretly dreams of being a successful, slim, and graceful ballerina. I have been extremely fortunate in having had numerous memorable and richly satisfying experiences singing especially sacred choral but also secular music. Most people confront physical limitations that leave them deficient in some respect relative to a single or a set of wished for attributes. An MtF woman though, whatever her physical characteristics, faces a different transparent wall of separation from the reality of physical potential, experiences, and aspirations of most other women. So much of music listening can help listeners contend with separation through a vicarious sharing of disappointment, frustration, or as a transporting distraction. The empathic journey possible through the beautifully expressed realm of emotions created by composers, arrangers, and performers calls the most adamant listener to move, at least temporarily, from her or his current static psychic state to a beautiful world of greater possibilities.

How Music Transforms

The advent of photography was welcomed by some and feared by others as portending an end to canvas and other graphic arts. The development of more sophisticated cameras increasingly gave almost anyone who could afford one the opportunity to capture and show to the world her or his view of it and, particularly, those things she or he found especially appealing and/or abhorrent. Just as refrigerators replaced iceboxes, Edison's phonograph might have been seen as, the technologically superior means of capturing and replaying the ultimate rendition of a composer's work. Society has not developed a similarly advanced method of enabling everyone with the financial means but little other effort to create, have performed, and preserve her or his tonal vision of things deemed of great value for either their intrinsic beauty or other significance. Even the best film and sound recordings of such attempts lack the three-dimensional reality of a live performance. The results of an effort to recreate a Lincolnesque automaton to recite excerpts from several of his speeches at the New York World's Fair in the 1965 was interesting to watch, but few if any viewers were impressed because they felt that they had actually been in Lincoln's presence.

For contemporary as well as time-honored compositions, though, the work itself, rather than its composer or other renditions of the work, is reborn with each live performance. It is not really born again in the sense of a cloned copy but, by having different parents and/or other inter-actors, it is born anew. This is far removed from viewing a dusty and stale mummified corpse of a vision seen by a long-dead composer. Each new performance of a work of one of the hallowed three "Bs", for example, might be more alive for listeners today than the composition's original debut was for its audience. A new performance would be more alive even than a recording of the work's original debut, were that possible, because audiences know more about some things and know other things differently today than did that earlier audience. For many such compositions, there is a catalog of previous performances for comparison and critique so listeners can learn more about the composer's vision and its interpretation.

Through most of the above, the idea of music as a medium is incomplete. Music seems to convey a composer's and a performer's message but it almost seems to have its own message as a moving and engrossing rather than a static entity. It further invites a listener's response as an answer or reply of emotional and intellectual participation. As different as each performer's and/or listener's response to a work or its rendition might be, each is an indication of how individualized and personal is that communication. Through most of my teens, the music most of my peers enjoyed did not seem to say the same thing to me that it said to them. If the overall message was the same, i.e. this is wonderful because it is not music to which your parents listened, my response was very much different from theirs. The fact that many of their parents did not enjoy much of the music I preferred did not matter either. Even those students who seemed to spend at least as much time and effort as I did studying music usually had preferences that were more contemporary than my own.

When I was a freshman attending an orientation-week dance, two other students and I left because the music was louder than any of us would tolerate. This rare moment of quasi-peer harmony seemed to exclude all of the other students who stayed at the dance. That same year, a senior theology major made my listening preferences seem less unusual when he introduced me to his growing, but still far short of his ambition, collection of Stravinsky's choral music. He heard in that music so much more than the immaturity of my musical taste would permit me to enjoy. Ten years later I was a member of a group of local singers preparing for a presentation of his *Symphony of Psalms* and was able to appreciate more fully the beauty, power, and complexity of some of Stravinsky's choral work. An impressively capable organ major also had a gift for interior design and had given his half of their dorm room a New England flavor thicker than the most dense of New Hampshire fogs. He and one of my fellow music theory students was enamored of anything written by J. S. Bach but was less inclined toward Stravinsky's work. Although I still felt as though I were a part of a small minority, it was becoming increasingly apparent that there were other, and more capable, members of that minority.

Music can be an unequaled force to motivate and inspire, to soothe or console, and to entertain or amuse. It heightens storylines on stage and in cinema and serves as a means of escape for a variety of listeners. Because of its multifaceted nature, "music" is no more specific a term than the graphic arts, dramatic arts, or literature. People who are drawn to music as a vocation or preoccupying avocation may have equally varied reasons for their commitment to it, and many may have started for one reason and continued for another. As an alternate means of communication, perhaps even between a subconscious and conscious self, some form or forms of music may be irresistible to every hearing rational being. If its power to communicate is the reason for the student's interest, then the color or style of music and choice of instrument(s) may be intimately linked to the body of thought communicated. Organists, for example, may have begun their study because of an interest in the instrument's association with houses of worship and then discovered the world of secular works for organ. In an extreme case, a talented researcher might discover that organists favoring secular works written in e major during the early 1700s tend to be left handed and to share an abiding concern for the welfare of dogs. As gratifying as that might be for one student in thousands, most music speaks to a far larger audience.

Again, music can be an unparalleled medium for conveying a sonic image of, or appreciation for, great beauty but that message is clearly not the intent behind all or even most musical compositions and/or performances. Some percussion-only works are an energetic and rhythmic celebration of life that seems primal in its appeal. Another body of work may convey an unreasoned frustration, confusion, or desire to escape from, rather than moving toward, distorted reality. Still other works, performed in a heavily amplified and almost violent style, convey a studied abandon exercised by its performers that is coercively rather than benignly oppressive for its audience. Such works, performed for receptive audiences, can be seen as a massive brutal aural assault met by the acquiescence of, and even encouragement from, its victims. Rather than perceiving this as a barely contained aggressive assertion of power or a ritualistic celebration of masochism, many in the audience vicariously identify with those conducting the assault. This twist by audience members must be the musical version of the "Stockholm syndrome." The fact that there is an underlying structure and organization means that such events even fail to be the ostensible tributes to license, anarchy, and mayhem that is often part of their packaging.

If many of the people who regularly attend such "concerts" also attend car-smashing events held for fundraising, their apparent penchant for pairing positive and negative energies would be an almost inescapable conclusion. Such people might argue that, either on a 1:1 or other ratio, any failure to recognize an intimate connection between opposing forces acting for well or ill is fundamentally unrealistic and dishonest. By this rationale, healthful diets would have to include "forbidden" foods, those attempting to live lives of monastic purity would have to take periodic debauchery sabbaticals, airplanes would regularly make some of their trips without leaving the ground, etc. So irrational a rationale would be an indulgence of imagination rather than an exercise of reason. Of particular interest, though, is whether attitudes among people in these groups differ according to honest gender. Those with female gender identities might view aural assaults by musicians and destruction of property for charity as laudable or, at least, legitimate acts when performed by everyone, women only, or only by men. Males might differ on any of those points and even question whether either matter involves an exercise of real power. It is unlikely but possible that there would be no gender identity-related differences in their responses.

The motivation of some groups of performers and listeners to choose certain music and whether that motivation is the same as, or significantly different from, what moves others is important because of what it reveals about those involved in this means of communication. Competent analysis may well provide valid indications of the nature of associations and relationships members of these groups would form, products and services they would use, and the way they would act in a variety of situations. Whatever analysis indicates about one's choices in music, it would be most surprising if valid conclusions could be drawn relative to the preferences of later-transitioning MtF women compared both to those who transition earlier and to non-transgendered people. If all MtF women, and only MtF women, responded negatively to a song about smashing automobiles, for example, diagnosing the condition would be far less complicated.

The Dramatic Arts

In a different but still powerful means of expanding each person's horizon, great works for the stage and on film have exposed humanity to a wealth of experience, understanding, and imagination that can be almost as real for each audience member as a vividly recalled dream or memory. Done well, presentation of the story makes its characters seem real to its audience. If the audience is drawn into a story and cares about its characters, those characters become people to be liked, admired, envied, or their opposites. Where music and drama share their nature as a means of communication, however, there is undeniable potential for abuse. Rather than a striving toward a goal to inform, elevate, and entertain its audience, a work may debase its art as propaganda, for prurient titillation, or some other base motive.

For a quiet evening's entertainment during a week-long trade association's banking school, two fellow students and I decided to see a film advertised in a local newspaper. We naively failed to realize that films with a certain rating may not be intended to tell, or even consider telling, the story suggested by their titles. If there is such a thing as good pornography, this was not it. During an early and poorly contrived scene of "intimacy", one of the other two banking students who had recently married said "It isn't like that". He found repugnant the film's coarse treatment of an act so important in the intimate personal life of his wife and himself, and an act, or repetitions of it, essential to the propagation of the entire human race. I asked if they wanted to leave, they did, and we left. We were offered a refund, but we did not want that money back.

The film had started with grand quotes extolling the benefits to a free society of unfettered artistic expression but the citations were from people who almost certainly would have objected to the film's content. The quotes might have been our first indication that the story or another aspect of the film was going to disappoint us but we still expected a story. The title and the film's opening suggested a plot involving an attractive female, a politician, and a story line as old as drama but any intent to develop that story soon was abandoned. One character after another became part of a couple exhibiting as much emotional attachment and mutual commitment as a motorist paying for gasoline. From the reactions of my classmates, their disappointment with that film was as great as my own and had no evident connection to my being transgendered. The reprehensible and almost studied disregard for the simple human dignity of any of the story's characters, or the "actors" playing them, seemed the primary intent of its director and/or whoever wanted the film to be made. Some people would suggest that no one can appear to others to be dignified while engaged in certain fundamental human activities, but the key here is "to others" because these activities are private by their nature. They have, or can have, the greatest meaning and dignity for those directly involved in them.

Hedonists would consider such an attitude "prudish" if they considered it at all and, even more than the Epicureans, would contend that people do themselves no good service by adding societal constraints that would limit the private or public enjoyment of great pleasure. If the true ideal were that there can be no such thing as an excess of the zealous pursuit of unlimited pleasure, then all canvases would be black as artists added ever more color to their work and symphonic scores would be unreadable blurs of black as composers continually added notes to build their aural towers. Gluttons would die young of acute obesity but still hungry as they consumed larger and more frequent portions of foods they found desirable. While enough water can quench a person's thirst too much of it can mean her or his death by drowning. Art in dance or a musical performance can be accurately described as an economy of motion with sufficient but not overtly excessive energy employed to convey all of a work's message. The performer must not become a distraction from that communication. In performance something that might be impossible for every member of an audience is often made to look almost effortless, "natural", and always graceful by the greatest performers.

At least one experience in each person's past probably has helped convince her or him that too much of something is unpleasant, however pleasurable it is in moderation. An excess of that thing may well have the effect of demeaning it so that it no longer has any value to us. I cannot promise that all of this went through our minds that evening as we sat in the theater so many years ago. What might have been fondly remembered as a most fulfilling, enlightening, inspiring, or simply entertaining evening of great film in a small but pleasant theater, however, was actually none of those. What I, and the other two bankers, remember most about the evening is our wasted time and effort in getting to the theater, our disappointment with the film, and our desire to leave. As unpleasant as this experience was, many other films have been its polar opposite. They are superbly entertaining, inspirational, informative, etc. and several even have tried to convey a sense of the transgendered condition.

In a strictly physical sense, the central characters in the films *Goodbye, Charlie* (Minnelli 1964)[81] and *Switch* (Edwards 1991)[82] represent the ideal for MtF women, because, if such a transformation would occur for them, their gender identities would finally be in harmony with their completely female bodies. In a perverse irony, these two stories created gender identity conflicts by placing male, rather than female, identities into female bodies. The previous lives of the unambiguously male characters, before their transfers, meant that they lacked any of the social, cultural, biological, and other life experiences that contribute to a woman's being who she is and that were an arguably essential but mostly missing element in each story. The films' creators unfathomably gave the "men" almost no story time to contend with or contemplate gender identity conflict. Numerous possibilities might explain the deficiency, but its existence may only have been troubling to transgendered viewers. Surely, an accurate portrayal of the conflict would have meant telling a very different story. The obviously contrived and supposedly comic instances of the male characters trying to be feminine essentially ignored the conflict and assumed an almost instant and intended adaptability by these "men" to the use of their new bodies, much as they might adapt to using a differently shaped toothbrush.

The awkwardness for a transgendered person in seeing how parts of these stories were intended to be funny is, to a small degree, akin to a blind person's perception of how her or his participation in a pratfall might be considered amusing. The glaring deficiency in each film is that the central characters were not treated as being transgendered in any conceptual sense even though each was, for most of each story, supposed to be a man who knew he had been seen as a man but suddenly found himself with the body of a woman. These two films have provided additional strong evidence of a common ignorance of gender identity and gender identity conflict where the most rudimentary conception of them would compel their inclusion. The films did not even pretend to the honesty of their storylines by having transgendered women, transvestite males, or female impersonators play the parts of the two transferred men.

While intending no slight to the obvious and considerable talents of Ms. Reynolds and Ms. Barkin, the person whose life experience would have prepared him to make each story's central point after each man returns as a physical female is an FtM man. Before he begins transition, an FtM man must really live as a person with a male gender identity in the body of a "woman." Although he would lack most of the life experience of the male character before his first death in the film, an FtM man would have imagined himself repeatedly living that role. Whether before or after transition, the FtM heterosexual actor would be playing a man "remembering" affairs as a man that were actually the actor's fantasies in real life. The reincarnated aspect means the FtM actor would be playing his life in reverse, i.e. physical male to female, rather than physical female to male. A physical male with a male gender identity would still be appropriate for the films' opening scenes where the central character first lived as a man with no conflicting gender identity.

A different version of the above *Switch* story cries out to be told with an unerring focus on the extremely difficult choices gender identity conflict poses for its main character. His options would include 1.) suppressing his identity for a time as he pretends to be his friend's wife and the pseudo mother of his and his friend's child, 2.) bearing the child and permitting its adoption, 3.) raising the child alone as its father, 4.) letting his friend raise the child as its father, 5.) aborting the pregnancy, or 6.) ending his own life and, possibly, that of the fetus. Assuming that gender identity conflict is as intense a reality for an FtM person as it is for MtF women, then being pregnant would be an intolerably acute dissonance no FtM man would abide. The *Switch* ending, when the central character becomes his best friend's wife and the mother of their daughter just before dying, is the powerfully poignant impossibility that demands a different ending. It wrongly asserts that a reincarnated man could ignore his gender identity and placidly accept being a wife and mother.

As well as Ms. Barkin played the part of a man being her character, there are at least hundreds of post-op transgendered people who would attest to the impossibility of doing that over time. Keen awareness of his gender identity would demand that he reject his role as wife and mother for the sake of his potential child, his friend, and himself. He would know that he could not be the biological father of the child he carries in *Switch*, nor of any other child; nor would his gender identity permit him to be the child's mother. That kind of harsh realization and an inability to find an acceptable alternative might well lead to a suicide like that of Ms. Reynolds' character in *Goodbye, Charlie* but there is certainly nothing amusing about such desperation. The sleepless contemplation of each possible outcome, as the character agonizes over and rejects each possibility only to continually revisit the alternatives knowing that a choice must be made, has to invite all too vivid memories for every transgendered person who has been through transition.

The apparently non-transgendered screenplay writers, pretending that a young or middle-aged male could quickly adjust to having suddenly found himself in a different and female body, seem to have had no sense of their own gender identities and, surely, the characters they created had none. *Switch*'s writers did permit their main character to agonize briefly over some physical differences, but his inability to express physically his male gender identity was either not considered important to the story or it was not considered at all. Even if he found himself in another male body, the character would not readily be able to accept it as his own. The different sex of the character's new body, his engaging in sexual intimacy as a woman, and then (in *Switch*) his bearing a child all demand that viewers suspend their own intimate knowledge of what it means to be human.

It is common for writers to utilize anthropomorphic trees, rocks, or other objects to make a literary or dramatic point. These two films attempted the reverse. To fit their storylines, the essence of who a person is or the whole of a person's identity was presumed to be as easily slipped into another body as an assembly line's interchangeable parts would fit into its product. Being human would mean little more than being one of those trees, rocks, or other objects. The goal of the screenplay's writers was to challenge the soul of a sexually active hyper-male by placing it into a woman's body and having the transformed man act and react as a woman. The humanness of a man's unwillingness and inability to do that is the essence of a story that should have been told. I am not suggesting that there was any intentional misrepresentation by these writers. However, two more potentially significant opportunities to help broaden and deepen the understanding for millions of viewers of what the whole of each person's identity really means to her or him, and especially to transgendered people, were squandered in another of countless iterations saying merely that there are differences between women and men.

Abuse as Entertainment

It is difficult to imagine a world without comedy, or at least to imagine such a world in which we would choose to live. Comedy takes many forms including dark, ironic, cynical, as well as slapstick, parody, satire, etc.; each usually employed to entertain and inform or persuade. While discussion and debate may be informative, they may also be sufficiently confrontational that an audience, as well as the participants, only hear what they wish to hear, continue to support their previously chosen position, and will not be persuaded. Proverbs 15:1 advises "A soft answer turns away wrath, but a harsh word stirs up anger" (National Council 1989).[83] Comedy can be that softer and less confrontational approach to attempting to help people better understand a topic about which they hold a poorly informed view.

Comedians may see transgendered people as possessing an inherently amusing condition, see the non-transgendered public as being uncomfortable or feeling threatened by the matter, or intend to convey enlightening information through humor. Whatever their goal, they rarely seem to understand or be sympathetic toward transgendered people. From the origin of the vocation, comedians have used some form of cross-dressing and/or affectations of manner as a means of addressing differences between genders and sexes with humor. In most, if not all, instances the modeled humor would target either conventional female or male identities and rolls, or their unconventional (and minority) counterparts. That first set is of little concern because excesses that mock a majority are usually controlled effectively and emphatically by that majority. Humor targeting masculine appearing women or effeminate men is of greater concern because it is likely to be construed as validating and strengthening extant bias. Targeting of transgendered people is even more problematic.

It is difficult to imagine how a comedian could represent visually a transgendered person. If a physically male comedian affects feminine behavior, unless he is portraying a woman, he is seen as mocking effeminate men. The reverse would be true for a comedienne. How either quickly could convey the concept of gender identity conflict in a way a non-transgendered audience would grasp and find amusing should be a worthy challenge for the most gifted of the profession's performers.

In an episode of the original *Star Trek* television series a female criminal takes over the body of William Shatner's character "Captain Kirk." The script did not allow any development of the sensations, emotions, and insights such a change of physical form would impart. Mr. Shatner's remarkable portrayal was convincing in his seeming to be a woman, and not an effeminate man, using the body she had just acquired as one might change a pair of shoes. While I thought the acting was impressive, I had expected much more to have been made of just how much different those shoes really were. Mr. Shatner's performance might be a guide for the above gifted comedian but finding an appreciative non-transgendered audience would be at least as daunting a challenge.

An even more challenging role would occur for the actor where the portrayal took a darker turn. Imperfections in performance would be more telling if they could not be seen as farce. Film efforts that do include transgendered characters usually have female actresses play MtF women. By trying to portray MtF women as whole women after transition, filmmakers expend an appreciated effort to reflect appropriate gender identity, but the portrayal necessarily will lack the life experience and perspective of someone who did not grow up as a woman.

About a month after the calamitous attacks of September 11, 2001, Tom Lyons' column included an "e-pal's" suggestion regarding a possible disposition of Osama bin Laden, if he were captured. The "e-pal" proposed that bin Laden be taken to a clinic where his sex would be changed and his beard removed. The writer did not suggest which result bin Laden might consider the greater loss. Bin Laden would then be returned to Afghanistan to live out his remaining days as a woman under the Taliban's oppressive rule (Lyons 2001, B3).[84] The "e-pal" obviously did not anticipate the Taliban's ouster. It is not clear, though, whether the suggestion even in jest, was intended more to be critical of sects and governments which oppress women or to seek a blurring of vengeance and justice in the handling of bin Laden. This variation on the wholly unoriginal idea of emasculating an enemy does offer an interesting twist on ways to torture that enemy. While I have no sympathy for bin Laden, I take exception to the suggestion for a different reason.

This was by no means the only, most egregious, or most strident expression of the concept of surgically altering a male's body, as punishment, for revenge, or for some other abusive or perverted goal. Any of these would be an horrendous abuse of a carefully designed process, and not a single event. That process was never intended to physically change one male into a different kind of male. Its purpose is to help an MtF woman resolve and heal her intrapersonal conflict and to facilitate a concert of her essential identity with her physical self. To advocate use of such a procedure as a form of torture is fundamentally inhumane and abhorrent. Serious advocacy of such abuse would constitute an appallingly careless disregard for judicial, medical, and moral thought and practice. So horrendous a perversion of the process would be akin to the butchery of Josef Mengele's experiments and the U.S. S. R.'s mental health system that chemically abused healthy political dissidents and others who failed to "appreciate" the flawless virtues and developing wonders of the promised Marxist Nirvana.

Telling the Conscience

During his life, Alexander Woollcott earned a national reputation as a theater critic and radio personality. He wrote as an enthralled fan both of live professional theater and of many of its players. Since the earliest Greek morality plays, the power of theater as a form of communication has served, not in the least, as an imperfect precursor of film and television but as a unique and enduring means of creating life-changing images and lifelong memories for its audience. As Woollcott wrote about an art form so dear to him, of well-written plays, powerful performances, and the performers about whom he cared, he was keenly aware of those less-urban Americans for whom such performances would require a greater commitment than a few hours out of their week and the price of admission.

In a 1934 article for the *Saturday Evening Post,* he explored the possibility of taking the stage experience to these people and the major, if not insurmountable, obstacles that would be encountered. Performers completing a long run of a great work would be loath to live from a suitcase during a national tour when they might be performing a new, and perhaps even greater, role in a major theater, he reasoned. The questionable adequacy of local theaters, a possibly hostile reception from established local providers of entertainment, and the cost of a ticket relative to other items in a household budget were other considerations (Woollcott 1934.)[85] Despite the decades that have passed since death silenced this theater advocate's voice in 1943, those who were alive and aware of the man and his work do still remember him.

In his wonderful biography of Alexander Woollcott, Howard Teichmann wrote about the forceful personality of the famed critic and "Algonquin Round Table" leader. He also addressed the apparent reluctance of three previous biographers to address forthrightly rumors about the great man's sexual orientation, as well as possible reasons for their perceived reluctance or timidity (Teichmann 1976, 12).[86] The daily assemblage at the "Round Table" of participants in and active observers of the continuing development of the richest examples of our culture's dramatic arts would be difficult to approximate in a contemporary form. Surely, no modern chat room could reasonably aspire to the ambiance, intimacy, immediacy, and stature of that group or rival its influence. Broad and continuing national interest in the gathering's musings attested to its importance to pre-television America. Today's plethora of readily accessible voices online, in print, on air, and through cable make it more difficult both for a particular voice to gain wide acceptance and for that acceptance to become influential, rather than merely responsive. Such competition for an audience also means that, if there is anything personal and potentially embarrassing that can be discovered about a person of note, the probability that the information will be discovered and aired is very high.

The absence in those earlier biographies of references to Mr. Woollcott's gender identity and partner preference may have been due to any of several factors. Lack of sufficient factual evidence and/or understanding of the psychology of Mr. Woollcott would severely impede a reputable biographer's work. Respect for the propriety of honoring the apparent wish, even of so public a figure, to keep some part of his life private, would arguably ennoble and commend the biographer and her or his profession. Absence of any indication that this personal area of Mr. Woollcott's life had any demonstrable bearing on his professional life, or some mix of all three factors would also explain and justify the subject's omission for many readers.

Mr. Teichmann wrote that he found no evidence that Mr. Woollcott ever had a homogendered relationship but that there was evidence of transvestism and inclinations in what was seen as the direction of homogendered preference. In captions showing Mr. Woollcott as a college student in women's clothing, Mr. Teichmann observes that somehow, after starting an acting group at the school, "Aleck" always played the part of a female in its plays. When author Anita Loos criticized the no-longer-functioning "Round Table" and Mr. Woollcott's part in it, he invited her to tea. After speaking about other matters Mr. Woollcott, suddenly and with obvious unease, presented a picture of himself dressed as a woman in one of those college plays. He told Ms. Loos that he had always had an obsession to be female and that "All my life I've wanted to be a mother". Ms. Loos apparently was unpracticed at hearing such admissions and never expected to hear this one from him; she found his confession most unsettling. Having shared so intimate a secret, Mr. Woollcott asked if they could be friends. Ms. Loos replied in something decidedly less than an enthusiastic affirmative (Teichmann 1976, 12, 72-3, 157-8).[87]

Readers probably never will know what reasoning led Mr. Woollcott to confide in someone who found his Algonquin position and behavior so objectionable. He might have thought that something he knew about her personally or because of her work meant that she was likely to understand, or at least be intrigued by, his revelation. He may finally have been ready to tell someone and that tea seemed the appropriate occasion. Knowing of her public criticism of him, he may have thought that he had taken the first step to resolution by telling someone who would tell others. Someone hearing of his disclosure would contact him, confirm his suspicions regarding the condition, and suggest his next step.

The experience of disclosure would certainly have been traumatic for him. There was apparently no evidence that he made such a statement to anyone else. If he told only Ms. Loos, to have her react so negatively must have been jarring and a horrible experience. His widely reported "dressing" at parties could have been presented or received in a variety of ways but the honesty and intimacy of Woollcott's admission while appearing as a male in a tea room has to have been a singular moment that showed courage and vulnerability. Ms. Loos' rejection must have made Woollcott feel more alone than he had ever before felt. His surviving the evening and continuing his career is a further tribute to his character. The moment of making each such disclosure is an indelible memory for each transitioned transgendered person. The preceding masculine references to Mr. Woollcott have been used only because the account of his admission to Ms. Loos is not sufficient to prove that "his" gender identity was female.

The possibility that a forensic psychiatrist or psychologist might determine that Mr. Woollcott may have been transgendered adds another facet to the gem of personality who so strongly influenced the dramatic arts in the first half of the twentieth century. We can infer, from early Greek and Roman history accounts of people who appear to have been MtF women, that there must have been tens or hundreds of thousands, and perhaps more, of transgendered persons since that time. Many, or even most, of them must have hidden the painful frustration of their gender identity conflicts for most or all of their lives.

The agonizingly slow trickle of knowledge about, and experience with, the condition has finally begun to be organized and made available to both its subjects and those who are trying to help. If Mr. Woollcott did share the condition, his achievements are even more impressive. That he may have failed both to resolve a gender identity conflict and to have augmented efforts to expedite and increase effective treatment for the condition are readily understandable and, in no way, diminish what he did accomplish. If his voice had been lent to the task of explaining the essence of a transgendered person's journey, however, it certainly would have heightened awareness and understanding of the condition.

Theater might seem a natural fit for a transgendered person. Fiction affords a means of escape from the reality of her or his compulsion of gender identity conflict but also provides a means of controlling every aspect of the lives of each character in a play to either be or not be transgendered. On stage, a character can be given a nearly infinite degree of culpability or innocence, encounter a tremendous range of experiences, and engage in discussions and behavior that are wrenching in their emotional content. If a character were written as being a suppressing transgendered person, perhaps only the author would know that secret. Being transgendered might be ascribed as a character motivation by a director, an actor, or even belatedly by a critic. The exquisite clarity or deliberate imprecision by an author on such a point must be one of the great joys of creating a well-written work.

The fact that his fourth biographer was writing thirty-years after Mr. Woollcott's death and still confused transvestite or possibly transgendered behavior with a homogendered state may be as compelling as Mr. Woollcott's possible struggle with the condition. A continuing confusion among the general public to this day about what each of these conditions does and does not tell society about those who have them must account for much of the suspicion, discomfort, and even hostility with which society regards them. Whatever the moral, medical, philosophical, or other considerations surrounding the issues, the persistence of the misconception that gender identity conflict is the same as, or a form of, homogendered status adversely affects people with the conditions, those who care about them, those who might study the conditions, those who might fund those studies, and many other people.

Having common adversaries has helped cement alliances among disparate groups that advocate for public policies that limit the harm caused by that confusion. The alliances then become a seemingly monolithic force allegedly pursuing privilege when the force's very different subgroups are merely seeking similar kinds of protection from prejudice that is based on ignorance or belief. Those who would deny common access to food, clothing, shelter, and other necessities to individuals they perceive as possessing a single characteristic that renders all other characteristics irrelevant are exhibiting an unconscionable and, in many settings, unconstitutional bias.

As each constitutional provision must coexist with the others, so no provision can be preeminent. Otherwise, a circuit judge might order the closing of his district's bars to enforce the U.S. Constitution, Eighteenth Amendment that banned intoxicating liquor because he believes it is more important than the Twenty-First Amendment that repealed prohibition. The First Amendment includes the words "Congress shall make no law respecting an establishment of religion or prohibiting the free exercise thereof..." (Kashner 2007, 504, 506-7).[88] Those who would argue that they have a preeminent right to be guided exclusively by their religious faith are missing the same point about coexistence.

Bias advocates and opponents might argue irreconcilably about the moral, ethical, philosophical, and religious worth of a justification for withholding or attempting to withhold food, clothing, shelter, employment, and other necessities from anyone because of a single prejudice against the latter's legal and constitutionally protected behavior. They might even argue about whether there should be a legal right to engage in such behavior or to exercise such a bias. The First Amendment's entire text would protect the right to think, conclude, and attempt to persuade others that an individual or group is right. The right to act as people worship and express their faith in free exercise of that belief is also protected, but none of the protections is absolute. A surgeon during a critical phase in a major surgery could not reasonably expect to be exonerated if she or he suddenly disengaged from the operation for purposes of worship and the patient died as a result. An attempt to use the First Amendment to deny rights to another person and especially her or his right to life is unlikely to be upheld by courts established to deter and punish that kind of behavior. The history of U.S. Supreme Court rulings upholding the constitutionality of everyone's civil rights, including its recent ruling in *Lawrence v. Texas*, shows that organized efforts to adversely affect or deny the civil rights of even the smallest minorities, sometimes even when they are engaged in an activity prohibited by state law, is not deemed permissible under the U.S. Constitution (*Lawrence v. Texas* 2003 .)[89]

11. A Room with No Door

The Journey of Hiding

Mental health professionals may point to numerous studies concluding that young children have a neutral sense of their own gender identities. Even if that were true of most children who have no gender identity conflict, and I am not willing to cede that point, it is not true of all, or even any, transgendered children. When I was four years old, I had two toy trucks of which I was particularly fond; each was about 18" long. The red tanker was a miniature version of the trucks used to refuel gasoline stations and the flat trailer was a model of a wider variety of trucks used to haul freight. I enjoyed sitting on the tanker, which was a little higher and more substantial than the flatbed, and scooting in counter-clockwise circles through our living room, hall, kitchen, and dining room. A three-step metal stool was kept in the kitchen beside the doorway to the dining room. A book of stories for children was a perennial favorite but it included an odd drawing of a wolf or large dog sitting up, holding a book, and seeming to read. During a tanker ride one winter Saturday afternoon, I vividly recall seeing not the drawn figure but a three-dimensional image of that storybook animal sitting on the stepstool in our kitchen. Dad was sitting in the living room with a newspaper he, unlike my apparition, actually was reading but I did not tell him what I had seen. It is not difficult to imagine that the guilt I felt about being transgendered could manifest itself in a perpetual fear of imminent punishment, even from an anthropomorphic vision of something from a book of stories for children.

Roughly one year later, I talked with my mother while wearing one of my older sister's dresses during an extended afternoon game of "Janet and Joanne." She said that my father did not like the fact that I was wearing my sister's clothes and that, if I continued playing this game as a child, I was risking development of a desire to cross-dress as an adult. For someone so young adulthood seems an impossibly distant time, but I thought the idea that I might still have the obsession as an adult was abhorrent. So many years after that conversation I still remember the feeling of dread and the dawning realization that becoming a father like my father was not inevitable. While I would later vacillate between acceptance and rejection of prospects of spending my vocational life in my hometown, the idea that I would lose the option to make that and other choices because of an irrepressible obsession was repulsive. Even as so young a child I would not have wanted to continue to live if I had thought that any public revelation of the conflict was the only alternative to remaining secretly conflicted. Neither possibility though seemed conducive to a worthy or desirable childhood.

However the obsession would end, I was sure it would end before or when I became an adult. I trusted that something about becoming an adult would make the obsession simply go away. Mother and I did not discuss the nature or even the existence of my desire to wear my sister's dresses. We each had accepted that the game was my sister's idea although I had at least acquiesced to my participation. The prevalent view in the 1950s was that, thanks in part to Pavlov's salivating dog and the work of the behaviorists, people were shaped by, as well as being contributors to, their environments. If that hypothesis had been correct I would never have had, or would quickly have outgrown, the obsession.

Our clothing discussion was more important to me even at that time than I thought my mother realized. Yet, I did not know how to tell her that there was more to the "dressing" game than she thought. I do not think she would have suggested a trip to a psychiatrist or psychologist even if I had attempted to elaborate. Our conversation was primarily one-sided because I neither knew the nature of my condition nor what might happen if I acknowledged and disclosed it. I went to my room and changed clothes.

I knew that our conversation probably meant that I was not going to be openly wearing my sister's clothes anymore, but I did not understand that it would be forty years before I would again feel comfortable when similarly attired in the presence of any other person. Had it gone differently, this terribly important conversation might have changed immeasurably the entire pattern of my life. Rather than a negative one based on fear of being who I really was and trying absurdly to escape that fate, I could have pursued an affirmative course to be the best woman I could be decades sooner.

Our talk had occurred too quickly and ineffectively in terms of resolving or even addressing my obsession. Any adult living with a child or children could live in near constant fear of being inadvertently complicit in so colossal a failure to help her or his child resolve a similar problem. A clairvoyant mother with phenomenal abilities of perception and understanding might have seen the conversation's significance and helped to arrange the counseling, feminizing hormones, socialization, and surgery that even prominent Johns Hopkins researchers asserted were unnecessary. It probably does not even occur to most parents that one or more of their young children might be harboring such a secret. I fervently hope one result of this work is that there will be far fewer instances of its happening.

Thoughts of a Child

As young children my sister and I, after we were in our beds each night, took turns reciting a common prayer of childhood. My older sister would recite aloud her version of the prayer and then I would recite mine. My version also began "Now I lay me down to sleep..." but always included the phrase "...and help me be a good boy tomorrow". The prayer's customary syntax had nothing to do with our variations.

One night after my discussion with Mother about my sister's clothes, I resolved to say the prayer quite differently. I prayed "...and help me be a good girl tomorrow". I said it apprehensively but in a normal voice, and waited for my older sister or a parent to say something. There was utter silence. No thunder or lightening, no flung tablet of stone casting me into "The Pit," no wail of disappointment, and no mocking slight that "I did not have the legs for it" ensued. An assertive "Did anyone hear what I said?" might have elicited a variety of unpredictable responses, but I did not consider asking that question. If there was a divine response, it was far from immediate, unless the answer was "No." When I asked recently if any of those family members remembered the incident, none did. It had been so very important to me that I say it at least once but, as disclosures go, the altered line of that prayer had been far too subtle to achieve a helpful or even disparaging response.

My obsessive thoughts about being female were incompatible with a positive self-image. As a child I often lulled myself to sleep imagining one, two, or more limbs having been broken or stoically enduring some other physical, but never sexual, abuse without being aware of or even particularly concerned about who was causing the injury. I realized much later that I was attempting to exact a psychological punishment for repeatedly thinking about something that I knew my parents had indicated and I believed was wrong and harmful. The obsession was clearly something that was happening inside me because there was no external influence encouraging apparent sex-inappropriate thoughts. The fixation was destructive to a sense of confidence, honesty, and self-worth but I had neither the knowledge nor the capacity to make it stop. Whether most or all transgendered people share that experience in childhood is unknown, although those who hide the condition from feelings of shame, fear, or embarrassment certainly feel some form of guilt however that guilt is expressed. Realization of the power this dreadful secret has to war against a child's sense of self is a clarion summons for the utmost efforts at remediation from anyone who truly cares about children.

During one of our "Janet and Joanne" episodes, my closest friend unexpectedly stopped by our house and saw me wearing one my sister's dresses. He said he was going to "tell" but my sister and I told him that the bathrobe he had put on also was hers and that we would have to share that knowledge with anyone he told about what I was wearing. Our tale of her simple cotton robe might even be embellished to include something as shameful as a ruffle. This unsubtle persuasion must have been effective because no one else ever mentioned the incident.

Such behavior with my closest friend and the deceit in arranging to wear my sister's clothes were evident signs that my perplexing obsession did not lend itself to forthright encounters with others and were clearly contrary to the imperative to be honest. Yet, it was the conscious fear of embarrassment rather than a sense of honor and conviction that left me determined never to be caught wearing such clothing again. Prior to the incident with my friend, I had not been consciously aware of any feelings of guilt about the "dressing" game with my sister even when wearing her clothes outdoors. I had been so comfortable appearing publicly in them that I have no recollection of having done so even after repeated assurances from my mother and sister that I did.

After the embarrassing incident with my friend and the conversation with my mother, my period of relatively innocent gender identity revelation had ended. The revelations could not have been entirely innocent, or I would not have needed the guise of a game with my sister. Accounts of those who understood and refused to suppress their gender identities might be nothing more than the result of theirs and their parents' initial reactions to those earliest disclosures. Applying the most powerful analytical tools I had acquired in my first six years of life, I could not divine the nature of my urge to present a feminine appearance but clearly understood the social and parental imperative to suppress it. I could not imagine how my constant obsession to "dress" would be expressed after learning, first, that it was not acceptable outside of the house and then, at all. The sensation was very much like a harsh confinement in a room with no door.

One morning, also at age six, I attempted to satisfy my obsession by wearing eight or more pairs of briefs under my other clothes to school. After spending the morning with so many layers of elastic pressing against my young waist, I came home for lunch with unanticipated pain in my abdomen. I made some excuse for needing to go to my room, and quietly but quickly removed the extra underwear. The moral discomfort of dishonesty and embarrassment with my friend and the physical discomfort from wearing inappropriate clothing were inescapable signs that living with my obsession would not be easy. In an earlier incident, I had clomped through the uncarpeted upstairs hall of our home wearing a pair of my mother's high-heeled shoes while she was dressing for an evening out. This experience was unusual because it stemmed more from idle curiosity than a response to my obsession. It may have been one of the most normal "kid" things I did.

A "Donning" Awareness

As a child, I had asked my parents to replace my twin bed with a set of bunk beds. Mother was still making our beds but I so desired the thrill of sleeping on a top bunk that I promised to put the sheets on the beds myself. In our smaller home for five people, flat surfaces could have taught magnets and black holes the real meaning of attraction. The lower bunk became the in-transit repository for the family's clean laundry that awaited further sorting and dissemination. This irresistible opportunity to borrow and wear clean clothes that were, primarily, my mother's was a thoroughly unplanned but most welcome bonus to having wanted bunk beds. Since I would not dare put any of these clothes on if my sisters or parents were in the house, there were few actual opportunities to surrender to my obsession.

During one such exercise, I had donned some of those clothes and was standing in front of an upstairs hall mirror when my older sister came home from school. She knew I should be home and asked where I was. I told her I was upstairs changing my clothes, which I never did after school. I changed into the clothes I had been wearing in a switch that might have exceeded Broadway standards and hurriedly forced Mother's things back into the stack of clothes on the lower bunk. I offered an excuse for going back to the high school and left the house before my sister could see that I was out of breath from the effort. Neither my unusual behavior nor the mussed clothes on the bed elicited parental or sibling comment, but I resolved to be even more careful about hiding my obsession in the future.

Suppressed gender identity conflict can manifest itself in a succession of incongruities. Whether as a child at "Little League" practice, swimming at the city pool, or riding my bicycle on a summer afternoon, I would suddenly imagine my appearing with hair and clothes like those of other girls my age. As a student attending a high school or college football game, I often felt an intense desire to be like the majorettes or cheerleaders but never to be a specific majorette or cheerleader. I still did not understand but the desire had nothing to do with any of those young women.

My fantasies continued long after high school and college. While strolling on a beautiful beach at sunset on an ideal day in Florida, I often became fully absorbed, not in the stimulating natural beauty of the surroundings but in imagining myself in my home secretly wearing some of my secret wardrobe. None of the activities had been undertaken as a means to evoking such thoughts. To the contrary the thoughts were an unbidden distraction from the activities. In retrospect though when gender roles were a significant part of almost any activity, I probably became more acutely aware of my gender identity conflict.

Contrasting fantasy images for a "presenting" female or male seem harshly dissonant with worthy and earnestly pursued virtues like honesty, integrity, and self-respect. My imaginings involved nothing of a prospectively aggressive, hostile, or violent nature toward anyone else. Any violence was inwardly directed and destructive to my own sense of worth. I never even imagined attempting to acquire any of the clothing, makeup, or jewelry illegally. Had anyone challenged the legitimacy of a purchase I simply would have left the store. Except for "borrowing" my mother's or my sister's clothes as a child, I wished to acquire things of my own that would help me express my identity. I had an intense desire to have physical characteristics that seemed impossible for me to obtain and to which those things would be more appropriate. That desire conflicted with my acceptance of an imperative to present and maintain a "male" façade that coincided with my decidedly male physical characteristics. Dressing secretly was the compromise but it was not a satisfying one.

It may seem immodest or overly modest to wonder how anyone survived her or his own experience. Yet, transgendered people endure not merely a single, or even numerous, cycles of obsession, release, and reproach, but they can live much of their lifetime engrossed in a conflict for which no one would reasonably wish. The lost time and energy consumed by the struggle, whatever its actual nominal value, must be staggering. There is in retrospect a third-person or removed sensation to describing the quasi stasis experienced before transition. Letting go of that previous psychic struggle probably is the only way a transgendered person can avoid a constantly recurring feeling of bitterness, disappointment, and depression. After transition trying to live two lives is no longer necessary and the reality of the earlier effort quickly fades.

The fact that it is important for everyone's mental health, perspective, and quality of life that they not see themselves as victims is apropos. Humans accept their past as forever being a part of them but that past need not bind them. Like other assets that past can be a useful tool for growth and greater understanding of what being human means. Someone wrongly convicted of a crime and freed after having spent decades in prison could reasonably be asked "Yes, your incarceration was horribly tragic but what are your plans for tomorrow?" The freed prisoner who has known no experience beyond her years of "treading water" in prison, whatever her other prison experiences might have been, has the gates closed firmly behind her and she must now try, in a sense, to swim on dry land. If she quickly learns to adapt to her very different environment, she can survive. Her ability to live freely depends primarily on the education and natural inclinations she has, her own fantasized life outside of prison, her observations of others living in prison and outside of it, and such superficial art and ability as she can readily assimilate and practice in her new environment. For the MtF woman, her long-affected male persona was that prison and transition is her release. Without faith that places all of this in perspective, her prospects for long-lasting success must be dim.

The Weight of Waiting

The accuracy of the water-treading analogy is not easily overstated. During 5th but especially 6th grade, I felt as though I were in a kind of dulling daze of sameness even though I liked my sixth-grade teacher and continued to do well academically. Having gone to the same school for half of my natural life, I seemed to lack the imagination to find a stimulating challenge in the routine of the school's subject matter, my avocations, or social interaction. Failure to make progress toward resolution of my secret inclinations must have been a large part of that fundamental disappointment and lack of committed involvement. I was not making any progress toward resolving a matter of primary interest to me.

Despite extant intellectual, social, or physical alternatives and challenges, no options for expressing or even discussing my suppressed gender identity presented themselves. My inability to simply waken one wonderful morning to being, and being accepted as being, female, the onus of appearing to be convincingly male, and the evident absence of anyone from whom I might seek effective remedial intervention were an equivalent burden weighing several times my own weight. Had I known I would wait more than forty years for that morning, I would have found the prospect unbearable.

While in 7th grade, I stayed home for several days fighting a bout of flu. When I was well enough and everyone else was out of the house, I dressed in one of my mother's girdles and a pair of her gartered stockings under my own clothes and went downstairs to watch daytime television. The meager offerings of our two local channels included *Truth or Consequences* (Davis 1950)[90] and *Art Linkletter's House Party* (Guedel 1952).[91] The cover of the newspaper's weekly television directory featured a young woman wearing slacks, seated in a relaxed manner, and looking pleasantly at the camera. I stared at the photo trying to imagine myself as being in that photograph. Wearing some of my mother's clothes, I sought more readily to imagine being the picture's subject, even though the woman in the photo was not wearing a girdle and stockings. I was not doing anything else differently as I sat watching television in those clothes, but I somehow felt an augmented ability to understand the women, men, and children I saw on the game shows, talk shows, and other programs. I could pretend to interact with those people from the safe distance of a television broadcast. I was attempting, in a desperately futile way, to reveal my gender identity to real people but to people I did not know and who I knew could not see and respond to the revelation.

This most unsatisfying means of telling, without telling, my secret to someone was another self-destructive assault on my sense of honor and honesty. It was also another reminder that the problem I was continuing to hide from everyone else was easily beyond my own efforts to resolve. There was almost a sense of drowning in invisible water so that getting out of that water or finding a place where the water was more shallow was impossible. I knew of no means to a satisfactory resolution of my conflict at least partly because I did not understand the problem.

My mother was the person in whom I most likely would have confided, but she had already told me years before that, except for a bleak future of wanting to wear women's clothing as an adult male, I had no choice but suppression. To have broached the subject again years later seemed no more likely to lead to a different outcome. The attempt would have meant taking the risk of revealing my shameful secret. I would have been disappointing my parents by not being the son I was trying to be, nor could I ever again be the same grandson to the grandmother I cared so much about if she knew. My unhappy encounter with my bathrobe-wearing friend had clearly indicated the possible social embarrassment that awaited sharing my secret with another friend and the prospect of discussing such a matter with anyone more distant seemed even less inviting.

The Family Shepherd

The same minister was pastor of the church my family attended from my earliest memory until after my graduation from college. I knew, and frequently saw, all the members of his immediate family. The minister and I had not formed the kind of relationship that would have been conducive to my sharing my secret with him but, once I felt the imperative to suppress it, I cannot imagine a relationship with anyone that would have encouraged its disclosure. It seemed as important to be the person the minister thought I was as it did to fulfill the expectations of all the other people about whom I cared.

He frequently reminded me, and usually in the presence of others, that when I was quite young and choking on a jellybean, he had pried the offending object from my throat. I was apparently too young to remember the event but I have not cared for jellybeans for as long as I can remember. I had thought my dislike was a matter of preference rather than self-preservation, but even a subconscious association or sublimated memory regarding the experience would reasonably induce aversion. The fact that the story meant enough to him that he never tired of repeating it is still a fond memory.

In addition to theology, this man's varied interests included the use and abuse of English, history, music, and foreign languages. Yet, these were only a few of the subjects whose study he enjoyed. Despite the high regard for scholarship he fostered among his own family, our church, and the community, there was never any indication that gender identity conflict had appeared among his favorite subjects. When talking with him after my transition and shortly before his death, he proved that my reticence with him and with so many others had been rooted in a baseless, but no less real, fear of shame and embarrassment. His sincerity and light humor were as they had always been, and he spoke with me as though nothing important about me had changed.

Had I asked him earlier about my obsession he might well not have known what next step to suggest but I believe his response would have been sincere and caring and that he would have tried to help. I had known this man for most of my life and I represented the congregation at a presbytery meeting when our church's long pastoral relationship with him came to its end. That life-long relationship and personal regard for him were actually an impediment to my seeking his help or the help of so many others in our community. If I would not seek assistance from anyone I knew and respected, I was even less likely to seek it from someone I did not know and respect. Any disclosure would imperil my false, but universally accepted, persona while seeming to offer no known or knowable substitute. Since even I accepted that persona as my identity, abandoning or escaping that "self" was unthinkable. To confide meant not just trusting someone who seemed unlikely to be able to help but confiding would empower someone with the capacity to shatter the only life I had known.

The Romantic Scene

Advertisers and dramatists often seem obsessed by a single theme. Through countless variations, the image of an attractive and youthful female dancing romantically with an equally attractive male, the couple elegantly attired, and their enjoying themselves and each other in an opulent setting has been endlessly repeated. Later scenes frequently show the couple wearing less clothing, if any, and being enthusiastically intent on getting even closer together. The overpowering suggestion is that each of them is enjoying the experience. From both a religious and philosophical perspective, the scenario, if extramarital and epicurean, might accurately portend a longer-term absence of happiness. Familiarity can make repetitions less exciting. The exceptional can become ordinary. An unintended pregnancy might mean a drastically altered life plan, especially for the mother.

The male who saw sexual intercourse as his primary interest in one woman may seek to repeat the routine with another woman. He fails to realize that a longer-term relationship could mean a different, far deeper, and more lasting kind of happiness. From a more mundane perspective, the intent of the creators of such scenes often is to appeal to a prurient interest among its viewers on an unreasoning or anti-reasoning but emotional level. When thinking about such scenes, a few people might take turns vicariously as the female and then as the male, but most would find being or identifying with one or the other person to be so reflexive as to have escaped conscious thought. She or he might favorably recall one or more such occasions that led to, or was an important part of, a long-term and warmly enriching relationship. Others would remember similar occasions that were part of a familiarization process that led to a certainty that the relationship should not and would not last much longer.

Whichever character non-transgendered people would imagine themselves playing in such scenes regardless of their authors' purposes, the experience for a suppressing transgendered person is quite different. While an MtF woman's immediate and nervously exciting reaction can be to imagine being female in either of the above such settings, there is a realization that the thought is incongruent with her physical appearance and the way others perceive her whole person to be. There appears to be no way to make such scenes become part of her life. She is frustratingly aware that her desperate longing for such experiences was never encouraged by anyone about whom she cares nor by anything she has read. Her failing to discover the origin and nature of the longing is perplexing. Frustration and confusion about why that longing is so intense, so unmistakable, and so persistent compound the unrest. While producers of such scenes attempt to suggest what is possible, the message to suppressing MtF women is a reminder of what seems, for them, to be impossible.

MtF women may choose, or be compelled, to pursue a life of importance to someone else. Whatever the merits of that effort, it is not a pursuit of the one answer MtF women must obtain. If they outlive the distraction, and even while they pursue that other life, their obsession will persist. Their unbidden imaginings will inevitably recur with an unpredictable frequency that is independent of their other thoughts and actions. However stubbornly it is pursued, suppression, as a strategy for contending with the transgendered condition, will fail.

12. A Time for Resolution

Moment of Crisis

My year of transition began after returning from a Christmas with my parents at their home in Florida. I had resumed my normal work and other life routine, including frequent, if not daily, episodes of dressing in my make-up and clothes. During the increasingly less satisfying spate of episodes, there was a greater than normal and more intense sense of disappointment and frustration. Even the bizarrely exciting sense of wanting to be seen and accepted as female but not recognized had changed. I knew that the overwhelming desire to be as physically female as I could be was not possible to achieve alone, without a potentially and probably fatal encounter with a very sharp and sturdy implement. I do not know anyone who attempted to satisfy that desperate urge on their own, but I understand fully the feeling that has led some transgendered women to attempt it.

I was accustomed to hiding the conflict, had continued to separate myself from any possible assistance in resolving it, and was aware of the existence of only a few people who had transitioned and were living relatively normal lives. I had previously been unwilling to explore the internet for serious treatment of the subject. The remote but real possibility of discovery by someone in my internet service provider's (ISP's) office or some other monitoring entity would have meant violating my stubborn obeisance to secrecy.

Transvestites, who discussed transient fulfillment of their compulsion, and a few transgendered people, who seemed to lead more stable lives, had appeared in the media and made reasonable cases for their living as they did. While understanding and envying their apparent transformations, I did not see an acceptable alternative to the stoic regret they seemed to share as they discussed their lives. There seemed no possible common ground between the lives they lived and the world of my male persona. The possibility of an embarrassing chance meeting with someone I knew as I explored library resources had always impaired my access to published works in college or local libraries. As an MBA student I frequently considered accessing the impressive resources of West Virginia University's library system for information about the transgendered condition. Fear of being recognized or of attempting to describe to anyone what I was looking for and why I wanted it was sufficient to prevent my doing so. Had I searched for and found the right pieces to my puzzle, I might have begun transition almost fifteen years sooner.

The false impression that there is a sudden impulse, without a life-long history of suppressed gender identity, in favor of transition devolves from an errant focus on the moment when an MtF woman resolves to take those steps leading to transition. That impression ignores or minimizes consideration of the whole span of the MtF woman's preceding conflict. The prologue to that moment does not diminish its magnitude. Still, the moment of decision, because sustaining the conflict is no longer bearable, is difficult to describe. It probably is without parallel in the life of each person who experiences it, as well as for those who never have had reason to make it. Unlike so many formal tests there is no gathering of people to sit for the same event, no list of questions, and no one else physically present to evaluate one's performance.

My moment arrived on a certain January evening. For the thousandth or ten thousandth time, my partial yielding to the familiar compulsion was traversing its familiar path of brief fantasy that would be followed by a return to the re-donning of the male façade. This time instead of the usual empty feelings of remorse, wasted energy, and lost time, there was a sudden, overwhelmingly deep, and final desperate exasperation. It heralded the no-longer-escapable realization that what I was doing was not, nor ever had really been, enough. Like the smallest acorn instantly becoming a huge oak tree or a star going from stellar gas to supernova, the outer shell was no longer remotely adequate to contain and represent the person I am. The power of that thought was an almost tangible blow. There was a stunning realization that the previous grossly insufficient and inadequate representation of myself had seen a psychical rending of its shell---a shattering of the decades-old barrier behind which a suppressed gender identity was believed to be securely restrained. Sporadic partial releases were no longer enough. I did not know how, but I was determined that coexistence with my obsession had come to its end.

The routine I had accepted of tolerating the behaviors, accepting the condition as a most unusual sort of hobby, and fantasizing almost daily about a miraculously accomplished transition in some vaguely distant future was no longer possible. I did not think that any of this was a matter of wanting to be all one thing more than the other, but I had arrived at the impasse where having a female gender identity and being physically male was no longer bearable. I had been able neither to resolve the conflict in favor of gender identity nor to accommodate my continued male appearance. I was still desperately seeking a solution that made more sense than rubbing two ice cubes together to start a fire, but I was unwilling to seek a chemical solution that might destroy my mind while preserving the body. The possibilities of quasi-religious programming or of being medically drugged into oblivion were only slightly less appealing than the equally considered option of suicide.

Some members of the community of faith would argue that, in rejecting religious programming, I was refusing to submit to divine will. This argument is another fundamental denial of the essence of gender identity conflict. What is really a contest between a person's innate gender identity and physical sex is seen incorrectly as the soul's battle between good and evil. Having struggled for decades with religion as it relates to the condition, I still considered the advice of several people whose opinion I valued regarding matters of religion. They were helpful in reassuring me, although that was not their intent, that the manner in which I had attempted to cage and restrain my obsession was actually the behavior that was inappropriate.

The Sublime Mr. Frost

From a sufficiently broad perspective, most human thought and action is far from original. Those who drive an automobile are acutely aware that the activity is a common, and perhaps too common, one. Yet, each person's use of, and experiences with, the vehicle she or he controls is unique. The "soccer mom," "cabbie," racecar driver, and commuter have something in common with other drivers characterized by their respective descriptor, but they do not think of themselves as engaged in a group activity when driving. In each case only one person is seated behind each vehicle's controls.

The same generalization applies to the crossroads that occur in the lives of people and nations. Few decisions can compare in import to the one made by General Eisenhower on June 6, 1945, but every adult has faced at least one decision that brought great change to her or his life. In his often-cited "The Road Not Taken," poet Robert Frost wrote eloquently about the process of deciding and a decision he made (Frost 1920).[92] Much of Mr. Frost's poem would apply differently to different readers but for a transgendered woman, the traveling of two roads and then finally choosing one, doubting a valid opportunity to travel the other, a lengthy pause for thought at the intersection, etc. reflects the turmoil felt before and at the beginning of transition. Having stood at one fork for over forty years, I could not see beyond the bend and undergrowth on the tangential road, but the path similar to the one I had been traveling led back where I had been and that was unacceptable.

In China and elsewhere when even the longest journey begins with that "single step," there is still a question of direction. Further, is the traveler prepared for the journey? Who else is on the road and how might brief encounters and meetings of longer duration go? Recurring questions of whether the change is really worth the disruption of others' lives, the strain on relationships, the commitment of time, effort, and other resources will not rest. When there is ultimately no acceptable alternative, there remains only one road to travel. The fact that nominally fewer people take the road I traveled is doubtlessly the result of their not having faced the same choice. I have spoken with fewer men about gender identity, but the women who have discussed it have consistently said that they always knew they were female and never wished to be, or thought they were, anything else, which is very much the nature of gender identity. The problem comes in recognizing it. Surely, people do not all face the same choices and, even when there seems to be no acceptable alternative, they might still agonize at Frost's diverging roads in the A...long I stood..." phase until deciding or letting someone or something else choose for them.

In the film version of *Oklahoma*, Aunt Eller seems prepared to impart a tested recipe for success to Laurey, who is about to marry someone of whom she is unsure. Aunt Eller tells her she will have to put all the positive things on one side and the negatives on another and then decide (Zinnemann 1955).[93] This pragmatic approach to life and life's inescapable and important pseudo choices is more profound than its simplicity would suggest. The listing of positives and negatives might be an interesting use of time where time permits. The exercise may even be instructive regarding an enhanced understanding of the subject. All of that effort, though, may ultimately be of little consequence when deciding upon the course of action. Exogenous factors, inertia tied to emotional history, concern for the opinion or feelings of others, or intuition may move the decision maker at a key moment to choose the road that everything else would proscribe.

Faith in Action

A cousin's husband told me he thought that, if there were anything sinful about transgendered people, it might be their failing ultimately to resist the force impelling them toward physical transformation. I would agree with that idea about resisting temptation to do something one knows she or he should not do, but I would argue that there is nothing for the transgendered person to resist. There is no external power, force, thought, etc. against which an MtF woman can fight. The engine driving her is her own gender identity. Those who believe mankind is made in the image of a triune God argue neither that there is more than one God nor that humans have more than one essential self. As intense as was my moment of cathartic desperation, I still based my decision to seek the assistance of a qualified and experienced psychiatrist on my extant understanding of the professional qualifications of, and appropriate role for, such a professional. I was not certain whether the problem was psychiatric, psychological, or biological in nature,. but I knew it was not metaphysical. If the matter were a question of faith, I would have sought spiritual counseling, but the incessantly recurring voice of my suppressed identity was my own and not that of malevolent tempting force.

However new and frightening the horizon, there was no possibility of returning to the familiar confines of my mental prison. An incredible journey had taken place without my leaving the room. A conventional mirror would not show what had changed but the "fantasy" side of the mirror had been united with its face. Whatever the path or paths forward, there was no question of whether to proceed. There was a sense of resolve but also of controlled panic. With no plan, no prospect for a sudden magical transformation, no marshaling of resources and practice for a carefully chosen contest, everything I was and had was at risk in pursuit of something defined only as being quite different from where I had been.

A Cathartic Search

As I tentatively began to explore related web offerings, I was amazed at the quantity and nature of its content. Although I had been using a personal computer for almost ten years and had searched the developing internet for other information, I had not dared to use it for so personal a matter. As I began to use this new and abundant source of information about the transgendered condition, it seemed as though I could do so almost anonymously. The wealth of information now seemed of far greater value than any possible danger of embarrassing discovery by anyone in my ISP's office. The internet, as a vast library of resources of varied quality that can be explored at will, may well represent society's greatest achievement since the Library at Alexandria. It does facilitate access to a seemingly endless, perpetually changing, and increasingly substantive body of information obtainable at the user's whim and discretion. It permits the user to speak in the new language of possible solutions.

Gender Identity Expressed

When adding to my secret trove of clothing and makeup, I had always attempted to minimize the risk of discovery by purchasing things as far from home as possible. If a stranger did guess the reason for a purchase, I would still be paying with cash and intended to leave no form of identification in the store. While purchasing a bra in a clothing store in a small town roughly one hundred miles from home, I encountered the gentleman who owned the store. As the clerk was handling the sale, the man persisted in a series of questions about where I worked, how long I had been in the area, if I liked the town, etc. His inquisitiveness vied both with the clerk's progress processing my purchase and my hastily fabricated life history in a tense contest that I felt but dared not reveal. I said I had just started at "the bank" but should have anticipated his asking which one. I had never been in that town before, and had not passed a bank getting to the store. I said we would be disappointed if he thought there were more than one bank. I said I thought I would see him again but fervently hoped that would not be so.

It did not occur to me then, that the man might have seen other transvestite or transgendered people making such purchases in his store. My impression had been that he was interested in establishing a continuing business relationship, but his questions were not about sports, the weather, or more casual conversation. If I had somehow indicated the real purpose for my purchase, he should have known I was not going to volunteer any accurate personal information. Since I never returned to that town and, given his age at the time of our meeting, I will never know what he really thought about our encounter.

Hypersensitivity and awkward self-consciousness always accompanied me because I felt guilt while buying such things. I was not, though, sufficiently paranoid to imagine someone's following me from the store, to my car, and even to my home. The anonymity of personal contact with strangers had seemed preferable to inquiry or making purchases by phone from my home. The new effort at an internet search was risking a small chance of discovery by people who knew my family and me. That discovery could lead to their acting without my having an opportunity to explain to them why I was visiting the sites I explored. The internet search effort was also different because I was finally beginning to confront the real nature of my conflict, rather than simply attempting to satisfy the latest episode of its manifestation. Previous efforts at research and self-analysis had not helped me resolve my persistent and obsessive compulsion, yet I had embarked again on a journey to discover the illusive hidden treasure of revelation and insight.

If my ISP reviewed the sudden change in the pattern of my web surfing or the apparent nature of many of the sites being accessed, the most logical motive to them would have been a prurient one, but that attribution would have been most incorrect. People I had known for years but did not see on a regular basis were associated with the parent company of the dial-up internet service I had been using. I often would wonder if the company's abrupt cancellation of all ISP service had anything to do with the sites I and other users were visiting. When I phoned their office, the only explanation offered was that the service was not profitable and was a distraction from their main business. I considered asking to speak to one of the people I knew, but rejected that option to avoid possible embarrassment to either or both of us. I did not ask if they had taken exception to some of the sites I had been visiting. Since their service was the medium through which I found my psychiatrist, it might have been appropriate for me to tell someone how critically helpful their service had been.

The information I had obtained before their terminating my service had been sufficient to help me chart a course for the first positive steps toward openly confronting my gender identity conflict. The relative ease of finding a new ISP did not assuage my concern about what the people I had known and liked might have thought they discovered. My snowball was beginning its rapid and irreversible descent down a very steep hill. The concerns that ball represented, as it grew, about where I believed I was headed, what others might think, and how I might act and react to them might embarrass an avalanche by comparison. My path was an unequalled threat to extant relationships precisely when the support of those relationships seemed of unrivaled importance.

Site offerings by, about, and/or for transgendered people ranged from those sponsored by reputable institutions, transgendered people with significant academic and/or professional credentials, clinicians, surgeons, and support groups to a quite different mix of spike-heel and leather undergarment clothiers, people interested in genital mutilation, purveyors of mechanical devices for self stimulation, and pornographers. Not only was being transgendered something that had happened for many people as a major part of their lives, but many of these people were living them in a decidedly un-closeted fashion.

They and those who cared about them were candid about what steps were involved in transition, and where and how the steps might be taken. None of the sites I searched addressed the condition as being a sinful state where resolution through faith alone was the only appropriate answer. Although some sites might have carried such a message, my search was problem-oriented. I found nothing indicating that faith alone had permanently resolved the conflict for anyone. My own faith did help me to and through transition, but it had been unable to resolve, or to help me resolve, the conflict.

Healing by Faith

Except for members of a small number of fringe sects, faith healing alone for some medical conditions would not reasonably be encouraged, nor would it seem likely to be effective. Faith healing and the use of the mind to heal or promote healing offer uneven histories ranging from spectacular successes to ineffectiveness or complications due to postponed conventional treatment. To attempt to apply either approach to heal gender identity conflict would suggest that the subject's gender identity or physical sex needed healing. Essential identity and physical self each was healthy but the two certainly were not compatible in one person.

Some faiths or philosophies would see the conflict as a manifestation of poorly aligned or poorly tuned sub-parts of the whole. Whether the soul, heart, mind, strength, and other human facets are discernibly separate parts, forms, or dimensions of each person has been exhaustively contemplated for ages. Various religions and philosophies profess the validity of their views, which is testimony to the absence of a consensus. These disparate views might contribute to a variety of imaginative explanations for gender identity conflict. Adherents who are not transgendered would almost certainly offer the most imaginative explanations. Like a large number of listeners hearing a poorly written radio play, each would "see" and understand the vexatious specter of festering conflict as a different psychical aberration to which only her or his method offered any real hope for resolution. Exercise, concentration, a pattern of thought, certain ingestible items, etc. would be recommended as the most appropriate means to gender identity harmony.

Consideration of the morality of the condition, if such conditions can be moral or immoral, centers on the fact that the only way presently known, and possibly the only ethically acceptable solution that will ever exist, to effectively resolve gender identity conflict is through changing the body. If it is immoral to change the foreordained physical sex of the body, then all surgery, medicines, and even "natural" remedies are immoral because of the changes they would cause. Nature itself could be considered immoral since age, the sun's radiation, and gravity also change the body.

Faith and prayer can reasonably be asked to accomplish much but asking God to alter the gender identity of one's essential identity is to seek to become someone completely unknown to that self and to God. If such an impossible wish were realized, suddenly being granted a male gender identity in middle age would be little different from finally approximating gender identity consonance through the slower process of transition unless a whole new set of life history, memories, and experiences were part of the gift. That impossible result still would mean that the previous self had no future and the wished for self had no real past. Prokofiev's *Lieutenant Kije Suite,* about a fictitious Russian Army officer created solely to be destroyed in the place of those who actually were responsible for a military blunder, would be wonderfully appropriate theme music for this concept. The idea of creating a new fiction and fraud to replace an existing one would be as desperate in its attempt as it would be tragic in its result.

My momentum toward resolution felt like a response to a force at least as immutable as gravity. The direction was irreversible because I would no more resist taking each next step than I would forsake a scheduled treatment in a battle with cancer or dispose of the world's greatest mystery novel before reading its last chapter. The most compulsive element of my essential self was slowly being revealed to an enthralled audience of one. I was, in a sense, both audience and partial author of a drama more than forty years in its making and its most climactic scenes were finally unfolding.

Hamlet's Bodkin

I had considered internet "hemlock" information and possible methods of suicide when I thought I might not be able to contend with transition. Having another alternative to the impossibility of continued suppression and the seeming improbability of transition restored a limited sense of control of my present and foreseeable future. Yet, searching desperately for another alternative was like trying to repair a flat tire on a car with a blown engine; the conflict that was no longer suppressible had to be resolved. Convincing oneself that there is no acceptable way to resolve, or survive, a crisis can lead to an all-too-common attempt to escape the seemingly intolerable fate by pursuing what would really be a worse fate.

Suicide as a response is rooted in a secular regard for humanity rather than faith in God. Suicide is not a specific answer to a single problem but merely an attempt to escape from the answer or from responsibility for trying to find it. I do believe that, with God's help, such a crisis is not only survivable, but it can be a phenomenally warm and enlightening experience with occasional exceptional moments that feel anything but warm and enlightening. To choose suicide and not that help is to refuse or deny God. To the agnostic or atheist I would offer my experience of having felt very alone and inadequate to pursue transition while relying solely on my own strength. Yet, that is the only option for someone fighting to keep an obsession or compulsion secret. Without the resource of prayer the agnostic or atheist facing the same situation must be in a much more perilous state.

My feeling of desperation initially abated after I began seeing the psychiatrist, understanding the process of transition, and anticipating a future in which my appearance would finally and appropriately reflect my gender identity. Prospects for the condition's successful remediation had brightened from dismal to more moderately bleak. The desperation returned when I wrestled with what seemed the more probable possibility that I might not become more fully female but remain a pathetic example of ineffectively resolved gender identity conflict. Appearing constantly as a kind of cartoon would mean not just being unable to live as before but being unable to exist as anything other than a marginalized oddity on the periphery of society. The condition's "treatment" then would be as bad as if not worse than the ailment.

In a mindset similar to that of an earlier chapter's "old soul," those who attempt suicide must have decided that there is no prospective or even possible conceivable joy worthy of the effort necessary to endure their unpleasant present. They must find their condition beyond remediation and either unbearable or a cause of pointless chronic suffering. These people know that they are a very small part of a vast universe that has existed, and will continue to exist, for an incomprehensively long time. Whatever time the current conscious state of these people shares in that universe already is relatively brief. The possibility of opting for an even more-brief sojourn would seem to demand their comparing what they think they know with the true nature of things known and unknown. This work's "Beyond Appearance" aspect of suicide included a contrast of one's desire to punish with a concern for loved ones. The concern here is also an obligation to oneself to consider one more thought, obtain one more fact, have one more interpersonal experience, view another bit of nature, etc. Even if any or all of these experiences would be unpleasant, something else might be learned. That knowledge will be imperfect and/or incomplete, but the need to acquire it is also part of what it means to be created in His image.

While their suicides might have occurred even if they had rejected transition or might have resulted from circumstances beyond those proximate to transition, some MtF women have found their post-transition lives unacceptable. The psychiatrist or psychologist, in conveying the history of such instances to her or his patient, is acknowledging, and requiring the patient to acknowledge, realistic limits on her expectations for life after transition. The process of transition does not purport to return time that has been lost, change past life experience, substantially alter one's physical stature, and/or alter essential interpersonal relationships. Contending with each of these realities must still be the patient's responsibility, with or without electrolysis, feminizing hormones, counseling, and surgery. There can be no all-encompassing life manual that guarantees pain-free transition for a transgendered person, nor can any competent professional provide a reliable guarantee for successful transition and a "...lived happily ever after" ending.

Inertia's Curse

A local support group established by and for transgendered women hosted one of the many responsible sites discovered in my search. Their site included the phone number of a psychiatrist who was trained for, and experienced in dealing with, transgendered people. Twelve years earlier, I had seen a support-group president with her father when they appeared on a morning talk show. Near the program's end, she provided the group's west coast phone number, which I wrote down and kept carefully hidden. I often thought about calling that number and, several years after seeing the program, actually dialed the number, but I hung up without giving anyone a chance to answer. Talking with a stranger had seemed unlikely to help address what I was sure was the impossibility of realizing my fantasy/obsession. The same pessimism prevailed each time I considered making the call. An actual call would have been my third acknowledgment to another human being in over forty years that my familiar, if uncomfortable, outward life might no longer be tenable. I could not imagine how to contend with everything that admission would mean. The conversations with my mother and with an Army social worker had not mentioned the concept of gender identity, yet this support-group call would have been about nothing else. Still confused about the matter, I resisted seeking help from those seemingly predisposed to a particular view, rather than an objective assessment, for their recommendation. I know now that I should have completed that call.

Surely, Thomas Jefferson did not have this specific problem in mind when he wrote A...all experience hath shown that mankind are more disposed to suffer, while evils are sufferable, than to right themselves by abolishing the forms to which they are accustomed" (U.S. Declaration of Independence).[94] He was referring, though, to a similarly inhibiting inertia. While some MtF women have followed the unwavering direction of their internal compasses at a much earlier age, I had postponed the inevitable for far too long. I had not been ready to make that earlier phone call but was finding it impossible not to call this psychiatrist. The Declaration's next line includes the words "...evinces a design to reduce them under absolute despotism..." (Kashner 2007, 496).[95] This also applies, in a sense, to transgendered people who have been forced by their inherited government and society, and not chosen by any act of their own, to live a life based on the physical sex indicated on their birth certificates, rather than the gender identity of their hearts and minds.

The "F" or "M" on a birth certificate, at present, neither requires nor permits any input from the person who is most affected by the designation when it is assigned. Some in the medical community would say that this is fundamentally a simple matter performed for the benefit of all concerned. Were any other medical matter, of arguably less significance, made without the consent, or even expressed views, of the person most directly affected, the practice would be prohibited. Without revisiting the English and Tory views of the American revolution, a strong case could be made not that the King's motives were those of an uncaring despot but that his benevolent design was simply intended to achieve the greatest possible good for Great Britain and all of the people of its Commonwealth. The nation-forming principle of consent recognized by the United States two centuries ago in matters of government still has not been applied to one of the most fundamental aspects of individual identity.

Those who argue that transgendered people should accede to the common-sense logic of their physical selves and should continue to live the role assigned by government and society also would argue that theirs was not a malicious view, but that a benevolent intent was behind their suggestion. Society's failure to comprehend the distress caused by the unrelenting and irresistible urge to manifest physically the gender identity of the transgendered person's essence cannot justify denial of its existence. Similarly, that failure cannot absolve government, and the society it represents, of its responsibility to alter the fallaciously founded system of continuing to attempt to assign gender based upon physical sex at birth. Time spent waiting for the American political machinery to approve an efficient and equitable regimen may be inconsequential from an abstract and theoretical perspective, but it seems an intolerable near-eternity in practice to those acutely aware of the anguish and frustration of gender identity conflict, and for those who have already been treated unfairly by U.S. courts.

The Right Doctor

Someone in my alma mater's psychology department had said that anyone seeking help should see a psychiatrist for a diagnosis of the problem, a psychoanalyst to find out why she or he had that problem, but a psychologist to bring about a necessary change. This overly-brief summary of the different disciplines glosses over qualifications, methodologies, and treatments, it is especially kind to psychologists, and it doubtlessly was intended to be so by the psychologist who offered it. The fact that practitioners in each area practice some part of the work of the other two was not the point. Certainly, the primary and fundamental difference between psychiatry and psychology was glibly summarized.

Several years before my phone call to the psychiatrist, I had attended an awards dinner where members of the county's mental health department also were present. Through the entirety of the main speaker's message, the department's workers each folded her or his name card into an intricate figure or tore it meticulously into variously sized and shaped pieces. No other person present was similarly preoccupied. It did not occur to me that, despite their unusual behavior, at least one of these workers might be someone with whom I should talk.

Family members and others had expressed disparaging views of people who did not seem able to manage their own problems. I had attempted my own means of behavior modification and realized that behavior alone was not the core of the problem. Although I knew of no friend or relative who ever had seen a psychiatrist, it became increasingly clear that I needed to see this one.

With a nearly paralyzing combination of hope and dread born of an awareness and determination that somehow my forty-something year struggle finally was going to change, I placed the call to the psychiatrist's office that I should have placed twenty or thirty years earlier. He answered his own phone, which removed even that last momentary opportunity to ask if I really intended to do this. I told him where I had found his name and that I thought I needed to talk with him. He briefly described the nature of his practice and what was involved in making an assessment. I said I wanted to think about his comments and we ended the call. Twenty minutes later, I had decided that I really had no acceptable alternative, needed to talk with this man, and might never find anyone better qualified. I called him again, said that I needed to meet with him, and we scheduled my first session.

At that first meeting, I began to release my firehose of futility and frustration at having hidden for so long a fundamental conflict that still seemed irresolvable. I suddenly felt angry that I had never believed before that there was anyone to whom I could reveal it. In retrospect, my willingness to make such revelations to someone I had never met, yet trusted because of his professional qualifications and reputation, was incredible. The act of actually talking aloud about my long-held secret to another person, and especially to someone who might be able to help me do something about it, seemed a therapy of its own. My massive genii had been released from its impossibly small bottle because its time finally had come, and returning it to that bottle was even less possible than it was desired. Like a dramatic alteration of my world's gravitational orientation, the thing I always had been least likely to discuss was now something I no longer was willing to hide, first, from the person who might help me resolve it, and later, from anyone else.

The situation of my being an apparent six-foot and 200-plus pound male who was no longer willing to be seen as a male still seemed a problem beyond any reasonable solution. Yet, anything I had done over my life to the point of this disclosure seemed a tragic farce because I had not been living for any of that time as the person I am. The sham of acting and living as a male without being one, because I could not be one, seemed like a rat's running in a maze with no exit.

I told the psychiatrist that I saw no bearable alternative to a transition that would mean my appearing, for the rest of my life, as an unamusing pseudo clown; as an apparent male wearing make-up and a dress. I asked him to tell me if there were another possible diagnosis or treatment. He said that the symptoms I was describing did not fit many other condition, that it was possible that I was transgendered, and that aversion therapy and other approaches were not effective over time. He also said, as he would each time I raised doubts about a successful transition, that the inevitability of my direction was not inescapable if I could accept an alternative.

The alternative to transition was simply not to do it. I could reveal the conflict to people about whom I most cared but simply go on projecting my masculine façade. I told him that I saw transition as unavoidable but that I thought its prospects for success were incredibly poor. He told me that twenty-six weekly sessions were necessary for him to have a sufficient basis for making his assessment, that I should begin electrolysis, and that I should arrange to see an endocrinologist to begin hormone therapy. While the steps to begin altering my physical appearance might be discontinued at any time for anyone less certain of her direction, I could not begin them soon enough. I saw them as tangible steps down the path I both dreaded and was eager to tread.

My pessimism regarding the effort's outcome would be raised and addressed repeatedly during the six months of our meetings and was usually expressed as one of three sometimes concurrent sentiments. I a) regretted having lived for so long a life of falsehood and wished fervently that I had begun transition decades earlier, b) wished there were an alternative and effective means of resolving the conflict such as medication or neurosurgery that would not require transition, and c) feared that the eventual outward manifestation of my female self would be spectacularly unsatisfying. Each time the third sentiment was expressed, I reverted to another search for an acceptable alternative and fail to find one. The superficial interest in a neurosurgical or medical approach other than sex-reassignment surgery had no basis in my wishing to remain physically male but rather only in my reaching an alternate effective resolution to the intractable conflict.

The least disruptive of alternatives was to stop the sessions, the hormone therapy, the visits to the electrologist, and to resume living the lie that was universally accepted, except by me. It should have been impossible for everyone I knew to accept me as a male when I no longer was willing to accept and project that male image. Before talking with my psychiatrist, endocrinologist, and post-op transgendered people, I was the only person who was beginning to understand that my gender identity was not male. It had become time for the lie to end. The electrolysis and hormone treatment would start and, after I could tell those people I wanted to tell about it, I would begin presenting a more gender identity-appropriate appearance.

Further sessions with my doctor dealt with various life experiences, aspects of my character, and dreams. In every instance, I was truthful and cooperative with him. Even though he probably would have immediately detected any deceit or reticence, either one only would have made his job of helping me more difficult. I fully had disclosed my life-long secret to him in our first session. I saw him not as a gatekeeper between conflict resolution and a previous stasis but as a qualified professional whose help was essential finally to resolve the conflict.

In Olive Drab

I had come close to revealing the whole of my gender identity conflict to a social worker in the Army. At that time I had thought or hoped my problem was just a desire to appear feminine, but I had no idea what that meant. The social worker probably had no better an idea what gender identity conflict was than I did. He was satisfied with his paramount conclusion that I had no interest in an homogendered relationship with any of the men around me, and that, at least, was accurate. He did attempt to note ways in which I was and was not adjusting to life in basic training, but he lacked the academic preparation, professional experience, and informed inclination to consider that the absence of other women in my environment might have something to do with my difficulty in living only with men as a man.

An Army psychiatrist I had seen earlier was only concerned about whether or not I was rational and mentally fit for service. His decision that I was and his failure to pursue the matter beyond those points meant that I had missed another opportunity to obtain a diagnosis from someone presumably qualified to provide it and to begin the process of resolving it. He actually was angry with me for having added to his over-burdening case load of people he deemed worthy of his help. That the condition could be so cavalierly dismissed or not even considered in my case means that it must also have been ignored in countless others. Establishing a regimen that would require qualified professionals to explore the general mental health and, especially, the gender identities of those having seemingly non-specific adjustment problems, or even no apparent problems at all would require the commitment of considerable additional resources this country might be unwilling to expend. Justification for that allocation though would be little different from that which established the current requirement that a general physical examination be performed in screening all candidates for military service. How else could President Trump's or anyone else's mandate to exclude transgendered people from military service be accomplished?

The difference, most practitioners probably would see between the two types of examinations is that patients usually come to physicians wanting to reveal their physical ailments in anticipation of their being returned to a state of good health. Those experiencing severe mental distress may exhibit unavoidable signs of abnormality that invite or compel professional intervention, but others may well attempt to hide their condition out of fear, shame, embarrassment, or for other reasons. A transgendered woman, unsure of the precise nature of her conflict and determined to avoid the presumed crisis of the condition's being revealed to her friends, family, and others, would surrender knowledge of that conflict only under a very limited set of circumstances.

The brief examination by a presumably qualified Army psychiatrist had failed to reveal my gender identity conflict due to his lack of time, inclination, and/or expertise necessary to discover it. His discovery would have meant a dramatically different life for me over the decades following military service, and for however many other suppressing transgendered women had the misfortune to encounter such a doctor who served the Army which paid him rather than his patients. If this situation is not considered a breach of medical ethics, one might be forgiven for wondering why not.

To Be a Wife

The psychiatrist I saw regarding transition did not share the conundrum of the Army doctor's loyalty and did have the requisite interest, inclination, and expertise to address my conflict. As I started the sessions with him, the previously irrepressible urge to "dress" vanished. The pulse-pounding interest in, and anticipation of wearing, any of the clothes, makeup, or any other vestige associated with my suppressed identity disappeared. Prospects for my finally becoming as physically female as possible quickly became a most satisfying substitute for the old cycle of suppression and partial release, even as anxiety regarding other aspects of transition persisted. There could not be a clearer indication that suppressing the conflict was the root of each of those decades of compulsive thought and aberrant behavior. I no longer had any interest in the wigs, inexpensive makeup, and cheap jewelry although some of the clothing remained as an active part of my wardrobe.

My imagined interactions in home, work, social, and other environments during and after magically being as fully feminine as possible had been unlimited by reality, like any other fantasy where its author seems to control its variables. I now readily moved beyond that fantasy to new consideration of a possible role as a real wife to my husband and even an adoptive mother to our children. These aspirations had been much more remote a possibility than the seemingly impossible fantasy of transition but they now were as pearls in an ever-straighter row. Each visit with my doctor was taking me a step closer to the possibility that such a future relationships could exist.

As an adolescent female, I might have regarded many men as possible mates and been thrilled at the prospect of spending time with them romantically as well as in cultural, educational, recreational, and other pursuits. The fantasized candle-lit dining room setting as I sat, wearing a full-length evening dress, opposite a nice-looking, well-groomed Mr. X in an expertly tailored suit, the deep-red wine contrasting with the white table linen, soft music, and pleasant conversation would all fly by much too quickly to reward adequately the effort of its imagining. There must be few enduring emotional memories as gratifying as being part of such an intimate experience and in a relationship with a person with whom one really wanted to spend time. The common motivational basis for becoming a part of such a relationship, both historically and from a religious perspective, is that each person is part of a whole couple who then share the, at least theoretical, prospect of becoming parents. For a variety of reasons, members of many couples know that their prospects for becoming natural parents are quite remote. For a transgendered post-transition woman, that prospect is presently not only remote but nonexistent.

As unlikely as might be the pairing of any "perfect" couple from the million and more extant possibilities, it seems even less likely that there exists a male whose desire for a spouse includes someone of my physical description, interests, and outlook who would also appeal to me on a similar basis. During a wedding I witnessed as a child, the minister said it was remarkable that, of all the women in the world, the groom had found his bride. Each of the couple was from our small town. I was certain that there must have been at least one woman on a remote island in Micronesia that the groom had not considered. That island native well might be my only prospective husband, and I have not even thought about how to get there to look.

Other transgendered MtF women have not only accepted the possible existence of one such mate, but they have discovered or convinced themselves that such males are legion. If an MtF woman finds affirmation of her own identity in the presence of one or more men who she believes accept her as being physically female without understanding who she really is, she may find their acceptance to be so satisfying and ingratiating that she is reluctant to disclose her past. When that past is discovered she not only risks the loss of the relationship with that man or men, but she loses the affirmation and acceptance of the person she longed to be and thought, for a time, she was. As I have consistently asserted, an MtF woman during and after transition is as much concerned about manifesting her true identity as she is determined to live as her essential self. This certainty is a consequence of the decades of struggle, of intellectual and psychological maturity, of cumulative life experience, and of other aspects of life for a later-transitioning MtF woman. It is not dependent upon the affirmation and acceptance of others and, as welcome as that experience is, self-awareness is not lost, impaired, or even threatened when others reject, or deny, essential identity.

The importance of each person's self-awareness and discovery, rather than reliance on the identity suggested by others, is difficult to overstate. The earlier work of mental health professionals who suggested the latter has done great harm to transgendered people and to all with whom they share a part of their lives. Drs. Diamond and Sigmundson have decried the persistence of the disproven myth that gender identity can be assigned (Diamond and Sigmundson 1997 298, 303).[96] The insidious myth is still widely accepted by the general medical community with the notable exception of the mental health disciplines. Yet even Dr. Money appears to have abandoned his hypothesis of assignable gender identity. In 1986, Dr. Money described gender identity, regardless of its origin, as something present in each person, separate from one's physiology, rooted firmly in one's psyche, and irreversible by any known means (Money 1986, 102).[97] That certainly was not his view when he first tried to help Bruce/Brenda/ David Reimer.

Other people would see themselves vicariously in the romantic scene quite differently. A bigendered person might identify with the interests of either, or both, of the female and the male in the scene. A homogendered female or male (with consonant gender identity and physical sex) would not identify with the aspirations of either person but would want each to have the same gender identity. A heterogendered FtM man reasonably would share the desires of the male. An MtF lesbian woman would wish for a female-to-female relationship. There are other possibilities but, for those who are honest with themselves, such imaginings manifest from, rather than determining, their gender identities.

Something about Dad

My father had dual carotid endarterectomies performed in a hospital near our valley homes during the autumn preceding my transition. The surgeries went smoothly, healed well, and made possible our family's celebrating an even more joyous Christmas. During the following January and February in Florida, Dad began developing a knot or swelling in his neck that we believed was related to his surgeries. His primary doctor in Florida did not think there was much reason for concern and said he suspected that an accumulation of fluid had resulted from one of the endarterectomies. When the swelling had not resolved in a reasonable amount of time, his doctor still was not concerned but recommended Dad's seeing a specialist nearby if Dad so desired. The specialist recommended Dad's returning to the doctor who had performed his surgeries as soon as possible to obtain an analytical biopsy. The second doctor was concerned but did not mention the possibility of cancer. We later decided that the specialist had probably been almost certain that it was cancer.

My niece was a senior at a university in Wisconsin and was pursuing a dual major in performance piano and English. Her senior recital was scheduled for April. Mother planned to fly to Wisconsin for the recital if I could return to Florida to be with Dad and their two bichon frises. I had resolved to tell both parents about my long-kept secret and the steps I was taking toward resolution after Mother returned from Wisconsin. They would be the first people I would tell who were not medical practitioners directly involved in the first steps of transition.

It was a strange sensation to know that I had begun taking feminizing hormones, hours of electrolysis, and sessions with my psychiatrist without mentioning any of this in phone calls with those closest to me. My understated telephone response that not much was happening was a bit more spin than even the most enthusiastic practitioners of that questionable art might abide. I certainly was not a child, but I had previously shared almost everything except my gender identity conflict with my parents. Having decided to reveal that secret as it became necessary, I found incredibly awkward the wait to tell them but saw no acceptable alternative.

Telling

The sessions with my psychiatrist and my progress on transition's path were interrupted by the spring trip back to Florida. When I had returned to my home from Florida after Christmas, I weighed more than I ever had in my life. As I began to see my psychiatrist and to progress toward a future that was becoming increasingly clear in the short term but much less clear thereafter, I also intentionally began losing weight. My weight-loss plan was not healthful but it was both simple and effective. I stopped eating most foods and accepted hunger as an indication of progress toward finally attaining an outward appearance more in harmony with the person I believed myself to be. I had lost over fifty pounds when I flew back to Sarasota less than four months later, and was surprised when my mother did not immediately recognize me as I descended the airport's escalator to the baggage claim area. I had told my parents about having lost weight in the intervening months but had not even considered that they might not recognize me. An explanation that I had been too heavy seemed to satisfy their curiosity.

Mother, Dad, and I celebrated her return from Wisconsin and my niece's impressive recital with dinner at a local restaurant as I again wondered how my parents would react to the revelation I was about to make. Details about my niece's recital, those who attended it, and events before and after it would have been far more compelling if I had not been thinking about what I was about to do. My two sisters and their husbands had attended the recital and Mother had brought a video tape home for her to hear again, and us to enjoy, the marvelous performance.

Everything seemed amazingly normal as we ate meals like ones we had eaten so many times before in that restaurant's very familiar setting with people we often saw there. I knew I was about to disclose something that would make that night very different for each of us. As well as I thought I knew my parents, I still could not imagine what the experience of hearing such news would be for either one of them, but I was about to find out what it was like to tell it. Waiting until after the Wisconsin trip had meant that Mother was able to enjoy her talented granddaughter's work and a wonderful week with the family, but there was no longer a reason for further delay. Each segment of the twelve-mile drive back to the house seemed to be passing too quickly and too slowly at the same time. Mother was driving their car so that I did not have even that distraction from anticipating the conversation that was about to occur. The feeling was oddly like that I had when I was acquiring or expecting to wear my gender-identity appropriate clothing.

We pulled into the garage and she removed the key from the ignition. I asked my parents to stay in the car for a moment. That in itself was unusual. After only a moment's breathless silence I asked if they knew what a "transsexual" was. I was not yet sufficiently familiar with talking about the condition to realize how inappropriate that term is. They asked why and I told them because I was one. They were not familiar with the term and asked what that meant. I answered that, among other things, it meant I eventually was going to begin to look different. I explained that my mind was not being changed chemically or through surgery. I told them that my psychiatrist had said it was precisely because of the inability to alter the mind's concept of gender identity that my body would be altered. All of this meant that, rather than my becoming someone else, I was finally going tobecome more fully the person I always had been.

I told them the doctor's explanation of the theory about something occasionally not changing in the development of a fetus so that the egg's gender identity remains female while the other changes that normally occur to create a physical male continue. The result is the birth of a physical male with a female gender identity. I also told them that, for the same theory to explain FtM men, only the gender identity portion of the brain would become male and the remainder of the fetus would remain female.

If the two conditions shared the same genesis, then it would be possible that determination of gender identity was not part of a process but a single event. The theory of abnormal estrogen levels in *utero* affecting establishment of gender identity in fetal development but having little impact on other aspects of development may be less intuitive yet quite valid. I explained the BSTc (the bed nucleus of the *stria terminalus)* study (Zhou, et. Al. 1995)[98] which found an area associated with sexual behavior in the autopsied brains of MtF women to be much more like that of other women than of heterogendered and of homogendered men. The brain area studied had previously been identified with sexual behavior. A subsequent effort confirming the 1995 study had not yet occurred (Kruijver, et. al. 2000).[99] It did not occur to me at the time to wonder if the nature of the small affected area of the brain being studied might be the result, rather than the cause of, transition, although this possibility was discounted by the researchers. I did tell my parents that, regardless of the condition's origin, my doctor had assured me that his diagnosis would be based on the evidence before him and that he would make his determination in my case after meeting with me for six months. Primarily because of my intervening trip to Florida, we would actually meet for 27 sessions over nine months.

When I told Mother and Dad about being transgendered, I was doing something without precedent. There had been very few times during my life when I told them something they did not expect to hear. No previous declaration had approached this magnitude, nor had it been something they so fervently wished were not true. Later that evening, Mother asked if there was anything she or Dad had done to cause the condition. Because the doctor's explanation described an *in utero* origin, and because it had always seemed so important to me to hide the condition, I said there was really no opportunity for either of them knowingly to have been responsible for it. We did not discuss long-past opportunities to have explored the condition when I was a child.

Our being largely unaware of the concept of gender identity meant that the discussion focused on the less accurate idea of brain sex. Appropriate knowledge and understanding are the absent raft by which I might have escaped my figurative stranding on the remote, featureless, and desolate atoll that is suppression of gender identity. I told my parents about some of the childhood, teen, and later "dressing" experiences that I had always been careful to hide. The human tendency to deny unexpected and unwelcome news may have helped my parents to recall instances of conventional masculine behavior they thought would somehow prove that what I was telling them could not be true.

Whether the condition is hereditary, is due to specific abnormal development of the fetus, or is caused by factors present or absent in the mother's biochemistry either at a key moment or throughout her pregnancy, the condition's innate origin strongly suggests a causative biological process that should be detectable. If the process has a genetic cause, then the condition might be an hereditary trait. One or more of my ancestors might have contended with gender identity conflict, and done so without the medical and surgical treatments or the literature and support groups that now help transgendered people and their families understand the condition. A compassionate spouse, suppression, and suicide would also have been choices open to these ancestors, if they could not "pass" in the society of their day.

An agrarian ancestor might have manifested her conflicting identity quite openly to farm animals and nature but then felt uncomfortable and even ashamed among people in her community. If there is an hereditary genetic trait, I may have had more in common with that agrarian ancestor than with my contemporary relatives. There is no family lore regarding an odd great-great "Uncle Alice." My paternal family's Daguerreotypes contain no hint of an ancestor who shared the transgendered experience. Had there been such an indication, my path to and through transition would almost certainly have been unchanged, since awareness and understanding are often associated by only the finest of threads.

After my disclosure our family followed an otherwise normal evening routine but on waking the next morning, I found that my mother had not slept all night. She asked how our fundamental relationship would change and I again attempted to assure her that it was precisely because I intended to be more myself than I had ever been that I really did not believe there would be a dramatic change. My formal education certainly would be unchanged, so too my sense of ethics and morality. The people I knew and with whom I had been associated were not expected to change unless they thought a change was necessary.

Later that afternoon Mother took some things she no longer wore from her closet and, for the next hour or so, I tried on various articles of clothing and jewelry that she thought I might use. A suit that she could not wear did fit rather well and I modeled it for her and my father. It had been forty years since they had seen me in gender identity-appropriate clothes, but this time it happened honestly and with understanding rather than from pretense and confusion. The experience was not embarrassing but I was still not ready to begin appearing in public that way. If my parents found this different appearance any more troubling than the things I had told them, they did not say so.

After again being assured there was nothing either of them had done intentionally that had contributed to my having a transgendered identity, Mother said they had decided to offer help with the expenses of transition. One caveat, she said, was that she wanted to be at the hospital during surgery. Dad's cancer had not been diagnosed at this time, and we knew of no reason why an eventual date for my surgery should conflict with anything on their calendar.

This incredible twenty-four hours progressed for the three of us with a hoped for and most welcome tenderness and sensitivity. Those sentiments were afforded in much smaller amounts, or were nonexistent, in the more trying experiences of other MtF women when they told their families and friends of their intention to begin transition. The nature of a person's no-longer suppressible gender identity is as uncompromising as the inability of some people to accept it. When those uncompromising natures belong to family members or friends, the unfortunate and unavoidable prospect is separation.

Home Again

After leaving Florida and returning to the valley, both parents attended one of my sessions with the psychiatrist. The doctor told them, as he had told me, about his understanding of the condition's genesis and answered several questions they posed. My parents confirmed that my gender identity revelation had been a complete surprise to them and that I had never given them any reason to question my gender identity. I do not remember that the doctor asked them if they believed I was transgendered or if they had difficulty accepting the possibility but I am almost certain that he did. If so, they would have said they believed what I had told them and that I would not be progressing toward transition if there were an acceptable alternative.

After beginning electrolysis, I met two other MtF women and their impressively large dog. The women lived and worked near my psychiatrist's office and he had suggested, during my first session with him, that I might contact them regarding the support group they had started. I met with them several times but I never attended any of the support group gatherings. During my first visit I drove with one of them to lunch at a nearby restaurant. I had never knowingly spoken with a postoperative transgendered person before and wanted to know how much different she thought my life during and after transition might be. We shared a pleasant meal, she told me about many of her experiences, and she answered several of my questions.

On the way back to their office/home we passed a nicely-dressed woman walking briskly on the sidewalk. I said, appreciating this first-ever freedom of expressing the thought to another human being, "I want to do that." My new acquaintance knew precisely what I meant and she said that at their support meetings they referred laughingly to the yearning as "vagina envy." This coarse twist on the disparaging term often used regarding women's efforts to shatter the glass ceiling or to fill positions previously held by men was especially ironic since MtF women could expect to experience an even more severe bias in employment.

My father accompanied me during at least one subsequent session with the psychiatrist. I had not been getting enough sleep and Dad was concerned that I might fall asleep during one of the lengthy trips to see the psychiatrist, the endocrinologist, or the electrologist since each practitioner's office was located roughly an hour's drive from home. I took Dad to meet the MtF women after he and I had attended a session. I was still wearing male clothing but their transitions were behind them and they were suitably dressed.

I introduced them to Dad and we discussed a variety of subjects in lighter conversation. One of them asked how Dad felt about having a transgendered daughter, because they also had fathers who did, and he said something about its being different. His saying anything less would have been denial and anything more might have been dishonest. He consistently appeared to accept the reality that my gender identity would no longer be suppressed. This was not the first time he had accepted and adapted to a reality that was far different from the one he wanted or for which he had planned.

Each of the MtF women had more difficult family adjustments to make during transition than I but, possibly because I was still dressing as a male, they seemed reserved about discussing their transitions with me. They did not assume that, because I had started along transition's path, I must be transgendered. They were even skeptical about the capacity of mental health professionals to diagnose correctly the condition we shared, even though each of them had obtained that diagnosis. They were firm believers in the Harry Benjamin Standards' one-year "real life test" whether or not they had waited that long before their own surgeries. Our cordial meeting lasted about a half hour, and Dad and I left their home to get ahead of the city's rush-hour traffic. Dad and I might have discussed any of a wide range of aspects to our meeting during that ride home, but our conversation touched lightly on their appearance and a bit more on the fact that they were actively and constructively living healthy and productive lives.

When my parents went with me to see my endocrinologist a couple weeks after our return to the valley, I was still a couple months away from beginning the "real life test". I wanted my parents to meet each of the doctors involved in my transition and thought the endocrinologist would like to meet them too. The discussion included mention of our awaiting Dad's biopsy results that were our first indication and confirmation that he had non-Hodgkin's lymphoma.

Dad was still referring to me as "he" and "him" when my parents and I were together, which he may have been doing from habit. I was still dressing as a male, though, and he still may have been thinking of me as his son. When he did this in the endocrinologist's office, the doctor corrected Dad. He told Dad he had another daughter. Until that moment, no other person had referred to me deliberately in a gender identity-appropriate manner, regardless of my appearance. The doctor's acknowledgment of the significance of gender identity, especially regarding, or because of, his other transgendered patients, was impressive. He was one of the small group in whom I had confided since I began seeing the psychiatrist. Each member of that group knew I was intensely serious about transition but none of them showed the slightest indication of expecting my transition to be either an unparalleled success or unequivocal failure. Throughout my transition, Dad's successful battle with cancer, and the intervening years of his recovery, his referring to me using masculine pronouns was infrequent at most, and always seemed inadvertent. An incident recounted later in this work suggested, at least momentarily, that might not have been true.

13. Stepping Out

What It Will Be

My mother told me repeatedly she was concerned that after surgery I might find the reality of my altered anatomy to be disappointingly different from what I expected. With each repetition, I replied that it could not be different from my expectation because I had no similar experience with which to compare it and I could not imagine how it would be. Each astronaut who walked on the moon must have anxiously anticipated his journey before launch and visualized actually being on that orb. Even after having practiced far more realistic simulations than I could approximate, the reality of their first lunar steps must have been exponentially more powerful for them than anything they expected, despite their extensive rehearsals.

The process of manipulating male anatomy to approximate a post-operative contour does achieve the desired cosmetic result, but that effect is far different from the result of surgery. It is as difficult to recall the reality of that pre-surgery physiology, despite having lived with it decades, as it was previously to imagine the post-op experience. I do not regret the surgery, wish it had occurred decades earlier, and wish it could have been even more complete.

Much is made in comedy and drama of the differences, inferences, and implications of genital anatomy precisely because most people only fully experience one set throughout her or his lifetime. I have heard many males talk about their own and female anatomy when they thought I was male. While few women would be surprised by much of the content of those conversations, I do not remember hearing a single comment that could remotely be construed as expressed or disguised envy. I was never able to contribute to these conversations. I did not share the inclinations of those males and dared not share my own with them.

Normal psychology blesses its owner with so strong a sense of the present that fantasies of what might be are a distinctly intangible construct. Mental images permit one to imagine, but not wholly experience, the sensory perceptions of sight, sound, touch, taste and smell. The pairing of the whole of that perceived reality with one's desires and expectations over time, and a person's determination to reconcile herself or himself with less pleasant aspects of that reality help set the parameters of satisfaction each person feels with her or his life. For many people, faith is the primary facilitator of that reconciliation.

Faith calls believers to attempt to influence constructively those things they are able to improve while helping them accept the things they cannot. The process of such considerations does not slow or stop during an MtF woman's transition but may be more intense than at any other time in her life. Gender identity conflict ultimately feeds the compulsion to pursue a life-altering unknown to achieve whole gender harmony because the dissonant present state no longer is tenable. Faith is a guide to accepting the need for resolution and an indispensable aid to addressing the anxieties that attend it.

The temptation to call the above perceptions "reality" is resisted by some who call that reality an illusion. Their premise is usually that the reason for human existence is not centered on, or even related to, that reality. Without attempting to explore the nearly limitless philosophical and psychological implications of this thought, adherents must have some explanation for, or conception of, their own sense of consciousness. However that entity is defined, transgendered people are evidence that it has a gender identity as one of its primary components and most fundamental characteristics.

Spreading the News

My younger sister had come home for a weekend visit after hearing of Dad's lymphoma diagnosis, and I planned to tell her about my transition at an opportune moment. While she and I were in the kitchen of my parents' home and I was preparing a late evening snack for us, Mother came into the kitchen. In the presence of this person who was so important to each of us, I told my sister using almost the same words I had used with my parents. I was surprised to see her tearful reaction as she said that she was just thinking, in characteristic empathy, about how unhappy I must have been.

Greater distance, difficulty traveling, and work scheduling meant that my older sister and her family would not come home to see Dad until after I had begun "presenting." While I would have preferred a face-to-face meeting for the disclosure, a flight for that sole purpose was not practical. The alternative, that people all over my hometown would know before she did, was unacceptable. With my parents present, I called her and told her I had some news. When she said that my birth certificate certified that I was male, I replied emphatically "I know, and 'they' got it wrong!" She asked if I was angry and I said "Not at you, but I might be able to work up a rather warm rage toward those responsible for the errant indication on my birth certificate." That would, of course, be ridiculous because medical science still lacks a test for gender identity nor a means to achieve one-hundred-percent congruence.

In the long months since deciding to meet with my psychiatrist, I had repeatedly experienced feelings of anguish, anxiety, guilt, joy, and many other emotions. I do not believe I had even thought about being angry at my circumstance until that moment. The fact that I had spent more than forty years trying to be what a piece of paper said I was had suddenly seemed to make anger a grossly inadequate descriptor for the sentiment. That path, though, offered no constructive prospect and the feeling subsided almost as quickly as it had arisen. It would not be constructive to see myself as the victim of an unintended universal conspiracy.

The absence of visual communication and the ability to touch during this conversation was deeply regretted. As intimately as I know the experience of conveying such information, I only know indirectly what it must be to receive it. Hearing such news over the telephone must be especially difficult. Like viewing an uncaptioned foreign-language film, its audience is keenly aware that an important, or even essential, part of the intended communication is not being received. Absence of physical presence while conveying such a message may give it an unreal quality so that, if the listener just broke the connection, the conversation and its reality might not have occurred.

There is another dimension to the unreality of that revelation. If there is a feeling of losing someone close during the call, the person missed was never wholly real. Rationally, the feeling would be like waking from a dream where Martians, dinosaurs, or "...one pearl of great value..." (Matt. 13: 46) were illusions firmly secured behind the veil of sleep (National Council 1989).[100] The danger, problem, opportunity, prized item, or other factual basis, if any, for the dream is part of a real present where one's talents, skills, intellect, and other resources can be employed to deal with the matter. The no-longer suppressing transgendered person is the essence or factual basis behind the fraud that had been portrayed, but the fraud was never a whole person. Each of the people I told, most of whom had known "me" all of my life, was being asked to make this kind of adjustment.

The First Day

When I began presenting a gender identity-appropriate appearance, I had not cut my hair in six months, had completed seventeen sessions with the psychiatrist and fifty-five hours of electrolysis, and three months of hormone treatment. There had to be a first day, but it had not seemed important to the psychiatrist or me whether it occurred after our first, tenth, or twentieth session. I had hoped that a dramatic change from the hormone therapy and electrolysis might make the appropriate time evident, but that never happened. There was no flashing green light, clanging opening bell, or shot from a starter pistol. Like the moment when suppression was no longer possible, the appropriate time seemed dependent on an internal clock. I had found transition inevitable and yet, had not felt prepared to take the next step. The link I was clinging to was to the only past I ever had known. Transition was a break from, rather than an extension of, that past. The fact that each person's present links her or his past and future seemed too short of particulars to apply. Ultimately, I was waiting for me.

My preliminary "dressing" day was a Sunday afternoon in late June. I took some of my clothes and makeup to my parents' home and dressed there. My parents, having talked with my psychiatrist and endocrinologist and seen me in Mother's extra clothing in Florida, were not surprised and said they thought I looked "nice." They had known this was coming but had no clearer sign when it would be appropriate than I did.

Mother asked if she might tell one of her close friends about my impending presentation and I said yes, if that person would not tell anyone else. Like many other MtF women in transition, I thought there might be an intimate group of people who would know. I still did not know how people would react, how I would react to their reactions, nor whether I should move to another community where each encounter would be new and unencumbered by the history of acquaintance with a fraudulent male persona. After telling my family, the people I intended to include in my group of informed intimates and the people they would tell quickly grew beyond any semblance of control. Keeping a list of people who knew quickly became as meaningless as it was futile. Still, the lifelong habit of not revealing my gender identity was not easily broken.

The first non-family member I told about my impending transition was my next-door neighbor whom I had known her for roughly twenty years. Before her husband died, these dear friends often spent warm and pleasant afternoons on their front porch alone or with members of their large family. I envied their weekend family gatherings that filled their home with playing children, pleasant conversation, and copious laughter. The tomatoes and peppers from the couple's backyard garden that they graciously shared always were delicious. Their banana peppers were an especially welcome addition to scrambled eggs.

As she sat on a front porch chair, we chatted about the weather, traffic, and other pleasantries until I told her I was going to begin looking a bit different. Although nervous, I explained that I had been seeing a doctor about the matter and that "presenting" was the next step. She got up from her chair and asked me to come toward her. Her hug was unexpected, warm, gracious, and unforgettably appreciated. She said she had noticed my longer hair and weight loss but had not guessed the reason.

A couple days after my preliminary gender identity-appropriate appearance in my parent's home, they and I agreed on a first outing to a favorite cafeteria thirty miles from our homes. In the late afternoon of a beautiful sunny Wednesday, and the same day I had told my neighbor, I stepped out of my back door wearing a blue dress and heels with nails polished, my hair carefully combed, and carefully-applied makeup. I expected to be nervous but was not, although I was quite self-conscious. I got into my parents' van and we had a pleasant forty-mile ride to a favorite cafeteria. As we waited in line to get, and then fill, our trays, I kept expecting everyone to be staring at me, but no one was. When we were seated and enjoying our meals, I casually but frequently glanced around the dining rooms. I was certain that someone must be aware that I was doing something I had never done before in my life. No one was staring at me, and no one suddenly and deliberately averted her or his gaze. Each person was simply enjoying a delicious meal.

After dinner, Mother and I shopped in a nearby mall where my radar of self-consciousness kept picking up false positives of laughter and whispered conversation about me. I was certain that someone would be pointing, giggling, or worse, but that was not happening. Those I had thought were focusing on me simply were more interested in their own lives. I was self-conscious and apprehensive, but I was not ashamed or embarrassed. When we repeated the shopping trip a week later, even my visit to a kiosk jeweler for ear-piercing did not stir untoward interest. I was behaving as normally as I could while doing things I had never done before. The anticipated masses of mockers never arrived.

When I got home on this "first" day, I removed the makeup, changed back to my customary male attire, and went over to my parents' home. The next day I also wore male clothing and no makeup but wondered why I seemed to be following the former routine of restricted use of gender identity-appropriate clothing. I have not appeared in male clothing since that day. Several months after sex-reassignment surgery, I put on a suit I had been saving for one of my brothers-in-law. I was intensely satisfied to find that I looked like a woman wearing a man's suit.

The Friday that I began "dressing" fulltime was another beautiful summer day, and almost all of our neighbors were outside when I walked over to my parents' home. It was absurd to think I could pass them unnoticed or to ask them to keep my appearance secret. As I walked my parents' two bichon frises, I saw, and was seen by, other neighbors. The list I had thought would be so important to keep was including an exponentially increasing number of who knew. It was soon evident that moving away was still possible but controlling who knew about my transition was not.

Much as nature "abhors" a vacuum, small and tightly knit communities must abhor secrecy because they have developed an amazingly efficient means to thwart it. One might imagine duly authorized representatives of nature and small towns formally deciding which things they shall abhor and which they will merely dislike. For town representatives, adolescents on skateboards doubtlessly would be an example of the former, probably ranked second after secrecy. Their list of dislikes would certainly include anything that threatened their sense of community.

In small communities, an ever vigilant, especially perceptive, or keenly observant person notices something, whether subtle or profound, and tells a friend who tells a friend, each of whom knows, knows someone who knows, or knows of the person to whom that something applies. What the method may lack in detail, perspective, or accuracy, it makes up for in speed. A similar process may begin in larger communities but the greater number of probable permutations reduces the mechanism's effectiveness. Whether from concern, curiosity, self-interest, a sense of obligation, or a mix of these, people in and around my hometown who knew little or nothing else about me quickly heard about my new appearance.

A regular session with my psychiatrist was scheduled for the Monday following my "first" day. I was wearing a summer suit and, after the session, I visited the electrologist's office and the MtF women I had met. None of them was surprised by my appearance because, during the several months I had been seeing them, I had talked with them about transition. The electrologist's office had been recommended by my psychiatrist. Its owner had relatives in my hometown and she thought, to allay any concern for confidentiality, I would be more comfortable with one of her associates. I could not imagine continuing to suppress my gender identity but appreciated her discretion. None of the people

I was seeing was either encouraging or discouraging regarding transition. They each seemed acutely aware that disclosure of suppressed identity after decades of suppression is a singularly intense private journey whose pace is set by the traveler. The help of others, though, is essential and appreciated.

After I began "dressing," it still made no sense to wear makeup for electrolysis sessions. Even after one hundred hours of electrolysis, there was still more than enough facial hair to be embarrassing if I had not shaved and applied makeup. Shaving, like makeup, made the electrologist's work less efficient and, therefore, more expensive. The few times I had a session with the psychiatrist after electrolysis, I applied makeup in the car before going to his office. I always wanted my appearance to reflect the importance it had for me, before and after transition, even if that meant applying makeup too soon after electrolysis.

My electrologist's office was on the second floor of a two-story building in a strip mall. The first floor included a popular restaurant and, as I hurried from my parking space toward the office door for a session, two hardhat-clad construction workers were headed toward that restaurant. After passing me, one of them said in a raised voice "*What*, the h***, was that?" He obviously did not care what I thought of his question but wanted everyone within hearing to know what he thought of my appearance. This presumably masculine male probably had seen other MtF women under similar circumstances. His defensive assertiveness suggests that he must have felt threatened by them. Though infrequent, such reactions are not unique.

Benchmarks

The restrooms that served the mall's second-floor offices were at the end of a long hall. My new appearance meant that I would no longer visit the facilities for men and now needed to use the electrologist office's key for the women's restroom. During my first legitimate visit to a women's restroom, I found that the water was just as wet, the paper towels were as absorbent, but the men's room had never been locked and the women's always was. My appropriate use of a facility intended for use only by women was not an overwhelming or thrilling experience but it was gratifying. Like so many other aspects of transition though, it was only new once.

The fact that I was no longer pretending to be a man did not, nor could it, cause anyone to regard me as female. While I could influence the reactions of others, I knew that I could not control those reactions. The manner in which I wished to be regarded would be seen, and either accepted or rejected, by those

I encountered. As I accepted my inability to control others, I became more resolved that I would no longer permit their reactions to influence the way I thought about myself. This crucial aspect of relationships probably seems elementary to most people as something they learned, perhaps painfully, in childhood or adolescence. For those who have spent decades avoiding a critical part of their own identities, however, the way a suppressing MtF woman is perceived by others who were and are important to her is, in some respects, paramount. Accepting her gender identity permits her to develop a more healthful attitude toward relationships. A more balanced perspective does not encourage callousness or dismissiveness but when repeated post-transition efforts to address or reach beyond an acquaintance's bias are rebuffed, reduced voluntary contact becomes inevitable.

In a lighter moment, Shakespeare suggested "The quality of mercy is not strained; it droppeth as the gentle rain from heaven…" (Shakespeare 1975/n.d., 222).[101] I might have accepted that statement in a literal sense before transition, but I did not fully understand its power until it became so much a part of my own experience. Those responding to my appearance during transition fell into three general categories. Some chose spontaneously and immediately to offer either a literal or figurative embrace, others were upset and recommended my seeking alternative counseling, and a third group were openly hostile and offered copious amounts of sarcasm or profanity to someone they saw as unacceptably different. Friends, neighbors, and life-long acquaintances frequently exhibited an apparently spontaneous and fundamentally honest perception that my expression of gender identity was genuine, or at least that I thought it was genuine. A few close friends fell into the second category. When I was on vacation with my younger sister near Colorado Springs, Colorado roughly 30 years earlier, I had reacted as badly as some of those in the third group.

On the no-longer existing Mount Manitou Incline, one of the two people riding on the tram seat ahead of us was in transition. I said, much too loudly to my younger sister, that "she" was fooling no one. For my sister's benefit, I was attempting to show what I thought was a masculine disdain for any non-natal female who might dare behave in anything other than a masculine manner. I was probably also attempting to convince my sister and myself that I would never appear that way, at least not in public. The two people in that forward seat graciously ignored my atrocious behavior, which helped fix that embarrassing moment even more firmly in my memory. While the incline no longer exists, the memory of my misbehavior has been much more enduring.

The process of transition does not automatically confer insight, wisdom, circumspection, or any other virtue upon those pursuing it. A transgendered person with a history of suppression, is acutely aware, however, how important and misleading constrained self-expression through affected appearance can be. While unable to resolve her conflict, her years of reflection, attempted self-diagnosis, and determined suppression harshly restrict unguarded emotional release. During and after transition, an MtF woman no longer requires the impersonal fraud of her male persona.

The ultimate primacy of gender identity over physical manifestation was shown wonderfully in the film "The World According to Garp". Actor John Lithgow plays an MtF ex-football player who has transitioned. The character uses her football skills to act against someone threatening another of the story's characters. The maneuver causes the character some physical discomfort but she was unreserved in the full use of her abilities to protect those around her. The casting of John Lithgow in that role was especially appropriate, not just because of his excellent acting ability, but also because of his physical stature that so powerfully illustrated how little one's decision for transition has to do with unalterable physical attributes.

The same heroic dedication and willingness for self-sacrifice was exhibited in the film "The Fisher King", which also starred actor Robin Williams. The transgendered or transvestite character who otherwise seems so excessively self-involved that "she" is barely able to function in society is not only willing, but unreservedly anxious, to help "her" friends. The generosity of spirit given to these characters might be attributed to the gratitude they feel in being able to openly express themselves in the presence of an accepting and caring group of close friends. More fundamentally though since they are not suppressing their honest identities, they can and do believe that at least some part of their own lives has value. In so doing they must, by extension of reason, value the lives of others and then value all life.

For curious neighbors, I became a somewhat reluctant but capable ambassador from the alien nation that is gender identity conflict. I was willing to answer questions about the condition for those who were trying to understand it, but I expected people who knew me to understand intuitively that the only reasonable explanation for my altered appearance was honest self-expression. The brief explanation I offered, when one seemed appropriate, was that the condition is not common, its origin is not yet understood, and its treatment options are limited. Several people told me they had difficulty understanding or accepting the concept of gender identity conflict. I told them that I had struggled with it all of my life, so I readily understood their difficulty.

For those who still could not or would not understand, I had less to offer. I experienced occasional bouts of frustration verging on anger at having been categorized inappropriately since birth based on apparent physical sex rather than gender identity. That frustration fed my conviction that I owed no one justification for expressing finally and openly my long-suppressed gender identity. I had been dealt a figurative hand of cards by the system that generated my birth certificate. I had not chosen the cards or the game. Part of this work's purpose is to encourage revision of the game.

One household located near my parents consisted of a grandmother, her daughter and the daughter's husband, and their daughter. The three or four-year old daughter was socially precocious and cute. I was concerned that my changed appearance might be a problem for her. I asked the mother and grandmother for their opinion and was pleasantly surprised that they did not believe there was a problem. They said they had noticed my seeming to be more serious or troubled over the preceding month before beginning transition and had wondered why.

The grandmother, who was about my age, complimented my appearance and said she wished someone would help her "...look real cute". She apparently thought that a support group or team of professionals had helped with my hair, clothes, and makeup. While it might have been advisable, I had not even considered seeking such help. Years of "dressing" secretly and of having been aware of the appearance of other women had provided all of the assistance I thought I needed. I had taken her comment as a compliment but she could have meant that kind of help was still needed.

Not Conforming

One of the town's less-conventional residents was a high school classmate of my older sister. He was one of the few students who studied Latin for four years in high school and his active mind continued to pursue a wide range of subjects through and after college. Although his perspective was often exceptional, his contentions were usually difficult or impossible to refute. He might have argued that, when people are the square pegs that do not fit round holes, it might be the holes that should be changed.

Soon after I began "dressing," he asked me if I knew the fellow who used to live in my house, and said that fellow had been a good guy. I appreciated his genuine effort to try to help. If a lack of self-confidence, emotional distress, or some other psychological impairment were the reason for my actions, such support would have been wonderfully reassuring. I said that I had known that guy far too long and that the resolution I was pursuing was right for me. When he asked what my neighbor had said, I wondered why he asked. I told him she seemed to understand and he asked, "But did she give you a hug?" His question was entirely unexpected but I could answer truthfully that she did.

During a subsequent conversation, I told him it was evident that my transition was proving rich fodder for the town's grapevine. He said that, since he had already fed it to the level of a demanding vintner's highest standards, my story was closer to a light snack. My appearance was very different from the fraudulent persona I had manifested all of my life, and townspeople quite reasonably wondered about the seemingly sudden transformation. My friend had some bitter experience with similar curiosity and seemed to wish some of it had occurred or resolved differently.

In the first months of transition, adults I encountered were nearly unanimous in avoiding overt signs of embarrassment or disdain. Younger children were usually much more open in their reactions. While shopping for a pair of shoes, I walked by a woman with two young children. The little boy, who had been staring at me, got very close to his mother and said "Look, look Mommy. That man is wearing a dress." "Mommy's" look at him, full of love, patience, and understanding, was priceless.

The heart-warming innocence and honesty of the young boy was reminiscent of my own youth. The child had referred a matter of something that just was not correct to the person in his world he thought had the ability to address it. His actions also showed how acutely aware of apparent and appropriate gender even young children are. The boy had not considered what remedial action his mother might take if any, but he did want her to do something. He might have expected her to use magic to make me disappear or for me suddenly to appear wearing other-gender clothing, but she chose the moderate position of partially ignoring him and gently suggesting that he be quiet.

Especially during those first transition months, a few local teens took peculiar pleasure in driving by my home and, when seeing me outside, offering such carefully considered and insightful remarks as "(expletive) queer". The words do not carry the same elegance in print they possessed when repeatedly hurled in full voice unison from teens in a rapidly passing car, but the sentiment survives. The teens would return occasionally for an encore performance, as though they feared I might have missed some nuance in their performance. Their action must have been predicated by immediate, if not considered, emotion since no suggestion of higher intellectual involvement was evident. Their zeal implied the dedication of another generation's Hitler Youth or the more recent religious police of some repressive theocratic régimes to enforcing acceptable appearance in public.

If there is a rationale behind such epithets and that method of delivery, it might be akin to the reasoning of a spear-shaking caveman who, on seeing the potential threat of an approaching stranger, attempted to show the stranger that the caveman was armed and dangerous. The stranger must flee or face great peril. The fact that the stranger held no weapons and was doing nothing more threatening than ambling across the savanna either would not register or would not matter. The emotion of feeling threatened by something one does not understand, however powerful that fear, must not be permitted to rule one's actions. It is not the human ability to reason but humanity's use of that ability that separates it from all other terrestrial forms of life. Some people feel that the mere existence of transgendered people threatens their conceptions of morality, religion, social order, etc. The nature of that perceived threat can, and probably should be, debated repeatedly in appropriate forums. Surely, when even the most careful of visual examinations shows that someone or something poses no overt threat, the reflexive human response is not reasonably one of emotional hostility but of reasoned curiosity.

I recounted an episode with the teens to my psychiatrist who replied that the experience of the encounter was probably new for them too, at least the first time they drove by; yet individual responsibility was a matter about which he also cared. I thought that the actions of these older teens should have been much more difficult to dismiss. Newness does not explain, and cannot justify, repeated verbal or physical abuse or any hostile reaction to a non-threatening individual. Of course, there is an important difference between explaining reactions and justifying or condemning them. I am sure the doctor was doing the former while I was concerned about the latter. Rude behavior might be expected as an expression of ignorance, but it cannot be acceptable that people would express themselves abusively in response to non-aggressive behavior. An MtF woman in transition is merely beginning to look like the person nature compels her to reveal. She is no more aggressive than a tree sprouting leaves.

The impetus to unease, distress, or hostility for many of these troubled souls is that they see the passive but consistent behavior of transgendered women as a threat even though it is not aggressive. Any behavior by transgendered people is seen as a challenge to the exclusive rightness of a single-model way of life that will abide no variations and tolerate no exceptions. As much as transgendered people might share their preference for that highly regarded model, they can neither accept the role they would play in it nor subscribe to the assertion that everyone must fit into it. For transgendered people, the model is based on illusions. It is rooted in the perception of exhibited physical appearances, rather than the equally real and much more important essence that separates people, as far as is known, from all other living things.

As I had considered and resisted any move toward disclosure and resolution, it repeatedly occurred to me that if I were to attempt to live as a female, I would do so in a world populated by other women who had spent their lives becoming the women they are. There can be few parallels to undertaking so different a manner of being. One might imagine a rabbit being saddled and entered in a horse race, or a child being given a surgical mask in preparation for its performing surgery. Neither example involves a full commitment of the anticipated years of one's remaining life spent in the new role.

The magnitude of that commitment is ignored or dismissed by lawyers, religious leaders, and others who argue that the process of qualifying for sex reassignment is somehow whimsical or capricious. Sex reassignment is neither. The rabbit's life probably would come to its sudden and unequivocal end when the jockey sat down, almost as the life of an MtF woman might end during or resulting from reassignment surgery. The child-surgeon would enjoy a greater chance for survival than the rabbit but surely not the child's patient.

A goal-oriented person would logically wonder whether transition is compatible with other things a transgendered person wants to accomplish in her or his life. Expressing one's gender identity is so important a part of life that, when the conflict no longer can be suppressed, it must be resolved. Those intimately involved in the decision must determine whether gender identity conflict really is the matter at issue, and some elements of the timetable on transition's path can be modified to accommodate reasonable doubt. Goal compatibility checks, however, like the concerns of a close friends or relatives, are as effective inhibitors to the desire for resolution as tissue-paper umbrellas beneath the falls of Niagara.

Adapting to Change

As the transition journey became my own, everything around me seemed different, yet unchanged. Familiar people and things were not changing but I was. Several months after beginning hormone therapy, I stepped up on the sidewalk near my parents' home. Part of me may have been in its own time zone but it did not stop when the rest did. The sensation was new and wonderfully satisfying but if it happened again, it had quickly become normal. As skeptical as I had been about the limited possibility for physical change, however, something clearly had changed.

Noticeable benefits from hormone therapy and electrolysis are finite. Continuing to take hormone medicines may be a threat to health. To declare completion and simply stop them is one way to end those parts of transition but I may never be ready to do that. It may be impossible, though, for an MtF woman to be at peace as a single self if she is not willing and determined to accept as finished an exhausted list of reasonable physical or external accommodation. Every day, however, presents opportunities for initiating or continuing non-physical changes.

Transition is only one of myriad reasons people make such changes, but it is unique in establishing a set of changes MtF or FtM people make. *Jeanne d'Arc* is an often-cited example of someone who moved or removed boundaries for herself and society. That may well be a misreading of the events. A more appropriate inference from her short life seems to be that it is possible to act without regard for, or despite, one's gender identity, rather than seeing gender as a determinant of what someone can and cannot do. A major difference between resolving gender identity conflict and attempting to alter the direction of a nation's history is one of identity (who a person is) versus occupation or avocation (what she or he does.)

Nearly six-hundred years ago, the clarity of "the Maid's" purpose not only overpowered every other concern for her own future but was persuasively inspirational to better educated and more politically powerful people of her time. Civilization will never know how much different might have been the history of France, England, and the world if Jeanne and others had not heeded her voices. If her determination to appear in masculine attire, even after having been sentenced to life in prison, was due to gender identity conflict, she may have been executed for being transgendered and refusing to suppress gender identity, rather than for heresy or treason. It is especially ironic that she may have been a martyr to the cause of gender identity expression since the same faith that executed and then canonized her still views the transgendered condition as a form of mental illness or defect. That view is examined with the views of other faiths later in this work.

Introspection and Introversion

In most instances, no healthy person would imagine that all, most, or even many of the people around her or him would interrupt their lives to focus solely on her or his appearance. Each person who would influence others is concerned about the impact appearance might have on those about whom she or he cares but is appropriately less concerned with its impact on others. The suppressing and transitioning transgendered person experiences a heightened concern regarding both situations. When a meeting with someone has special significance, the suppressing person's presented image is intended not only to convey her or his intent but to conceal the slightest hint of the suppressed identity. During transition, a transgendered person has the dual task of conveying the meeting's intent in a gender identity-appropriate manner and attempting to avoid or minimize embarrassment for either or any of those present.

Initially, my perception during transition was that any comment within sight and/or sound, and especially one that elicited laughter, was about me. The presumed content of the casual conversations I partially overheard was never a fantasy of effusive flattery, but anticipation of unmitigated scorn. After my mother repeatedly suggested that I seemed hypersensitive to the reactions of bystanders, I usually found that, if I could follow the thread of their conversation, what I had been certain were comments of criticism or derision about me actually had nothing to do with me. The discovery that the lives of others could actually transpire uninterrupted in my presence was always gratifying. I had been taking hormone supplements for only four months, had been letting my hair grow for six months, and I was still losing weight, but I was not the pyrotechnic attention-garnering spectacle I had thought was inevitable.

My pessimistic expectations were fed both by my apprehension regarding transition and a few instances of real and unflattering comments to and about me. The most embarrassing of those instances occurred at a local restaurant about one month after I began transition. My mother and I had ordered a carryout dinner for my father who was undergoing his first round of chemotherapy. While waiting for the meal, my mother and I overheard the restaurant's hostess tell several people in the kitchen that there was a man at the counter wearing a dress. For the next several minutes, successive young workers opened the kitchen door, stared briefly at me, and returned to the kitchen to more giggles and whispers. I do not remember how many other people were seated nearby or were waiting in the adjacent lobby to be seated, but an attempt to collect names and phone numbers for a civil suit became more tempting with each repetition.

During a subsequent visit to that restaurant, I spoke with a manager about the embarrassing experience. She assured me that their policy was to encourage employees to treat all customers with respect. She said that their proximity to a large amphitheater often meant after-concert visits by fans who presented a less-conventional appearance. While kitchen workers would reasonably be otherwise occupied, no waitress or waiter could reasonably expect to be generously tipped by people to whom she or he had been deliberately and unexpectedly rude. The difference between her statement of policy and the practice of several employees during my previous visit was not explained, but I never had another similar experience at that restaurant. If there had been a repetition I would immediately have brought the matter to a manager's attention. I had understood my psychiatrist's point that encountering a transgendered person in transition was a new experience for many people with whom I would come in contact, but I was becoming increasingly less willing to abide rude behavior from anyone whose position demanded a reasonable degree of courtesy or civility.

A year after I had begun appearing in a gender identity-appropriate manner, I told a friend about a few of the awkward encounters I had experienced. He said that he was sure that I must have expected some verbal or other abuse from people intent on displaying either spontaneous or considered displeasure in a number of possible settings. I had become so comfortable with my own identity, though, that his comment did not immediately remind me of the reservations I had felt for so long about appearing to be a man wearing women's clothing. When I had contemplated possible failure to appear to be acceptably female to myself and to others, I had thought in terms of personal embarrassment or of my embarrassing others, of social settings where my presence would be upsetting or a distraction, and about the possible adverse economic consequences from client reactions. I had imagined that my only possible prospective employment might be as a "graveyard" shift worker where no personal meetings with customers and the public and only incidental encounters with co-workers would occur. It had not occurred to me that I might experience verbal and/or physical abuse from people so disturbed by my mere presence that they would feel compelled to act. Several years before the attack on The World Trade Center and the Pentagon, I believe that naiveté was a delusion commonly shared by most Americans.

Instead of agreement, my friend's comment evoked surprise that he had expected some part of the calculus of my transition to include concern for the possible uncivil reaction of other people. It may well seem prudent, especially at a time of an ongoing war on terrorism, to consider whether each person is presenting too easy a target for someone exhibiting unrestrained bias to the point of violence. That prudence does conflict with what demonstrably has been an essential element of this nation's robust character.

While I was an undergrad, one of the school's French language teachers wrote a letter to the school paper about Americans walking boldly and aggressively from point to point at an often hectic pace, and how easily such behavior might lead to one's slipping on an icy sidewalk. The quintessential Frenchman, he wrote, would prefer the more steady and sure-footed ambulation of the donkey who looks downward constantly to carefully place each hoof. There is self-evident merit in avoiding unnecessary danger where nothing might be gained from a potentially violent encounter, but a total aversion to risk at any price is fundamentally incompatible with a dynamic economic system that can richly reward investors and a confidently extroverted society. Historians will record whether terrorists successfully altered this nation's collective temperament to the detriment of the economic and cultural system they so despise. Even before the heinous Towers attacks of September, 2001 caused some people to redefine or reconsider their acceptable level of risk, I thought that ordering my life after transition to avoid being seen by anyone other than family and friends would be unhealthful. Doing so would border on, if not actually be, paranoia. I did not seek confrontations with people who might be upset by the mere fact of my presence, but I would not hesitate to enter any setting where I had a legitimate purpose. Decades of doubt that I could ever appear acceptably female vanished as if by divine expiation. In the remaining void resided self-confidence firmly rooted in a single identity whose projected appearance and gender identity had become one.

The evolutionary path from self-doubt to self-confidence was not always smooth. It included such obstacles as a post-op phone call with my younger sister acknowledging the limitations of surgery and a post-op visit to my psychiatrist's office after my father's cancer returned. An important part of post-transition self-confidence is a maturing of understanding regarding the internal and external parts of one's identity and the limitations humans share in interacting with a wondrously varied world of similarly constrained human beings.

What should reasonably be expected from a society that has been informed, with increasing clarity, about the nature of the transgendered condition can be divided into the areas of research, education, screening, counseling, and legislative relief. People of science have known about the condition for centuries, yet they still know little about how it occurs, how frequently it occurs, how to discover it at its earliest-possible stage, and how best to intervene medically for an optimal outcome. That gaping void should make researchers most uncomfortable. It is difficult to imagine a parallel for the extant tolerance of the historic and current lassitude regarding transgendered people who are suppressing their gender identities. The people they care about, and those who care about them, unknowingly await the inevitable crumbling of the carefully maintained façade MtF women constructed in childhood on an inadequate foundation of dreams, hopes, confusion, shame, and fear. In noting how much work remains for researchers, I am not attempting a general appeal for altruism. Rather, the goal is to stir the conscience of those who profess a dedication to their chosen fields of scientific study or government and to move them to greater efforts to remediate contemporary treatment of the transgendered condition. Those who are still unsure of the gender identities of MtF women must recognize the essential nature of gender identity and the inherent rightness of accommodating it.

Even while some still argue about some aspects of gender identity conflict, including its cause or causes, its nature, and its remedy, there can be no reasonable doubt about the fact that it exists. At age-appropriate levels, school students should be taught, from a natural science and humanities perspective, that transgendered children do exist, that they are not deserving of condemnation or ridicule, and that they have the same potential to make important contributions to society as any other students. Transitioning children and teens who are merely expressing their innate identities have the same potential to be loyal and caring friends as any other young people. They also exhibit, however, an evident aspect of their humanity that makes them vulnerable to the same uncivil and unacceptable treatment that too frequently is visited upon people who are seen as "different".

Suppressing MtF women may have performed meritoriously in combat, risked their own lives to save others as police officers or firefighters, and performed other tasks in an heroic or exemplary manner prior to their transitions because, rather than despite, their being transgendered. If they risked their lives to save others, their actions were heroic regardless of their motivation. The threatening prospect of a premature end to the life of a suppressing MtF woman, however, could be ameliorated by the certainty that her gender identity conflict also would end. If she is attempting not merely to suppress but to deny her gender identity, she might risk her life to make the pretense of her male persona appear more convincing to herself and/or others by saying, in effect, "I must be a man because of what I did". Anyone rescued or who witnessed her heroism would be unlikely to challenge the rescuer's gender identity. A compromised aversion to death and an attempt to continue her masquerade are certainly less altruistic motives than risking her life on principle, but the intensity of the obsession summoned by gender identity conflict can make most other considerations secondary.

Feeding the Beast

When her slumbering obsessive urge to "dress" unpredictably reawakens for its ten-thousandth time and calls her to engage in her favorite, yet despised, pastime, the suppressing MtF woman might still postpone the exercise for any of several reasons. A temporary delay would occur if necessitated by the prime imperative of preserving secrecy. A lack of sufficient privacy, distance from clothes and makeup, or more pressing vocational, social, or family obligations could also require postponement. However long the delay, the change always meant delay, not cancellation. The depressing frustration of inevitably yielding to the obsession could be a powerful motivational force for a suppressing transgendered person to accept a higher level of mortal risk, especially for what seems to be a worthy goal and meritorious death. Such a choice emphasizes the importance of the distinct difference between who someone is and what she or he does.

Authentic goals and aspirations rooted in each person's talents, interests, and abilities are difficult or impossible to discern when suppressing so critical a part of one's essential self as gender identity.   I had not seen my obsession as an honest basis for charting my path. The suppressed obsession had demanded a projection of self that was incompatible with my affected persona. As it became increasingly clear that the direction I had taken in seeing my psychiatrist was likely to lead to my realizing what had previously seemed a fantasy, I could finally try to think of myself as a potential wife and adoptive mother. This was a grossly belated attempt to experience dreams or imaginings similar to those of most young girls, but it was harshly tempered by the knowledge that medical science still could not permit me to become a biological mother.

Permitting my mind to contemplate a future uncompromisingly foreign to my affected male persona was a liberating experience. I began to accept that the woman, and possible wife and mother, I am must contain the set of spiritual, emotional, intellectual, and other characteristics I possess and can acquire, rather than those I might wish I had. The whole experience of common female maturation contrasts sharply with mental constructs of conscious thought subconscious aspiration sporadically assembled by an MtF woman over decades. Still, such thoughts now carried none of the feelings of shame, anxiety, or compulsion that had preceded or accompanied each of my countless episodes of temporary gender identity release.

Relatively New

I had been "dressing" for less than two weeks when my two sisters and their families visited for Independence Day weekend. My older sister's family and I had agreed to meet at the airport baggage claim and I waited a short distance from the escalator they would use. The fleeting moment's delay in their recognizing me was gratifying. I had been thinking in terms of my appearance finally reflecting the person I am, but that also meant not wanting to look like the male persona I had affected for so much of my life. The instant of indication that I was not the person they expected could favor any of several explanations, but I had been projecting a male image during our last meeting and I do not believe they saw that image at this one. A different reaction from even these special people would not have altered my course of transition, yet their response was exactly as I might have wished. I did not have a similar opportunity to gauge the reaction of my younger sister and her husband because they made the trip home by car.

As my direction became increasingly clear, I contacted a highly recommended surgeon regarding his procedure, the arrangements, and costs. He provided the information I requested, said he had a date available in late September, and reminded me that I would need a second qualified opinion before he could do the work. Several possible sources were decidedly uncooperative regarding the second evaluation because I had only been "dressing" full time for one month. I was disappointed by the adherence of these people to a guideline and their questioning, in effect, the clarity of the vision I now held with certainty. I finally found a qualified person near home who shared my understanding of the guideline as something intended to help patients, rather than its being part of a form into which patients must fit. I met with him before and after the final session with my psychiatrist and was gratified by his confirmation of a diagnosis that I believed was irrefutable.

A Change of Name

After I began wearing gender identity-appropriate clothing in public, it no longer seemed reasonable to continue using the official records of someone with the name of a male. The name never represented who I really was and now no longer fit the person I appeared to be. A couple weeks after my first "dressing" day, I checked with our County Clerk and found that the process of changing my name was not complicated. State law required that the purpose and time for the Court's hearing of my case be advertised, but the Court Clerk would not set a time for the hearing until the legal advertisement had appeared. I addressed this circular logic in the advertisement by writing that the date and time of the hearing could be obtained by contacting the Court Clerk.

When no other interested parties appeared at the hearing, the judge, a stenographer, my mother, and I were able to complete the process in a setting that seemed timeless, dignified, and efficient. I was pleased that the presiding judge was someone I knew by reputation. He had been part of a firm with which the bank had previously done business and he had decided two widely publicized cases that affected the entire state. He had held that the state's funding of education was inequitable and that real estate throughout the state was not being assessed fairly.

Despite his vast and varied experience, he had not previously dealt with a case involving an impending change of sex. During his consideration of my petition, he stated that he saw proper function of the law as being a facilitator, rather than an inhibitor, to those engaged in the lawful pursuit of life, liberty, and happiness. My mother's presence for the hearing and the absence of any objections to my change of name facilitated his issuing the order. During the brief but cordial discussion following his granting of my petition, he asked several questions about the nature of the condition and the process of transition. His genuine and caring concern reinforced my conviction that our legal system can and does attract considerate, conscientious, and capable people to positions of responsibility and power.

Copies of the judge's order were necessary for most of the changes of name on my accounts and records. The change on my license to drive was easily accomplished along with a new photo. There was a slight stir, though, over my needing the first two names changed, rather than the last one. The designation of sex could not be changed legally without the medical certification that was also necessary to change my birth certificate. As far as the state was concerned, I could drive a car as a male named "Brenda." The fact that I was not, and had never been, a male in the most meaningful sense of the term is still not the state's relevant standard   I would have sought legal representation if it had been needed to accomplish any of these changes but it ultimately was not.

Shortly after the court hearing for my change of name, I sustained what I would realize two months later was a gallbladder attack. After an hour of severe pain, I called the county's emergency medical service. By the time the technicians arrived, the pain had subsided, my vital signs were normal, and I tentatively accepted their explanation that I probably had a painful bout of indigestion. Two days later a gifted cousin died. We had often visited her and her parents in Syracuse, New York and they had visited us in New Jersey and at home. She wrote several plays while she was in high school, but I do not know if any of them ever was performed. She did not major in drama or journalism, and I often wondered why she did not pursue her interest in writing. I did not have an opportunity to discuss the transgendered condition with her but would have been interested in what she might have written about it.

An Autumn of Loss

Roughly two months after I had begun "dressing," an aunt died. I had known and been fond of this special aunt for most of my life, although my uncle did not marry her until after I graduated from college. We had visited with them every summer for almost twenty years when we visited Dad's parents, his other brother, and that brother's family. Dad's chemotherapy kept my parents from attending her funeral, just as it had prevented their going to my cousin's funeral in Syracuse. Because of my altered appearance, I told my uncle that, if he would rather I did not attend, we certainly would understand. He said that if it would not be a problem for me, then it would not be one for them either.

Two days after my final session with the psychiatrist, I flew to Kingston, N. Y. for my aunt's funeral. The flight, motel stay, funeral, and visiting with relatives involved innumerable firsts. I told my MtF acquaintances that I had worn slacks long enough as a "male" and did not expect ever to wear them again. I kept that promise for most of the first year except when gardening, corralling autumn leaves, or doing other work for which heels were impractical.

Such previously routine activities as packing a suitcase, getting in and out of a vehicle, and stepping over a curb were now new. They were not difficult but were different, and I was gratified that each one could not have seemed more appropriately so. I had stayed in motels during a brief stint with a bank-consulting firm, and packing suits each week had become a habit. For this trip though, I was packing things I had never had reason to take anywhere before. Despite otherwise careful preparation, I had failed to anticipate arriving in a torrential rainstorm and had not even packed a rain bonnet.

My younger sister met my flight, seemed unfazed by her third sighting of my feminine appearance, and graciously shared her most welcome umbrella. She walked with me to my rental car and I followed her for the fifty-five-mile drive to our motel. The next morning, my sisters, their husbands and I drove our rental cars to the funeral home. The relatives all now knew about my having begun transition, but the weight loss, hair, clothes, and makeup meant that I did not look like the person most of them had seen one year earlier.

The brief service at the funeral home was followed by a final viewing, Mass at a nearby church, and a gathering at the cemetery. The tears that followed my leaving the funeral home were the first I had experienced in over thirty years. Realizing and expressing such emotion was coupled with an awkward awareness of its happening. Under other circumstances, I might have been embarrassed by my sisters' caring concern, but this time it was very much appreciated. The moment left its indelible imprint and we proceeded by caravan to the church for a beautiful service. There was no sign of the previous night's drenching rain, and the procession to the cemetery was accompanied by a gorgeous September day. The solemn placing of flowers on the casket was as tender a farewell as we could offer to this loved and lovely woman.

More than one hundred relatives and friends attended the luncheon that followed. Women easily outnumbered men and most of them seemed to be in the restroom when I was. None of them appeared to mind sharing those facilities with me and, while there was no reason for anyone to, I had wondered if someone might object. Later my older sister revealed that she had come to the restroom in case someone did object. My psychiatrist had given me a letter stating that I was under his care and that he could be contacted if there were a question. Other practitioners have issued such letters but I do not know if any patient ever has needed to present one. I did not have occasion to present mine, although merely having the letter provided reassurance.

Following the luncheon my sisters, their husbands, and I visited with my uncle, two other aunts whose husbands were no longer living, and my cousins and their families. My uncle was particularly sympathetic and concerned about why, how, and what I was doing. I tried to answer his questions as thoroughly as possible and hoped the discussion would provide at least a momentary respite from his grief. While sharing my father's ability quickly to address the heart of a matter, he always has been easy to talk with, and he was so for this discussion.

While visiting another cousin, her sisters, and her family in Kingston the year before transition, I had met their delightful son. One year later and ten weeks after I began "presenting," I saw the boy again at my aunt's funeral. Because of my different hairstyle, clothes, makeup, and a 50-pound weight loss, he did not remember having seen me the year earlier. After the funeral, my cousins had some photos of our visits as children. The boy said he wanted to see the photos too. When he quickly recognized his mother and her two sisters, one of his aunts asked if he could guess which one I was. I waited breathlessly as he carefully studied the pictures before pointing to a young girlfriend of one of my cousins. I put my hand on his shoulder and thanked him without explanation. I thought this impromptu experiment had gone on long enough and had concluded in a most satisfactory manner.

This very full weekend sped by filled with the funeral components, visiting with relatives, seeing old photos, and wonderfully supportive conversation. When my older sister and I realized we would be sharing a flight back to Pittsburgh, we changed seat assignments so we could sit together. We reviewed the weekend's events, especially noting the irony that so sad an occasion could pass pleasantly in such warm and gracious company. We also discussed the game of dress-up that I had played with her in our youth and the few things that are known about the transgendered condition.   My mother met our flight and the four of us had time for a brief visit before my sister and brother-in-law flew back to Wisconsin.

The next two weeks flew by as Dad's chemotherapy continued. The last Sunday in September was the day before my flight for surgery. Mother and I attended church. The service seemed to proceed normally until the first stanza of the last hymn. Whether from concern about Dad's illness, my impending surgery, the prospect of her caring for everything at home until my return, or all of this and more, I saw her crying for the first time since her mother's death almost twenty years earlier. She quickly regained her composure but it was evident that many of the costs of transition could not be counted in dollars.

The Badger State

My flight to Wisconsin made a connection in Detroit. While waiting in the terminal for my connecting flight, I used a payphone to pay a bill I had intended to pay before leaving home. This most ordinary of financial transactions when carried out back at home was anything but ordinary when performed in that setting only a few hours before my meeting with the surgeon. As I walked outside toward the plane, the steady breeze, my wrap skirt, purse, and travel case engaged in a comical battle with modesty with modesty faring a poor second. The commuter plane that completed the flight was noisy and cramped but these were minor distractions as I thought about where I would be in two hours.

During the short taxi ride to the doctor's office the driver attempted cordial and casual conversation, but my questions about the community and his answers and observations seemed more ironic comedy than conversation. I might have asked how many MtF passengers he had conveyed to the doctor's office, but that would have altered the casual color of the conversation. He helped me with my small suitcase, I thanked him, and I entered the doctor's waiting room.

Since the cost of the procedure had been paid in advance, there were no financial matters to discuss with the office staff. I had arrived about an hour early for my appointment, so I had ample time to peruse the periodicals, flyers, and other literature in the waiting room. A few patients came in and left before my name was called. The doctor's spacious office with dark rich colors was almost oppressively masculine and I felt oddly out of place. I think he asked if I were ready for surgery and I replied that I was, if he was. He told me to disrobe. After complying, I reluctantly signed the release he presented for the photos he took and then left for the short walk to the hospital.

The cool, cloudy, and windy day might have seemed ominous but I had no second thoughts about undergoing the procedure. I found my room and read or listened to audio cassettes when there was no other distraction. A nurse brought the beverage whose use consumed much of the evening. I understood the need for the cleanest-possible operating field. No perforation of the intestine was expected but I had made an autologous blood donation and appreciated all reasonable precautions to minimize the risks of surgery. Since no one else was assigned to my room I went to bed at the earliest opportunity.

Shortly after being wakened the next morning I received pre-anesthesia. Two women arrived with a razor and I asked if they were starting the surgery.

They seemed to appreciate my attempt at humor. The doctor's work apparently went as planned, although I may have responded too well to the anesthesia. My older sister had driven ninety miles from their home to see me. She was told repeatedly that I should awaken soon but I did not waken until the following morning.

My roommate following surgery had previously had sex-reassignment surgery but required, or had elected, a modification. She said she was an American Indian and an agent for the Federal Bureau of Investigation. She always was awake before I was and was much more active than I for as long as we shared the room. She attributed much of her stamina to heredity. Whatever its source she possessed great vigor and I envied her capacity for almost constant activity. My instructions had been to stay in bed, and I was most willing to comply. The odor of iodine solution seemed to be everywhere, including on or around the food. Except for ingesting anti-nausea medication, eating became another of the routine activities I did not perform well.

My sister returned, and was a most welcome visitor. She told me about having made the trip to the hospital and back home for information she could have gotten by phone. She asked why I had been "out" so long but I do not know why she thought I would know the answer. I asked an anesthesiologist about that sometime later, and he said a practitioner's primary responsibility is to keep the patient in a deep sleep during surgery.   Recovery from the anesthesia is a secondary, or even non-existent, concern.

A favorite younger cousin from Louisiana phoned. I had not spoken with him for a couple years but we did correspond regularly. He said he had heard about my surgery and wanted to know if everything had gone well. I said I thought it had and that it was good to hear his voice. I had not been expecting his call and was very pleasantly surprised to receive it.

Three days later, both sisters and their husbands brought a cake and we celebrated my birthday in a setting quite different from any other. My younger sister's lengthy trip from Michigan, partly by ferry, was especially appreciated, and they made the return trip the following day. There was no ready morale-building substitute for the visit of these close relatives. Each of them had other things to do during that time and I fully realized they could not be doing them while they were visiting with me.

While they were present, something caused my first sneeze since arriving at the hospital. A moment later, my older sister left suddenly to find a nurse. I did not realize that one of the stitches had broken but the resultant bleeding required attention. My relatives left the room and the nurse applied pressure to stop the flow. He said he knew the technique was supposed to work but this was his first opportunity to try it. He must have been a good student because the bleeding quickly stopped.

The seventh day after surgery, I saw the surgeon for the second time. He removed the bandages and gauze, examined the work he had done, and seemed pleased by the result. I was glad that he did not seem disappointed, but I knew that he had performed many such surgeries. This was my first, of course, and I had nothing with which to compare it. A couple hours each day for the next several months would be required to keep the surgeons work from being countered by my body. I might have been expected to feel an emotional response, as though something was missing, added, or radically different. More broadly, I might have felt elated or depressed. None of those occurred to me. It was terribly important to have the surgery, almost as one might want desperately to have a malignant tumor removed. Hating the tumor would be a foolish waste of emotion, so too, though differently, would be mourning its loss. With the surgery done, my interest and focus turned to recovery and the trip home.

His orders were that I should get out of bed, take a shower, have a prescription filled at the hospital pharmacy, and move to my accommodations at a nearby inn. None of these steps sounded difficult but each was. As I showered, whatever energy I might have stored during that week in bed quickly dissipated. There was an emergency call button in the shower and I used it. I could not differentiate between weakness from the surgery and the week of inactivity in bed, but I was most grateful when help arrived. The return to my room was a brief respite. I dressed, had a chair ride to the pharmacy, and then waited for the taxi ride to the inn.

The walk across the inn's lobby seemed to take hours. The clerk at the reservation desk later told me that I was so pale she had wondered if I would survive the stay. She thought the only color in my face came from the makeup I had used. The elevator ride to my room also occurred in slow motion. I wanted to fall into bed but knew I needed something to eat. The line of least resistance also was the least healthful, but the pizza I ordered was delivery and I did not have the energy to go anywhere. I wanted to change clothes for bed but wanted also to be dressed when the delivery person arrived. He seemed unusually anxious to complete his task, but it was not difficult to imagine why he was uncomfortable. I hurriedly ate some of the pizza but felt guilty about wasting so much of it. Still, I could not get to bed soon enough.

The following day after the third two-hour trip from her home that week, my older sister arrived. She spent the nights of the next five days in a room adjoining mine. She tried repeatedly and valiantly to get me out of the room for a walk, but I just wanted sleep. She described a beautiful spot at a nearby lakefront where I could enjoy the view, get some sun, and breathe fresh air. I did go with her to a restaurant for lunch one day but that was my only outing. I seemed almost to lack the energy even to think. I was waiting for energy restored by rest rather than creating stamina by testing and stressing my body. My five days at the inn were passing too quickly and the flight home grew increasingly daunting.

Back to the Valley

The first leg of my homecoming was another commuter flight from the small local airport. Despite the wheelchair request on my reservation, none was provided until after I checked in at the ticket counter. The ticket agent was also the boarding agent and she even helped load some of the baggage onto the plane. The range of tasks she performed was impressive and I almost expected her to be part of the flight crew. The return to Detroit was at least as noisy and cramped as the departing flight had been, and I was eager to descend the plane's steps to the wheelchair for the shuttle ride to the connecting flight. The shuttle driver left me at the foot of a flight of stairs to the next boarding area. A door attendant said that, if no one came to help me to the boarding area, he would do it himself. When no one else came, he finally took me to a hidden elevator, but when we got to the gate my flight had just left.

I was re-ticketed for a later flight by a supervisor who could not have been more helpful. She called Pittsburgh to notify my mother of the reason for the delay and made a second call to confirm that the page had been answered. Despite her performing other duties, she made it seem as though there were nothing more important than getting me on that later flight. The obvious disparity between employees who were doing so much more than their assigned duties and those doing much less was of more than passing interest from a variety of standpoints, but I did not have the energy to dwell on them. This Sunday already had seemed much longer than any previous one and I yearned for it to end.

Gratifyingly, my skycap in Pittsburgh was one of the over-achievers. He took me to the baggage claim, helped me get my suitcase, pushed the chair to the rendezvous point with my mother, and then took me to her van for the ride home. I slept fitfully on the van's reclining bench-seat during the ride, but thoroughly enjoyed the chicken dinner we had that evening. Like the day of the restaurant outing with my sister, this day also had consumed all of my regained strength. Two weeks after major surgery, I was back in my own home, but I am certain that my FBI roommate would not have been impressed. Had she been met by a skycap and wheelchair, she might have insisted that he ride in the chair!

When it Pours

Three days after getting home, my second gallbladder attack occurred. I awakened with a severe pain that I thought must be related to the recent surgery, but this pain was not like anything I had experienced in Wisconsin. I phoned the emergency squad, the pain was still severe when they arrived, and they took me to a local hospital. A conscientious neighbor saw me being lifted into the ambulance, realized that I probably had not called my mother, and she phoned my minister. I had wanted my mother to get what rest she could because she had been taking care of Dad and coming to my home to help me. The minister called her and asked if she knew that I had been taken to the hospital. That was one of the last things I wanted to have happen but I was very pleased to see her when she and the minister arrived.

An impressive set of test results indicated the nature of the attack. At my request, the emergency room physician referred the case to a surgeon who had helped my father. The obligatory chest x-ray necessitated a gurney ride to radiology. My conversation with the gurney attendant turned to gender identity and she stated that she had always known she was wholly female. I was surprised that she had even thought about the subject because so few people with consonant physical gender and sex seem to be aware even of the concept of gender identity. I replied that life was difficult when gender identity and physical sex are in conflict. The minister took my mother home, she returned with their van, and I had my second ride home in it that week.

Two weeks after this second attack and one month after my Wisconsin surgery, I had a second major surgery. Two days later, I left the hospital and went to my parents' home where my mother had set up a rented hospital bed on their first floor. I wasted no time putting it to its intended use and spent much of the next week there. She had decided, and I had concurred, that my using the rented bed would be far easier for her than my staying at my own home waiting for her to make judiciously rationed visits.

By the end of the second week I had not only resumed my normal routine but was helping with Dad, their dogs, and such incidental tasks as the shepherding of fallen leaves to their proper place at the curbs in front of my parents' and at my home. I had resumed attending church services and during the Christmas Eve service, I was surprised to see someone I had not seen since we were in high school. When I attempted to speak with him after the service though, he obviously did not recognize me and I did not pursue the matter. There is an awkward sensation at such moments, especially during transition, when the temptation to renew a friendship is restrained by doubt that the other party is similarly inclined. After transition, there is a certainty and confidence that comes from self-acceptance and it usually is apparent to people we knew before transition. Whether someone is receptive or not is entirely in their hands and about who they are. Rejection by someone whose prejudice prevents cordial or even civil conversation is unpleasant and unfortunate but certainly not shattering. Later, my classmate's mother told me he had mentioned the incident regarding someone he did not recognize, and she had told him who I was. I was grateful both that he had accepted me as being the woman I presented and that he had not known that I was the person about whom many people in town were talking.

There continue to be occasional awkward and difficult moments but they were easily outweighed by instances of extraordinary support and concern. I received an unexpected phone call from someone in town that I did not know well. She said she had heard innocent comments about my transition but also had heard disturbing things said by people who did not, could not, or would not understand the condition. She wanted me to know that those comments were upsetting to her because she shared neither their disseminators' views nor the vehemence with which they were expressed. If it might help me to know that there were other people in town who empathized with how difficult suppression and transition might be, she wanted to be certain that I knew it. A friend with whom I had shared twelve grades of public school said it more colorfully in a card of encouragement that cited Isaiah 40: 31 "...they shall mount up with wings like eagles..." (National Council 1989).[102] Other friends, neighbors, and church members were also supportive through greeting cards, casual conversation, warm smiles, and more.

Dad's treatment seemed to have gone well and he was considering undergoing the "precautionary" radiation treatments recommended by his oncologist. As my parents anticipated a January return to Florida, the year was nearing its end. Our family had been stressed and drained in some respects, but it also was stronger, more resilient, and even felt blessed.

14. The Condition and its Future

Science and the Conflict

Even children learn that, since only human females can produce human ova, masculinization of the ova requires their interaction with sperm from a male. Given their physical origin, if (female) ova have gender identities, they would presumably be feminine unless altered by a still unknown process. Medical science is far from understanding thoroughly the entire process of embryonic and fetal development of the brain, especially regarding determination of gender identity. The assumption has persisted that, if any part of a nascent human was not caused to become male, that part would "remain" female. If that were true, the gender identity of MtF women could be an unswitched remnant of an otherwise switched male. In 1997, Dr. William Reiner was referring to this hypothesis when he wrote A...the absence of prenatal androgen exposure ...may render the brain to the default, or female, position" (Reiner 1997, 225).[103] For one or more possible reasons, the various changes or processes normally occurring to produce male children have been thought occasionally to miss the portion of psycho-biochemistry and physiological development *in utero* that establishes congruent gender identity. For an MtF woman, the result would be a physically male person born with a sense of self that is innately feminine. Although widely, if tentatively accepted, this hypothesis still has not been tested and cannot be theory.

The hypothesis faces an immense hurdle. For it to explain the development of FtM men, the process would require finely-focused spermatic activity that only masculinized the embryo's or fetus's gender identity. It is far easier for even the most error-prone humans to believe that during a plethora of changes, only one might have been missed than to believe that all of the changes that should happen were missed except one. For the FtM condition, this hypothesis would require the equivalent of a continuously bouncing ball in a room full of switches to strike only the switch that causes masculine gender identity. The relative rareness of FtM men relative to MtF women supports this concept.

Some recent work suggests that there may be many switches and that they do not express at the same time. If there were very high ratio of MtF women to each FtM man, this hurdle to the "switch" hypothesis would be substantially less powerful. The anecdotal indication from current research, however, is that the actual ratio may be closer to 1:1. The evident likelihood that the rare incidence of gender identity conflict equally affecting both females and males may be fatal for the premise that gender identity has a "default" position. The counterintuitive and waning possibility that gender identity conflict for MtF women is caused by a different process than that for FtM men cannot yet be dismissed, but an absence of data supporting this alternative cannot be encouraging for its supporters.

Another popular hypothesis is that the maternal hormone levels in and around the embryo's environment at a critical moment in, or phase of, its development alters or prevents altering the embryo's gender identity. Like white cotton with red flannel in a hot-water wash, gender identity would receive, or fail to receive, a sufficiently strong rinse to change it figuratively from pink to blue. An attractive aspect to this hypothesis is that it would explain a rough equivalency in the frequency of occurrence of MtF and FtM people. This hypothesis has been dealt a severe or fatal blow, however, by the existence of sets of twins who, of course, shared the same embryonic environment throughout a pregnancy and where one, but not the other twin, is transgendered.

The death knell for the "default" gender position, "switch" flipping, and the color-changing hypotheses may have sounded in "The Golden State." In a recent study, genetic gender differences in mouse embryos were detected before physical sex had developed. At the University of California, Dr. Eric Vilain found that 54 genes work differently in female and male mouse embryos shortly after conception and before the embryos' sex hormones are even produced. If embryonic development, alone, did not account for that difference, it still may have been influenced by the hormone level of the fluid surrounding the embryo. Dr. Vilain's work indicates that, since gender-related gene differentiation occurs before the embryos' physical sex begins to form, that gender identity development cannot have been caused by the mouse embryo's own sex hormones (Pinholster 2005.)[104]

Science may well find that, at the time of conception, various characteristics of an embryo and fetus are established as parts of an interconnected whole, that none of the parts can easily be changed, and that any alteration will dramatically affect the whole.   In an interview, Dr. Vilain stated that there is action that causes the genes either to express as female or to express as male, so there really appears to be no "default" position (Vilain 2004, under "...default sex in development.")[105] Obviously, what is true of mouse embryos may not be true of all, or perhaps any other, life forms. If it is only true of mice, though, something of even greater significance might be learned from that uniqueness.

A recent study of fruit flies was conducted in Austria. In a series of experiments, manipulation of a single "switch" gene could cause or prevent exhibition of male courtship behavior in both female and male fruit flies (Demir and Dickson 2005 785, 791).[106] The study indicates that the sexual behavior of fruit flies is genetically determined before the flies are born. It does not indicate, however, how the flies felt about their gender identities.

If establishment of gender identity ultimately proves to occur independently of any other part of embryonic or fetal development, that proof will almost certainly include a demonstrable means of recognizing that identity. Medical science would still face the unresolved question of how best to accommodate the conflicting physical sexual identity where potential conflict occurs. The genesis and provenance of the sex gene in Demir and Dickson's work, but especially that same information regarding the gene in a naturally-occurring transgendered fruit fly, would seem to be near the core of the biogenesis of gender identity conflict, at least for fruit flies. A test for the presence of a predictive or associated coding could be the elegant diagnostic for early detection of the transgendered condition that would be of inestimable value to transgendered children and their families. Altering that coding *in utero* could mean elimination of any trace that potential conflict ever existed. A case for the ethics of altering an embryonic or fetal miscoding would reasonably be more persuasive than a case for prenatal alteration of gender identity or physical sex.

Neither mouse embryos nor fruit flies can possess and express the innate gender identity so frequently referred to throughout this work. American society certainly would not sanction performance of either of the above experiments using potentially human embryos or fetuses. The research is important, though, because it advances knowledge about other forms of life, improves the technology and process required for present and future study, and guides research that is applicable and suited to human pathology.

A search of over 120 peer-reviewed studies and journal articles published since 1981 and more than 160 other works published since 1963 shows an evolution of thought away from a skeptical analysis of "deviant" behavior to a clearer and less biased understanding of gender identity. An MtF woman once thought to be rejecting her "appropriate" gender identity, which was presumed to be unambiguously indicated by "his" physical sex, has increasingly been seen as expressing awareness of her own distinct gender identity that differs from her physical sex. Recent studies look at the separateness of gender identity as an aspect of each person's essential self, at its interaction with her or his physical self, and at that person's interactions with family members and others.

This trend in thought coincides with increased study of a still insufficiently understood area of the brain's development, the mind and physiology. While earlier gender and gender identity studies appeared at a nearly constant rate of four per year, peer-reviewed journal articles in my search increased from only eight from 1982-1989, to sixty-nine from 1990-1999, and to fifty-four from 2000 through 2003 or an arithmetic equivalent of one-hundred-eight for 2000-2009. Whatever factors have contributed to the increasing rate of apparent academic interest, the result will almost certainly be a better understanding of the unique human characteristic that is gender identity.

Earlier works treated gender as a set of behaviors each person exhibited relative to her or his presumed physical sex. Their authors, too, seemed unaware of the importance of gender identity or unconcerned about gender identity conflict. Crudely, a person's behavior either was or was not appropriate to societal expectations for that person's known natal physical sex. Someone whose physical sex at birth was male but who behaved in a manner different from other males simply exhibited an inappropriate gender. Since people can and will adopt behavior that facilitates their living as they deem necessary, the older concept of gender as observable behavior was clearly prone to error. Continuous exhibition of "typical" male behavior does not necessarily indicate the presence of a male gender identity. Since behavior can be imitated, and it certainly would be by suppressing transgendered people, whether a person believes her or his behavior honestly reflects innate gender identity may not be discernable. This is especially true regarding expressions of sexual preference. Despite distressingly frequent public perceptions, however, few qualified and experienced mental health professionals would confuse gender identity with sexual preference.

The Persistence of Sex

Drs. Reiner and Gearhart have followed the cases of sixteen genetic (forty-six XY) males for as long as ninety-eight months. Surgical treatment of a rare birth anomaly led most of the subjects to be raised as females. While eight of the sixteen declared themselves to be male (versus two of fifteen cited in an earlier article (Reiner 1997, 225),[107] all sixteen exhibited mild to strong typically male attitudes and interests (Reiner & Gearhart 2004, 333).[108] The later study's table showing duration of the subjects' follow-ups suggests that there is an overlap between the 1997 and 2004 populations. If five or six more of the study's subjects were more willing to reveal their gender identities by 2004 than in 1997, the latter study is also evidence of the persistence of the guilt-ridden or stasis-preserving tendency to suppress one's conflicting gender identity even though the subjects were part of a study of that very issue. Each subject must have been afforded numerous opportunities to reveal his gender identity but several chose to continue to suppress it. That tendency must be far more powerful and enduring among transgendered people who have neither sought, nor been given an opportunity to receive, professionally competent assistance to address their conflict.

What Drs. Reiner, Gearhart, Diamond, Sigmundson, and others have explained is that an intersex baby can be "given" a sex, and even assigned a gender but the baby cannot be given its gender identity. Yet the myth persists. An effort to form medical consensus regarding treatment of intersexed children includes the recommendation that, following expert evaluation of newborns at an appropriate facility, the child should be assigned a "gender" (Hughes et al. 2006, 150).[109] In its children's health issues section under "genital defects", a Merck manual states that experts advocate quickly but carefully assigning a child's sex to promote parental bonding and to avoid gender identity disorder (Beers 2004a).[110] Although he has argued that children know their gender identities, in 2005, Dr. Reiner said that gender "must" be assigned at birth for legal and social purposes (Pinholster 2005).[111] Near the end of an ABC 20/20 program segment that aired April 19, 2002, the reporter said, AWhat all sides do agree on is that an intersex baby should be given a gender identity from birth and raised unambiguously as a boy or girl" (Sherr 2002, 16).[112]

To the transgendered eye, there is a disturbing inference, intended or not, that where gender identity exists it must be consonant with, or even part of, each person's predominant physical sex when physical sex is ambiguous. The unacceptable corollary is that gender identity conflict is not rooted in innate gender identity that conflicts with the physical sex of a normal physical female or male. Each of the four assertions above was offered in the context of restraint regarding the possible assignment of physical sex for intersexed children. Yet, incredibly, they each appear to advocate, or unreservedly support, the arguably more grievous abuse, however careful the preliminary assessment, of assigning gender. The reasoning seems to be that physical sex is more important than an innate gender identity that may not even exist. Utmost caution, deliberation, and even the child's informed consent, they argue, should precede surgery, but gender as the single aspect of identity that will most influence, and be reflected in, the child's every thought, action, and interaction can, and even must, be quickly assigned. Yet the above cited Merck manual also states that gender identity is fully established by or between eighteen and twenty-four months of age (Beers 2004b).[113] Dr. Reiner has said in 1997, 2000, and did so two sentences before the above Pinholster citation, that each, at least intersexed, child ultimately knows her or his own gender identity (Reiner 1997, 225,[114] Hendricks 2000,[115] Pinholster 2005).[116] Ultimately, there is a difference between the knowledge one has of the gender assigned to her or him, and that person's knowledge of her or his own gender identity, regardless of whether they are consonant.

There apparently is no economic cost to mis-assigners of gender. If true intersex births are one in three-thousand and transgendered births are one in fourteen-thousand, the probability that an intersex child is also transgendered might be one in forty-two million. The intersex and transgendered conditions are almost certainly unrelated, however, so the probability for an intersex child also to be transgendered must be the same as for the general population. The small probability of being wrong and the societal history of gender assignment would exculpate any mis-assigner in court. The assignment, though, still would not have been based on gender identity and assignments not based on gender identity are, at least in this author's view, unequivocally and morally wrong.

Every transgendered person's existence, but especially her or his transition, is additional confirmation of the medical inability to assign gender identity. Assignment efforts have been spectacularly and tragically unsuccessful. The effort at Johns Hopkins to convince a male that he was female was purportedly successful until David Reimer proved unequivocally that it was not (Colapinto 2000).[117] Failures to convince Christine Jorgensen, Jan Morris, and other MtF women that they were or are male, similar accounts of FtM men regarding their transitions, and an increasing amount of research data have shown consistently and unequivocally that gender identity cannot be assigned. These case histories should have sounded an at least cautionary warning to the medical community. When faced with an infant's ambiguous or malformed genitalia, that community has been historically, and remains, tempted to do more than the minimum amount of surgery medically necessary for the infant's immediate physical health.

The misconception that gender identity can be imposed and enforced is especially harmful for parents. Parents may easily see a transgendered child or homogendered child as the parents' failure to reinforce and demand certain behavior. As onerous as are parental responsibilities for things they can change, parents need to know they cannot be responsible for the gender identity of their child. When I was in grade school, there were occasional tabloid stories about a parent or parents forcing a child to cross-dress. These sensationalized stories were never sympathetic to the possibility of a supportive parent attempting to help a transgendered child. As compelling as I thought these stories were, I was certain that each story's subject was rewarded by everyone outside the home for behavior deemed appropriate to the child's natal physical sex and harshly punished for any incongruent behavior. I always responded to the accounts with feigned indifference or with as masculine a dismissal as I could muster.

What Can Be Disproved

Opposing advocates confronting each other in loud and emotional disagreement is distressingly common in the political arena but is wholly inappropriate to defining and attempting to resolve a medical condition. Proponents of alternative views of the transgendered condition who lack an intimate familiarity with the condition should rely on peer-reviewed published results of objectively stated and properly tested hypotheses. Again, extant such literature includes numerous accounts of failed attempts to assign gender following surgery to assign sex. Those infants and children were not transgendered at birth but their gender identities conflicted harshly with the physical sex assigned to them. In these cases, well-intentioned efforts to correct one problem created a different problem that was even more traumatic. Some would argue that attempts to impose surgically and psychologically an opposite gender and physical sex are not entirely unlike the horrible experiments of unparalleled cruelty conducted by Nazi physicians regarding the possibility of manufacturing post-birth Aryans. Clearly though an important difference exists between a sincere therapeutic intent only to serve each patient, however erroneously contrived, and its opposite of attempting to alter entire populations of demonstrably healthy people for the sake of racial bigotry. Medical science would magnify the tragedy if it ignored the important results obtained at such great personal cost from unsuccessful attempts to assign gender identity.

Drs. Milton Diamond and Keith Sigmundson extensively reviewed an unambiguous and spectacular failure to assign gender under the auspices of

Johns Hopkin's Dr. John Money. Despite surgical, hormonal, and sociological
efforts expended by this leading research institution's qualified practitioner
and his outrageous assertions that efforts to assign gender were succeeding;
the subject's male gender identity was ultimately uncompromising and
uncompromised. The reviewers were particularly concerned that the reported
"success" at reassignment was widely heralded and that its influence has been so
pervasive and enduring (Diamond and Sigmundson 1997, 298, 303).[118] Humans
learn, throughout the journey of their lives, about the person each one is in terms
of things that bring fleeting, and others that provide lasting, peace and happiness;
but that knowledge comes from, rather than determining, one's essential identity.

Each of us must regret that at least once we failed to show the kindness,
thoughtfulness, generosity, and/or other favorable attributes we expected
always to be present in our nature and behavior. On other gratifying recalled
occasions though we did or said precisely what was most appropriate and
helpful. Such thoughts and actions stem honestly, from one's essential self, or
falsely, from efforts to suppress that self. Surely, not all honest instincts, actions,
and reactions are inherently good, nor will every action of an affected self be
bad or evil. The association between each person's essential self and her or his
thoughts and actions though either helps that self grow or diminishes its sense of
conscience and virtue.

Reliable scientific evidence and knowledge regarding the brain
components and processes that determine gender identity, gender identity's
operation relative to thoughts and actions, and the influence of exogenous factors
is weak or nonexistent. If, at some future time, increasingly detailed fMRI does
reveal a single small area of the brain that correlates highly with gender identity,
when and how that area was formed and whether it can be altered still may
remain unknown and unknowable. There may be only one area, parts of several
areas, or a process-component common to all brain areas that correlates highly
with determining gender identity. That correlation may also be different for
females and males, younger women and older women, pre-transition and post-
transition MtF women, etc. Testing for a wide range of variables regarding MtF
women may be problematic because of the apparent infrequent occurrence of the
transgendered condition. In their significant study, Drs. Kim and Jeong have
shown an association between free testosterone and sexual arousal in FtM men[119]

The BSTc peer-reviewed study published in the journal *Nature* was based
on a small sample (Zhou et al. 1995).[120] Yet, its replicable findings do show a
marked similarity between at least one critical identity-related brain area in MtF

transgendered women and women whose natal physical sex was female. Even if application of this study were accepted as conclusive indication of the presence of the condition however, its diagnostic utility is obviously marginal since it relies on post-mortem microscopic examination of brain tissue. An MtF woman "dying to know" the results of such a test should not have to be taken literally.

The nature or nurture contest regarding the transgendered condition's origin continues with little, if any, case history supporting the nurture side. Biases strengthened by perversity in the face of contrary findings must be unacceptable in the scientific community where concepts or aspects can be subjected to rigorous objective testing. The persistent hypothesis that the transgendered condition occurs suddenly and subjectively, despite histories recounting decades of suppression, is an example of such bias. Some who reject an innate origin of gender identity conflict assert that the condition is, or results from, either a preference for, or an aversion to, a perceived gender role. The choice is deemed merely one of many along an implied continuum between identity and preference. However, no such continuum exists. Identity, whether fabricated, suppressed, or ardently manifested, is identity. Preference, however confidently or tentatively held, flows from one's sense of essential identity.

People versus Magnets

Before transition, I would not seek a lasting romantic relationship with anyone. Although I did not understand the whole of my conflict before seeing my psychiatrist, the obsession was chronic, and I could imagine no one with whom I might discuss it. I had reached a bearable stasis with my cross-dressing but, as satisfying as the episodes were, what they suggested about partner preference did not make sense. My assigned gender was male, and I had no romantic interest in pairing it with another. The obsession was a challenge to my assigned gender, but I did not understand that the compulsion must be an honest expression of myself and that it was my assigned gender that was dishonest. Whether or not I found someone attractive, that person could not be attracted to, or even aware of, the gender identity I suppressed. However strong the physical, emotional, and/or intellectual interest in anyone else, my gender identity remained hidden behind a persona that was unworthy of and unwilling to seek mutual commitment.

Possessing and hiding the trappings of my suppressed identity warred against my masculine persona and its sense of pride and confidence, yet I continued to be obsessed by the desire to have and wear them. Despite periodic efforts either to rationalize and subdue the condition or to eradicate it and dispose of the clothing, the obsession always resurfaced with at least as much power as before. Its persistence and magnitude were as perplexing as they were inescapable. Genuine aspirations to be part of my own traditional family were thwarted by a mystifying inability to know what part I would have in it.

Transgendered people pose no threat to those who revere traditional family life, especially when so many MtF women long to become wives and mothers in traditional families of their own. The only way society acquires transgendered people, whether they suppress or reveal their gender identities, is by birth, and almost certainly into a traditional family. Similarly, society's only means of preventing the condition, at present, would be to prevent birth. Gender identity conflict can be discovered only in those who have it; transgendered people can be neither recruited nor infected. A person might be induced to smoke, gamble, or drink alcohol. She or he cannot reasonably be persuaded to become naturally blonde, to be left-handed, to belong to a different race, and certainly not to change gender identity. As hundreds or thousands of transitioned transgendered people can attest, each person is born with certain unalienable characteristics and among the most fundamental of these is gender identity. However their identities are revealed and analyzed, transgendered people are not magnets and their gender identities cannot accurately be determined by, or inferred from, the gender and/or sex of those to whom they are attracted.

Because of the innate imperative of humans to reproduce, society discourages deviations from a norm that does not encourage progeny-affirming nuclear families. Again, MtF women do not seek innately to change that model but to address the status of those for whom the model is, as current law is applied, an unattainable goal. Ironically, society initiates and perpetuates gender identity suppression by assigning gender based on medical certification of natal physical sex, but it continues that practice despite the medical community's recognition of gender identity conflict. The irony is that the medical community has been given unlimited power to assign and attest to every infant's legal sex-at-birth but not fully to correct mis-assignments that resulted because the most important component of human sexuality was not even considered.

The compound problem of my having been raised as a male and not having experienced those childhood and adolescent years being treated as a female must be something like a blind person's being raised in a school for the deaf. A suppressing MtF woman's life experience is oriented to a male persona she is treated as being, but she is not and cannot wholly be that persona, despite the intensity of her effort and the length of time she tries. However late her physical self and appearance finally begin to reflect and project her released feminine gender identity, many of the patterns of behavior that most women habitually exhibit as they act in, and react to, their worlds were never learned, or they were learned differently from the way most women acquire them. Many of the experiences and aspirations, the disappointments and limitations, and the petty and significant victories and failures unique, yet similar, to those of other women are not, and never can become, part of an MtF woman's life. Even the most dedicated woman seeking to know more about men could not wish to do so at the expense of her own identity without becoming irreparably lost. The transgendered woman declared to be male at birth comes quite late to the opportunity for choice when, as an adult, she can no longer suppress her identity. At that late time, she is confronted by a harshly limited choice. She must choose, finally, to be who she is but she can never fully be the woman she might have been.

Women with a Past

In 1966, sexologist Dr. Harry Benjamin published his seminal work *The Transsexual Phenomenon*. He wrote about his forty years of experience with transgendered people who attempted to reconcile their gender identity with an incongruent physical sex. Benjamin also wrote of his visits with Dr. Magnus Hirschfeld, a fellow native German, in the 1920's and of the latter's work to differentiate characteristics that defined the transvestite, homogender, and transgender conditions (Benjamin 1966, Ch. 2).[121] In an appendix to Benjamin's work, Dr. Richard Green wrote of numerous examples of apparent transgendered behavior through time and across cultures (Green 1966).[122]

The life and transition of Christine Jorgensen is one of the most widely publicized histories of a transgendered person in the United States. Echoes of her widely heralded return to this country after surgery abroad even broke into the muted roar of news from outside the river valley of my youth. What little I did hear about her made her experience seem as fantastic as the plans for those involved in the then nascent space program. Her transition seemed a fascinating, enticing, but exceptional possibility. I saw no way to pursue a similar course, still hoped the condition would somehow resolve itself, and dared not appear too interested in someone who seemed so different from my male persona. Nothing about her exceptional journey said to me "Gender identity conflict is the problem and this is the best solution available. Transition though was not only possible but for me it was inevitable!" I do wish I fully had grasped that message decades earlier but the inertia of suppression still was overwhelming.

Whatever her other attributes Ms. Jorgensen was an exceptionally courageous person dedicated to resolving her conflict. She was willing to confront every obstacle that would thwart her progress and she was willing to help others understand why her transition was essential. Legal, medical, psychological, social, and other impediments obstructed the untrodden public path she blazed for American MtF women in her determined efforts to be herself. With substantial help, she wrested grudging accommodation from society and its systems that still do not acknowledge the full power and importance of gender identity.

As humans developed or were given a sense of self-awareness, gender identity must have been an integral part of each primal self. Gender identity must have affected then, as it does today, each person's development and shape each of her or his social interactions. Thousands at least of transgendered people since that primal ancestor have faced a choice similar to that of Ms. Jorgensen. They resisted braving transition's path all of their lives, started tentatively down it by modifying their clothing and behavior, tried self-mutilation in a desperate lurch down the path, or fled its prospect through the escape of suicide. The Harry Benjamin Standards of Care now afford a prescribed treatment for the condition that would have been among the most ardently desired but unrealizable fantasies of those past generations of transgendered people.

Adoption of the standards, development and use of feminizing hormone therapy, and continuing advancement in surgery has enabled the medical community to offer a comprehensive course of treatment. While that treatment is not and may never be perfect, it does afford the possibility of greater physical sex and gender identity harmony than any known alternative. Had this treatment been available centuries earlier, those countless thousands doubtlessly would have sought it.

Dr. Benjamin cited examples throughout history of "men" who would not accept their conventional societal role but lived, as much as possible, as the MtF women they were. An unknowably large number of instances went unreported and it is often unclear in cases that were recorded which of the subjects were transvestites, transgendered, or exhibiting symptoms of another condition. Yet, it would have been every bit as important to the MtF women of their day and in their culture to have lived, to the greatest extent possible, in concert with their gender identities as it is for MtF women today. Inability of earlier MtF women to achieve or even aspire to the most rudimentary surgical accommodation may have led some of them rigorously to suppress their conflict. They might have exhibited aggressively overt "masculine" social behavior that astonished their contemporaries. In earlier centuries, those who did perform, or obtained from others, the removal of their external male anatomy did so without today's antibiotics, general anesthesia, and contemporary surgical implements. The painful experience was probably followed quite often by sepsis or other infection, shock, and death.

While Dr. Benjamin described numerous historical examples of apparent gender identity conflict in the work cited, one historical account is especially compelling. Cassius Dio Cocceianus a politician and historian, recounted with unbridled disdain the intense desire for death-defying surgery sought by one of Rome's emperors. Cassius wrote about the physically-male Sardanapalus (also known as Heliogabalus, Elagabalus, Avitus, etc.), whose brief rule occurred during the historian's lifetime. I refer to her as female, not because I arrogantly "know" she had a feminine gender identity but because *she* repeatedly indicated that she did. A murderer herself, Sardanapalus was murdered at the age of 18 in A.D. 222 after having ruled the empire for fewer than four years. Born in Syria, she dared elevate her local god Elagabalus above Jupiter as the high god of Rome. As part of her worship, Sardanapalus slew boys, or ordered them slain, for sacrifice. Cassius apparently did not record how the boys were selected, whether they knew they would be killed, and whether they held a favorite pet or object as they were slain. Such acts are so abhorrent that they might approach, in nature if not in number, those of Hitler, Amin, Saddam Hussein, and other more recent incarnations of evil. While Cassius clearly believed many of the emperor's excesses were wrong, it is not clear why Sardanapalus was uninhibited by conscience, although her age and culture must have had some bearing. She reportedly even offered human genitals as feed to animals in Elagabalus' temple (Cassius Dio ca. A.D. 250/1914, book 80).[123]

Sardanapalus married at least five women and, Cassius alleges, "he" had sexual intercourse with women outside of these marriages primarily to imitate more closely the behavior of women when sleeping with men. She dressed as women of her time, repeatedly behaved as a harlot, and married as a woman the male slave Hierocles. She had affairs with other men, sought and received punishment from her husband for this adultery, and then had additional affairs with other men. At an unspecified time during this turmoil, she offered her surgeons great wealth if they would create a vagina in her body. Cassius did not record what, if any, surgical resolution Sardanapalus attained. After adopting a cousin who was almost her own age as her "son", she named the boy her successor. When she began to distrust him, she conspired against him. Near the end of her brief reign, Sardanapalus offered her life to save Hierocles, and both briefly were spared. After another plot against her cousin/son disintegrated, she and her mother were slain by her Praetorian Guard, which sided with the cousin she had adopted (Cassius Dio ca. A.D. 250/1914, book 80).[124] Cassius may not have been wholly objective. Had he written more favorably about the slain emperor, he might have been killed by Sardanapalus's successor. Yet he did not have to write anything and many details in his account could be verified.

In other times, Sardanapalus's abuse of her position or her example as an absurdly indulged teenager would serve as examples of those excesses. Her rapid rise to power might be at least as instructive. This fascinating account, though, of someone with the power and resources of a Roman emperor apparently attempting to resolve her gender identity conflict dramatically shows the insatiable and uncompromising nature of the obsession. At a time when the empire's rulers rose to, and retained power with, the support of the army, Sardanapalus garnered that support. Initially, Sardanapalus was able to fulfill enough of her responsibilities as leader to retain the loyalty of those troops. Her later efforts to contend with gender identity conflict apparently became her all-consuming desire. Beyond Cassius's obvious and understandable contempt for her, and not minimizing, in the least, the horrors of her excesses, Sardanapalus exhibited extraordinary desperation to attain the unobtainable. Her desire to be punished for being unfaithful to Hierocles, whom she apparently loved, seems an acknowledgement that despite her great power as emperor, she could not fully satisfy any aspect of her obsession. Her willingness to relinquish power to become Hierocles's wife, her pursuit of surgery, and other aspects of the historian's account are an indication of the eagerness and passion with which Sardanapalus would have pursued a contemporary transition.

This brief journey through Dr. Benjamin's work, Christine Jorgensen's life, and the nearly 2000-year-old account of Sardanapalus are further evidence of the power and persistence of gender identity conflict. As each person directly and indirectly contended with the conflict, she or he did so with different abilities and resources. Their efforts have produced a wealth of knowledge about some of the condition's characteristics, even as a few academically qualified specialists and non-professionals continue to dispute its essence. The worth to science of that dispute is a further testing of each previously tested hypothesis that has become theory. The destructive aspect of that dissent is its support of unreasoned bigotry and its harmful impact on transgendered people and those around them. Publicly aired challenges to the process of transition mean further suppression of suppressed identity, delayed or denied treatment, and more strident opposition to a greater systematic diagnosis and treatment of the condition. Such challenges, however, may also serve as additional impetus to further research.

A Common Bond

MtF women's shared experience of having fought much of their lives with gender identity conflict gives them a far stronger common bond than might have been conferred by any more tangible physical characteristic. While the sum of individual differences easily will be far greater than that common bond, there remains for many MtF women a powerful sense of kinship at having shared decades of similar mental and emotional conflict. Although some MtF women may have engaged in immoral, illegal, or unethical behavior, those who did are not representative of all, or even most, MtF women. They did not engage in that behavior solely because they are transgendered.   Given the passion of those who consider transgendered people to have yielded to moral and ethical weakness, temptation, and sin, the absence of credible evidence showing any abnormal sexual propensities among the transgendered population clearly cannot be due to anyone's reluctance or failure to search for it.

The bias others have against MtF women being around children as their teachers, pediatricians, daycare workers, etc. has extended to opposition to the adoption of children by transgendered women. That bias purportedly comes from a slightly less malevolent but more insidious concern that such women are harmful role models. Not only can MtF women professionals help teach non-transgendered children about the harmful and limiting consequences of unfounded bias, but they can help transgendered children seek the professional help each one needs for addressing her or his own conflict.

MtF women, by virtue of transition, do not become imbued with new characteristics that qualify them as role models for every occasion. They have been able though to muster the internal resources necessary to acknowledge the existence of a significant problem that is far beyond their own capacity to resolve. They have committed themselves to the full course necessary for resolution, including the shattering of a persona they had affected their whole lives. Where these characteristics of courage and commitment are appropriate for role modeling, post-transition transgendered people are as fitting examples as anyone else who has contended with a traumatic set of experiences, seen them through to resolution, and learned from the experience. Nothing about the experience of transition would harm the character of a transgendered person. Each one's sense of morality, integrity, and ethics is unchanged, if not dramatically enhanced, because they wholly are no longer suppressing their identities and perpetrating the fraud they have, through transition, emphatically rejected. They may also have enhanced, through the lessons of experience at having honestly revealed their true selves, their understanding that other people can be as worthy of trust and confidence as they are of the trust and confidence of others.

Transgendered people, especially because of their own experience with identity conflict, are keenly aware of the importance to a child of her or his own perception of innate gender identity. Transgendered people also are very much aware of the requisite effort expended during childhood in the continuous attempt to meet intrinsic and extrinsic expectations for fulfilling the role of one's assigned sex. The roots of fundamental familial and other expectations must pre-date civilization since the primacy of preserving and perpetuating families links our present to humanity's past and future. Extrinsic expectations include not only family and the community, but especially those of like-aged peers, whether those peers are liked and admired or crude and unfriendly. Some of that peer pressure, in the aberrant logic of youth, seeks to challenge each child's physical sexual maturity. A strong sense of one's essential self is the surest defense against those assaults but gender conflict makes that especially challenging.

Tangible Diagnostics

Numerous (fMRI) studies of problem solving between groups of female and male subjects have shown identifiable and substantial differences in the areas of the brain each group utilized for various tasks. One study found significant differences in female and male brain organization for working memory (Speck et al. 2000)[125] and more recent studies with working memory led by Dr. Goldstein was mentioned earlier (Goldstein et al 2005).[126] It should be useful to know to what extent scans of MtF women fit the typical female model. MtF women's brains exhibit patterns that are typically female in most respects, in some respects, or typical only of other MtF women. Their patterns may be unique, closely approximate those of FtM men, look like those of normal males, or even resemble those of typically gay or lesbian people, although the BSTc studies previously cited suggest that the last alternative is unlikely. Men, whether homogendered or heterogendered, would be expected to share a common fMRI general pattern, if gender identity is the primary determinant of pattern type. Similarly, lesbian women and heterogendered women should exhibit the same female pattern.

Determination of gender identity may result from, cause differences in, or be independent of these brain activity patterns. Studies regarding sex difference in brain activity have been conducted with regard to the concept of gender identity but suppressed conflicting gender identities would distort study findings or, if the tests failed to detect the conflict, indicate that researchers were only finding what they expected to find. Failure to acknowledge the importance of gender identity can compromise even this important work.

Genome research should determine if there is a coding or miscoding unique to transgendered women and how it differs from that of other women and men. If coding is different, whether and to what extent reasoning, emotional, and other active and reactive mental processes are impacted might be determined. If there is a range of affected processes and even of kinds of gender identity, the importance of that information and its implications would not easily be overstated. A range of gender identity coding might influence the intensity of interest each person has in starting a family, as well as determining which parent she or he should be. The coding for gender identity conflict may not occur in the DNA *per se* but in a higher ordering of nucleosomes or other structure yet to be discovered. Progress toward resolution of these uncertainties may provide an interim key to greatly improved treatment as well as highlighting the path to eventual prevention or correction of the condition before birth.

None of this true research constitutes a threat to transgendered people because they know their gender identities are real, however they were formed. While advocates might fabricate, massage, distort, and interpret data as evidence of conclusions they reached long before generating their "findings," such efforts are not the practice of science. Whatever extant causative or descriptive components yield to accurate analysis, the whole of its nature still is immutable. As more becomes known about the condition's in utero formation, the availability of earlier effective intervention and treatment should increase. Researchers must pursue this worthwhile goal for the benefit of future transgendered people and all of society.

In the absence of an extant and objective diagnostic test of DNA, amniotic fluid, blood, or other substance showing presence of the transgendered condition, comparing brain-use patterns from fMRI studies indicate the condition's presence in living individuals. A funding source and willing participants continue to be needed for further studies to determine a discernable and useful pattern. Such a conclusive pattern for adult test subjects, should prove its potential effectiveness for children and adolescents. The value of a reliable and valid test used at the patient's earliest possible age would be enormous. Each day a child lives without the scourge of gender identity conflict is one day less of suffering, pretense, and self-reproach; and it is one more day of that child's living and growing as a whole person.

A sufficiently distinct fMRI pattern for MtF women and girls also should prove to be a valuable tool in helping to resolve a variety of cases for patients who present a puzzling array of what could be gender identity related conflicts. Whether the exhibited pattern was the product of an innate gender identity or resulted from environmental factors and learning should be apparent in pattern comparisons. Since I have never had such a scan, I may never know whether a childhood, adolescent, teen, or other pre-transition pattern, and a more recent pattern would have been similar. This same consideration would apply to comparisons of women before and after puberty, marriage, and bearing children. If longitudinal studies of patterns for women were unchanged by any of these events, the patterns might confidently be said to have been independent of any one or any set of them. If larger differences as compelling as the small area of the brains examined in the previously cited Zhou and Kruijver studies appeared with sufficient clarity in fMRI studies, the medical community would finally have a tangible diagnostic tool that could indicate, perhaps in the patient's early childhood, whether transition should be facilitated or discouraged. A discernable diagnostic pattern might still be of little practical use if the scan's cost, health risk, or availability to patients were prohibitive.

A Leading Institution

As already stated, Dr. Benjamin wrote about the work Dr. Hirschfeld was doing 100-years ago. These two doctors were not the only two people attempting to increase the depth of human knowledge regarding a subject critical to the meaning of being human and to human procreation. Germany's Richard von Krafft-Ebing, Britain's Dr. Havelock Ellis, and Americans Alfred Kinsey, Dr. William Masters, Margaret Mead, and Virginia Johnson were pioneers in the field of gender and sex research. As significant as was their pioneering work, it is disappointing in its failure to have analyzed, detected, hypothesized, or even anticipated the existence and importance of innate gender identity. If researchers did not know about gender identity, though, they would be unlikely to look for it or to recognize it. Like the early writers of sacred texts, these pioneers would unavoidably hear accounts of the experiences of their subjects through the filter of their own non-transgendered experience. Because of the condition's infrequent occurrence, transgendered people would have comprised a small part, if any, of that early work. Without the ability to discuss their condition with other transgendered people, subjects in early research would have had difficulty explaining the nature of their conflict. For that and other reasons, absence in early literature of gender identity analysis is not surprising. Whatever the reasons, the resulting delay in addressing the condition has been devastating for those transgendered people who might have been helped.

As part of a leading U.S. research and teaching institution, the Johns Hopkins Hospital (JHH) has had substantial resources that could be committed to explore the transgendered condition and treatment of sex ambiguity in infants. Like other institutions, JHH might have attempted to avoid controversy regarding the still poorly understood phenomenon of gender identity conflict. It would have done so at the costs both of society's knowing even less about the condition than is now known and of greatly delayed prospects for relief for the thousands of transgendered people who have been helped. That does not mean, however, that JHH fully embraced the Benjamin Standards of Care nor that it clearly has separated cases of ambiguous natal sex from those of gender identity conflict.

Doubtlessly aware of the work of pioneering behaviorist Dr. John B. Watson at JHH and behaviorist proponent Dr. Burrhus. F. Skinner at Harvard University, Dr. John Money co-authored a 1955 article regarding evidence of human hermaphroditism delimiting, at least for its authors and many of the work's readers, the false concept of psychosexual neutrality at birth (Money et. al. 1955, 301-319).[127] In 1960, JHH began performing sex-reassignment surgery. In the 1970s, it established a more elaborate system of screening and protocol but continued performing the surgery. Dr. Paul McHugh became director of the Department of Psychiatry and Behavioral Sciences at JHH in August, 1975 and retained that position for twenty-six years (McHugh 2001).[128] In 1979, a study by Dr. Jon Meyer, director of the sex-unit at JHH, questioned the benefits of reassignment surgery and JHH stopped performing the surgery (Duffy 1999, under gender-change issues).[129]

Still, JHH's attempt to assign gender to young children born with ambiguous genitalia implied that, once firmly established, gender identity would not change. Thus, even rejection of gender identity's innate origin did not mean that researchers believed established gender identity could be altered. Sex-assignment surgery performed to resolve a purely physical anomaly relatively soon after birth, according to Dr. Money's model, would be followed by enforcement of the assigned sex and gender. Because this approach ignored, discounted, or rejected the primacy of innate gender identity, the treatment actually was likely to create gender identity conflict, as it did for David Reimer. Dr. Meyer's study did not address the critical essence of innate gender identity. That primary screening criterion for both assignment and reassignment surgery was not, and still may not be, even considered in JHH's treatment of gender identity disorder.   Since gender identity does not lend itself convincingly to detection by contemporary means, those who deny its existence can disregard it. No one reasonably can hope to solve any problem where its cause is ignored. Symptoms might be treated but the cause of the problem must be addressed when the problem will not resolve itself.

From 1975 through 1979, simultaneous gender and sex assignment and reassignment at JHH for both intersexed and transgendered patients can be seen as an attempt to determine the superior method for resolving gender identity disorder. Before JHH discontinued its sex-reassignment program, that pursuit might also have been seen as an immodest assertion that the medical community could therapeutically alter the mind, the body, or both. The theoretical foundation of behaviorism certainly would support that view. The work of Watson and Skinner mentioned above indicated that sufficient training or reward and punishment could bring about effective therapeutic modification of essential self and behavior.

In 1975, Dr. McHugh's initial assessment of the department was that it was disorganized and that it attempted to see too many sides of the same elephant. As the department's director, he instituted a four-tiered classification system for patient evaluations differentiating them as either 1.) suffering from a medical condition affecting their brains, 2.) having a weakened "mental constitution" that might be strengthened, 3.) having acquired a destructive habitual pattern of behavior, or 4.) having experienced some significant or even traumatic event with which they were having difficulty contending. He instituted this classification system for the diagnosis and treatment of patients rather than tolerating the department's continued use of a seemingly endless array of analytical approaches, styles, and methods. Dr. McHugh's system could move patients through a process with a beginning, middle, and an end. That approach focused on how a condition was affecting each patient's life, rather than labeling the patient by the name or nature of a problem and attempting a variety of treatments to resolve the condition (McHugh 2001).[130] The rigidity of the classification and phase structure must have seemed excessively restrictive to some and ambiguous to others who expected a research hospital to accommodate and encourage practice of conflicting approaches and treatments. JHH apparently considered its obligation to improve measurably the lives of its present patients paramount and worthy of this compromise even though it ignored essential and unmalleable identity.

Whether sex-reassignment surgery, as an essential part of one therapeutic approach, did not fit within the McHugh model or the concept failed to satisfy a different set of expectations, Dr. McHugh decided he could not support such surgery at JHH In 1992, more than a decade after JHH stopped performing reassignment surgery, Dr. McHugh criticized sex-reassignment for MtF women by rhetorically asking why surgery would be performed on the bodies of men with a mental problem (McHugh 1992, III).[131] Obviously, his use of the word "men" meant that the MtF patient's physically male sex at birth was preeminent in determining that the child wholly must become a man. JHH became oriented to bringing the person's mind into concert with her or his physical sex. McHugh's view, decades after Dr. Money's 1955 work, that MtF women were men rests uncomfortably with the latter's assertion that a person is, or becomes, the person she or he is trained to become. Neither position, of course, would accommodate an innate dissonant gender identity.   Dr. McHugh was undoubtedly aware of Dr. Money's work. Even though sex-reassignment surgery had continued at JHH for four years after Dr. McHugh's arrival, his determination to attempt to change the patient's mind rather than the body, especially in light of Dr. Meyer's study but following Dr. Money's work, became the JHH approach. (Duffy 1999).[132]

When there is no valid indication that a transgendered patient's gender identity can be altered, ruling out remedial surgery, hormone treatments, and electrolysis to resolve an MtF woman's conflict would leave the transgendered patient in a continual unresolved and conflicted state of torment for the remainder of her life. She might be convinced to return to a life of suppression, but suppression is far different from resolution. Having revealed her conflict to experts who were unable or unwilling to help could leave an increasingly desperate patient with no constructive options. She might turn to substance abuse, self-mutilation, and/or suicide to escape her irresolvable conflict. The more fortunate MtF patient, though, would seek assistance from one of the many other qualified and experienced practitioners who offer treatment more closely conforming to the Benjamin Standards of Care.

When presented with the ambiguous or malformed genitalia of a newborn, doctors usually have surgically assigned a female sex. Doctors have been extremely reluctant to leave intact, or attempt to construct, a phallus that would be unlikely to perform adequately during sexual intercourse. This willingness to assign sex is rooted in the widely accepted belief that, as Money concluded above, infants have no psychosexual predisposition at birth and that, as children, they will not develop a healthy self-image if their genitals appear to be abnormal. The neutrality-at-birth idea was supported by behaviorist theory but especially by the work of Dr. Money and his colleagues. Drs. Diamond and Sigmundson cited articles by Dr. Money as author or lead author bearing dates from 1955 through 1972 as helping to establish the assumption of neutrality and the primacy of assigned and reinforced gender. Garnering special attention were those asserting the behaviorists' view that one's essential gender is not dependent upon genes and hormones (Diamond and Sigmundson 1997, 298).[133]

Drs. Diamond and Sigmundson wrote critically of the attempt to raise one male as though he were female. The subject of that attempt had refused to continue to live in his gender-assigned role and had lived, at and after his earliest opportunity, as a male. The authors wrote that, while Dr. Money moderated or repudiated some of his early and influential work in 1994, nearly forty years had passed since the publishing of that precedent-shaping and even standard-setting work. Based largely on that widely accepted early work, medical practice and attitudes were established that assumed gender identity neutrality at birth. Those attitudes still persist and support imposition of an inappropriate female sex upon males for whom a gender identity-appropriate remedy should have been, or should be, attempted (Diamond and Sigmundson 1997, 298).[134] Elapsed time since birth was deemed critical. At JHH, renowned urologist Dr. John Gearhart was referring to boys like David Reimer when he said that, in a similar situation today, no one would attempt to reassign his gender (Gearhart 2000.)[135] He might have said that, even if JHH does not do sex-reassignment surgery to help resolve gender identity conflict, at least he and his colleagues would be less likely to create gender identity conflict when attempting to repair a physical defect. Unfortunately, neither statement can be read as wholehearted acceptance of innate gender identity as the basis for gender identity disorder.

When a pseudo penis can be constructed for FtM transgendered men, surely a similar or identical procedure could be used for male infants born with ambiguous genitalia. The infant's gender identity still should be the primary consideration. It would be ironic if an expensive and painful remedial surgery were performed on an infant based on "his" apparent physical sex only to discover, after she endured a traumatic struggle with gender identity conflict, that her gender identity is feminine. The apparently low incidence of the transgendered condition makes that possibility remote, but until a routine gender identity test becomes the basis for every medical and governmental determination of physically appropriate sex, that chance remains.

I do not know from personal experience about any of the actions, methods, or motives of Dr. Money, and no practitioners have acknowledged to me that he influenced their acceptance of the concept of gender neutrality at birth. That concept appears to have been promulgated when little serious study regarding gender identity was underway in the United States. Why the need for additional study largely was ignored and why the neutrality concept gained wide acceptance without further rigorous testing are unanswered questions. A large part of the answer well may be a prudish American reluctance to support, or even tolerate, research into matters regarding gender identity and sexual orientation. Such research regarding children must be especially problematic since the knowledge, inclination, and interest of children is presumed to depend on the onset of puberty and parents likely would be unwilling to submit their children for testing. Yet, every parent knows, through observation and experience, that girls and boys are acutely aware of their own differences at a much earlier age. In the face of resistance to research in this area, the courage and dedication of anyone undertaking a serious study are praiseworthy. The terrible cost of neglecting such study is a continued blundering perpetuation of fallaciously founded half-truths and ignorance that underlie custom, medical treatment, and law. That cost is borne directly by those who suffer conditions that are not treated properly and indirectly by everyone who encounters those with the conditions.

Society, through its political instruments, should acknowledge its responsibility for mis-assigning gender, stop the practices by which that abuse continues, and support reasonable efforts better to address, and ultimately eliminate, the transgendered condition. Though unlike any other, the transgendered condition certainly is not the only matter desperately in need of additional research. For the sake of its children, our society should demand a deeper understanding of such abominations as parental incest with children, sexual relations among children, child pornography, and pedophilia. Society, for its own sake, must not fail to protect its children from such abuse. Surely, the goal of, and best use for, any additional knowledge gained from these studies is elimination of the behavior. Yet, some unfathomable logic resists such work as something that would somehow imply approval of, and cause an increase in, repulsive behavior; or even argue that parental rights to raise their own children are being infringed. While a few problems may be virtually self-correcting among resilient children, the history of this reprehensible behavior is that it has not responded favorably to neglect. All evidence indicates that, in matters where victims are unable to protect themselves, neglect favors the perpetrators of abuse.

The only "benefit" of society's disdain for this research is that the lack of data may mean that the incidence of these problems is grossly understated. Those most vocal in their condemnation of aberrant and abhorrent behavior are often absent from efforts to gain the political, financial, academic, and other resources necessary for the requisite increased research. If some of the inhibiting strident zealousness of those who would "protect" children were applied to promote the highest standards of ethical practice and stringent and sensitive controls in increased levels of research, substantial reduction in repulsive behavior might be realized.

The transgendered condition is not a target of, but is adversely and severely affected by, the reluctance to permit and encourage necessary gender and sex research. The almost incredible persistence of inaccurate conclusions reached in an environment where research is so challenging is symptomatic. The absence of more accurate information means that whatever does seem to be known, however inaccurate, incomplete, and incredible, will be propagated. For forty years or more, the assertion that a person's gender identity could be determined or assigned by those around her or him has been accepted by far too many medical practitioners. Society will never know the full cost of that tragic error.

The statement that "knowledge is power" was not intended to suggest that the exercise of such power was necessarily either beneficial or harmful. People have power if they decide they have it and resolve to use it, whether they act from knowledge or ignorance. When actions are based on firmly held but incorrect beliefs, exercise of that power will necessarily be destructive. Jefferson's view of the people as sovereigns suggests that they can cede to, and reclaim from, those to whom they grant power. Granting it is an exercise of power by the grantor, and confers great responsibility upon its representative. A social order that irresponsibly permits others to act for it ultimately is still responsible for the results. This certainly is true of society's persistent and fallacious assignment of gender. When inadequately grounded opposition prevents or impedes research that is needed to alleviate and, ultimately, eliminate substantial suffering, it is society's obligation, as it is also in that society's enlightened interest, to permit and secure the necessary research.

A Fable of Advocacy

Most fables are problematic in some respect. The following one does not pretend to challenge Aesop's reputation, but it does illustrate what could happen if researchers in the study of gender identity conflict or any subject appropriate to scientific endeavor approached their work from the standpoint of advocacy rather than science.

A magnet situated near the smoke department's compass let someone in the department observe and conclude that true north might really be east. When someone or something outside the department moved the magnet, unseen by the smokers, the smokers observed that true north now seemed to be west. The smokers concluded that there really must not be any such thing as true north. They based that conclusion on their observations of what had always been a reliable instrument, but they had not subjected their decision-making process to rigorous scientific testing. Since they now believed that every compass point had equal validity and could be called "true north", the smokers thought they could choose one compass point and steer their charges in that direction.

Later, through the smoker-influenced work of some surprised and uncomfortably warm aspiring arctic explorers in Tahiti, it became apparent that the smokers were wrong about true north and that its direction was indeed subject to a fundamental and natural, rather than an arbitrarily subjective, force. Further, the community decided that, should the smokers or anyone ever acquire the ability to move true north, the authority and responsibility to approve use of that ability must rest with a different department called ethics. Ethics may well determine that changing true north's location, though now possible, is an unacceptable option with unknowable implications and that the solution must be to fit the compass into a more appropriate container so that magnets have no misdirecting effect on it.

Rather than attempting to alter so fundamentally the essence of anyone's essential self, the medical community appropriately pursues harmony between gender identity and physical sex by altering the body to conform to honest identity. Changing a person's gender identity, should that ever become possible, would mean fundamentally changing who that person is without perfect knowledge of that person's potential before and after the change. Calling such action "ethical" would mean abandoning any reasonable definition of the word. Even with the patient's "informed" permission, the change would be a variant of assisted suicide where the patient could not know who her or his remains would become.

A Pragmatic View

Certainly most, if not all, physicians have chosen their professions primarily as a means of helping establish conditions that improve the quality of their patients' lives. The primary obligation first to do no harm is the corollary by which physicians obligate themselves to refrain from acting if they are unable to improve the quality of their patients' lives. Trained and tested in their laboriously acquired skills, physicians frequently must encounter situations that seem to cry out for application of their skills. A medical journal's jarring image of an infant born with ambiguous genitalia clearly shows the reader why any caring medical practitioner would feel compelled to act, but it also shows that the medical practice of assignment of physical sex without determining gender identity is still disturbingly common and accepted today (Karam and Baker 2004, 393).[136]

Great concern for the infant's prospective ability to experience a normal childhood with other children and her or his family is a compelling motivation in such cases. The child's ability to process solid food and liquids, her or his ability to evacuate waste, and parental ability to care for the child are more immediate reasons for medical intervention. Waiting until the child is sufficiently self-aware to make known her or his gender identity may not be possible before some surgery is medically necessary. In such instances, the procedures performed must be the least necessary to promote physical health and hygiene until the patient's gender identity can be determined. Other intersex conditions, such as Mosacicism, micropenis, Klinefelter, or Turner Syndrome, may mean that a child has enviably focused years to manifest innate gender identity.

In the same issue of the medical journal just cited, Drs. Reiner and Gearhart wrote of their findings regarding a study between 1993 and 2000 of 16 children ranging in age from five to sixteen years who had a rare neonatal genital abnormality. The abnormality exclusively affects the size, shape, and/or condition of the phallus. Fourteen study participants had been surgically assigned and were initially raised as sexual females; the parents of the other two children had refused to permit reassignment surgery. Following the cases for between three and eight years revealed that all 16 showed "interests and attitudes" of typical males, although five of the children were living as girls. Eight of the study's subjects identified themselves as males during the study. Drs. Reiner and Gearhart concluded that routine reassignment of physically male patients as females needed to be reexamined (Reiner, Gearhart 2004, 330-341).[137]

This work is additional confirmation of what Dr. Diamond and Dr. Sigmundson, had done, earlier work by Dr. Reiner, and the efforts of many others. It is further evidence that gender identity exists, that it is a separate matter from one's apparent physical sex, and that many in the medical community have continued to ignore gender identity when treating children who are transgendered or whose physical sex at birth is ambiguous. Such mistreatment of these patients occurs at tremendous cost to the children, the children's families, and the society that permits this abuse.

Of particular concern should be the five children in the study who adamantly insisted that they are female despite their consistently showing attitudes and interests typical of males. Part of the agreement between the children's parents and the study's researchers stipulated that the children would not be told of their condition at birth, and that they would be told they were and are the girls they seem to be. Most people who never have experienced gender identity conflict are ill-prepared to imagine the effect on a child of such an insistence from the adults she or he is forced by nature to trust as caring parents. If the gender identity of the five children is male, then their insistence that they are female is a desperate attempt to convince themselves and others that their fraud is reality and that the immutable reality of their suppressed gender identity does not exist. The parents and researchers being aware of their effort to alter innate gender by not telling the children was the exact opposite of my experience and the experience of most children who attempt to suppress their gender identities.

My parents never were part of such a study and never agreed to such an insidiously destructive pact. They thought they had every reason to believe that I was the male child indicated by my physical sex and birth certificate. They never had heard of gender identity nor gender identity conflict. Their having followed their perceptions in my rearing made them complicit in, or coauthors of, the unintended fraud of which I was the central character. The fraud was perpetrated on, as well as by, me and all who knew me before transition. Such a fraud is the inescapable result of the extensive abuse of society's power and responsibility to act for the good of all of its members, and will continue so as long as the practice of assigning gender based on physical sex at birth continues.

The five children above who essentially insisted that their parents had not lied to them and that each is the girl "her" family has helped "her" to become should surprise no one. No reasonable adult who has grown up in a caring family would expect a child to be skeptical innately about the insistent assertions of the parents and family that have fed, clothed, and nurtured her or him from earliest memory. The amazing performances were the eight who insisted they are male, and at so early an age. Their actions are what shout so forcefully to those who will hear that gender identity is the unerring essential compass that must help each of us chart the course of our lives. It is as much a fundamental element of each person's essential self as is any other unalterable aspect of each person's true self.

It is a bizarre irony that slightly increased knowledge about a subject would make some people less able to understand it. Whether by intent or methodology, many of those professionals who do not regularly treat transgendered people seem frustratingly eager to discard the work of their fellows in favor of unproven and even untested descriptions of the condition that happily conform to their bias. This same frustration must be felt keenly by intimates of other fields who are exhaustively familiar with subjects foreign to the knowledge of much of the rest of humanity.

Problems of physical health, even when a condition's symptoms are due to an extremely rare condition or disease, usually present tangible symptoms that can be tested or compared to define the problem. When those whose gender identity and physical sex have always been consonant are confronted by an instance of extant dissonance, they may logically wonder if the concept of gender identity is valid for everyone, only valid for those who are transgendered, or if there is an explanation other than gender identity conflict for the professed dissonance. Such curiosity and/or skepticism is useful and productive if it fosters further careful research. When the response of qualified professionals is to eschew the foundation of their profession and to assert their own belief that the world simply was not put together that way, they dismiss the work of competent and careful researchers as having reached an impossible or unacceptable result. These people betray the commitment they have made to their field, diminish the valuable tool that is science, and, if they prevail, would compromise the integrity, effectiveness, and worth of their profession.

Trusting the Method

Given the tenet that the Creator's hand will be evident in whatever He creates and that He created man; it follows that God created the best of art and science since those things would not exist without man. If its methods are honestly applied, the gift of medical science will permit discovery of the cause of, and improved treatment for, gender identity conflict. That confidence is not based on faith, alone. As a college student home on Christmas break, I saw a map of the floor of the Atlantic Ocean I had not seen when the magazine first arrived (National Geographic Society 1968).[138] The continental shelf of Africa's west coast matched precisely the shelf of the Americas extending from Brazil to Maine, Greenland seemed to have been attached to Quebec, and there were other apparent pairings. When I returned to school, I asked a geology professor if there were an explanation for how those huge landmasses could have been connected. He said that roughly ten percent of geologists accepted the idea, that a number of hypotheses had been generated to explain it, but none of them was persuasive.

By studying the work of other geologists, comparing soil samples, utilizing sensors to detect continental drift, and other measures, the discipline's students and practitioners have now come to accept plate tectonics and a history of continental separation and connectedness by a margin similar to the one by which the theory previously had been rejected. Innate curiosity must make life extremely difficult for those who lack confidence in the discipline of science that so imperfectly but relentlessly pursues truth and ultimately rejects falsehood. While a few scientists may see such an elegant tool for attempting to make sense of the universe and all it contains as undeniably manmade, most other scientists and many non-scientists do recognize that this, too, is a gift of the Creator.

This gift, like so many others, often is abused but especially so when scientists become advocates. As children know intuitively, their telling the whole truth sometimes means including things they would rather omit. Scientists who massage some data and selectively overlook other data may strengthen the case for their hypothesis, but they do so at great risk to their reputations and to the value of their profession. Their "findings" not only mislead others who follow their misdirection but would deflect research from potentially more productive paths. Where that misdirection is deliberate, no richly deserved punishment can rectify the potential harm that could result.

The founders of our current judicial process for handling criminal matters concluded that, since almost any point can be argued persuasively in the absence of contradiction, the greatest opportunity for arriving at the truth rests in having two opposing sides each present their strongest possible argument of the case. The scientific method however eschews advocacy in favor of skepticism so that the true scientist attempts to disprove his own case and other presumed "truths". Scientific truth is what remains, however tenuously, when exhaustive efforts to disprove that truth have failed. When a judge must decide a matter in the absence of advocates, she or he may best serve the cause of justice by adopting the scientific approach. It is most unlikely, however, that reliable science would be the result if scientists acted as advocates in an adversary system and attempted to prove their hypotheses, rather than striving to disprove them.

The pivotal conversation I had with my mother while I was a child, after which I became determined to hide and to attempt to suppress my gender identity, coincided with publication and acceptance of behaviorist work asserting that gender identity was learned and not innate. Had my mother sought and obtained professional guidance on my behalf, she almost certainly would have been told that the latest work by "experts" had determined that simply discouraging any cross-dressing and overtly feminine behavior and encouraging overtly masculine behavior would be sufficient and should be effective in resolving the problem. Of course, the Pavlovian approach to so intrinsic a matter as gender identity could not have resolved the conflict.

The "carrot and stick" approach would have meant family and professional encouragement that augmented my continuing attempt to suppress my gender identity. It would have meant my living the same way I did by suppressing all overt signs of femininity and appearing to be as normal a male as possible when other people were present. Someone aware of Dr. Benjamin's approach, however, would have recommended a vastly different solution. I never can know what effect an earlier attempt at transition would have had on its course, but if only because I would have avoided decades of identity suppression, my life would have been much different.

Practitioners and Progress

Some of the important work done by psychiatrists and psychologists does not lend itself to quantitative analysis, but that characteristic is grossly inadequate as an indication of the worth of these essential disciplines. Difficulty in the precision of assessments extends to clinical methods and practice. Psychiatrists, of course, can prescribe medication as part of their practice. In some cases, practitioners find that therapy and medication are better than either tool used alone. Although some psychologists have been licensed to prescribe psychotropic medication, others have not sought prescriptive authority because of their belief that counseling is at least as effective in the treatment of some disorders. Further, psychotherapy does not carry the increasingly well-documented risks posed by medication nor is a relapse likely if that medication is withheld. My attempting to summarize the complexity of disorders, options for treatment, standards for professionals, aggravating and mitigating patient characteristics, public and private funding mechanisms, etc. is beyond the focus of this work. While mental health professionals seek to improve their disciplines, accounts of patients who have benefited from capable mental health treatment are legion.

Skeptics question the ability of mental health professionals to determine and treat patients by any means. One might as reasonably question whether any duly licensed professional is ever really capable of accomplishing the work to which s/he has dedicated themself, sought and obtained the requisite credentials, and acquired an extensive amount of experience. The alternatives skeptics propose usually offer far fewer objective prospects for success. The regimen they suggest for establishment and maintenance of high professional standards is far less rigorous. Some in the medical and mental health communities have taken decades to begin to acknowledge the horrendous burden caused by mis-assignment of sex, and others have yet to acknowledge that burden and their role in causing or exacerbating it. This history shows both the fallibility of the profession's practitioners and the imperfect, yet ultimately effective, mechanisms for correcting their failings.

Gender identity conflict continues to occur because of the absence of a proven and efficient means to assess genetic determination of gender identity, and to intervene medically to prevent the conflict. Even if an fMRI or other post-birth diagnostic testing could indicate essential identity with validity and reliability, that test still would require a subject to be old enough to respond to questions. The child, then, would already be aware of, and might be determined to hide, her or his conflict. Without even that problematic diagnostic, society, but especially transgendered people and their families, remain dependent on voluntary disclosure and the skill of practicing psychiatrists and psychologists to help identify and resolve the conflict. Members of those professions fail themselves and society when they ignore work with which they disagree, assert that something is true when it can be proven false, or claim something is false when it cannot be disproved. These professionals can do great harm to their patients, themselves, their profession, and society. It is encouraging, though, that there may be none more aware of this potential for harm than a substantial portion of each profession's own members.

Society's continuing reliance on apparent sex-at-birth for assignment of both gender and sex, especially when the two are in conflict, causes its medical, legal, mental health, and other professions to utilize a lexicon of categories and subsets inappropriately with people who always should have been categorized their gender identities. While there is an undeniable physical aspect to sexual intercourse, even the most hedonistic advocate must acknowledge that at least a minimal amount of mental and emotional commitment or awareness is part of the process. Anyone who would argue that the act only involves two people responding to a fundamental biological imperative would dispute the whole history of culture and advanced civilization. Even offering the argument utilizes faculties that would never have been needed if people only experienced purely physical relationships. The gender identity of that non-physical component is fundamental to any meaningful discussion regarding the relationship between the individuals involved. The exception to this, of course, is rape or other sexual assault

In the current absence of reliable and valid tests to determine gender identity, physicians continue to assign each infant's gender even though no attempt has been made to assess it. In an effort to recognize this insensitivity or inability, transgendered people in and outside of the mental health field have sought changes in policies and practices regarding classification and treatment of the transgendered condition. Gender identity conflict is described as a disorder in the American Psychiatric Association's DSM IV, but that does not mean it will always be so characterized (American Psychiatric Association 2000).[139]

Shortly after my diagnosis and surgery, a different view gained currency. Some assert that the identities of transgendered people are sound and it is their conflicting bodies that cause dissonance. The American Psychiatric Association has also considered that whatever its origin, the transgendered condition may not really be a disorder but an elective orientation on a spectrum of personality to which certain people are inexplicably drawn. Any revision of the manual might be changed to reflect either or both of these views until a future edition. Surely, no transgendered person would describe her or his condition as a choice, nor would she or he accept that characterization. A mental health professional who would knowingly facilitate surgical sex reassignment for a reason other than true gender identity conflict, called a disorder or not, betrays one's self, patient, and profession. Use of imprecise and/or widely inaccurate terminology unnecessarily complicates the practice of anyone charged with this responsibility.

Skeptics who question the condition's classification might opine glibly that "Having a female gender identity is quite normal for roughly four billion people on the planet. Therefore, It hardly can accurately be described as a disorder". That absurd inference ignores the fact that more than ninety-nine percent of those four billion people were born physically female and have no gender identity conflict. How any condition that so significantly impairs the normal socialization, social interaction, romantic life, and other gender-related activity appropriate to an MtF woman's gender identity and physical sex would not be considered a "disorder" is almost incomprehensible. If the standard is set by looking only at people with similar outward symptoms, then the sociopath who behaves like other sociopaths is "normal". If gender identity conflict is not a disorder, the term "disorder" has an unfathomable, illogical, and, hence, useless meaning. Unlike other mental disorders however, gender identity conflict is not solely, or even primarily, in the mind but between a consonant mind and its diverging body.

When I talked with my psychiatrist about another matter several months after my sex-reassignment surgery, he told me of the serious consideration being given to reclassifying the condition and he wondered what I thought about the possible change. My spontaneous, if defensive, response was that I had no objection because, while I was suppressing my gender, I was able to function in a rational manner both personally and professionally. I should have responded, though, by saying that I thought those promulgating that view should be vigorously challenged.

My sister, a speech pathologist, and I discussed what constituted a clinical problem in her field. Her profession employs precise terms that minimize the gray area between a person's qualifying or failing to qualify for remedial speech services under that person's health insurance plan, or federal, state, or local government programs. A mildly distracting mannerism or vocal impediment irritating to some listeners is not deemed to require clinical attention unless the distraction impedes clear communication of the speaker's thought. While I was seeking a theoretically pure definition that would reinforce an inflexible standard of correct speech, the fact that some speakers, especially in commercial television, use nonstandard speech devices to garner greater attention for themselves and their message should be obvious. Some speakers have had spectacular careers despite, or even partly because of, their unusual speech mannerisms. The definition I would prefer has no practical utility in an established profession where diagnosable problems and their prescribed treatment regimens, at a reasonable cost, enjoy the dedicated attention of experienced practitioners like my sister.

The desire for precise terminology is far from universal. Confusion can facilitate mis-characterizations and blurred distinctions especially regarding conditions among vulnerable minorities. The consideration of suppressed gender identity conflict as anything other than a major diagnosable medical condition is distressing for this and other reasons. I had decided, too quickly, that the condition was not a disorder because its victims are not prevented from affecting "normal" behavior, nor does it cause her or him to be a physical threat to other people. In retrospect, I was thinking about a distinction like the one that typically separates neuroses from psychoses. Those conditions, though, are disorders, even if not all neuroses require treatment.

The fact that a suppressing MtF female is desperately engaged in a nearly constant effort to maintain her male and masculine façade means she is struggling with an horrendous conflict few people are prepared to face. Technically, each effort to protect and project her masculine façade is dissociative relative to her suppressed gender identity. Practitioners who suggest that such a problem is not a disorder and that suppressing transgendered people are not in desperate need of help is an abrogation of their obligation to relieve suffering.

Of course, if the condition were not a disorder, it would not require treatment. That expedient must be attractive from a budgetary perspective to boards and executives attempting to allocate limited resources. Similarly, practitioners facing excessive workloads might be relieved of a whole class of cases. A variation of these considerations probably applies to many conditions that might be seen as chronic rather than acute, so that only acute conditions tend to be addressed. Unfortunately, as much blood might be lost from one-hundred smaller cuts as from a single large wound. The suffering will continue if its cause is not addressed.

Whether the condition is or is not classed as a disorder is much more than a question of semantics. Were diagnostic manual classifications reserved to professionals whose sole use of them was to aid their patients, it probably would not matter if the transgendered condition were called a chocolate bar. The condition, in my case, meant experiencing unusual early-childhood thoughts and behavior with attendant feelings of low self-esteem. Later, I tried to understand why I did not wish to be with "attractive" women but to be like them. My sexual fantasies never included my performance as a male and I knew that definitely was not the sentiment expressed by the males around me. I repeatedly experienced the expense and dishonesty of acquiring and then purging sex-inappropriate attire, and the inevitable reacquiring of clothing that would permit me to present myself, at least privately, as a pseudo female. My intellectual struggle to understand what was happening included desperation to see interviews, films, and documentaries about transgendered people. I experienced unrelenting feelings of guilt regarding the obsession. My climatic search for resolution meant meeting the standards of two qualified mental health professionals, sharing the experience of finally revealing who I was to my parents, then sisters, relatives, neighbors, clients, friends, and complete strangers. It also meant enduring hundreds of hours of electrolysis, and the expense and life-threatening risk of major surgery.

To assert that any of this, much less all of it, was because of a whimsical choice I made and kept making and is not a disorder is to have made up one's mind without understanding the evidence and to greatly underestimate mis-identify the experience. The assertion is a denial of innate gender identity, for which their does appear to be increasing evidence. The conviction standard in a criminal case may be "beyond reasonable doubt", but if the above does not transform suspicion into conviction, it can only be because someone is unwilling to be convinced.

If someone is unable to reconcile two apparently irreconcilable but true ideas (called "cognitive dissonance" during my undergraduate introduction to psychology) she or he will fabricate a rationale that permits accepting both ideas as being true or, less often, will discard the one that is deemed less true. If two ideas are irreconcilable but apparently true, the dissonance should lead to greatly increased knowledge and understanding. Those who would assert that they understand gender identity conflict but believe it is a phase or a choice either have had too little personal experience with the condition or they refuse to accept its true nature. For many suppressing sufferers, the condition's contrast with their own sense of acceptable religious, moral, or ethical behavior makes acknowledging and embracing its *in utero* genesis unacceptable. They have struggled mightily in ultimately having accepted that conclusion, but they have accepted an erroneous one. That conclusion comes from explanations of others who do not understand the conflict. If a person has spent a lifetime in water even to the point of near drowning, she is unlikely or irrationally willing to accept a desert dweller's definition, however well-intentioned and well-schooled, of the word "wet." Water is different from gender identity conflict in most respects of course, but decades of intimate experience with each one is a powerfully convincing provider of certitude. Assertions about water that exclude the fact that it is, or ever has been, wet cannot be accurate or constructive. For MtF women, including those attempting to suppress their conflict, anyone's denial of her condition's origin ultimately must be acknowledged as fatally flawed.

I had struggled with attempting to understand the pulse-pounding obsessive thoughts, compulsive behavior, and inevitable self-reproach from earliest memory through more than forty years of introspection. The scant relevant material I had studied failed to facilitate an accurate self-diagnosis and to indicate the surest path to resolution. As the possible revision of the diagnostic manual and the moratorium on sex-reassignment surgery at Johns Hopkins suggested, even some professionals today do not yet understand or accept the likely origin of, and appropriate treatment for, the condition. Since transition, I understand far more thoroughly how I failed to assess the conflict correctly and why I postponed as long as possible seeking competent professional diagnosis and treatment.

The essence of the inability to understand my own gender identity conflict earlier is that it was a very long and frustrating journey of suppressed identity. I contended constantly with a fundamental failure to be the person I had so thoroughly convinced others I was, but I did not know why and how I had failed. The experience was like trying to inflate a balloon (the outer surface or façade an MtF woman presents to her world,) but the balloon had no opening, I lacked the appropriate substance with which to fill it, and inflating and keeping that balloon inflated was the preeminent purpose for my existence. Maintaining that façade seemed important both for my own sake and others as the manifestation of my only accepted identity. It seemed essential to be the person everyone I knew and cared for thought I was. Mental health professionals and researchers who work to help eliminate those horribly wasteful and destructive façades do an incalculable beneficial service both to suppressing transgendered people and to all with whom those people come in contact.

Gender Anatomy

If differences among the samples in the Zhou and Kruijver BSTc studies previously cited were caused by environmental, familial, behavioral, dietary or other external causes, they could not have been part of each subject's essential self before birth. Dr. Vilain's earlier cited mouse-embryo work is a preliminary indication though, that the hypothesis of gender identity as an essential part of each person's earliest development yet may find irrefutable scientific validity. The transgendered person's "knowing" that gender identity is a fundamental part of each person's essence is far different from being able to demonstrate that knowledge in a clinical sense. The former provides essential self-awareness for transgendered people through and beyond transition and the latter is essential support for the professionals whose help transgendered people and others must rely. The extent to which gender identity determines each person's self-image is an important aspect of this and other accounts of suppression, transition, and reflection.

The fact that only one corroborative BSTc study, whose authors included some of the initial study's team members, supports the original BSTc study should not be viewed with excessive suspicion. Given the small subject area of the brain studied, the difficulty of obtaining suitable specimens, and the fringe status of the entire transgendered population, it should surprise no one that there is a dearth of conclusive studies supporting the existence of a genetic or other causative brain anomaly related to the phenomenon. Funding sources for such research are not available in uncontested abundance. Unless transgendered or other concerned persons are inclined and able to do self-funded research, or the research is funded by transgendered persons or organizations acting on their behalf; divining the condition's cause and perfecting the earliest possible means of wholly remedial intervention may remain beyond the grasp of medical science.

Leaders of at least one major religious denomination have suggested that sexual intercourse without even the remote possibility that a child could result is a perversion of God's gift of that aspect of an important human relationship. By extension, sexual activity that did not envision the possibility of conception also would be a perversion. Post-reassignment transgendered women, like women who have had radical hysterectomies, must know that the remote possibility of their conceiving is on a plane with fantasy and the unlikeliest of miracles. Today's most skilled surgeons do not have the ability to create the full physical anatomy of female reproduction, to alter the coding for the requisite DNA , and to impart a female life experience to complete an MtF woman's transition. Even if all of that were possible, the cost of the procedures would be prohibitively high. Medical science may never have the capability to enable a post-operative transgendered woman to bear her own children, however fervently she might wish it.

Many cis-gendered women cannot bear children but most or all did not grow up knowing of that inability, and they still were raised as women. Conventional heterogendered couples may decide before marriage that they do not intend to have children, even if they believe that capacity to be present. Again, each wife would have matured certain that her gender identity and physical sex represented the potential to become a mother. That potential, whether physically remote or purportedly undesired, must be an unknowably large but significant part of spousal relationships.

The expectations any male has for his wife must be tempered, preferably early in the relationship, by the realization that his wife will also have expectations regarding her husband. When they marry, each spouse does not promise to satisfy all of her or his spouse's expectations and in the anticipated manner but to dedicate each one's whole self to the other in an exclusive relationship. A key point must be each spouse's voluntary, rather than coerced, commitment.   Separation and/or divorce is the likely outcome if one or both spouses find that the original commitment no longer can be kept, that the couple strongly disagrees about what the promises really meant, or that there were important expectations that should have been, but were not, part of their vows.

Each spouse grows in her or his relationship with the other finding new ways to fulfill, and be fulfilled in, their mutual commitments.   My parents were married for more than 60 years. The marriages of my older and younger sisters are tracking toward a similar number. These six people have experienced dramatic changes in their lives, and they have done so as couples who have grown in their mutual commitment through or despite those changes. Even if each person were wholly the person her or his spouse thought she or he married, each one must have changed in unanticipated ways. Their respective acceptance of those changes was not a matter of chance but of a commitment each made long ago and has held inviolate.

Many MtF women have been married to women before their transition. Their highly stressful, traumatic, and heart-wrenching struggle with gender identity was much more than an unsought or unanticipated opportunity for growth. Disclosure of their conflict meant an end to the previous stability of a seemingly conventional nuclear family devolving from the "husband's" having made a promise she was incapable of fulfilling. I knew that I could not promise to be a husband and expect to fulfill the entirety of that promise. While I might have learned intimately about parts of the spousal relationship and my desired role as a natural parent by marrying as a male, the tuition cost in human terms for living as a male in that relationship would have been unacceptably high. I do not write this from a judgmental perspective or as an assertion of self-righteousness but as an acknowledgement of my lack of capacity to become a whole husband and father. If anyone would argue that being a spouse and parent is the primary goal and that which spouse or parent she or he is does not matter, transitioned people who married before their transitions should be convincing evidence that which spouse one becomes not only matters but is preeminent.

To a suppressing MtF woman, the woman she married must be little different from an exaggerated sort of roommate and not her life-mate. As a husband before her transition, an MtF woman must know, at some level, that she lacks the potential to provide the masculine and male components of completeness implicit in a traditional heterogendered relationship, even as she had committed to providing essential aspects for her wife. Married to another woman, the MtF woman has no husband who could become the father of her children. The relationship between these two women would have had far greater prospects for success if it were based on homogendered interest, but neither spouse had that intent because they married as people of opposite gender. Still, neither spouse had the requisite gender identity to be a husband and father.

The knowledge that the MtF woman cannot be a natural mother or a whole father, in the full sense of either term, and the absence of childhood fantasies shared with girlhood friends about when and how many children her family might have are insurmountable obstacles for the suppressing MtF woman who marries as a man. The satisfaction that she would expect from sexual intercourse would not have even the remote possibility of producing a child at its core since she would imagine her wife as the child's father. No one reasonably would contend that post-menopausal women, women who have had hysterectomies, men who have had vasectomies, and others who presumably cannot procreate are never moved to have sexual intercourse. In each of these instances, though, there would have been the opportunity in their past to have had sexual intercourse where the possibility of a pregnancy was present. This may seem like a "straining at a gnat and swallowing a camel" concern for a post-operative MtF woman, but it is supported by the accounts of other MtF women. The above considerations devolve from the gender identity, regardless of her or his natal physical sex, of each person who is part of each of the relationships.

The Teenage View

I never had a sexual fantasy of being with a woman as a man, with a man as a man, or as a woman with another woman. My fantasies of a typical heterogendered female and a general knowledge regarding the preferences of homogendered people should have made self-diagnosis of my condition straightforward, but I did not understand that my essential self is a feminine female. The accounts of "normal" sexual activity and interests "typical" males shared with me were, of course, foreign to me. Since adolescence, the plethora of images of women in what were intended to be provocative poses elicited a yearning for their experience or a curiosity about what their experience would be. High school, college, military, and other social instances of exposure to, or discussions of, such activities always left me at a decided disadvantage. The experience was much like someone's telling a terribly amusing story where the punch line was in a language I alone could not understand.

During a high school gym class, its teacher provided a description of a certain activity in which, he said, most teen-aged males engage in the privacy of their own homes. His information was sufficiently descriptive that the activity to which he referred was unmistakably clear. Never having had such an experience though, I did not understand why anyone would engage in it. When I told my father what the teacher had said and that I would not want him to think that I would do such a seemingly disgusting thing, he seemed skeptical. It is odd and quaint that I even mentioned the subject to anyone, including my father, but the teacher's remarks had included his saying that knowledge of the activity would not come as a complete surprise to most parents. I had interpreted his comments as detailing a guilty-till-proven innocent situation where I really was naively innocent. Fundamental biochemistry and human development apparently do allow for variations. It would be more than ten years before those stirrings and my cross-dressing would come together and mis-direct me toward a very poorly self-diagnosed clothes fetish. If I had to live as a male, I apparently had resolved that my affected male persona would be celibate.

Long after that gym class met, President Clinton's Surgeon General dared to discuss the same topic. She proved unequivocally she not only had touched an allegorical "third rail" of public discourse, but that she had done so in a manner that soon led to her becoming an ex-Surgeon General. Since the transgendered condition is uncommon and since other transgendered people must also struggle with the biochemistry of their physical selves at and after puberty, I have included my own quintessentially personal experiences at that time.

Except for possible exacerbation of my wanting to cross-dress, succumbing to hormonal urges or periodic releases of my suppressed identity never inspired pursuit of a sexual relationship with anyone. Like other students in high school of a certain age, I increasingly became aware of the biochemical dynamics of maturation. I knew it would be considered quite normal or even inevitable that I would marry a woman and, with her, create a family. The interests of other students and prospects for their relationships were obviously and inescapably related. However, contending with my own gender identity conflict was so confusing, yet acutely secret, that I was unable to share and express the urge influencing most of my contemporaries, much less the rest of civilization. If I had "fathered" a child in whatever context, as have many MtF transgendered women before their transitions, I would have had grave reservations about being the child's mother or father. Still, I would have intended to be among the most committed of parents. The shade of pink that colored my glasses made it impossible for me to experience the joys and pain of all that goes into establishing and being a part of my own family.

My interest in political science devolved, at least partly, from wanting to learn about the non-biological fundamental forces that move people to structure a society that preserves and perpetuates itself. If someone had no spouse and/or children, romantic love and procreation would not be her or his primary reason for living. She or he still would have great interest in an advanced social order because life, liberty, and the pursuit of happiness are still important in each person's own life. Many of my interests, motives, and views were different from those of other people my age. I did not share the interest of my classmates in contemporary culture, nor did I share their preoccupation with dating. How these and other differences among people might be accommodated while basic principles are protected in law also fed my curiosity about political science. How current laws have been established, whether the underlying matters were appropriate to legislative action, and what the procedures and resources necessary to change laws that should be changed are does matter to me and should matter to everyone affected by those laws.

In high school, one of the students organized a "politics club" with a very broad scope. A guest instructor from a local college spent nearly an hour one evening talking to the club about the Sino-Soviet rift and its significance for U.S. foreign policy. At that time, few topics were more important in international politics but asking the speaker to address so broad a topic in one evening was certainly unfair. Another meeting might have focused on changes to the mundane process for electing class officers. Learning about the difference between breadth or scale and details or specifics was an important indirect part of such sessions. Unlike much of our academic work though, club membership meant an opportunity to select and share perspectives on governmental matters of common interest.

The "politics club" met briefly one afternoon to review applications for membership beginning the following school year. Other predominantly male members began discussing names and commenting about which girls were sufficiently attractive to "qualify" for membership. I decided to object to the next girl's application based on the club's inadequately defined criteria for reviewing applications. The next application, of course, belonged to the classmate who would become our class homecoming queen. Fortunately, my objection was quickly dismissed and she promptly was selected for membership. I learned that politics not only consists of procedures and policies but also, if not preeminently, of personalities and judgment. This episode was an overdue, unmistakable, and unforgettable lesson in the importance of the third and fourth elements of politics. Policies and process are of little value if they produce a poor result. These views and experiences are not offered simply as an explanation, an excuse, or as additional biographical data. They show some of the individual and societal costs of unaddressed and unrelieved gender identity conflict suppression that desperately demand to be redressed.

15. The Law and the Church

Friend or Foe

From the hunter/gatherer ancestors subsisting at the dawn of civilization to contemporary law enforcement and military personnel fighting the war on terrorism, the ability of humans quickly and accurately to identify friend or foe has been essential to survival. Refining that ability has meant honing perceptions to a fine, though certainly not flawless, edge. When considering the difference between appearance and other characteristics, we can acknowledge inevitable bias where it exists, and attempt not to compensate for it but to go beyond it by looking for positive characteristics and abilities offsetting or outweighing ones deemed less desirable. That effort may be time-consuming and fraught with uncertainty, but making it whenever possible is an obligation humanity owes itself.

It is far quicker and easier to generalize that, because one was once offended by someone with blue eyes, that we must view all blue-eyed people with suspicion. Quicker and easier, yes, but reliance solely on such physical characteristics is obviously an inefficient, unreliable, immoral, and often illegal basis for the assessment. Adverse bias is at least as likely to significantly and adversely affect its practitioner as it is to harm the people toward whom it is directed. Unfortunately, the burden of sustaining bias seldom is acknowledged by those who hold it.

The Nation recognizes the great work of Dr. Martin Luther King at least annually. As a persistent but nonviolent advocate, Dr. King forged a far stronger nation by helping to release all of the human gifts of a suppressed segment of American society. He helped relieve the suppressors of their self-imposed burden of suppressing. He helped millions of people experience greater fulfillment of this nation's promise of liberty. Most aspects of Dr. King's work directly or indirectly affected and continues to affect every member of American society.

Dr. King called for a national awakening. The nation could not reasonably expect to end its destructive and senseless racial bias unless it learned from its past. While most of America's history is replete with the laudatory, altruistic, and heroic motives and actions of its people, part of that history was far less worthy. Many colonial and other Americans not only denied the right of people brought to America by force to live free, have liberty, and pursue happiness, but they even questioned whether such people were fully human. Americans of similar ilk who have exploited those who entered the United States illegally would deny to them the rights of citizenship. Exploiters who profess to favor citizenship know that they will pay a very small share of the associated costs of services provided to their workers and the workers' families.

One might expect that only a rationale based on superiority would permit one people to enslave another, but world history shows the contrary. Jewish slaves in Egypt, Greek slaves in Rome, and, more recently, indentured white immigrants in early U.S. history are examples of servitude with that different basis. Whatever the excuse, history shows an appallingly unfortunate tendency of some people, and even whole societies, to treat other people as undeserving of the same rights they have guaranteed themselves by their system of government. Prior to the establishment of the Hammurabic Code, uniform civil rights were not recognized as belonging to all humans. They were granted or withheld by capricious circumstance and secured by the power to dominate. Those early wielders of power, however that power was acquired, enslaved others because they could, not because they deemed their own humanity to be inherently superior to that of people who were less powerful. In a tacit admission of not being wholly superior, Romans adopted elements of the cultures of those they enslaved. Enslavement based on one or a set of particular physical characteristics crosses a line even other enslavers resisted. Representative government, equal rights, rule of law, and equal justice form the fragile barrier that separates American society from the crude, abusive, and destructive system of those earlier days.

The benevolent condescension evident in an earlier century's rationale of the "white-man's burden" shows that, while no society is qualified to judge its ancestors because it cannot be their peers, an enlightened society can and must reject some of their views. Each American who is not wholly dedicated to the ideals of Dr. King shares a society of real, intense, and often unbidden sensory richness that informs her or his thoughts. One's perception of that reality may lead to the saving of her or his own life or the lives of other people, but it also can mislead that person and cause the taking of innocent life. If race, height, age, or any single feature of appearance is the exclusive determinant of friend or foe status, the decision is certain to be incorrect in one or more, if not all, instances.

Answering the friend or foe question is compounded by the shades of possible responses, the time available to decide, the person or people making the decisionto be incorrect in one or more instances.is the exclusive determinant from its past, and the education and technology utilized. These and other variables can cause the seemingly simple question of accurate identification to be excruciatingly difficult to answer. Concern for self-preservation that results in everyone being deemed a threat unless or until proven otherwise verges on unrelenting paranoia. Presuming that everyone is harmless unless or until she or he presents indisputable indication of intent to harm abrogates responsibility for security. A balanced approach preserves appropriate concern for security while minimizing abuse of those who are not threatening. From a practical standpoint, that balance may be impossible to achieve.

Security of its citizens, assets, and interests is the first concern of most governments. Addressing that concern requires the dedication of limited energy, time, and other resources. Each nation reviews carefully and constantly whether it has assessed accurately the threats it is facing and has allocated the resources necessary to meet them. That calculus certainly applies to the war on terrorism. Unfortunately, organized terrorism is an effective and efficient means of forcing resource allocation, even though terrorism fails to strengthen its originators and seems inevitably to bring about their defeat. Civil society's reasonable response to terrorism, beyond its unwavering commitment to subdue that scourge, is the balance society strikes between preserving the values terrorists wish to destroy and the methods used to destroy the terrorists.

On an interpersonal level, a similar balance must be found. Reasonable efforts to protect life and property from real and likely perils are an obligation of self-interest and stewardship. Yet, resources squandered in opposition to nonexistent threats serve no useful purpose and can cause great harm. Whether considered by government, organizations, or individuals, reasonable people must realize that transgendered people pose no threat to civil society.

The Theoretical Case

Humanity can be seen as essentially evil or essentially good, or it can be seen as devoid of an essential nature and subject entirely to the influence of other persons and things. Individually and collectively that view bears on expectations as people encounter strangers, order their own lives, and choose their political system and leaders. What people believe about their own nature must be part of this calculus unless they would consider their individual natures unique.

Those seeing mankind as having a darker nature seek the protection of a firm and restraining hand of an all-powerful central government. Like seventeenth century theorist Thomas Hobbes, these people would save themselves from humanity's aggressively hostile nature by accepting absolute subjugation under one civil authority. Hobbes's saw the natural state of man as engaged in horribly harsh competition and subject to unrelenting anxiety as each person would struggle to glean and protect those things essential to preserving her or his life. In nature, the absence of a central authority with sufficient power to establish and enforce rules means that each person would possess only what she or he could defend. Hobbes saw the desire and logic of ending fear and incessant vulnerability as sufficient to cause every person to yield everything to their sovereign so the sovereign would have the resources necessary to establish and maintain peace and safety (Martinich 1999, 146-7, 157, 228).[140]

I wrote earlier of each person's wholly understandable tendency to surrender to the frustratingly unfair and destructive expedient of using simple characterizations, or mental slots, to label and contain any new acquaintance. The same unfortunate tendency exists when considering the authors of political thought cited throughout this work. Students of their recorded thought know that these authors lived exceptional lives even by contemporary standards. Further, these political theorists seriously considered a variety of alternatives and expressed opinions regarding them. It is far too easy to remember these extraordinary people virtually in a word-association sense. My intent in citing the intriguing concepts they presented is to compare some of their relevant ideas and not to attempt to summarize the entirety of their work.

Dr. Martinich's wonderful analysis describes Hobbes's rich trove of religious, philosophical, and political thought. Apparently assuming that natural man is ruled more by emotion than reason, Hobbes argued that fear was a sufficiently strong force to impel all people to relinquish their liberty to obtain security. With the possible exceptions of the Athenian democracy and the Roman Republic, absence of an extant or historic enduring democracy let Hobbes believe that divergent forces in a contentious non-autocratic system would prevent an effective consensus regarding threats to that system's union. Founders of the United Nations (U. N.) expected, or at least hoped, that the common interest of avoiding another world war would be greater than the ebb and flow of shorter-term conflicting self-interests of U. N. members.

Today's opponents of U. N. preeminence in international relations see the harsh competition and concomitant dissension of Hobbes view as inevitably fatal to the success of the U. N.'s primary mission. A naïve optimist might say that the U. N. founders and Hobbes were each correct and that overwhelming fear would cause requisite consensus. The point is especially apropos regarding Middle East stability and the war with terrorism. Tremendous disparities among U. N. members may prevent those members from sharing a common perception of a common threat, especially when the threat is not seen as uniform. The U. N. was not formed, and cannot be relied upon, to act against a threat that seems to confront only one or a few of its members. Some nations seem inexplicably unaware of the threat to them constituted by Wahhabist Fundamentalism.

While fear is an undeniably powerful motivator for people facing an immediate threat, fear was not the sentiment that led America's founders to challenge British rule. Patrick Henry's speech to the Second Virginia Convention on March 23, 1775, included the famous and stirring words, "Is life so dear, or peace so sweet, as to be purchased at the price of chains and slavery? Forbid it, Almighty God!" (Kashner 2007, 496).[141] The questionable logic of Hobbes's assertion that humans would give to their sovereign an unlimited authority to take their lives in order to save them could not differ more from the view that inspired so many who sacrificed greatly to achieve American independence. Propounded by an acknowledged leader in the thought of his day and eloquently presented in the work of Dr. Martinich, Hobbes's premise could hardly present a more stark choice. Hobbes would urge a people to surrender their liberty to preserve their lives, while Henry would implore them to risk their lives to preserve their liberty.

Model governments that would fit between those extremes are legion. Who decides what is virtuous or worthy continues to be a question of politics today but it is often far less cumbersome for the philosopher. Nomadic and opportunistic early ancestors known as "hunter/gatherers" did not need to contend with such matters until they moved to form associations much larger than their tribe. As humans became members of a more complex social order, the shape of that order became paramount since it determined who received which scarce resources and how those resources would be provided.

Some systems, almost universally autocratic, would focus on an idealized national identity, a crushingly costly military, or rigorous religious study. Nazi Germany, North Korea, and Saudi Arabia are examples of such systems. These governments would not encourage development of independent identities that might conflict with the established collective purpose. An individual's divergence from the national purpose could be treason. In a fascist system, the person pursuing a separate goal could be convicted and imprisoned for treason and/or theft of government property since she or he has effectively rejected the social contract that binds her or him to the state.

Closer to Mr. Henry's view, Ayn Rand insisted that each person had not only the right, but the obligation, to pursue her or his own potential based on a "sense of life" and augmented by a "conscious philosophy of life" (Rand 1969, 36).[142] The latter, she would add, should be objectivist philosophy. Far from self-indulgent Hedonism or Epicureanism, the "objectivism" or egoism she advocated was firmly rooted in philosophy and characterized by self-reliance and self-direction. Throughout her work, Ms. Rand firmly rejected the collectivism that is inseparable from communism, socialism, and fascism. She opposed repressive systems primarily because they methodically prevent citizens from making the decisions necessary to live their own lives. For their societies, repressive regimes thwart the value-oriented discipline of free markets.

A less generous model than Ayn Rand's might engender the limited and accountable government favored by John Locke. A properly constituted government acceptable to his theoretical view was a system responsive to the changing demands of its citizens who, by their nature, would demand of it and pursue for themselves what they deemed best for them. The government that abuses its authority or fails in its responsibility to protect individual rights while preserving the public good makes opposition to that government legitimate. Locke's concern for balance would not permit that statement to stand alone. He would add that government has an almost unlimited legitimacy in pursuing the public good (McClure 1996, 242-3).[143]

Aristotle was much more concerned with both the rule of reason over emotion and the pursuit of virtue than he was in anything approaching the American concept of freedom. Aristotle would define freedom as the unencumbered opportunity to choose what is virtuous or good and he saw that as mankind's natural inclination. He was so averse to a rule of emotion that he favored enslaving those who would be so ruled (Bradley 1991, 17).[144] Choosing a thing that was harmful to oneself and/or others was seen not as an exercise of freedom but of license.

The American system of government preserves liberty, not only by guaranteeing or recognizing specific rights for each person, but by its making and enforcing laws prohibiting certain bad choices by one or more people that would unjustly injure the person and/or property of anyone else. Freedom from fear of robbery, for example, is promised to citizens by an established government that enacts laws, enforces them, and punishes those who commit robbery. These legislative, administrative, and judicial functions theoretically work together for the common good, check each other's excesses by protecting their powers, and answer to an electorate that jealously guards its unalienable rights to liberty. The fact that robberies still occur means that the system is not perfect, but it also means that perfection may be too high a standard for system that also values other freedoms.

Other systems, presuming a favorable view of natural man, might favor a benevolent government dedicated to maximizing every citizen's potential. All public and private education, including apprenticeships, internships, and private study, would be offered non-competitively to every citizen. From the standpoint of representative government relying upon an informed electorate, this benevolent government might be an extension of the rationale for America's current mandatory public schooling. The power of government to provide a service, though, is not easily separated from its power to control other aspects of that service. Government monopoly of education would be at least as great a potential threat to liberty as any other government monopoly. Initially, a system that provided unlimited educational opportunities to its citizens would face unlimited pressure and temptation to influence the content and delivery of that education. Later, the system ostensibly established to permit each person to pursue her or his own goals would become a government that permitted little, if any, deviation from prescribed thought.

The Arts Proxy

Government support for the creative arts might be seen as a test for disproportional influence and control, especially for work that escapes the discipline of market valuation. Regardless of its structure, government support requires that an executive agency decide which works will be funded. Further, that support is a transfer of wealth from taxpayers to selected artists. The perception that such support would favor disproportionally, if not exclusively, affluent citizens in urban areas made that support seem like a grossly unneeded subsidy. These concerns and an inevitable controversy over which works would be funded are major reasons why, for much of America's history, such support was not provided. Artists had to find a market for their work, find patrons to support them, or subsidize their own work. Absence of government support often meant art was not available to the general public, artists had greater difficulty acquiring skill and building an audience, and American democracy functioned largely without the benefits of artistic enlightenment.

Prior to the 1960s establishment of the National Endowment for the Arts and its sister endowment for humanities, the American economic system attempted to balance need and availability. Impresario Sol Hurok proved that, under certain conditions, great works capably performed would find large and appreciative public support. He exposed the insidious and odious myth that only a social or economic elite were interested in great art. Inescapably hollow when offered by repressive regimes, a society's functional means of strengthening and broadening the best of its artistic life is an unerring indication of the health of the entire society. Much worse than children "playing hooky" from school, societal elements resistant to the best elements of their culture are intellectual anarchists who would starve the root system of their society. Far from simple escapist entertainment or an earlier generation's "do your own *thang*," great art inspires and invites every member of society to strive for that society's highest ideals.

For many, the language of that expression, if not the ideals themselves, is divine inspiration. The message of each work is life and faith affirming. Like individual limbs of a tree of life, each work is both separate and attached. The work's own message and the message of the whole are not a fleeting moment of satisfaction, but a resonating honest depiction of wholeness and the means to lasting happiness. The Bible, Dr. Elbin's *Paradox of Happiness*, and other works tell their readers that they can never satisfy the need for the classical definition of happiness directly. Satisfying that need comes from the things people do constructively with their lives. Happiness is not achievable when it is the only motive or goal. Deep, enduring, and satisfying happiness is the shadow cast by sincere and confident pursuit of something worthwhile.

As stated previously, an MtF woman is not directly seeking impossibly illusive happiness when she seeks to resolve her gender identity conflict nor is she trying to avoid pain or to escape unavoidable conflict. Escapism and the happiness paradox are woefully inadequate excuses offered by those who do not understand gender identity conflict. Just as Martin Luther discovered that penance for its own sake was not a path to salvation, an MtF woman eventually discovers that enduring the silent and unrelenting frustration of her conflict is pointless. Whoever is credited or blamed for the origin of each person's essential self, she or he ultimately cannot hide from that self. Discovery of that self is not an inconsequential waypoint along the path of human life. Postponing the discovery is a futile and tragic folly.

While not so naive as to believe they could adopt a system that would eliminate greed, envy, a lust for power, etc., America's founders did decide to err on the side of favoring, rather than restricting, individual liberty. A long list of historic events has invited our revisiting that decision including the unforgettable acts of September 11, 2001, but we remain committed to protecting the rights of each person to pursue happiness (Aristotle would argue that means virtue) while acknowledging each person's obligation to afford our fellow citizens those same rights. The U.S. Constitution, Preamble does not state flippantly that the government is being established because there needs to be one. In describing a continuing process, it provides a marvelous and concise list of six objectives, ending with "...secure the blessings of liberty..." (Kashner 2007, 499)[145]

Some would argue that there is an abiding American conflict between the pursuit of liberty and the pursuit of virtue. The previously discussed classical thought characterizes that as a false choice. It is an illegitimate use of governmental power to sanction the exercise of liberty in pursuit of anything other than virtue. In theory, liberty is not an end, but a means to an end. Again citing the Preamble, the American system protects pursuit of "...a more perfect union..." (Kashner 2007, 499)[146] in form and effect, and does so at least as successfully as any other governmental system in history. It is in the light of this understanding of government's legitimate role that most transgendered people seek justice. They seek recognition in law of their fundamental natural right to be the people their hearts, minds, and souls, tell them they are and that qualified and licensed professionals have verified that they are. Transgendered people seek that same recognition in law that has been denied to them by numerous courts and yet is recognized for every other citizen, whether or not she or he can produce expert certification of gender identity.

Stellar Minds

Locke and Hobbes are stellar examples of the capacity of the British educational system of their era to enable some gifted students to develop more fully their impressive abilities. Because of the absence of comparable universal public education in their time, civilization can never know how powerful the ideas and significant the discoveries were that were lost to mankind, nor can it know how a more inclusive system might have influenced the people whose work survived. Locke and Hobbes were each sufficiently confident of his own abilities to author works which fed, as well as responded to, political unrest. Hobbes advocated a strong monarchy despite its reduced popularity among some members of parliament and a lessened role for clerics accustomed to relative civil independence and support from parishioners. Locke advocated an accountable government selected by its sovereign citizens when French royalists feared chaos in the absence of a king. Given the relatively lower literacy rates and difficulty of producing books at the time, it is amazing that such men could be as influential during their lives as they were.

Given that each normal human is born with a mind and soul of unknown capacity, research and debate regarding the extent to which abilities, morality, behavior, and other characteristics are either learned or innate undoubtedly will continue. The delineation will be of limited utility, however, because those aspects of each human are inextricably linked. The ability to influence them is appropriately tempered with the knowledge that much of human curiosity and creativity, as well as the capacity for cruelty and destruction, springs from their interaction. Whether from nurture or nature, each person's virtues are either exposed and enhanced, or significantly diminished through that person's interaction with society. Each society and government enforce requisite prohibitions of undesired actions as they attempt to provide encouragement for worthy thoughts and actions before, or when, they are needed.

This pragmatic view can be independent of the continuing quandary regarding mankind's essential nature, but it would be of little use when attempting to persuade a people of their need for, and the rightness of, revolution. Nurture proponents see each person as born with a mind like an immaculately clean sheet of paper waiting for its first mark. They see each infant as devoid of any innate inclinations to act for good or evil, judgmental conception of morality, sense of fairness, or knowledge of their Creator. Each of these, they would argue, is a manmade construct formed for a sinister, benevolent, or simply logical preference for social order. People who create a god as an opiate or other form of escape worship an inherently flawed and ultimately ineffectual deity incapable of moving believers to an enduring pursuit of individual and collective religious worth. They do not accept the omniscient, omnipresent, and omnipotent God that Christians and some others see as the Creator of mankind. Devoid of a truly religious purpose, pursuers of such alternative constructs as manmade gods necessarily lack a convincing focus. They offer an unfortunate rationale of harshly limited secular worth but usually one demanding a sense of obligation. Such alternatives are an invitation to return to Plato's allegorical cave rather than to pursue an enlightened and unending life for the soul.

Political implications of the restraints, inducements, and rewards offered by the U.S. economic and political system of government appear differently depending upon the filtering biases of the country's widely varied citizenry. Those who see government as a necessary restraint on the baser instincts of a dark human nature are comforted by vigorous enforcement agencies of government, laws and mechanisms intended to "keep people honest", and societal pressure to abide by law and to conform to accepted norms of behavior. This group's ideal enforcer would arrest immediately anyone making an incorrect decision or choice.

People having a less harsh view of human nature, especially those seeing each person as possessing a divinely created and wholly active soul, are less comfortable with a system that includes a relatively large array of powerful and passionate regulators whose dedication may be diametrically opposed to their own. For them, enforcers are reluctantly accepted protectors who represent stifled creativity and imagination and are a potential threat to liberty. This group supports mechanisms intended to encourage people always to be their best selves and to perform to the highest level of their potential as a matter of personal integrity. Some of these optimists must welcome as manna opportunities to strive energetically and enthusiastically for new and better solutions to the challenges of their surroundings.

Many people have one foot in each camp depending on the issue at hand, or have both feet in each camp at different times in their lives. Each group confronts different implications of their views for themselves and others. Since each group might see the other as detractors or rivals, agreement on a set of rules and the procedure for changing those rules is essential for each to live in an ordered society. The U.S. Constitution, including its Bill of Rights and other amendments, enumerates some of these rules and rights and provides a procedure for giving formal recognition to other rights.

Constraining Partner Preference

Whether addressed by custom, in law, or both, society does not ignore conditions of aberrant gender identity and sexual preference. In a society that bases its laws on majority rule with unalienable rights rather than on religious doctrine, not all behavior considered by many, or even most, people to be objectionable or morally wrong will be illegal. One of the reasons the U.S. is engaged in a war against Islamic extremists is that the extremists would establish systems based on subjective and ever-changing interpretations of religious texts rather than clearly delineated civil rights. Afghanistan's Taliban did not merely ignore widely accepted civil rights, it was openly hostile to them. Liberty is unacceptable to those opposed to religious freedom precisely because a system guaranteeing true liberty must require that civil law cannot favor one religion over another. People of non-Islamic faiths, too, would establish systems of government based on their religious beliefs. Their systems also would be hostile to civil rights conflicting with their views and to a secular means of resolving those conflicts.

Other things being equal where freedom is defined as the right to choose the right, repressive regimes, including theocracies, are "free" because the state chooses what is "right." In such systems, the state assumes responsibility for compelling, and has unlimited power to compel, citizens to act rightly. Where freedom is defined only as the right to choose, while recognizing fundamental unalienable rights of all citizens, the individual has the same right to choose as everyone else and bears responsibility for her or his choices. The distinction between liberty based in law and more subjective morality is that not all things that are legal are necessarily moral, and not all things that are immoral necessarily should be illegal. Among other freedoms, the U.S. Constitution, First Amendment protects each person's right to practice her or his beliefs and to attempt to persuade other people of the virtue of those beliefs (Kashner 2007, 504).[147] Inherent tension between morality and law continues to fuel debate concerning what is and what should be legal. The wisdom reflected in systems prizing freedom is that these systems accommodate debate while preserving the process for determining what is legal. All parties have a stake in safeguarding the process since it protects their right to attempt to persuade others in future contests.

Not all critically important rules of process are written. The U.S. Senate sets its rules and some are set by tradition. In 2005, a few senators suggested considered employing an almost unprecedented use of the filibuster to block Supreme Court nominees with whom they had ideological differences. Since a supermajority would be required to end the filibuster, the U.S. Senate effectively would be changing substantially the number of senate votes necessary to confirm nominees. When the majority threatened to reciprocate by changing the number of senators needed to end a filibuster, a bipartisan group of senators acted to impede either change. In this microcosm, the Senate reflected the American regard for preserving process, the rule of law, and the means by which contentious matters should be resolved. That resolve was especially tested and vindicated in the exceptionally close Presidential Election of 2000. Religious faith also has a bearing on contentious public discourse. Those who believe that everyone shall ultimately face the same arbiter and that His judgment is the one that most matters can approach each contest with greater patience. All of this bears directly on the framework for considering such matters as appropriately accommodating gender identity conflict and the preferred gender identity of one's prospective partner.

The Judicial Record

Cases such as *Corbett v. Corbett* in England, and *Anonymous v. Weiner* (New York) and *Littleton v. Prange* (Texas) in the U.S. have shown the latitude inherent in the interpretive powers and responsibilities of the courts due to the inadequacy of legislative clarity regarding transgendered people (*Gardiner v. Gardiner* 2001, I-E).[148] The rulings in these cases have been written by conscientious, well-schooled, and predominantly male judges who apparently have had little personal knowledge of, or extensive relevant discussions with, transgendered relatives, friends, or acquaintances. If any did have such knowledge or experience, it is not evident it their rulings. They have held that the matter of sex for legal purposes is primarily one-dimensional. Courts have looked, almost exclusively at each principal's natal potential capacity to participate in biological reproduction as the unequivocal and immutable determinant of that person's legal sex.

In the above cases and numerous other judicial attempts to contend with matters regarding transgendered people and their marriages, each court's reluctance or inability to grasp the reason sex-reassignment surgery is medically sanctioned caused it to miss the essence of those essentially heterogendered unions. Courts fail to acknowledge that, because her gender identity is female, an MtF woman must ultimately reflect her identity as fully as possible. Since they do not understand or will not accept the nature of gender identity, courts and others search for another valid explanation of the transgendered condition, but they inevitably fail to find it. A court's refusing to accept a post-operative MtF woman as female because of her natal physical sex is as reasonable as its refusing to accept as a living person a cardiac patient who survived heart transplant surgery.

No court would reasonably accept the argument that, because the heart with which someone was born is no longer functioning, that person must be legally dead. Imagine the numbing shock the patient would feel when told by an appellate court judge that, regardless of the contrary medical testimony, personal experience, or demonstrable capabilities presented, she or he is now and forever legally dead. The right of the patient to marry and to adopt children would be denied. The court would find cohabitation distasteful, if not illegal. Health department regulations might require that the legally deceased body must be cremated or buried. Despite ubiquitous references to the things people know, feel, or believe in their hearts, the essence of each person clearly and demonstrably does not reside in that organ's chambers. Each person's intellect, character, personality, and innate sense of morality cannot function without use of some areas of the brain, but those characteristics do not depend on any other known component of physiology.

Acknowledging syntactic deficiencies or other imprecision in extant law without the court's applying gender identity-conscious criteria, supported by expert testimony, is equivalent to a court saying that it cannot, or will not, fulfill its responsibility to protect the rights of the transgendered person or people in the case at hand. Judicial recognition of constitutional protections in other cases has been seen by varying groups as "legislating from the bench" or creating case law in place of, or even contrary to, enacted legislation. The courts, though, have become the jealous guardians of the rights promised to all by the social contract that is the U.S. Constitution. This does not mean, of course, that every application is flawlessly construed, that the balance struck between conflicting principles is always correct, and/or that each matter was decided citing the most applicable provisions. Many matters previously decided favoring one direction in cases testing church and state separation are falling another way based on protected speech. If not perfect in every instance, the judicial system clearly has worked well enough to spark strong reaction against those who would change it substantively. Today, even the regular replacement of retiring U.S. Supreme Court justices usually is contested with a vigor once reserved to presidential elections. Despite extant support for the current judicial system, however, poorly reasoned rulings invite strident demand for change.

The fact that human reproduction is important is undeniable. The view of most courts, however, has meant that people were treated as mere bodies with empty or absent minds and souls. This illogical tyranny of physiology forces people into one of two classes regardless of their female and male biology. It would deny to every person her or his heart, soul, mind, or spirit and the gender aspect of each one of them. Humanity, in this harshly restrictive and coldly secular view, is in its essence not significantly different from amoebae, viruses, or algae where the primary or only reason for existence is procreation.

The excuse that legislatures have failed to address adequately the essential, and even dispositive, role of nonphysical characteristics in determining gender identity has been accepted by most appellate courts as demanding a rubber-stamp application of *Corbett's* natal sex standard from case law. Less restrictive U.S. rulings include the New Jersey Superior Court (*M.T. v. J.T.* 1976)[149] and the Supreme Court of Vermont (*In RE: B.L.V.B.* 1993),[150] but their being seen as departing from, rather than building on, precedent left them awkward leaders of an army of two. In its finding for J.T.'s ex-wife, the New Jersey court was persuaded by evidence showing that applicable precedents relied on a grossly inadequate definition of sex. The antiquated standard, based on a harshly restrictive and fatally flawed definition, did not give appropriate weight to preponderant opinion of qualified professionals. Its reliance on the role M.T. aspired to fulfill with her husband, however, virtually ignores the essential role of gender identity. The court's assertion of physical wholeness following surgery overstates the case for surgical success.

There is no indication that anyone in the Vermont adoption case was transgendered. In a unanimous ruling, however, the court was the first state supreme court to uphold adoption by a same-sex partner while leaving the birth parent's rights intact. It held that when society changes what is, and is not, acceptable, courts must apply extant law consistent with its purpose while adjusting to those changes. The court noted that there was no indication that continuing to live with the parents who were raising them was harmful to the children. Citing precedents in lower courts and a ruling by the Superior Court of Washington, D.C. in 1991, the court held that taking a child from its birth mother who was in a stable and loving relationship with another woman was both "unreasonable and unnecessary" (*In RE: B.L.V.B.* 1993, 369).[151]

U.S. courts and the courts of many other countries have consistently decided cases concerning transgendered women primarily on the basis of the inability of MtF women to become pregnant asserting that they are merely applying statutes which define women and men strictly in terms of their potential role in procreation. The courts have effectively ignored all other, and arguably much more important, aspects of a person's living her or his fullest-possible life in every other respect because they can characterize such matters as the sole province of a disinclined legislature. This is the equivalent of the courts acting as an informed but determined "flat earth" society after repeatedly being told of Newton's Laws of Planetary Motion and Galileo's discoveries through his telescope.

From the standpoint of political theory, citizens in a representative democracy would prefer the legislature's exercising its deliberative, inclusive, and representative responsibility regarding controversial matters than to see those matters resolved in court. No transgendered woman, however, can be pleased with an American legislative system that has so thoroughly failed to affirm the validity and preeminence of her medically attested gender identity. Further, it has been America's political tradition that its courts have tended to be the protectors of last resort for the rights of minorities, and it is difficult to imagine a much smaller and consistently aggrieved minority before courts in the United States than the transgendered community. To date, though, U.S. courts have failed to uphold the equal rights of MtF women.

The Gardiner Remand

In its May, 2001 reverse and remand ruling in *Gardiner*, the Court of Appeals of the State of Kansas challenged that "flat earth" view of sex in law. The circuit court had ruled against J'Noel Gardiner regarding possible inheritance of her intestate husband's estate on the patently false suggestion of an extant wholly female / wholly male dichotomy. The decision of the appeals court cited Julie Greenberg's work that described common human variations, many of which might be elementary for high school biology students (*Gardiner v. Gardiner* 2001, Conclusion).[152] In addition to six physical measures, Dr. Greenberg included the two additional measures "assigned gender and gender of rearing," and "sexual identity" (Greenberg 1999).[153] These more amorphous criteria were an acknowledgement that measures of physiology alone may not be sufficient to access accurately the status of any human regarding so important and fundamental a part of her or his being human. Although typically the same as "assigned gender or gender of rearing," "sexual identity" appears to have been included as a separate category to show a potential for the two to be in conflict. Parents who decided that their son or intersexed child was, or could be, their "daughter" would ignore all aspects of physiology, their child's protests, and his behavior that strongly indicated "she" was really their son. In that instance, their "daughter" by the "assigned gender and gender of rearing" standard would still be male by the "sexual identity" standard.

Dr. Greenberg's work focused on "intersexuality", but she included a definition of gender identity conflict and described the David Reimer case history showing the extent of complexity that attends discussion of any person's gender, gender identity, and sex. Like transgendered people, intersexed people have encountered substantial difficulty in their treatment by presumed experts. Precisely because of their ambiguous physiology, however, most intersexed people have no gender identity conflict. They may want their bodies to reflect their gender identities more fully, but most, if not all, intersexed people see their physical selves as predominantly consonant with their gender identities. Unfortunately, discussion of gender identity conflict in an article about the intersexed condition might lead some to believe that gender identity or "brain sex" differing from one's predominant natal physical sex is also an intersexed condition, which it is not.

Predominant medical opinion would be considered dispositive regarding Ms. Gardiner's status for almost any other condition, but the medical records cited by the circuit court were deemed insufficient to prove Ms. Gardiner was sufficiently female to satisfy Kansas law. Mental health professionals might have made the case for gender identity as the most important aspect of any person's true sex, but they did not. Like a questioned placement in an absurd game of horseshoe law, Ms. Gardiner was deemed just not quite female enough to count. The indignity of such a process is barbarously inhumane. To suggest that an intelligent responsible person with undiminished faculties must permit others to determine her or his sexual status is unconscionable. The court might well have held that so shocking a legal requirement was an unconstitutional invasion of privacy.

Clearly, the historic and intended basis for each state's marriage statutes has been the preservation and perpetuation of a nuclear family consisting, at its inception, of a woman and man as wife and husband respectively, but they have not defined "woman" and "man". The physical attributes listed by Dr. Greenberg can be assessed by qualified professionals using tests that yield consistent and verifiable results. Such assessments would strongly suggest the potential for two sexually opposite people to be able to produce their own child or children. Many people would consider such a test a requisite, if not the exclusive, requisite test for legal marriage. However, such tests would not indicate whether the gender identity of either parent was consistent with her or his presumed status. Readily accessible characteristics are almost irresistibly seductive to those who would favor their expanded or exclusive use as a legal standard, but such people fail utterly to understand the nature and importance of gender identity.

A case regarding the legal status of a transgendered woman should never be about any aspect of her physical sex. Physical characteristics and affected or imposed gender are wholly unsuited and entirely inappropriate to matters regarding any individual's innate gender identity. Most, if not all, MtF women would readily agree that their apparent natal physical sex was male, because mental conflict with their physical sex was at the heart of their desire for resolution. The fact that the appeals court in *Gardiner* was not prepared to render summary judgment based on gender identity is an indication of the extreme and continuing deficiencies in consideration of matters of identity, gender, and sex, even at the highest levels of a state's judicial system. For most MtF women, assigned gender, gender of rearing, and sexual identity are a continuation of the fraud that began with the impersonally and erroneously assigned imposition, however benign the intent, of the "F" or "M" entered on her original birth certificate. Even those three softer measures are inadequate to access gender identity and the transgendered condition. Still, the appeals court did not directly confront the matter of Ms. Gardiner's legal sex. It found that the manner in which the lower court had reached its decision was critically deficient. Mr. Gardiner took the matter to the Supreme Court of Kansas which upheld the circuit court's finding. Ms. Gardiner appealed to the U.S. Supreme Court which declined to hear the case.

The appeals court did acknowledge the court's responsibility to apply extant law in its review of relevant statutes and case law while considering relevant information supplied by qualified sources. Yet, the court also tacitly acknowledged the responsibility of a court to define terms not adequately defined in the law when it cited Dr. Greenberg's work. Courts deciding matters such as those in *Gardiner* have resisted doing so, but they must recognize that the terms "woman" and "man" in law are only appropriately applied when gender identity is the primary basis for the decision. If legislators, judges, pastors, teachers, or other responsible parties deny the primacy of gender identity then, regardless of the other criteria they would use purporting to define "woman," "man", and their union, they cannot accurately characterize the whole of those relationships. If a physically male "man" has a female gender identity, "he" still might father a child, and throughout history an unknowably large number of such "men" have done so. "He" is assuredly not a man in the most important sense of the word, however, regardless of what the statutes, case law, and physiology indicate that "he" is. Similarly, FtM men who bear children cannot be whole mothers, however diligently they may try.

To the biologist, rancher, or veterinarian, the mechanics of reproduction are fundamentally simple, even if specific instances are problematic. Breeding mares and stallions, heifers and bulls, and various other animal pairs has been quite successful without concern for the gender identities of the animal participants. Society attempts to impart to its members a nurturing family role for each parent so that the most imaginative interpretation of terms such as man, male, father, and woman, female, mother connote profound essential differences between beings who also share many physical characteristics. The final judicial rulings in such cases as *Littleton* and *Gardiner* were that each MtF woman could not be considered a woman in her respective state by applying narrow definitions that animal breeders and veterinarians would readily recognize but are horribly inappropriate to people aware of their own identities. Like cattle, they are virtual rejects from an auction that found them incapable of producing children. By failing to include, and acknowledge as preeminent, nonphysical attributes in their analyses, their respective courts failed to recognize these women even as being fully human. Mmes. Littleton and Gardiner had promised to be the wives of their husbands and had heard their husbands like commitments to them, just as have millions of married couples before them. These MtF women, their families, and others saw those mutual commitments demeaned as inconsequential. The sanctity of their marriages was denied by the highest courts in their respective states.

The courts in these cases construed the laws of their states as having been written, not for thinking, feeling, and caring people, but for soulless, merely physical, and sexually-ruled pseudo animals. By their acts, two more of the nation's highest state courts exacerbated an abhorrently repressive and erroneously contrived assertion that certain women cannot be recognized as the people they are until new legislation specifically including them is enacted. A similar assertion is implicit in the recent finding of the Chief Counsel of the Internal Revenue Service that disallowed a tax deduction for the costs of sex-reassignment surgery, despite overwhelming unequivocal professional opinion that the surgery was medically necessary. The Chief Counsel was persuaded, not by the accepted standards of the American Psychiatric Association's manual of diagnoses, the Harry Benjamin Standards of Care, and the International Classification of Diseases, but by a non-peer reviewed article from the previously mentioned Dr. Paul McHugh. Either of the established standards describes a condition clearly falling within the memorandum's cited pertinent regulation for deductibility (Treas. Reg. § 1.213-1 (e)(1)(ii) which includes, "…for the prevention or alleviation of a physical or mental defect or illness" (IRS 2006).[154] In none of these instances has the legislature acted to rectify the abuse apparently because no consensus has been reached regarding the urgency of that need.

Treating MtF women differently from other women under law is almost as arbitrary as deciding that drivers born on Tuesdays are not like people born on any other day of the week and that those people shall not be licensed to drive unless the legislature enacts law specifically to include them. One person in seven, or fourteen percent of the population, is a far larger minority than is the transgendered population, but size is no guarantee against arbitrary repression. Strict adherence to the principle of equal justice under law is its surest guarantee. In successive cases throughout the United States, courts have failed to provide equal protection to MtF women. A society that repeatedly abandons the principle of equal justice regarding one minority sees an inevitable weakening of the reliability of each of its legal protections. Parallels to the societal adversity that necessitated Lincoln's Emancipation Declaration, the U.S. Constitution's Fourteenth Amendment regarding equal justice, and its Nineteenth Amendment granting women's suffrage should be apparent (Kashner 2007, 505-6).[155] These momentous federal actions were responses to systematic adverse classifications of blacks in the first two cases and women in the third despite the substantial size of their populations.

The Texas and Kansas supreme courts established or reinforced an adverse classification on their own, in the absence of what they considered legislative specificity, and they asserted that new legislation of indisputable clarity would be necessary to reverse it. The fact that the legislature did not enact provisions barring MtF women from marrying their husbands did not matter to the courts. In the face of testimony before the courts, absence of a legislative prohibition should not have kept the courts from recognizing the essence of the matter before them. If the legislatures wished to attempt to treat transgendered women differently from other women, they could do so by writing new discriminatory legislation that surely would be tested in subsequent litigation and, in a just court, dismissed with prejudice.

Unequal Protection

The U.S. Constitution, Fourteenth Amendment includes the words "... No State shall make or enforce any law which shall abridge the privileges or immunities of citizens of the United States... " (Kashner 2007, 505)[156] Ratified following the Civil War, these words could be read at that time both as an affirmation that the people of each state are all citizens of the same country and that the United States consists of only one class of citizens. Increasingly, though, that section has been understood to mean what it says. The right to equal protection is an important safeguard of each person's constrained freedom to act regarding other people. Each citizen's freedom to exercise her or his own rights must be concomitant with the knowledge that those same rights belong to all citizens. Cases testing "equal" in this context have turned on the question of relevant equality. Despite real and significant differences between females and males, whether one group could justifiably deny suffrage to the other might have been tested on this principle. A Reconstruction Era U.S. Supreme Court that applied the amendment's contemporary construction might have held that women could not be denied the right to vote, and it might have done so fifty years before the Nineteenth Amendment specifically recognized that right to suffrage. When some rights are capriciously denied to some citizens, each right may eventually be denied to every citizen.

Courts have repeatedly denied that MtF women are wholly legally women. MtF transgendered women have the same gender identity as other women. Until or unless there is sufficient and incontrovertible evidence indicating that a valid and substantive basis exists for denying or abridging their rights, equal protection should apply to all women. With few exceptions, though, courts have consistently resisted using gender identity as the primary determinant of whether someone is a woman or a man under law. They may resist because of an inability to understand gender identity, because they have not heard sufficient unequivocal and professionally qualified testimony to establish its primacy, or because they were reluctant to attempt to establish a precedent that would be overturned.

The assertion by these courts that some women would require different legislative action than other women is contrary to gender protections in civil rights law and the U.S. Constitution, Fourteenth Amendment guarantee of equal protection (Kashner 2007, 505).[157] Even asking if MtF women are women is little different from asking if a person is human, but the question would have to be at issue so that the Court could address it. By relying primarily upon problematic physical descriptions indicating normative differences between groups of transgendered women and groups of women who were physically female from birth, courts and others are certain to make generalizations, especially about the second group's norms, that would be opposed by women in both groups. Courts might rule as arbitrarily that, unless judges personally find the person appearing before them to be sexually attractive, "she" cannot be female. The most perfectly defined physical female, applying the most rigorous set of norms or other criteria, will fail to satisfy the whole roll of fulfilled female, wife, and/or mother if her gender identity is not female. Incredibly, though, that fact is still not reflected in a decision by any high U.S. court.

Many of the legal questions regarding transgendered persons could be answered much more quickly and consistently if gender identity could be shown clearly on an x-ray or other objective diagnostic tool, and such a tool may be on, or just over, the horizon. However, development of a reliable mechanism to identify consistently and accurately a subject's gender identity, and of a means to indicate the powerful influence gender identity has in each person's life, has been agonizingly slow. Lack of a widely accepted single test has facilitated actions of zealots who cite incorrectly interpreted religious dogma to argue that gender identity does not exist, that it is insignificant or inconsequential, or that it can be altered. The previously cited studies of autopsy slides have indicated that gender-related parts of brains of MtF women seem like those of other women. MtF women, though, would consider a test requiring their autopsies for determination of their legal status to be unacceptably harsh. Functional magnetic resonance imaging (fMRI) studies have been useful for showing a variety of brain differences in test subjects but they do not appear to have been used successfully to identify transgendered people.

Checks and Balances

The U.S. Constitution's framers gave each branch of government checks on the other two, but recognized that ultimate legitimate power rests with the people. Each branch not only jealously guards its powers, but seeks constantly to expand them either at the expense of the other two or of the people. Unchecked rule by judges was anathema to America's founders and, by deliberate and careful design, a court's actions can be countered, usually by the passage of new legislation. Particularly egregious judicial behavior can be redressed by impeachment or recall. Some states make their judiciary even more accountable to the electorate by regularly asking if certain judges shall be retained in office.

The key role of the judiciary in preserving the same rights for minorities that are enjoyed by the majority also protects the courts. Since every person's majority or minority status can change on any given issue, people will not support removal of principled judges for what the U.S. Declaration of Independence in a similar context called, "..light and transient causes..." That key role is both a legitimate power and a responsibility. If the courts cannot or will not invalidate a distorted legislative result, legitimate rights and interests are denied. If the courts fail to protect the rights of minorities where those rights, based on the principle of equal justice, are legislatively infringed, the future of all rights is jeopardized.

With the fate of a nascent nation in the balance, the U. S Constitutional Convention reluctantly deferred a decision regarding the buying and selling of human beings. The Convention's failure to reach a peaceful compromise, because none was possible, merely postponed resolution of the matter that ultimately led to an horrendously-costly civil war. Had slaves, former slaves, and slave owners, alone, been empowered to reach a legislative compromise, law based on deeply rooted conscience, conviction, and experience would have resulted. To some, such a process would be little different from giving murderers, executioners, and murder victims (represented by people who loved them) similar legislative responsibility. The result of that process, though, would be an informed and substantive legislative content based not on theory or polemics, but on stark reality and crafted by those who had grappled directly with many aspects of each issue on extremely personal terms.

Acutely interested people providing legislative substance might approximate the educational function of lobbyists, but their motivation would be deeply personal conviction rather than the lobbyists' presumed dispassionate compensated advocacy. The capacity of non-transgendered people to legislate for so small and unique a population is questionable. As appealing as it may be to have only those most directly affected by legislation involved in its passage, this unworkable approach would require a new legislature for each matter considered and invite endless debate about which people were most qualified to be its members. Further, in a system based on representative government, any legislation so constructed could not apply to all of society if significant parts of its population were not represented during the legislation's formation.

A representative legislature is intended to provide a broader perspective so that concerns of even the least affected parties are appropriately considered. In practice, though, influence often is not proportional to the rights and legitimate interests of those most directly affected by the legislation. Majority rule with minority rights, as practiced in the U.S., means that those least affected by legislation may have far greater influence on its construction if there are enough of them or if they are intimately familiar with the relevant levers of power. Primarily reflecting the will of the majority, the legislature, if it fails to protect the rights and legitimate interests of minorities, leaves the adversely affected minorities the options of the courts, forbearance, a campaign of education, or rebellion. A substantial American judicial history shows, in many instances of infringed minority rights, that the courts can and will act to restore balance. Frederick Douglass, Elizabeth Cady Stanton, and Dr. Martin L. King were exceptional people who proved that a campaign of education can bring meaningful change in a system resolved to oppose it. While such efforts may be insufficient to sway the majority, they have been effective in causing a change in policy.

A World less Flat

On February 21, 2003, the grossly inadequate legal standard of natal physical sex in case law was tested in a Florida court. Judge Gerard O'Brien Jr. of the Florida 6th Circuit, rendered his opinion in the *Marriage of Michael v. Linda Kantaras*. The court considered whether an FtM man could legally marry a woman and be the father of their children. Found to be a case of first impression in Florida, Judge O'Brien treated this case in a far more circumspect manner than have dogmatic judges in matters of sexual status in other states. Unprecedented courtroom testimony of expert witnesses was presented in court where it could be challenged under oath by opposing counsel and questioned by the court. Over 800 pages in length, the ruling included a thorough and unprecedented presentation and review of relevant contemporary expertise by people who have studied, diagnosed, and treated the transgendered condition. It also included a thorough review of relevant state statutes and extant case law. Frequent use of the term "gender identity" throughout the court's finding is a tremendously refreshing contrast to the final rulings in *Corbett, Anon. v. Weiner, Littleton, Gardiner,* and others (*Kantaras v. Kantaras* 2003a).[158]

Judge O'Brien's extensive work, exhaustively researched and reviewed, should have been a seminal challenge for the court that would consider the inevitable appeal. The caliber and content of Judge O'Brien's opinion, his findings of fact, his interpretation of law, and his circumspection reflected the finest qualities of anyone in his profession. His finding that no fraud had occurred because Michael's wife knew of his surgery before their marriage was similar to most other such cases, but especially to the previously cited New Jersey Supreme Court ruling in *M.T. v. J.T.*

Judge O'Brien determined that Michael Kantaras satisfied Florida's definition of a sexual male in law. He based his opinion on extant law while considering the gender identity standard attested to by expert witnesses. He exercised appropriate deference to the precedents of similar cases and noted how interpretations of relevant law had emphasized anatomical or physical sex even though experts repeatedly expressed a contrary opinion regarding the primary significance of gender identity (*M. Kantaras v. L. Kantaras* 2003a, 771).[159]

The appellate court, by a three-zero vote, reversed Judge O'Brien's ruling on the sexual status of Mr. Kantaras based on the tired standard of natal physical sex (*L. Kantaras v. M. Kantaras* 2004).[160] An appeal to the Supreme Court of Florida was denied (*M. Kantaras v. L. Kantaras* 2005b).[161] The reversal doubtlessly pleased strict constructionists regarding their limited reading of

Florida law. Despite the professional competence and clarity of the explanation provided at trial, the Court of Appeal failed utterly to acknowledge that gender identity is the most important component of anyone's sexual identity. Its horrendously flawed ruling meant that despite Mr. Kantaras's counseling, hormone therapy, and extensive surgery, his living continuously as the man he is since transition, his own declarations and daily life as a man, his being the only father his two teenage children have ever known, etc., he may only legally marry another man, or at least someone whose natal physical sex was male, in the state of Florida. Like other jurisdictions that rely on the natal physical sex standard, Florida will only permit a transitioned transgendered person legally to marry another person presenting the same gender. That surely is not the intent of supporters of heterogender marriages. Opposing the heterogender marriage of a transitioned transgendered person is at its core like opposing any other heterogender union to, and including, that of Eve and Adam. Natal physiology is obviously a grossly inadequate standard for marriage.

Judge O'Brien's *Kantaras* ruling is a seminal judicial effort in American courts, to acknowledge what overwhelming expert testimony indicated about transgendered people and, by inference, all of society. In contemporary vernacular, Judge O'Brien "got it." Many others in the U.S. still have not accepted gender identity as the ultimate determinant for whether someone is female or male. Deference to potential legislative action that may be postponed for decades regarding acknowledgement of a fundamental constitutional right will ultimately be seen as egregious a wrong as past failures of the Supreme Court to protect the rights of other minorities.

Some people discomfited by Judge O'Brien's ruling feel threatened by transitioned transgendered people who live their normal lives in honest harmony with their gender identities. Ideologues doubtlessly would prefer a judicial system for resolving matters regarding uncomfortably "different" people that more closely resembles that of Afghanistan's Taliban or Iran's Mullahs. Such systems are based on subjective interpretations of selected scripture propounded by religious zealots, rather than careful constructions of enacted and case law. Further, these people would cede indisputable authority to whoever placed the initial "F" or "M" on a birth certificate and they would forbid official consideration of efforts to resolve the conflict it caused. An "F," they would assert, must stay an "F" because they "know" that is what God wants. Adherents to this kind of thinking have continuously resisted advances of science and political thought that differed with what they chose to believe. If careful and objectively reasoned advances in science, philosophy, the social sciences, and elsewhere do not support their specific beliefs, they would assert, those advances must be wrong. The current war against Western Civilization and, some would argue, civilization as a whole is predicated on such a view.

Consequences of rule by belief are not limited to the substantial losses likely to be incurred by a transgendered party in a lawsuit. The greater loss inures to the thousands of transgendered people, their families and friends, and others where the anguish of suppressed identity means half-lived lives. That loss is also society's loss, and society must bear responsibility for the system that perpetrates and perpetuates these grievously errant assignments. Older rulings where courts did not have the benefit of the growing body of research supporting the existence and power of gender identity could still have been constructive in recognizing the humanity and essential identity of the transgendered party in each case. Rulings in more recent cases, however, have been rendered by courts that were aware of the research but still decided cases on a natal physical-sex standard. Excusing those courts is more problematic.

The appropriate alternative to the constructions of these more recent courts is to hold that the primacy of gender identity, as established in Judge O'Brien's court and supported by increasing relevant literature, must be dispositive regarding matters of identity. Courts employing that standard would have recognized the certifications of status by medical professionals and the mutual commitments openly made in marriage in the cases before them. They would have found that Christie Littleton and J'Noel Gardiner were each legally married to their husbands. These women would have been deemed fully entitled to the rights, as they willingly had been bound by the responsibilities, of marriage.

A mundane implication of rulings such as *Littleton* and *Gardiner* is that an MtF woman using a public restroom in Texas or Kansas might be subject to arrest for its inappropriate use, but the decisions were much more important. In *Littleton*, Christie Littleton was prevented from officially challenging the cause of her husband's death. In *Gardiner*, J'Noel Gardiner lost the right to a sizeable inheritance and the use of that wealth to further her husband's and her own interests. More broadly, if sexually assaulted in either state, an MtF woman's attacker might be charged only with simple assault as prosecutors sought to lessen the risk of an acquittal based on a successful challenge of the victim's legal status. When MtF women live as their gender identities compel them to live, society increasingly has treated them as the women they are, except in its courts. *Littleton, Gardiner*, possible assaults, and a myriad of human interpersonal interactions show the unjust ramifications of a judicial system that fails to adjudicate based on gender identity. Courts have continued to assert that establishing that basis resides in the province of the legislature. In their courts, judges are the arbiters of justice under the law, and they are well aware of the prerogatives and responsibilities of their positions. When they perpetuate bias and stereotypes, they promote injustice despite their oath to uphold its opposite.

The fact that consonant gender identity and natal physical sex is the natural state of non-transgendered people does not mean that the gender identities of either group are insignificant. Rather, it is their gender identities, and not their physical sex, that helps make them the people they are. If noticing the cart is laudable, ignoring the horse is inexcusable. The natal-sex standard without regard for consonant gender identity is the epitome of that backwards cart. Continued reliance on that standard, which ignores gender identity, is perversity in the extreme. Increasing awareness of the transgendered condition and the essence of gender identity conflict mean that continued rearing of children by a natal sex, rather than gender identity, standard is barbarous. It must end.

The Continental View

Ten European countries, including the United Kingdom, marked establishment of the Council of Europe with a formal signing in London on May 5, 1949 (Council of Europe 2003).[162] The Council's "Convention for the Protection of Human Rights and Fundamental Freedoms" went into effect September 3, 1953 with the Grand Chamber of the European Court of Human Rights (ECHR) as its final arbiter (European Court of Human Rights n.d.).[163] On July 11, 2002, the ECHR found the United Kingdom to have violated that convention regarding Christine Goodwin and "I". In a stellar departure from the flat-earth view of legal sex, the ECHR's seventeen judges held unanimously that British law violated Convention Articles Eight and Twelve in its treatment of transgendered persons (*Goodwin, Christine v. United Kingdom* 2002a,[164] *I. v. United Kingdom* 2002a).[165] With language reminiscent of parts of the U.S. Constitution, Fourth and Fifth Amendments, Article Eight states:

"1. Everyone has the right to respect for his private and

family life, his home and his correspondence.

2. There shall be no interference by a public authority

with the exercise of the right except such as is in accordance with the law and is necessary in a democratic society in the interests of national security, public safety or the economic well-being of the country, for the prevention of disorder or crime, for the protection of health or morals, or for the protection of the rights and freedoms of others," and Convention Article 12 states:

"Men and women of marriageable age have the right to marry and to found a family, according to the national laws governing the exercise of this right" (Council of Europe 1950).[166]

The ECHR previously had considered similar questions regarding transgendered people, including at least three cases regarding the United Kingdom, and had not found the member states involved to have violated the Convention. By July 11, 2002, however, twenty of the Council's thirty-seven contracting members specifically recognized the marriages of their post-transition transgendered people while only six clearly did not and the position of the remaining nine was not clear (*Goodwin v. United Kingdom* 2002b, 57[167] and *I. v. United Kingdom* 2002b, 40).[168] The ECHR saw that recognition as a response to increasingly persuasive peer-reviewed data and changing social attitudes occurring since the Court's earlier rulings. The ECHR acknowledged a need to respect precedent, but saw that regard as intended to augment, and never to supersede, its charter to protect human rights (*Goodwin v. United Kingdom* 2002c, 74)[169] and *I. v. United Kingdom* 2002c, 54).[170]

It is ironic that a founding signatory to the Statute of the Council of Europe was adjudged by that Council's highest court to have violated the very principles on which the organization was based. Yet even as the United Kingdom worked legislatively to bring the country into compliance with the ECHR holdings in *Goodwin* and *I.*, it still teetered at earth's flat edge by continuing to uphold its position in *Bellinger v. Bellinger*. On April 10, 2003, Lords of Appeal of the House of Lords agreed with two lower courts that Mrs. Bellinger's physical sex at birth was preeminent (*Bellinger v. Bellinger* 2003).[171] These British courts, like many U.S. courts, focused on what could be changed rather than on what could not. They failed to see transition as an acknowledgement, and not an alteration, of the essence of sex and gender identity.

That focus, at least to the principles and their supporters in the case, must have seemed vindictive when another appeal to the ECHR was the likely outcome of an adverse ruling. That appeal was not necessary because the United Kingdom adopted the Gender Recognition Act 2004 with its Royal Assent July 1, 2004 (Department of Constitutional Affairs 2004).[172] The judiciary's determination consistently to follow precedent regarding extant law that has been found to be unjust, until the law is changed, seems an odd perversion of the concept of blind justice. Even if the Kingdom-wide practice is vigorously to apply every law and to prosecute every violation without exception, such devotion to law, or its interpretation, that a higher court has found to be unjust seems arbitrarily capricious and a harsh abuse of power. However problematic the procedure by which fundamental human rights are recognized, the *Goodwin* and *I.* seminal cases decided against the United Kingdom portend an increasingly enlightened awareness of who transgendered people really are, not only in the United Kingdom, but throughout the world.

Church Views

If there were a major religion that did not hold a concept of the soul as one of its central tenets, its god would have to be quite bored, otherwise occupied, or not alive. Central to most of the world's religions is the belief that the soul, the essential part of who each person is, leaves the body at death. In the presence of the body of a deceased loved one before, during, and after a funeral, mourners are well aware that the essence of the person with whom they interacted no longer has a form with which conscious interaction is possible. Whether that person still has a gender identity after death may be unknowable, but that identity was a key element of her or his existence before death.

As people experience audio and/or video recordings of loved ones who are no longer alive, they remember who those people were. They recall shared instances of warmth, humor, sadness, and other intensely human life experiences. Yet, the bodies and remembered images are not that for which these people most yearn. Grief at having lost the physical presence of someone dear to them even causes some people to forsake what they had previously accepted as a matter of faith. These bereaved would deny the only condition that accommodates continuation of their loved one's essential existence. It is equivalent to asserting that "if the person does not exist physically in my presence, that person cannot exist". They are really saying that their grief will not permit the person they loved to exist in a form whose presence does not immediately and tangibly include them. That is at least as immature as the naiveté of which skeptics often accuse believers.

When my paternal grandmother died, my grandfather, in a heart-rending, deeply personal, and tender expression of love, allowed himself a last kiss before leaving her in her casket at the funeral home the night before her burial. I never asked him how hard it was to experience that additional brutal aspect of the harsh reality of her passing. Their marriage of more than fifty years had given them a oneness whose physical existence ended with her death. As hard as each surviving spouse knows that experience of parting to be, living daily with the physical absence of who we thought that person was must be still harder. It is the absence of the living manifestation of a real and complete person, whatever the physical attributes and deficiencies of that self, that is haunting and, occasionally, overwhelming. Again, that essence of a living person is largely absent from the rulings of most of the court cases previously cited.

In January, 2003, the Catholic Church's Congregation for the Doctrine of the Faith circulated a document declaring that the transgendered condition is incompatible with leadership positions in the Catholic Church. If an ordained member of an order transitioned, that person must be expelled from the order. A transitioned person must not seek membership in an order, but if she or he did, the application must be rejected. Even if civilian birth records were corrected, baptismal records showing natal physical sex were not to be changed (Sidney Morning Herald 2003).[173] Not only did the document question the state of a transgendered person's mind, but it found medicine's best efforts insufficient to alter that person's natal sex (Donovan 2003, 8).[174] Questioning the mental state of transgendered people stems from a mindset that does not accurately grasp, or will not accept, the concept of gender identity. This view is similar to the myopia described above regarding the British courts in *Bellinger*. There is common ground here, but only one side recognizes it. To the best of current medical knowledge, a person's gender identity cannot be changed and it cannot be forced, coached, coaxed, or otherwise altered to fit a conflicting body. That is the rationale for altering the body, which can be changed, causing it to conform more closely to the person's mind.

I do not question the intent and commitment of such dedicated theologians to attempt to understand and comply with the Will of God, especially regarding their understanding of the ordering of His Church. By "His Church,"

I do not a mean specific building or set of them, a particular denomination, or a group of people who might call themselves by that term. Its use here does not refer to anything that humans have given or can give to God. It refers to something God has given to, and shares with, humanity.

The sincere devotion of some followers may well be so selfless that they might lose, in a sense, their innate connection to humanity as they pursue the greatest possible emersion in His Word, though they began and will end their earthly lives as humans. That separation, though, was also common to the people who were instrumental in approving the Spanish Inquisition, the granting of Papal Indulgences, treating Galileo's work as heresy, tacit acquiescence in the Holocaust, failure to alert parishioners regarding pedophile priests, and denial of the gender identities of transgendered people. Far from being part of a sweeping indictment of His Church, these periods through history show the potential for great harm when a lack of circumspection can mean an incomplete hearing and/or application of His Word by devout believers in it. They, like most transgendered people and those who would help them, have prayed, studied scripture, and accepted the gift of salvation. If only one, or neither, population can accept the assertions of the other, they still share a bond that should be far stronger than any matter that would separate them. Their Savior does not forsake those who do not forsake Him.

The Bible, to those who believe it, is the inspired word of God. While welcoming and considering what others say it says, believers dare not ascribe to anyone else the authority to determine what it says. The Bible contains no book, chapter, or verse specifically referring either to gender identity conflict or to transgendered people. Because the concept has been foreign to the experience of most humans, gender identity conflict almost certainly was not understood by those recording scripture, even if any of those people attempting to do the recording were transgendered. An MtF person of that time would have assumed that her gender identity conflict was a terrible and persistent temptation that must be confessed in prayerful silence and suppressed in the presence of others. Surely, any effort to reconcile the condition's obsessive and compelling thoughts with an understanding of the Word of God would conflict harshly with what she had learned as a "male" and what she thought God said. Her experience would certainly be beyond most or all of the people around her who had no intimate experience with the transgendered condition.

Believers accept that God speaks to them but, because they are human, they are fallible and hear Him through the filters of their knowledge, imagination, and experience. Their hearing is imperfect, not because of Him, but because of them. They may implore Him to whisper to them about the splinter while He shouts to them about the log, but they do not hear Him. The rarity of the transgendered condition's incidence means that many of those in the Church and in society who have the authority to, and have assumed the responsibility for, establishing limits on the activities and opportunities available to transgendered people must find the very concept of gender identity conflict well beyond the scope of their personal experience and comprehension.

The hierarchy of the Church must hear God too, but since they are mortal, their hearing also is imperfect. Just as these men have perpetuated a priesthood that excludes women *en masse*, so they would also exclude all MtF women from fulfilling their roles in the Church as women. The Church will undoubtedly survive without the services MtF women might have provided as priests or nuns, but no one ever can know how much stronger the Church might have become with their full inclusion. It is reasonable to ask the same questions and to apply the same tests of faith to transgendered members as to other people who are called to serve. To proscribe the service of certain members because of their honestly disclosed gender identity, however, is to deny the part of God's message that would speak through their service.

Active supporters of civil rights, proponents of the Equal Rights Amendment, those in favor of affirmative action, and others certainly should not be surprised by another instance of separation of, and discrimination against, one group by another based on a characteristic the former has shared since birth. To those with an irrational bias, that single characteristic becomes preeminently dispositive regardless of the individual's demonstrable talents, abilities, achievements, and factors such as intellect, character, maturity, or other qualifications. Everything else becomes irrelevant. Such prejudice is illegal in most instances for governments and corporations throughout the industrialized world, but it still is practiced by many private organizations, individuals, and third world countries. It is especially distressing that leadership in the Church would take such a position when it purports to prize highly the worth of the individual human soul. The victory of a clearer vision must await a brighter day, but its advent, as surely as people of faith believe in inexorable enlightened human advancement through grace, is inevitable.

The Body Preeminent

To some supporters of the final rulings in *Littleton, Gardiner, Kantaras,* and others, each person's natal anatomy, as the product of Divine Will, is holy. In their view, all humans are, at birth, created as God intended them and, with the caring nurture of parents, teachers, and His help, infants become the adults they were meant to be, unless they sinfully choose a contrary path. Many proponents of predestination reluctantly accept some medical intervention to treat children with birth defects, physical injuries from accidents, and evident diseases, but do so primarily as part of their obligation to nurture children. Something about gender identity conflict is unacceptably disconcerting to many of these people. In their view, God created the universe, dark matter, earth and humanity, and even medical science, but He could not, would not, or simply did not create, and would not permit to exist, such incongruity. My efforts in correspondence and discussions with warm, well-educated, well-intentioned, and devout people whom I like and respect, to elicit a rationale for their certainty of this peculiar divine limitation have been unsuccessful. Their answer consistently has been that they "know" it because they believe it, and they believe it deeply.

The earthly leadership of the Roman Catholic Church (but certainly not all Catholics) decried a "blurring" of physical differences between women and men to the perceived detriment of the traditional family (Ekklesia 2004).[175] That "blurring" is not something society is creating, but merely recognizing. It is caused, or at least nourished, by a failure to acknowledge the existence, persistence, and power of gender identity. Female gender identities are always female whether they exist in natal female or male bodies. Male gender identities are always male whether they exist in natal female or male bodies. It is the inability to see or acknowledge that characteristic of essential identity that is responsible for the perceived "blurring." The terrible irony is that for the Church to insist that MtF women must be treated as men is to assert that the body must be preeminent over the mind and soul. Dedication to a bias so extreme that it supersedes a central tenet of their faith is unworthy of people who call themselves Christians, and especially so among those who are leaders in or teachers of their faith. Even some Muslim clerics in theocratic and repressive regimes have perceived gender identity as an expression of a true self in conflict with its natal physical sex (Stack 2005, 8-A).[176]

Those accepting the notion of reincarnation might argue that an MtF woman is carrying forward the female gender identity she retained from a previous life. The conflict's origin would stem from a more elemental self that is separate from the present incarnation's mind and body. Why that would be the only aspect of an earlier life to cause conflict with her different body, however, should be difficult to explain. Each previous self would certainly have had different family relationships, a different formal education, and realized a whole other life experience. The idea that an MtF woman would suddenly waken to discover her essential self in a body inappropriate to her gender is almost unimaginable. Those offering this explanation might argue that family, education, and life experience are ancillary aspects of the existence of one's essence. They see the primary purpose of that existence, however, as advancement. Without vivid recollection of having learned gender-related life-lessons, that essential self arguably could experience little or no real advancement.

Some philosophies see the soul, or other essence, not only as having experienced past lives, but as having experienced lives in one or more nonhuman form(s). Dr. Jaime Stover Schmitt, author of *Every Woman's Yoga*, said that two of the quartet of components that make up the discernible "antar karana" (inner instrument) are "chitta" (the memory of past lives) and "ahamkara" (the sense of self or identity) (Schmitt 2005.)[177] Assuming that the essential self has a gender identity, it might have been in consonance and dissonance with its respective physical sex through repeated incarnations. Gender identity, as a characteristic of that essence, probably has not been explored by proponents of these philosophies because absence of its conflict among the vast majority, if not the entirety, of its leaders and those who influence them would mean they are unlikely to be aware even of the existence, much less the importance, of gender identity.

Male writers of the Bible's Old Testament, through transference, would reasonably assume God must be male because they "heard," as males, the all-powerful God speak to them. Christ's reference to His Heavenly Father or "Our Father Who art in heaven…" suggests that those writers were correct in their characterization, but for a very different reason. Since any but the most bizarre conception of God would ascribe limitless power to Him, the only logical reason for His having a gender identity is that it says something about who He is. Made in His image, each human would also have a gender identity that is part of who she or he is.

Whether rooted in Islam, Buddhism, Judaism, Christianity, or another religious philosophy, the rejection of, or an assigned inferior status given to, MtF women based on ignorance of the condition and/or poorly construed interpretations of sacred texts ill-befits followers of any faith. For those who would deny the validity of the concept of gender identity, there remains only an unthinking, and even emotionless, stunted view of physical sexuality. If these deniers reject the evident outward manifestations of other people and the proof of their own experience regarding the part of each self that cannot be directly observed, they should also relinquish their pretense of belief in the human soul since it, too, cannot be seen. For these skeptics, a natal physical male must mate for life with a natal physical female. No other pairing is acceptable. For countless millions, this pattern has required no more conscious thought than does one's pulse or breathing. Normal pairing is simple compared to making a lifelong marriage work. So wonderfully simple a pattern is clearly the essential history and foreseeable future of most of civilization, but there are some for whom the pattern, however much they might desire it, will not fit.

In the view of single-pattern proponents, though, anyone who does not fit that pattern must be irreparably defective, broken, warped, corrupted by sin, etc. They see pattern-averse people as leaning over "the pit" with both feet on banana peels and their hands grasping desperately for the finest of threads that are not attached to anything. If observable facts do not fit their model, proponents would assert, those facts must be wrong, incomplete, or misunderstood. If pattern proponents do accept the existence of gender identity, they would argue that gender identity must be the servant to, rather than the master of, one's natal physiology.

By the same errant reasoning, if each person's natal physical sex immutably determined her or his true gender, then a transgendered person could only exist if her or his mind were transplanted into a body of the opposite natal physical sex. The subject's transgendered condition would be short lived, though. By definition, as soon as she or he realized the nature of the new body's sex, her or his new gender would immediately be realized and accepted. The mere suggestion might have tempted Hitler's Dr. Josef Mengele to perform such a surgical experiment, but no reasonable application of medical ethics would permit that experiment today. For an MtF woman having her essential self magically transplanted into the donor body of a natal physical female has been one of her most cherished fantasies, second only to having been born physically female. That surgical process, though, would be the antithesis of the gender identity skeptic's fallacious reasoning because it would actually resolve, rather than to create fleetingly, gender identity conflict.

Body-preeminent proponents contend that couplings other than two natal physical opposites are a "homosexual" aberration. The aberration, they argue, is caused by something awry in the brain that medical science just does not yet know how to repair. Whether the errant component is the result of an object striking the head, a high fever, an allergic reaction, the result of some unfortunate process of thought, misaligned stars, etc., gender identity skeptics argue it is the brain that must be changed because sex-reassignment surgery is an immoral abuse of medical science. Despite a meager number of heralded instances of self-professing "cured" homogendered people, there appear to be no instances involving a reliable and valid testing of the hypothesis regarding "cured" transgendered people.

If a patient in need of bypass surgery were given a choice of surgical repair, taking sugar pills, or ignoring the problem, the rationale of gender identity skeptics, often offering an excuse of religious belief, would require ignoring the problem since there are no obvious visible symptoms. Though gender identity conflict has a major physical component, the condition is not characterized by demonstrable visible symptoms. When considering medical or alternative options for a life-threatening physical condition, those who consider themselves faithful stewards of their bodies will seek medical treatment in the belief that God gave talent, ability, and dedication to the medical practitioners from whom they seek treatment. There need be no conflict between faith and medicine when the two fields, as complements, have been applied so successfully even if there will be conflicts with or among some medical practitioners.

A few medical professionals deny that any of their aptitude, talent, or skill has a divine origin. For them, medicine is just another reasonable result of the emergence of the first creatures that slithered from primordial ooze. Medical professionals who do not acknowledge the divine source of, and limits to, their art believe that they, alone, can make things happen medically. They do not see their work as part of a process intended to promote or aid healing with God's grace. As much as any believer might be inclined to avoid such a practitioner, she or he would tempt fate and faith by avoiding entirely the gift of the medical arts that God has granted.

Some would forbid medical remediation of the transgendered condition. These people of faith exhibit a condescending arrogance that their understanding and perceptions are superior to those of corrupted transgendered people and the medical community. They would say, in effect, an MtF woman cannot be saved as the woman she is. She must become the male façade she has affected, and then pursue salvation. Those who are certain that transgendered people are "lost" might recall that they, nor any humans, have the power to grant or deny salvation. Christians believe that the One who has that power has given it through expiation and propitiation to those who will accept the gift.

16. Popular Misconceptions

Unboxed Thinking

Those who would ground their alternative explanations of the transgendered condition in a contemporary pseudoscience may well have no more ill intent than most philosophers, moralists, ethicists, or people of faith. They have a greater potential to do harm, however, because this nation's legislators and courts usually rely on science and medicine for guidance on matters of physical and mental health. Despite the condition's lengthy history, a growing library of anguished personal accounts, and increasing peer-reviewed volumes of serious scientific inquiry, those who are not intimately familiar with gender identity conflict continue to generate an amazing variety of hypotheses to justify their rejection of a theory they find troubling. For them, gender identity conflict is so difficult to accept that they resort to fallacious explanations that are even more problematic. While observation is the appropriate basis for forming an hypothesis, gender identity conflict continues to be detected indirectly. Like black holes and distant planets, presence of the conflict can be inferred. If presence of the condition were indicated clearly and unequivocally on an x-ray or similar diagnostic tool, there would still be debate about how it got there and the manner in which it should be treated.

Since it is far easier to observe indicators of physical sex, the *lingua franca* of these creative hypothesizers is that MtF women actually are and must remain men. Oddly, these creative explainers have been less concerned about the transgendered condition in FtM men. A bias-based and absurd creative hypothesis for this lopsided interest is that every rational person, whether natal female or male, would prefer to be a stereotypical male. Unfortunately, these hypothesizers share an insistence on the preeminence of natal physical sex to determine gender and that has given them great capacity to do harm. Because of that realized and unrealized potential, the most common of these ersatz hypotheses are addressed in this chapter.

Given the cacophony of contemporary voices offering alternative explanations for the condition, it should not be surprising that transgendered people who are attempting to resolve their suppressed gender identities would have difficulty discovering which, if any, of the voices is correct. When the "gender of rearing" or imposed-gender myth was perpetuated, enthusiastic repetitions of that essentially unchallenged single erroneous answer was at least as unhelpful as too many possible answers. Only through awareness of her or his own identity can a transgendered person find the anchor that secures her or his position through the storm of transition when she or he makes that inevitable journey.

As essential as is the support of family for a child or adolescent taking the first tentative steps toward transition, that support is a grossly inadequate substitute for the assurance that is the essence of self-awareness. In the absence of the certainty of gender identity, gender identity conflict would be transitory. True gender identity is an expression of essential identity. There may well be an especially and appropriately difficult afterlife for the counselor or gatekeeper who would say to a conflicted child "I am not going to help you pursue transition. I am simply not convinced that your conflicting gender identity is real." If that potential "help" were predicated on any of the following alternative and erroneous hypotheses, withholding it actually could be a harshly delivered boon to the child who would find more enlightened help elsewhere.

An extant bias in these alternative hypotheses usually precedes or is concurrent with their proponents' observations. Humans, through a mixture of perverse temperament and enthusiastic curiosity, often show an amazing capacity for attempting to prove that down is up, fantasy is reality, vice is virtue, etc. Despite the honest effort in these pages, some would say that is what I have done, but that would be further evidence of their bias. Those who deny the existence and power of innate gender identity, unfortunately including some in the mental health community, would argue that it is innate gender identity that is the perverse and fallacious hypothesis. They would argue that transition and sex-reassignment surgery are not the best-available or even an acceptable answer to a decades-long identity conflict, but that a perverted conscious or subconscious desire for surgery is the real genesis of a recently fabricated "conflict." This dismissive rationale is addressed later, but the matter is not about *ad hominem* attacks by imaginative proponents. Honest, capable, and proper scientific inquiry differs sharply from a dishonest, less-capable, and improper spontaneous determination to prove a belief. The latter behavior may be accepted and even encouraged in some creative arts, but it must be unacceptable when working at the limits of science.

As wondrous as are the imaginings of some writers of science fiction, those whose work usually is most intriguing still have grounded it, if only by the finest of filaments, in theories that have not been disproved. Ancients who thought the earth was flat must have originated fascinating explanations for why the oceans did not run dry during draught as the seas spilled over the edge of the world. Flashes of insight, original approaches to old problems, applying established principles in new ways, etc. can be priceless fruits from the labors of those who stay demonstrably on the side of reality near the line separating it from fiction. Their patience, diligence, and dedication have resulted in magnificent scientific advances.

There is an important difference between thinking "outside of the box" and forgetting that there is a box. Those practicing the latter may be heeded for amusement or entertainment, but following their work as though it were science, when these "scientists" have eschewed a diligent practice of the tool's methods, is folly. Decking halls with boughs of the stuff might be harmless, but society dares not call it science or it would be welcoming the chaos that would inevitably ensue.

Addiction

Psychiatrists and psychologists who focus much of their practices on the conditions of gender identity conflict and substance abuse must find the similarities and differences between the two conditions compelling. The ground not merely similar, but common, to both afflictions is an apparent unsustainable elation resulting from an altered reality, both anticipated and realized, that is an almost constant presence in the minds of their victims. Those regularly counseling patients who present with one or both afflictions must be especially well trained, experienced, and adept at discerning between authentic and feigned attempts to reveal and conceal aspects of their conditions and at thwarting those who attempt to manipulate people they believe might help them. While experienced diagnostic professionals are acutely aware of the significant differences between the conditions, others may believe that the similarities are far more convincing, if not dispositive.

For the MtF transgendered person who has not resolved her conflict, each anxiously anticipated temporary manifestation of her gender identity can provide an ephemeral realization of her obsession. The substance abuser may realize her or his intensely desired fantasy or altered perception of the present with increasing amounts of the abused substance. While some substance addictions worsen so that no amount is sufficient, the moderately suppressing transgendered person can reach the stasis of a bearable routine where each expression or release is followed by renewed suppression. The boundaries of the routine's plateau are stretched by varying the fantasies, acquiring different clothing and/or makeup, and altering one's behavior while dressed.

Thoughts of any such changes can feed an intense pulse-quickening desire to realize that change. However satisfying the result, the satisfaction is short lived and incomplete. A search for the next variation is inevitable. Individually and cumulatively, her episodes of "dressing" and makeup fail to end her compulsion to reveal her suppressed gender. In the same sense, an addicted person who swallows pills, receives injections, or drinks alcohol pursues a futile search for the final bit that will trip an internal switch that eliminates her or his desire for the state of altered consciousness induced by the abused substance. Despite possibly vehement denials, people with either or both conditions must be acutely aware that the relief they experience is temporary, however great the cost of that relief. Each repetition is one more bit of fuel to the unquenchable fire. Each successive episode of the behavior not only fails to extinguish, but does not even diminish, the urge to repeat that behavior.

Manifestations of the persistence of conflicting gender identity are erroneously seen by some as both growing from and bringing about the next of the transgendered person's successive episodes of expressed gender. View proponents would argue that manifestation and suppression are two halves of a self-perpetuating cycle that must be broken. This view cannot accommodate the existence of innate conflicting gender identity. If MtF women merely had an addiction to patterns of thought and behavior akin to the dependence of someone using illegal drugs or alcohol, abstinence from the behavior would eventually diminish the desire and ultimately end the obsession. Detoxification camps might be established by view proponents for people "addicted" to the transgendered condition. The camps would enforce the inability to practice the behavior and attempt to prevent "addicts" from experiencing stimulating episodes of inappropriate thought. These camps might be modeled after the "reeducation" camps established by repressive government régimes around the world, and they would seek to reduce or eliminate the condition's overpowering obsession.

During lengthy periods in my past, the privacy I required to express my suppressed gender identity was unavailable. Those successive months or years never reduced the intensity of my suppressed gender identity. Thoughts of varying intensity about manifesting my identity were nearly always present and were singularly unhelpful when I was with groups of males. Whether with Boy Scouts, "Little League" players, other students in a men's dorm, etc., I was reminded continually of the ways in which I was very much different from those boys or men.

Although a profusion of case histories will show that individuals have attempted exhaustively and failed utterly to end their obsessions, clinical evidence of successful instances of conflict resolution in favor of one's natal physical sex is sparse or nonexistent. Some people profess to have succeeded in extinguishing their conflict through alternative means. It is unclear, however, whether diagnosis by a qualified professional would have shown that these people were transgendered before they undertook their professed cure and if they would be diagnosed as continuing to suppress a transgendered condition after their "cure." Functional MRIs have demonstrated that the minds of women and men are different. Innate gender identity may be a fundamental part, and even the most important part, of that difference. It is likely, then, that any "cure" that so fundamentally altered a person's brain, assuming she or he survived the procedure, would also have changed fundamentally and powerfully who that person was.

Among the rich variety of matter comprising the universe are objects that produce visible light and other objects that reflect it. Although objects of each type may appear bright in a dark night's sky, they are fundamentally different things. An addicted person's condition comes from a dependency on something outside of the self. If the substance had never been introduced, the addiction could not have occurred. The suppressing transgendered person's behavior stem's from a conflict she or he struggles to, but cannot, resolve. Her or his behavior comes out of that conflict. This comparison is not merely a matter of extrinsic versus intrinsic characteristics nor of one set of things being green and another purple. The transgendered condition and addiction are, in essence, at least as different as they are similar.

Apotemnophilia

An intense compulsion to attempt to have one's body conform to an uncommon but intensely desired mental picture of oneself, which is the essence of the term's definition, demands attention and relief from the community of professionals to which society has given, and which has accepted for itself, responsibility for providing them. The intense and obsessive desire to relieve oneself of a normally functioning healthy limb because one's mind finds that limb's presence unbearable is, by any reasonable and compassionate definition, a condition that richly deserves whatever assistance the medical community can provide. Some, however, have attempted to compare this desire to gender identity conflict. Nothing about the Benjamin Standards of Care would help someone fervently desiring amputation of a healthy limb.

The transgendered person's compulsion to achieve a more consonant self differs substantially from the apotemnophile wishing for an amputation both in motivation and the nature of the desired physical change. University of Minnesota bioethicist Carl Elliott wrote that "Clinicians and patients alike often suggest that apotemnophilia is like gender-identity disorder and that amputation is like sex-reassignment surgery" (Elliott 2000, III-9).[178] Whether that was or is Dr. Elliott's view, the statement typifies the apparent sentiment of many who would prefer any option other than sex-reassignment for attempting to resolve gender identity conflict. Dr. Elliott is described as an ethicist, and not someone who is intimately familiar with the treatment of gender identity disorder. Presumably, a medical ethicist would challenge the appropriateness of an heroic treatment if more modest efforts would achieve an equally satisfactory or superior result. The "if" is crucial, though, because medicine does not, and may never, offer an effective alternative treatment for the transgendered condition.

A medical ethicist's cautionary message would reasonably be intended for the medical community and those who influence or constrain it rather than for prospective transgendered patients. The most basic understanding of the condition, though, would assure the community that if those patients could not be treated in the U.S., their condition would impel them to seek treatment abroad. Reservations regarding the physician's oath not to harm the patient should be especially troubling for anyone who would consider removing a healthy limb or organ that functions within normal limits. That is far different, however, from what happens during sex-reassignment surgery.

The unbelievable absurdity of a comparison between apotemnophilia and gender identity conflict, regardless of who suggests it, is staggering. The two may be related in the same way that trees and amoeba are living things, but the two forms of life have more and important differences between them than they have similarities. One might suggest that Abraham Lincoln and Adolph Hitler were alike because each was a national leader whose first name begins with the letter "A," that filet mignon and arsenic can each be ingested, or that a child's balloon and Jupiter share a pivotal relationship to gas. The horrendous loss of three limbs that former U.S. Senator Max Cleland experienced in Viet Nam or the heart-rending experience of a child who loses a limb to cancer might be compared to an apotemnophile's surgery. Even if amputation in the third case were considered medically necessary, the physical etiology of the first two conditions so sharply differs from the third that equating them is patently absurd.

The fact that crude removal of the external male anatomy of an MtF transgendered woman would leave insufficient tissue from which her surgeon could fashion her new organs should be obvious. No MtF woman would desire so irremediable a loss. A second flaw in the "hypothesis" is that an MtF woman seeks to cause her anatomy to conform, as nearly as possible, to that of more than half of the world's physically normal population. Clearly, that cannot be said of anyone who desires removal of a healthy and fully functional arm, leg, or any combination of appendages. Further, neither apotemnophiles nor those who treat them have indicated that the condition has anything to do with gender identity.

An MtF woman's desired role as wife, mother, or even infatuated lesbian is one sought by other women with a female gender identity, and has been so, from all evidence, since the dawn of recorded history. Those who see MtF women and other women as two groups who merely share a common trait of desire (one legitimately, and one not) are focused only on a tangible aspect that they can see, test, or measure. Their myopic fixation is on physical sex at birth. They refuse to see the common essence of the individual identities of all woman who share a female gender identity.

Someone who has no idea what gender identity is or who is aware of, but will not accept, the concept cannot hope to understand its conflict. A desire for a consonant physical self that more closely approximates one's gender identity does not mean the transgendered person finds certain physical appendages unbearable or even unattractive. Those physical characteristics are only appropriate to a particular gender identity. If one's physical characteristics and manifested self are not appropriate to her or his gender identity, they are a constant reminder both of the unremitting conflict and an absence of the reinforcing sense of oneness that devolves from their being alike.

Autogynephilia

Transgendered people can readily empathize with those struggling with a puzzle for which they can find no solution. That empathetic inclination rapidly diminishes when those who would be its objects repeatedly reject gender identity conflict's parameters despite increasingly persuasive peer-reviewed evidence supporting them. Rejection of the nature of the transgendered condition is a rejection of the essence of the life-long struggle of people who are suppressing and those who no longer suppress their gender identities. That rejection is especially harsh when it comes from mental health practitioners of a discipline supposedly predicated on scientific theory.

People desperate for any explanation that rejects the existence of gender identity conflict could suggest that the transgender condition stems from mothers who wore green more than once a week, sunspot radiation present at the moment of conception, a being from another dimension meddling in fetal development, fathers who wore shoes that fit too tightly, etc. Each of these explanations would be more plausible than the pseudo hypothesis called "autogynephilia" (Blanchard 1989, 616-23).[179] The term presumably would apply to women obsessed with self-stimulation, but that is neither for whom it was intended nor how it has been applied. It was coined to refer to men, if there are such men, who would seek sex-reassignment surgery from male to female. The term apparently does not even consider FtM men whose incidence apparently is even less frequent than that of MtF women.

Autogynephiles would seek to satisfy themselves in a psychosexual sense by becoming physically female while retaining and satisfying their male gender identities. The men to whom such work purportedly applies are so desperately dedicated to their gender identity's passion for self-gratification that they would convince licensed mental health professionals they are transgendered women (and not men) under the Benjamin care standards. They would undergo electrolysis and hormone therapy, live the "real life" test, and then submit to sex-reassignment surgery. By attempting to manipulate and deceive the very practitioners who might provide some of the help they so desperately need, these men would harm that profession, themselves, and those for whom the Benjamin Standards are appropriate. Autogynephiles would cause caregivers to become unwitting accomplices in their escalating attempts at self-gratification that are, by definition, wholly destructive.

The recent work of Dr. Bailey, suggesting that the term may describe all transgendered MtF persons who are not young effeminate males wishing to remain physically male, further strains the imagination (Bailey 2003).[180] Whatever the methodology of this work, the hypothesis and conclusion are incredible. A male gender identity in a physically female body is the exact opposite of the natural state of an MtF woman, but precisely describes the state of an FtM man. The physical state that becomes unbearable for FtM men supposedly is the ideal state desired by an autogynephilic man.

It is difficult to understand how any male fitting this description could convincingly appear to have the background common to MtF women who have suppressed their gender identities. As a male with a male gender identity, the autogynephilic male could not, by definition, have a female gender identity. His condition would not manifest itself in early childhood female role-playing since he had no interest in being seen by others as a woman. Further, since he would be attempting to become his own ideal female, the autogynephile would have to assume that the physical female he wants to become would find him attractive and someone with whom she was infatuated or even in love. Narcissus was a pathetically inexperienced amateur with a grossly limited imagination compared to the "men" of this absurd model. The complex effort of their attempting to satisfy two opposite aspects of the same person would have to be incredible, and in the most literal sense, it certainly is.

If there is such a person as the autogynephilic super-male who seeks realization of his fantasy of self-stimulation through sex-reassignment surgery, that person certainly is not motivated by gender identity conflict and would not qualify for sex-reassignment surgery under the Benjamin Standards. His goal would not be resolution of conflict, but to provide for himself what he believes no other person can provide. He would be both quarterback and receiver in a season-winning sexual football game. Resolving identity conflict by becoming either wholly woman or wholly man may well be beyond comprehension for those who never experienced gender identity conflict, but it is very much at the center of the transgendered person's quest.

The Benjamin Standards were adopted as a means to resolve an internal conflict by bringing the body into harmony with the mind. Medical science lacks the ability to cause the mind to conform to the body, and the ethics of so fundamental an alteration of the mind would be questionable, at best. For someone with a male gender identity to seek sex reassignment would stand the process on its figurative head. A gender identity previously in concert with his physical sex would be brought into dissonance for prurient and fleeting desire, but the surgery is permanent. Such an abominable assault on the worthwhile and necessary proper use of the procedure would almost justify the overzealous defenders of the Benjamin Standards as necessarily inflexible and absolute.

The autogynephilic rationale does not fit the life experience of MtF women. The view suggests a characteristic of failure to fulfill expectations in male role-playing, but that rationale fails to explain earliest and pre-pubescent memories of gender identity conflict that MtF women had before they had an opportunity to fail in a male role. The rationale's emphasis on sexual motivation does not explain my playing as my sister's girlfriend that had much to do with my gender but nothing to do with sex. It affords no explanation for MtF women's annoyance at the suggestion that they want to become women, because they do not seek a different identity. MtF women want to be recognized as the women they are, and they seek the only known procedure for resolving gender identity conflict. The autogynephilia rationale also offers no explanation for the monogamous nature of the friendships of my youth.

Autogynephilia does not begin to explain my sexual fantasies. I never had an interest in, nor fantasized having, sex as a male with a female or male. I lacked the anatomy necessary to have sex as a female with a male, but I desired and fantasized no other kind of relationship. In those sexual fantasies, the males were always unrecognizable. Contrary to the argument's rationale, my interest and fantasies regarding the matter disappeared for months after surgery. My interest, like that of most women, was and remains in being with one heterogendered man that I find attractive and who wants to be with me.

Autogynephilia could be given a more useful definition. It might describe the desperation of MtF transgendered women who attempt to force their bodies to fit their gender more accurately by performing some part of the surgery themselves. Accounts of this drastic action show that it was done from anguish and desperation, rather than from an interest in self-stimulation. The preoccupation of these women was a condition that they could no longer bear, rather than a desire for an erotically exciting but fleeting episode of self-indulgence. I did consider trying what aptly could be called "the ultimate do-it-yourself project," but I thought it probably would prove fatal either from loss of blood or from infection. If that meant the real goal of the act was suicide, it also meant that the only perceived acceptable alternative to continuing to live with gender identity conflict was death. I had no desire to put those I most cared about through such an experience. The possibility of surviving the attempt or of a lingering death following it were even less desirable potential outcomes.

Trying to explain having committed what is essentially a desperate act of self-mutilation, assuming anyone were willing to listen, would make even the most challenging accounts of "How I Spent my Summer Vacation" pale by comparison. If self-inflicted harm was actually an intermediary step to a transgendered person's finally talking with someone about her or his own poorly understood identity conflict, it clearly would be more reasonable and expedient to skip the act of desperation and move directly to a search for qualified help. The emotions of frustration and desperation at such times, compounded by the real or perceived unavailability of qualified help or financial considerations that make the option unaffordable may well preclude one's undertaking that search. The power of such inertia, or the paralysis of indecision, is incredibly effective in prolonging suppression. While I fully can understand the desperation that would move an MtF woman to attempt her own surgical resolution, even as it inhibited her pursuit of a better reasoned action, I do not understand how anyone could consider the gender identity underlying that emotional conflict to be male. A similar torment must plague an FtM man regarding a different part of his anatomy.

Emotion over Reason

This position's proponents contend that transgendered people were already "messed up" before transition, using illegal drugs, suffering depression, and/or otherwise behaving irresponsibly. Proponents are really arguing that the driving force for transition emanates from a mind given over to addiction and excesses of emotion, and one that resists reason. Proponents often will reluctantly agree that treatment for drug dependency and psychoses should be attempted, but they assert that if one or more self-indulgent excesses is treated successfully, a new one, new ones, or a relapse to familiar behavior inevitably will follow. The transgendered condition, they argue, results from permissiveness and is characteristic of a pattern of surrender to self-indulgent and addictive behavior. Proponents may reluctantly agree that it is expensive, but necessary, to try to help such perpetually flawed people, if only to try to strengthen society or because there is a bond of humanity obligating everyone to help those less fortunate than themselves. Still, they would argue, it is likely that such efforts will fail, that those who are helped will never produce anything of value, or that the value of what is produced will be exceeded by the greater cost of the treatment. This is not really an argument based on economics but an expression of bias. Proponents refuse to see that the other problems many transgendered people experience are either independent of her or his gender identity conflict and probably would have occurred anyway, or were the result of contending with, and repeatedly failing to resolve, so persistent a conflict. A decades-long unresolved personal conflict about so central a matter as gender identity should demand any conceivable means of escape, however that attempt might be viewed by the rest of society.

For some proponents the rule of emotion hypothesis also suggests that the claim of gender identity conflict is essentially either a.) the result of someone's spontaneous emotional response to a stimulus, b.) a seduction, perversion, or contamination by a malevolent person or spirit, or c.) a problem devolving from a different corrupting process to which a weak-willed or, more generally, weak-minded person too readily succumbs. The next errant rationale's proponents also assert that transgendered people only discover their childhood manifestations retrospectively, and make that discovery through a lens distorted by their decision to be, or their failure to resist being, transgendered. The fact that most, if not all, of those who have primary responsibility for distinguishing the transgendered condition from a behavioral addiction have not found its origin to be anything other than prenatal development should give pause to even the most ardently biased critics. As bias darkly triumphs over reason, though, proponents of several alternative rationales offer an essentially circular argument that all such conditions and disorders only affect weak-minded people, and only people predisposed to an addiction or to becoming ill are susceptible to dependency or disease. For them, people "become" weak because they always have been weak.

A Fabricated History

Some who dispute gender identity's innate origin assert that transgendered people recount a lifetime of emotionally wrenching identity conflict that is actually a poorly remembered, misconstrued, or ambivalent past. That past was concocted in a desperate attempt to justify their recent "choice" of repugnant behavior. These proponents know that, if the transgendered person's conflict has seamlessly existed from earliest memory or even from birth, then it could not have resulted from choice. Since their argument is critically dependent on choice, proponents must allege that the remembered history is false, misunderstood, or inaccurately remembered. This is like saying that, since the numbers needed to win the lottery are different from mine and I believe I won the lottery, the different numbers must be the ones I have. This conundrum, where something that, from all empirical evidence is certainly false but has to be true to support an hypothesis of choice, confronts those working in areas of mental health, moralists/theologians, and others who reject the condition's innate origin.

Those who believe it should be difficult, if not impossible, for transgendered people to end their conflicts by altering their bodies might consider how their own lives would unfold under a gender identity-based system. If expressed gender identity were the sole determinant of the female/ male dichotomy, those who rejected gender identity would have no gender status. These deniers would be isolated from identified females and males to prevent imposition, assumption, or inadvertent mis-assignment of their gender. Socially isolated deniers would mature and live out their days as gender-neutral beings. Their sense of who they are would be grounded in vapor without any sense of themselves or their real relationships to other people. This cruel scenario is slightly more generous than society's current treatment of transgendered people because it would avoid mis-assignments that are reinforced by every social contact including family, friends, and the whole of society. In practice though, the scenario would be unlikely to occur since even the most ardent of gender identity opponents would soon admit or exhibit her or his gender identity.

The few comparisons I have been able to make between my past and those of other transgendered women have shown that our earliest memories always included attempts to manifest our female gender identity at a very early age. If the condition were a matter either of adult or childhood "choice" for whatever reason, it still would be no less an enduring and substantive problem worthy of serious efforts toward resolution by, or with the help of, competent practitioners. The chronic and life altering impact of a suppressed gender identity that no longer can be hidden still would be just as powerful. To accommodate an hypothesis of "choice," though, those years or decades of suppression simply would be denied.

A transgendered person has no need or desire to generate fabricated or misconstrued memories as an essential part of acknowledging and justifying a very real and ultimately irrepressible self. Her or his focus, before transition, is not primarily on a troubled past, but on an unacceptable present and the imperative to suppress gender identity. The childhood memories and experiences I related to my doctor were only one aspect of a multi-faceted problem that I was no longer willing or able to suppress. Family and social relationships, the decades of secret behavior, the irrepressible wishes, and the condition's other aspects would have been no less substantial a problem without those early recollections. I sought resolution of the entirety of the conflict. If a virus, food allergy, vitamin deficiency, or other cause had been responsible for the conflict, it would have been no less real, but its cause would have been more easily proven and resolution would be less controversial. Honestly related and reliably corroborated childhood memories and experiences did not cause, but were part of, the life of my essential identity. There was never a reason for me to create or embellish my memories whose simple honesty and detail could make the experiences almost as real in recollection as the events were when they occurred.

The need for recently fabricated or wrongly remembered memories originates with those who assert that such is their origin. A quasi solution predicated on choice cannot succeed where that choice was never made. Logic requires that if a false assumption underlying an hypothesis must be true for the hypothesis to be true, then the hypothesis must be false. While having sympathy for those caring enough to generate and advocate this hypothesis, there must be little value in an approach that would stand on wishes, false assumptions, or emotion, but it cannot stand on reason. Repressive governments and societal acquiescence can sustain such thought, often for distressingly long periods. The gulf that exists between an hypothesis that can be tested and an opinion that has not been tested feeds cultures that "know" but do not verify differences among truths, half-truths, and falsehood. Cruelly enforced by unchecked power, the worst such systems have thrived as tyranny throughout history. Persistent disciplined inquiry, free expression, and representative government have been the surest defense against that tyranny.

Iowa by the Sea

As previously stated, in 1992, Dr. John McHugh questioned the practice of sex-reassignment surgery writing "Why amputate the genitals of those poor men? Surely the fault is in the mind, not the member" (McHugh 1992,).[181] Nine years later, columnist John Leo cited that quote in a column questioning media coverage of civil rights advocacy on behalf of transgendered people. Mr. Leo argued that a public forum is an inappropriate place to attempt to deal politically with a matter he thought should remain between a doctor and her or his patients (Leo 2001, 20).[182]

It is indeed appropriate for a transgendered person to seek professionally competent and confidential help for an accurate diagnosis of her or his condition. While that is a reasonable and necessary course for transgendered people, however, following that course does nothing to remedy the fraud of assigned gender that society continues to perpetrate by relying on natal physical sex for the issuance of birth certificates. Unless the political system itself is altered, systemic problems and abuses can only be redressed through the mechanisms that system provides. When their happy consonance of gender identity and natal physical sex leaves them devoid of intimate experience with the transgendered condition, waiting idly for legislators to act only promotes further inaction. History indicates that successive societies have failed utterly to address the condition appropriately, beginning long before America was founded.

JHH, as one of the country's leading research institutions, has had the varied history noted earlier regarding treatment of transgendered people. Ambiguity can be an unfortunate consequence of courageous, if incautious, exploration. The skull of one animal found near the cervical vertebrae of another was long accepted as the remains of a third prehistoric creature that never existed. With respect to the transgendered condition, seeming clinical evidence propounded by qualified professionals who do not always practice good science feeds the hunger of those predisposed to accept their work. This is especially true of subjects and/or disciplines that mysteriously attract the critical attention of those whose religion or philosophy compels them to question the product of some science while eschewing its methods. The U.S. Constitution, First Amendment protects the right of such people to propound their views, but it does not explain why anyone would listen to them (Kashner 2007, 504).[183] When results, or inaccurate inferences from them, become more important than the method used to obtain them, ultimately the results and the method will suffer.

Some have decided that, if the mind and body are in conflict, the mind must be at fault. Dr. McHugh's assertion that MtF women must have a mental problem is, in a sense, like a Hawkeye booster's insistence that, if the ocean exists, it must be in Iowa. There are not two distinct warring identities in the mind of the MtF woman. There is no female self who is engaged in a desperate struggle with a male self. Neither does she feel any dissociative split between her mind and her body. That oneness is the source of her conflict. The factor contrasting with, rather than reflecting, her gender identity is her own anatomy. While she might wish to have her mind stay figuratively in Des Moines while her physical self is removed to Ocean City, the daily commute would be problematic at best.

Dr. McHugh apparently had little clarifying personal experience with transgendered people, despite his obvious expertise and experience in his field. Dr. John B. Watson, behaviorist founder and Dr. McHugh's predecessor at JHH, doubtlessly would have agreed that, in the absence of demonstrable proof of the existence of gender identity, Dr. McHugh must be deemed correct. This view of the condition as the result of a failing mental compass is similar in many respects to those who argue the condition is a matter of gender preference or of sexual preference. It can be seen, however, as a denial of the innate nature of identity, or one's soul, and of that essential identity's gender component. The best evidence favoring this contrary view of essential identity is the successive generations of people, and especially transgendered people, who have lived since the dawn of man.

Reversing History

Many of the misconceptions regarding transgendered people, and even the disgustingly dismissive argument about the alleged ease and inadequacy of sex reassignment, would be strengthened if some significant number of post-transition people sought a reversion to their natal physical state. However inadequate the procedure is deemed by its critics, the process does not involve the attachment of buttons, snaps, or zippers. There is nothing ambiguous about the extent and permanence of the changes made during sex-reassignment surgery. They will remain for the balance of each transgendered person's life. There permanence is precisely the appropriate goal of anyone seeking that surgery.

To a society accustomed to money-back guarantees, the "real life" test of the Benjamin Standards could seem like a new car "test-drive." Its purpose, though, is not to rate likes and dislikes as if considering the purchase of a luxury sedan, but to see if the transition an MtF woman anticipated all of her life is really a matter of her gender identity and to gauge her capacity for adjustment to the social stresses of transition. I never thought of those months as a test. Returning home after my "debut," I took off the makeup and clothes as I had done countless times before in anticipation of each next "dressing" episode. The next day, I realized that what I was doing was no longer, if it had ever been, a partial realization of fantasy, but it was an acknowledgement and manifestation of essential identity. I would no longer need the "guy" clothes in my closet.

I dressed as appropriately as possible for whatever I intended to do each day, but the clothing would be appropriate to my gender identity rather than to my natal physical sex. When I began "presenting" as female, I had not cut my hair in six months and was combing it differently. It was shorter than I wanted it to be, but it would lengthen. I still had many hours of electrolysis ahead and I resented having to shave before applying makeup. These things were certain to improve. Each improvement, however slight, was cheerfully encouraging, yet far short of the dramatic change I desired. The seeming enormity of desired change could be depressing both because it contrasted sharply with current limitations on the physical changes that are feasible and because it was not possible to relive one's entire life in a gender identity-appropriate manner.

Gloria Hemingway attempted to revert to her life of suppression, although others would say she was courageously admitting her mistake. After her transition, she reverted to dressing as a male and even attempted to remarry someone about whom she obviously still cared (Miller 2003).[184] It should not be difficult to understand any transgendered person's desire to be "normal" and that person's reaching for a largely imagined, rather than a selectively remembered, past stasis as a whole part of a pre-transition relationship. An MtF woman, who lived for decades being seen by everyone else as her or his opposite gender, has only that set of memories and life experience to help her contend with the present and anticipate her uncertain future. Having finally and openly expressed her gender identity and progressed to and through transition to resolve her conflict, her life of suppression fades in memory or is conveniently compartmentalized. In a moment of melancholy, she longs to regress and revives her old wish that she might somehow become the fraudulent self of her male persona.

Before transition, in my recurring fantasies of realizing a female self, I had imagined relocating and beginning a new life where no one else would know about my "male" past. People in a new location might presume that I had one, but they would not know what it was. As I began transition, I realized that relocation would prevent any possible daily recurrence of being called by my former name. Having to hear people use inappropriate pronouns when referring to me while talking with a third party would also be less likely. Further, everything else's being new could augment the realization of my no-longer suppressed gender identity.

Some of that sense of newness, though, was false. I both was, and was not, the same person who had grown up in our family, attended the same schools, and shared my work and other life experience. It would be impossible and redundant to prove retention of the capabilities of my pre-transition self by attempting to relive every test and trial of my past. Transition does involve an exchange, but it is one of fraud for truth. Whatever was relinquished in abandoning the pretense of my affected male persona has been more than replaced by the honesty and sense of wholeness that gender and gender identity consonance provides. Experiences with all of the people I had known before transition would be impossible to recreate for a female self because those people also changed. While some of their changes were substantial, none could approximate the experience of suppression and transition.

As much as I would wish for all of the female gender identity-appropriate aspects of a female past, that also is impossible. In the unalterable unidirectional nature of life, undertaking a drastic change of environment is fundamentally a life-altering choice many people choose every day, but they plan to take themselves, as themselves, with them. My relocating would have meant moving away from the support and familiarity of friends, family, and the community. The value of that familiarity and support, though intangible, is incalculable.

Our family had an abridged version of the experience of relocating when we shared my sister's restorative summer at the New Jersey shore. Like millions of others, I first experienced a solo version of relocating when attended a college hundreds of miles from home. I anxiously anticipated the independence my attending college so far from home would bring. Yet, I was ambivalent about the unrealistic expectations I would leave behind in one sense and internalize in another. It was easy to dismiss as fantasy the possibility of my simply appearing on campus as a female version of the person who was enrolled and whose parents had brought "him" to school. There was no honest way to attempt a transition without telling someone. My roommate and room assignment in a men's dormitory meant that my new "independence" was limited. In retrospect, the family's gathering for my paternal grandmother's funeral that year would have made telling someone, without telling everyone, practically impossible.

As a child, I had almost promised myself that I could not possibly carry the baggage of my peculiar preoccupation into adulthood. I had believed and expected that something about the unfathomable process of moving from adolescence to adulthood or the experience of college would be the gate through which my obsession could not pass. Surely the abilities and responsibilities of adulthood were incompatible with so insistent, yet undesired and perverse, a preoccupation. One more prayer, another religious service, some biological clock's tick, something I would learn, or the "special someone" I had been virtually assured I would meet and want to marry; one or a combination of these was certain to slay my phantom. All I had to do was wait. This illogical logic was even more a fantasy than my unspoken desire to attend class wearing a dress. Not knowing the nature of gender identity conflict means that such futile wishing effectively becomes a surrogate for action that has real, and not merely imagined, potential to be effective. Suppressing the condition and hoping it will "go away" is a poorly reasoned excuse for doing nothing.

Never having trusted anyone with my secret at home meant that sharing it with anyone in a new college community of strangers was even less likely. The prime imperative of secrecy was so ingrained that telling anyone about the conflict, even as a precursor to the possibility of resolving it, was not remotely possible. I was acquiring extensive familiarity with the condition from the narrow perspective of personal experience, but I knew nothing of the experience of other transgendered people. In self-reinforced isolation, a young transgendered person's understanding of the condition could be compared to what someone with angina might learn about cardiology. I had no premonition regarding the inevitability of my transition. There was no evident logical or titular companion, friend, or campus counselor in whom to confide as a first step which, of course, precluded my taking a second one. I had never heard of the "real life" test, and I would have had difficulty imagining it because it would requires disclosure. Advancing to the "real life" test would have meant telling everyone, which was incompatible with my dedication to secrecy.

The college health center was staffed by a general practitioner and a nurse. Although the psychology department offered a wide range of classes, I do not believe that any of its staff evaluated and counseled students. The college chaplain seemed decidedly unconventional, and I never heard of anyone's approaching him, or any of the theology department's professors, with such a problem. If there had been someone with whom to violate my prime imperative, resolution was still unlikely. At that time, professional consensus regarding achieving resolution was farther from unanimity than it is today. It is unlikely that I would have found anyone who could speak authoritatively about the importance and preferred method of resolving the conflict.

After transition, one's worldview is not the same and yet, not entirely different. Anyone who has returned to an alma mater, a previous place of employment, somewhere that used to be home, or become reacquainted with a friend or relative following a lengthy separation has encountered this sense of things being familiar but different. The familiarity is with things, and no longer with a continuity of vital interpersonal relationships. The bond of mutual connectedness in an important shared experience has been broken. Understanding this situation rationally is far different from feeling it emotionally. The sense of purpose and belonging that was part of our earlier experience was centered on the people with whom we shared that locale. On returning, there is a sense of belonging but, for an MtF woman, not being the person who belongs or did belong.

These sensations and observations have been my experience in numerous settings, including my returning to my college alma mater before transition, but not after it. High school students and college students probably do not know their respective classmates in the same way for a variety of reasons.

Such differences as the stage in their intellectual and emotional development, their being somewhere they chose to be, greater independence, etc. promote homogeneity in college with a basis other than compulsory attendance and geography. Since I have not shared a reunion experience with college classmates before or after transition, I cannot compare it to the wonderful experiences of the several high school reunions I have attended. Being more honest with these people than I had been so many years before meant not only discovering who each of us has become, but a much belated acknowledgment that the person they thought they knew, regarding any matters of gender, had been a fraud.

Famous father or not, being married, "fathering" children, having a problem with alcohol, being a doctor and a writer, etc.; any or all of these could be a welcome distraction from some of the above conflict. Gloria Hemingway might have had an unpleasant, or an especially challenging, life even if she had transitioned as a child or teenager, but she would have done so as a more complete person. Her seeking the solace of familiarity, even after sex-reassignment surgery, was a quintessentially human thing to do. That solace's illusion is an emotional, and not a reasoned, need to become again someone projecting a grossly incomplete persona to whom others would relate. Her reversion would be even more difficult than her pre-transition existence because she is more acutely aware of her gender identity. Regression would not be to something real and comfortable, but an attempted escape from herself. While I did try on some of my old "guy" clothes long after surgery, from curiosity rather than nostalgia, I was pleased to discover that I thought I looked like a woman wearing men's clothing. Having realized the futility of gender identity suppression before I understood the nature of the conflict, I would not now wish, under any circumstances, to revert to that state. I do understand, though, how Ms. Hemingway's yearning for the way some people reacted to her affected male persona could entice her to attempt to reprise the role.

Homosexuality

When I was a teenager, my older sister showed an article to me about two men who intended to be "married." We each laughed when I replied that I wondered which one would wear the dress. My laughter was defensive, though, because I had no conception of the nature of their relationship nor of the term "homosexuality." The term, itself, is further confirmation of the world's preoccupation with, and custom of reliance on, natal physical sex to define relationships. A couple with the same natal physical sex but opposite gender identities is not, and would not be, together because of that physiology but because one of them is transgendered and intends for her or his physiology to be changed. In common parlance, for a single-sex couple to be a "homosexual" couple, they must have the same gender identity, but people applying that term do not even consider gender identity.

Couples with the same gender identity, regardless of the status of their physiology, are described more accurately as homogendered.   It is more accurate because it describes each partner's preference relative to her or his own gender identity. If the couple cannot satisfy each other's gender identity preference, neither person will find fulfillment in their relationship. Since gender usually refers to perceived appearance and manner, application of "homogendered" can also lack precision because suppressing transgendered people project a persona of opposite gender. Still, it has been used throughout this work because its intended use refers to expressions of honest gender identity.

As some non-transgendered people try to understand the transgendered condition, their limited experience with homogendered people, transgendered people, and peer-reviewed literature regarding the two conditions permits them to conclude that they are far more alike than dissimilar. Unfamiliarity underlies confusion about the distinct differences between addiction and gender identity conflict and most of the misconceptions about the transgendered condition. Even among "experts" in mental health, the belief persists that since an MtF woman must really be a man, "he" must be using a fictional excuse called "gender identity" to rationalize, garner support for, or otherwise facilitate "his" sleeping with another man. By extension, the same argument would mean that an FtM man must be a woman wanting to sleep with other women. This fallacious rationale is especially appealing to advocates of the autogynephilia hypothesis, except that the "woman" the subject wishes to sleep with is his own alter ego.

The most glaring fallacy of the homosexuality hypothesis is that it is based on preferences for sleeping partners rather than each person's own identity. View proponents must believe either that MtF women have no identity of their own or that their maleness is more easily but erroneously denied than acknowledged because they do not wish to acknowledge the nature of their peculiar aspiration. A second problem with this view is that, after sex-reassignment surgery, MtF women lack the physiology necessary for them to have the kind of physical relationship with men its advocates believe MtF women desire. A heterogendered MtF woman actively pursues transformation of her physiology away from that desired by homogendered men.   She honestly has no interest in being with a man who wants to be with another man.

Non-transgendered homogendered people have gender identities consonant with their physical sex and they desire a relationship with someone of their same gender and physical sex. Transvestite males also have no gender identity conflict because they do not desire to change their sex, whether they seek a heterogendered or homogendered partner. Most hermaphrodites or "intersex" people have no gender-identity conflict. They perceive both their gender and their bodies to be female, although their feelings and desires regarding their unusual anatomy are varied. They may desire a sexual relationship with a male, a female, or profess to have no preference regarding their partner's gender identity or sex. Intersex people may even claim to be ambivalent about their own gender identities, but that almost certainly has more to do with preference than their own gender identity. Each of these three conditions, with its unique set of characteristics, differs substantially from the transgendered condition.

It is no more likely that transgendered MtF women are homogendered men than it is that homogendered men have female gender identities. An unwillingness to acknowledge the great difference between the nature of gender identity and sexual preference evinces the extant gulf separating transgendered people from those who will not or cannot accept the existence of innate gender identity. This is especially true of those who read and interpret passages, but not the whole, of scripture, but they do not read and understand, or they refuse to accept, relevant peer-reviewed studies. The willingness in such circles to avoid precision in the use of appropriate terms applied to each very different condition stems partly from religious or moral conviction that all such subjects fall wholly on the wrong side of a distinct and unvarying line. That disdain bespeaks an apparent intellectual laxity regarding the rudimentary foundation necessary for any meaningful discourse and strongly suggests that no such discourse is desired. A cynic would interpret this dismissiveness as meaning, "Don't trouble us with thought, fact, or theory because we know what we believe."

Without common agreement on the meaning of basic terms, prospects for a positive outcome from any serious discussion, if it did occur, must be exceedingly dim. Absence of reasoned discussion is especially harmful to members of groups offering such opposition. Since conditions randomly arising from innate causes, however infrequently they occur, inevitably affect every population, those who do not accept the nature of the condition will be so affected. Like any other innate condition, the transgendered condition's incidence has nothing to do with divine justice from a wrathful god, but everything to do with what it means to be human.

An unwillingness to challenge their own averse biases in closed groups or societies means that people in them who experience unpopular conditions can be executed for their "crimes," expelled from their communities, or forced to suppress their identities. The unrelieved stress of suppression inevitably will lead many or all of them to end their own lives or otherwise separate themselves from their communities. Ironically, Islamists in some repressive systems accept the need for surgery to address the transgendered condition, but they would only abide homogendered men who aspire to sex-changing surgery. Such men probably do not exist. Those who would approve and even advocate so inappropriate a use of sex reassignment surgery fail utterly to understand either condition. Gender identity and sexual preference are as much related as a woman who is short and her preference for green.

Despite the acute self-awareness and frustrating confusion many, if not all, suppressing transgendered people feel about the nature of their compulsion, there is much more certainty about what that condition is not. A woman who does not know she needs size ten shoes can still be certain she does not wear size seven. However difficult and perplexing my struggle with gender identity conflict became, it never involved an interest in, aspirations to, or fantasies of my being one of two men or two women in a romantic relationship. There may be another way to define homogendered relationships, but common physical sex is clearly the most prevalent. Common gender identities, though, is a more accurate characterization.

My romantic interest, like that of most MtF women, is to be with a man who finds me desirable as a woman. Honest attraction flows from, rather than helping to establish or define, each person's essential identity. Homogendered women and men would provide their own accounts, but their interest in, and desire toward, their partners is probably, for them, virtually identical to what members of heterogendered couples feel and profess for their partners. For a variety of social and personal reasons, however, finding those partners may be much more difficult. By noting the significant differences between the homogendered and the transgendered condition, I am not suggesting that members of either group should feel superior to the other, especially when some people are members of both groups.

I have experienced three expressions of interest by gay men in sharing a physical relationship. The first two incidents were long before transition and the third was more than one year after transition. Each instance was entirely unanticipated, occurred in a different setting, and involved a man who seemed quite different from the other two. There may be a language of, or ritual to, communicating receptiveness to that interest but if so, it is foreign to me. I do not know if three instances is a larger or substantially smaller number than most transgendered or most non-transgendered people experience. There is probably no way to know how often an average person might have such an encounter since, in most instances, only two people know that it occurred.

The first instance involved a talented friend whom I respected and with whom I continued to share many common interests and views. Perhaps I should have known of his firmly-established preference, but I did not. I briefly considered responding to his invitation in a defensive/aggressive manner as though it was deemed insulting, at least partly because I thought my male persona demanded it. I knew his intent was anything but disrespectful, however, and his disarming embarrassment at its rejection garnered almost immediate sympathy. Although I had known him for several years, he had suddenly dared to reveal a personal aspect of his nature in apparent anticipation of a favorable response that I could not provide. He told me that he had decided about his orientation while he was in college and, when sexually involved with a female student, had found the experience amusing and unsatisfying. I said I thought his interest could be construed as a compliment, but if so, it was an unwelcome one. He asked if I were sure and I said I was. We remained friends, but did not discuss that evening again.

A few years later, the second instance occurred during an arts management conference. I had just met his wife and him during one of the sessions. The three of us and roughly one hundred other attendees had just enjoyed a wonderful New England lobster dinner baked in an open pit at a beautiful and historic setting. My "single" hotel room was a hastily-converted reception room that was much larger than their room. I invited both of them to it to continue our discussion about several of the conference sessions we had attended and the arts in general. When he came to my room, he said his wife had decided to stay in their room. We continued our discussion of the week's events until he subtly, but unmistakably, suggested an interest in something else. This incident was at least as unexpected as the first had been, but I did not even consider a hostile response. When I quipped that we would have to be married first, he quickly changed the subject and soon left. I reviewed our discussion and could find nothing I had said or did that might have been misunderstood. I had enjoyed talking with his wife too, and, although he was more actively involved in the arts than she, they both had actively participated in our earlier conversation and I had assumed that would continue.

The third instance occurred more than a year after my transition when a stranger said he had seen me in a local grocery store. He said that he thought I was a man attempting to "pass." It is certainly possible that a man would attempt to appear female to attract the attention of another man. In a dominant/submissive homogendered dichotomy, he would be proclaiming his preference. To the extent he was attempting to elicit interest from a heterogendered male, his enterprise would be grossly dishonest. He would be attempting to begin a relationship he was woefully incapable of continuing. Since each MtF woman is acutely aware of her gender identity and must ultimately express it, his deceit would be immensely troubling. An MtF woman may spend decades living as an imposed persona while she suppresses her gender identity until she can no longer abide the unrelenting conflict. She would be appalled that a man who had no such conflict would willingly fabricate an opposite-gendered persona to deceive another man merely to satisfy the first man's sexual appetite.

This experience was by far the most unpleasant of my three encounters. It suggested that, to at least one person with whom I apparently shared no common interest, the extensive efforts I had undertaken to resolve my conflict and to end the fraud I had helped to maintain for most of my life were seen as a mere substitution of a new and different kind of deceit. The stranger had supposedly recognized me as he was driving by my home and had waited for an opportunity to attempt a liaison while his wife was away. I wanted to feel sympathy for this person because of his evident confusion and aberrant interest, but found the incident so unpleasant that I simply wanted him to leave. If he really was married, I wondered what kind of a relationship he had with his wife. If he was merely acting as a devoted husband, was she attempting to be his accepting and loving wife? Did she know about his orientation? He evidently had perceived my honestly being myself as dishonesty and was not repulsed by it.

The art and skill actors employ to portray characters quite different from themselves as a means of telling a story is far different from their employing those abilities to deceive people around them and, perhaps, to delude themselves in life. They, more than most people, may be keenly aware of when they are being themselves and when they are playing a role. At the other extreme, it is disturbing for anyone to find that the person she or he honestly and earnestly presents to the world is not readily and correctly perceived by others. It is far worse to have that projected self perceived as unsavory, inviting of an indecent proposal, and suggesting a willingness to acquiesce or even to encourage infidelity. Someone conservatively dressed and innocuously engaged in grocery shopping or leaf raking would not be projecting this latter and unflattering self-image, and no person can bear an unlimited responsibility for the invalid perceptions of others. As strong as was the urge to take a hot shower with strong soap, there was neither water hot enough nor soap sufficiently strong to expunge so unpleasant an experience

None of the three above instances would be appropriately interpreted as evidence of an above-average incidence of homogendered people in the arts. I had known the fellow in the first incident for several years before it occurred. He obviously had not initially presumed a homogendered predisposition on my part. The man in the second incident had an interest in the arts but was neither a musician nor an artist. The third incident could not have had less to do with music. It resulted from my innocently shopping for groceries and raking leaves. Music can be a communication medium of incomparable power, but who uses it and how it is used cannot reasonably be attributed to the medium.

During the struggle to understand and resolve their conflict, transgendered people may consider sexual preference as an indication of the nature of their condition. Some may even attempt homogendered liaisons as a means to clarifying their conflict. If they do so, they make themselves victims of the same confused ignorance that persists in society at large. The liaisons must inevitably fail to resolve their gender identity conflicts. The probable result of those affairs is an exacerbated sense of overwhelming conflict. MtF women are likely to experience greater confusion regarding their sexual preferences. They will almost certainly feel a further lowering of their self-esteem for having engaged in socially proscribed behavior that did not clarify their conflicts. Concern for, and the risk of contracting, sexually transmitted diseases, would exacerbate their feelings of general anxiety. Greater confusion regarding emotional commitment and its connectedness to physical intimacy and the straining of extant family relationships are also likely to occur. The primary reason I was never tempted to participate in such a liaison may well be that I was never confused about the kind of physical relationship I desired. Still, a prospective partner's physical sex is clearly unrelated to whether a person is transgendered.

A Troubled Man

Those who assert that an MtF woman is really a man seeking resolution of a different psychological problem by the specious means of counseling, hormone therapy, and surgery are simply restating the most serious flaw in their argument. The MtF woman seeking resolution of her gender identity conflict was never a man in the true sense of the word. Ultimately, MtF women pursue alteration of their bodies because their essential selves compel them to appear as the women they are. The fraud of their affected male persona is no longer sustainable.

Every person may do things or behave in ways that may reflect who that person is, but those actions or behaviors determine neither that person's identity nor any of its components. Authentic actions, and not those borrowed in mimicry or performed solely to satisfy others, flow from each person's interests, goals, and ideals. Each of those is colored by who she or he believes, and ideally, knows her or his essential self to be. Christians and others believe each person's essential self is known to God. A very large part of the calculus of that essence, flowing so effortlessly and naturally from it that many people have never contemplated a divergence, is gender identity. By suppressing her gender identity, an MtF woman may be defying the Will of her Creator.

Who each person really is, without pretense or artifice, is an intrinsic matter that informs and limits the person she or he may become. What individuals do and how they interact with other people are extrinsic matters on which there may be a variety of other influences. It is astonishing that people whose strong avocational, if not vocational, life is primarily concerned with less tangible matters of the mind, heart, and soul blithely ignore those key aspects of every person's identity regarding transgendered people. When I was strongly resisting disclosure of my secret, I would have argued as forcefully as I could that a man cannot be a woman, but I did not fully understand what that meant. I repeatedly failed to recognize that my own and anyone else's gender identity will not, because it cannot, be determined by her or his physical sex.

No religious person could reasonably argue that the body must rule the mind, heart, and soul when it should, and must ultimately, be the opposite. A woman is a person whose female gender identity must be manifested in a physically female body, or she will be obsessed continually by the alternative's dissonance. Recognition of that dissonance impels mental health and medical professionals to change the physically alterable aspects of a transgendered person to reflect more accurately her or his essential self that cannot be altered without destroying that self.

The assertion that transgendered women are men who want to be women is, from increasingly persuasive research and the reality of my own experience, entirely false. Anyone might wish to be younger or more attractive, to have greater wealth, to be a better athlete, to be more healthy, to get along better with family members, to be married to someone else, or to be divorced from her or his current spouse. None of those desires approximates the driving force that impels a transgendered person toward and through transition. MtF women realize that transition is the final battle in which their lengthy and arduous contest with gender identity conflict will be resolved to the greatest extent medically and reasonably possible. They are no longer willing to suppress their identity in any setting. This quintessential fuel powers an MtF woman's determination to surmount any impediment that obstructs her path to resolution.

During the first meeting with my psychiatrist, I was not predisposed to attempting to become physically female, but I was no longer willing to suppress my identity. If there was another diagnosis and/or other treatment that would resolve my conflict, I wanted to know about it. As desperately determined as I was to find resolution, I was pessimistic about my prospects for a successful transition if one was attempted. If transition meant that I would be shunned, ridiculed, or pitied, limited resources of time, money, and effort would have been wasted. Transition would have produced a "cure" that was almost as unpleasant as the disease. My goal was to end the incessantly repeating cycle of anticipation, "dressing," fantasy, and relief, that were followed by self-loathing or reproach, depression, and then stoic fatalism that awaited the next iteration of the cycle. To frame that struggle as a desire for transition is to confuse action with its reaction or cause with its effect. That errant assertion is the exact opposite of the reason I, and most or all other post-op transgendered people, sought professionally competent help and then welcomed transition.

False Memories

There is a distressingly persistent view toward MtF transgendered women that could be expressed as the following:

> "I am not saying you are lying, but you are
>
> mistaken. The decision you made to change your
>
> sex involved both your developing a different
>
> perspective on very common childhood
>
> occurrences and your creating

a set of false memories. Your deciding to become

a woman is no

different from your deciding to become a rabbit

or a car. Whatever its

cause, there is obviously a problem with your

mind and that is what must be

changed. You must accept the body and natal

physical sex

that God gave you and abandon the notion of

gender identity, which

only exists in your imagination."

This statement itself is incorrect in so many ways that the transgendered person's immediate response is incredulity. There is no possibility that transgendered people from around the world and across thousands of years have conspired to concoct a common history. Far from being a belated excuse, manifestation of an enduring and compelling gender identity conflict is the force that ultimately drives a transgendered person to and through transition. Hundreds or thousands of MtF women have transitioned in their forties and later after decades of gender conflict and deceit. They acted with the help of professionally competent counselors who found them qualified for surgery. No sudden whim prompted them to act. The absence of cars and rabbits that have become people shows that there is a major difference between gender identity conflict involving aspirations rooted in underlying reality and the critics' proffered pseudo reality rooted in fantasy.

While it was possible to postpone acting to end the conflict for decades, that postponement would erroneously be construed as an adjustment or accommodation that can permit an MtF woman to live her own life before transition. However thorough or incomplete her understanding of her condition, the MtF woman knows her identity does not conform to her masculine features. Altering that mind chemically or through an intense "programming" course with an inescapable physical component would create a new person different from the one who began treatment. There might be a fine line between helping someone to resolve a problem and fundamentally changing who that person is, but there is an enormous moral and ethical difference between the two sides of that line. Any legal entity that would sanction the latter poses a challenge to the most basic of human rights, with or without the subject's consent.

Other issues of religion, politics, philosophy, esthetics, etc. pale into obscurity compared to the significance of altering so fundamental an aspect of a person as her or his gender identity. Even if that change were or might become possible, it would be embraced at an horrendous cost to the core values of society. Fundamentally altering anyone's essential self would be quintessentially barbaric. Whatever brutal acts might have been committed during humanity's most barbaric past, aggressors and those attacked lived and died as the people their Creator ordained. Any society that condoned so draconian a change of anyone's being would sanction destruction of someone it did not create to create someone of unknowable dimensions. That society would devalue the human soul. Surely, even the most callous and least principled observer would note that such a society would richly deserve its unenviable fate.

Preferring Orange

Those who contend that transgendered people have chosen a "lifestyle" fail by a huge margin to understand a condition beyond their own experience and, apparently, even their imagination. The manner and routine of desert-crossing nomads, seafaring New England fishermen, contemplative monks, research scientists, touring pop musicians, and other stereotypical examples could be termed "lifestyles." Being right-handed, five-feet tall, native-born American, or having a female gender identity is not adopting a lifestyle. Far from choosing their identity, many MtF women have chosen to fight against it and to suppress it for much of their lives. After decades of unsuccessful effort, I realized that my female gender identity could no more be forced to become male than an orange might become an apple. The orange might become more ripe, bigger, sweeter, juicier, or it could even be painted red and a stem attached. As long as it exists in a recognizable form, though, its essence remains that of an orange.

The experience of hundreds or thousands of transitioned transgendered persons is that gender identity conflict is not something they chose or to which they were recruited. I know of no MtF woman who will admit, acknowledge, or even accept that any aspect of the condition is optional. If an MtF woman did assert that she chose her condition, she would have great difficulty explaining her innate feminine gender identity. At least as rare is an MtF woman's assertion that she was convinced by, or contracted her condition from, another

MtF woman. In the studies I have reviewed, none has suggested a plausible explanation for transgendered recruitment or contagion.

People of such determined orientation that ultimately nothing is more important to them than the resolution of a no-longer bearable conflict have pursued and achieved transition after decades of suppression. Examples such as the Jorgensen transition and the Reimer reassignment failure are notorious and compelling instances of the ultimate futility of attempting to induce or enforce an assignment of gender identity that conflicts with the subject's own. The sisterhood of MtF women who have transitioned since adoption of the Benjamin Standards of Care and the previously cited casework of Dr. Reiner are further evidence of the innate origin of the transgendered condition.

As difficult to describe as are the sensations, confusion, and compulsion of gender identity conflict, the effort is likely to be received as if spoken in an alien tongue. How someone who has not studied the condition, endured her or his own, or shared someone else's experience could understand it is unfathomable. It is amazing, then, that some "normal" but inexperienced people will state with amazing certainty that they know what the condition is. These people usually do not view favorably what they contend is a choice, and a wrong one. While their inability to grasp the whole of the condition's reality is understandable and even expected, their apparent unwillingness to seek valid answers before they decide they do understand it is not. The vehemence with which some deny the essence of a transgendered person's conflict might lead one to suspect that the deniers are, themselves, conflicted about their gender and sex identities and are suppressing, instead of acknowledging and expressing, their own conflicts.

Before transition, I exercised a similar exaggerated aversion when asked about public displays of attraction between two men. Concern for perpetuating my male façade was so overpowering that I could not simply say that all excessive public displays of an essentially private mutual affection, whether heterogendered or homogendered, were boorish. My aggressive rejection of the propriety of such displays was primarily defensive. I sought to deflect or defeat any perception of ambiguity about who I was by reacting the way I assumed most men would. Suggesting that two men who publicly and enthusiastically expressed mutual affection should be punished was similar to my exercising the unsympathetic self-loathing I sometimes felt about my own conflict.

A more appropriate answer would have been that, even if I were empowered to draw a line for appropriate public behavior, few would be likely to observe it. If one person really loves another, though, shouting the fact from a rooftop would only seem necessary if the other person were not also on the rooftop, was near but hard of hearing, or could not read the first person's handwriting. However boorish elaborate, public, and attention-seeking displays may be, the theoretical basis for making them illegal is weak and conflicts starkly with America's common regard for individual responsibility and liberty. Some people are especially adept at expressing their disdain for infractions of social mores. They will tactfully, but firmly and unmistakably, remind offenders that a healthy concern for other people in public places reasonably constrains behavior in public. For those people unwilling to observe even today's modest constraints, the force of law is unlikely to provide the desired result. Fines and/or jail can be powerful tools when applied judiciously. Those tools would be abused if applied to minor transgressions against common courtesy and decency.

In a second instance of aversion more than 20 years ago, I was inconsiderate regarding an MtF woman during or soon after her transition. While riding in a public conveyance with my younger sister, we were seated behind an MtF woman and her supportive male companion. Certain that my sister also had noticed the woman, I told my sister that I was sure the person ahead of us was fooling no one. The MtF woman certainly was not attempting to fool anyone, but had acted to end a charade. I had seen her as embodying the potential futility of my own obsessive, but still suppressed, interest in transition and she was doing so in the presence of a sister for whom I was still attempting to be a caring and protective brother.

Each of these and other persona-protecting excesses was a pathetic attempt at role-playing. My constantly jeopardized male façade dared not show empathy, objectivity, tolerance, or even courtesy regarding matters where equivocation could be misconstrued. No list of key issues, no manual of prescribed responses, and no classes for exemplary bigotry supported people who reflexively defended their weak affected male personas. Any list would have been useful to delimit the bounds of necessary and excessive indignation, but there was a steep learning curve and there were several instances of single-incident lessons. As awkward as these occurrences were, there seemed no acceptable alternative to confronting them. Other suppressing transgendered people may also have exhibited similar excesses of defensive behavior to preserve their personas. Memories of these unfortunate acts were probably much more fleeting for the other people present, but they remain like scars from self-inflicted wounds for their perpetrator. Understanding why such things were done does not erase them from memory nor, many people would add, should it. Such defensive excesses may be among the least harmful consequences of unresolved gender identity conflict, but they will remain part of the conflict as long as the conflict remains.

Sexual Perversion

Some people who do not understand the condition suggest that transgendered people are simply expressing a promiscuous desire that fuels, and feeds on, an insatiable quest for sexual relationships. They allege that because each transgendered person is very much concerned about her or his own gender identity, she or he must be motivated by an unremitting desire for sexual intimacy of any kind with anyone or anything. As stubbornly as this perception persists, there is no valid evidence to support it and substantial indirect evidence to refute it. The same sweeping baseless allegations have been asserted regarding people with a same-gender partner preference, but homogendered and heterogendered people alike have exhibited a similar propensity to maintain caring and enduring relationships with their partners and families (American Psychological Association 2004).[185] Apprehension regarding all transgendered people and an alleged abnormal interest in sex with multiple partners, animals, and even children is at least as unfortunate and unfair as it is unfounded.

Arguably, the most heinous perversion of sexual interest involves abuse of children. Even though the abuser may have no direct sexual interest in her or his victims, it is certainly abuse of each child. It is likely that, even if she or he wanted to, no other person could imagine the whole of the life of a pedophile or the misery that must attend anyone's interest in child pornography. Like the histories of other abusers, the past of those who abuse children often includes periods when they were the subjects of, or witnesses to, similar abuse when they were children. Those seeking to understand the behavior might ascribe the psychology of perpetrators to an insatiable lust for power, a desperate desire for money, or a displaced yearning for revenge. Like bigots, abusers of children may not even see their victims as human.

The motivation for consumers must be rooted in emotion because there is no obvious tangible benefit derived. Surely, no abuser could imagine a child as the mother or father of another child. To the contrary, likelihood of capture and punishment suggests that any perceived benefit could not reasonably be considered worth its costs. The fact that such acts are perpetrated by those who have previously been imprisoned for the same or similar crimes indicates that reason has little, if anything, to do with the abuser's decision to commit them. Attempting to understand the motives of any of these people is far different from suggesting that abusers, purveyors, and/or customers should not be punished severely for their actions. The primary reason for greater understanding is to prevent further abuse.

In an almost unbelievable case, parents participated in the criminal abuse of their own children (U.S. Customs 2002).[186] At least one of the thirty-seven abused American children was only two years old and the oldest child was fourteen (CNN 2002).[187] The horrendous betrayal of trust, the exploited vulnerability, and the complete victimization of children that devalues or denies their humanity place such crimes in a virtually unparalleled category of reprehensible human behavior. Perhaps because of my own family, I cannot imagine the thinking and emotions of an adult who would betray so deliberately and completely the trust, love, and responsibility inherent in being a parent. Nothing about the transgendered condition would cause an MtF woman or FtM man to abuse a child. If anything, the condition would help transgendered people identify with its victims who were intimately involved in a critically important matter that was beyond their control.

It would be only slightly less heinous a wrong to accuse someone falsely of having sexually abused a child. Those who would suggest that transgendered people are any more likely to commit such crimes fail utterly to comprehend the nature of gender identity conflict and the nature of abusers of children. Further, such accusations or suspicions do nothing to enhance the safety of children. To the contrary, when such accusations are disproved or cannot be proven, prosecution of people who are abusers can be made more difficult.

Nothing in the accounts of the above case of horrible abuse indicates that any of the adults, either directly involved in the acts or who bought or sold the images, was transgendered. That observation may seem like noting, with relief, that a serial killer was from a different hometown, was reared in a different religious faith, or spoke a different language. Yet, transgendered people, like homogendered and bigendered people, are often and unjustly suspected of a propensity to a variety of aberrant, and even abhorrent, behavior without reliable evidence to support the contention. Extant evidence does suggest both that most MtF women, like most other heterogendered women, do not have abnormal sexual appetites, and that some seemingly normal heterogendered people exhibit a propensity to irregular and even abhorrent behavior.

Many post-op MtF women quite publicly practice the professions of medicine, law, and education, and still others work in the fields of music, government, and business. I know of none who has ever been involved in child abuse or any other illegal activity. There may be some transgendered people involved in criminal activity, but there is nothing about gender identity conflict that compels them to be so involved. MtF women who are still suppressing their identities would be loathe to act in a manner which might subject them to rigorous scrutiny or would interfere with their private attempts to realize their secret identities.

If, as increasingly seems likely, the transgendered condition's genesis is proven to occur before birth, then the condition probably has no more to do with a person's propensity for sin or salvation than does race, physical sex, or having blue eyes. In *utero* physical elements of newly forming bodies are the beginnings of the homes in which people will live out their earthly lives. The structure may be surgically modified and, under normal conditions, it will grow, but the limits of that home's fundamental parameters are, to the best of contemporary medical knowledge, unalterable. One such parameter must be the biochemical mechanism that determines or represents each person's gender identity. Clearly, that early development could not have resulted from, or coincided with, behavior in which the unborn person has not even been able to engage.

Shunning the Role

Some men, because they have male gender identities and have always seen themselves as men, see a physically masculine appearing MtF woman as being another man who is merely refusing to accept that he is a man. My experience before transition was always that of being seen as a male and having to contend with internal and external expectations regarding an acceptable role for me as a male in society. That experience has given me an unusual vantage point from which to view how men see their interests, desires, and obligations regarding marriage, their families, and their lives.

The knowledge most men glean from a conventional rearing is a useful guide as they attempt to live their lives fulfilling aspirations to be the best possible husbands and fathers. Despite their intent, some men find themselves unequal to the challenge. For those who step away from continued acceptance of their roles through divorce, abandonment, or suicide, the emotional trauma for their families and themselves must be wrenching. There is little merit in praising such men for having at least attempted to meet their responsibilities. What support is usually available focuses on finding a way for the remnants of the family to redefine its relationships and to establish new achievable goals.

An MtF woman who had started a family before transition is probably seen by such men and others in much the same light as men who fail to preserve their family, although the ability of an MtF woman to achieve those aspirations was always critically compromised. An MtF woman who did not commit to attempting to be a husband and father could be seen as preemptively asserting failure because she did not even attempt to accept "his" conventional sex-appropriate role. The primary difference between the broken relationships of the man in the first instance and the MtF women who do or do not marry is that, however much an MtF woman might wish to be a parent, she lacks the essential understanding, inclinations, intuition, perspective, and other attributes essential to becoming a whole husband and father. Ironically, because she was raised as a male, the later transitioning MtF woman also lacks much of the understanding, perspective, and experience that would help her be a whole wife and mother. This has nothing to do with innate emotional or intellectual ability but everything to do with society's persistent attempt to assign gender based on natal physical sex.

The benefit of gender consonance is not easily overvalued. Yet, even with the advantages conferred by consonant gender, some biological mothers and fathers with healthful upbringings abuse their children and otherwise fail in their relationships while whole, healthy, and successful adults have come from decidedly disadvantaged backgrounds. An MtF woman is deficient as a parent in at least one respect, but she acquired that deficiency precisely because of her cross-gendered life experience before transition. Her view of being a wife and mother cannot be informed by the childhood games she played with dolls and with other girls, but it has been enriched by the observations, perspective, and stronger male influences that were her experience. Transition is not pursued as a promising journey to perfection because transition is far from that. Beyond essential identity, every person is also the sum of a lifetime of learning and experience. Transition cannot replace a gender-specific past and, even if it could, the memories would not fit reality. The need for gender identity-appropriate life experience is part of the reason every transgendered person should begin transition at the earliest possible time.

Men who did expend considerable effort, and achieved no small success, in sharing their lives as wonderful husbands and fathers, have contributed generously to my understanding of how families develop and maintain healthy relationships. The model that has been so intimate a part of my own experience is one that has been, and doubtlessly will continue to be, the predominant manner by which strong families are perpetuated. Transgendered people generally would not challenge the foundation, efficacy, or any other aspect of that model. Few, if any, would suggest that the gender conflict path presents a preferable alternative to accomplish the same thing. If I had become a natural parent before transition, I would have intended to be as committed and caring a "father" as anyone with a female gender identity could be. After transition, of course, becoming a natural parent is no longer possible.

Although I have never been a parent, I was raised in a family that surely could serve as a successful model. The matter of MtF women as real or potential fathers is essentially one that would not disparage or advance any particular model. That potential has everything to do with the identities of the people who are trying to fit, or are strongly encouraged by most of society to fit, the traditional model. Any expectation that a suppressing MtF woman should attempt to "father" a child as her affected male persona is fatally flawed. It presumes that official records based on natal physical sex, the history of her persona's acquaintances, and/or her physical appearance prove that the whole of her person, and not just the image she fostered, accepted, and perpetuated, is male. People sharing this view are not prepared to accept that they were victims of a most convincing, but unintended, deceit. They had never considered that the "man" they thought they knew could be female, and she had never given them reason to doubt her affected persona. The set of attitudes and beliefs that induce men who are whole and who are fully dedicated to being men of strong character do not understand or cannot accept that people they know who have bodies so much like their own have gender identities that are female.

The concept of conflicting gender identity is so alien to the lives of such men, and their sense of who and what a man is, that they do not realize their perception actually helps explain the extent of their differences from MtF women. The chasm over which an MtF woman would attempt to explain, to such men and to others, the essence of her gender conflict is not fundamentally one involving ethics, morality, or religious belief. That chasm is what separates anyone whose gender identity and physical sex have always been in concert from transgendered people who, before transition, have only known those two aspects of themselves to be in conflict.

One of the most glaringly offensive accounts that did not acknowledge even the possibility, much less the primacy, of gender identity occurred in a report attributed to the Associated Press regarding the death of Gloria Hemingway. The article's consistent use of masculine pronouns, its referring to her as Ernest Hemingway's son rather than his daughter or child, and its mention of "his" death in a women's prison cell ill befit so highly regarded an institution in its treatment of this unfortunate death (Spencer 2001).[188] To attempt to summarize so large, if imperfect, a life in these pages would merely add further insult. Yet, her struggle with the many problems she and her family shared during her tumultuous life are instructive. In 1958, she had asked her oldest daughter, author Lorian Hemingway, how she would feel if her father were (or became like) her mother, but Gloria did not have sex-reassignment surgery until 1995 (Quittner 2001).[189] Although I never knew Gloria Hemingway, it is interesting to know that some part of her intervening thirty-seven years before transition, primarily her suppression of gender identity, must have been much like my own.

Gloria Hemingway is presumably beyond caring about superficial and harsh treatment of any aspect of her life. Her friends and family may have acquired a defensive insensitivity to any treatment of the talented person, medical doctor, and author whose father had earned an international acclaim, but they would certainly not be beyond caring about the abuse. Jealousy or resentment may inure to anyone perceived to have been more fortunate, in one or many respects, by accident of birth. None of these is at all satisfying as an explanation for the press having provided, and the public's having accepted, so sensationalized and inaccurate a portrayal of gender identity conflict. Following in Ernest Hemingway's footsteps might have been a daunting role for anyone, and a task far more easily eschewed than accomplished. It is the failure to acknowledge each person's responsibility to live her or his own life, however, that permits role-shunning proponents to misunderstand fundamentally the transgendered condition.

A Crisis at Midlife

"Normal" women and men are each capable of the introspection that naturally and appropriately assesses their self-satisfaction and fulfillment in family relationships, vocational achievement, social status, etc. regardless of physical age attained or state of health. In midlife, the examination occurs from beyond a well-remembered and seemingly recent youth, but many of the prerogatives of that earlier period either were exercised or are no longer viable. Adults realize that many of the decisions they made, or that were made for them, precluded possibilities that were, or are still, attractive. A welling of dissatisfaction occasionally leads to an inhibiting melancholy, rebellious spontaneity, or rekindled ambition that tips the adult beyond the inertia of familiar routine to pursue a change of employment, divorce, plastic surgery, relocation, etc. Argument proponents suggest that this desperation for change causes a few men to seek reassignment of their sex. Other aspects of the presumed "crisis" are beyond the scope of this work, but as a rationale for seeking sex reassignment, this argument too is seriously flawed.

To a person who struggled with gender identity suppression for decades, the argument is even less reasonable than a physically healthy person saying, "Since I was already in the hospital to visit a friend, I thought I would have coronary bypass surgery." Some people see all humans as drifting in an ever-changing sea of crosscurrents, given almost totally to caprice or whimsy, or motivated solely by whatever appeals to them at the moment. That view is a denial of the existence or significance of one's essential self. With no essential guidance rooted in self-knowledge and core beliefs, all people can be perceived almost as sub-humans who are oriented only to seeking pleasure and avoiding pain. Even animals will defy so simplistic a model when they sacrifice to care for a mate or offspring. This general indictment of the argument clearly bears on more than gender identity conflict, but the existence of an essential self and the nature of that essence's earthly gender identity is at the heart of resolving the condition's conflict. Psychiatrists and psychologists might consider, perhaps appropriately, that this refutation is more a matter of philosophy than of mental health yet, each of those disciplines would define the nature of the human condition and must ultimately reach common ground.

Several fallacies common to three other errant hypotheses also apply to this one. Assertions of a fabricated childhood and adolescent history, insistence that MtF women are men, and denial that memories of sex-inappropriate behavior are accurate memories of real events are prerequisites for this argument's allegation that an otherwise normal midlife male might decide to be transgendered. Those three fallacious hypotheses are no less flawed because they are prerequisites for a fourth. Failure to explain instances of MtF women who begin transition in their teens or twenties further weakens the "midlife crisis" argument.

Any man's pursuit of sex reassignment as a response to melancholy or as a form of midlife rebellion would not be rational. Either motivation could move a man to change his life but his attempting to manifest a female gender identity would mean denying his own identity. He might decide he hates life or hates his own life, but he would still be the central identity at the core of that sentiment. An urge to melancholy or rebellion does not stem from one's essential self but from what its subject has, and/or has not, done toward achieving her or his life-goals. While what each person seeks to accomplish is important, that is separate from the self-awareness and knowledge of identity that are a crucial part of the essence of being human.

As a response to a sense of crisis, men could not reasonably hope to improve their familial, financial, social, or other post-transition lives, through sex reassignment. Present post-transition physiology does not lend itself to prospects for an MtF woman to give birth. A "man" who wishes to be a wife and mother arguably does not have a male gender identity. The historic reality of lower average wages for similar work done by women would make the financial argument challenging. As the social status of women continues to evolve, women have proven that theirs should not be, of its nature, inferior to the status of men. However, women have not attained a national status of superiority to which a desperate midlife male, or any person with a male gender identity, would aspire. While one of these reasons would logically invite hesitation, they collectively comprise a forceful, but only supplemental, argument against inappropriate transition.

Someone with a male gender identity becoming physically female for any reason is beyond a logical rationale or emotional motivation. The continued existence of his male gender identity in a man's post-transition life would mean that his prospects for success after surgery, however he would define success, would be severely impaired by a gender identity conflict that was not present before transition. His post-transition mental state would be like the natural state of FtM men before their transitions. The state of his natal physical sex, though, would be the opposite. His new transition-induced gender identity conflict would cause him to long for his original physical state, but his natal physiology could never be completely regained.

Dissatisfaction, doubt, a sense of fading youth, and general anxiety can precipitate a sense of desperation and "crisis" at any age. If a person in that emotional state happens to be middle-aged, she or he is said to be having a "midlife crisis," but attained age may have nothing to do with the sudden questioning of personal priorities. The geophysics of the widely accepted theory of "plate tectonics" or "continental drift" explains that a huge mass seeming to move inexorably in one direction can encounter something that causes that direction to change, but the new direction can be calculated and anticipated. Comparison of this phenomenon to human existence suggests that human behavior is not, in all or even many respects, capricious. An MtF "man" in midlife who begins transition does so because her innate gender identity is, and always has been, in conflict with her body. She moves to end the conflict when suppressing it is no longer bearable.

The Tumbleweed Hypothesis

Among mental health professionals, one popular explanation for gender identity conflict is an hypothesis that transgendered people are normal people whose gender identity mutated. Some see gender identity and/or sexual preference as possibilities each person faces anew each morning. Tumbleweed proponents often seem to see identity and preference as very similar things or as things influenced by, or subject to, the same controlling forces. They argue that, like the capricious wheel of Carl Orff's *Carmina Burana*, fortune may impart to any individual at any time a different predisposition that she or he immediately finds impossible to resist. The hapless individual is like a rootless weed drawn into a blazing prairie fire. She or he has no essential identity that directs, and is fed by, belief and reason. Proponents would argue that the woman who knows her gender identity is female and whose sexual preference is to be with another woman is mistaken and may merely be attempting to rationalize a newly awakened aspect of herself. She has accepted, for any of several possible excuses, a new understanding of who she is.

Tumbleweed adherents would argue that an apparently well-adjusted and happily married father of two children can waken one morning believing that his identity has always been female. He may believe that his sexual preference is to be with other women as a woman. Sometime after divorce, transition, and a relationship or relationships with one or several women as though he was a woman, the wheel may spin again. With this spin, he discovers that he was mistaken about his identity or that it changed again, and that he now longs for the life and family he formerly felt compelled to leave.

The fact that so incredible an explanation is beyond my experience and almost beyond imagining does not mean it has never occurred. There may be some small set of unfortunate souls whose gender identity is given to endless wandering. It is far more likely, though, that sexual preference might vary than that gender identity could. While sexual preference is fundamentally straightforward and extrinsic in terms of the manifested characteristics of the person with whom one wishes to be, gender identity is intrinsic and a part of each person's essential self. Although inanimate objects lack gender, virtually every thought and act of each person has a greater or lesser gender component. Regardless of affected gender or a drifting sense of undefined self-awareness, for most if not every person, each person's gender identity is a core element of that person that does not change.

17. A Call to Action

The Case for Acting

No caring parent would knowingly but passively and dispassionately watch her or his seemingly "male" child struggling with, and even dreading, her future of hiding a desire to wear feminine clothing and manifesting, to the greatest extent possible, an appearance appropriate to "his" physical sex, but inappropriate to her gender identity. Children are engaged in that struggle today as surely as other children have been so engaged throughout history. The parents of these children may be unaware of the problem or, worse still, unable or unwilling to pursue its resolution. It is usually erroneous to assume that any situation or condition is without parallel, but it must be at least as fallacious to assume that one situation must be exactly like another in the most meaningful sense. I have recounted a childhood of confusion, shame, self-loathing, and more because, when suppressing the transgendered condition has been so much a part of my past and that of countless others, it must be happening for hundreds or even thousands of young people today. It would happen differently, though, in the life of each one of them.

When a transgendered child is inappropriately raised as having the gender identity indicated on her or his birth certificate, it is almost never the result of malicious intent, a willful abuse of authority, an exercise of perverse ideology, or a result of clinical malpractice. The "almost" qualifier would apply to principals who were aware of extant gender identity and chose to attempt to impose an opposite one. There is no nebulous "they," however, who are responsible for mis-assignment when it occurs. A licensed physician, probably known to both parents, to the community, and to other medical professionals, complies with applicable statutes and requisite medical training. She or he applies the "female" or "male" label deemed appropriate, by training and practice, for each newborn. The physician, alone, has been no more responsible for the mis-assignment than is any other responsible adult unless, again, the transgendered person's gender identity was willfully ignored. The parents rely on the doctor, the doctor relies on training and the law, and educators and legislators have acted as they believe their respective professions required.

"They," in this instance, are a large, but finite, number of people against whom a transgendered person might bring legal action, but the suit's responsible outcome would be far from certain.

Given the transgendered condition's long history and the growing awareness of gender identity in the medical and general community, it should be increasingly more difficult to argue that the intent behind application of the label really is benign and that mis-assignment is inadvertent. At some point, ignoring gender identity must be deemed willful, and those who do ignore identity should be held liable for the suffering they cause. So blatant a need for statutory remediation should already have brought the matter before the legislature of its own weight. Most states have taken small steps toward addressing some aspects of the deficiency, but no state has made gender identity its relevant standard. Universal official recognition of the primacy of gender identity is probably inevitable, but it is coming at a pace that makes tectonic plates seem like racecars.

Any responsible person, but especially a student of political science and business administration, must be concerned about the point at which what society demands of itself exceeds what that society is able to provide. The American legal system, based on core principles, was designed to be fluid and dynamic, and that design is certainly one of its greatest strengths. As the system is continuously pushed and pulled by ever-changing factions in perpetual pursuit of incremental or sweeping change, the worth of each change should be carefully weighed against its potential to irreparably harm the very mechanisms necessary for that system's existence. Responsibility for this ersatz impact survey must rest with the whole legislature, but it should also be a responsibility and concern of those who advocate the desired change.

Society would raise irresponsibility to a high art if it would stress its system of government to its breaking point without the knowledge and ability to bring about a superior or even equivalent replacement. Excessive demands invite anarchy and violate every citizen's obligation to promote and participate in responsible self-government. Some might argue that a system sufficiently fragile that its continued existence would be so jeopardized is no longer worthy of support and should be replaced. That is akin to suggesting that if a thing can be broken it should not exist and could be said as easily regarding anything made by man and much of nature.

History is replete with examples of the relative ease with which something carefully constructed has been destroyed far more quickly and with much less effort. A brief encounter with someone abusing a match or hammer could easily destroy many of civilization's greatest works of art. The abject poverty of soul and the barbarous cruelty shown by those who conceived and acted in the destruction of the wonders that were The World Trade Center Towers is one example. Using as their tools two similarly marvelous aircraft, the terrorists caused immense harm to thousands of victims, their families and friends, as well as to the world's most productive economy in an unforgettable and even singular exhibition of coarse destruction.

The infant who smashes two toys together shows the same poverty of creative energy and misdirected mental effort that is understandable in a child, but inexcusable in a presumably competent adult. It has always been much more difficult to build or create something useful and durable than to destroy it. This partly explains why society so values art, grace, beauty, functionality, and many other favorable attributes of the work of talented and capable artisans. It is difficult to imagine how a world might work where building or creating demanded little effort but destruction required great commitment of time, energy, and effort. In such a world, terrorists would have to create something of significance in order to attempt to destabilize a system they opposed. That, alone, might make such a world worthwhile.

To suggest that only those things which might be perfect and which cannot be destroyed are worthy of consideration is to argue for repressed creativity, imagination, and ambition. It would eliminate everything from sandcastles to ice sculptures. Insistence on permanence and perfection would be an insurmountable impediment to each person's responsibility to exercise the gifts she or he has been given. Callously disregarding the adverse implications of one's advocated action, though, would be at least as irresponsible.

To remain silent in the face of despicable wrong, at tremendous personal cost for those continuing to suppress their inappropriately assigned genders, cannot be acceptable. The responsibility for restraint in what its citizens ask of their government does not require acquiescence to the perpetuation of the current fraud and abuse of our society's having assigned, and its continuing to assign, gender identity based on physical sex. Ending this insidious wrong is entirely constructive. Government must adopt and implement the steps necessary to discover the gender identity of each newborn. By implementing a program of gender identity discovery, rather than gender imposition, government and its society would acknowledge that nothing important about assessing identity could be as simple as administering a cursory glance and assigning an "F" or "M" status on a birth certificate.

The 4-Step Plan

A four-fronted assault on the scourge of suppressed gender identity is intended to provide establishment of respectful, tactful, caring, and sensitive procedures that permit and encourage children, however few, to reveal their extant transgendered condition and to begin participating in a remediation process before the onset of the physiological changes of puberty. Government and society have a responsibility to act regarding suppressing transgendered people that they do not have in many other areas. However inadvertently, the United States has established and it maintains a system of laws that perpetrates a lie which victimizes transgendered people and all with whom they come in contact. Government issues and requires use of documents that perpetuate that lie.

Advocates for this plan must anticipate the assertion that government bears no legal responsibility for the suffering its actions have caused under the legal principle that "the king can do no wrong", because the king decides what wrong means. Obviously, kings have done great wrong. That argument has been offered as a governmental absolution for other abuses of fundamental human rights. Whatever the outcome of any contest regarding legal responsibility, ethical and practical implications of government's cognizance and continued perpetration of a system of fraud remain. Continuing social and economic costs for present and future suppressing, and eventually transitioning, transgendered people, for their families, and for all of society should constitute sufficient impetus to effect remedial action. The plan's design, adoption, and implementation should have begun aggressively decades ago when Christine Jorgensen, Harry Benjamin, and others very publicly presented their generation's evidence of the condition's enduring presence.

The plan includes:

1.) implementing a program of public awareness focusing especially on the parents of young children but also including academic boards, administrators, teachers, students, legislators, employers, and then the general public,

2.) federal, state, and local governmental review of all statutes and their resultant mechanisms that continue to perpetuate an assumption, and/or facilitate an assignment, of gender based on physical sex. The "m" or "f" designation on a birth certificate and on any other official document that was not based on gender identity must be acknowledged to have the unacceptably harmful effect that has so tragically complicated the lives of people for whom the assigned label was inappropriate,

3.) enlisting a sufficient number of qualified and capable screeners to establish and maintain a means of identifying and treating each child who has been mislabeled according to her or his physical sex at birth, rather than appropriately identified by her or his conflicting gender identity,

4.) dramatically increasing efforts to identify the responsible DNA markers, proteins, prions, and/or other biochemical processes that cause an infant to be born transgendered. Discovery of a means to eliminate gender identity conflict, preferably before birth, must be found.

The Awareness Step

The primary purpose of the awareness step is to identify, and facilitate treatment for, those who are attempting to suppress their gender identities. This effort is especially important for transgendered children who are nearing the age of puberty. These children desperately need to discuss their condition with someone qualified and capable to help them a.) understand, and become more comfortable with, who they really are, b.) gain assurance that the condition is treatable, c.) realize that they did nothing to cause the condition to happen to them, d.) develop the sense of self and adopt a regimen that will see them through difficult situations with classmates and others who do not understand the condition, and e.) know that there are other children, and many productive and successful adults, who have struggled with the condition.

When the onset of puberty can no longer be delayed for these children, parental consent for surgery also means agreeing to irreversible sterility for their child or adolescent. This harsh choice would be readily, if remorsefully, accepted by an MtF adolescent who must know she can never be a whole father. The decision might be far more difficult for parents to make. Each parent has known the unparalleled elation of holding her or his own infant, has carefully noted the beauty and wonder of every delicate feature, has felt intense and unlimited devotion to the infant, has been acutely aware of the infant's innocence and vulnerability, and has resolved to be, to the fullest possible extent, that infant's mentor, protector, and provider. The infant is each parent's seemingly limitless link to future descendents. Accepting surgical sterility means breaking that link and denying all of the aspects and experiences of a natural parent to one's adolescent.

The fact that the adolescent's gender identity was never compatible with her or his physiology, though, means she or he was never able to be a whole natural parent. The decision for sterility is, in the truest sense, a false one. It is not a choice, but an acknowledgement. Every responsible parent knows from reason and experience that being a mother or father is far more than the biological act of human reproduction. Most transgendered natural parents have attempted to be the best possible mothers or fathers to their children, but the parental roles were reversed. The MtF natural father could watch her wife become the mother she, herself, longed to be. She could attempt to be the best father any woman could be, knowing that she lacked the gender identity necessary to be a whole father. Surely, no parent would wish this for her or his adolescent.

A transgendered parent faced with the choice for her or his adolescent's surgery would know the anguish of suppression and identity conflict. The knowledge of gender-inappropriate upbringing permeated every facet of her or his life before transition. She or he would know intimately the impossibility of whole natural parenting. For the transgendered parent, the decision for surgery would be less difficult.

This step's second purpose is to encourage adults who are still suppressing their gender identity conflicts, legislators throughout government, the general electorate, and others to support the program including, but not limited to, allocation of requisite public funds. As each of these constituencies becomes more aware of their own gender identities, their understanding of the condition would grow. Similarly, as they better understand gender identity conflict, they should become more aware of their own gender identities. A litany of understanding should include the facts that there are standards of care for treating the condition and there is a lack of adequate legislation to protect the rights of transgendered people to live normal lives appropriate to their gender identities.

Further, there may be an hereditary genetic predisposition toward the condition. If so, parents not seeking the earliest possible detection of the condition not only condemn their children to additional days, months, and years of identity conflict and gender-inappropriate socialization, but they risk the probability that successive generations will also have to contend with the same conflict. Even if non-transgendered siblings might transmit an hereditary transgendered trait, the propensity would intuitively be greater for the transgendered sibling. Parents would be tempted to decide that it is preferable to risk having transgendered descendants than to have the certainty of fewer or no descendants. The danger of transmission may not be overwhelming to these parents, but they should also be aware of the grim future facing their own adolescent as a natural parent. If research would permit timely *in utero* correction of gender identity conflict, then the decision of parental consent for surgical sterility for her or his adolescent would not be necessary.

It should not be surprising that many people would be ambivalent, if not hostile, toward greater efforts to rectify society's established bias of attempting to assign gender. Their own absence of gender conflict does not lend itself to intuitive insight. The reality of gender identity and its occasionally being opposite to one's natal physical sex are concepts so alien to the experience of most people that their existence seems almost beyond comprehension.

Oddly, though, most people readily accept that one's soul or spirit is separate from her or his body. Otherwise innocuous dictionaries, at least those written by non-transgendered people, promote the confusion by treating the words "gender" and "sex" as synonymous. When discussing an intersexed child, many in the medical community will speak in terms of assigning a gender. They do not seem aware that the child already has a gender identity as surely as she or he has any other characteristic of essential identity. If they assign an inappropriate gender, they create a tormenting fundamental conflict.

Writings by, and statements of, "experts" and others have been less than enthusiastically supportive in clarifying the difference. As noted earlier, columnist John Leo wrote critically of media treating as a civil rights issue something he considered a personal matter of mental health (Leo 2001, 20.)[190] The primary problem with the column is its incredible confusion about the fundamental differences among MtF transgendered women, homogendered men, and autogynephilic men. That problem is aggravated by a similarly disturbing confusion between the nature of gender identity and the matter of sexual preference. Again, each MtF woman has a female gender identity that is, at present, unalterable by any known method. MtF women may be heterogendered, homogendered, bigendered, or agendered. The gender identities of the people with the other two conditions are not feminine, but masculine.

For MtF women, society's imposition and perpetuation of a superficial masculine gender commensurate with an apparent male sex creates and sustains a dreadful conflict that eventually becomes unbearable. The innate origin of the transgendered condition has not been readily apparent to parents, doctors, or society. Yet, the condition's long history means that elements of society have long been very much aware of its existence. In that light, society's continued sanction of gender assignment based on natal physical sex is unconscionable.

While society is clearly no more responsible for the existence of the transgendered condition than it is for any other innate condition it cannot correct, it is very much responsible for having established a system that, however inadvertently or benignly, caused and continues to reinforce the mis-assignment of gender that causes gender identity conflict. Society might have deigned to assign no sex and no gender or to base the assignment solely on gender identity, but it has thus far chosen to do neither. Asserting that gender mis-assignment and the traumatic conflict caused by attempting to suppress true gender is not caused and sustained by society is an attempt to escape appropriately-fixed responsibility. To suggest that transgendered children and adults are responsible for their own suppressed gender identities is to blame the car for where it has been driven or a missile for the target it strikes. Mr. Leo's question regarding the appropriateness of politics as an arena for resolution must be answered in a resounding and unequivocal affirmative because the political process is the only way to attempt to halt the system of mis-assignment, stop its concomitant harm, and seek remediation for that system's victims.

Allegations of body-hatred and rejection of sex are simply incorrect. They result from a failure to acknowledge that male physical characteristics of a human body are obviously inappropriate to a female gender identity. By attempting to present to others, to the greatest extent possible, the sex and body appropriate to her gender identity, an MtF woman does not reject her sex and hate her body. She seeks to exhibit honestly, like any other whole person, a physical manifestation of the person she is. Were there any hatred involved, an MtF woman would erroneously direct it at her obsession before transition. During and after her transition, she might more appropriately feel a deep and abiding hatred for that part of the system that horribly abused her since birth by mis-characterizing her identity. The abuse continues as society only reluctantly permits to exist a jumble of steps she must pursue, without emotional and financial help from that system, in an attempt to rectify her mis-assignment. The system that caused and reinforced her mis-assignment accommodates, but does not facilitate, its rectification. It is virtually impossible to sustain feelings of bitterness, however, when transition is accompanied by the gracious support of family, friends, and even strangers. Increasing general awareness of the nature, conflicts, and implications of the transgendered condition should increase public support for the plan's other three steps.

The Legislative Step

Extant relevant law and proposals purporting to encourage heterogendered marriage are glaringly deficient. Marriage has been, and continues to be, defined in terms of natal physical sex by some courts that ignore gender identity. This practice is akin to the odd custom common among newspapers to carry lengthy descriptions of the bride's attire, as though the event reported were a fashion show instead of a wedding. Perhaps the assumption is that if the description of the gown is sufficiently enticing, women will seek divorces so they can remarry wearing a similar gown. That assumption would be as reasonable as the decision that the only or primary requirement for marriage is that each partner must be of opposite natal physical sex. Given that prime requirement, as Florida confirmed in the Kantaras case, a post-operative MtF woman can still legally marry a post-operative FtM man. On the license, though, the wife would be cited as the husband, and the husband listed as the wife. The couple certainly would have mixed feelings toward that document and those who issued it. Similarly, an MtF lesbian woman married before transition could remain legally married to her wife in states purportedly prohibiting lesbian unions. The potential for such unintended results has always been present, but legislatures continue to ignore gender identity and to see such unintended possibilities as rare aberrations not worthy of their limited time.

An increasing preponderance of peer-reviewed findings regarding gender identity continues to be resisted, probably uniquely, in enacted and common law. These findings are not resisted because of the quality and reliability of the same science that has produced other immensely valuable results. They are resisted because they make people who have had insufficient intimate experience with the transgendered condition uncomfortable. Opponents believe things about the condition that simply are not true, and they have unconscionably sought to impede the ability of the small number of its victims to resolve devastating conflicts. Earlier generations dealt with those deemed unacceptably different by institutionalizing, exiling, executing, or otherwise separating such people. While some groups would still prefer a draconian solution, a better understanding of some of these differences has enriched society and expanded its knowledge of the human experience. Gender identity is at that tipping point today, but with only sporadic support from the courts.

Legislative relief is desperately needed to end society's imposition of inappropriate gender based on natal physical sex. Like all "normal" people, the transgendered population seeks ultimately to be seen as the people they are. When they do so under society's current standard of natal physical sex, transgendered people encounter a plethora of legal impediments from enacted law and court findings that continue to perpetuate a bias against their being treated according to their gender identities. Post-transition transgendered people who suppressed their gender identities for decades would argue vigorously that, as a fundamental characteristic of every human, innate gender identity must be expressed and appropriately accommodated in law.

Those who have opposed historic legal bias against women have attempted to achieve gender and sex neutrality in law even where those changes would seek to prohibit consideration of real and relevant differences. Most people would agree that the ideal of equal justice under law means government is aware of, but exercises completely unbiased neutrality regarding, indicators of gender and sex that do not have a legitimate bearing on the legal issues before them. Legitimate bearing is, of course, subjective and if society were anywhere near the ideal, efforts like the Federal Aid to Education Act's Title IX regarding public education and the Equal Employment Opportunity Commission would be unnecessary.

Rather than that extant tilt toward neutrality in law, the legislature should establish a gender identity legal standard to set unequivocally the primacy of its importance in all matters where that characteristic has a bearing, and there are few matters where it has not. If specific law or practices that recognize gender differences are unjust, those certainly should be changed. Ideally, new legislation for this step would simply require that an established DNA test for the transgendered condition become part of standard prenatal care. When the test indicated the condition's presence, the body of the embryo, fetus, or infant would be altered utilizing improving capabilities of medical science and gender identity conflict would no longer occur.

In the absence of that elegant solution, a gender identity legal standard is essential. In any instance where gender identity is challenged and, until a definitive objective diagnostic tool is developed, the finding of the subject's qualified mental health professionals should be made dispositive. Although not as clear as some bone fractures on x-rays, licensed professionals specializing in the treatment of transgendered patients would argue that their assessment process is objective. They would assert that, if two or more specialists properly apply the same techniques in evaluating the same patients and if other influences are unchanged, those specialists will obtain the same results. The practice of science and the important work of these professionals demands that reliability.

Deference to expert judgment is wholly consistent with the established practice of leaving most health matters, including matters of mental health, to the patient and her or his doctor. The European Court of Human Rights held that an appellate court did not have "...sufficient information and medical expertise...to assess..." the cause of an MtF woman's condition (*Van Kuck v. Germany* 2003, 62).[191] Specifically, any document issued by the subject's qualified psychiatrist or psychologist approving that person's sex-reassignment surgery, supported by the opinion of a second qualified mental health professional, should be deemed sufficient indication of the subject's true gender identity or mental sex for every legal purpose including proof of the subject's need for medical remediation.

As obvious as should be the need to recognize the primacy of gender identity, navigating appropriate enabling legislation through the legislative process might make Captain Bligh's incredible post-mutiny voyage from H.M.S. Bounty seem like a trip to the corner market. A major impediment even to its consideration is a lack of awareness of, or acute skepticism regarding, the existence of gender identity common among legislators and the general public. Common consonance of gender identity and physical sex makes it difficult for most, if not all, legislators and others to comprehend the nature of gender identity conflict.   Having convinced their constituencies that they share important common interests, legislators are ill prepared to write law constraining people with respect to a distinctly uncommon condition. This systemic characteristic does not disparage in the least the essential work of conscientious legislators.

The trite "ship of state" analogy could be used and abused in a variety of ways, especially regarding accumulated rust, a less capable crew, a missing rudder, the relative strengths of other vessels, the peril of a stormy sea, etc. The analogy, though, is especially illustrative in addressing the matter of accommodation of a nation's transgendered population. If the effort to cause government to change is compared to attempting to alter the direction of a large ship at sea, the people engaged in the effort would not be passengers on the huge craft, but the crew of smaller vessels sharing the same sea. The vessel of state, powered by the inertia of its history, is constrained by the strictures of its form, the demands of a varied and incessantly changing population, and an inescapable competition of ideas and economic challenges emanating from a world of differently configured, but similarly dynamic, rivals. The leviathan moves relentlessly through a crowded sea populated by an almost infinite number of smaller vessels, each with its own power source and each struggling valiantly to alter, even as each is affected by, the course of the behemoth to which it is inextricably linked.

Of incredible variety, many of the lesser vessels appear and disappear like the flash and bang of a firecracker. Others, like the stalwart American Civil Liberties Union and National Rifle Association, are supported by large memberships of enthusiasts that perpetually power their vessels near the leviathan's bow usually, of course, on opposite sides. Among the least of the lesser vessels have been those that attempt to establish the primacy of gender identity over biological sex in all relevant matters of law and society. A larger flotilla of these lesser vessels, formed in determined union, could and must move the vessel of government toward the more perfect sea of a gender identity legal standard.

In an additional and even more controversial effort, the legislature should prohibit gender assignment. Parents should demand this for the health of their own children. Surely, no caring parent would want, nor should society permit, assignment of the wrong gender to any infant. From ignorance, though, that is precisely what has caused gender identity conflict and led to identity suppression. Since gender identity before, at, or soon after birth still has not been detected by any known means, birth records should omit any suggestion of gender and refer only to each newborn's size, weight, hair and eye color, etc. Although it would be virtually impossible to enforce, society should not permit parental, social, and official recognition of gender until each child has clearly revealed her or his gender identity. Some mental health professionals dispute the existence of gender identity in infants and very young children, but that is almost certainly due to inadequate tests to discover it. Eventually, the transgendered condition will be detected and corrected, if possible, before birth. When that is accomplished, each newborn will have a consonant gender identity and natal physical sex. The temporary effort to refrain from assigning gender would no longer be necessary.

In a further legislative step, committees should conduct a thorough review of relevant law to discover all references to gender and sex that are not based on gender identity. Those references have established, enforced, and perpetuated the raising of suppressing transgendered people and have governed their legal adult activities as though they had a gender identity opposite to their essential selves. To end this unconscionable abuse, such laws must be changed. Until medical science can prevent transgendered births, suppressing, transitioning, and transitioned transgendered people of all ages will be part of society. They must seek justice from legislative, executive, and judicial systems that not only have treated women differently from men when that difference is not relevant, but still treat MtF women differently from other women in matters where their shared status could not be more relevant.

In a society where its citizens cannot presently, and may never be able to, agree on the extent to which general differences between women and men should be accommodated in law, this cannot be surprising. Yet, that treatment should garner a much higher level of public concern and advocacy among people whose conscience calls them to act than occurs at present. The U.S. Supreme Court may eventually rule that MtF women must be treated under law in the same manner as all other women, perhaps as a construction of the U.S. Constitution, Fourteenth Amendment, although there has been no indication it is eager to do so (Kashner 2007, 505).[192] Even if the Court were to recognize that status of MtF women, the legislative review would still be necessary to recognize gender identity as the most important and fundamental aspect of anyone's sexual identity.

The level of enthusiasm for effecting desperately needed legislative remediation was evident in a statement by the then-incoming President of the Florida Senate. He said that he did not know the merits of "transsexual" marriage and lacked sufficient knowledge to speculate about its prospects in the legislature, but thought its being considered was unlikely (Chachere 2004).[193] An optimist could read his quoted statement as meaning that the Senate intends to address a matter of critical interest to transgendered people, to the families and extended families of transgendered people, and to others as soon as it has dealt with something about flying pigs from Neptune. A pessimist would read it as meaning that the speaker does not know anyone who is transgendered, does not want to know anyone who is transgendered, and is as anxious to see the matter addressed in the Florida Senate as he is to move to Alaska, which might become necessary if he were to support the effort.

The political considerations for this influential servant of many masters include the strong possibility of alienating an overwhelming large, occasionally vocal, and potentially generous part of his constituency over a matter of benefit to a relatively small part of that group. He is unlikely to win plaudits for facing such odds-on principle, especially if that principle is one with which he is not entirely comfortable. Given this political calculus, it is amazing that there actually has been some legislative progress in rectifying the harm done by the current practice of assigning gender, but the primacy of gender identity still is not acknowledged in law. Especially for the transgendered population, that legislative step is long overdue.

The Screening Step

The plan's third strategic objective is the methodical and caring screening of students in all public schools to offer help to suppressing transgendered students. The effort would be the polar opposite of an earlier generation's Army draft physical examination. Psychological rather than physical assessment is its focus. Promoting individual health instead of enhancing collective security is its purpose. The program's primary objective is to help those people who will accept help. This step's benefit to society, though a secondary objective, would be substantial. Since, at best, every country is a nation of the individuals it comprises, successful efforts to help students who are transgendered, who have learning impairments, or who are "normal" but facing abnormal situations must make that country stronger. Opponents willing to forsake aid to students in the latter two groups because they are averse to helping those in the first would richly deserve the weaker society that would follow but, surely, the students would not.

In the absence of an objective test, the screening effort for gender identity conflict would require a phalanx of qualified and skilled mental health workers adept at working with children and trained to discover the gender identity of a suppressing transgendered child. A key component of that training would be the knowledge that there must be nothing confrontational, accusatory, or intimidating about the screening process. Few things could be less appropriate to the discovery effort than even the appearance of attempting to impose inappropriate gender. Errant reassignment would actually create gender identity conflict where none had existed. If development and universal application of an objective diagnostic test were accomplished, counselors would still be needed to assist students to and through transition and to treat other students. Many schools and school systems do have mental health professionals available, but their primary responsibility, if all of their time is not spent administering tests, is to help students with treatable learning problems. Qualified personnel are not available in anything approaching the numbers needed, and with the training necessary, to implement this step effectively on a national scale.

In a continuing comprehensive screening program, a mental health professional would see each student at least twice each year throughout twelve years of public school. The amount of time each screening would take would vary depending upon the skill and experience of the interviewer and the level of cooperation or the reticence of each student. Assuming a 180-day school year and a 7-hour daily screening period, one professional could see each of 420 students for a one-hour session twice each year and have one half-hour

per student each year to summarize and review the most recent and previous
sessions. Additional service days might be required to assemble summaries
in support of continued or additional funding. So brief a period per student
is intended to provide for a preliminary assessment and a referral for further
diagnosis and possible treatment, if necessary.

Those twenty-four total hours of meetings for each high school senior
would constitute less than one-fifth of one percent of the time she or he spent in
school, but could be among the most important and life-changing hours of her or
his life. For 50 million public school students, more than 119,000 professionally
competent counselors would be needed to do this work. The National Association
of School Psychologists reports that 10,777 school psychologists are certified
members of the Association (National Association of School Psychologists n.d.).[194]
While other school-based mental health professionals may carry different licenses
and certifications, the U.S. is apparently far short of having 119,000 of them.
Assuming approval for hiring 100,000 mental health professionals to achieve
the 420:1 student to counselor ratio for screening and a $50,000 average annual
salary, new annual staffing for nationwide school-based mental health centers
would cost $5 billion. This program might be coordinated with, but would be in
addition to, current efforts to help students with treatable learning problems.

The 420-student caseload would allow time for neither follow-up
counseling nor classroom presentations. Some counselors, in systems that have
them, might look enviously at a reduction to a potential 420-student caseload
while others would consider that load impossibly high and flee any system
proposing it in favor of private or corporate practice. The numbers used in this
illustration are intended only as an hypothetical approximation of the additional
resource commitment necessary to address this critical need for screening.

The U.S. Department of Education estimates that $852 billion was spent
on all public education in the 2003-4 school year and the Department's fiscal 2004
appropriation was $63.3 billion or less than 7.5% of total education expenditures
(U.S. Dept. Education n.d.).[195] The $5 billion estimated additional staffing cost
for school-based mental health centers is less than .6% or roughly one-half of one
percent of total outlays for public education. Since the education act's Title 1 and
Medicaid provide some mental health services, parts of program funding might
appear under several governmental umbrellas. Offsets in anticipated reduced
incidence of juvenile crime might be claimed as an additional source of funds.
Despite the program's relatively low cost, federal legislation adopting a national
program to establish these centers would still be required. Intense opposition to

this critically important legislation from certain groups is inevitable.

Some opponents would argue that the cost of school-based mental health centers is unbearably high, despite its relatively low cost. Those opponents should weigh that cost, however, against the benefit to transgendered people and their families of being spared the stresses and pain of festering conflict and the postponed but unavoidable revelation of true gender identity. A larger benefit would inure to all of society as it would begin to redress its system of mis-assigning gender and improving the psychological health of all students willing to be helped. The tragedy of teen suicides is an alarming indication of the unanswered need of some students for professional intervention. When the cost of intervention to discover such problems can be less than one-half of one percent of total public school funding, failing to meet that need is inexcusable.

A survey of 15,000 American adolescents found that 16.67% of them had seriously considered suicide in the last year, but only 27.28% of that 16.67% had sought qualified help (MedlinePlus 2003).[196] One promising effort to identify suicidal teens does not rely on interpersonal evaluation. Columbia University's "Teenscreen" program assesses suicide risk beginning with the participant's responses to a fourteen-question test lasting roughly ten minutes. Depending on test answers, assessment by a mental health professional may be necessary (Columbia University Teenscreen 2004)[197] This objective indication and measure of propensity to suicide would seem like manna to parents of a child whose life was saved. Incredibly, concerns for privacy, mis-diagnoses, and the costs of counseling necessitated by positive test results have been used as excuses to keep some school systems from adopting a system-wide testing program. Program flaws, if they exist, should be addressed, but they must not be permitted to justify discarding the program. Forsaking such a program would be little different from refusing help from the policeman who was left-handed, swimming away from a lifeboat that had only one oar, or removing one's parachute because it was getting too close to the ground. Concerns for privacy, counseling costs, and false positives can be addressed in a variety of ways. No amount of belated counseling will revive students who have killed themselves. Their loss to society is irretrievable. Complicit responsibility for that loss, where it was reasonably preventable, should be inexcusable.

The same mental health professional, if available to each student throughout her or his twelve years of public school, would provide continuity and promote trust and confidence. The ubiquitous practice of placing children and teens in separate schools and normal staff turnover would make this model unobtainable for many students. Mental health professionals would work with, but not replace, social workers and child welfare agencies in cases of parental abuse, of student substance abuse, of students engaged in criminal conduct, and in other situations where use of additional resources is necessary. The emphasis in most counseling sessions would be psychology, rather than abnormal psychology, and every student would meet with a mental health professional at least twice each year throughout the duration of her or his public-school tenure. "Normal" students would be more inclined to share both larger and lesser problems with a mental-health professional they saw as a regular part of their school experience.

To maximize effectiveness of personnel and to protect individual privacy, a meeting site other than the public school might be deemed preferable. Surely, the least awkward and least intimidating setting would mitigate anticipatory discomfort associated with screening. The personal and private nature of each consultation might be difficult to accommodate in a school setting. Yet, the apparent advantages of a separate setting can also be their weaknesses. A student outside of her or his school environment may act and react differently. The rapport the school's mental health professional might want to establish as part of each student's "normal" life could be more difficult to achieve or revive in an off-campus setting. The counselor's ability to present class lessons on a variety of subjects might be reduced if she or he were not part of the regular school environment. Finally, parental suspicion of, and resistance to, an off-campus setting might imperil the program's efficacy and/or existence.

Broad public knowledge of the exact screening process necessary for obtaining accurate diagnoses would compromise its reliability and validity yet, parents would demand assurance that screenings are neither accusatory nor confrontational. The rationale and politics of screening for conditions such as acute depression, bi-polar disorder, and eating disorders are not the purpose of this writing. Yet, it is only as a part of a wider endeavor to address a broader range of mental health issues that a large-scale effort to help younger suppressing transgendered people is likely to be seriously attempted. Assurance of the professional competency and high ethical standards of counselors would be critical to acceptance and continuation of the program. Enforcement of those standards would be at least as important for counselors as for any other group of school system employees.

A well-documented increase in the prescription of psychoactive medications is influencing the behavior of children. For the ten-years 1987 through 1996, a doubling and trebling of prescribed drugs was observed among different age, race, and gender groups of youths under age twenty but with a greater rate of increase beginning in 1991 (Zito et al. 2003).[198] The increase might be due to improved diagnostics, better marketing by drug companies, or greater efficacy of the medications. It may also be due, however, to the urging of budget-conscious payers or administrators who encourage drug treatment over therapy, to the aversion of parents or students to psychotherapy, or to an excessive mental health staff caseload that precludes the option of therapy. Medication may be the only available option in many school systems. In this environment, adding system responsibility to screen for otherwise healthy transgendered students, without a concomitant increase in resources, would almost certainly meet substantial resistance.

ABC News reported that five major universities saw a twenty to fifty percent increase in the need for mental health services since 2000, without an evident commitment of resources or available personnel to provide those services (Norris 2002.)[199] While the Shankar report indicating an increase in medication usage could not prove that a shortage of qualified mental health workers was a factor contributing to the increase, it is difficult to accept that study and the ABC News story as unrelated. If responsible parties are unwilling or unable to accommodate the cost of critically needed psychotherapy, then a worsening shortage of qualified therapists and the elimination of therapy as an option are virtually inevitable.

The Elegant Step

The program's fourth step is a commitment to discover the dichotomous DNA or other sets that code for gender identity and for physical sex. Following that discovery, a process by which those sets can be made consonant must be developed. The condition's sublime cure will almost certainly be a response to the routine DNA analysis of every fetus performed at the earliest sign of pregnancy. Dissonant codes for gender identity and physical sex and codes for other serious conditions almost certainly will be repaired through refined application of still-evolving techniques of genetic engineering.

To those engaged in genetics and research, this may seem like assuming the answer to an unsolvable puzzle. Author Michael Crichton has written critically, consistently, and convincingly about the naïve optimism that permits society blissfully to expect science to resolve complex, if not impossible, questions and especially those that society itself has created. The transgendered condition's history, however, suggests that its origin is neither a recent phenomenon nor one spontaneously instigated by man. Like those concerned about other serious health problems, people acquainted with the transgendered condition reasonably and appropriately look to researchers in the medical community for an elegant answer or, at least, one that is far superior to the current practice.

In little more than a generation, society has seen such wonders as the unanticipated rapidity with which the human genome was mapped, widespread use of ever-faster generations of microprocessors, increasing miniaturization and portability of technology, and discovery of much of what is currently known about life sciences, physics, and astronomy. The rapid pace of such advancements encourages an optimistic aspiration that twenty-fourth century medicine actually may be available much sooner. Yet, if the goals of this elegant step's search were likely to be attained in the near future, the program's other three steps would be unnecessary. It is more probable, though, that decades will pass before such measures are available. That probability makes the earliest possible implementation of each of the program's four steps essential.

Attempts to better define, diagnose, and treat the condition have included the confirming BSTc study (Kruijver et. al. 2000, 2034-2041)[200] continuing gender-related brain scans, further work in genetic research, and the previously cited work done by Dr. Vilain. Dr. Vilain's work cited earlier indicates that the genesis of embryonic gender identity, at least in mice, may precede that of development of physical sex. While transgendered people would find this intuitive, its affirmation through research involving humans would be gratifying. If the reverse is true in humans so that gender identity was determined after physical sex was determined, then even if the conflict becomes discernable in utero, achieving gender identity and physical sex consonance before birth may not be possible. Objections to attempting to change gender identity have already been stated. When sufficient data are available to show the extent to which gender identity is a fundamental part of the heart, mind, and soul of every human, it is inconceivable that medical ethicists, moralists, philosophers, and enlightened religious leaders would permit development and use of any medical procedures to alter it.

States have required testing of newborns, but not fetuses, for decades, primarily to address conditions that are much less severe for the patient and far more easily treated if discovered at their earliest stage of development. Few conditions better fit that description than gender identity conflict, and it richly deserves this elegant step. If treatment could begin before a child were even aware of the conflict, the transition to gender and sex harmony that non-transgendered people know as a matter of their fundamental nature would also become the life experience of transgendered people. When a genetic test is finally available, it might be applied forensically to show which powerful leaders, other historical figures, entertainers, athletes, authors, and others were transgendered, and how each contended with the obsession. The earliest possible diagnosis is essential to facilitating the most effective transition with the least emotional harm. That should be the goal of immediate and substantial efforts to discover and help those who suffer from the condition.

Some might argue for an odd ideal in which each child is raised without the slightest regard for and reference to gender. Since gender is an essential component of our identities, to suggest that such an element be ignored is to ask humans to deny their humanity, and in a matter as important to them as their understanding of themselves, the raising of their own children, and their interactions with every person they encounter. However worthy might be deemed the results of so cruel an experiment, anyone who approved the raising of a child as though she or he were a genderless thing, perhaps even raised by machines using artificial intelligence, would be committing a moral, ethical, and religious crime not just of un-human or inhumane, but of inhuman proportions. For the incomplete person who endured the test, her or his connection to all of the civilization that had preceded and produced her or him would be missing. Although there would have to have been a natural mother and father, the matured child could not fully or adequately be either parent for her or his own child. Its role in propagation would be uncertain because, regardless of physiology, the caring, nurturing, protecting, educating, and other connections to its own child would come only from mere chance and whatever remained of instinct but not from the personally imparted warm experience of a rich familial and cultural heritage.

The life experience of every person helps shape that individual even as each person influences her or his environment. Since children, by definition, lack the knowledge, understanding, and perspective of age, each formative experience of youth must be much more powerful for them. In some respects, the power of each experience is inversely proportional to the child's ability to influence the result. This could be seen as both the blessing and curse of innocence. The nature of the relationship means it is even more important that early experiences should be appropriate to each child's gender identity. For those who acknowledge the primacy of gender identity as a component of each person's essential self, development of medical procedures to alter the body, as early as possible, to cause physiology to conform to that identity becomes essential. Ultimately, until the conflict becomes preventable, the essence of the transgendered condition must be acknowledged for the unbidden revelation of gender identity that it is.

18. Following the Plan

Ethics and Change of Sex

If diagnosis and treatment for gender identity conflict *in utero* is still not possible in medicine's next generation, it might be possible to utilize stem cells or other tools to enable an MtF woman to bear her own children after her earliest possible transition and sufficient maturation. Like other women who have attempted but been unable to become biological mothers conventionally, MtF women who desire that capacity would consider such a gift of medical science to be of inestimable value. Ideally, though, providing that capacity before birth would be accomplished so early that MtF women would never know they had not always had it.

In a case of Jules Verne meets Josef Mengele, one might imagine a pre-transition MtF woman donating sperm, going through a transition that included stem cell-assisted organ generation and/or transplant of a donated womb, and using *in vitro* fertilization with a donated egg and/or her own cells for cloning. She would become both mother and father of her own child. Sufficiently early transition, though, would preclude her sperm donation and the donor womb-generated or donated egg would mean she was not, in the fullest sense, the child's mother. It is unlikely that medical professionals willingly would participate in so garish a use of a procedure intended to help struggling couples become natural parents. Still, so extreme an example of possible abuse undoubtedly would be used by opponents to try to prevent medical professionals from affording MtF women the ability to become natural mothers. Enabling an MtF woman to give birth, by any method, would give her what some courts, legislatures, churches, and others have argued prevents her from really being a woman. With substantial medical assistance, she would finally have the ability to become what too many girls in their early and middle teens have become with distressing ease and frequency.

A Center in Practice

In Bennington, Vermont, an elementary school principal and board of education arranged with a dentist, a psychologist, and a pediatrician to provide in-school services for its 440 pre-kindergarten through 6th grade students. More than half of the students are members of families with low incomes (Am. Youth Policy Forum 2001.).[201] The school's comprehensive approach to helping students improve their ability to learn means that the program's mental health professional can observe students in normal school related activities and the students' interactions with fellow students. Students who would otherwise be unlikely ever to see a mental health professional can overcome learning problems and developmental barriers that have separated them from knowledge and the potential that knowledge represents.

A search of the Health Professional Shortage Areas database indicated that for all regions, all states, all metro areas, and all types, there were 5,680 *designated* and *mental health* areas of the U.S. lacking adequate services (U.S. Dept. H.H.S. 2005.)[202] Broad support exists among politicians, school professionals, and mental health professionals for establishment of school-based mental health centers as an efficient means of addressing this need. In its final report released July 22, 2003, The President's New Freedom Commission on Mental Health included among its recommendations that schools work with parents to support screening and initiate early intervention where warranted, mental health centers be a part of all school health centers, and the federal government fund mental health services (The President's New Freedom Commission 2003, 63).[203] Not surprisingly, attempting to reach suppressing transgendered students was not mentioned in the report, but that must become a meaningful part of this effort.

By helping children become better students, school-based mental health centers may prevent or reduce the incidence of suicide, self-destructive behaviors such as drug abuse and smoking, externally expressed violence bred from the frustration and desperation felt by failing students, and, eventually, incidence of adult crime. Early intervention not only offers immediate direct benefits to each counseled student and indirect benefits to her or his classmates, but also means a greater collective potential for success for all of these people as adults. Acute conditions treated while students are young may well be the critical difference between their becoming contributors to, instead of a burden on, society.

Even efforts as broad as Bennington's program might not offer their mental health professionals a legally and ethically acceptable opportunity to discover the one or two suppressing transgendered children who might be present among the "normal" children in the school. While being adept at perceiving the gender presented, most licensed mental health workers are not trained to detect and treat suppressing transgendered students. As part of licensing, license renewal, or continuing education, counselors should be required to demonstrate proficiency in this critical area. Bennington's program could serve as an appropriate and supportive foundation on which to build a pilot study within an established framework to screen for gender identity conflict. A proactive program of screening students for a variety of conditions should accomplish three important goals. It should discover, and indicate possible treatments for, threats that imperil each student's ability to learn, discover underutilized capabilities, and help students cope with distractions that interfere with pursuit of their goals. One of the most important steps in each student's assessment is evaluation of extant consonant or dissonant gender identity.

Arbitrary Priorities

Whatever the possible source and however high the potential level of spending for school-based mental health centers, that number is finite. In 2002, the Florida electorate approved an amendment to the state's constitution that, if not repealed or altered by a subsequent amendment, will require spending as much as $27 billion over the next eight years to build additional classrooms, adjust class scheduling, change teacher contracts, increase vouchers, etc. to achieve class maximums of 18 students for grades K-3, 22 students for grades 4-8, and 25 students for grades 9-12 (Kallestad, 2003).[204] In the same election Florida reelected Governor Jeb Bush, who vigorously opposed the class size amendment during his campaign, and the state rejected, by a comfortable margin, his Democratic challenger who enthusiastically supported it. This important issue redirecting allocation of scare funding for the entire public education system in Florida apparently had broad, but not deep, support.

Before passage of the amendment, the State's increasing population was its own impetus to classroom construction, so that building new classrooms to comply with the size limitation would mean even more work for a thriving industry. What may become a substantial subsidy to an already robust sector of Florida's economy must have seemed a most welcome boon to the State's suppliers, contractors, builders, and others. A cynical and inexpensive approach to amendment compliance would entail hanging a curtain of inexpensive material to divide each classroom. Teachers would teach as before or apportion their time between the two sections.

The approach doubtlessly anticipated by amendment supporters was the hiring of more teachers and construction of additional classrooms. Not only would less capable teachers be retained, but the need to hire more teachers would make the process less selective. The Florida Education Association's lobbying power doubtlessly would be enhanced by the addition of thousands of new dues-paying members. Additional contributions to pension plans could help ensure the retirement benefits of retired and soon to retire teachers, but they also increase the plan's future liabilities. The swelling of plan assets would also increase the political and economic power of its managers.

Class-size reduction would ease the workload for each teacher already employed if she or he were required to teach fewer students each year. Employing more teachers and building more classrooms, though, comes at the horrendous cost of reduced funding available for extra-core subject offerings, student services, and other program support and enhancements. Mandated class-size reduction conflicts with such other needed improvements as salary incentives to reward better teachers (however better is defined) and attempting to identify and improve "failing" schools.

There is a reflexive aversion by many teachers to achievement awards because there is inherent subjectivity and ambiguity in the assessment of teacher performance. The same difficulty applies to assessing student progress, but students are not required to teach. Two teachers with essentially identical backgrounds will almost certainly see different outcomes among their classes because their own humanity and that of their students affects learning. Good teaching occurs where learning occurs and attempting to influence that complex interaction does not readily lend itself to the use of financial incentives. How well a student learns and makes use of that knowledge is often beyond the teacher's control and cannot be fully assessed even at the end of the student's, much less the teacher's, life.

One view of the difference between a profession and an occupation is the effect of rewards on measured performance. In theory, a "professional" is unaffected by incentives. Those who believe that manipulating others is an important part of their lives know that teachers are more likely to wear hunter-orange shoes if they are paid one thousand dollars each year to do so. By attempting to control others, a manager, supervisor, or teacher assumes responsibility for the actions of others. This is one of the surest means of increasing one's level of undesired stress. Providing focus and direction toward desired results and helping those for whom one is responsible is a different approach toward obtaining the same results that encourages initiative and creativity while reducing undesired stress. Creating an environment where teachers knew that their hunter-orange shoes would improve student performance, if that were true, would achieve a similar result without the coercive element. Inducing stress that demonstrably detracts from achievement of stated goals is inhumane, unnecessary, inefficient, and irrational.

Were memorization of a set of facts substituted for orange shoes in the above example, more teachers probably would help students memorize those facts, but memorizing is a different mental activity from thought. It is difficult to imagine how Socrates might have altered his method if he had been promised financial incentives. He was apparently unmoved to alter the nature and content of his work even at the cost of his life. Most teachers do not face his choice, but it is unfair and unreasonable to assume they do not care about their work. If a general-assessment examination indicates a higher level of performance in one class of 22 students than in a different teacher's class of 35 students, there might be an inferred difference in the capability of each teacher, but differences in students and classroom settings may also explain much of the outcome. Florida voters would apparently attribute the difference solely to the size of each class. Some of the most challenging teaching may occur with students and in environments where learning might seem impossible. Those very challenges may give students a thirst for knowledge and achievement that is absent in other schools.

If enough classes in one school are measurably behind similar classes in another, that school may be deemed to be failing. Florida had been energetically pursuing a program to close failing schools, and may continue to do so, but that effort also conflicts with reducing student/teacher ratios. The idea that each of 27 students in a class would improve her or his individual level of achievement if three or four fellow students were not there, but nothing else changed, is absurd. That notion is unworthy as the sole rationale for a massive redirection of available public funds. Simply building a new classroom cannot help even one child learn if there is no capable teacher and are no desks, educational materials, and supplies in that room. More importantly, for those students struggling with problems that significantly impair their ability to learn, if those impairments are not addressed every other effort may be futile.

Stated differently, since The Florida Constitution now requires the legislature to dedicate substantial resources to the reduction of class size, those same resources cannot be available to address class sighs or even class thighs. While addressing size may have an infinitesimal impact on each of millions of students, the sighs and thighs matters may be symptoms of conditions severely impact the students who have them. Funds that might have been used for additional counseling to improve student performance and to avoid or ameliorate destructive behavior are one casualty of the class-size mandate. Allocations for athletic programs to improve the physical fitness of exceptional students is another. More experienced teachers at or near retirement age might choose retirement rather than participate in a system that would sacrifice curricula, professionalism, and student welfare on a concrete block altar to new construction. These professionals would be no more anxious to see longer school days, wider use of vouchers for private schools, or increased incidence of home schooling. Possible alternative uses for scarce education funds are almost limitless.

Into the Trenches

The task of winning support for, and implementation of, the entire plan but especially the establishment of childhood and adolescent mental health screening would be daunting for the most ardent of activists. Ideally, a sufficient number of qualified professionals willing to undertake the effort would marshal the human, financial, and tactical resources necessary to obtain public support and to secure enabling federal and state legislation to implement the plan. These professionals probably would include child and adolescent mental health experts, experts in relevant law, public school administrators, and pharmaceutical manufacturing representatives. Members of the Presidential Commissions previously cited and other people involved in efforts to secure mental health reform legislation could be immeasurably helpful in drafting and winning passage of enabling legislation and effecting administrative rule-making. Those involved in winning passage of the latest iteration of federal aid to education also could be immensely helpful in this work.

Philanthropic support, especially from foundations dedicated to improving adolescent mental health and from manufacturers of youth-oriented products, would be essential to the effort. Natural allies would include a wide variety of child welfare and law enforcement agencies whose work with disadvantaged youth and youthful offenders makes them intimately familiar with the difficult lives of some transgendered adolescents. Many civic organizations, as well as public and private foundations, should welcome the opportunity afforded by the plan to strengthen their communities and eliminate a potential source of decades of needless suffering for transgendered children and adults.

The simple rightness of ending the imposition of inappropriate gender should appeal to civil rights advocates and much of the religious community.

No major religion is based on a literal concept of body preeminence over the soul and mind. To the contrary, major religions call followers to moderate, delay, or deny their own physical gratification for the sake of others and their own souls. Most of the religious community understands that the primary message they have received and they proclaim does not disparage or devalue each person's essential self but seeks to elevate it. Transition has nothing to do with physical gratification, but everything to do with manifestation of one's essential self. If a large segment of the community of faith will understand that transition is entirely in harmony with their message, that population should support the four-step plan.

Most mental health researchers, school psychologists, and private practice psychiatrists and psychologists are already aware of the need for a better way to help transgendered people. Transitioned transgendered people, legislators who share any or all of these concerns, caring parents and family, and many others should also be willing to help end the scourge of imposed gender. While an effort to obtain legislative relief only for suppressing transgendered youth might not be successful, its prospects should be brighter as part of a larger effort to secure funding for school-based mental health centers. In addition to the plan's secondary benefits, successful adoption and implementation of the plan would mean discovery of the one or two suppressing transgendered people in hundreds or thousands, and an eased transition for each one of them into as complete as possible gender identity harmony with her or his physical sex.

Efforts to implement the four-step plan will be met, most unreasonably, by strident opposition. A sharp increase of contributions to, and membership in, opposition groups to a perceived threat to children and traditional families should be anticipated. These groups will allege that a devilish plot to lure children into a depraved homogendered lifestyle is the inadvertent, if not intended, basis for the plan. So absurd a characterization should fail utterly to garner public support but it almost certainly will. These emotional, false, and malicious, assertions must be vigorously countered by qualified mental health professionals, the greater medical community, post-op transgendered people, and especially caring parents of transgendered children. Since the first widely publicized case of transition in America, increasing numbers of transitioned MtF women and FtM men have shared publicly their experiences with gender identity conflict. Their accounts have helped mental health workers, the greater medical community, other transgendered people, and those who care about them understand the conflict far more thoroughly. Transgendered people and all of society owe them a debt of gratitude.

Since the program would facilitate the transition of hundreds, if not thousands, of young transgendered people, opponents would contend that these "converts" were created and not discovered. Most opposition groups would have little regard for peer-reviewed literature that conflicts with their firmly held beliefs. For them, peer-reviewed means little more than that something was seen from a platform over water or that people with whom they already disagree have agreed with a new work's author. Their stunted view of religion means that those who honestly, seriously, and devoutly hear God differently must be wrong. Their intolerance has more in common with the Taliban and Iran's mullahs than they would like to admit. Opponents would contend that the plan would force impressionable children and adolescents to make a false choice, because their sex and, therefore, appropriate gender identity is obvious. Government, they would argue, is not virtuous if it encourages, or even forces, minors to consider forsaking their natal sex and transitioning inappropriately to being nether-sexed half-persons. The proper role of public education is enlightenment, and not corruption, of young minds. Corruption and inappropriate transition are diametrically opposite to the plan's goals, of course, but opponents would still make that allegation.

People who are skeptical or dismissive of the entire mental health field also would be expected to oppose the plan. While reservations regarding specific practices, procedures, or medications might be expected, eschewing the entire fields of psychiatry and psychology is as unreasonable as forsaking any other discipline with enforced standards of professional competency and rigorous requisite testing for licensure. One might as prudently attempt to launch a spacecraft while ignoring essential principles of physics. With motors ignited and restraints released, the craft would either collapse into a rapidly expanding mass of flame or lift slightly before exploding into wildly whirling chunks as too little or too much fuel was consumed at a catastrophic rate.

Like proper application of the disciplines necessary for a successful launch, appropriate use of mental health sciences are essential for those whose bio-medical or behavioral conditions would otherwise make their lives, and the lives around them, far more difficult or impossible. Mental health conditions aggravating a person's ability to live her or his life are not an absolution for poor choices. Once aware of a condition requiring treatment, responsibility for failing to seek that treatment, for failing to follow prescribed protocols, and for the chosen direction of one's life must remain with the person making those choices. I have never met a mental health professional who would assign that responsibility differently, but mental health care critics, cynics, and skeptics often assert that all mental health care professionals would abrogate personal responsibility. Suppressing transgendered youth and their parents would not be acting responsibly if they rejected the assistance offered them by the plan.

As reelected politicians continually prove, the easiest way to oppose effectively an ambitious new program is to assert that it will do, in purpose or effect, something that is blatantly abhorrent. This may be the most common adversarial tactic employed in political public discourse. The plan, of course, does not include confronting, encouraging, forcing, or challenging anyone to change identity. Its purpose is to discover and reveal suppressed identity conflict only to the person suppressing it and not to create gender identity conflict. Encouraging inappropriate transition would be at least as antithetical to the plan's purpose as society's initial imposition of inappropriate gender.

The Benjamin Standards of Care are a set of hurdles jealously guarded by those who have helped to establish and maintain them and by most of those who have traversed them. The standards can be said to grudgingly permit transition rather than to facilitate it. For standards defenders, willingness to persist in carefully clearing each hurdle is a requisite shibboleth to the rite of transition. If the protocol for any other condition perpetuated so studied a tedium, practitioners and patients probably would demand radical revision. Even so, psychiatrists and psychologists do have some latitude in applying transition standards to their patients. Far from encouraging anyone to pursue transition, part of the counseling required for transition attempts to determine whether the patient can accept not transitioning.

For a transgendered person who reveals her or his gender identity after a lifetime of suppressing it, reverting permanently to the old façade and secret of suppression after transition would be at least as unwelcome as returning to the grave after having received new life. After transition, transgendered people are closer to being whole persons than they were at any earlier time in their lives. As should be intuitively obvious, the sooner such wholeness is achieved, the sooner transgendered people can begin living as whole people and can stop living with suppressed conflict. Earlier transition also means an earlier end to perpetration of an insidious fraud that harms its direct victims, their family, friends, and associates, and then their spouses and children, if transgendered people marry before finally committing to resolution of their conflict. Skeptics questioning each of these points may become avid plan supporters when reminded that sufficiently early transition almost certainly prevents possible transmission of a transgender hereditary gene or trait if one exists.

Other potential impediments to program implementation and success are substantial. Despite exhaustive efforts by teachers, administrators, and counselors, some students doubtlessly would see transitioning students as unacceptably different, inferior, and deserving of ridicule, ostracism, and other abuse. The sarcasm and ridicule likely to attend any student's perceived failure to display convincingly a congruous gender identity and natal physical sex are potentially life-threatening to a student in transition. Further, the financial burden of seeking the haystack's needle, or the absence of discovering any needles in some smaller populations, would be weighed critically against programs of equal or lower cost that would afford different benefits to non-transgendered children. The parents of a child who shows no clinical signs of gender identity conflict probably would consider the value of that finding to be negligible compared to the child's being able to spend more time in a computer lab. The parents of a child found to show signs of conflict might side angrily with their suppressing child against the mental health professional and the school system's assessment program. Only a consistently determined effort to find and help suppressing transgendered people would transcend such powerful impediments and afford the faintest prospect of achieving the plan's goal of ending gender identity conflict.

Successful discovery of, and adequate transition assistance for, a suppressing transgendered child would ultimately have inestimable value to that person and her or his family. The appropriate level of service that constitutes "adequate" might be defined differently in each system, but should certainly include counseling and provision for a protective and nurturing environment for the child as she or he works to resolve the conflict. The program's other benefits would include affirmation of non-transgendered status for most students, discovery of other learning and behavioral problems in screened students, and society's moving toward the U.S. Constitution, Preamble's "... more perfect union..." (Kashner 2007, 499)[205] by its ending the scourge of sex-based imposition of gender.

In the cold light of the politically possible, the central financial argument in favor of federal and other public funding for the program is that it affords to governments greater prospective tax revenue and lower healthcare and criminal justice expenditures. The more productive and less troubled lives of detected and treated transgendered people would result from helping those people. Secondary program beneficiaries with other detected and treated conditions also would reasonably increase tax revenues and decrease expenditures.

This financial, social, and political argument is unlikely to be seen as overwhelming by legislatures facing a steady clamor for scarce current public funds. Further, the principled argument of attempting to right the wrong of government-sanctioned sex-based mis-assignment of gender is likely to find few receptive legislative ears. The music of a judicial resolution becomes frustratingly more seductive if played by an amenable court, but each such ruling is one more instance on the list of failures of the legislature to meet its constitutional responsibility to adhere to, and build upon, the founding and central principles of American government.

The alternative to establishing an effective plan of discovery and treatment is to leave suppressing transgendered people to their lives of conflict. The most troubled of them will continue to permit their lives to be defined by the expectations of others with those expectations based on an inappropriately assigned gender. As MtF women seek fulfillment by pretending to be the "boys" and then "men" others think they are, they can be neither the fiction they are portraying nor the whole person their gender identities call them to be. There is ironic humor in the masochist who is pleased when the abuse stops. The humor comes from people seeing instances of similar behavior in themselves and others. For the suppressing transgendered person, however, that self-abuse may abate but it never stops, even during innumerable fleeting episodes of cross-dressing.

Likely Outcome

Advocates for the plan and others waging battles for health-related problems that confront children probably would not see a surge of support similar to that of their opponents because many supporters are already active in, and committed to, efforts to address such problems. The following scenario is an example of the nature of confrontations likely to occur between plan advocates and opponents:

> On street corners of an intersection near a large
> metropolitan board of education building where the board
> is meeting to discuss possible support for implementation of
> a Gender Identity Health Assurance Amendment to an act
> establishing school-based mental health centers, supporters carry

signs saying:

"Save Our Children", "Health Care Now", and "Prevent Psyche Pain". The opponents' placards read "Hands Off Gene's genes", "Don't Let Perverts Pervert Our Children", "God Made Me A Boy" (carried by a pre-kindergarten child obviously too young to have printing skills,) and "Mental Health Care Is Sick".

The edge in signage probably would favor opponents, especially when the inertia impeding change is much greater than the resources of those attempting to establish a new program for necessary spending. The American political system was designed to provide numerous opportunities to resist change to prevent passage of legislation that was poorly reasoned or inappropriate to law. In a different context, the U.S. Declaration of Independence referred to similarly unworthy matters as "...light and transient causes..." (Kashner 2007, 496)[206] Advocates reluctantly accept the difficulty of obtaining needed legislative relief because they know that other advocates face the same hurdles, that the arduous process may improve each legislative result, and that alternative systems throughout history have proven capricious and ultimately harmful to their societies.

Understanding the difficulty of the challenge they face would provide additional motivation to parents and others concerned about the welfare of all children, especially those who are transgendered, and the hypothetical confrontation continues as one protestor confronts a supporter saying:

"Keep your professional hands off Johnny's genitals!"

The supporter replies:

"Thanks for providing the coarse in today's discourse. When Johnny leaves her wife and kids, puts on one of her dresses, rents her body for sex to get funds for surgery to become Joan, and dies from AIDS, then look in a mirror and see if you can celebrate your efforts at having opposed this program."

If national media carried that or a similar such confrontation, a broad constructive discourse might ensue. Some would assert that being an MtF woman happens randomly to the "son" of any mother and father. Others would assert that MtF women are the result of parents who failed to provide sufficiently stern, masculine, and fundamental religious training to their young impressionable boys. Still others would allege that MtF women are boys who were otherwise sick, weak, or unusually susceptible to a flawed system of thought.

Such views would be part of that broad discourse. Whether they are discussed publicly or not, knowledge of such views are certain to be part of the deep and consuming sense of guilt, shame, and failure felt by each of these MtF "sons".

The primary benefit of school-based mental health centers for most of society would be the indirect learning impairments discovered and treated in non-transgendered students. The life-altering benefits for successfully diagnosed transgendered young people and their families, though, would be immeasurable. These benefits, as a clear offset to program costs, would not readily accrue to the entities that establish and support it. Absence of immediate and demonstrable success might threaten the program's continued existence. Competition for allocating finite resources might even lead to the use of volunteers, inexperienced interns, practitioners proficient in other aspects of mental health counseling, and mental health professionals who are unable or unwilling to detect the parameters of the affected façade presented by a suppressing transgendered person. Such concessions for the sake of minimizing cost would almost certainly compromise the program to the point of failure, at least in specific instances.

Those who have had no personal experience with transgendered family, friends, or associates are unlikely to understand the condition and to be sympathetic to the four-step plan. Information from sources other than peer-reviewed professional journals may have led these people to believe that the condition is something far different from gender identity conflict. These innocents may follow religious zealots and a few mental health "experts" who cling to narrow belief and unsupported hypotheses above the whole of religious teaching and the cumulative work of peer mental health professionals. They would dispute the fundamental and unequivocal nature of gender identity and almost certainly will continue to support a status quo that imposes gender and resists mitigation efforts regarding the resulting identity conflict. Unconstrained by the whole of the work to which each is supposedly dedicated, the well-funded opposition these people would offer is unlikely to be swayed by the content of this book. No amount of reason or evidence, in part or in sum, will be sufficiently compelling to move everyone who offers that or other mischaracterizations of the transgendered condition. Despite a vociferous advocacy by those who do not accept the existence of gender identity and gender identity conflict, it is incumbent on society and its government to halt and rectify the imposition of inappropriate gender.

Again, frustration with, or intimidation by, the legislative process has led many people to seek a remedy through the courts. Obtaining a desired result by avoiding the legislature feeds cynicism toward that body and thus weakens a critical, though also flawed, division of government. Efforts to win through the courts what legislatures seem largely to have ignored have failed in cases such as those brought by Christie Littleton and J'Noel Gardiner. MtF and most other women would sympathize with another woman whose gender identity is questioned and especially so after marriage by MtF women to men who knew their wives' life history.

Courts in other matters seem almost anxious to act where the legislature has not spoken, or has spoken insufficiently, and been criticized for "legislating from the bench." Yet, despite a wife and her husband having accepted the MtF woman's gender identity and documentation of her condition, courts have been reticent to concur. Such seemingly selective reticence, especially by a male dominated judiciary is almost unbearable. Following the death of her husband, Ms. Littleton lost the ability to address his alleged wrongful death and legal recognition of her marriage when the Supreme Court refused her appeal (*Littleton v. Prange* 2000).[207] Similarly after the death of her husband, Ms. Gardiner lost both her legal status as a widow in the state of Kansas and her husband's estate valued at more than two million dollars (*Gardiner v. Gardiner* 2002).[208] After these and other such judicial decisions, transgendered women throughout the nation have lost confidence in a system where supposedly clear-thinking and well-educated people with substantial authority and responsibility have declared very publicly that under law MtF women are not women. Courts have so ruled despite the fact that the process by which MtF women have been officially documented as being women is the same as for other women, i.e. a medical doctor's certification of her status at birth. Still, in a representative system of government, a legislative remedy is the theoretically superior solution.

Rearing by Identity

Absence of a genetic test confirming feminine or masculine gender identity means that caring parents must look for and track the slightest verbal and non-verbal hints of conflict in their infant and child. The child must be given every opportunity freely and honestly to express her or his gender identity, even as parents help to mold their child's character. The challenge of being a loving and effective parent is sufficiently difficult without the additional burden of trying to eliminate or minimize possible influences on the child's gender identity. Any child sensing a lessening of parental gender support is likely to manifest immediately a stronger affected version of the behavior the child thinks is expected. Whether intending to or not, siblings, other children, and other adults will influence the child's perceptions of gender despite parental efforts to the contrary. Acknowledging the difficulty or impossibility of attempting to raise a child in a gender-neutral environment, however, must not be an acceptable excuse for attempting to impose inappropriate gender based on the child's natal physical sex.

As young children begin to realize that people they encounter exhibit, and are seen as being, one of two genders, they begin deciding, if they do not already know, to which group they belong. It would be maddeningly frustrating for any parent resisting reinforcement of gender to have attempted to remove all influences on gender formation only to discover that the child is well aware of her or his own gender identity and the expressed gender identities of other people. Withholding of reinforcement for expressed innate gender is not the same as discouraging its expression. The appropriate goal of attempting to remove gender influences is discovery of innate identity; not the rearing of a gender-neutral being. The absence of clues in the child's environment would almost certainly cause the child to be even more keenly aware of her or his innate identity. Whether revealed in early childhood or suppressed for decades, innate gender identity will be expressed. Rearing according to carefully elicited or observed revelation, though, rather than to perceptions, preference, expectations, or their absence is of preeminent concern for the child's future well-being and happiness.

Even if valid, reliable, and irrefutable evidence were found showing that transgendered people could live a full and fulfilling life through faith, self-discipline, or some other mechanism accommodating gender identity suppression and denial while maintaining their opposite-gender personas. Even if that were possible, it would still be morally and intellectually dishonest, but it might be acceptable as a practical expedient to caring people of conscience. The deception would continue with each subject made a more culpable accomplice in an even more morally offensive fraud. Thankfully, no such compromise is possible. Rather than perpetuating frauds to which anyone directly involved could attest, the voyage of the lives of transgendered people individually and of society generally can be more open, honest, and healthy when the primacy of gender identity is recognized. If revealed gender identity becomes the basis for assigning whole sex, lives lived in confusion, loneliness, desperation and fear of discovery, the inevitable repeated surrendering to an obsessive urge to cross-dress, and being ashamed of one's own inability to approximate normal sexual behavior will be avoided. This superior theoretical and practical goal is attainable, but it requires establishing a national screening regimen for gender identity conflict in children.

Whether a more elegant means of detecting the condition becomes possible and practical, diagnosis at present still requires careful examination by a qualified professional mental health care professional, usually over several visits. Calling for intervention to discover transgendered people as early as possible, and especially before puberty's devastating assault on their psychosexual selves, is in no way intended to recruit or entice any confused child to change who she or he is. To the contrary, the notorious evidence indicates that, while apparent gender might be altered for a short time, it is not possible wholly to reverse anyone's gender identity. That is central to attempting to resolve gender identity conflict. Where gender identity matches natal physical sex, even the most confused child has a core, or essential psychic center, that a qualified professional is trained to discover. Where gender identity and natal physical sex do not match, though, the person's essential identity is even more important, if that is possible.

Regarding intersexed children, Dr. William Reiner wrote that children can, and must be afforded the opportunity to, identify themselves because the brain is critical to psychosexual adaptation and development (Reiner 1997, 225.)[209] Three years later, Dr. Reiner's grasp of innate gender identity, at least for intersexed children, appears to have grown stronger. He realized that the children he was seeing were not deciding to which group they belonged. They had always known their identity as an existential aspect of their beings (Reiner 2000).[210] The view of a professional who is primarily involved in psychiatric or psychological research may be considerably different from that of a mental health care provider. While research is essential to discover optimal interventions for future cases, practitioners must attempt to provide appropriate care for present cases. Dr. Reiner's 1997 editorial acknowledged that the scientific understanding of gender identity is in its infancy and suggested that the brain may not know its gender. He asserted, though, that the brain is more important than the body as the ultimate determinant of that gender. I would have preferred Dr. Reiner had written "to discover" rather than "...to predict..." gender, but I could not agree more with his assertion that the brain is the appropriate focal point. Dr. Reiner characterized the "nature or nurture" question as pre-natal or post-natal bias, and noted that behaviorists are careful to preserve the, at least theoretical, possibility that identity can be influenced (Reiner 1997, 225.)[211] If that intended influence is inappropriate, as the case of David Reimer (Colapinto 2000)[212] shows has occurred, great suffering will ensue. Dr. Reiner noted that work by Drs. Diamond and Sigmundson was in marked contrast to earlier published reports about the case (Reiner 1997, 224).[213] His observation shows great concern by at least one mental health professional for the harm his colleagues and practicing surgeons can cause by inappropriate assignment of gender and sex. That sensitivity to revelation of identity, however, is incompatible with a program that refuses to support appropriate sex reassignment.

Clearly, most MtF women represent a challenge to the behaviorists because, as my history and that of many of MtF women clearly indicate, there was never reinforcement of, or encouragement for, our affecting either subtle or overt feminine behavior as children or adolescents. To the contrary, we were aware of the harsh social consequences of those seen to be unacceptably different. The socializing carrots dangled before my nose before transition always encouraged masculine behavior, however broadly that behavior was defined. From the accounts of many of other MtF women, their early life-experience with the expectations of others was similar to my own.

Given the jaundiced view of skeptics and cynics regarding contemporary scientific and medical capability, it might be surprising that advanced degrees and licenses are still granted for practitioners in those professions. Student ambitions and appropriate mechanisms, though, continue to provide an adequate, though far from abundant, stream of qualified practitioners in these critically important fields. In the absence of a plausible alternative that would diagnose and treat the transgendered condition with reliability and validity, society would choose appropriately to assist families that will contend with the condition using the Benjamin Standards of Care. Even the most ardent supporters of that assistance, though, would admit that it is difficult, if not impossible, to help someone who has little confidence in the field and/ or practitioners expected to provide that help. Like a kite that would eschew its string, those who reject utterly the best treatment yet devised to alleviate suffering will not be free of suffering, but would succumb to it.

An accurate appraisal of the success or failure of sex reassignment must include an assessment of the changes in the nature of the life lived by each transgendered person. The ease with which I discuss appropriately with any reasonably receptive person a subject I had so carefully concealed, with such earnest intensity from the time of that early conversation with my mother until I began transition, has an intangible and inestimable value. The reserve that impeded my honest interaction with people I did not know well is gone. There is far less reason to be concerned about the candor of others, whether legitimate or questionable, when I am no longer concerned about hiding the gender identity component of my essential self.

At a high school reunion a few years after transition, a classmate I had not known well said he thought my post-transition self was "better" than the one he remembered. I am certain that he was referring to my being far more relaxed around other people. The reticence he must have remembered was a defensive sheltering of my male façade. Anxiety about possible discovery of my persona could have been masked by extroversion or introversion. I chose the latter. Absence of that anxiety is probably one of the first things anyone would notice about a post-transition MtF woman who had carefully hidden an essential part of her identity. That earlier inhibition had made formation of honest and lasting relationships difficult, if not impossible. Stunted relationships is another form of the costs to the individual and others of society's imposition of inappropriate gender.

Critics would argue that it is unreasonable and extravagant to test thousands of children to find the few who might be transgendered. It is more unreasonable, however, to permit knowingly to exist a governmentally established and sustained system that imposes gender expectations based on natal physical sex. Society generally, and prospective parents particularly, will eventually demand *in utero,* and even *in vitro,* DNA testing of fetuses or embryos. Those tests will reveal the high probability or certainty of any of a wide variety of genetic propensities to specific diseases and/or conditions that will occur without remedial intervention. Since the birth of the first child from an *in vitro* embryo, techniques have markedly improved. The process of embryo screening now permits elimination of roughly seventy percent of known possible chromosome-based defects (McKenzie 2002).[214]

In vitro labs may provide an increasingly selective screening process that permits virtual elimination of hereditary and congenital birth defects and diseases. Screening could eventually include filters for higher probabilities of increased aptitudes in math skills, verbal skills, the arts, or for exceptional general intelligence. *In vitro* fertilization might become preferable to natural conception. Expectant parents with average or lower family incomes would be loath to cede the benefits of screening capabilities only to wealthy parents. If family economic wealth were the primary or sole determinant for which families could realize this benefit, not only to eliminate undesirable characteristics but to secure various heightened aptitudes and intelligence for their children, the resulting and unsustainable two-tiered social structure would virtually guarantee revolution. The majority would seek to eliminate or subjugate the gifted minority. A standard screening with limited discretionary factors for inclusion would have to be available to all prospective parents.

Standard pre-natal care will probably eventually include that universal DNA or higher screening with strict confidentiality of the results assured for parents and the child. Economies of scale should reduce each screening's cost, and much of the program's cost would be more than offset both by increased quality and quantity of productive life and by the decreased medical expenses and reduced suffering that would ensue. The politics of apportioning the cost of screening and allocating its benefits would not be new to federal and/or state legislatures.

A search for the DNA or other coding associated with potential gender identity conflict must become part of that standard pre-natal screening. The search cannot begin, of course, unless and until the associated genetic expression for the transgendered condition is found. From a non-scientist's perspective, that coding probably would be ascertained by comparing a statistically significant number of transgendered MtF women's donated DNA or other samples to those of a like number of non-transgendered women and men. For greater clarity in the study, the transgendered group would consist of separate groups of MtF and FtM people divided between those who had, and who had not, had sex-reassignment surgery. These four groups might be further divided based on their heterogendered or homogendered sexual preference. Samples from non-transgendered groups would be separated on the same basis. Each of the groups might be further divided to test for a plethora of variables. Codings common among the groups, matter already identified only with non-gender related functions, and those apparently left over from an ancient human past and having no identifiable function would be discarded to isolate the codings of primary interest.

Codings common to, and confirming physical similarities between, heterogendered men and heterogendered MtF women and codings related to brain similarities between other women and MtF women would be of, at least, inferential value if specific markers for MtF women could not be identified. If specific codings unique to MtF women and to FtM men, regardless of their sexual preferences, are found, researchers would want to exclude the possibility that coding was somehow concurrent with or resulted from, rather than having caused, gender identity conflict. The conflict's changing DNA might be compared to a computer that changes its own wiring, and is probably even less likely.

If no significant unique codes for gender identity conflict are found, comparison of general coding for brain development approximating the typical female model and coding for physical development approximating the male model would strongly suggest that the two are, at least for transgendered people, independent. If the study's findings support independence, screening for MtF transgendered people simply would look for the diverging whole brain and whole-body genetic sets, rather than a single genetic indicator. If no pairing exists for coding for brain development between the groups of non-transgendered women and MtF women (contradicting the BSTc studies previously cited,) then a different prenatal basis for gender identity and a different direction for the research would be indicated. My own life experience, the brain studies cited, the foundation for the Harry Benjamin Standards of Care, and professional psychiatric opinion prevalent at the time of my transition all point to either the condition-specific set or the sets for divergent brain and body developmental independence hypothesis.

The primary reason for differentiating people, whether transgendered or non-transgendered, based on heterogendered or homogendered preference is to refute or confirm a genetic basis for either condition, and its relationship, if any, to the transgendered condition. While I have argued for the innateness of the transgendered condition and its separation from sexual preference, confirmation in an extensive genetic study would be gratifying. Further, because of the infrequent incidence of the transgendered condition, inclusion of findings regarding sexual preference means greatly enhanced prospects for the widest possible reception of the study's findings.

It is unimaginable that any caring parent would willingly permit her or his child to be born transgendered if the condition were preventable. When it becomes possible, if embryonic or fetal screening indicated a high probability for the condition, the DNA or other coding would be altered to effect gender consonance, the physical sex of the child would be altered to conform to the child's gender identity, or the pregnancy would be aborted. Given society's traditional preference for males, if gender identity could be made consonant with a coding for male anatomy, it probably would be. Any changes to essential identity, however, would cause a very different person to be born. The possibility of such changes should be earnestly debated by medical ethicists, the religious community, and others.

If altering the child's DNA or other coding would mean achieving gender identity consonance, the alteration might also mean the child would be more likely to be a musician instead of a doctor, left-handed rather than right-handed, prefer ground beef to fish, and/or a myriad of other possibilities. A still more advanced medical capability, employed primarily because of ethical concerns, may alter coding to trigger, leave unchanged, or even reverse fetal biochemistry to make physical sex consonant with gender identity. The harmony sought by all transgendered people will occur without any knowledge on their part that life-altering conflicts have been avoided. Transgendered people will cease to be born. Their bodies may well not conform in every case to the size, shape, coordination, etc. they might wish, but their gender identities and physical sex will be consonant. The waste of physical, emotional, and intellectual energy, time, and other resources each transgendered person would have expended will be used in other pursuits. As utopian as may seem a future without gender identity conflict, with adequate research it may well become reality even before the end of the twenty-first century.

However near might be that better future, society must act to help the extant and the intervening transgendered populations. With each new dawn, those in, and others entering, puberty are beginning to experience physical changes that are inappropriate to their gender identities. Each of the changes, once made, becomes much more difficult and expensive to alter. Every passing day of suppressing one's gender identity is another day lived as a shadow, as a continuing fraud, and of not living and learning as a whole person. Like so many prospective medical advances, the potential to prevent and eradicate a devastating health problem for which there has never been a truly effective treatment lies tantalizingly beyond reach. For MtF women today, their condition remains one for which there is a range of just adequate and very expensive, but incomplete, feminizing steps. Correcting the condition before birth would mean never having to diagnose and treat it in someone who has already begun to contend with gender identity conflict.

In the interim, an effort to confront the condition comprehensively should include a continuing and substantial effort to inform parents. Surely, no parent worthy of the description would reject a daughter or son because of a physical or mental health condition saying, in effect, AI can only love you if you are or do this and refrain from being or doing that." Such an acknowledgement in no way disparages the need for parental discipline. Overwhelming evidence indicates that children and adolescents, perhaps from an innate tendency, will test constantly the limits of the rules under which they live. That testing may be an awkwardly expressed desire that the child's parents demonstrate their continuing concern and affection by clarifying, reestablishing, or reaffirming the parameters of expected and acceptable behavior. Just as that testing is not inherently disrespectful and/or a denial of the child's love for her or his parents, a parent reasonably would not assert that continued parental love is contingent upon the child's strictly delimited behavior. As most parents know, awareness of unconditional parental (or guardianship) love is a critical part of the self-esteem necessary for children to choose rightly in a society that knows choices ultimately are and must be each person's responsibility. The difference, though, between choice or behavior and essential identity is critical. Where this calculus conflicts with gender identity though, the result must exceed its universe and cannot apply.

The natural bond between parent and child is such a source of pride for the parent and confidence for the child that there are few relationships more important. Hiding the transgendered condition is endemic to the condition, at least partly, because of the obligation children feel as a part of their families, and the danger that they might irretrievably alter or destroy that unique bond. The child's determination to suppress quickly becomes so strong that most parents are unlikely to know about it, and they are unlikely to discover their MtF child's gender conflict while she still is a child. Because of fear of disappointing their loved ones or themselves, an abiding and deep sense of embarrassment, and/or basic human insecurity, suppressing transgendered children are determined not to reveal their conflict.

A nationwide effort to discover and begin treating transgendered children would be a massive undertaking. Having the screening performed by practicing mental health professionals, whose goal is helping patients, contrasts with the work of researchers, whose goal is discovery and development of more effective treatment. To the extent that individual practitioners fail to make an accurate diagnosis and that the profession fails to improve and promulgate its diagnostic tools, mis-diagnoses and undiagnosed cases will occur. These unfortunate consequences of the practice of an imperfect art are regrettable and should be actionable as a necessary discipline to the profession, but they should not be an acceptable justification for failing to implement and support the most effective screening possible.

Free at Last

It is an almost indescribably wonderful and enlightening experience finally to have shattered completely and irreparably the figurative glass wall from behind which I was living my life. Much of my childhood was as pleasant, enlightening, and supportive as my parents, teachers, and other caring adults thought they could make it. Children raised in broken homes, who experienced serious illnesses themselves or in their families, had clinically remote or depressed parents, or who faced other difficult and challenging circumstances might envy those nurturing aspects of my childhood that I so fondly remember. The whole of society might be quite different if everyone experienced at least as supportive an upbringing.

Yet, most if not all transgendered people will live their lives as a lie until their gender conflict is resolved. This central and immutable fact means that anything else contributing to that person's upbringing may have, in a real sense, great import, but in a larger sense that thing is like a bucket of water for someone who is already drowning or firewood for the fireplace of someone whose home has burned to the ground. Unless early and significant intervention addresses the transgendered child's gender identity conflict, that conflict quickly and almost certainly is going to become the child's most closely guarded secret at the earliest hint of bias or sign of disapproval. That child's determination to hide the secret means that those expending all of the other effort necessary to raise a child may fail to recognize one of the primary and central characteristics of the person to whom the effort is addressed.

The ability of an MtF child to hide her condition would be easily understated, just as the harm to the child and those closest to her from hiding it would be difficult to overstate. Many parents would confidently assert that their child could not hide such a secret from them. They might think that my parents must have been unusually distant, not concerned enough about their own children, or so preoccupied with their own lives and the family as a whole that little details like a child's hidden gender identity were easily missed. None of this was true of my parents. The memory of my childhood friend's threat to "tell", my mother's warning regarding a future propensity to cross-dress, and her admonition that my father would prefer that I did not wear my sister's clothes helped to establish my determination to suppress my secret self. Early comments and behavior of my peer-aged friends confirmed it. I cannot imagine the successful technique a skilled professional might have used, much less a parent unskilled in this art, to elicit the secret I was determined to hide.

While the natural process of maturing transfers legal responsibility for her suppressed identity from her parents to the MtF woman, it clearly cannot be the responsibility of a minor to discover, analyze, and reveal or resolve her secret. That is precisely where the difficulty lies. There is no extant mechanism to accept or share that responsibility for the suppressing and troubled transgendered child. Nothing prepares new young parents to expect that their ardently desired and wholly dependent infant will begin suppressing a conflicting gender identity at the first sign of behavior deemed "inappropriate."

A better solution is still not at hand. It is terribly important for all currently suppressing transgendered children and adults that society establish an effective regimen to identify them, or to encourage them to identify themselves, as candidates for competent analysis and counseling at the earliest possible time. Young transgendered people who have resolved to hide their conflicting gender identity should be the primary focus of any such effort. Transgendered children are still young enough that the biology of their bodies has not yet begun to further compound remediation of their conflict. Each passing day also exacerbates the emotional trauma and increases the difficulty of corrective action by effecting a socialization that rewards manifestation of an inappropriate gender and harshly punishes disclosures of her or his true gender.

As individuals and as a society, each person's past both informs the present and guides the future whether or not it is recalled accurately. For an MtF transgendered child, her past before transition provides a set of keys that will not open the locks she must open. She acquires the tools to react to her environment as masculine-gendered people around her might act, but those tools are not appropriate for her. While the nation seeks equality of opportunity and justice before the law for women and men, it seeks neither to make them be, nor pretends that women and men are, the same. Their histories are not, and should not be, interchangeable.

It is unfortunate that the best-intentioned specialist cannot actually look into someone's essential self. The task is sufficiently difficult when a subject is willing to participate. Early experiments in the use of genome mapping and gene therapy suggest that, if some variation in DNA is the condition's cause, successful analysis of each person's genome will indicate a genetic probability or certainty that she or he will be transgendered if the sequence is not altered before birth. When science discovers the condition's precursor(s), testing for it or them should become part of each state's mandatory infant screening. A likelihood of gender identity conflict may be part of a profile resulting from personal DNA surveys.

The dawning era of "personal genomics" holds dynamic potential for indicating an increasing variety of prospective health problems for which preemptive action might be taken (Rae-Dupree 2002, 62).[215] If the determinant is not inherently flawed DNA, but some other biochemical process(s) in utero, the earliest possible intervention to address the condition is still necessary. The glacial advance of knowledge from recorded history's first indications of the presence of the condition to the present is finally hinting toward a complex innate determination of gender. Yet, insufficient but increasingly unassailable evidence of the conflict's from-birth origin and the continuing inability to diagnose and resolve the matter in utero still leave psychiatry or psychology, hormone treatments, electrolysis, and surgery as the MtF woman's only recourse.

The hidden anguish a suppressing transgendered person experiences and the official sanction of gender assignment based on physical sex persist. Society, through its institutions, is complicit in, and perpetuates the presence of, that anguish because it caused the original mis-assignment and has not established a procedure to help alleviate the suffering it caused. As a country, the American people create, enforce, and perpetuate a system of natal sex-based mis-assignment of gender. The elegance of the allegory of Plato's cave teaches that even if a philosopher-king could be persuaded to return to life in the cave and to explain the truth to those who see only shadows, those who do not know the truth would be unlikely to accept the truth. In a vicious twist on this allegory, society places dark glasses over the eyes of an infant and tells the young MtF girl throughout her life that she must not remove them.

When she does remove the glasses, or when they fall away from their own weight, the MtF woman will not live one more moment of her life behind them despite the most strident of howlings in society and friction from some of its institutions. She has frightfully few alternatives either to her living among those who will not accept the clarity of her sight or to confronting the impediments that governments and others have set in her path. Melancholy may induce a selective recollection of fond moments from her earlier affected life in disguise, but she will realize prudently that what she thinks might be missing from her life was never, and cannot be, real. She cannot capture again something that was not real and never truly existed.

Effects of Transition

Later-transitioning transgendered women have probably reached an age and/or set of circumstances that signals an emphatic and permanent end to their willingness to hide their gender identity. Far from making these MtF women less capable of functioning productively in society, though, the very public confrontation and resolution of gender conflict greatly enhances their ability to recognize the humanity in those around them. They have a newly freed ability to interact honestly with those closest to them and everyone else. Whatever hesitation there may have been to identify with the honest and unrestrained expression of real affection between two people who love each other, that hesitation no longer impairs a self whose appearance more faithfully reflects who that person is.

In *On The Beach,* Nevil Shute's grim tale about a devastating nuclear exchange, the author also painted an ironically wondrous vision of the certainty with which the story's characters would pursue their ultimate aspirations. His auto race, where amateurs let their ambitions exceed their abilities leading to virtually instant death, only meant that those deaths preceded by a slight margin the impending nuclear cloud's ending the lives of every person remaining on earth. The certainty of nearing death suffused most of Shute's characters not with a fatalistic depression but with a single-minded determination to be with the people they loved, to do the one thing they most yearned to do, or to otherwise realize a small taste of something they had yearned to spend years savoring(Shute 1957).[216] Searching for and then tending a particular tree, rather than wandering wistfully through a diseased forest, might compare to the difference between an overwhelming concern for the health of one person and concern for the plight of all humanity. The proximate end to all human life on earth could move people to do today only that which would satisfy them today however they, and they alone, would choose to define that satisfaction.

For a suppressing MtF woman on Shute's beach, the dilemma of skewed priorities would pit continuation of her affected male façade for her few remaining days against the now-or-never urge finally to appear openly, yet far from completely, as her previously hidden self. Her suddenly abbreviated longevity would not only mean acceptance of the reality that the often fantasized and coveted transition would never occur but that even the partial steps of surgery and hormone therapy would not be possible. The choice made by most such women probably would be based on proximate relationships.

Those who were part of geographically close and loving families would sigh and reflect that, when they were able to live their lie for so many years before death's nearness threatened, their sense of obligation to those they love and their unwillingness to add to the emotional difficulties already present were overpowering. Their gender identities would remain hidden. Denying the ultimate honesty of revealing themselves to those people most important to them would be a bearable sacrifice for love. Other MtF women who lacked such familial bonds or whose close friends and/or family members all chose to remove themselves in pursuit of their own last-chance priorities would race to the nearest department stores and begin acquiring anything their own previously-secret collections lacked. The store counters would be unattended because the impending fatal cloud of radiation meant there was no longer a reason for commerce. As these women dressed carefully and then appeared confidently in public perhaps for the first time in their lives, they would feel a deep melancholy for the opportunities past and future they might have had as the women they now permitted themselves to be. They would try very hard to live as much of their remaining life as fully and honestly as they could. They would attend religious services and parties, engage in whatever avocational activities seemed inviting, and even attempt to establish new friendships as they finally, but belatedly, permitted themselves to stop hiding.

Egg in Santa's Beard

Several years after transition, I was having breakfast at my parents' home. My father said something to my mother and referred to me using a masculine pronoun. Concerned that it sounded deliberate, I was surprised and said something about it. Dad replied with sudden evident irritation, "You will *never* be a woman to me". Years after transition, surgery, and my living as fully as possible as the woman I am, I found his statement jarring. He had attended meetings with my doctors and with other transgendered people, participated in those discussions, and seen the literary and video information I had acquired regarding the transitions of other people. It was possible that my father still did not understand, or would not accept, the concept of gender identity, or that he was disputing my gender identity. It also was possible that he could not or would not deny his apparent sensory image of hearing and sight or his memory of who I had seemed to be in favor of a genuine acceptance of his transgendered daughter. At that moment I realized the estrangement other MtF women have felt regarding former close family, friends, and acquaintances who either did not understand, or would not accept, the existence of gender identity conflict; or they might accept its existence but not its preeminence. I told him that I certainly was not a man and had never wholly been one, but I continued trying to understand what he had said and why he had said it.

His forceful statement was completely unanticipated and I suddenly knew how I might resolve never again to see or talk with my father. The certainty one's self-knowledge, rather than self-deception, imparts means that, in such a moment, the completely spontaneous genuine reaction to that rejection is the confident awareness that the implicit characterization is incorrect. I was tempted to respond that "If you cannot accept me as the woman I am, then I can no longer accept you as my father". His response might then have been "When I was your father, you were my son. Whoever you are now, I am not *your* father". This is more of a discussion than declarative fathers usually share, and I would realize soon after that his statement had resulted from a sudden flash of irritation and not from any lengthy deliberation. In that heated moment, he was not rejecting the part of my transition he had shared. He had made innumerable transition-related trips with me for no other reason than to be present if he would be needed. He was acknowledging that the experience had been, and continued to be, difficult for him, too. Since my father no longer is living, I trust that he would not object to my sharing this instructive conversation.

A comparable "never" assertion, however, would be a father's telling his adult son "You will *never* be a man to me!" It is not difficult to imagine such an exchange as the basis for a rift that would never be bridged. Dad was a part of countless memories, including his kneeling beside his three or four-year old "son" as I stood facing the camera in my favorite photo of us. It is disquieting to know that such harm can come to important relationships yet, it is precisely because the bonds are so important that its members have such great potential to harm.

Daughters often accept their fathers as a standard for, or prototype against which to measure, their prospective husbands. For me, Dad had seemed suddenly to be deficient in a major respect. It is difficult to imagine a woman who would be interested in a man who said to her "Darling, that dress is most becoming; it almost makes me think of you as a woman". If I had accepted Dad's flash of irritation as considered and deliberate rejection, his previous care when referring to me, his support and concern throughout transition, and his consideration of everything he had heard about the condition would have to have been a carefully crafted deceit, unless he had decided only recently on a new and unalterable course.

One might suggest that such a deception would be no more severe than the one I had practiced when my parents had thought I was their son. Yet, there can be no equivalency between the sex-based imposition of gender and system of childrearing that parents, acquaintances, and society are complicit in perpetrating, however inadvertently, on one hand and a single, sudden, but determined deliberate choice to deceive, on the other. A fraud victimizing innocent children who then reluctantly attempt to live with what they have been taught might be compared to one's struggle with a surgically attached but nonfunctioning extra limb. That extra limb would be visible, though, while the fraud of enforced inappropriate gender is hidden. Even so, that fraud is far different from one intentionally contrived and practiced by an adult whose intent was always to deceive. If I could not trust my father to understand and accept my gender identity, it would be that much more difficult for me to trust any man in a meaningful and potentially lasting relationship.

Such thoughts rest comfortably in a failure to perceive and interpret, or to distinguish correctly between, momentary flashes and deliberative expression. Those abetted failures have to be a bane to continuation of the most powerful of human relationships. Yet, some people live as though such failure is inevitable and beyond their ability even to influence. They do not intend to be misunderstood, but they do not expend, from habit, the effort necessary to minimize those instances of misunderstanding. Others are so averse to the danger of serious misunderstanding that they avoid discussion when possible and express themselves only in short declarative statements. That very unwillingness to engage in discussion, though, lends itself to misinterpretation. This characterization is not intended to summarize any aspect of my relationship with my father, but to encourage those families who have a transgendered member to engage in mutually honest and considerate communication.

It is almost inconceivable that any MtF woman would continue a daily relationship with a person who rejects her gender identity. A willingness to accept such abuse is akin to admitting that, on some level, the abuse is deserved. A person to whom honesty was paramount might live daily with another who continuously called her or him "liar." Honesty, honor, piety, nor any other characteristic, however, approaches the intimacy that essential identity shares with gender. To live daily with anyone who would question that essential self would be to question one's own right to life.

The intensity with which an MtF woman ultimately accepts her gender identity and would not abide its rejection suggests how she must perceive anyone's refusal, whether overt or implicit, to accept her. Since the overwhelming majority of people are not transgendered, most of them have never questioned their gender identities, nor even realized that vital and central component of themselves does exist. Each person knows that her or his conception of self is not merely what they see in a mirror and what others tell them they are, but they fail to realize that the essence of that self has a gender identity on earth that may continue after death. For transgendered people who have lived for decades acknowledging but suppressing that gender identity, they have denied a key part of their lives. From microbes to viruses, insects, animals, weeds, and, especially, humans, there is an extant history of the tenacity and resilience of life. So fundamental a force must ultimately compel the transgendered person to begin transition. It finally permits her or him to become fully alive. Rejection of that newly revealed gender by those they care about or who matter to them is, for them, as harsh an action as questioning their right to life.

A parent or sibling might well despise anyone who would take her or his family member away from them suddenly and irretrievably, but the revelation of a fictitious relationship, especially by a person who was part of that relationship, invites a direction of that hatred toward the very person missed. The discussion between an MtF woman and her relative might take the following form:

> Relative: "I hate you for taking away the person I
>
> loved. I need time to mourn the loss."
>
> MtF woman: "But I still am the essence of
>
> that person. Did you love the person or the
>
> relationship you thought you had with me? I
>
> cannot help you mourn something that did
>
> not exist, however much you thought it did,
>
> especially when the part of that person that was
>
> real is still part of me. I feel more alive now than
>
> at any earlier time in my life!"
>
> Relative: "You were my son (or brother.)"
>
> MtF woman: "No, I was not and I am sorry that
>
> you thought I was.
>
> I tried very hard to be that person, but it was a lie
>
> and I will
>
> no longer try to be that person in our
>
> relationship.

I am still the person you knew, only more so now

than either of us had realized I could be."

Relative: "I am going to have to give this a lot of

thought."

MtF woman: "Take all the time you want, and if

you have any questions for me, just ask. I finally

have valid answers for them."

The form is not important, but the discussion is about the emotional tension of love and hate, disappointment, loss, curiosity, and of having been part of the deceit. The transgendered person and the relative have each been perpetrators and victims of the fraud. That confusing mix of sensations for a relative favors denial and does not yield easily to acceptance. The feeling that, with discovery of a fatally flawed detail, reality can be ignored and the prior relationship restored wars against acceptance. Ultimately, the decision of acceptance or rejection applies not to the wish for the restored relationship, but to the person who is transgendered. Rejection of the resolved and newly revealed gender identity is rejection of the essence of who that person really is. The decision might be postponed, but once made, it must be unequivocal.

Being a Victim

After transition transgendered people, who have endured years or decades of wrenching challenge to their reason and emotion, can choose to live the balance of their lives feeling like victims. They can choose to anticipate hostility, pity, or derision from every new acquaintance or feel always regretful for the life lived, and the life not lived, before transition. They could choose to be bitterly resentful of a governmental system and society that has treated them in accordance with a cursory examination of their bodies at birth, and which frequently persists in upholding the initial error in matters of law, marriage, and family.

Transgendered people must realize that such a decision is a choice they make. It has a self-fulfilling aspect; those who feel remorse or a deep and perverse sense of guilt are likely to be perceived as having done something for which those feelings are appropriate. When honestly and simply being the people they know themselves to be, transitioned people cannot be responsible for the actions, and especially reactions, of others. They were not the authors of their former status, but they have been the initiators to its remediation. Remediation began when they truthfully acknowledged that they are transgendered.

That self-knowledge can also be a starting point for a different sense of self. The tremendous baggage of shame and deception, if it ever was appropriate, is certainly no longer so. Resilience is an application of character. Adjustments necessitated by a long-held onerous burden are counterproductive when the burden is gone. During and after transition, no affectation of a fraudulent male persona is necessary or appropriate. The ability to honestly and openly act and react that was always present but carefully controlled can be exercised to the limits of reason.

19. A Closing Word:

Both nature and nurture proponents probably will have found much in this book to reinforce their view regarding the causes of the transgendered condition. Nurture proponents will find solace in their disagreement with many of its assertions. It has not been my intent to persuade or convince, but to explain what has happened in my life as forthrightly as possible and to explore the condition from the perspective that experience has afforded.

During an exceptional 60-Minutes program segment regarding a brain cancer oncologist and his treatment of a teenage victim, the young girl being treated said that she might not live as long as she and others had expected, but that she was living as full a life as she could (Black 2002).[217] The final heroic treatment did not stop the tumor's growth and the exceptional girl, mature beyond her years, died. Her recognition that the number of years or of precious days lived and, by extension, the physical possessions and/or apparent social status attained during one's lifetime is of little, if any, lasting importance. Surely, the greatest tragedy of September 11, 2001 is not the physical loss of airplanes, buildings, and other material assets, but the loss of the potential of the unlived lives of the victims and their unborn progeny compounded by the missed interaction of otherwise intersecting lives. That loss was the loss of the above young teenager but multiplied exponentially both in terms of the direct and indirect victims of that singular event and the fact that organized human action deliberately caused the loss even as other heroic acts kept that loss from being larger.

Responsibility for that loss and the suffering of the events' direct and related survivors would be an unbearable burden for anyone who professed a worthy concept of morality. If justified by a different concept, then morality and immorality in it must be synonymous, rather than polar opposites. The heinous crime was not committed only against the people irreparably harmed, but against the god in whose name perpetrators supposedly acted, because their behavior ended the opportunity for that god to act in the earthly lives of the murdered victims. It clearly was their will they were exercising, and not the will of their god.

Every human life may have a purpose where the doctrine of "free will" means accepting or rejecting that purpose. If so, a transgendered person's lifelong suppression of gender identity is a rejection of that purpose, just as it is a rejection of a large and fundamental part of one's essential self. Had I not lived to experience transition, I would have missed a wonderful opportunity to see how kind, understanding, and caring would be the spontaneous reactions of so many people; of family, neighbors, friends, and others. Finally confronting the conflict, experiencing transition, and living openly as the person I had so diligently kept hidden now seems to have been a major purpose for my life. Graduation from that suppressing self was an essential step to learning much more about my true self and the lives of others.

During and since transition, every encounter with someone has been an opportunity for me to form an identity-appropriate relationship. These encounters also have been opportunities for others to test their own beliefs and biases. These people could grow in their understanding of who they and other people really are and what is, and is not, important to and about them or cling to their biases and beliefs and reject the honest expression of identity they encountered. With few exceptions, those who have been uncomfortable with my transition were gracious and caring. Their most common concern also has been expressed by supportive relatives and acquaintances who have suggested that I might regret having chosen an unalterable path. For most, if not all, MtF women, though, that prospect would be less reasonable than someone blind since birth receiving the gift of sight and then wishing again to be blind. Not a belief in, but knowledge of gender identity precludes the prospect of reversion and regression.

Many of the experiences I have described must have seemed familiar or even common to many people. Even the extraordinary experiences might seem common in the sense that each person's life is uniquely her or his own. I might have attempted to include only those aspects of my life that I thought were uniquely related to gender identity conflict, to the extent they were discernable, but without context, that effort would be like trying to describe a sunset without mentioning color. As powerfully influential as contending with that conflict has been in my life, the struggle has shaped, but has not controlled, my existence. Each obsessive thought and compulsive act had to contend with, as well as influence, my sense of honor, integrity, ethics and morality. I can imagine what my life would have been without that conflict but doing so is exactly like imagining myself as having been someone else.

I cannot say that I sailed my ship through a troubled sea without so much as a wrinkled sail. The occasional thoughts of abandoning the voyage and the ship entirely were trying, but not stellar, moments. The analogy is also apt in terms of imagining how someone else might have captained my ship, or if the ship had been, or had been configured as, any of countless other vessels. In sharing much of my actual voyage, I have attempted to focus on the events themselves rather than on how each event shaped and was shaped by me. I believe that providing this account was necessary and fervently hope others will benefit from it. The wonderful support I have had from every member of my family is something I would wish for anyone encountering difficulty and, especially, for every MtF woman as she contends with her gender identity conflict and the experience of transition. Without detracting in the slightest from the immeasurable value of that support, faith and its importance to each person's self-awareness and confidence are at least as important.

The faith element was strengthened immeasurably for me on that previously described, unforgettable, and unparalleled night in the allegorical and actual winter of my transition year. After an increasingly frantic sense of desperation at failing to find suitable alternatives to transition, I had been praying without the form of prayer. My thoughts were of urgently seeking, but failing to find, a solution that was better than the no-longer bearable tension of gender identity conflict. I wondered how I could disclose the secret I had so closely guarded all of my life. I dreaded the reactions of those closest to me when I told them what I had been hiding. I feared what impending transition would mean to relationships with family, friends, clients and others. I did not see how I could live as a woman in a community that thought it knew me, but had never seen me as female. I doubted that I could be accepted as female especially by people who had been, and been seen as being, female all of their lives. In pursuing transition, I would be forsaking my carefully tended façade with its attributes of capacity and capability, and I had no confidence in whatever would take its place. During the whirlwind of such ominous thought, the voice that came, and which I accept as divine, was instantly assuring, calm, and caring beyond description as it said with stunning clarity "It will be alright", and so it has been. With His help, it will be so for others.

20. Definitions and Conventions Used In This Work

"dressing": a transgendered person's appearing in a
manner that reflects her (MtF) or his (FtM) gender identity
rather than her or his natal physical sex before transition.

FtM: an abbreviation of female-to-male, referring to a
transgendered man whose gender identity is male and
whose natal physical sex was female.

gender: the broadest possible range of behavior
that is still identifiable as typical of most females (feminine
gender) or most males (masculine gender) and which
invites reaction or response as though the person exhibiting
that behavior is female or male. A suppressing MtF woman
exhibits a masculine gender but has a female gender
identity. *Pseudo gender* may be suggested or imposed.
Society has consistently imposed gender based on the natal
sex designation entered on each person's birth certificate.
Affected gender is displayed by suppressing transgendered
people and by other people for different reasons. A
homosexual male may present a feminine gender to
suggest or show submissiveness. *Honest gender* reflects the
unsuppressed female or male gender identity of the person
exhibiting it and indicates whether that person's essential
self is female or male.

gender identity: the set of apparently innate and

unalterable nonphysical aspects of each person's essential self that may be revealed or suppressed, but which ultimately determine, like a true bearing from an unwavering compass, whether that person is female, male, partly female and partly male, or neither (please see "sex" below). As a component of each person's innate essential self, gender identity is no more likely to be missing in any person than is any other aspect of that person's identity. There is no way to alter any person's gender identity currently known to medicine. If unobstructed by conscious or subconscious inhibitions, gender identity informs all human actions, preferences, thoughts, and every other aspect of consciousness. It relentlessly demands, for each person, expression of her or his essential self as she or he defines that appropriate expression. That definition may not be wholly identical for any two humans.

he/him (intentionally applied to a transitioning or post-transition MtF woman): probably perceived by the MtF woman as an insufferably boorish comment suggesting that, despite her best efforts to indicate the contrary, the person making the comment knows the MtF woman's gender identity better than she does. The ignorance and apparent arrogance of the observer, however well intentioned, suggests that all of the years of effort at self-analysis, of rationalizations and frustration, and final revelation and acceptance, certification by qualified

professionals, tested through potentially life-threatening
surgery, etc. are inconsequential compared to the observer's
own greater powers of perception and/or gift of religiously
inspired insight. Ideally, pronouns are always used to refer
to the subject's true gender identity, regardless of her or his
apparent sex.

homogendered: the ultimate partner-preference of a
person with a feminine or a masculine gender identity
for someone with the same gender identity, regardless of
either person's current physical sex. This term accurately
describes the relationship to which the general public is
usually referring when it employs the term "homosexual."
Regardless of the state of her or his physical sex, the term
refers to the honestly manifested appearance and manner of
each partner in a couple.

homosexual or "gay" male: in common parlance,
a grossly inadequate term intended to describe the
relationship between two apparently physical males but
which ignores their gender identities.

homosexual or "lesbian" female: in common parlance,
a grossly inadequate term intended to describe the
relationship between two apparently physical females but
which ignores their gender identities.

human female: used accurately, a person whose gender
identity and physical sex inform the individual and those
whom she encounters that she is a woman. In common

usage, her gender identity has been assumed, if it is even considered, to be the same as her physical sex.

human male: used accurately, a person whose gender identity and physical sex inform the individual and those whom he encounters that he is a man. In common usage, his gender identity has been assumed, if it is even considered, to be the same as his physical sex.

intersexed: the condition where natal physical sex is deemed by the attending physician to be ambiguous, regardless of the infant's gender identity. An appallingly arrogant professional standard has permitted surgical alteration of the clitoris or penis without anyone's attempting to discern the child's gender identity, her or his opinion, or occasionally, even the wishes of the child's parents.

MtF: the abbreviation of male-to-female refers to a transgendered woman whose gender identity at birth was female and whose physical sex at birth was male.

post-op: for a transgendered person, having experienced surgical reassignment of physical sex. For an MtF woman, briefly, the skin that once surrounded the penis has been inverted to form a neo-vagina.

purging: the cycle of futile attempts, by an MtF woman before transition, to rid her mind of the obsession to appear feminine by discarding and replacing the obsession's manifestations of sex-inappropriate attire.

sex (human): that set of purely physical characteristics of
an individual having to do with the part the individual
would play presumably in biological reproduction if no
higher brain involvement, and spiritual, emotional, or other
nonphysical activity were involved.

sex reassignment (male to female): the process of using
feminizing hormones, electrolysis, and surgery (sex-
reassignment surgery or S. R. S.) to attempt to conform the
patient's physical self to her gender identity.

transgendered woman: a woman whose feminine
gender identity, or whose conception of her essential self, is
opposite from her natal physical sex.

transgendered man: a man whose masculine gender
identity, or whose conception of his essential self is
opposite from his natal physiology.

transgendered person: a person whose gender identity is
different from, and causes an obsessive and unrelenting
conflict regarding, her or his natal physical sex.

transitioning: the process of wearing gender-identity
appropriate clothing and generally appearing, to the extent
possible, in accordance with one's gender identity rather
than that appropriate to one's physical sex.

transperson (transpeople *pl.*): a broad term including
transgendered women and men, but also including
transvestites and intersexed people. Because of its breadth
and possible confusion, it was not used in this work.

transsexual: a term appropriately used to describe a person whose apparent biological or anatomical sex as a conventional female or male is ambiguous to the casual observer and, occasionally, even to the medical community. The term more commonly used for the condition of ambiguous sexual anatomy is "intersex." Use of the term "transsexual" avoids reference to the person's gender identity, in the same sense that a use of language would ignore thought. The term is inappropriately, but frequently and even assertively, used when referring to transgendered persons to suggest that their gender identity conflict has a primarily physical, rather than a nonphysical, genesis. Its use suggests that the biological or anatomical sex of the body must be preeminent, rather than the gender identity of that person's essential self. Since the term ignores her of his essential identity, the transgendered woman or man usually finds the term offensive.

transvestite male: a man whose gender identity is masculine and physical sex is male and who wears clothing and make-up to present a feminine appearance for self-gratification. The term does not imply a sexual preference.

21. Index

J

K

L

M

N

O

P

T

U

V

W

Y

Z

22. Endnotes

1. World Professional Association for Transgender Health. 2012. Standards of Care for the Health of Transsexual, Transgender, and Gender Nonconforming People {7th Ver.} https://www.wpath.org/publications/soc

2. Shrier, Abagail. 2020. Irreversible Damage: The Transgender Craze Seducing Our Daughters. Washington, D. C.: Regnery Publishing Div., Salem Media Group.

3. Batty, David. 2004. Mistaken identity. SocietyGuardian, July 31. http://society.guardian.co.uk/health/story/0,7890,1273045,00.html?'rss (accessed Nov. 20, 2006). 3 World Professional Association for Transgender Health.

4. Central Intelligence Agency. 2004. World factbook [sic]: United Kingdom. http://www.cia.gov/cia/publications/factbook/geos/uk.html (accessed July 15, 2004).

5. Kashner, Zoe, ed. 2007. The world almanac and book of facts, 2007. New York: World Almanac Education Group.

6. Niebuhr, Reinhold. 1950. *The a. a. grapevine.* January. Quoted in S. Platt, ed., *Respectfully quoted: A dictionary of quotations requested from Congressional Research Service.* Washington DC: Library of Congress, 1989.

7. Money, John. 1986. *Lovemaps: Clinical concepts of sexual/erotic health and pathology, paraphilia, and gender transposition in childhood, adolescence, and maturity.* New York: Irvington Publishers and Buffalo: Prometheus Books.

8. Goldstein, Jill, Matthew Jerram, Russell Poldrack, Robert Anagnoson, Hans C. Breiter, Nikos Makris, Julie M. Goodman, Ming T. Tsuang, and Larry J. Seidman. 2005. Sex differences in prefrontal cortical brain activity during fMRI of auditory verbal working memory. *Neuropsychology* 19 (4): 509-519. http://www,brugganabdwinebs,irg/ConnorsCenter/Research/Images/Articles/Sex%20differences%20in%20prefrontal%20cortical%20brain%20activity.pdf (accessed March 18, 2007).

9. Kashner, Zoe, ed. 2007. *The world almanac and book of facts,* 2007. New York: World Almanac Education Group.

10. Lubin, Arthur, director. 1943. *Phantom of the opera,* from Internet Movie Database. http://www.imdb.com/title/tt0036261/.

11. Sears, Fred, director. 1956. *The werewolf,* from Internet Movie Database. http://www.imdb.com/title/tt0049944/.

12. Fleming, Victor, director. 1941. *Dr. Jekyll and Mr. Hyde,* from Internet Movie Database. http://www.imdb.com/title/tt0033553/.

13. Fisher, Terence, director. 1959. *The mummy,* from Internet Movie Database. http://www.imdb.com/title/tt0053085/.

14. Stevenson, Robert, director. 1959. *Darby O'Gill and the little people,* from Internet Movie Database. http://www.imdb.com/title/tt0052722/.

15. Julian, Rupert, Lon Chaney, Ernst Laemmle, and Edward Sedgwick, directors. 1925. *The phantom of the opera,* from Internet Movie Database. http://www.imdb.com/title/tt0016220/.

16. Rand, Ayn. 1943/1993. *The fountainhead.* 50th anniversary edition with afterward by Leonard Peikoff. New York: Signet.

17. Rand, Ayn. 1943/1993. *The fountainhead.* 50th anniversary edition with afterward by Leonard Peikoff. New York: Signet.

18. Lubin, Arthur, director. 1943. *Phantom of the opera,* from Internet Movie Database. http://www.imdb.com/title/tt0036261/.

19. Brahm, John, Alfred E. Green, James B. Kern, et al., directors. 1955. *The millionaire,* from Internet Movie Database. http://www.imdb.com/title/tt0047758/.

20. London, Jack. 1903. *The call of the wild. Online Literature Library,* 1995. http://www.literature.org/authors/London-jack/the-call-of-the-wild/index.html (accessed June 8, 2004).

21. Edinburgh Scotland Tourist Information. *Greyfriars Bobby.* http://www.beautiful-scotland.co.uk/Edinburgh.htm.

22. Byron, George Gordon. 1808. Epitaph to a dog. *"Poetry-Lord Byron."* http://www.davidpbrown.co.uk/poetry/lord-byron.html (accessed May 6, 2004).

23. Morse, Hollingsworth, Oscar Rudolph, George B. Seitz Jr., et al., directors. 1949. *The lone ranger,* from Internet Movie Database. http://www.imdb.com/title/tt00410038/.

24. Blair, George, John English, Christian Nyby, et al., directors. 1951. The Roy Rogers show, from Internet Movie Database. http://www.imdb.com/title/tt0043225/.

25. Davis, Eddie, Leslie Goodwins, Lambert Hillyer, et al., directors. 1950. *The Cisco Kid,* from Internet Movie Database. http://www.imdb.com/title/tt0042093/.

26. Copelan, Jodie, Oliver Drake, Richard C. Kahn, et al., directors. 1951. *Sky King,* from Internet Movie Database. http://www.imdb.com/title/tt0043232/.

27. Russell, William D. and Peter Tewksbury, directors. 1954. *Father knows best,* from Internet Movie Database. http://www.imdb.com/title/tt0046600/.

28. Bellamy, Earl, Jerrold Bernstein, Lawrence Dobkin, et al., directors. 1958. *The Donna Reed show,* from Internet Movie Database. http://www.imdb.com/title/tt0051267/.

29. Satenstein, Frank, director. 1955. *The honeymooners,* from Internet Movie Database. http://www.imdb.com/title/tt0042114/.

30. Vogel, Virgil w., Bernard McEveety, Paul Henreid, et al., directors. 1965. *The big valley,* from Internet Movie Database. http://www.imdb.com/title/tt0058791/.

31. Claxton, William F., Lewis Allen, Leon Benson, et al., directors. 1959. *Bonanza,* from Internet Movie Database. http://www.imdb.com/title/tt0052451/.

[32]. Sale, Richard and William F. Claxton, directors. 1958. *Yancy Derringer,* from Internet Movie Database. http://www.imdb.com/title/tt0051329/.

[33]. Archainbaud, George, Douglas Heyes, Fred Jackman Jr. et al., directors. 1956. *Circus boy,* from Internet Movie Database. http://www.imdb.com/title/tt0048855/.

[34]. Bare, Richard L., Alan Crosland Jr., Paul Guilfoyle, et al., directors. 1958. *Lawman,* from Internet Movie Database. http://www.imdb.com/title/tt0051290/.

[35]. Meston, John, Andrew V. McLaglen, Harry Harris, et al., directors. *Gunsmoke*, from Internet Movie Database. http://www.imdb.com/title/tt0047736/.

[36]. Beaudine Jr., William, Earl Bellamy, James B. Clark, et al., directors. 1954. *Lassie*, from Internet Movie Database. http://www.imdb.com/title/tt0046617/.

[36] World Professional Association for Transgender Health. 2012. Standards of Care for the Health of Transsexual, Transgender, and Gender Nonconforming People {7th Ver.} ttps://www.wpath.org/publications/soc

[36] Shrier, Abagail. 2020. Irreversible Damage: The Transgender Craze Seducing Our Daughters. Washington, D. C.: Regnery Publishing Div., Salem Media Group.

[36]. Batty, David. 2004. Mistaken identity. SocietyGuardian, July 31. http://society.guardian.co.uk/health/story/0,7890,1273045,00.html?'rss (accessed Nov. 20, 2006).

[36]. Central Intelligence Agency. 2004. World factbook [sic]: United Kingdom. http://www.cia.gov/cia/publications/factbook/geos/uk.html (accessed July 15, 2004).

[36]. Kashner, Zoe, ed. 2007. The world almanac and book of facts, 2007. New York: World Almanac Education Group.

36. Niebuhr, Reinhold. 1950. The a. a. grapevine. January. Quoted in S. Platt, ed., Respectfully quoted: A dictionary of quotations requested from Congressional Research Service. Washington DC: Library of Congress, 1989.

36. Money, John. 1986. Lovemaps: Clinical concepts of sexual/erotic health and pathology, paraphilia, and gender transposition in childhood, adolescence, and maturity. New York: Irvington Publishers and Buffalo: Prometheus Books.

36. Goldstein, Jill, Matthew Jerram, Russell Poldrack, Robert Anagnoson, Hans C. Breiter, Nikos Makris, Julie M. Goodman, Ming T. Tsuang, and Larry J. Seidman. 2005. Sex differences in prefrontal cortical brain activity during fMRI of auditory verbal working memory. Neuropsychology 19 (4): 509-519. http://www,brugganabdwinebs,irg/ConnorsCenter/Research/Images/Articles/Sex%20 differences%20in%20prefrontal%20cortical%20b rain%20activity.pdf (accessed March 18, 2007).

36. Kashner, Zoe, ed. 2007. The world almanac and book of facts, 2007. New York: World Almanac Education Group.

36. Lubin, Arthur, director. 1943. Phantom of the opera, from Internet Movie Database. http://www.imdb.com/title/tt0036261/.

36. Sears, Fred, director. 1956. The werewolf, from Internet Movie Database. http://www.imdb.com/title/tt0049944/.

36. Fleming, Victor, director. 1941. Dr. Jekyll and Mr. Hyde, from Internet Movie Database. http://www.imdb.com/title/tt0033553/.

36. Fisher, Terence, director. 1959. The mummy, from Internet Movie Database. http://www.imdb.com/title/tt0053085/.

36. Stevenson, Robert, director. 1959. Darby O'Gill and the little people, from Internet Movie Database. http://www.imdb.com/title/tt0052722/.

36. Julian, Rupert, Lon Chaney, Ernst Laemmle, and Edward Sedgwick, directors. 1925. The phantom of the opera, from Internet Movie Database. http://www.imdb.com/title/tt0016220/.

[36]. Rand, Ayn. 1943/1993. The fountainhead. 50th anniversary edition with afterward by Leonard Peikoff. New York: Signet.

[36]. Rand, Ayn. 1943/1993. The fountainhead. 50th anniversary edition with afterward by Leonard Peikoff. New York: Signet.

[36]. Lubin, Arthur, director. 1943. Phantom of the opera, from Internet Movie Database. http://www.imdb.com/title/tt0036261/.

[36]. Brahm, John, Alfred E. Green, James B. Kern, et al., directors. 1955. The millionaire, from Internet Movie Database. http://www.imdb.com/title/tt0047758/.

[36]. London, Jack. 1903. The call of the wild. Online Literature Library, 1995. http://www.literature.org/authors/London-jack/the-call-of-the- wild/index.html (accessed June 8, 2004).

[36]. Edinburgh Scotland Tourist Information. Greyfriars Bobby. http://www. beautiful-scotland.co.uk/Edinburgh.htm.

[36]. Byron, George Gordon. 1808. Epitaph to a dog. "Poetry-Lord Byron." http://www.davidpbrown.co.uk/poetry/lord-byron.html (accessed May 6, 2004).

[36]. Morse, Hollingsworth, Oscar Rudolph, George B. Seitz Jr., et al., directors. 1949. The lone ranger, from Internet Movie Database. http://www.imdb.com/title/tt00410038/.

[36]. Blair, George, John English, Christian Nyby, et al., directors. 1951. The Roy Rogers show, from Internet Movie Database. http://www.imdb.com/title/tt0043225/.

[36]. Davis, Eddie, Leslie Goodwins, Lambert Hillyer, et al., directors. 1950. The Cisco Kid, from Internet Movie Database. http://www.imdb.com/title/tt0042093/.

[36]. Copelan, Jodie, Oliver Drake, Richard C. Kahn, et al., directors. 1951. Sky King, from Internet Movie Database. http://www.imdb.com/title/tt0043232/.

36. Russell, William D. and Peter Tewksbury, directors. 1954. Father knows best, from Internet Movie Database. http://www.imdb.com/title/tt0046600/.

36. Bellamy, Earl, Jerrold Bernstein, Lawrence Dobkin, et al., directors. 1958. The Donna Reed show, from Internet Movie Database. http://www.imdb.com/title/tt0051267/.

36. Satenstein, Frank, director. 1955. The honeymooners, from Internet Movie Database. http://www.imdb.com/title/tt0042114/.

36. Vogel, Virgil w., Bernard McEveety, Paul Henreid, et al., directors. 1965. The big valley, from Internet Movie Database. http://www.imdb.com/title/tt0058791/.

36. Claxton, William F., Lewis Allen, Leon Benson, et al., directors. 1959. Bonanza, from Internet Movie Database. http://www.imdb.com/title/tt0052451/.

36. Sale, Richard and William F. Claxton, directors. 1958. Yancy Derringer, from Interne

37. Clark, James B., Robert Gordon, Albert S. Rogell, et al., directors. 1956. *My friend Flicka,* from Internet Movie Database. http://www.imdb.com/title/tt0048887/.

38. Salkow, Sidney, Lesley Selander, and Ray Nazarro, directors. 1955. *Fury,* from Internet Movie Database. http://www.imdb.com/title/tt0047734/.

39. Bellamy, Earl, Charles S. Gould, Douglas Heyes, et al., directors. 1954. *The adventures of Rin Tin Tin,* from Internet Movie Database. http://www.imdb.com/title/tt0046576/.

40. Conrad, William, Alan Crosland Jr., Eddie Davis, et al., directors. 1958. *Bat Masterson,* from Internet Movie Database. http://www.imdb.com/title/tt0050025/.

41. Carr, Thomas, Don McDougall, George Blair, et al., directors, 1958. *Wanted: dead or alive,* from Internet Movie Database. http://www.imdb.com/title/tt0051327.

⁴². De Toth, Andre. 1954. *The bounty hunter,* from Internet Movie Database. http://www.imdb.com/title/tt0046801/.

⁴³. Boetticher, Budd, William F. Claxton, Lawrence Dobkin, et al., directors. 1958. *The rifleman,* from Imdb. com at http://www.imdb.com/title/tt0051308/.

⁴⁴. McLaglen, Andrew V., Richard Boone, William Conrad, et al. directors. 1957. *Have gun – will travel,* from Internet Movie Database. http://www.imdb. com/title/tt0050025/.

⁴⁵. Adreon, Franklin, William Hale, Douglas Heyes, et al., directors. 1955. *Cheyenne,* from Internet Movie Database. http://www.imdb.com/title/ tt00447720/.

⁴⁶. Post, Ted, Andrew V. McLaglen, Stuart Heisler, et al. 1959. *Rawhide,* from Internet Movie Database. http://www.imdb.com/title/tt0052504/.

⁴⁷. Ray, Nicholas, director. 1960. *The savage innocents,* from Internet Movie Database. http://www.imdb.com/title/tt0053244/.

⁴⁸. Swift, David, director. 1960. *Pollyanna,* from Internet Movie Database. http://www.imdb.com/title/tt0054195/.

⁴⁹. N.O.A.A., National Weather Service Forecast Office. n.d. *The greatest storms of the century in the greater Washington-Baltimore Region.* http://www.erh. noaa.gov/er/lwx/Historic_Events/StormsOfCentury.html (accessed September 24, 2003).

⁵⁰. Council of Economic Advisers. 2003. *Economic report of the President,* February. Table B-3: Quantity and price indexes for gross domestic product, and percent changes, 1959-2002. http://w3.access.gpo.gov/usbudget/ fy2004/erp.html (accessed September 27, 2003).

⁵¹. Kashner, Zoe, ed. 2007. *The world almanac and book of facts,* 2007. New York: World Almanac Education Group.

⁵². Jefferson, Thomas. 1774. A summary view of the rights of British America. *The papers of Thomas Jefferson,* ed. Julian P. Boyd, et al. (1950) cited in *The Columbia World of Quotations,* eds. Robert Andrews, Mary Biggs, Michael

Seidel, et al. (New York: Columbia University Press, 1996). *Bartleby.com.*, http://www.bartleby.com/66/91/30891.html.

53. Kennedy, John F. 1961/1997. Inaugural address of John F. Kennedy from *The Avalon project at Yale Law School:* Inaugural *speeches page,* 1997.

http://www.yale.edu/lawweb/Avalon/presiden/inaug/kennedy.htm.

54. Morris, Jan. 1974. *Conundrum.* New York: Harcourt, Brace, Jovanovich.

55. National Council of the Churches of Christ U.S.A., Division of Christian Education. 1989. The Holy Bible: New Revised Standard Version. Nashville, TN: Thomas Nelson.

56. National Council of the Churches of Christ U.S.A., Division of Christian Education. 1989. The Holy Bible: New Revised Standard Version. Nashville, TN: Thomas Nelson.

57. Hawks, Howard, director. 1941. *Sergeant York,* from Internet Movie Database. http://www.imdb.com/title/tt0034167/.

58. de Sales, Francis. n.d. Prayer of St. Francis de Sales under *Francis de Sales B. Doctor* (RM). Washington DC: *Saint Patrick Catholic Church.* http://www. saintpatrickdc.org/ss/0124.htm (accessed January 18, 2007).

59. Kipling, Rudyard J. 1902/1950. Just so stories for little children: How the elephant got his trunk, in *Better Homes and Gardens* storybook selected by Betty O'Connor, 101-5. Des Moines: Meredith Publishing, 1950.

60. Asimov, Isaac. 1974/1956. The last question, in *The best of Isaac Asimov.* Garden City, NY: Doubleday, 1974.

61. Dotson-Lewis, Betty L. 1972. Author's note in *Oral history interview with Larry Conn.* AppalachiaCoal. Com. http://wwww.appalachiacoal.com/Oral%20History,%20Larry%20Conn,%20 Buffalo%20Creek%20Flood,%20Logan,%20WV.htm.

62. Kashner, Zoe, ed. 2007. *The world almanac and book of facts,* 2007. New York: World Almanac Education Group.

[63]. Kashner, Zoe, ed. 2007. *The world almanac and book of facts,* 2007. New York: World Almanac Education Group.

[64]. *Lawrence v. Texas,* no. 02-102. 2003. U.S. Supreme Court: 539 U.S. 558. http://www.supremecourtus.gov/opinions/boundvolumes/539bv.pdf.

[65]. *Lofton, Steven et al. v. Secretary of the Department of Children and Family Services,* no. 01-16723. 2004. U. S. Court of Appeals for the Eleventh Circuit: 377 F.3d 1275.
http://www.ca11.uscourts.gov/opinions/ops/200116723ord.pdf.

[66]. Elbin, Dr. Paul Nowell. 1975. *The paradox of happiness.* New York: Hawthorne Books. Repub., _______. *Making happiness a habit.* Nashville: Abingdon Press, 1981.

[67]. Henley, William Ernest. ca. 1900. Invictus. From *The Constitution Society.* http://www.constitution.org/col/Invictus.htm.

[68]. Reiner, William G. interviewed by Sadie F. Dingfelder. 2004. Gender bender: New research suggests genes and prenatal hormones could have more sway in gender identity than previously thought. APA *Online: Monitor on psychology* April, http://www.apa.org/monitor/apr04/gender.html.

[69]. Reiner, William G. and John P. Gearhart. 2004. Discordant sexual identity in some genetic males with colacal exstrophy assigned to female sex at birth. *New England Journal of Medicine* 350 (January 22): 333-41.

[70]. Culotta, Elizabeth. 2005. What genetic changes made us uniquely human? *Science.*
http://www.sciencemag.oeg/gi/content/full/309/5731/91.

[71]. Diamond, Milton and Keith Sigmundson. 1997. Sex reassignment at birth: Long-term review and clinical implications. *Archives of Pediatric and Adolescent Medicine* 151 (March): 298-304.

[72]. Colapinto, John. 2000. *As nature made him: The boy who was raised as a girl.* New York: HarperCollins.

73. Kashner, Zoe, ed. 2007. *The world almanac and book of facts*, 2007. New York: World Almanac Education Group.

74. Elbin, Dr. Paul Nowell. 1975. *The paradox of happiness.* New York: Hawthorne Books. *Repub..Making happiness a habit.* Nashville: Abingdon Press, 1981.

75. National Council of the Churches of Christ U.S.A., Division of Christian Education. 1989. The Holy Bible: New Revised Standard Version. Nashville, TN: Thomas Nelson.

76. Cleveland Clinic, Department of Otolaryngology. 2001. Laryngotracheal: For your information. *The Cleveland Clinic.* http://www.clevelandclinic.org/otol/laryn/hello.htm (accessed August 9, 2002).

77. Logan, Joshua. 1958. *South Pacific,* from Internet Movie Database. http://www.imdb.com/title/tt0052225/.

78. Sidney, George. 1951. *Show boat,* from Internet Movie Database.

http://www.imdb.com/title/tt0044030/.

79. Curtiz, Michael, director. 1954. *White Christmas,* from Internet Movie Database. http://www.imdb.com/title/tt0047673/ (accessed January 17, 2007).

80. Koster, Henry. 1961. *Flower drum song,* from Internet Movie Database. http://www.imdb.com/title/tt0054885 (accessed January 17, 2007).

81. Minnelli, Vincente. 1964. *Goodbye, Charlie,* from Internet Movie Database. http://www/imdb.com/title/tt0058154/.

82. Edwards, Blake. 1991. *Switch,* from Internet Movie Database. http://www/imdb.com/title/tt0103016/.

83. National Council of the Churches of Christ U.S.A., Division of Christian Education. 1989. The Holy Bible: New Revised Standard Version. Nashville, TN: Thomas Nelson.

[84]. Lyons, Tom. 2001. Anti-terrorist tactics take shape via e-mail – and they make sense. *Sarasota Herald-Tribune,* Oct. 10.

[85]. Woollcott, Alexander. 1934. Miss Kitty takes to the road, from the *ScreamOnline.com.* http://www.thescreamonline.com/essays/essays2-3/Woollcott.html.

[86]. Teichmann, Howard. 1976. *Smart Aleck.* New York: William Morrow and Co.

[87]. Teichmann, Howard. 1976. *Smart Aleck*. New York: William Morrow and Co.

[88]. Kashner, Zoe, ed. 2007. *The world almanac and book of facts,* 2007. New York: World Almanac Education Group.

[89]. *Lawrence v. Texas,* no. 02-102. 2003. U.S. Supreme Court: 539 U.S. 558. http://www.supremecourtus.gov/opinions/boundvolumes/539bv.pdf.

[90]. Davis, Phil, Stu Phelps, Bob Lehman, et al., directors. 1950. *Truth or consequences.* http://www.imdb.com/title/tt0143074/fullcredits (accessed January 16, 2007).

[91]. Guedel, John, producer. 1952. *Art Linkletter's House Party.* http://www.imdb.com/title/tt0047714/fullcredits (accessed January 16, 2007).

[92]. Frost, Robert. 1920. The road not taken. From *mountain interval. Bartleby.com.* http://www.bartleby.com/119/1.html (accessed June 30, 2002).

[93]. Zinnemann, Fred. 1955. *Oklahoma* from Internet Movie Database. http://www.imdb.comhttp://www.imdb.com/title/tt0048445.

[94]. Kashner, Zoe, ed. 2007. *The world almanac and book of facts,* 2007. New York: World Almanac Education Group.

[95]. Kashner, Zoe, ed. 2007. *The world almanac and book of facts,* 2007. New York: World Almanac Education Group.

96. Diamond, Milton and Keith Sigmundson. 1997. Sex reassignment at birth: Long-term review and clinical implications. *Archives of Pediatric and Adolescent Medicine* 151 (March): 298-304.

97. Money, John. 1986. *Lovemaps: clinical concepts of sexual/erotic health and pathology, paraphilia, and gender transposition in childhood, adolescence, and maturity.* New York: Irvington Publishers, Inc. and Buffalo: Prometheus Books.

98. Zhou, Jiang-Ning, Michael A Hofman, Louis J. G. Gooren, and Dick F. Swaab. 1995. A sex difference in the human brain and its relation to transsexuality. *Nature* 378 (November 2,): 68-70.

99. Kruijver, Frank P. M., Jiang-Ning Zhou, Chris W. Pool, Michael A. Hofman, Louis J. G. Gooren, and Dick F. Swaab. 2000. Male-to-female transsexuals have female neuron numbers in a limbic nucleus. *The Journal of Clinical Endocrinology & Metabolism* 85 (May): 2034-2041.

100. National Council of the Churches of Christ U.S.A., Division of Christian Education. 1989. The Holy Bible: New Revised Standard Version. Nashville, TN: Thomas Nelson.

101. Shakespeare, William. 1975/n.d. *The merchant of Venice,* act iv, sce. 1. From *William Shakespeare: The complete works.* New York: Gramercy Books.

102. National Council of the Churches of Christ U.S.A., Division of Christian Education. 1989. The Holy Bible: New Revised Standard Version. Nashville, TN: Thomas Nelson.

103. Reiner, William G. 1997. To be male or female-That is the question. *Archives of Pediatric and Adolescent Medicine,* 151 (March): 224-5.

104. Pinholster, Ginger. 2005. New research casts doubt on surgery for infants born with male and female traits. *American Association for the Advancement of Science.* News release (February 18). http://www.aaas.org/news/releases/2005/0218gender.shtml.

105. Vilain, Eric interview. 2004. Biology of sex and gender: Expert interview transcripts. From *Rediscovering biology.* Annenberg/Corporation for Public Broadcasting.

http://www.lerner.org/channel/courses/biology/units/gender/experts/vilain.html.

106. Demir, Ebru and Barry J. Dickson. 2005. Fruitless splicing specifies male courtship behavior in drosophila. Cell, 121 (June 3): 785-794. http://download.cell.com/pdfs/0092-8674/PIIS0092867405004071.pdf.

107. Reiner, William G. 1997. To be male or female-That is the question. *Archives of Pediatric and Adolescent Medicine,* 151 (March): 224-5.

108. Reiner, William G. and John P. Gearhart. 2004. Discordant sexual identity in some genetic males with colacal exstrophy assigned to female sex at birth. *New England Journal of Medicine* 350 (January 22): 333-41.

109. Hughes, I. A., C. Houk, S. F. Ahmed, and P. A. Lee. 2006. Consensus statement on management of intersex disorders. *Journal of Pediatric Urology* 2: 148-162. http://www.intersex-tr.org/documents/Consensus%20%statement%20on%20 management%20of%20intersex%20disorders.pdf.

110. Beers, Mark H., ed. 2004a. Children's health issues: Genital defects. From *Merck Manual Home Edition.* Reviewed/revised Gregory S. Liptak, April, 2006. http://www.merck.com/mmhe/print/sec23/ch265/ch265d.html.

111. Pinholster, Ginger. 2005. New research casts doubt on surgery for infants born with male and female traits. *American Association for the Advancement of Science.* News release (February 18). http://www.aaas.org/news/releases/2005/0218gender.shtml.

112. Sherr, Lynn. 2002. A different sex, in *ABC NEWS* 20/20. New Hudson, MI: ABC News Videos/Burrelle's Information Services, item: T020419.

113. Beers, Mark H., ed. 2004b. Mental health disorders: Gender identity. From *Merck Manual Home Edition.* http://www.merck.com/mmhe/print/sec07/ch104/ ch104b.html.

114. Reiner, William G. 1997. To be male or female–That is the question. *Archives of Pediatric and Adolescent Medicine,* 151 (March): 224-5.

115. Hendricks, Melissa. 2000. Into the hands of babes. *John Hopkins Magazine September,* http://www.jhu.edu~jhumag/0900web/babes.html.

116. Pinholster, Ginger. 2005. New research casts doubt on surgery for infants born with male and female traits. *American Association for the Advancement of Science.* News release, February 18, http://www.aaas.org/news/releases/2005/0218gender.shtml.

117. Colapinto, John. 2000. As *nature made him*: The boy who was raised as a girl. New York: HarperCollins.

118. Diamond, Milton and Keith Sigmundson. 1997. Sex reassignment at birth: Long-term review and clinical implications. *Archives of Pediatric and Adolescent Medicine* 151 (March): 298-304.

119. Kim, GW, Kim, SK, Jeong, GW. 2016 Neural Activation-based Sexual Orientation and its Correlation with Free Testosterone Level in Postoperative Female-to-male Transsexuals. Surgical and Radiolgic Anatomy 38 (2) (March) 245-52.

120. Zhou, Jiang-Ning, Michael A Hofman, Louis J. G. Gooren, and Dick F. Swaab. 1995. A sex difference in the human brain and its relation to transsexuality. *Nature* 378 (November 2): 68-70.

121. Benjamin, Harry. 1966. *The transsexual phenomenon.* New York: Julian Press, from Electronic Books. http://www.symposion.com/ijt/benjamin/chap_02.htm)

122. Green, Richard. 1966. Appendix c in *The transsexual phenomenon,* by Harry Benjamin. New York: Julian Press, from Electronic Books. http://www.symposion.com/ijt/benjamin/appendix_c.htm.

123. Cassius, Dio Cocceianus. ca. A.D. 200. *Roman history:* Book 80. Trans. by Earnest Cary, Greek and English 1914 Loeb Classics Edition. http://www.brainfly.net/html/books/diocas80.pdf.

[124]. Cassius, Dio Cocceianus. ca. A.D. 200. *Roman history:* Book 80. Trans. by Earnest Cary, Greek and English 1914 Loeb Classics Edition. http://www.brainfly.net/html/books/diocas80.pdf.

[125]. Speck, Oliver, Thomas Ernst, Jochen Braun, Christoph Koch, Eric Miller, and Linda Chang. 2000. Gender differences in the functional organization of the brain for working memory. *Neuro Report* 11 (August): 2581-2586. http://www.hawaii.edu/mri/additional%20pdfs/Recently%20 downloaded?Speck%20(NeuroReport%202000).pdf.

[126]. Goldstein, Jill, Matthew Jerram, Russell Poldrack, Robert Anagnoson, Hans C. Breiter, Nikos Makris, Julie M. Goodman, and Ming T. Tsuang. 2005. Sex differences in prefrontal cortical brain activity during fMRI of auditory verbal working memory. *Neuropsychology* 19 (4): 509-519. http://www,brugganabdwinebs,irg/ConnorsCenter/Research/Images/Articles/ Sex%20differences%20in%20prefrontal%20cortical%20brain%20activity.pdf (accessed March 18, 2007).

[127]. Money J., J.G. Hampson, and J.L. Hampson. 1955. An examination of some basic sexual concepts: The evidence of human hermaphroditism. *Bulletin of Johns Hopkins Hospital* 97: 301-319.

[128]. McHugh, Paul R. 2001. Adventures in academic psychiatry. *Hopkins Medical News* (Fall). http://www.hopkinsmedicine.org/hmn/F01/top.html (accessed July 18, 2002).

[129]. Duffy, Jim. 1999. Sexual healing. *Hopkins Medical News* (Winter), under Gender-change issues, http://www.hopkinsmedicine.org/hmn/W99/top.html (accessed July 18, 2002).

[130]. McHugh, Paul R. 2001. Adventures in academic psychiatry. *Hopkins Medical News* (Fall). http://www.hopkinsmedicine.org/hmn/F01/top.html (accessed July 18, 2002).

[131]. McHugh, Paul R. 1992. Psychiatric Misadventures. *The American Scholar* (Autumn.) http://www.lhup.edu/~DSIMANEK/mchugh.htm.

132. Duffy, Jim. 1999. Sexual healing. Hopkins Medical News (Winter), under Gender-change issues,
http://www.hopkinsmedicine.org/hmn/W99/top.html (accessed July 18, 2002).

133. Diamond, Milton and Keith Sigmundson. 1997. Sex reassignment at birth: Long-term review and clinical implications. *Archives of Pediatric and Adolescent Medicine* 151 (March): 298-304.

134. Diamond, Milton and Keith Sigmundson. 1997. Sex reassignment at birth: Long-term review and clinical implications. *Archives of Pediatric and Adolescent Medicine* 151 (March): 298-304.

135. Gearhart, John. 2000. Interview in Into the hands of babes, by Melissa Hendricks. *Johns Hopkins Magazine,* (September). http://www.jhu.edu/~jhumag/0900web/babes.html.

136. Karam, Jose and Linda A. Baker. 2004. True hermaphroditism. *New England Journal of Medicine* 350 (January 22): 393.

137. Reiner, William G. and John P. Gearhart. 2004. Discordant sexual identity in some genetic males with cloacal exstrophy assigned to female sex at birth. *New England Journal of Medicine* 350 (January 22): 333-341.

138. National Geographic Society. 1968. Atlantic Ocean floor map. Supplement in *National Geographic Magazine* June.

139. American Psychiatric Association. 2000. *Diagnostic and statistical manual of mental disorders,* fourth edition, text revision. http://www.psychiatryonline.com/resourceTOC.aspx?resourceID'1.

140. Martinich, A. P. 1999. *Hobbes: A biography.* Cambridge: Cambridge University Press.

141. Kashner, Zoe, ed. 2007. *The world almanac and book of facts, 2007.* New York: World Almanac Education Group.

142. Rand, Ayn. 1969. *The romantic manifesto,* Cleveland, OH: The World Publishing Co.

143. McClure, Kristie M. 1996. *Judging rights: Lockean politics and the limits of consent,* Cornell University Press.

144. Bradley, A. C. 1991. Aristotle's conception of the state, in *A companion to Aristotle's politics,* David Keyt and Fred D. Miller, Jr. eds. Cambridge, MA: Basil Blackwell, Inc.

145. Kashner, Zoe, ed. 2007. *The world almanac and book of facts,* 2007. New York: World Almanac Education Group.

146. Kashner, Zoe, ed. 2007. *The world almanac and book of facts,* 2007. New York: World Almanac Education Group.

147. Kashner, Zoe, ed. 2007. *The world almanac and book of facts,* 2007. New York: World Almanac Education Group.

148. *Gardiner, J'Noel v. Joseph M. Gardiner,* no. 85030. 2001. Court of Appeals of the State of Kansas: 29 Kan. App. 2d 92, 22 P.3d 1036. http://www.kscourts.org/kscases/ctapp/2001/20010511/85030.htm (accessed August 1, 2002.).

149. M. T. v. J. T., no. 140. 1976. New Jersey Superior Court 77: 355 A.2d 204. http://loislaw.com/pns/index.htp (subs. required).

150. *In RE: B.L.V.B. and E.L.V.B.,* no. 92-321. 1993. Vermont Supreme Court: 160 VT 368, 628 A.2d 1271 (June 18). http://loislaw.com/pns/index.htp (subs. required).

151. *In RE: B.L.V.B. and E.L.V.B.,* no. 92-321. 1993. Vermont Supreme Court: 160 VT 368, 628 A.2d 1271 (June 18). http://loislaw.com/pns/index.htp (subs. required).

152. *Gardiner, J'Noel v Joseph M. Gardiner,* no. 85030. 2001. Court of Appeals of the State of Kansas: 29 Kan. App. 2d 92, 22 P.3d 1036. http://www.kscourts.org/kscases/ctapp/2001/20010511/85030.htm (accessed August 1, 2002.).

[153]. Greenberg, Julie. 1999. Defining male and female: Intersexuality and the collision between law and biology. *Arizona Law Review* 41 (Summer): 265-328.

[154]. Internal Revenue Service, Office of Chief Counsel. 2006. Request for Chief Counsel advice: Medical expense deduction. *Internal Revenue Service,* memorandum 200603025, http://www.irs.ogv/pub/irs-wd/0603025.pdf.

[155]. Kashner, Zoe, ed. 2007. *The world almanac and book of facts,* 2007. New York: World Almanac Education Group.

[156]. Kashner, Zoe, ed. 2007. *The world almanac and book of facts,* 2007. New York: World Almanac Education Group.

[157]. Kashner, Zoe, ed. 2007. *The world almanac and book of facts,* 2007. New York: World Almanac Education Group.

[158]. *M. Kantaras v. L. Kantaras,* no. 98-5375CA. 2003a. Sixth Judicial Circuit Court of Florida: (not recorded). http://www.transgenderlaw.org/cases/kantarasopinion.pdf

[159]. *M. Kantaras v. L. Kantaras,* no. 98-5375CA. 2003a. Sixth Judicial Circuit Court of Florida: (not recorded). http://www.transgenderlaw.org/cases/kantarasopinion.pdf

[160]. *L. Kantaras v. M. Kantaras,* no. 2D03-1377. 2004. 2nd District Court of Appeal of Florida: 884 So. 2d 155. http://www.2dca.org/opinion/July%2023,%202004/2D03-1377.pdf.

[161]. *M. Kantaras v. L. Kantaras,* no. SCO4-1953. 2005b. The Supreme Court of Florida: 898 So. 2d. 80. http://www.loislaw.com/pns/index.htp (subs. required).

[162]. Council of Europe. 2003. Chart of signatures and ratifications of a treaty: General agreement on privileges and immunities of the Council of Europe. *Council of Europe,* http://conventions.coe.int/treaty/EN/searching. asp?NT'002&CM'1&DF'16/03/03 (accessed March 16, 2003).

163. European Court of Human Rights. n.d. The Court: Historical background. *European Court of Human Rights,* http://www.echr.coe.int/ECHR/EN/Header?The+Court/The+Court/History+of+the+Court/ (accessed March 7, 2007).

164. *Goodwin, Christine v. United Kingdom,* no. 28957/95. 2002a. European Court of Human Rights, Grand Chamber: [2002] ECHR 588 (July 11). http://hudoc.echr.coe.int/Hudoc1doc2/HEJUD/200207/Goodwin%20-%2028957jv.gc%2011072002e.doc.

165. *I. v. United Kingdom,* no. 25680/94. 2002a. European Court of Human Rights, Grand Chamber: [2002] ECHR 592 (July 11). http://hei.unige.ch/~clapham/hrdoc/docs/echrIcase.doc (accessed March 12, 2007).

166. Council of Europe. 1950. Conventions for the protection of human rights and fundamental freedoms as amended by protocol no. 11. *Council of Europe,* http://conventions.coe.int/Treaty/en/Treatoes/Html/005.htm.

167. *Goodwin, Christine v. United Kingdom,* no. 28957/95. 2002b. European Court of Human Rights, Grand Chamber: [2002] 57 ECHR 588 (July 11). http://hudoc.echr.coe.int/Hudoc1doc2/HEJUD/200207/Goodwin%20-%20 28957jv.gc%2011072002e.doc.

168. *I. v. United Kingdom,* no. 25680/94. 2002b. European Court of Human Rights, Grand Chamber: [2002] 40 ECHR 592 (July 11). http://hei.unige.ch/~clapham/hrdoc/docs/echrIcase.doc (accessed March 12, 2007).

169. *Goodwin, Christine v. United Kingdom,* no. 28957/95. 2002c. European Court of Human Rights, Grand Chamber: [2002] 74 ECHR 588 (July 11). http://hudoc.echr.coe.int/Hudoc1doc2/HEJUD/200207/Goodwin%20-%20 28957jv.gc%2011072002e.doc.

170. *I. v. United Kingdom,* no. 25680/94. 2002c. European Court of Human Rights, Grand Chamber: [2002] 54 ECHR 592 (July 11).

http://hei.unige.ch/~clapham/hrdoc/docs/echrIcase.doc (accessed March 12, 2007).

171. *Bellinger v. Bellinger,* UKHL 21. 2003. House of Lords, Lords of Appeal: [2003] UKHL 21,
http://www.publications.parliament.uk/pa/ld200203/ldjudgmt/jd030410/
bellin-l.htm.

172. Department of Constitutional Affairs. 2004. Legislation: The gender recognition act 2004. *Crown.* http://www,dca.gov.uk/constitution/transsex/
legs.htm.

173. Sidney Morning Herald. 2003. Vatican moves to ban all sex-change priests, nuns. *Sidney Morning Herald,* February 2.
http://www.smh.com.au/articles/2003/02/01/1043804574455.html (accessed February 5, 2003).

174. Donovan, Gill. 2003. Vatican says sex changes don't change one's gender. *National Catholic Reporter,* January 24.
http://www.findarticles.com/p/articles/mi_m1141/is_12_39/ai_97173570/print.

175. Ekklesia. 2004. Vatican issues statement on men and women. *Ekklesia,* February 8,
http://www.ekklesia.co.uk/content/news_syndication/article_04082vat.shtml (accessed August 4, 2004).

176. Stack, Megan K. 2005. In Iran, some clerics promote sex-change operation. *Los Angeles Times* appearing in *Sarasota Herald Tribune,* January 30.

177. Schmitt, Jaime Stover. 2005. The Yogic inner instrument. Personal communication, May 20.

178. Elliott, Carl. Dec., 2000. A new way to be mad. *Atlantic Monthly* 286 (December): 72-84.

179. Blanchard, Ray. 1989. The concept of autogynephilia and the typology of male gender dysphoria. *The Journal of Nervous and Mental Disease* 177 (10): 616-623, from
http://www.genderpsychology.org/autogynephilia/male_gender_dysphoria/.

180. Bailey, J. Michael. 2003. *The man who would be queen*. Washington, D.C.: Joseph Henry Press.

181. McHugh, Paul R. 1992. Psychiatric Misadventures. *The American Scholar* (Autumn.) http://www.lhup.edu/~DSIMANEK/mchugh.htm.

182. Leo, John. 2001. The sex change boom: Is politics the appropriate arena for this discussion? *U.S. News and World Report,* March 12.

183. Kashner, Zoe, ed. 2007. *The world almanac and book of facts,* 2007. New York: World Almanac Education Group.

184. Miller, Carol Marbin. 2003. Gender of Hemingway's son at center of feud. *The Milwaukee Journal Sentinel,* September 29. FindArticles.com, http://wwwfindarticles.com/p/articles/mi_qn4196/is_20030930/ai_n10909778.

185. American Psychological Association, Public Policy Office. 2004. A.P.A. briefing sheet on same-sex families and relationships: What does the psychological research say about same-sex families and relationships? APAonline (June), http://www.apa.org/ppo/issues/lgbfamilybrf604.html.

186. U.S. Customs Service. 2002. 45 children rescued, 20 arrests in U.S. Customs, Danish police investigation of global child-molesting, pornography ring. *U.S. Customs Service,* press release August 9, 2002, http://www.customs. ustreas.gov/hot-new/pressrel/2002/0809-00.htm (accessed August 15, 2002).

187. CNN. 2002. Web child porn ring broken: International ring included parentes abusing own children. *CNN.com,* http://www.cnn.com./2002/US/08/09/internet.child,porn.bust/index.html (accessed August 16, 2002).

188. Spencer, Terry. 2001. Ernest Hemingway's son Gregory dies. *The St. Augustine Record,* Oct. 5, 2001. Staugustine.com, http://www.staugustine.com/stories/100501/sta_192253.shtml (accessed March 19,2007).

189. Quittner, Jeremy. 2001. Hemingway's son Gloria: When Ernest Hemingway's son died in prison, the world learned he had been a troubled man who found the strength to live his life as he saw best—as a woman. *The Advocate*, Nov. 20. http://www.advocate.com/html/stories/851/851_hemingway.asp (accessed April 6, 2002).

190. Leo, John. 2001. The sex change boom: Is politics the appropriate arena for this discussion? *U.S. News and World Report*, March 12.

191. *Van Kuck v. Germany*, no. 35968/97. 2003. European Court of Human Rights, Third Section: 62 ECHR 285 (June 12,). http://www.worldlii.org/eu/cases/ECHR/2003/285.html.

192. Kashner, Zoe, ed. 2007. *The world almanac and book of facts*, 2007. New York: World Almanac Education Group.

193. Chachere, Vickie. 2004. Court: Floridians who have sex changes can't marry as new gender. *Tallahassee Democrat, Tallahassee*, FL, July 23,

http://tallahassee.com/mld/tallahassee/9227312. htm?template'contentModules/printstory.jsp (accessed July 25, 2004).

194. National Association of School Psychologists. n.d. Standards: Background information on the standards. *National Association of School Psychologists*, http://www.nasponline.org/certifications/standards.html (accessed February 2, 2005).

195. U.S. Department of Education. n.d. The federal role in education: Overview. U.S. Department of Education, http://www/ed.gov/about/overview/fed/role. html?src'ln (accessed February 13, 2005). http://www.ed.gov/about/overview/fed/role.html?src'ln

196. MedlinePlus. 2003. Few suicidal teens seek professional help: Report. *Reuters*, April 18, 2003, National Library of Medicine and National Institutes of Health. http://www.nlm.nih.gov/medlineplus/print/news/fullstory_12429.html (accessed May 5, 2003).

197. Columbia University Teenscreen. 2006. Teenscreen program: How the program works. *Teenscreen.org,* http:www.teenscreen.org/ (accessed March 18, 2007).

198. Zito, Julie Magno, Daniel J. Safer, Susan dosReis, James F. Gardner, Laurence Magder, Karen Soeken, Myde Boles, Frances Lynch, and Mark A. Riddle. 2003. Psychotripic practice patterns for youth: A ten-year perspective. *Archives of Pediatrics and Adolescent Medicine* 157 (1): 17-25. http://archpedi. ama-assn.org/cgi/content/full/157/1/17.

199. Norris, Michele. 2002. Campus crisis: Some students' mental health needs go unmet. World News Tonight, February 12. *ABC News.com,* http://more.abcnews.go.com/sections/wnt/dailynews/ college_mentalhealth020211.html (accessed December 27, 2002).

200. Kruijver, Frank P. M., Jiang-Ning Zhou, Chris W. Pool, Michael A. Hofman, Louis J. G. Gooren, and Dick F. Swaab. 2000. Male-to-female transsexuals have female neuron numbers in a limbic nucleus. *The Journal of Clinical Endocrinology & Metabolism* 85 (May): 2034-2041.

201. American Youth Policy Forum. 2001. Is the concept of full service community schools ready for federal support? *American Youth Policy Forum,* (March 9), http://www.aypf.org/forumbriefs/2001/fb030901.htm (accessed December 30, 2002).

202. U.S. Dept. H.H.S., Bureau of Health Professionals. 2005. Shortage designation branch home page: Health professional shortage areas: Ad-hoc database query results. *Health Resources & Services Administration,* U.S. Department of Health & Human Services, http://belize.hrsa.gov/newhpsa/ newhepsa.cfm (accessed February 8, 2005).

203. The President's New Freedom Commission on Mental Health, Michael F. Hogan, Chm. 2003. Achieving the promise: Transforming mental health care in America. *Mentalhealthcommission.gov* July 22. http://www. mentalhealthcommission.gov/reports/reports.htm (accessed March 19, 2007).

204. Kallestad, Brent. 2002. University presidents discuss concerns about class-size amendment. *Naples Daily News* August 16. http://www.naplesnews.com/02/08/florida/d808988a.htm (accessed March 22, 2003).

205. Kashner, Zoe, ed. 2007. *The world almanac and book of facts,* 2007. New York: World Almanac Education Group.

206. Kashner, Zoe, ed. 2007. *The world almanac and book of facts,* 2007. New York: World Almanac Education Group.

207. *Littleton v. Prange,* no. 00-25. 2000. U.S. Supreme Court 531 U.S. 872. http://www.supremecourtus.gov/opinions/boundvolumes/531bv.pdf.

208. Gardiner v. Gardiner, no. 01-1853. 2002. U.S. Supreme Court 537 U.S. 825. http://www.supremecourtus.gov/opinions/boundvolumes/537bv.pdf.

209. Reiner, William G. 1997. To be male or female-That is the question. *Archives of Pediatric and Adolescent Medicine,* 151 (March): 224-5.

210. Reiner, William G. interviewed by Melissa Hendricks. 2000. Into the Hands of Babes. *Johns Hopkins Magazine* (September). http://jhu.edu/~jhumag/0900web/babes.html (accessed August 7, 2006).

211. Reiner, William G. 1997. To be male or female-That is the question. *Archives of Pediatric and Adolescent Medicine,* 151 (March): 224-5.

212. Colapinto, John. 2000. *As nature made him: The boy who was raised as a girl.* New York: HarperCollins.

213. Reiner, William G. 1997. To be male or female-That is the question. *Archives of Pediatric and Adolescent Medicine,* 151 (March): 224-5.

214. McKenzie, John. 2002. Improving the odds: Prescreening IVF embryos results in greater success. *ABCNews.com* August 13. http://abcnews.com/ (accessed August 14, 2002).

215. Rae-Dupree, Janet. 2002. Know your genes, know yourself: A coming era of personal genomics could bring DNA profiling to the masses. *U.S. News and World Report,* May 27.

[216]. Shute, Nevil. 1957. On The Beach. Mattituck, NY: Amereon House.

[217]. Black, Taylor interviewed by Ed Bradley. 2002. Desperately fighting cancer. 60 Minutes, *CBSNews.com* April 4. http://www.cbsnews.com/stories/2002/04/04/60minutes/main505402.s html.

23. Works Cited

Literature

American Psychiatric Association. 2000. Diagnostic and statistical manual of mental disorders, fourth edition, text revision. http://www.psychiatryonline. com/resourceTOC.aspx?resourceID'1.

American Psychological Association, Public Policy Office. 2004. A.P.A. briefing sheet on same-sex families and relationships: What does the psychological research say about same-sex families and relationships? APAonline (June), http:// www.apa.org/ppo/issues/lgbfamilybrf604.html.

American Youth Policy Forum. 2001. Is the concept of full-service community schools ready for federal support? American Youth Policy Forum, (March 9), http://www.aypf.org/forumbriefs/2001/fb030901.htm (accessed December 30, 2002).

Asimov, Isaac. 1974/1956. The last question, in The best of Isaac Asimov. Garden City, NY: Doubleday, 1974.

Bailey, J. Michael. 2003. The man who would be queen. Washington, D.C.: Joseph Henry Press.

Batty, David. 2004. Mistaken identity. SocietyGuardian, July 31. http://society. guardian.co.uk/health/story/0,7890,1273045,00.html?'rss (accessed Nov. 20, 2006). 217 World Professional Association for Transgender Health.

Beers, Mark H., ed. 2004a. Children's health issues: Genital defects. From Merck Manual Home Edition. Reviewed/revised Gregory S. Liptak, April, 2006. http://www.merck.com/mmhe/print/sec23/ch265/ch265d.html.

Beers, Mark H., ed. 2004b. Mental health disorders: Gender identity. From Merck Manual Home Edition. http://www.merck.com/mmhe/print/sec07/ ch104/ch104b.html.

Bellinger v. Bellinger, UKHL 21. 2003. House of Lords, Lords of Appeal: [2003] UKHL 21, http://www.publications.parliament.uk/pa/ld200203/ldjudgmt/ jd030410/bellin- l.htm.

Benjamin, Harry. 1966. The transsexual phenomenon. New York: Julian Press, from Electronic Books. http://www.symposion.com/ijt/benjamin/chap_02.htm)

Black, Taylor interviewed by Ed Bradley. 2002. Desperately fighting cancer. 60 Minutes, CBSNews.com April 4. http://www.cbsnews.com/ stories/2002/04/04/60minutes/main505402.shtml.

Blanchard, Ray. 1989. The concept of autogynephilia and the typology of male gender dysphoria. The Journal of Nervous and Mental Disease 177 (10): 616-623, from http://www.genderpsychology.org/autogynephilia/ male_gender_dysphoria/.

Bradley, A. C. 1991. Aristotle's conception of the state, in A companion to Aristotle's politics, David Keyt and Fred D. Miller, Jr. eds. Cambridge, MA: Basil Blackwell, Inc.

Byron, George Gordon. 1808. Epitaph to a dog. "Poetry-Lord Byron." http:// www.davidpbrown.co.uk/poetry/lord-byron.html (accessed May 6, 2004).

Cassius, Dio Cocceianus. ca. A.D. 200. Roman history: Book 80. Trans. by Earnest Cary, Greek and English 1914 Loeb Classics Edition. http://www. brainfly.net/html/books/diocas80.pdf.

Central Intelligence Agency. 2004. World factbook [sic]: United Kingdom. http://www.cia.gov/cia/publications/factbook/geos/uk.html (accessed July 15, 2004).

Chachere, Vickie. 2004. Court: Floridians who have sex changes can't marry as new gender. Tallahassee Democrat, Tallahassee, FL, July 23, http://tallahassee. com/mld/tallahassee/9227312.htm?template'contentModules/print story.jsp (accessed July 25, 2004).

Cleveland Clinic, Department of Otolaryngology. 2001. Laryngotracheal: For your information. The Cleveland Clinic. http://www.clevelandclinic.org/otol/ laryn/hello.htm (accessed August 9, 2002).

CNN. 2002. Web child porn ring broken: International ring included parents abusing own children. CNN.com,
 http://www.cnn.com./2002/US/08/09/internet.child,porn.bust/index.html (accessed August 16, 2002).

Colapinto, John. 2000. As nature made him: The boy who was raised as a girl. New York: HarperCollins.

Columbia University Teenscreen. 2006. Teenscreen program: How the program works.
Teenscreen.org, http:www.teenscreen.org/ (accessed March 18, 2007).

Council of Economic Advisers. 2003. Economic report of the President, February. Table B- 3: Quantity and price indexes for gross domestic product, and percent changes, 1959- 2002. http://w3.access.gpo.gov/usbudget/fy2004/ erp.html (accessed September 27, 2003).

Council of Europe. 1950. Conventions for the protection of human rights and fundamental freedoms as amended by protocol no. 11. Council of Europe, http://conventions.coe.int/Treaty/en/Treatoes/Html/005.htm.

Council of Europe. 2003. Chart of signatures and ratifications of a treaty: General agreement on privileges and immunities of the Council of Europe. Council of Europe, http://conventions.coe.int/treaty/EN/searching. asp?NT'002&CM'1&DF'16/03/03 (accessed March 16, 2003).

Culotta, Elizabeth. 2005. What genetic changes made us uniquely human? Science. http://www.sciencemag.oeg/gi/content/full/309/5731/91.

de Sales, Francis. n.d. Prayer of St. Francis de Sales under Francis de Sales B. Doctor (RM). Washington DC: Saint Patrick Catholic Church. http://www. saintpatrickdc.org/ss/0124.htm (accessed January 18, 2007).

Demir, Ebru and Barry J. Dickson. 2005. Fruitless splicing specifies male courtship behavior in drosophila. Cell, 121 (June 3): 785-794. http://download. cell.com/pdfs/0092-8674/PIIS0092867405004071.pdf.

Department of Constitutional Affairs. 2004. Legislation: The gender recognition act 2004. Crown. http://www,dca.gov.uk/constitution/transsex/legs.htm.

Diamond, Milton and Keith Sigmundson. 1997. Sex reassignment at birth: Long-term review and clinical implications. Archives of Pediatric and Adolescent Medicine 151 (March): 298-304.

Donovan, Gill. 2003. Vatican says sex changes don't change one's gender. National Catholic Reporter, January 24. http://www.findarticles.com/p/articles/mi_m1141/is_12_39/ai_97173570/print.

Dotson-Lewis, Betty L. 1972. Author's note in Oral history interview with Larry Conn. AppalachiaCoal. Com. http://wwww.appalachiacoal.com/Oral%20History,%20Larry%20Conn,%20Buffalo%2 0Creek%20Flood,%20Logan,%20WV.htm.

Duffy, Jim. 1999. Sexual healing. Hopkins Medical News (Winter), under Gender-change issues, http://www.hopkinsmedicine.org/hmn/W99/top.html (accessed July 18, 2002).

Edinburgh Scotland Tourist Information. Greyfriars Bobby. http://www.beautiful- scotland.co.uk/Edinburgh.htm.

Ekklesia. 2004. Vatican issues statement on men and women. Ekklesia, February 8, http://www.ekklesia.co.uk/content/news_syndication/article_04082vat.shtml (accessed August 4, 2004).

Elbin, Dr. Paul Nowell. 1975. The paradox of happiness. New York: Hawthorne Books. Repub..Making happiness a habit. Nashville: Abingdon Press, 1981.

Elliott, Carl. Dec., 2000. A new way to be mad. Atlantic Monthly 286 (December): 72-84.

European Court of Human Rights. n.d. The Court: Historical background. European Court of Human Rights, http://www.echr.coe.int/ECHR/EN/Header?The+Court/The+Court/History+of+the+Court/ (accessed March 7, 2007).

Frost, Robert. 1920. The road not taken. From mountain interval. Bartleby.com. http://www.bartleby.com/119/1.html (accessed June 30, 2002).

Gardiner v. Gardiner, no. 01-1853. 2002. U.S. Supreme Court 537 U.S. 825. http://www.supremecourtus.gov/opinions/boundvolumes/537bv.pdf.

Gardiner, J'Noel v Joseph M. Gardiner, no. 85030. 2001. Court of Appeals of the State of Kansas: 29 Kan. App. 2d 92, 22 P.3d 1036. http://www.kscourts. org/kscases/ctapp/2001/20010511/85030.htm (accessed August 1, 2002.).

Gearhart, John. 2000. Interview in Into the hands of babes, by Melissa Hendricks. Johns Hopkins Magazine, (September). http://www.jhu. edu/~jhumag/0900web/babes.html.

Goldstein, Jill, Matthew Jerram, Russell Poldrack, Robert Anagnoson, Hans C. Breiter, Nikos Makris, Julie M. Goodman, Ming T. Tsuang, and Larry J. Seidman. 2005. Sex differences in prefrontal cortical brain activity during fMRI of auditory verbal working memory. Neuropsychology 19 (4): 509-519. http://www,brugganabdwinebs,irg/ConnorsCenter/Research/Images/Articles/ Sex% 20differences%20in%20prefrontal%20cortical%20brain%20activity.pdf (accessed March 18, 2007).

Goodwin, Christine v. United Kingdom, no. 28957/95. 2002a. European Court of Human Rights, Grand Chamber: [2002] ECHR 588 (July 11). http://hudoc. echr.coe.int/Hudoc1doc2/HEJUD/200207/Goodwin%20-%2028957jv.gc%20 11072002e.doc.

Green, Richard. 1966. Appendix c in The transsexual phenomenon, by Harry Benjamin. New York: Julian Press, from Electronic Books. http://www. symposion.com/ijt/benjamin/appendix_c.htm.

Greenberg, Julie. 1999. Defining male and female: Intersexuality and the collision between law and biology. Arizona Law Review 41 (Summer): 265-328.

Hendricks, Melissa. 2000. Into the hands of babes. John Hopkins Magazine September, http://www.jhu.edu~jhumag/0900web/babes.html.

Henley, William Ernest. ca. 1900. Invictus. From The Constitution Society. http://www.constitution.org/col/Invictus.htm.

Hughes, I. A., C. Houk, S. F. Ahmed, and P. A. Lee. 2006. Consensus statement on management of intersex disorders. Journal of Pediatric Urology 2: 148-162. http://www.intersex-tr.org/documents/Consensus%20% statement%20 on%20management%20of%20intersex%20disorders.pdf.

I. v. United Kingdom, no. 25680/94. 2002a. European Court of Human Rights, Grand Chamber: [2002] ECHR 592 (July 11). http://hei.unige.ch/~clapham/ hrdoc/docs/echrIcase.doc (accessed March 12, 2007).

In RE: B.L.V.B. and E.L.V.B., no. 92-321. 1993. Vermont Supreme Court: 160 VT 368, 628 A.2d 1271 (June 18). http://loislaw.com/pns/index.htp (subs. required).

Internal Revenue Service, Office of Chief Counsel. 2006. Request for Chief Counsel advice: Medical expense deduction. Internal Revenue Service, memorandum 200603025, http://www.irs.ogv/pub/irs-wd/0603025.pdf.

Jefferson, Thomas. 1774. A summary view of the rights of British America. The papers of Thomas Jefferson, ed. Julian P. Boyd, et al. (1950) cited in The Columbia World of Quotations, eds. Robert Andrews, Mary Biggs, Michael Seidel, et al. (New York: Columbia University Press, 1996). Bartleby.com., http://www.bartleby.com/66/91/30891.html.

Kallestad, Brent. 2002. University presidents discuss concerns about class-size amendment. Naples Daily News August 16. http://www.naplesnews.com/02/08/ florida/d808988a.htm (accessed March 22, 2003).

Karam, Jose and Linda A. Baker. 2004. True hermaphroditism. New England Journal of Medicine 350 (January 22): 393.

Kashner, Zoe, ed. 2007. The world almanac and book of facts, 2007. New York: World Almanac Education Group.

Kennedy, John F. 1961/1997. Inaugural address of John F. Kennedy from The Avalon project at Yale Law School: Inaugural speeches page, 1997. http://www. yale.edu/lawweb/Avalon/presiden/inaug/kennedy.htm.

Kim, GW, Kim, SK, Jeong, GW. 2016. Neural Activation-based Sexual Orientation and its Correlation with Free Testosterone Level in Postoperative

Female-to-male Transsexuals. Surgical and Radiologic Anatomy 38 (2) (March) 245-52.

Kipling, Rudyard J. 1902/1950. Just so stories for little children: How the elephant got his trunk, in Better Homes and Gardens storybook selected by Betty O'Connor, 101-5. Des Moines: Meredith Publishing, 1950.

Kruijver, Frank P. M., Jiang-Ning Zhou, Chris W. Pool, Michael A. Hofman, Louis J. G. Gooren, and Dick F. Swaab. 2000. Male-to-female transsexuals have female neuron numbers in a limbic nucleus. The Journal of Clinical Endocrinology & Metabolism 85 (May): 2034-2041.

L. Kantaras v. M. Kantaras, no. 2D03-1377. 2004. 2nd District Court of Appeal of Florida: 884 So. 2d 155. http://www.2dca.org/opinion/July%2023,%20 2004/2D03-1377.pdf.

Lawrence v. Texas, no. 02-102. 2003. U.S. Supreme Court: 539 U.S. 558. http:// www.supremecourtus.gov/opinions/boundvolumes/539bv.pdf.

Leo, John. 2001. The sex change boom: Is politics the appropriate arena for this discussion? U.S. News and World Report, March 12.

Littleton v. Prange, no. 00-25. 2000. U.S. Supreme Court 531 U.S. 872. http:// www.supremecourtus.gov/opinions/boundvolumes/531bv.pdf.

Lofton, Steven et al. v. Secretary of the Department of Children and Family Services, no. 01- 16723. 2004. U. S. Court of Appeals for the Eleventh Circuit: 377 F.3d 1275. http://www.ca11.uscourts.gov/opinions/ops/200116723ord.pdf.

London, Jack. 1903. The call of the wild. Online Literature Library, 1995. http://www.literature.org/authors/London-jack/the-call-of-the-wild/index.html (accessed June 8, 2004).

Lyons, Tom. 2001. Anti-terrorist tactics take shape via e-mail – and they make sense.

Sarasota Herald-Tribune, Oct. 10.

M. Kantaras v. L. Kantaras, no. 98-5375CA. 2003a. Sixth Judicial Circuit Court of Florida: (not recorded). http://www.transgenderlaw.org/cases/ kantarasopinion.pdf

M. Kantaras v. L. Kantaras, no. SCO4-1953. 2005b. The Supreme Court of Florida: 898 So. 2d. 80. http://www.loislaw.com/pns/index.htp (subs. required).

M. T. v. J. T., no. 140. 1976. New Jersey Superior Court 77: 355 A.2d 204. http://loislaw.com/pns/index.htp (subs. required).

Martinich, A. P. 1999. Hobbes: A biography. Cambridge: Cambridge University Press.

McClure, Kristie M. 1996. Judging rights: Lockean politics and the limits of consent, Cornell University Press.

McHugh, Paul R. 1992. Psychiatric Misadventures. The American Scholar (Autumn.) http://www.lhup.edu/~DSIMANEK/mchugh.htm.

McHugh, Paul R. 2001. Adventures in academic psychiatry. Hopkins Medical News
(Fall). http://www.hopkinsmedicine.org/hmn/F01/top.html (accessed July 18, 2002).

McKenzie, John. 2002. Improving the odds: Prescreening IVF embryos results in greater success. ABCNews.com August 13. http://abcnews.com/ (accessed August 14, 2002).

MedlinePlus. 2003. Few suicidal teens seek professional help: Report. Reuters, April 18, 2003, National Library of Medicine and National Institutes of Health. http://www.nlm.nih.gov/medlineplus/print/news/fullstory_12429.html (accessed May 5, 2003).

Miller, Carol Marbin. 2003. Gender of Hemingway's son at center of feud. The Milwaukee Journal Sentinel, September 29. FindArticles.com, http:// wwwfindarticles.com/p/articles/mi_qn4196/is_20030930/ai_n10909778.

Money J., J.G. Hampson, and J.L. Hampson. 1955. An examination of some basic sexual concepts: The evidence of human hermaphroditism. Bulletin of Johns Hopkins Hospital 97: 301-319.

Money, John. 1986. Lovemaps: clinical concepts of sexual/erotic health and pathology, paraphilia, and gender transposition in childhood, adolescence, and maturity. New York: Irvington Publishers, Inc. and Buffalo: Prometheus Books.

Morris, Jan. 1974. Conundrum. New York: Harcourt, Brace, Jovanovich.

N.O.A.A., National Weather Service Forecast Office. n.d. The greatest storms of the century in the greater Washington-Baltimore Region. http://www.erh.noaa. gov/er/lwx/Historic_Events/StormsOfCentury.html (accessed September 24, 2003).

National Association of School Psychologists. n.d. Standards: Background information on the standards. National Association of School Psychologists, http://www.nasponline.org/certifications/standards.html (accessed February 2, 2005).

National Council of the Churches of Christ U.S.A., Division of Christian Education. 1989. The Holy Bible: New Revised Standard Version. Nashville, TN: Thomas Nelson.

National Geographic Society. 1968. Atlantic Ocean floor map. Supplement in National Geographic Magazine June.

Niebuhr, Reinhold. 1950. The a. a. grapevine. January. Quoted in S. Platt, ed., Respectfully quoted: A dictionary of quotations requested from Congressional Research Service. Washington DC: Library of Congress, 1989.

Norris, Michele. 2002. Campus crisis: Some students' mental health needs go unmet. World News Tonight, February 12. ABC News.com, http://more. abcnews.go.com/sections/wnt/dailynews/college_mentalhealth020211.ht ml (accessed December 27, 2002).

Pinholster, Ginger. 2005. New research casts doubt on surgery for infants born with male and female traits. American Association for the Advancement of Science. News release (February 18). http://www.aaas.org/news/releases/2005/0218gender.shtml.

Quittner, Jeremy. 2001. Hemingway's son Gloria: When Ernest Hemingway's son died in prison, the world learned he had been a troubled man who found the strength to live his life as he saw best–as a woman. The Advocate, Nov. 20. http://www.advocate.com/html/stories/851/851_hemingway.asp (accessed April 6, 2002).

Rae-Dupree, Janet. 2002. Know your genes, know yourself: A coming era of personal genomics could bring DNA profiling to the masses. U.S. News and World Report, May 27.

Rand, Ayn. 1943/1993. The fountainhead. 50th anniversary edition with afterward by Leonard Peikoff. New York: Signet.

Rand, Ayn. 1969. The romantic manifesto, Cleveland, OH: The World Publishing Co.

Reiner, William G. 1997. To be male or female-That is the question. Archives of Pediatric and Adolescent Medicine, 151 (March): 224-5.

Reiner, William G. and John P. Gearhart. 2004. Discordant sexual identity in some genetic males with cloacal exstrophy assigned to female sex at birth. New England Journal of Medicine 350 (January 22): 333-41.

Reiner, William G. interviewed by Melissa Hendricks. 2000. Into the Hands of Babes. Johns Hopkins Magazine (September). http://jhu.edu/~jhumag/0900web/babes.html (accessed August 7, 2006).

Reiner, William G. interviewed by Sadie F. Dingfelder. 2004. Gender bender: New research suggests genes and prenatal hormones could have more sway in gender identity than previously thought. APA Online: Monitor on psychology April, http://www.apa.org/monitor/apr04/gender.html.

Schmitt, Jaime Stover. 2005. The Yogic inner instrument. Personal communication, May 20.

Shakespeare, William. 1975/n.d. The merchant of Venice, act iv, sce. 1. From William Shakespeare: The complete works. New York: Gramercy Books.

Sherr, Lynn. 2002. A different sex, in ABC NEWS 20/20. New Hudson, MI: ABC News Videos/Burrelle's Information Services, item: T020419.

Shrier, Abagail. 2020. Irreversible Damage: The Transgender Craze Seducing Our Daughters. Washington, D. C.: Regnery Publishing Div., Salem Media Group.

Shute, Nevil. 1957. On The Beach. Mattituck, NY: Amereon House.

Sidney Morning Herald. 2003. Vatican moves to ban all sex-change priests, nuns. Sidney Morning Herald, February 2. http://www.smh.com.au/articles/2003/02/01/1043804574455.html (accessed February 5, 2003).

Speck, Oliver, Thomas Ernst, Jochen Braun, Christoph Koch, Eric Miller, and Linda Chang. 2000. Gender differences in the functional organization of the brain for working memory. Neuro Report 11 (August): 2581-2586. http://www.hawaii.edu/mri/additional%20pdfs/Recently%20 downloaded?Speck%20 (NeuroReport%202000).pdf.

Spencer, Terry. 2001. Ernest Hemingway's son Gregory dies. The St. Augustine Record, Oct. 5, 2001. Staugustine.com, http://www.staugustine.com/stories/100501/sta_192253.shtml (accessed March 19,2007).

Stack, Megan K. 2005. In Iran, some clerics promote sex-change operation. Los Angeles Times appearing in Sarasota Herald Tribune, January 30.

Teichmann, Howard. 1976. Smart Aleck. New York: William Morrow and Co.

The President's New Freedom Commission on Mental Health, Michael F. Hogan, Chm. 2003. Achieving the promise: Transforming mental health care in America. Mentalhealthcommission.gov July 22. http://www.mentalhealthcommission.gov/reports/reports.htm (accessed March 19, 2007).

U.S. Customs Service. 2002. 45 children rescued, 20 arrests in U.S. Customs, Danish police investigation of global child-molesting, pornography ring. U.S.

Customs Service, press release August 9, 2002, http://www.customs.ustreas.gov/
hot- new/pressrel/2002/0809-00.htm (accessed August 15, 2002).

U.S. Department of Education. n.d. The federal role in education: Overview.
U.S. Department of Education, http://www/ed.gov/about/overview/fed/role.
html?src'ln (accessed February 13, 2005).

U.S. Dept. H.H.S., Bureau of Health Professionals. 2005. Shortage designation
branch home page: Health professional shortage areas: Ad-hoc database query
results. Health Resources & Services Administration, U.S. Department of
Health & Human Services, http://belize.hrsa.gov/newhpsa/newhepsa.cfm
(accessed February 8, 2005).

Van Kuck v. Germany, no. 35968/97. 2003. European Court of Human Rights,
Third Section: 62 ECHR 285 (June 12,). http://www.worldlii.org/eu/cases/
ECHR/2003/285.html.

Vilain, Eric interview. 2004. Biology of sex and gender: Expert interview
transcripts. From Rediscovering biology. Annenberg/Corporation for Public
Broadcasting. http://www.lerner.org/channel/courses/biology/units/gender/
experts/vilain.html.

Woollcott, Alexander. 1934. Miss Kitty takes to the road, from the
ScreamOnline.com. http://www.thescreamonline.com/essays/essays2-3/
Woollcott.html.

World Professional Association for Transgender Health. 2012. Standards of Care
for the Health of Transsexual, Transgender, and Gender Nonconforming People
{7th Ver.} https://www.wpath.org/publications/soc

Zhou, Jiang-Ning, Michael A Hofman, Louis J. G. Gooren, and Dick F. Swaab.
1995. A sex difference in the human brain and its relation to transsexuality.
Nature 378 (November 2,): 68-70.

Zito, Julie Magno, Daniel J. Safer, Susan dosReis, James F. Gardner, Laurence
Magder, Karen Soeken, Myde Boles, Frances Lynch, and Mark A. Riddle. 2003.
Psychotropic practice patterns for youth: A ten-year perspective. Archives of
Pediatrics and Adolescent Medicine 157 (1): 17-25. http://archpedi.ama-assn.org/
cgi/content/full/157/1/17.

Cinema

Curtiz, Michael, director. 1954. White Christmas, from Internet Movie Database. http://www.imdb.com/title/tt0047673/ (accessed January 17, 2007).

Edwards, Blake. 1991. Switch, from Internet Movie Database. http://www/imdb.com/title/tt0103016/.

Fisher, Terence, director. 1959. The mummy, from Internet Movie Database. http://www.imdb.com/title/tt0053085/.

Fleming, Victor, director. 1941. Dr. Jekyll and Mr. Hyde, from Internet Movie Database. http://www.imdb.com/title/tt0033553/.

Hawks, Howard, director. 1941. Sergeant York, from Internet Movie Database. http://www.imdb.com/title/tt0034167/.

Julian, Rupert, Lon Chaney, Ernst Laemmle, and Edward Sedgwick, directors. 1925. The phantom of the opera, from Internet Movie Database. http://www.imdb.com/title/tt0016220/.

Koster, Henry. 1961. Flower drum song, from Internet Movie Database. http://www.imdb.com/title/tt0054885 (accessed January 17, 2007).

Logan, Joshua. 1958. South Pacific, from Internet Movie Database. http://www.imdb.com/title/tt0052225/.

Lubin, Arthur, director. 1943. Phantom of the opera, from Internet Movie Database. http://www.imdb.com/title/tt0036261/.

Minnelli, Vincente. 1964. Goodbye, Charlie, from Internet Movie Database. http://www/imdb.com/title/tt0058154/.

Ray, Nicholas, director. 1960. The savage innocents, from Internet Movie Database. http://www.imdb.com/title/tt0053244/.

Sears, Fred, director. 1956. The werewolf, from Internet Movie Database. http://www.imdb.com/title/tt0049944/.

Sidney, George. 1951. Show boat, from Internet Movie Database. http://www.imdb.com/title/tt0044030/.

Stevenson, Robert, director. 1959. Darby O'Gill and the little people, from Internet Movie Database. http://www.imdb.com/title/tt0052722/.

Swift, David, director. 1960. Pollyanna, from Internet Movie Database. http://www.imdb.com/title/tt0054195/.

Zinnemann, Fred. 1955. Oklahoma from Internet Movie Database. http://www.imdb.comhttp://www.imdb.com/title/tt0048445.

Series Television

Adreon, Franklin, William Hale, Douglas Heyes, et al., directors. 1955. Cheyenne, from Internet Movie Database. http://www.imdb.com/title/tt00447720/.

Archainbaud, George, Douglas Heyes, Fred Jackman Jr. et al., directors. 1956. Circus boy, from Internet Movie Database. http://www.imdb.com/title/tt0048855/.

Bare, Richard L., Alan Crosland Jr., Paul Guilfoyle, et al., directors. 1958. Lawman, from Internet Movie Database. http://www.imdb.com/title/tt0051290/.

Beaudine Jr., William, Earl Bellamy, James B. Clark, et al., directors. 1954. Lassie, from Internet Movie Database. http://www.imdb.com/title/tt0046617/.

Bellamy, Earl, Charles S. Gould, Douglas Heyes, et al., directors. 1954. The adventures of Rin Tin Tin, from Internet Movie Database. http://www.imdb.com/title/tt0046576/.

Bellamy, Earl, Jerrold Bernstein, Lawrence Dobkin, et al., directors. 1958. The Donna Reed show, from Internet Movie Database. http://www.imdb.com/title/tt0051267/.

Blair, George, John English, Christian Nyby, et al., directors. 1951. The Roy Rogers show, from Internet Movie Database. http://www.imdb.com/title/tt0043225/.

Boetticher, Budd, William F. Claxton, Lawrence Dobkin, et al., directors. 1958. The rifleman, from Imdb. com at http://www.imdb.com/title/tt0051308/.

Brahm, John, Alfred E. Green, James B. Kern, et al., directors. 1955. The millionaire, from Internet Movie Database. http://www.imdb.com/title/tt0047758/.

Carr, Thomas, Don McDougall, George Blair, et al., directors. 1958. Wanted: dead or alive, from Internet Movie Database. http://www.imdb.com/title/tt0051327.

Clark, James B., Robert Gordon, Albert S. Rogell, et al., directors. 1956. My friend Flicka, from Internet Movie Database. http://www.imdb.com/title/tt0048887/.

Claxton, William F., Lewis Allen, Leon Benson, et al., directors. 1959. Bonanza, from Internet Movie Database. http://www.imdb.com/title/tt0052451/.

Conrad, William, Alan Crosland Jr., Eddie Davis, et al., directors. 1958. Bat Masterson, from Internet Movie Database. http://www.imdb.com/title/tt0050025/.

Copelan, Jodie, Oliver Drake, Richard C. Kahn, et al., directors. 1951. Sky King, from Internet Movie Database. http://www.imdb.com/title/tt0043232/.

Davis, Eddie, Leslie Goodwins, Lambert Hillyer, et al., directors. 1950. The Cisco Kid, from Internet Movie Database. http://www.imdb.com/title/tt0042093/.

Davis, Phil, Stu Phelps, Bob Lehman, et al., directors. 1950. Truth or consequences. http://www.imdb.com/title/tt0143074/fullcredits (accessed January 16, 2007).

De Toth, Andre. 1954. The bounty hunter, from Internet Movie Database. http://www.imdb.com/title/tt0046801/.

Guedel, John, producer. 1952. Art Linkletter's House Party. http://www.imdb.com/title/tt0047714/fullcredits (accessed January 16, 2007).

McLaglen, Andrew V., Richard Boone, William Conrad, et al. directors. 1957. Have gun – will travel, from Internet Movie Database. http://www.imdb.com/title/tt0050025/.

Meston, John, Andrew V. McLaglen, Harry Harris, et al., directors. Gunsmoke, from Internet Movie Database. http://www.imdb.com/title/tt0047736/.

Morse, Hollingsworth, Oscar Rudolph, George B. Seitz Jr., et al., directors. 1949. The lone ranger, from Internet Movie Database. http://www.imdb.com/title/tt00410038/.

Post, Ted, Andrew V. McLaglen, Stuart Heisler, et al. 1959. Rawhide, from Internet Movie Database. http://www.imdb.com/title/tt0052504/.

Russell, William D. and Peter Tewksbury, directors. 1954. Father knows best, from Internet Movie Database. http://www.imdb.com/title/tt0046600/.

Sale, Richard and William F. Claxton, directors. 1958. Yancy Derringer, from Internet Movie Database. http://www.imdb.com/title/tt0051329/.

Salkow, Sidney, Lesley Selander, and Ray Nazarro, directors. 1955. Fury, from Internet Movie Database. http://www.imdb.com/title/tt0047734/.

Satenstein, Frank, director. 1955. The honeymooners, from Internet Movie Database. http://www.imdb.com/title/tt0042114/.

Vogel, Virgil w., Bernard McEveety, Paul Henreid, et al., directors. 1965. The big valley, from Internet Movie Database. http://www.imdb.com/title/tt0058791/.

www.ingramcontent.com/pod-product-compliance
Lightning Source LLC
LaVergne TN
LVHW021146140726
843272LV00042B/987